For Steve,
With best wishes

Mark

THE MUSLIMS OF
VALENCIA

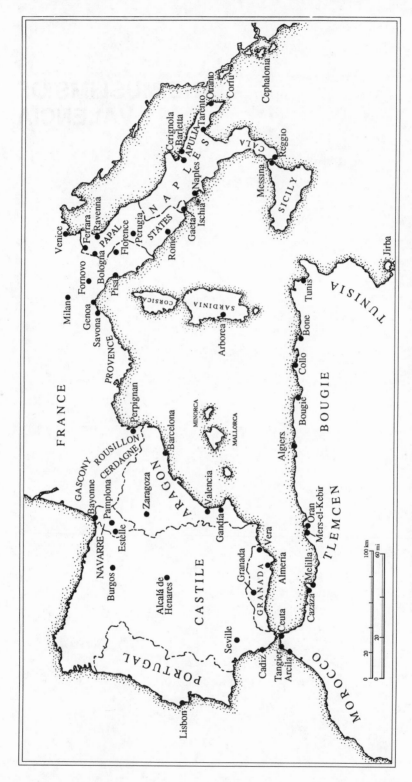

Map 1. The Mediterranean during the Reign of the Catholic Monarchs before 1492.

THE MUSLIMS OF VALENCIA

IN THE AGE OF FERNANDO AND ISABEL: BETWEEN COEXISTENCE AND CRUSADE

Mark D. Meyerson

UNIVERSITY OF CALIFORNIA PRESS

Berkeley   Los Angeles   Oxford

University of California Press
Berkeley and Los Angeles, California

University of California Press
Oxford, England

Library of Congress Cataloging-in-Publication Data

Meyerson, Mark D.
    The Muslims of Valencia in the age of Fernando and Isabel:
between coexistence and crusade/ Mark D. Meyerson.
        p.   cm.
    Includes bibliographical references and index,
    ISBN 0-520-06888-2 (cloth: alk. paper)
    1. Mudéjares.   2. Muslims—Spain—Valencia (Province)—History.
3. Valencia (Spain: Province)—History.   4. Valencia (Spain:
Province)—Ethnic relations.   I. Title.
DP302.V205M49   1991
946'.763—dc20   90-35502
                                                                      CIP

Printed in the United States of America

1 2 3 4 5 6 7 8 9

The paper used in this publication meets the
minimum requirements of American National
Standard for Information Sciences—Permanence of
Paper for Printed Library Materials, ANSI Z39.48-
1984

*To my father, for giving
so much in so little time.*

Contents

Tables

Acknowledgments

Like many first books, this one began as a doctoral dissertation, and as such owes much to the fine teachers I had while a graduate student at the Centre for Medieval Studies, University of Toronto. I had the good fortune of writing the dissertation under the supervision of Jocelyn Hillgarth of the Pontifical Institute of Mediaeval Studies. His profound understanding of medieval Spain in all its diversity, his patience, and his sense of humor made the writing of this work a rich, rewarding, and largely pleasurable experience. The late Frank Talmage of the University of Toronto, with whom I had studied Sephardic history and who impressed me in so many ways with his love of learning, impeccable scholarship, and humanity, read the dissertation carefully and made many incisive comments. John Boswell of Yale University offered much advice and encouragement both before I departed for Spain to begin archival research and after the dissertation was completed. Robert Burns, S.J., of the University of California, Los Angeles, was kind enough to read the dissertation and to make a number of helpful suggestions, of a kind that only he, with his great knowledge of Valencian history, could make. My colleague at Notre Dame, Greg Dowd, a historian of American Indians with a particular sensitivity to cross-cultural questions, also read the manuscript and provided insightful comments.

The staffs of the Archivo de la Corona de Aragón and the Archivo del Reino de Valencia were always kind and helpful, making working conditions as pleasant as possible for a young historian. Sr. Rafael Conde, now director of the Archivo de la Corona de Aragón, did the great service of pointing me toward the archival treasures of Valencia, although at the time I could not imagine ever leaving Barcelona. The Ontario government generously provided me with the funding necessary for sixteen months of research abroad, and The Lady Davis Fellowship Trust kindly granted me a postdoctoral fellowship at the Hebrew University of Jerusalem. Muna Salloum of the Centre for Religious Studies, University of Toronto, did a wonderful job of typing the final draft of the dissertation in the eleventh hour, and the staff of the Steno Pool of the University of Notre Dame kindly typed the revised manuscript.

On a more personal note, there are a number of people without whom this book would not have been possible. Friends in Barcelona and Valencia gave me a feeling and an appreciation for the Països Catalans and their peoples that could never have been gotten in the archives. Larry Simon, then, like myself, a graduate student researching in Barcelona, shared with me his enthusiasm and insights. I owe special thanks to my cousins, Karen and Dick Grimm, Doug, Eric, and Gia, and to my in-laws, Sid and Ruth Ross. The love and encouragement of my wife Jill were matched only by her patience as the Mudejars became part of both our lives.

Note

In order to minimize confusion, I have numbered the kings according to the Aragonese numeration, rather than Valencian or Catalan numeration—thus, Pedro IV (rather than Pere III) and Alfonso V (rather than Alfonso IV). Also, I have used the Castilian instead of the Catalan forms for toponyms. Personal names for the most part have been left in the form in which they were found in the documents. In particular, the Romance distortions of Muslim names rendered it practically impossible to transliterate all of them into their Arabic originals in any consistent and uniform manner.

Regarding the *Furs*, the law code of the kingdom of Valencia, I have utilized both the 1482 edition of Lambert Palmart and the modern edition of Germà Colon and Arcadi Garcia. Recourse to the Palmart edition was necessary because the Colon and Garcia edition is not yet complete.

The currency of the fifteenth-century kingdom of Valencia consisted of *diners*, *sous*, and pounds. One *sou* was worth twelve *diners*, and twenty *sous* made up one pound. The abbreviations "s" will be used for *sou* and "d" for *diner*.

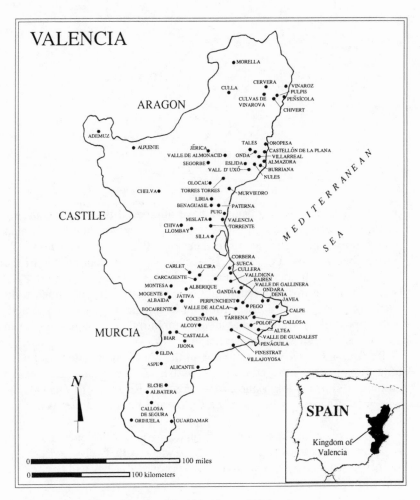

Map 2. The Kingdom of Valencia

Introduction

"Coexistence" and "crusade," the terms employed in the title of this study, suggest two contrary modes of thought and action and point to the fundamental tension existing in the relations between the religious groups of medieval Iberia. I use "coexistence" here as an approximate translation of the term *convivencia* (both terms will be used interchangeably throughout this study), a term that Américo Castro coined to describe the more or less peaceful "living together" of and cultural interchange between Christians, Muslims, and Jews in the Christian kingdoms of medieval Spain.[1] The crusade, a holy war aimed at the conquest of territories under the control of the ideological enemy, or "infidel," is manifest in Iberian history in the centuries-long Christian *reconquista* of the greater part of the peninsula from the Muslims who had conquered it in the eighth century. Although coexistence and crusade appear to concern distinct aspects of Christian–Muslim relations—the former being descriptive of the benign interaction of religious groups within the Spanish kingdoms, and the latter of the bellicose relations of those kingdoms with Islamic polities—neither one lacked elements that might be considered more characteristic of the other. In other words, the history of Christian–Muslim relations in medieval Spain presents the historian with a variety of situations on both the domestic and international fronts for which neither "peaceful coexistence" nor "fanatical belligerence" are accurately descriptive.

While the Christian *reconquista* appears to have been a perpetual crusade against the Muslims of al-Andalus, warfare with Islam was actually more intermittent than constant. This was especially the case

1

during the years between the midthirteenth century, by which time Aragon and Castile had made their major territorial acquisitions in Valencia, Murcia, and Andalusia, and the final push for the conquest of the sultanate of Granada (1482–1492). Realpolitik and commercial interests often prevailed over crusading fervor. Thus Christian kings and Muslim sultans not infrequently formed alliances against their respective coreligionists in an attempt to maintain a balance of power in the western Mediterranean. During periods of peace Christian and Islamic states engaged in commerce and merchants from both sides freely crossed the frontier to conduct their business. During the fourteenth and fifteenth centuries (until 1482) in particular, the Christian kingdoms were usually too involved in their own conflicts and civil wars to devote much energy to the struggle against Islam. In sum, the Spanish crusade against Islam, although always existent at least as a potentiality, was often far more apparent than real, and forms of international Muslim–Christian coexistence were not at all unusual.

It was, of course, the Islamic *jihād* (holy war) and the Christian crusade that gave rise to medieval Iberia's religiously plural societies. Because the Muslim and Christian conquerors did not expel, annihilate, or forcibly convert the subject populations, some form of coexistence or modus vivendi between the conquerors and the "infidel" conquered was necessary. Muslim and Christian rulers each dealt with the subject populations in accordance with theological considerations, political and economic pragmatism, and historical precedent.

The treatment of Christian and Jewish minorities in Islamic Spain was governed by the *dhimmah* contract, which accorded protection to the adherents of those religions with a revealed scripture considered by Muslims to be divinely inspired. In return for religious freedom and communal autonomy, the *dhimmīs* (as the beneficiaries of the *dhimmah* contract were called) had to acknowledge the domination of Islam, materially expressed in the payment of the *jizyah* or special poll tax. The *dhimmah* contract had its Qur'ānic (Koranic) foundation in the text (IX: 24): "Fight those who do not believe . . . until they pay the *jizyah*."[2] In other words, the *jihād* was to cease once the unbelievers had been subjected to Islamic rule. Given the vast populations of non-Muslims the Muslim conquerors incorporated within their empire, their policy could hardly have been otherwise. While Islamic law afforded the *dhimmīs* security, it nevertheless subjected them to civil and legal disabilities and excluded them, theoretically at least, from positions of political power. Regarding the protection of the *dhimmīs*, the letter of the law was not always followed, as evinced in the Almohad persecution of Mozarabic Christians and Jews. Still, such instances were a relatively rare exception to the rule of harmonious coexistence in al-Andalus.

In Christian Spain the legal structures governing the relations of the Christian majority with the Jewish and Muslim minorities were sufficiently similar to the *dhimmah* contract in their granting of freedom of worship and autonomy to each religious community to suggest that Christian rulers borrowed the *dhimmah* model and adapted it to Christian norms. However, there was a crucial difference between the Christian and Islamic systems. Whereas the *dhimmah* contract was sanctioned by revelation and was therefore universally applicable and essentially stable, the Christian system was based primarily on a series of surrender treaties and compacts concluded between Christian monarchs and individual minority communities, and was consequently more subject to change. Robert Burns points out that in one sense the new Christian model was an advancement of its *dhimmah* antecedent, because it was "the product of a community's rational manipulation of experience rather than . . . application or acceptance of a religious structure."[3] Although it is true that the compacts' initial formulations obeyed political and economic realities and at times were later modified in favor of the minority communities, the greater instability inherent in the Christian system—where minority privileges could be withdrawn by royal fiat in response to social, economic, and political pressures—more often than not boded ill for the minorities and resulted in the steady erosion of their security.[4]

Thus, in both Islamic and Christian societies there existed a form of institutionalized tolerance of religious minorities. Yet because this tolerance was institutional, an artificial governmental creation, it by no means guaranteed a harmonious intermingling of religious groups. Even though the state of war between Muslims and Christians was ended with conquest and the conclusion of surrender treaties, the religious animosity that, along with political and economic concerns, had motivated the military conquests was not immediately or ever completely extinguished. Owing to the continual, although sporadic, confrontation between Spain's Christian kingdoms and their Islamic adversaries— however much this was tempered by commercial treaties and political alliances—that fundamental odium and mistrust felt for the ideological enemy, so necessary for the mobilization of crusade and *jihād*, was sustained within the religiously plural societies despite the quotidian contact between Muslims and Christians. This tension, usually subliminal, occasionally gave rise to overt expressions of hostility, either official—as in the expulsions of the Mozarabic Christians by the Almohads and the Moriscos by the Christian authorities, both minorities being politically suspect—or popular—as in the anti-Muslim riots in Valencia in the 1270s or in 1455. Moreover, the very protection and autonomy granted to minority communities was also designed to isolate them from the majority, rendering each group strange to the other and fostering mutual aversion. Therefore, intrinsic to the institutional forms structuring Iberian Christian—Muslim—Jewish coexistence was a latent ideological antagonism. It follows that the concept of *convivencia* as peaceful coexistence must be modified to include this ever-present potentiality for religious and ethnic violence. Only then can *convivencia* have any applicability as a term descriptive of the reality of medieval Spain's plural societies.

The present study focuses on the Muslim minority of the kingdom of Valencia during the reign of Fernando II (1479–1516), some 240 years after that kingdom was conquered from Islam by Jaime I of Aragon. The decision to study the Valencian Mudejars (Muslims living under Christian rule) of this era originated in a desire to comprehend more fully the reasons for the breakdown of *convivencia*, which for the most part occurred under the Catholic Monarchs, Fernando and his wife, Isabel I of Castile. It was the Monarchs who set about taking care of Spain's "Jewish problem," first by establishing a national Inquisition (1478–1483) intended to eradicate from Christian society those converts from Judaism (Conversos) still adhering to their ancestral faith, and then by expelling the Jews from all of Spain (1492) as a means of preventing them from further contaminating the Conversos. In the same year that the expulsion was ordered Fernando and Isabel also completed the conquest of the sultanate of Granada, the last Islamic polity on Iberian soil. After some ten years of living under Castilian rule as Mudejars, the Muslims of Granada were given the choice of baptism or expulsion, as were the Mudejars of Isabel's Castile (1502). By the end of Fernando's reign only the Muslims living in the lands of the Crown of Aragon still retained their dissident religious status.

While the Jews and Conversos, and the Muslims of Granada and Castile, have all received some treatment by historians, the Mudejars of the Crown of Aragon curiously have been left untouched. Yet it would seem that a full understanding of the religious policy of the Catholic Monarchs, on whose shoulders the responsibility for the dissolution of *convivencia* must be placed, demands consideration of the situation of those minorities who, with royal sanction, remained non-Christian as well as that of those who by force or otherwise became members of the Catholic Church. Tidy explanations of the Monarchs' policy as a drive for the religious unity of the Spanish State remain untenable as long as Fernando's treatment of his own Muslim subjects remains unexplored. Efforts to sweep the question of Aragon's Muslims under the rug by pointing out the probable seigneurial resistance to any royal plans for their conversion, while accurate to the extent that the nobles indeed would have resisted had any such plans existed, nevertheless are not fully convincing. For it is evident in Fernando's imposition of the Inquisition on all his kingdoms, against considerable local resistance, that seigneurial complaints would not have deterred him had the religious unity of Aragon and Castile been his intention.

Thus far, precious little work has been done on the Mudejars of the fifteenth and early sixteenth centuries, particularly on the question of royal policy toward them. There are, however, the valuable studies of Miguel Gual Camarena and Leopoldo Piles on the Mudejars of the kingdom of Valencia and that of Francisco Macho y Ortega on their Aragonese counterparts. Although these studies provide important information on the internal organization of the Muslim aljamas (communities), the Muslims' economic life, and their taxation by the Crown, they do little to elucidate the vicissitudes of royal policy and do not take into account the changing political, social, and economic conditions that might have affected the Mudejars' situation. For the Castilian Mudejars we have the useful work of Miguel Angel Ladero Quesada, which includes 152 edited documents concerning the Muslims of Granada and Castile from 1492 to 1503. These documents shed valuable light on the views of the principal Christian actors in the drama: Isabel, Fernando, Cardinal Francisco Jiménez de Cisneros, and Hernando de Talavera, the first archbishop of Granada. However, Ladero's historical introduction to the documents does little to explain why the Monarchs acted as they did and attempts rather unsuccessfully to absolve Isabel of the charge of having forced the Granadan Muslims to receive baptism. Most important, Ladero fails to make the essential connection between the Monarchs' Jewish policy and their Mudejar policy, both of which were rooted in the same concerns.[5]

Most analyses of the Monarchs' religious policy have centered on their treatment of the Jews, the Inquisition, and the expulsion. Various hypotheses concerning the Monarchs' motives in expelling the Jews have been advanced. Stephen Haliczer has suggested that the powerful Converso elite, who, he maintains, controlled the urban governments of Castile, pressured the Monarchs into expelling the Jews in order to defuse Inquisitorial suspicions about their own contacts with Jews. Henry Kamen has proposed that the Castilian nobility was behind the expulsion. Such explanations, whatever usefulness they might have for an understanding of Castilian society, ultimately fail because they ignore Fernando's priorities in the Crown of Aragon and thereby suggest the unlikely scenario of one or another Castilian social group dictating to the king the policy he would follow in his own realms. Others, looking at Spain as a whole, have argued that it was Reason of State that moved the Monarchs to establish the Inquisition and expel the Jews; that is, in their drive toward a centralized monarchy they could not brook the existence of dissident groups. This last argument appears especially tenuous when one considers the simple fact that Fernando permitted the Mudejars of Aragon to remain Muslims. The consensus among most historians now seems to be that in expelling the Jews, Fernando and Isabel were motivated mainly by religious concerns, that is, by the concerns they themselves enunciated in the edict of expulsion—to prevent the Jews from contaminating the Christian faith of the Conversos. Maurice Kriegel has presented this viewpoint most convincingly while effectively refuting other opinions.[6]

However, if religious concerns, or the goal of religious unity, motivated the Monarchs, how can we explain the glaring exception of Aragon's Mudejars? Perhaps the greatest stumbling block to finding a consistent thread in the Monarchs' minority policy is the assumption that this policy, with its various conversions and expulsions, was preconceived, a fixed idea in the minds of Fernando and Isabel that needed only to be acted upon. While this may have been true of their Jewish policy—for there was a compelling logic in the movement from the establishment of the Inquisition to the expulsion, especially considering the clear role of the Inquisitors in the decision to decree the expulsion—it was not the case with respect to their Mudejar policy. As will be demonstrated in the first chapter of this study, Fernando had every intention of maintaining Mudejarism in his kingdom, and the same probably can be said of Isabel in Castile. The Mudejar "policy" that evolved out of the events of 1499–1501 was really not a policy at all but a somewhat confused reaction to the rebellions in the Albaicín and the Alpujarras and their aftermath. The decision to convert or expel the Muslims of Granada and Castile was, indeed, based on religious concerns— namely, on a fear that the Muslims might contaminate those Muslims who had converted to Christianity in the course of the rebellions. This was not a decision designed to create religious unity in the Spanish State (a concept in itself somewhat questionable) but a measure meant to prevent the corruption of the beliefs of the Monarchs' Christian subjects. In all of this Fernando's uneasiness contrasts rather markedly with Isabel's apparent satisfaction, as does his determination to maintain Mudejarism in Aragon with his acquiescence to Isabel's methods and measures in Castile. This study will put into relief the differences between Fernando and Isabel on the question of the religious minorities.

Methodological considerations have determined the chronological and geographic scope of this study. I thought it important to begin my archival research with the year 1479, the commencement of Fernando's reign, for it was in the early years of the reign that the monarch had to confirm or withdraw the privileges granted to Muslim aljamas by his predecessors. On the basis of such confirmations or revocations of privileges one can both assess the extent to which the king acted in accordance with tradition and conclude whether he intended significant modifications of the Mudejars' status. The terminal date for my research of 1503 was chosen because previous to 12 February 1502 the fate of the Granadan and Castilian Mudejars had not yet been decided. If this study is to have any comparative value vis-à-vis the Monarchs' differential treatment of the Mudejars in Castile and Aragon, then Fernando's distinct policy toward his own Muslim subjects must be traced at least until the time of the conversion of Isabel's Castilian and Granadan subjects.

The weightiest consideration in my decision to focus on the Valencian Mudejars was the simple fact that the kingdom of Valencia had the largest Muslim population—30 percent of the total, as compared to 20 percent for Aragon and less than 2 percent for Catalonia. Moreover, because of Valencia's geographic position—located on the Mediterranean coast and much closer to Granada and North Africa than Aragon—the situation of the kingdom's Muslims was much more affected by the Crown of Aragon's relations with Islamic states, a factor that seems to lend their story greater interest. Finally, it was events in the kingdom of Valencia—namely, the revolt of the *Germanías* with its attendant anti-Muslim violence—that led Carlos I to command the conversion of the Crown of Aragon's Muslim subjects. Hence, it was Valencia that would weigh most heavily in Fernando's formulation of a Mudejar policy and in the determination of the Muslims' ultimate fate.

The historian of the Mudejars under Fernando II can hardly ignore the substantial body of scholarship on the Moriscos (Muslim converts to Christianity), whose story in Valencia begins in 1525.[7] Certainly the Moriscos' situation was in some respects a continuation of that of the Mudejars, so that the findings of Morisco scholarship can be utilized to shed light on Mudejar life in certain areas, such as demography (taking into account the postconversion migration from urban areas to rural seigneuries), the relationship of Muslim vassals to Christian lords (although the bargaining position of the Morisco vassal worsened), the role of the *faqīh* (jurist) in Muslim community life, and the question of the Muslims' language. Nevertheless, great caution must be exercised in the application of the conclusions of Morisco studies. One must be wary of equating the Mudejars' status with that of the Moriscos and should take into account the modifications of the Muslims' position that conversion entailed. For instance, in the case of the Mudejars the mechanisms for acculturation were largely informal, whereas in the case of the Moriscos acculturation and assimilation were formal programs imposed from above by the royal and ecclesiastical authorities. In order to maintain their Islamic culture intact, the Moriscos were forced to take a more vehement anti-Christian stand both culturally and socially. The establishment of Catholicism as the norm governing cultural and social behavior gave the Old Christians (Christians without Muslim or Jewish ancestry) certain expectations as to how the Moriscos should conduct themselves. Failure to meet the Old Christians' expectations meant for the Moriscos social ostracism and Inquisitorial investigation. The Mudejars had been a social and religious minority; the Moriscos formed a marginal society, anomalous and anachronistic. The fundamental shift from a plural society, in which Islam was granted legal recognition and was an accustomed fixture on the social landscape, to a unitary Catholic society demanding conformity radically altered the state of Muslim–Christian relations. To see the particularly pointed hostility between Moriscos and Old Christians as indicative of the state of affairs before the conversion is to attach to the modus vivendi arrived at by Muslims and Christians after more than two centuries of coexistence the characteristics of a plural society rudely distorted.

In this study I have tried not to go over ground already expertly plowed by other scholars. Thus I have not treated in any detail matters such as the thirteenth-century Mudejar treaties, which can be found in Fr. Burns's works, or the basic Mudejar rights, which receive ample treatment in John Boswell's work.[8] However, a certain amount of repetition is unavoidable. Attention must be given to the organization of aljama government and to the taxation of the Mudejars, questions that are fundamental to an understanding of Mudejar life. And, as will be seen in chapters 3 and 4, even in areas such as these there was change from one century to the next, so that a careful reconsideration has considerable value. Likewise, chapter 5, which treats the operation of Islamic and Christian legal systems long in place, delineates more clearly than was hitherto possible how the two systems divided judicial labor and how the Muslims pursued justice in Christian courts.

Owing to the nature of the documentation available in the Archivo del Reino de Valencia, I have been able to explore some areas of Mudejar life that have been left largely untouched by scholars working in earlier centuries. By analyzing the Mudejars' role in the regional economy and their economic interaction with Christians of all walks of life, I have attempted to show that the economic basis for *convivencia* consisted of far more than the seigneurial exploitation of the Muslim masses. Moving further still from the model of colonial exploitation, I suggest how some Mudejars were able to adapt to fifteenth-century conditions and prosper by taking advantage of increased opportunities. I question the assumption of a continuous decline in the Mudejars' economic position since the thirteenth century and attempt to dispel the notion that fifteenth-century Mudejars and sixteenth-century Moriscos lived under the same material conditions.

The documentation has also made it possible for me to handle to some extent the more elusive problem of Mudejar family structure and social mores. In the final chapter I suggest that these structural factors were crucial for the Mudejars' maintenance of a Muslim identity and group cohesiveness. Extremely helpful in dealing with these matters was the work of Thomas F. Glick, who has shown how factors such as social structure and language act as cultural boundary-maintaining mechanisms that slow or impede the process of acculturation. Also, Pierre Guichard's study of the social structures of the Muslims of al-Andalus was essential for furthering my understanding of the behavior of the Mudejars.[9]

As has been suggested above, the reign of Fernando and Isabel presents special problems of its own. Not the least of these is how the Catholic Monarchs would treat their Muslim subjects while Aragon and Castile were engaged in crusades against the sultanates of Granada and North Africa and with the Ottoman Turks looming menacingly on the eastern horizon. Not since the thirteenth century did the crusade against Islam play such an important role in the history of the Spanish kingdoms. What this crusade would mean for the survival of Muslim-Christian coexistence in Aragon is one of the questions this study will attempt to answer.

1

Fernando II and the Mudejars: The Maintenance of Tradition

> *In the said year of 1481, the king Don Fernando and the queen Doña Isabel went with all their court to Aragon, Catalonia, and Valencia to be received as kings and lords of the land, and to take possession of those kingdoms and county of Barcelona. . . where they made for them very solemn receptions, and gave them very grand presents and gifts, both the councils of the cities and the knights and merchants, and the Jews and the Moors their vassals.*
> —*Andrés Bernáldez,* Memorias del reinado de los Reyes Católicos[1]

Anyone familiar with the history of Spain's religious minorities would recognize in Bernáldez's description of the Catholic Monarchs receiving homage from Christian, Jewish, and Muslim vassals a scene that the rulers of Aragon had been acting out for centuries. At the same time, the reader might suspect that the chronicler either was not privy to royal plans or was indulging in a bit of ironic foreshadowing, founding these suspicions on the knowledge that in little more than a decade Spain's plural society was to be abruptly and irrevocably transformed by the expulsion of the Jews in 1492, and then, a few years later, by the conversion or expulsion of the Muslims of Granada and Castile (1500–1502). Historians have interpreted these events, and the Monarchs' establishment of the Spanish Inquisition (1478–1483), as part and parcel of a preconceived plan to institute religious uniformity within the Spanish kingdoms. It is thought that the Catholic faith, with the Inquisition as its institutional arm, was utilized as a tool of the state to impose some semblance of unity on the otherwise diverse Crowns of Aragon and Castile.[2]

There was, however, one important exception to the sequence of conversion, Inquisition, and expulsion, namely, the large Muslim population dwelling in the lands of the Crown of Aragon, which maintained its dissident status throughout the reign of Fernando II (1479–1516). This suggests that Bernáldez's account was a matter-of-fact and accurate assessment of the Monarchs' real intentions toward the religious minorities in 1481. In other words, Fernando and Isabel, particularly the former in his own realms, did not have any plan to transform Spain's religiously plural society into a totalitarian Catholic state; rather, their minority policy was the sum of a series of responses to particular sets of circumstances and events as they unfolded. While it is true that the form these responses took was limited by certain fixed religious and political notions held by the Monarchs, there is a substantial difference between this admission and the postulate that they had a grand design for the transformation of Spanish society.

Still, there must be found a consistent thread unifying the discordant elements of the Monarchs' minority policy—establishing an Inquisition, expelling the Jews, converting or expelling the Muslims of Granada and Castile, and sanctioning the Muslims' continued presence in Aragon. This thread lies in the Monarchs' attempts to deal with the controversial problem of the neoconverts from Judaism (Conversos) and Islam (Moriscos). It was precisely this *converso* problem that added a new and destabilizing element to the already tense coexistence of Christian, Muslim, and Jew. The resolution of the problem demanded of Fernando and Isabel novel and extraordinary measures that ran counter to the general tone of their reign, characterized by recent scholarship as being marked much less by innovation and change than by the continuation of medieval traditions and the enforcement and extension of the legislation of their predecessors. The Monarchs' minority policy was a curious blending of the traditional with the innovative—and destructive.[3]

Until the eve of the expulsion the Monarchs continued the customary protection of the Jews and their communal autonomy. By themselves, the Jews did not present the Monarchs with a particular dilemma; it was the Jews' relations with the Conversos, or New Christians—ostensible Catholics, many of whom continued to practice Judaism—which caused them concern. So long as Jews were clearly distinguishable from Christians in terms of religious identity, Judaism was not perceived as a threat. However, when the boundaries between Jews and Christians became blurred, when black and white merged to form a large gray area, as had been the case since the forced baptism of approximately one-third of Sephardic Jewry in 1391, then Judaism acquired the character of a cancer threatening Christian society not from without, but from within. Therefore, the anti-Jewish measures taken by the Monarchs had as their primary goal the separation of Jews from Old and New Christians. In 1478 they reinaugurated the process of establishing a national Inquisition, an idea already conceived by Enrique IV of Castile, for the purpose of eradicating from Christian society those New Christians adhering to their ancestral faith. Fernando and Isabel enforced the legislation of the Castilian Cortes of 1480, calling for a stricter physical separation of Jews and Christians. In 1483 the Jews were expelled from Andalusia, where the problem of judaizing Conversos was most acute. The failure of these measures to terminate Converso judaizing, along with the contrived case of the Holy Child of La Guardia, in which the Inquisition supposedly proved that Conversos and Jews together had crucified a Christian child in the manner of Christ and engaged in necromancy to induce the downfall of Christianity, finally moved the Monarchs to pronounce the edict of expulsion in 1492. As Maurice Kriegel has concluded, one must take at face value the reason for the expulsion offered by the Monarchs: to prevent Judaism from further contaminating the faith of the New Christians.[4]

The essential difference between the Monarchs' Mudejar policy and their Jewish policy lay in the fact that until 1501 the complicating factor of a large number of Moriscos, Muslim converts to Christianity, did not exist. Because there was still no confusion between Muslim and Christian identities, and because Christianity was not menaced by an Islamic contamination, there was no pressing need to alter the traditional Mudejar policy. Fernando, as we shall see, encouraged Mudejarism in the lands of the Crown of Aragon throughout his reign. In contrast, the Mudejars of Castile were forced to convert or emigrate in 1502. While this difference may be explained in part by Isabel's greater intolerance, it was due primarily to the fact that in December, 1499, Cardinal Francisco Jiménez de Cisneros set in motion a train of events that resulted in the creation of a large body of Muslim converts in Granada. Although the Monarchs, especially Isabel, were responsible for sending Cisneros to Granada, they were not at all pleased with his hasty and violent methods of proselytizing. Nevertheless, as accepted theological opinion stipulated, the effects of baptism could not be erased. In essence, the Monarchs were now faced with the same dilemma the Jews and Conversos had presented: a large number of neoconverts dangerously straddling the chasm between Christian and non-Christian worlds. Instead of allowing for the coexistence of Muslims and Moriscos, an unacceptable alternative as the Converso problem had demonstrated, the Monarchs decided that all Muslims in Granada and Castile must become Christian or emigrate. Aragon's Mudejars were forbidden entry into Castile, lest they bring with them Islamic influences. It was hoped that in time the Moriscos would become sincere Christians. Similarly, after the *Germanías* of Valencia forcibly baptized a number of Mudejars (1521–1522), Carlos I followed the example set by his grandparents. By 1526 Aragon, too, had only a Morisco population.[5] As long as Christians, Muslims, and Jews remained in clearly definable socioreligious strata, religious pluralism continued to be a workable social formula in Spain. When, with the creation of substantial Converso and Morisco populations, the three strata seemed to merge into one, thereby bringing into question the very definition of Christian identity, all doubt and all possibility of religious alternative had to be removed for Spanish Christianity's own sake. The means of removal were Inquisition and expulsion.

Therefore, the Monarchs' treatment of the Jews and Conversos is of particular relevance to any consideration of royal Mudejar policy. That the treatment of the Muslims at the hands of Fernando and Isabel and their Hapsburg successors followed a pattern of forced baptism, Inquisition, and expulsion—closely paralleling the Jews' earlier experience— was not adventitious. The Monarchs' Mudejar policy was based not only on the legacy of Mudejarism bequeathed to them by their predecessors but also on the conclusions they themselves had reached after wrestling with the problem of the Jews and Conversos.

Tradition and Authority

As successor to the Crown of Aragon Fernando II inherited a longstanding tradition of Mudejarism, the royal sanctioning and protection of subject Muslim populations within Christian realms. The Mudejar pattern had been established in a series of surrender treaties reached between the Aragonese kings and the conquered Muslims of Aragon-Catalonia in the twelfth century (Zaragoza in 1118, Tudela in 1119, Tortosa and Lérida in 1148, Teruel in 1170, and so on), and, in the 1230s, was applied on a considerably larger scale in the new kingdom of Valencia by Jaime I. The treaties guaranteed to the Muslims their religious, judicial, and communal autonomy. In other words, the Mudejars could practice Islam, maintain their mosques with their adjoining properties (*waqf* endowments), rule on litigations between Muslims in Islamic courts according to Islamic law, and select their own officials for the governance and administration of their communities, or aljamas. The Muslims' sustenance was ensured by the terms allowing them to retain their homes, lands, and movable goods. By and large, the Crown consistently adhered to the capitulations, each king shrewdly balancing religious scruples with fiscal necessity. Mudejarism survived, not out of deference to an ideal of tolerance, but because the Muslims were valuable to the Crown as a source of taxation and as the agricultural and industrial substrata of local economies. This was especially the case in the kingdom of Valencia, where the Muslims always represented a substantial portion of the population, the majority, in fact, until the late fourteenth century.[6]

By the late fifteenth century the lands of the Crown of Aragon had experienced significant demographic change, so that in Aragon, Catalonia, and even Valencia the Christians formed a clear majority. Owing to recurrent plague, the wars between Aragon and Castile, Christian settlement, and Mudejar emigration, the Muslim proportion of the population had steadily diminished. During Fernando's reign the Muslims of Valencia constituted roughly 30 percent of the population, while in Aragon proper and Catalonia they formed only 20 percent and 1.5 percent, respectively.[7] Nevertheless, in Valencia, and to a lesser extent in Aragon, the Mudejars continued to play a vital economic role, and were viewed by both the king and the nobility as an important source of revenue. The royal–seigneurial competition to attract Muslim vassals to their respective lands, to be discussed at length in this chapter, bears out this assertion.

The large majority of Mudejars resided on seigneurial lands. There, local lords collected taxes and feudal dues from their Muslim vassals and exercised varying degrees of judicial authority over them. The Crown retained direct lordship over only a small number of urban aljamas. In Catalonia the royal aljamas were Tortosa and Lérida, and in Aragon they were Zaragoza, Huesca, Teruel, Daroca, Calatayud, Borja, Belchite, Albarracín, and Tarazona. In the kingdom of Valencia royal aljamas were located in Valencia, Játiva, Alcira, Murviedro, Castellón de la Plana, Villarreal, Alcoy, Jérica, Monforte, Onda, Liria, and Castellón de Játiva. Despite this distinction between royal and seigneurial Muslims—an important one, since it determined to whom the Mudejars paid their taxes—the Crown still possessed ultimate jurisdiction over all the Muslims in its realms. It was the Crown, in both Aragon and Castile, that decided the fate of its Muslims and Jews, variously converting them, expelling them, or defending their dissident status. As his predecessors had done, Fernando referred to the Mudejars as "our coffers," "our patrimony," or "servants of our chamber."[8] Under Fernando, royal supremacy in Mudejar affairs was more than a theoretical claim; it was a royal prerogative invoked and exercised.

With respect to his own Crown of Aragon, Fernando was an absentee ruler, spending less than three years in Aragon proper, just over three years in Catalonia, and only six months in the kingdom of Valencia. However, this did not prevent him from attending to the business of his kingdoms through a team of Catalan and Aragonese secretaries; in fact, he successfully strengthened royal authority at the expense of local powers. Fernando overcame strong local opposition in all of his kingdoms to institute a Crown-controlled Inquisition. He effectively imposed royal control over the principal cities of his realms, Zaragoza in Aragon, and Barcelona in Catalonia. In the city of Valencia the king exerted influence over the municipal government by appointing local magistrates, and he was able to exact substantial loans for royal enterprises, although with ruinous effect on the city's economy, as Ernest Belenguer Cebrià has shown. Still, ruling from a distance posed difficulties, causing delays in the royal response to local problems and necessitating a perhaps excessive reliance on the alacrity and diligence of local officials.[9]

In the kingdom of Valencia royal authority over the Mudejars was delegated to a handful of officials. The lieutenant general (*llochtinent general*), or viceroy, acted as the king's alter-ego and was invested with full royal power. While it may be assumed that the viceroys usually acted in the best interests of the Crown, at times their measures displayed an imprudence stemming from unfamiliarity with the local situation.[10]

Most important in Mudejar affairs was the bailiff general. Because he was the superintendent of the royal patrimony, of which the Mudejars formed a part, he exercised supreme authority over the kingdom's Muslims. All Muslims wishing to bear arms, beg for alms, travel within the kingdom or to Islamic lands, emigrate, borrow money, or practice prostitution were required to possess a license from the bailiff general. Any Muslims caught without such a license were summarily prosecuted. The bailiff general saw to it that Muslims paid their taxes and debts, or, conversely, pardoned them for debts and crimes. He supervised the sale of all Muslim slaves and captives, as well as their manumission. His court had criminal and often civil jurisdiction over all Muslims residing in royal *morerías* (Muslim quarters) and on the lands of the Church. In sum, the bailiff general was the executor of royal Mudejar policy, and, for the most part, his actions may be considered an accurate reflection of royal wishes. The holders of the bailiwick during Fernando's reign, Honorat Mercader (until 1485) and Diego de Torres (from 1485), seem to have fulfilled their duties conscientiously. Fernando sometimes relied on their expertise in Mudejar affairs when he formulated policy.[11]

Each royal city and town had a local bailiff to whom the bailiff general's powers were delegated. At the level of daily life, royal Mudejars dealt most frequently with this official. The bailiff functioned as the Muslims' judge and protector against the abuses of municipal govern-

ments, although at times Muslims suffered from the bailiff's own unscrupulous behavior. Thus, it was of utmost importance that the Mudejars
were able to turn to the bailiff general as a court of final appeal.[12]

The governor played a more limited role in Mudejar affairs. He was
competent to hear cases involving seigneurial Muslims, although the
lords themselves often administered justice to their vassals. A frequent
problem during Fernando's reign was the governor's attempts to over-
step the boundaries of his jurisdiction over Mudejars, which brought
him into conflict with the bailiff general. Although the governor at times
acted as the royal deputy regarding Mudejars, and his court had jurisdiction in specific Mudejar litigations, the general supervision of all
the kingdom's Muslims was always the bailiff general's special
prerogative.[13]

While Fernando's absenteeism compelled him to entrust considerable
power to these officials, it does not follow that he restricted his concerns
to only the broad contours of Mudejar policy. The king managed to find
time to attend to the particular grievances of his Muslim subjects as they
arose, and this was the case regarding seigneurial as well as royal vassals. Fernando's ability to intervene in seigneurial affairs is indicative of
the strength of royal authority and of its ultimate jurisdiction in matters
involving the religious minorities.

Individual seigneurial Muslims and entire aljamas, when wronged by
the nobility, would turn to the king for succor. Muslims who moved
from Chova to Eslida complained that the lord of Chova had violated
the governor's orders by seizing the fruits from their lands and other
possessions they still had in Chova. Fernando commanded the governor
to see to it that the Muslims' property was restored.[14] The lord of Malejám, in Aragon, received a royal order that he release the goods of his
Muslim vassals, who claimed that their lord had occupied their properties under the pretense of Malejám's entry into the *Hermandad*
(Brotherhood) of Borja.[15] The Christian councils and the aljamas of
Alcocer, Alberique, and Alasquer brought to the king's attention the
fact that their lord had altered the customary apportionment of irrigation water to their lands.[16]

Fernando's efforts to control the feuding of rival nobles tended to
benefit their Muslim vassals, who were often the victims of the nobles'
reciprocal depredations. When the Rocamoras murdered two Muslim
vassals of the Rocasfulls, Fernando tried to prevent further escalation of
the conflict by prohibiting the Rocasfulls from taking revenge on the
assailants. Instead, the governor of Orihuela was to apprehend and punish them.[17] In the dispute between the lords of Carlet and Alcudia and
their respective Muslim and Christian vassals, from which "wounds,
deaths, scandals, and evils" had already resulted, two royal officials

were sent to Carlet to punish the malefactors.[18] It is difficult to determine whether royal vigilance successfully curbed seigneurial feuding, or if it was always the case of the king demanding reparations for the broken bodies and destroyed property of the victims. Even if the latter were true, royal action still might work in favor of victimized Mudejars, as when Fernando commanded the governor of Aragon to see to the release of two Muslim prisoners whom the men of Argavieso had captured when they looted Novales.[19]

In general, Fernando's Mudejar policy can be described as a continuation of that of his predecessors. He envisaged no significant departures from the established precedent, and he readily confirmed the privileges granted to the various aljamas by previous kings. At the request of the aljama of Játiva, Fernando required his officials to observe the provisions of Alfonso V and Juan II, placing the *morería* under royal protection.[20] He confirmed the privileges and immunities his father had conceded to the aljama of Valencia as an aid to its recovery after the debacle of 1455,[21] and likewise ratified Juan II's creation of a *morería* in Alcoy,[22] and Juan's upholding of the rights of Daroca's Muslims to rent their butcher shop to a Christian and to graze their animals in surrounding pastures.[23]

In his governance of individual communities Fernando was guided by established usage, and he discouraged any innovations that local governments might wish to make. When the Christian council of Terrer planned to modify their arrangement with the local Muslims on the use and guarding of village common land without consulting the aljama, the king enjoined, "you should neither do nor innovate anything with respect to the abovesaid in derogation of their [the Muslims'] privileges, uses, and ancient customs observed between you and them; rather, you should maintain them."[24]

Fernando even found himself having to revoke his own enactments when he realized that they contravened those of his predecessors. He usually left the final ruling on such matters to the expertise of royal officials and lawyers versed in the local law. In the first year of his reign Fernando had provided that the *mustaçaff* of Játiva could inspect the weights and measures in the market of the local *morería*, a duty that normally pertained to its own *mustaçaff* (or *çalmedina*). When the aljama pointed out that this violated earlier privileges, and that a final decision on the question had been pending since 1428, the king ordered a return to the status quo prevailing before his provision.[25] He unwittingly raised other difficulties when he permitted the lord and Christians of Mislata to build their own oven, for Alfonso V had conceded to the Muslims of Mislata and their lord (the Muslims and the Christians had different lords) the exclusive privilege of possessing the town's oven.

Two years later, a compromise was reached through the offices of the governor and Valencian lawyers, allowing the Christians their oven, but forbidding Muslim access to it.[26]

A young king, particularly an absentee one, would have found the mastery of such intricacies of local custom one of the more difficult, and tiresome, aspects of royal administration. Although Fernando sometimes stumbled through a process of trial and error, his intention to tread on the path laid out by his forbears emerges clearly enough.

Augmenting the "Royal Treasure"

Fernando's exertion of monarchical power, his attention to detail, his accessibility to his aggrieved subjects of all faiths, and his deference to tradition all tell us more about Fernando as a leader and his style of rulership than about the specifics of his Mudejar policy. Given the importance of the issue of the religious minorities, for both Fernando's contemporaries and modern historians, it would be of significance to state simply that with respect to the Mudejars Fernando fully intended to maintain the status quo. This, however, was not quite the case, for from the outset the Catholic Monarch embarked on a program to augment substantially the populations of the royal *morerías* in the kingdom of Valencia. Implicit in the pursuit of such a program was Fernando's assumption that his Muslim subjects were a more or less permanent fixture on the Valencian and, by extension, Arago-Catalan scene.

Yet one must not attribute to Fernando any special enlightenment, nor should one presume that he had a moral stake in religious pluralism per se. Concretely, it boiled down to a matter of hard-nosed fiscal politics. By increasing the number of royal Muslim vassals Fernando was widening his own tax base. The Crown's financial needs were considerable, owing to Aragon's Italian entanglements and Castile's wars in Granada and Africa. Fernando's endeavor to augment his Mudejar treasure corresponds well with his exaction of numerous loans from the city of Valencia.

The royal program had three facets: (1) drawing Muslims away from seigneurial lands to royal *morerías*; (2) creating new *morerías* or instilling life into declining ones; and (3) settling Muslims from the conquered sultanate of Granada on Crown lands. All of these had precedents in the Mudejar policies of previous kings.[27] Because of the lack of detailed studies of this question for other reigns, it is difficult to say whether Fernando was any more avid or successful in his quest for taxable Mudejars.

Fernando was able to pursue the first course of action, inducing seigneurial Muslims to occupy royal *morerías*, because Mudejars could legally change their vassalage, moving from baron to king, from king to baron, or from one baron to another. However, on some seigneuries five or ten years of personal residence were required before the bonds of vassalage could be dissolved. In any case, the Mudejar was always someone's vassal. Unlike the Christian citizen and the urban corporation of the *universitas*, the Mudejar and his corporate aljama had no independent political status. The precondition to the Mudejar's dissolving the bonds of fealty to his lord was the settling of all accounts with the lord; that is, the Mudejar had to pay all feudal dues and whatever other debts he owed. Once this was done, the Mudejar could swear homage to his new lord, or king, promising to abide by the terms of the feudal relationship as stipulated by the lord. These terms were primarily of a fiscal nature. By the late fifteenth century Mudejar vassalage in Valencia was largely devoid of obligations of military service.[28]

Normally, the Muslim informed the bailiff general or the local bailiff of his desire to become a royal vassal. The bailiff would then see to it that the process of changing vassalage was expedited as smoothly as possible, mainly by instructing seigneurial officials to settle accounts justly with the departing vassal. For example, when Abdolaziz Abedua, a vassal in Tabernes de Valldigna, decided to move to the royal *morería* of Valencia, he informed the aljama officials there of his wish, and they then "presented" Abdolaziz to the bailiff general. The bailiff, treating the Muslim's change of vassalage almost as a fait accompli, wrote to the seigneurial officials of Valldigna "that [Abdolaziz] has been registered as vassal in the said *morería* [of Valencia] and is ready and prepared to settle accounts with you . . . And after he has settled accounts and has paid what he owes . . . he wishes to come and stay and live in this *morería* just as the other vassals of the said lord king." The bailiff was careful to remind these officials that Abdolaziz was now under royal safeguard and that he should be permitted not just to sell his property in Tabernes and liquidate his debts from the proceeds but also to collect any debts owed to him. For the bailiff the crucial point was that Abdolaziz, as a royal vassal, would be paying taxes to the Crown; hence, any failure to cooperate by Valldigna's officials would be tantamount to an assault on the royal patrimony. The bailiff concluded his letter with a warning: "if you should thus refuse to act, taking into account that the said Moor is being made a vassal of the said lord king, it will be necessary for us, for the preservation of the taxes of the said lord king . . . to provide on the matter as we determine ought to be done."[29]

Historians have assumed that the conditions of life in royal *morerías* were intrinsically better than those obtaining on seigneurial lands.[30] Yet it is not at all clear that this was the case, for, were it so, one would have expected the streets of royal *morerías* to have been inundated with new vassals. While a tendency for Mudejar movement from seigneurial to royal lands is discernible, it nowhere approached the proportions of a deluge. In terms of the Muslims' ability to make public manifestations of Islamic worship and to buttress their Islamic cultural integrity effectively, many probably preferred seigneurial *morerías* to royal towns. In the royal towns, even if the tax burden were lighter, Christian officialdom and clergymen tended to be touchier about ritual displays of Islam, and the Muslims' communal life suffered more from Christian interference or mere presence. The quality of Mudejar life on seigneurial lands varied from lordship to lordship, so that general comparisons between royal and seigneurial *morerías* are tenuous.

Because there were not large numbers of Mudejars clamoring for entry into royal towns, the Crown had to offer inducements to make vassalage to the king more appealing. In order to repopulate Alcira, Juan II had offered a royal safeguard against prosecution for crimes and debts to all Muslims, Christians, and Jews who would come to reside there.[31] Fernando followed his father's example, and, in order to fill the vacant Jewish quarter of Borja after the expulsion, freed new Muslim occupants from the tax of the *morabatí* for one year.[32] He granted to any Muslim who became a royal vassal in Játiva a ten-year exemption from the payment of the *besant*, or annual hearth tax paid by all Muslims. However, if the Muslim moved from Játiva before the expiration of the ten years, he then had to pay the *besants* for the years he had dwelled there.[33] Whereas in Aragon Fernando could legally threaten with penalty of death his Muslim vassals who were swearing homage to barons,[34] in Valencia his means of coercing Muslims to remain in royal *morerías* were limited to pecuniary penalties applicable during only the initial few years of their residence. Therefore, the king had to ensure that the circumstances of life in his *morerías* continued to be favorable. Herein lay the importance of the royal confirmation and protection of the privileges the Crown had previously conceded to royal aljamas. At the very least, Fernando had to prevent any encroachment on these privileges, for any marked deterioration in the Mudejars' situation could have as a consequence their abandonment of the royal *morerías*. Indeed, flight en masse was the Muslims' usual response to impossible tax burdens or to consistent harassment by local officials, and, of course, barons were more than willing to receive them on their lands.

A letter from the bailiff general to Fernando (1 March 1483) advising the king what measures he ought to take in the administration of his aljamas gives some sense of how delicately the king had to handle his Mudejar vassals. The aljama of Játiva had shown to the bailiff an order of Fernando (3 December 1482) establishing one royal mill that all local

Muslims would have to use. The king was hoping to earn 100 pounds annually from the rent of this utility. The bailiff delicately suggested that the king perhaps ought to reconsider, for when the construction of the royal mill recently commenced, so did the depopulation of the *morería*. The problem was that Fernando's measure contravened a privilege granted by Pedro III in 1283, which allowed the Muslims of Játiva to use whichever mill they pleased. Fernando's new mill would only serve to destroy and not to augment the royal patrimony. Besides, it would also be detrimental to the Minorite monastery that exercised lordship over the majority of Játiva's mills. In this same letter the bailiff reminded the king that the population of the *morería* of Alcira had increased from 25 to more than 100 households. Unfortunately, the municipal officials of Alcira were detracting from this achievement by forcing the Muslims to contribute to the *peyta*, in violation of the aljama's privileges. The bailiff recommended that Fernando put a stop to this activity, again in the interest of the royal patrimony. The bailiff added one final word of advice: "Because the counts, barons, and others who have vassals favor their vassals . . . much more ought to be favored the Moorish vassals of your Royal lordship."[35] In this competition between Crown and nobility for Muslim vassals the bailiff general recognized the necessity for prompt attention to Muslim grievances.

However eager the Crown might have been to acquire new Mudejar vassals, it still would not, and indeed, owing to seigneurial opposition, could not countenance the vassalage of Muslims still indebted to their former lords. Thus, when it was discovered that Azmet Ballester, a royal vassal in Alcira, owed his former lord, Pere Bosch, 30 pounds, the bailiff general ruled that Azmet and his wife Johar should be relinquished to Bosch if they could not pay. Muslims in the position of Azmet were considered to have committed the crime of "flight," for which the *Furs* demanded punishment.[36]

Because the system allowed Muslims to state their intention of becoming royal vassals before actually settling accounts, some, burdened by heavy debts to their lords, took advantage of that system and simply abandoned seigneurial lands, with the hope that by enlisting the support of royal officials unaware of their financial status they could evade their noble creditors. Ali Gombau, a vassal of and tax farmer for Don Joan de Vallterra in Areñol, escaped from Areñol without having squared accounts with Vallterra and became a royal vassal in Castellón de la Plana, successfully evading prosecution for almost one year.[37] Such abuses elicited loud complaints from the nobility in the Valencian Corts of 1488, resulting in legislation prohibiting the abandonment of seigneurial lands by Muslim debtors.[38] Nevertheless, the problem recurred. In 1492 the lords of Sellent, Cuart, and Turís protested that their Muslim vassals had departed insolvent, and that the local bailiffs had the temerity to demand that they come to town to settle accounts with their own fugitive vassals.[39]

At times Mudejars proved to be quite cunning, and criminally so, in their exploitation of the right to change vassalage. Juçef Çabot hoped literally to get away with murder by leaving Valldigna and becoming a royal vassal in Játiva. He returned to the valley, stabbed to death a Muslim enemy there, and then, as a royal vassal, sought the protection of the bailiff general.[40] With less sanguinary thoughts, Muslims of the barony of Torres Torres became royal vassals in Murviedro but continued to reside on the barony. Not only was the baron unable to collect feudal dues from them, but also, when the Muslims committed crimes or created disturbances on the barony, they were protected by the jurates (councillors) of Murviedro and took refuge in the court of the governor. Worse still, other vassals of the baron, realizing that while in this state of legal limbo they could disobey the baron with impunity, were swearing fealty to the king in Murviedro.[41]

It may be that local Crown officials and townsmen, motivated by economic interest and hostility toward the nobility, connived at bringing seigneurial Muslims to their lands and towns. Fernando had to rail at and threaten with deprivation of office unscrupulous royal officials who "with the favor and authority of [their] offices" were transferring Muslims from royal *morerías* to their own lands. He declared that royal Mudejars could not be received into other lordships until they had spent at least four years on royal lands.[42] This final stipulation suggests that the officials were directing their persuasive efforts at new royal vassals. Ultimately, seigneurial lands, the source of the new vassals, received the most damage.

Still, a much greater problem was seigneurial resistance to the Mudejars' legal change of vassalage. The departure of vassals was, of course, detrimental to the lord's finances, and this was especially the case in fifteenth-century Valencia, where a scarcity of labor, due to the toll taken by recurrent plagues, rendered each vassal a still more valuable asset. Two additional considerations explain why the lords felt these losses so keenly. First, those Muslims who could afford to take up residence in royal *morerías*, that is, those who possessed the wherewithal to pay all their dues and debts, were men of means, at least in comparison to those Muslims rendered immobile by insolvency. The lords, therefore, were being deprived of some of their most reliable and, one might presume, enterprising rent-payers. Second, when a Muslim transferred his fealty and residence from a barony to a royal town he did not thereby relinquish rights to the lands he rented in the barony. In Valencia there was a crucial distinction between the status of tenant and that of vassal. This meant that the new royal vassal, living and working in town, could continue to cultivate and reap the fruits from the lands he still rented on the estate of his former lord. He was obliged to pay to his former lord only the rent required of a tenant. He was now freed from the feudal dues incumbent on a vassal; these he now paid to the Crown. Consequently, the erstwhile lord was faced with the long-term occupation of his lands by absentee tenants who paid rent but not the more lucrative seigneurial dues. He was thus unable to exploit his lands to their maximum potential.

Taking into account these factors, it is not difficult to comprehend why the lords were so intent on preventing their vassals from altering their status. Seigneurial opposition on this score was not a problem peculiar to Fernando's reign; lords had been placing obstacles in the way of Mudejar transference to royal *morerías* throughout the fifteenth century. Fernando's efforts to remove such obstacles scarcely differed from those of Alfonso V and Juan II. Regarding the protection of new Muslim vassals in Castellón de la Plana and Alcoy, he simply reissued their commands.[43] Although it seems that the Crown was usually able to overcome seigneurial resistance, the lords, through a variety of tactics, often made the Mudejars' change of vassalage a long and litigious process. The officials of the lord of Valldigna, the Cardinal of Valencia, tried to nip the entire matter in the bud by proclaiming that any Muslim who was a vassal in the valley and then became a vassal of another lord, including the king, had to revert to his original status within eight days or lose all of his property in the valley. The bailiff promptly disabused these officials of the idea that they could enforce such a decree.[44]

Because the settling of accounts was the precondition to the Muslim's final release from vassalage to his lord, the first tack taken by the latter was to avoid the vassal trying to discharge his debts. Don Franger Ladro, seigneur of Turís, gave to Yuçeff Jacob b. Çahat the lame excuse that he did not have his account book with him. The Crown countered by notifying Don Franger that the 40s Yuçeff owed were being deposited with the bailiff general's office and that he could collect it only after he released Yuçeff's goats, wheat, and beehives to a Crown official.[45] At times evasion hardened and took crueler forms. When Abdalla Lopo went to Cuart to settle accounts with the Countess d'Aversa, he was imprisoned and physically abused.[46]

The lords' second line of resistance, once all accounts had been squared, was to hinder the new royal vassals from tilling and harvesting the lands they were still renting in the lordships. Some argued, perhaps justifiably so, that, according to the privileges attached to their lordship, tenants had to reside there personally.[47] It would follow that the Muslim resident in a royal *morería* thereby forfeited all rights to his lands. Other lords dispensed with the legal niceties. The officials of Mislata tried to force a Muslim widow to pay feudal dues on the house and property she possessed there, knowing full well that she was a royal vassal in Valencia.[48] Çahat Atzuar returned to Mascarell to cultivate his lands, only to discover that other vassals had since occupied them.[49] Açen b. Maymo Jaffiol had worse luck. Instead of being allowed to attend to his properties, he was imprisoned and had 60 pounds extorted from him by the lord of the Vall d'Artana.[50] In all three cases the bailiff general invoked the rights of the Muslims as royal vassals and demanded that the lords in question permit them to dispose of their properties as they wished.

The effects of such seigneurial aggression ramified beyond the lives of individual lords and Muslims and aggravated the tensions between the citizenry of royal towns and the neighboring nobility. Some towns welcomed the arrival of new Mudejar inhabitants, hoping that their enterprise would benefit the local economy. The citizens resented and resisted the unscrupulous measures taken by the lords against their former vassals. In effect, the general royal–seigneurial competition for Muslim vassals manifested itself at the local level in a tug-of-war between the nobility and the urban folk. The issue of Mudejar vassalage, only one of several that would lead to the antiseigneurial violence of the *Germanías* (1519–1522), by itself had the potential to cause considerable disorder. When the lord of Bechí imprisoned the wives and confiscated the goods of Muslims residing in Castellón de la Plana in an attempt to convince the anxious husbands to return to Bechí, the jurates of Castellón beseeched the bailiff general to intervene, and added that if he did not, the people of Castellón would themselves march on Bechí. They further pointed out that Murviedro and other royal towns, as well as Castellón, were already accustomed to taking into their own hands the correction of barons and knights.[51]

Fernando was fully aware of the blackmail of his Muslim vassals by lords struggling to maintain the financial equilibrium of their estates, and he seems to have understood its wider implications in the trajectory of the conflict between town and landed nobility. It probably was not a mere coincidence that during precisely the same month when the above tensions arose between Castellón and the lord of Bechí, Fernando commanded all officials, royal and seigneurial as well, to observe the provisions of Alfonso V and Juan II meant to curb the barons' misdeeds in the area.[52] He also issued a directive to all royal bailiffs in the kingdom regarding the appropriate response to the problem of seigneurial resistance:

we understand that by some barons and others in the kingdom of Valencia who have Sarracen vassals there is attempted this oppression and iniquity, namely, that after someone who was previously their vassal departs from the said barons and knights and comes to live and, at the same time, becomes a vassal in the said *morería* of Játiva or another royal [*morería*], they [the barons] seizing them or their lands, do not allow such vassals, presently ours, to return to their lands and possessions nor to cultivate their lands and to procure and receive the fruit.

Fernando continued, emphasizing that such actions could "result in the prejudice and damage of our *morerías* and of the royal curia," and he concluded by ordering the bailiffs to see to it that the seigneurs, on pain (penalty) of 1,000 gold florins, allow their erstwhile vassals to attend to the lands that they were still renting from them.[53] Later, the king made a point of expressing to the representatives of the military estate his displeasure at their treatment of Muslims wishing to become royal vassals.[54]

The pattern of landholding prevalent in Valencia, where the farmer rented small parcels in a number of localities, both royal and seigneurial, was a source of uncertainty as to whom any particular tenant was bound as a vassal.[55] Also, because vassals, by virtue of their dispersed landholdings, might have economic interests in other communities, their respective lords frequently conflicted while pursuing their vassals', and therefore their own, interests. Fernando asserted monarchical power on behalf of Muslims of Játiva when he learned that seigneurial vassals, both Muslim and Christian, were indebted to them. The bailiff was instructed to demand payment from the lords of the debtors in question, and, that failing, to confiscate enough of the debtors' property to satisfy the creditors.[56] Another document demonstrates that Fernando was less concerned with the welfare of his Muslim vassals per se than with filling his own purse. In response to the lords who were collecting feudal dues from royal Mudejars renting lands on their estates, the king, rather than simply putting a stop to this activity, decided to exact royal taxes from seigneurial Muslims farming Crown lands. The seemingly twisted logic Fernando employed in explanation of his decision—"so that our Sarracen vassals do not enjoy less prerogatives or rights than vassals of whatever persons, nay rather let them be treated equally"—is actually quite transparent.[57] The king and the seigneurs remained on an equal footing, while the vassals of both were fleeced.

Throughout the fifteenth century the kingdom of Valencia as a whole, the city of Valencia being a notable exception, suffered from chronic underpopulation. In the latter half of the century the population steadily diminished, a consequence of recurring epidemics of plague.[58]

As suggested above, this factor enhanced the rivalry between Crown and nobility for the labor of Mudejar vassals. One Crown response to underpopulation, which added to this royal–seigneurial rivalry, was the attempt to reconstruct and repopulate towns particularly devastated by pestilence. The Mudejars, renowned for their skill and energy as farmers and artisans, were integral to some of these reconstruction plans. In 1468 Juan II endeavored to resuscitate the town of Alcoy, the population of which had been halved from 600 to less than 300 households. At the request of its Christian council, Juan provided for the construction of a *morería* with 100 houses and a mosque. The council hoped that Mudejars would occupy and rebuild the homes in disrepair, and buy land in the area, thereby increasing property values. The king was, as always, attracted by the prospect of an increment in his revenue.[59]

Fernando's establishment of a Muslim aljama in Castellón de Játiva was motivated by much the same interests, although this time it was not done at the request of the town's Christian populace, who, nevertheless, in no way objected to the royal project. In the document detailing the creation of the aljama the king's fiscal concerns emerge quite clearly: "Just as other men strive to promote whatever is useful for them and to drive away misfortunes, so it is fitting that kings and princes occasionally seek ways of preserving and augmenting their patrimony and employ a method by which the increase of benefits is directed more easily to it." He pointed out that since "mortalities and other adversities" had reduced Castellón's population from four hundred to only ninety households, a new aljama would be just the thing to revitalize the town while replenishing the "revenues and profits for our patrimony."[60] Fernando was careful to attend to the necessities of the nascent Muslim community: the setting aside for it of a special part of town called "Lo Pedro," the constitution of its corporate aljama, the annual election of an *amīn* and *adelantats*, the establishment of a special Muslim butcher shop, and, of course, the taxes the inhabitants would have to pay to the Crown. In sum, the new aljama was to enjoy the same privileges and immunities as the aljama of Játiva.[61] The king also appointed a bailiff for the *morería*, Pere Caldes, who, like other bailiffs, would administer civil and criminal justice in cases involving the *morería*'s residents (although not in civil suits between Muslims) and see to the collection of taxes.[62]

Fernando shrewdly stipulated that all new Muslim residents must pay a fee of 50s for right of entry or vassalage, and that they could not transfer to Castellón from other royal *morerías* without royal license.[63] The newcomers, then, would not be destitute, and the populations of the other royal *morerías* would be maintained. The losers in this scheme would be the nobles of the region of Játiva.

As we might expect by now, the new aljama had its growing pains.

First, it was revealed that Christians owning homes in the part of town designated for the *morería* were taking advantage of the royal project and asking exorbitant prices for them. Concerned that potential Muslim buyers might be scared off, Fernando instructed royal and local officials to determine suitable sale prices.[64] The seigneurs in the area proved to be as troublesome as ever. Muslim residents of Castellón were prevented from picking the leaves from their mulberry trees in Alcocer; instead, the leaves, essential for the raising of silkworms, were taken by Muslim vassals of the lordship.[65] The knight Perot de Castellvi accused Ali Mançor of having abandoned his lordship, Benimuslem, for Castellón without settling accounts. After the bailiff general ruled on the suit in Ali's favor, Castellvi turned Ali's family problems to his own advantage. Apparently Ali's wife had been reluctant to move from Benimuslem and had demanded that her husband hand over her bridewealth. Ignoring the bailiff, who had jurisdiction in a case involving a royal vassal, Castellvi turned to the governor, who then had 100 head of Ali's sheep confiscated on behalf of Castellvi and Ali's wife.[66]

Establishing a new aljama was a risky business. There was the distinct possibility that it would sink into the existing welter of competing interests and jurisdictions. The following case, in which Castellón's bailiff, Pere Caldes, found himself in jail, is suggestive of this danger. Problems began when Mahomat Bonafort appeared before Caldes requesting to be made a vassal in Castellón. Caldes could permit this only after he, acting on Mahomat's behalf, and the lieutenant governor "beyond the Júcar River" had agreed on a settlement regarding Mahomat's wounding of another seigneurial Muslim. Despite the settlement, the lieutenant governor still attempted to have Mahomat seized, but Caldes, who was protecting Mahomat in his own house, would not allow it, pointing out that Mahomat, now a royal vassal, fell under only the bailiff's jurisdiction. Unfortunately, Luis Ferrer, the lieutenant governor of the entire kingdom, got wind of the affair. It so happened that the Muslim whom Mahomat had wounded was the vassal of one of Ferrer's relations. Ferrer complained to the bailiff general about Caldes, but to no avail. Later, when Caldes went to Játiva to pay the remainder of the settlement, the lieutenant governor threw him in jail and then proceeded to Castellón. There he and his men broke into Mahomat's house and made an inventory of the property they intended to confiscate on behalf of one of Mahomat's creditors. Worse still, when the other Muslim residents of Castellón witnessed these events they became very uneasy and began wondering about their own security, while other Muslims intending to move there changed their minds.[67] Eventually the matter was set right, and the new aljama managed, if not to prosper, at least to survive.

Whatever success Juan II and his son might have had in forming the new aljamas of Alcoy and Castellón de Játiva, it is doubtful if the income derived from these aljamas offset the losses sustained by the Crown in 1455 when the *morería* of the capital was sacked and largely depopulated. Valencia's Muslims had been notable for their prosperity and commercial activity. In the first half of the fifteenth century of the 170 Mudejar merchants conducting business with the sultanate of Granada, 118 were from the capital.[68] In contrast, during the years 1479–1491, of the 32 Mudejars engaged in commerce with Granada and North Africa, only seven were residents of Valencia's struggling *morería*, and three of these were agents of the powerful Bellvis family.[69] Juan II had attempted to rebuild and repopulate the *morería* by enjoining the aljama's creditors to reduce the amounts the aljama owed, and by permitting the aljama to pay to the Crown a simple annual lump sum of 25 pounds instead of the usual royal taxes. Fernando followed suit and confirmed the privileges conceded by his father.[70] Their efforts were not futile, for there is evidence that the *morería* attracted new vassals during Juan's reign,[71] and under Fernando between thirty and forty Mudejars took up residence there. However, the aljama never regained its former prosperity, since artisans had replaced the long-distance merchants.[72]

Because there simply were not enough bodies to populate both baronies and royal towns sufficiently, the Crown's policy of promoting the growth of its own aljamas could, after all, have only limited success, and since the new royal vassals were acquired from seigneurial lands, that policy could not be pursued too aggressively lest the nobility be dangerously alienated. Of course, the fluctuations of population were out of the king's control and depended on biological and epidemiological factors. However, the conquest of the sultanate of Granada presented Fernando with a situation in which he could direct the fate and, more importantly, the settlement of a large conquered Muslim population. As a means of preventing the complete ruination of Granada's economy, Fernando and Isabel reproduced the Mudejar pattern throughout the conquered sultanate. The large majority of Granada's Muslims remained in their homes as the vassals of the Crown of Castile and Castilian lords. Yet Fernando managed to secure some Granadans as vassals of his own Crown of Aragon.

More than three years before the conquest of the sultanate was completed Fernando began permitting the entry of Granadan Muslims into the Christian kingdoms as royal vassals. Some of these early immigrants, from Almería and Baza, seem to have been Fernando's agents. The Almerians, at least, expressed their fear of the sultan and of the city's other Muslims, probably on account of their own treachery.[73] At the request of the *faqīh* of Valencia's aljama, who hoped to expedite the escape of his relations from Almería before its fall, Fernando conceded a safe-conduct to the *faqīh*'s sister-in-law and niece, "and all their family and company . . . to come to live in our city of Valencia and become our vassals."[74]

The majority of the immigrants came from Vera and Almería, the part of the sultanate closest to Valencia. It was with these cities, especially Almería, that the Mudejars had maintained the most extensive commercial and family ties.[75] Fernando even went so far as to allow Muslims from Vera, who had first emigrated to Oran, to return and become royal vassals in Valencia.[76] Other immigrants originated from Málaga, Baza, and Granada itself.[77]

The Granadans settled in a variety of localities. Some made their new homes in royal *morerías*, such as Játiva, Alcira, Valencia, and Calatayud in Aragon.[78] Others became seigneurial vassals and joined the aljamas of Manises, Novelda, Elche, Bétera, Valldigna, Cocentaina, and others. The majority of the latter were captives from Málaga who had first been sold in the kingdom as slaves and subsequently were ransomed by the seigneurial aljamas.[79]

On occasion Fernando settled the Granadan Muslims in specific locations. He rewarded his bailiff "beyond the Jijona River" with a number of Muslim households to populate lands the latter possessed near Orihuela. These Muslims were not slaves, for they made a feudal contract with their new lord, promising to remain on his lands as vassals for a period of five years.[80] Still, in general, the king was content with the fact that the Muslims had come voluntarily to live in his kingdoms and was not too particular as to where they settled. In one instance, Queen Isabel bade the bailiff general to place Muslims from Vera on the lands of the Cardinal of Valencia: "work with them [the Muslims] in a manner that they accept their residence in the said baronies and in no other area."[81] One month later Fernando countermanded his wife's order, instructing the bailiff not to force the Muslims to live on the Cardinal's lands, but to allow them to settle where they wished, preferably "in our royal cities and lands rather than in any [other] lands."[82] In another case, the councillors of Montalbán had requested that the king send Muslims to settle in their town, but Fernando wrote them that his hands were, in effect, tied, "inasmuch as in their submission to our obedience we promised them and gave them freedom to go where they wish and, thus, for the sake of justice, they cannot be forced to live in some place against their will."[83]

Of course, there were strings attached, namely, that wherever a Granadan Muslim chose to settle he would have to pay the accustomed taxes, just like the other Mudejars of Valencia. When some Almerians maintained that the king had granted them exemptions from these taxes, Fernando replied, "we are surprised that they would claim such a thing, because we never would grant them anything that was contrary to the taxes of that kingdom."[84] The royal "milch cows" might graze where they liked, but they still had to produce milk.

It is extremely difficult to assess how many Granadan Muslims were incorporated into Valencia's Mudejar population. It is unlikely that their numbers were very great. Those Granadans unable to endure Christian rule would have emigrated to the Maghrib, and those who remained in Granada did so because of their attachment to their still recognizably Islamic homeland. Valencia, long transmogrified by a Christian impress, offered them little attraction. Only after Cisneros set in motion a sequence of rebellions and more or less forced conversions (1499–1502) would Valencia have appeared a haven, but by then it was too late, for the kingdom of Granada had been effectively cordoned off from the territories of the Crown of Aragon. The Granadan Muslims who made their way to Valencia did so either because they had kinfolk there, as was the case with a number of Almerians, or because they came in through the back door as slaves who, once ransomed, stayed on, or as refugees who were disenchanted with life in the Maghrib and could not return home.[85] Whatever their numbers, the salient point is that Fernando was willing to accept them as vassals. With one eye on his purse and the other on the example of his forbears, the king concluded that the perpetuation of Mudejarism had its benefits.

With both Crown and nobility, including ecclesiastical prelates, striving to maintain the population and productivity of their lands, Mudejar emigration to North Africa was correspondingly restricted and usually completely prohibited. When Mudejars were permitted to emigrate, they had to pay a passage duty of 13s 4d. Jewish emigrants paid far less, only 3s 4d, which reflects the greater economic importance of the Muslims in Valencia.[86]

Emilia Salvador has traced the increasing stringency of the emigration policy from the time of the thirteenth-century conquest until the midsixteenth century. The ten-year suspension on the issuance of emigration licenses enacted by Pedro IV at the request of the Corts (1370) became a perpetual prohibition under Martin I (1403). No doubt demographic change and a diminishing labor supply were considerations guiding the imposition of these restrictions. In the Corts of 1488 Martin's prohibition was reiterated.[87]

Despite such prohibitions, monarchs sometimes, in individual cases, conceded licenses for emigration or permitted the bailiff general to do so. This was a means of getting ready cash from the passage duties the Muslims had to pay. Juan II (1477) allowed the bailiff general to issue licenses, as did Fernando at the outset of his reign.[88] In 1486 this was still described as one of the bailiff general's duties.[89] Other officials who licensed Mudejars to emigrate were reprimanded for having encroached on the bailiff's special prerogative.[90] It seems that even after the Corts of 1488 the bailiff continued to grant emigration licenses, for which reason the military estate expressed considerable dismay.[91] Valencian Muslims who could not cross to the Maghrib from the port of Valencia might have been able to do so through Tortosa in Catalonia.[92] Before 1498 there is no record of how many Mudejars emigrated to the Maghrib, and after 1498 none of the emigrés were Valencians.[93] In any case, by 1492 Fernando had definitely deprived the bailiff general of the prerogative of licensing Mudejar emigration. Consequently, the bailiff's lieutenant had to be compensated for the revenues he had been receiving for his labors in the emigration procedures.[94] In 1493 the king expressly forbade the emigration of a rich Muslim of Játiva.[95] There is little other indication in the documentation that Valencia's Mudejars desired to emigrate. This became the case only during the troubled years after 1500.[96] Even if emigration had been desired, it was only infrequently permitted. It would have made little sense for the king to have exerted such effort to attract Mudejar vassals only to allow them to slip through his fingers.

The criterion by which the success of Fernando's program to augment the population of royal aljamas may be evaluated is the degree to which the aljamas grew. The *besant* lists of certain royal aljamas (the *besant* was the hearth tax paid annually by each Muslim household) allow for an assessment of the aljamas' population size on a yearly basis. It should be pointed out, however, that the *besant* lists have only a relative value. Not all Mudejars paid the *besant*; some were excused for reason of poverty, and others, as in Játiva, were exempted for a number of years as an inducement to their becoming royal vassals. Of course, the Crown was mainly interested in those Muslims who could pay their taxes. Population increase need not have been due to immigration; it might have been merely the result of other demographic factors, in the case of the *besant*, the departure of adult children from their parents' home to their own dwelling in the same *morería*. Likewise, population decrease was not necessarily caused by the flight of Mudejars to seigneurial lands, but by the normal rate of mortality or by an abnormally high rate due to plague.[97]

Taking these factors into consideration, the *besant* lists suggest that Fernando's program had moderate success (see table 1). The *morerías* of Alcira, Castellón de la Plana, Murviedro, and Monforte all show an increase in population, but without any extraordinary surges forward. From other sources, we know that at least six seigneurial Muslims joined the aljama of Liria, with the same number taking up residence in

Table 1. Besant *Lists*

Year	Alcira[a]	Castellón de la Plana[b]	Mur- viedro[c]	Játiva[d]	Mon- forte[e]	Castellón de Játiva[f]
1479	81	28	—	446	25	—
1480	83	28	—	—	25	—
1481	77	28	—	—	28	—
1482	58	30	—	—	—	—
1483	—	30	13	—	—	—
1484	—	30	10	—	25	—
1485	—	30	—	—	25	—
1486	—	30	9	—	25	—
1487	—	30	7	—	25	—
1488	92	30	8	—	25	—
1489	101	27	8	—	25	—
1490	102	27	—	356	30	—
1491	109	27	10	—	30	—
1492	112	29	10	—	—	—
1493	97	27	10	341 (out of 384)	—	—
1494	105	28	9	346	—	15
1495	116	30	5	353	—	15
1496	103	30	5	353	—	13
1497	103	32	11	—	—	—
1498	91	32	21	340	—	10
1499	92	41	21	—	—	—
1500	93	48	21	325	—	—
1501	93	43	21	—	—	7
1502	93	47	21	321	—	8
1503	93	45	—	—	—	—

[a] ARV: MR 942–960.
[b] ARV: MR 2469–2491.
[c] ARV: MR 4016–4034.
[d] ARV: MR 3052–3062.
[e] ARV: MR 4567–4574.
[f] ARV: MR 3052–3062.

Villarreal, and at least thirty Muslims doing so in Valencia's *morería*.[98]
Valencia, as a commercial center with a growing and dynamic population, held obvious attraction for the ambitious Mudejar. Although some
Mudejars moved to Valencia from considerable distances, the usual pattern was for the Mudejar to move to a royal *morería* near his former
place of residence. This allowed him to attend more easily to landholdings and other business interests concentrated within a specific region.
The one important exception to the success of Fernando's program was

the aljama of Játiva, the largest in the kingdom. It seems to have experienced a steady decline in population, to which the oppressive administration of the local bailiff likely contributed (see below). Plague also seems to have played a role. Given the kingdom's overall decline in population, the resistance of lords to their vassals' change of status, and the varied circumstances militating against a Mudejar's mobility (insolvency, preference of seigneurial lands for the comparative isolation they afforded Muslim communities, and so on), it was no small achievement that Fernando had any success at all in augmenting the population of his aljamas.

Protecting the "Royal Treasure"

Historians have emphasized the solicitude of Aragon's kings, and of their bailiff generals, for protecting their Muslim subjects. While the efficacy of royal protection is itself debatable, still more troubling is the avoidance of the question of why Mudejars so often felt compelled to turn to the king for aid against their oppressors.[99] Many of the difficulties Mudejars experienced derived from their membership in a turbulent and conflictive Valencian society, and, lacking comparative data for other social groups, it would be risky to posit that Muslims necessarily suffered more than Christians or Jews. Nevertheless, it is equally true that much of the hardship Mudejars endured inhered in their peculiar status as Muslims in a Christian society.

Modern observers would deplore the fact that the Mudejar was not, in either juridical, political, or social terms, on an equal footing with his Christian counterpart. The Mudejar, however, did not expect parity in treatment any more than did the Christian and Jewish *dhimmī*s in Islamic societies; nor did he strive to effect social change or to achieve social advancement, for not even substantial wealth could alter his inferior status vis-à-vis Christian society. The price the Mudejar paid, and was willing to pay, for his adherence to Islam was social inferiority and a lack of political status or power. Although Mudejar inequality was not an issue in fifteenth-century Valencia, the terms on which that inequality was based were, for the Mudejar, the source of numerous problems.[100]

Muslim survival in Valencia had been founded on a series of surrender treaties reached between the conquered Muslims and King Jaime I of Aragon. Every right the Mudejar enjoyed—the ability to practice Islam, own property, and so on—was set forth in a specific royal privilege or concession. There was no higher law guaranteeing the permanence of Mudejar existence or their enjoyment of particular rights; all depended on the royal will, at times quite capricious, and privileges could be as easily withdrawn as confirmed. The only source of protection for the Mudejars against the aggressions of nobles, clergy, local officialdom, or the Christian mob was the king. The king confirmed privileges and provided protection not because he was morally bound to do so—indeed, purely religious considerations advised against this course of action—but because the Mudejars' assiduous toil was beneficial for the kingdom's economy. Crown, nobility, clergy, and urban oligarchies all suffered the Muslims' presence out of economic interest, and all expected to profit from it. Although Mudejar vassals were sought after and the competition for them sometimes ameliorated the conditions of their vassalage, they were nevertheless perceived by their lords primarily as exploitable labor. If the Mudejars did not produce, there was nothing else, and least of all their religious affiliation, to justify their presence. If revenue could not be squeezed out of the Mudejar legally, then the interested parties were quick to resort to methods of extortion. Because the Mudejar professed an inferior religion, the Christian offender experienced little compunction for his crimes. Royal protection of the Mudejar rarely entailed the punishment of the culprit. Usually only restitution of the victim's property was demanded, which underlines the economic aspect of the problem, for restoring to the Mudejar what he had lost ultimately redounded to the benefit of the Mudejar's lord, either king or nobleman. The Mudejar, as individual or corporate aljama, was not really the main concern.

Valued as a dependable source of labor and conspicuous by virtue of their faith, the Mudejars tended to suffer acutely from the kingdom's socioeconomic dislocations. Thus, when labor was scarce, the Mudejars were more sought after by nobles and royal towns, but being the object of their rivalry also meant that they were frequently the victims of injury by the antagonistic parties. Either guarded as a precious resource despite the fact they were Muslims, or subject to the brutalities and extortions of a Christian majority because they were infidels, the Mudejars' position was a precarious one.

We have seen, regarding the issue of Mudejar vassalage, that the disputes between towns and neighboring lordships could become quite heated. Municipal governments and noblemen might clash for any number of reasons,[101] and in each case the interests of the local inhabitants, both Christian and Muslim, were implicated. Rights to land and water usage were vital questions. Alcira's modifications of the irrigation system that served it and the adjacent baronies in favor of the landowners of its own *huerta* prompted complaints from the councils and aljamas of Alberique, Alcocer, and Alasquer.[102] The effort of Don Manuel Lançol, lord of Gilet, to appropriate lands located within the boundaries of Murviedro was the cause of considerable hostility between the Christians of Murviedro and Don Manuel's Muslim vassals, taking the form of a breakdown in trade between Gilet and Murviedro and much "murmuring" on both sides.[103] The competence of municipal officials to collect taxes from seigneurial vassals in the surrounding countryside was also a point for debate. Orihuela's collection of the *sisa del carn* (sales tax on meat) from the vassals of Albatera raised objections from their lord.[104]

Hypothetically, Muslims should not have been affected any more than Christians by these disputes between town and nobility, for the matters of controversy—rights to land and water and to taxation—had little to do with the Mudejars' status as Muslims or as vassals of a particular lord. However, because Mudejars were so highly valued as vassals, the disputants seem to have reasoned that the most effective way of inflicting damage on one's opponent, and thereby lending weight to one's own argument, was to proceed immediately against the persons or property of the opponent's Muslims (a royal town's Muslims would have been royal vassals). This reasoning was given greater force by the Christians' disdain for the Mudejar as an infidel, by the inability of a minority to resist the majority's perpetration of outrage,[105] and by the Christians' confidence that for a crime against a Muslim punishment, if ever doled out, was unlikely to be severe. Thus, when the officials of Gandía arbitrarily raised the amount of the *sisa* they collected from the lordships located within the town's general limits, their first act was the confiscation of Azmet Vaquel's two mules as security for the payment of the *sisa*.[106] During their ongoing controversy with the lord of Gilet, the jurates of Murviedro violently threatened to exact the *peyta* from his Muslim vassals.[107] The officials of the barony of Corbera attempted to settle whatever scores they had with Alcira by making off with goats from the aljama's flock,[108] and by waylaying and robbing a Muslim transporting his olives from Alcira to a nearby mill.[109] The lex talionis as practiced by municipal and baronial officialdom was not "an eye for an eye," but a Muslim for a Muslim. When the bailiff of Alcira was questioned as to why he had seized two Muslim vassals of Valldigna, he responded with the justification that the officials of Valldigna had previously detained Açech Quilis of Alcira.[110] Indeed, the Cardinal of Valencia, Valldigna's lord, made his presence felt in Alcira and Játiva by his maltreatment of the king's Muslim vassals, clamping Offri Negral in irons for not paying a tax on wheat,[111] holding others in his custody for alleged crimes,[112] and summarily hanging two Muslims who had committed theft in Játiva.[113]

Barons and burghers both, jockeying for power and asserting their claims to land and resources, viewed their rivals' Muslims as the ideal target for their initiatives and reprisals. Essential to both as a source of labor and revenue, dispensable to both as Muslims, the Mudejars found themselves fought over, robbed, and physically abused, a state of affairs that the king, by displaying similar attitudes and by demanding the mere restitution of Muslim persons and property,[114] could not prevent but only referee.

The Muslims of urban *morerías*, even when safe from the depredations of local barons, still had to contend with the misdeeds of municipal governments. It may seem strange that the same town councils that had frequently struggled with the nobility in an effort to attract and protect new Muslim vassals should have violated the rights of those vassals. One must consider the fact that the towns desired Muslim inhabitants as a means of accelerating the growth of their local economies. Yet, because it was the Crown that collected most taxes, rents, and judicial fines from the royal aljamas, the towns profited only indirectly from the Mudejars' presence, that is, only to the extent that Mudejar enterprise increased local productivity. The towns had a political status independent of the Crown and were not always content to see the king reap all the immediate benefits of Mudejar settlement. Consequently, municipal authorities sometimes resorted to their own dubious means of squeezing revenue out of the Mudejars, revenue that would be deposited in their own treasuries. Furthermore, because the towns were themselves subject to royal taxation, the jurates might have concluded that extorting money from the Mudejars, the king's special wards, was one way of retrieving from him a portion of the taxes Christian citizens had paid.

Alcira was the locus of the most controversy between municipal government and royal aljama. The central problem was the jurates' illegal collection of taxes from the aljama. In blatant disregard of the bailiff general's command they proceeded "rigorously" to tax the aljama (1482),[115] and later (1492), their arbitrary exaction of new *sises* and *peytes* was impelling Alcira's Muslims to abandon the *morería* for seigneurial lands.[116] When taxation bore little fruit, the jurates tried to force the Muslims to labor in the town's public works (1493),[117] and in 1499 they were still making mischief, entering the *morería* and confiscating the property of Muslims for unspecified reasons.[118] The occurrence of these incidents over a seventeen-year period suggests that the aljama of Alcira was subject to consistent harassment by an apparently undeterred town council.

The experiences of other urban aljamas were variations on the same theme.[119] The aljama of Játiva took the wise precaution of seeing to it that Fernando confirm the provision of Juan II (1479) forbidding the justice and jurates to enter the *morería* and make executions on Muslim property for whatever reason.[120] This seems to have kept Játiva's jurates at a distance, although, as we shall see, the aljama had far greater difficulties with the local bailiff.

Apart from the question of taxation, two other points of controversy soured relations between the aljamas and the municipal authorities. One was the administration of justice, the problem here being the attempts of municipal justices to rule on cases involving Muslims so that any monetary fines would be paid into their courts. For this reason impediments were placed in the way of the trying of cases between Muslims in the *qāḍī*'s court in Valencia.[121] Játiva's public prosecutor had the same idea when he wrongly brought Muslims and Jews before the governor's court, instead of the bailiff's court.[122] Controversy also revolved around the Muslim butcher shops, which were royal monopolies. Valencia's aljama complained that the Christian guild of butchers was imposing restrictions on how much meat the Muslim butcher could slaughter, perhaps hoping to force the Muslims to buy meat from them.[123] The jurates of Castellón de la Plana feigned religious scruples when they forbade Christians to buy meat from the Muslim butcher shop, where they could not collect the sales tax (*sisa*). The jurates then went so far as to exact the sales tax illicitly from the Muslims as well.[124]

Albarracín (Aragon) was the scene of some interesting financial maneuverings involving the king, town council, and aljama. Fernando had conceded to the aljama the privilege of having its own store for the sale of bread, salted fish, oil, and other staples to all Muslims residing in or visiting the *morería*. The proceeds from the sales were to go to the aljama, which was in financial straits and had scarcely enough funds to pay taxes. The council, more concerned about the town's economy than with the royal patrimony, refused to allow the Muslims to open their store, obviously preferring that they do business with local Christian merchants.[125]

It is difficult to say how far the town councils would have gone in their fleecing of local aljamas if they had not been held in check by the king and his bailiffs. Probably they would have realized, as the Crown had long ago, that the depletion of an aljama's financial resources was, in the end, detrimental to their own interests. Certainly the depopulation of the *morería* would have meant an economic setback for the town. However, since the Muslims were not under their supervision and they did not necessarily identify the aljama's interests with their own, the councils were content to welcome the Muslims to their towns and then to exact from them what little else they could.

At the local level, the bailiff was the overseer of royal interests and, therefore, of Mudejar affairs. As the Muslims' judge and protector his office was of crucial importance, particularly in light of the transgressions of town councils. Although most local bailiffs seem to have fulfilled the duties of their office with the king's and the aljama's interests in mind, Joan Dezpuig, the bailiff of Játiva, which housed the kingdom's largest aljama, was a glaringly important exception. On one hand, Dezpuig and his surrogates seem to have guarded the aljama from the trespasses of others. The necessity of the bailiff's protection was demonstrated when the governor's officials, who had come to the *morería* to inventory and take pledges from the goods of Mudejar debtors, molested Muslim women and stole their belongings. Fernando responded with the command that no one could enter the *morería* without the bailiff in attendance.[126] This problem or similar ones involving Játiva's jurates did not arise again, so that it may be presumed that someone was doing his job. On the other hand, it seems that Dezpuig protected the aljama from others only so that he himself might interfere in its affairs and treat it as part of his own personal patrimony. Thus it follows that while the aljama of Játiva had the fewest problems with the municipal authorities, it suffered far more than other aljamas from the unscrupulousness of its own bailiff.

We first encounter Dezpuig just after his return to Játiva from an extended absence (1483). During his absence Luis de Fevollet, the lieutenant bailiff, had seen to the aljama's business and had ruled on a variety of matters. Dezpuig's first act was to annul Fevollet's provisions arbitrarily, perhaps because he perceived them to be inimical to his own interests. This act not only violated Fevollet's prerogatives but also seemed sure to burden the aljama with more costly litigation.[127] Although Dezpuig was reprimanded by the king for this, he still was not finished with Fevollet. Because the aljama was paying Fevollet a salary for his services, Dezpuig's next move was to confiscate securities (*penyores*) from the treasurer of the aljama so that the payment could not be made. He also incarcerated the aljama's *çalmedina* for an unknown reason, perhaps because the *çalmedina* had attempted to stop him.[128]

Two other cases, in which the aljama of Játiva was not involved, provide a bit more information on Dezpuig and how he operated. As bailiff of Játiva, a knight, and lord of Alcantera, Dezpuig was a powerful man in the region, and a well-connected one. In the first case, Çaat Melich, accused of the murder of Ali Dabbau of Ayelo, was incarcerated in the bailiff's jail. When the victim's family dropped the charges against Çaat, Dezpuig refused to release him because of his own kinship tie with the victim's lord. Çaat continued to languish in jail dying of hunger, which indicates the kind of justice Dezpuig was intending to administer.[129] Dezpuig was also involved in several litigations with the lord of Cárcer. The latter maintained that he was unable to receive a fair hearing in the governor's court, because the governor's surrogate was Dezpuig's nephew and the governor himself was only concerned that his son, married to Dezpuig's daughter, become Dezpuig's heir.[130] The bailiff of Játiva, then, appears an ambitious man willing to rise above the law and to utilize his considerable power and family connections to attain his ends.

Dezpuig employed like tactics in his dealings with the aljama. The antagonism between the bailiff and the aljama came to the fore in a litigation that lasted for at least fourteen years (1486–1500). The point of dispute was 13 pounds 11s, which, Dezpuig argued, the aljama had to pay to him annually, beyond his regular salary, for services rendered. The 13 pounds 11s was a translation into cash of a gift of linen to Dezpuig's wife, one sheep given to the bailiff himself, 110s for the lieutenant bailiff, and another 100s for Dezpuig's labors in farming out the *sisa* collected from the aljama. The aljama had made these gifts to the bailiffs in the past, but in 1486 refused to do so, apparently on the good advice of the lieutenant bailiff, Fevollet. Dezpuig responded by abrogating the privilege of the aljama to elect its four *adelantats* (jurates) and appointed *adelantats* favorable to his own interests, "less suitable and sufficient, and little zealous for the benefit and increase of the said aljama . . . so that you [Dezpuig] can extort from the said aljama the money not owed to you, as is said."[131] Fernando foiled the bailiff's plan, but the suit continued. Dezpuig argued that the bailiff of Játiva's right to the 13 pounds 11s had been established by the provisions of Alfonso V and Juan II, and that, after all, he ought to be recompensed for the labors he exerted on the aljama's behalf. The aljama countered that there existed no such royal provisions and that their gift of the 13 pounds 11s to Dezpuig had not been obligatory; rather, it had been given voluntarily and gratuitously. As for Dezpuig's services, the aljama pointed out that Dezpuig was living in Valencia, was never in Játiva, and had done absolutely nothing for the aljama. Therefore, the aljama had decided that the bailiff no longer deserved the gifts. By 1500, after one of the bailiff general's assessors had decided in the aljama's favor, and then another assessor in Dezpuig's favor, the outcome of the case was still uncertain. What is more certain is that Dezpuig treated the aljama as if it were bound to him personally, obliged to pay him regardless of whether he fulfilled his duties. Throughout the fourteen years of litigation the aljama complained of being subjected to the bailiff's harassment and molestations. That the population of Játiva's aljama experienced a marked decline may well have been in part due to the oppressive administration of Joan Dezpuig.[132]

Dezpuig was not the only one in a position of power over Mudejars to have abused his authority. For example, the archbishop of Zaragoza interfered in the elections of that city's aljama,[133] and attempted to have the ecclesiastical tithes collected from the seigneurial Muslims of Aragon, an unprecedented act.[134] There were certainly others crueler than Dezpuig. In one instance, after charges had been dropped and a settlement reached between feuding Mudejar families, Luis Bou, the lieutenant governor, nevertheless proceeded to the home of two previously accused brothers, and there seized not the brothers, but their eighty-year-old crippled father, who clearly was incapable of any crime. Bou hung up the old man by his feet and threatened to stone him. The victim's anxious friends and family agreed to pay 3000s to Bou for the old man's release. Bou was not punished; he only had to return the money thus exacted, that is, if the settlement he had reached with the elder's family was not "well made."[135]

Given the fact that men such as Dezpuig were permitted to retain their offices, and given the patent unwillingness of the king to castigate crimes against Muslims seriously, one must question those historians who have applauded the protection afforded the Mudejars by the Crown, although protection is clearly what they needed. The restoration of a Muslim's stolen property, if robbery were the only outrage to which he had been subjected, was an insufficient means of either deterring potential malefactors or repairing the damage done to the victim's human dignity. Still, the king at least recognized that leniency toward the Christian offenders had to be balanced by an attendance to Mudejar needs and grievances if he did not wish to be left with vacant *morerías*. Also, there were conscientious officials, such as Luis de Fevollet, Pere Caldes, and the bailiff generals, whose efforts on the Muslims' behalf perhaps offset the excesses and brutalities of others.

Islam: The Royal Outlook

We have seen that, contrary to the expectations evoked by the establishment of the Inquisition, the expulsion of the Jews, and the fate of the Muslims of Granada and Castile, Fernando was determined not only to maintain the Mudejar communities of his kingdoms but also to increase the Crown's share in the financial benefits accruing from Mudejar vassalage. Hence, one might conclude that in Fernando's mind fiscal considerations carried greater weight than religious ones, and that in the chemistry of the Catholic Monarchs' union the cool cynicism of Fernando managed to control but not extinguish the flames of Isabel's religious zeal. These conclusions are, to a certain extent, tenable. Certainly Isabel's religiosity was more extreme, and she was more willing to use the Catholic faith, in its mutations of Inquisition and crusade, as a blunt tool with which to hammer the Iberian peninsula, if not the entire Mediterranean, into a crude shape of religious uniformity. It is also safe to say that Fernando was the subtler one of the couple, adroitly balancing the seemingly disjunctive demands of Church, royal treasury, and Mediterranean empire. Nevertheless, it would be a mistake to assert that the king did not find the concerns of the Church and Christian society equally compelling. The main difference between Fernando and Isabel was not that the king was less interested in the promotion of the faith and the proselytizing of non-Christians, but that he was not willing to employ quite the same means as the queen in achieving those ends. Fernando had the perspicacity to realize that the majority of Mudejars were not about to abandon Islam voluntarily and embrace Christianity, and, as we shall see below, he had no desire to force the issue. At the same time, it was clear to him that an expulsion of the Mudejars would seriously debilitate the kingdoms of Valencia and Aragon. Fernando, then, accepted these two basic premises, that the Mudejars must continue laboring in their fields and shops, and that they would also continue praying in their mosques. Royal Mudejar policy consisted of pursuing the optimal fiscal benefits under these conditions.

Given that Fernando seems to have felt compelled to accept the Mudejar's adherence to Islam, which is evinced by the simple fact that the Mudejars' religious status remained unchanged until the subsequent reign, it is still essential to understand more precisely Fernando's outlook on the Islamic presence in his kingdoms, on the relations between Muslims and Christians, and on the possibilities of assimilating that Muslim body into Christian society through baptism. Such an understanding is necessary not simply because the history of the Jews and Castilian Mudejars raises the question but also for the reason that whatever economic importance the Mudejars had, it would have made little difference had Fernando indeed been intent on the eradication of Spanish Islam. The early history of the Inquisition speaks eloquently enough on this point. Very much aware of the economic havoc the Inquisition would and did wreak by decimating the Converso community, the Catholic Monarch still unhesitatingly forced the Holy Office on all of his kingdoms to stamp out the judaizing heresy.[136] Although material concerns significantly influenced Fernando's handling of the minorities, the factor of religion was ultimately decisive.

The most fundamental of all the privileges accorded to the Mudejars was the freedom to practice Islam, and this freedom Fernando never disputed. However, religious sentiments were such that the Mudejars' practice of Islam raised other delicate issues, namely, whether Islamic worship should be allowed to manifest itself publicly, and, if so, what kind of limitations were to be imposed so as to render it less offensive to Christians.

Since the time of the conquest the Crown had recognized the importance of mosques for the Muslims' religious and communal life, and thus allowed the Mudejars to retain them, along with their cemeteries and pious endowments.[137] From the Christians' perspective, the mosque was the physical symbol of Islam, just as the church was representative of their own religion. Fifteenth-century Valencian Christians begrudged the Mudejars their mosques and could take some comfort in the fact that, as a result of demographic change, mosques were greatly outnumbered by churches. While Mudejars might maintain and renovate the mosques they already had, the construction of new ones was quite a different matter.[138] Some Christians perceived this as an insult to their own faith and an unwanted increase of the Islamic presence.

Fernando himself was sensitive to this issue. When he established the new *morería* in Castellón de Játiva it seems that he purposely did not provide for the building of a new mosque there. Not every Mudejar community had its own mosque, and the king probably supposed that Castellón's Muslims would pray in the mosque of nearby Játiva. Yet, by 1493 Castellón's Mudejars had built or set aside a particular house for a mosque. The matter concerned Fernando, and he ordered an official investigation to determine if the mosque had been built recently—it probably had been, considering that the *morería* itself dated only from 1480—how long it had been standing, and whether there had been a mosque there in the past.[139] Perhaps he was willing to give the Mudejars the benefit of the doubt if some preconquest antecedent to the mosque could be found, but his queries suggest that he was not comfortable with the idea of the Christians of Castellón being subjected to the public display of Islam by an aljama of his own creation.

Similar sentiments prompted the king to relocate the mosque of Zaragoza from a site near a plaza "where the Christians socialize and . . . receive from it [the mosque] much offense" to "another area more convenient, closer to the *morería*, or inside of it."[140] Fernando was not questioning the right of Mudejars to worship as Muslims; he was, in his mind, protecting Christians from excessive exposure to Islam's ritual manifestations.

In another case Fernando's opinions emerge less clearly. The scene of conflict was the Vall de Ayora, where the lord of the town of Ayora, the Marqués de Zanete, was constructing a new *morería* and mosque in an effort to attract to the town Muslims from the surrounding communities of the valley. Don Gerubin de Centelles, the lord of the valley, strenuously objected, arguing that since the conquest the town had been populated by only Christians. Now, with this new mosque, the town, which had only heard the invocation of the name of Jesus Christ, would resound with the Muslims' call to prayer and the name of Muḥammad. Centelles, obviously trying to strike a nerve here, demanded that the king put a stop to the Marqués's initiatives, which were so detrimental to the faith. Fernando reacted by ordering the Marqués to cease construction pending a hearing of both parties. This measured reaction may be attributed to the rumor that the Marqués had procured a papal bull allowing him to construct a new mosque. Also, there was much more at stake than a new mosque; there was the additional question of conflicting seigneurial jurisdictions and the Marqués's prerogatives.[141]

As the preceding case suggests, what Christians found objectionable was not so much the existence of the mosque itself as the call to prayer five times daily from its minaret. Christians referred to the Muslims' call to prayer as the çala, employing this term for both the call (adhān)— "Ashhadu anna Muḥammad rasūl Allāh" ("I testify that Muḥammad is the messenger of God")—and the prayer itself (ṣalāt), although clearly it was the former that vexed them. It is interesting that Centelles remonstrated against the name of Muḥammad being invoked in Ayora, for the public chanting of the adhān had long been forbidden, although perhaps to little effect in seigneurial areas, if Centelles's word can be relied upon. Taking their cue from Pope Clement V at the Council of Vienne (1311), the Aragonese kings—Jaime II (1318), reinforced by Martin I (1403) and Alfonso V (1417) after the leniency of Pedro IV— had enacted a series of prohibitions, so that by Fernando's reign Muslims could be notified of the hour of prayer only by the sounding of a horn, and even that was prohibited in the city of Valencia. Since what the Church deplored was the public chanting of the name of Muḥammad, Fernando did not think it necessary to add to his predecessors' restrictions. After all, if the Mudejars were to be allowed to practice Islam, they needed to be apprised of the proper time for prayer.[142]

However, some of the more intolerant elements in Valencian society had other ideas. In 1477 placards had been posted in the capital calling for the tearing down of the minarets of all mosques.[143] The Inquisitors, whom the king had thrust upon Valencia, came to represent the forces of religious extremism. In 1506 they threatened with excommunication and monetary fine (500 gold florins) all seigneurial officials in the region of the kingdom south of the Jijona River who permitted the Muslims to make the call to prayer, even "indirectly" with a horn. The Inquisitors, it seems, were not satisfied with extracting the judaizing cancer from within the Christian body; they desired to "Christianize" the entire kingdom, which entailed the suppression of Islam. On this score they differed with Valencian clergymen, or at least with those who had Muslim vassals and seemed content with the existing arrangement. It is revealing that all three estates—military, royal, and ecclesiastical—complained to Fernando that the Inquisitors had violated the *Furs*, of which they had little knowledge. They noted that even canon law did not object to the Muslims' use of a horn. It is unlikely that Fernando would have supported the Inquisitors' initiative. The events of the crisis of 1500–1503 (see chap. 2) advised against further upsetting the Mudejars, who might have resorted to mass flight, utterly ruining barons, prelates, and towns.[144]

Along with the restriction of the ritual expression of Islam, the Crown also deemed it necessary to censure any demonstrations of disrespect toward the Catholic faith by Muslims. Alfonso V had demanded that Mudejars be punished for blaspheming in the name of Jesus Christ or the Virgin Mary, and during Fernando's reign legal procedure was taken against a number of Muslims, such as Ali Castellano of Alcira, who had to pay a fine of 50s "because he swore by the unclean parts of our Lord God."[145] Muslims were also expected to make overt displays of their respect for Christianity by kneeling or turning aside when the Host was carried through the streets, and by ceasing work on Sundays and feast days, although they were permitted to labor in their fields on many of them.[146] Fernando took great exception to the insolence of Mudejar blacksmiths and shoemakers in Tarazona who labored in public on Sundays and other feast days. When the priest elevated the Host during the Mass, the Muslims did "not cease hammering, striking iron, cutting and sewing," and even when Christian processions bearing the Host passed by the Muslims did "worse in the same manner without any respect or reverence, which is a bad example and by it service is done neither to our Lord God nor to us [the king]." Exasperated because he had already commanded that Muslim shops be removed from Christian areas of Tarazona, the king threatened to deprive the city's bailiff and jurates of their offices if they did not remedy the situation.[147]

Fernando favored a strict spatial separation of Islamic and Christian cults, so that his Christian subjects would not have to bear the affront of seeing mosques and hearing the Arabic chant of the *mu'adhdhin*, or of witnessing the Muslims' impudent disregard of their Lord. In other words, Islam was to keep a very low profile. No doubt the Church applauded Fernando's policy, or the enforcement of his predecessors'. Yet it is less clear that he acted in these matters in response to widespread popular demand or that the generality of his Christian subjects were as sensitive as he to these alleged insults to their faith; in Ayora and Tarazona, at least, it appears that they were not.[148] In fact, Fernando found the occasional manifestations of laxness and tolerance by his subjects to be shocking.

Much to the king's chagrin, the church of the Virgen María de la Rapita, located within the limits of his own city of Tortosa, was the site of a display of understanding rarely seen along the Christian–Muslim interface. With the cognizance of the authorities, presumably both ecclesiastical and civil, Muslims from Valencia, Aragon, and Catalonia were congregating in the church on Islamic holy days for prayer and ceremony. As far as Fernando was concerned, this was far worse than the building of a mosque in a Christian town or the labor of Muslims on Sunday; this was the violation of a church's sanctity by what were to him the ungodly and unclean rites of Islam. His reaction to the news, shock followed by intense anger, shines through the formulaic rhetoric of the document:

> Not without great astonishment and (?) we have learned of the tolerance which until now has been given in allowing the Moors of the said king-doms to enter the church of the Virgen María de la Rapita, which is estab-lished and built within the limits of that city of Tortosa, to ululate and to venerate the festivals and things required of them by their Mahometan sect and diabolic custom, which is done and consented to in the greatest disservice of our Redeemer Jesus Christ and of his most glorious mother, our Lady.

Fernando fumed, perturbed "that in the temple ordained for veneration and honor of the Divine cult there is permitted to be done another thing that is manifestly repugnant to the order of the Holy Church and Chris-tian religion." The king was determined to act decisively "as pertains to the service of our Lord Jesus Christ and of his pure mother, our Lady, and to the exaltation of the Catholic faith and the oppression of the disorders of the pestiferous and infernal Mahometan sect." The severity of the threatened punishment corresponded with Fernando's opinion of the gravity of the offense. Officials who permitted Muslims to enter the church were to be fined 1,000 gold florins, while the Muslims themselves who violated the royal prohibition were to be given capital punishment or made slaves of the king. Also, whoever had the keys to and custo-dianship of the church was to lose his life if he allowed Muslims to pray or leave votive candles there. The king further enjoined that the church undergo a symbolic cleansing. In the part of the church where the Mus-lims made their devotions—perhaps the part they used as a *miḥrāb* (a niche indicating the direction of Mecca)—the window was to be covered and on the window were to be painted images of Christ and the Virgin, "so that by them [the paintings] all impurity may be purged and abolished."[149]

Because Fernando viewed the faith of Islam with such obvious aver-sion, particularly when it threatened to intrude on the religious consciousness of the Catholic faithful, close social relations between adherents of that faith and Christians caused the king dismay. His opinion that the rites of Islam were somehow unclean implies that he feared Christians would be morally contaminated by extensive social interaction with Muslims. Fernando's sentiments were rooted not in a scorn for the Muslims as a distinct race, for there was little or no difference in the physiognomies of Spanish Muslims and Christians, but in a disdain for the religion that defined the Mudejars' ethnicity. There were, nevertheless, practical limitations to the institution of a rigid policy of social segregation. The Crown's encouragement of Mudejar economic activity—which meant their participation in most sectors of the economy and not just as servile agricultural laborers—militated against such a policy, for daily contact between Muslim and Christian in the workplace and market fostered a certain level of rapprochement that made social relations both possible and inevitable. If the king desired that the royal aljamas grow and prosper, he could not expect the Mudejars to remain in asphyxiating and impoverishing isolation. Religious concerns thus clashed with the Crown's fiscal interests. The contradictions or ambivalence perceptible in certain of Fernando's decisions are a reflection of this dichotomy.

The conditions stipulated by Fernando in his creation of an aljama in Castellón de Játiva are indicative of the state of affairs he deemed most preferable. He unequivocally commanded that the Muslims must inhabit a distinct *morería* and not mix in with the town's Christian residents.[150] Ideally, this was what many Christians and Muslims would have desired, but sometimes necessity advised otherwise. To help make ends meet, Mudejars of the struggling and underpopulated *morería* of Valencia sold to Christians houses located within the *morería*. The issue here was not whether Christians could purchase houses located within a *morería*—this Fernando did not question—but whether they had to pay the taxes incumbent on the *morería*'s Muslim residents.[151] Even when Fernando was intent on enforcing segregation, established local practice and relative indifference sometimes confounded him. While staying in Tarazona, he had decided that Jews and Muslims must be prohibited from having their homes and shops in Christian neighborhoods, "in order to avoid scandals and damages which could arise from it." Although the Jews and Muslims had dutifully returned to their respective quarters, Fernando was incensed when he learned that after his departure they had returned to live among the Christians "even more profanely than they were accustomed." Six years later word reached him that Mudejar craftsmen still had their shops outside of the *morería*, and that they worked in them on Sunday. It is significant that it was not an outcry from the Christian populace of Tarazona which had reached

Fernando's ears, but the complaint of only one citizen, Ferrando de Matalebreras.[152]

Because Muslims and Jews ritually slaughtered their animals as prescribed by their dietary laws, the Christians' purchase of meat from their butcher shops assumed religious implications. Fernando and his bailiff general seem to have ignored these implications on account of fiscal concerns, or at least that was the case initially. Thus, when the jurates of Castellón de la Plana forbade the Muslim butcher shop to sell meat to Christians, primarily because they themselves did not collect the sales tax on the animals slaughtered by the Muslim butcher, the bailiff general demanded that they revoke the prohibition since it was prejudicial to the Crown, from whom the Muslim butcher shop was rented.[153] The Inquisitors, however, did not take royal revenues into consideration when, in 1488, they preached in the see of Valencia that Christians should not dare to eat meat slaughtered by Muslims and Jews, under penalty of excommunication. Predictably, this elicited a protest from the lords of Mudejar vassals, and they enlisted the influence of the bishop of Segorbe in Rome to get a papal bull exempting their lands from the Inquisitorial decree.[154] There is no evidence that Fernando was privy to this Inquisitorial offensive, although his subsequent action in Alcira indicates that he at least approved of and so acted in accordance with its substance. By 1492 Fernando decided that Alcira's Muslim butcher shop did not need to be provided with as many sheep as before "inasmuch as now it is prohibited [that] the said Christians buy meat from the said [Muslim] butcher shop."[155] Owing to the resistance of the nobility, it seems that the zeal of the Inquisitors was felt less on seigneurial lands than in royal towns.

If Christians and Muslims were going to mingle, and realistically this could hardly be prevented, then it was important that Muslims at least be easily identifiable. At the behest of the Fourth Lateran Council (1215), Spanish monarchs had included in their legal codes legislation demanding that Muslims wear distinctive clothing, although this legislation was only intermittently enforced. Fernando attempted to correct the previous laxness, bidding the bailiff general of Aragon to see to it that the Mudejars wore their special apparel.[156] In the kingdom of Valencia Juan II had called for the enforcement of Jaime I's ordinances demanding that all Muslims dress in distinctive blue garb; however, in return for a 60-pound payment he had exempted the Muslims from having a special tonsure. Fernando followed suit and in 1482 issued a royal proclamation that Muslims and Jews must wear their special clothing in the city of Valencia. Yet, four years later Fernando was expressing dismay that his father's orders were being disobeyed and that Muslims were dressing "like Christians, and many of them in silk doublets and

fine clothing."[157] The king's interests in the enforcement of this legislation were partly political—so that incognito Muslim enemies could not
kidnap Christians (see chap. 2)—and partly social. Regarding the latter, Fernando was anxious to prevent "inconveniences and scandals" of
a sexual nature, especially relations between Muslim men and Christian
women. His fears were not unfounded, for the documentation attests to
the not infrequent violation of this sexual taboo.[158] When the jurates of
Zaragoza were outraged because Muslims visiting the fonduk (hostel) of
the *morería* brought Muslim women there with them—actually their
daughters—Fernando bade the jurates to let the Muslims be, "so that
those Moors will abstain from having anything to do with Christian
women."[159] In any case, it seems that despite the king's expressed concern to prevent such illicit relations, the Mudejars still were not forced
to wear the special clothing. This is indicated by the absence of any
record of the penalization of a Muslim for violation of the dress code
and by the near impossibility of regulating Mudejar dress outside of the
few royal *morerías*.[160]

Fernando's anxiety about immoderate intimacy between Christians
and Muslims may be considered within the context of the Catholic
Monarchs' efforts to reform Spanish Christian society. Their program of
reform for the Spanish Church, especially the religious orders, is well
known. They were also preoccupied with the moral laxity of their subjects. In Valencia Fernando took measures to regulate prostitution and
to prohibit gambling, profanity, sorcery, and usury.[161] Still, this general
interest in Christian morality does not minimize the fact that the comradeship of Muslims and Christians was perceived as a moral evil in
itself or as the root of others. It is understandable how Fernando could
have jumped to such conclusions, since Muslims and Christians were
often found together partaking in Valencia's riotous tavern life. For instance, there was the disreputable Hostal del Palomar in Albaida, which
Fernando wanted razed, because "there are committed many evils and
damages, since many men of evil life and practices congregate there,
and since it is found that Moors sleep with Christian women."[162] In
another tavern Muslims were fined for gambling with Christians.[163]

Despite its decline in population and wealth, the *morería* of Valencia
still maintained its reputation as a center of lowlife. Orders were issued
prohibiting gambling there and restricting the activities of Muslim
prostitutes to the *morería*'s bordello.[164] Muslim residents of the *morería*
who received as guests in their homes intoxicated Muslim vagabonds or
Christian men and women, thereby encouraging "scandals, fights, and
disorders," were to be fined 10s.[165] The Crown attempted to prevent
such disturbances from spreading beyond the confines of the *morería* by
forbidding Muslims to drink their wine in any place other than the royal

tavern.[166] Also, Muslims and Jews visiting the city of Valencia were required to lodge at the royal fonduk in the *morería* and not at Christian inns.[167] The same applied to other royal *morerías* that had their own fonduks. These restrictions had a double motive. On one hand, confining Mudejars to the royal tavern and fonduk curtailed the "many and great inconveniences, scandals, and other perils which arise from the cohabitation of Sarracens, Jews, and other infidels with the Christians."[168] On the other hand, the restrictions ensured a steady flow of income from these royal monopolies.[169] The repeated proclamation of them attests to the frequency with which they were violated.[170]

Fernando's measures to limit the public display of the Mudejars' religion and to promote the social segregation of Muslim and Christian all had their precedents in the legislation of previous monarchs, and it would be difficult to argue that the Catholic Monarch was more hostile than his predecessors toward Islam. In some areas where the king expressed concern, such as the Mudejars' distinctive clothing or their confinement to *morerías* and royal taverns for residence and recreation, the concern was not translated into consistent enforcement of proscriptive legislation. In others, such as the relocation of Zaragoza's mosque or the forbidding of Alcira's Muslims to sell meat to Christians, royal action was more decisive and in line with the views held by the aggressively anti-Islamic Inquisition. In any case, it is patent that Fernando, whether merely remonstrating or acting conclusively, desired to impede the mixing of Christians and Muslims, but without challenging the religious status of the latter.

Yet, considering the above instances of close and amicable relations between Muslims and Christians in Valencia, Aragon, and Catalonia, it seems that Fernando, in his desultory attempts to segregate Mudejars, was fighting a losing battle. Indeed, one might pose a disjunction between royal (and ecclesiastical) attitudes and those of a substantial portion of the Christian populace. Fernando's segregationist stance was inspired by a concern for the moral and spiritual well-being of his Christian subjects. His subjects, however, were probably not nearly as preoccupied with the state of their souls as he would have liked. Their concerns often were far more mundane. If their neighbors happened to be Muslims, it was perhaps easier to befriend them than to shun them. Christians in the capital knew Muslims of the local *morería* well enough to testify as character witnesses in their behalf.[171] Making a living might mean cooperation with the Muslim tilling the adjacent plot of land, or selling goods to a large Muslim clientele, or even a business partnership with a Muslim.[172] A Muslim of Alcira's acknowledgment of his debt to a Christian, written in Arabic and translated by the *qāḍī* general, indicates the direction in which some business relationships might tend: "I Ageg, son of Çahat Ageg, confess to you [my] singular and good friend, en Jacme Barbera, how I owe you twelve pounds."[173] Alasdrach of Buñol and Ali Alcayet of Chiva preferred to lodge at the "Hostal de Angel" when they were in Valencia, because they were acquainted with the hosteler, Joan Jeroni.[174] Deeper friendships between Muslims and Christians might flourish. Açen Muça's defense counsel tried to disqualify the testimony of the tailor Miguel Serra in favor of the plaintiffs, the family of the murdered Ubaydal (or Abdalla) Çentido, because Serra "was a very great friend, like a brother, of the said Ubaydal Çentido and is a very great friend of the sister of the said Ubaydal."[175] Another friend of Ubaydal was the farmer Domingo Roda. While visiting his sister and attending to his lands in Mirambell, Domingo dined at the house of Ubaydal's sister with Ubaydal and another Muslim, Alfiquinet. After dinner, the three of them went for a stroll and talked, mainly about a Christian woman who had run off with some Muslims. (The defense impugned Domingo's testimony as well. That Domingo might have perjured himself for the sake of Ubaydal's family is impressive in itself.)[176]

When leisurely pursuing pleasure Muslims and Christians let questions of faith recede into the background. Taverns brought Christians and Muslims together just as surely as churches and mosques separated them. Even the capital's colorful Corpus Christi Day processions, in spite of their being a clear expression of the Catholic faith, attracted Muslims from all over the kingdom. And the Christians found nothing unusual in this; nor did they expect the Muslim onlookers to kneel and show obeisance. In fact, Muslims and Christians set out for and watched the processions together.[177]

That some Christians had no qualms about mingling so freely with Muslims was not the result of their having somehow come to terms with the religion of Islam, for on the theological plane there could be no Mudejar–Christian rapprochement. These Christians probably did not see themselves as somehow compromising their own religious beliefs. For them such interaction with Muslims was simply a way of life, a life in which secular pursuits often obscured spiritual concerns. In Valencia the pursuit of peace, the pursuit of wealth, and the pursuit of pleasure all frequently involved dealing with Muslims. Given the size of the Mudejar population, it could hardly have been otherwise. In his efforts to reform Christian society, Fernando was essentially asking his subjects to lead more spiritual lives. Success here might have rendered his segregative measures more enforceable. The failure to segregate the Mudejars was partly the consequence of the unwillingness and the inability of most Christians to live completely in accordance with the dictates of the Church.

The Question of Conversion

Nevertheless, Fernando was not alone in desiring a fuller separation of the Mudejars from the Christian population. There certainly were elements in Christian society who viewed the Muslims with resentment and fanatical hatred. They were willing to go much further than the king to solve the Mudejar problem. They advocated either the expulsion or the baptism of the Mudejars. Both methods would have the same result: a wholly Christian society. Economic and political considerations combined with the weight of tradition advised against the former course of action. The history of the Conversos strongly argued against the latter. Since 1391, when widespread anti-Jewish pogroms saw approximately one-third of Spain's Jews forcibly baptized, Spanish society had been plagued with the problem of Conversos. The Conversos either refused to assimilate and continued practicing Judaism, or, when they sincerely sought assimilation, Old Christian society rejected them on the grounds of their Jewish origins. From the 1440s until the reign of the Monarchs the issue of the Conversos was hotly debated, particularly in Castile, where acute social and religious discontent gave rise to numerous anti-Converso riots. It was the gravest of problems, to which the Monarchs responded with the establishment of the Spanish Inquisition, hoping to separate true Christians, both Old and New, from the crypto-Jews. When this proved impossible, to a large extent because of the persistent contact between the Converso and Jewish communities, the Jews were expelled from the peninsula.[178] This was not, however, part of a larger plan to impose religious uniformity on Castile and Aragon; rather, it was a measure meant to solve a widespread socioreligious problem, of which the Mudejars were not a part. Even though these initiatives against the Conversos and Jews might have suggested to some that the conversion or expulsion of the Mudejars was the next step, Fernando himself did not entertain such designs. The Converso problem had shaken Castilian urban society to its very foundations and had raised serious questions about the premises on which Christian identity was based. It is highly unlikely that Fernando had the intention of creating a new class of Moriscos, thereby reenacting the Converso–Jew–Old Christian scenario. Whatever distaste Fernando had for Islam, his eyes were open wide enough to see that the Mudejar clung to his faith as stubbornly as the Jew.

Fortunately, the existence of a few documents in which Fernando speaks clearly on the question of Mudejar conversion enables us to move to more solid ground. One incident, in 1498, involved a young Muslim of Zaragoza (*moratiço*) who had expressed to the archbishop his desire to convert to Christianity. Rather than urging the immediate baptism of the Muslim, Fernando hesitated, requesting further information. He inquired whether the Muslim was of the age of discretion, that is, whether he was old enough to make a reasoned and sound decision in so important a matter as the abandonment of Islam for Christianity. He also wanted to know whether the Muslim had the consent of his parents or guardians to convert. Fernando did not wish to see an adolescent accept baptism on a whim, only to revert to Islam years later upon the realization that he had foolishly erred. The king reasoned that without parental consent the young proselyte would constantly be under familial pressure to abandon Christianity. Furthermore, Fernando was concerned that if the baptism were administered too hastily to an adolescent against the wishes of his family, the Mudejar community would perceive it as a form of forced conversion and, consequently, would be all the more opposed to Christianity. As the king summed up: "because if the said *moratiço* were baptized not having years of discretion against the will of the abovesaid [parents] it would be an exemplary case for all the others [Mudejars]. We would not allow such a thing to be done without considering it well."[179] It is probable that Fernando had the Conversos in mind when he pondered this decision. It was notorious—certainly by 1498, when the Inquisition had already brought to light so much information on Converso practices—that adult Conversos often resumed a wholehearted observance of Judaism after having been raised as Catholics, and that the Conversos' crypto-Judaism was rooted in a closely knit family and communal life.[180]

Fernando's other enunciations on the proselytizing of Mudejars stem from his efforts to shield them from the attacks of overly zealous Christians. In one case, a preacher of the crusade was inciting the Christians of Zaragoza against the local Muslims with his inflammatory sermons. Fernando admonished him to preach without mentioning the Mudejars, pointing out that by defaming the Mudejars and provoking the Christians against them he would not make much progress toward their conversion. The king added significantly:

> if you know some things that ought to be done with respect to the said Moors concerning their satisfactory and tranquil coming to the zeal of the holy Catholic faith, those things you should tell secretly to our governor so that he may provide in the matter, or you should intimate them to us by your letters.

That Fernando was interested in the conversion of the Mudejars there is little doubt; the crucial point is that he demanded peaceful methods in the attainment of that end.[181] This is corroborated by the stance taken by Fernando in the years 1500–1503, when, after the rebellion and conversion of Muslims in Granada, rumors were spread in Valencia, Aragon, and Catalonia to the effect that the king planned to convert all Mudejars, by force if necessary. Fernando firmly repudiated such plans and proclaimed that: "our holy Catholic faith in the conversion of the infidels admits neither violence nor force but [only] full freedom and devotion."[182] The survival of the Crown of Aragon's Muslim communities intact throughout Fernando's reign is testimony to the king's sincere opposition to forced conversion.

As has been indicated, Fernando was pleased to accept the voluntary conversion of Mudejars. When the Marquesa de Moya, one of the queen's ladies-in-waiting, sponsored her Muslim slave Casamito, who had expressed his intention of converting and marrying a Christian woman, by apprenticing him to a Christian dyer of Valencia, the king approved of the idea. When, after four years of apprenticeship, Casamito had a change of heart and ran off with Muslim companions, Fernando ordered Casamito seized and turned over to the Marquesa.[183]

Whereas the king gingerly handled the case of the young Muslim of Zaragoza in order to avoid upsetting his parents and community, he had no doubt that Muslim children bereft of family and legal guardians were valid objects of proselytizing. After learning that Valencian Mudejars had bought a number of captive Malagan children ranging from three to ten years of age, Fernando commanded the bailiff general to take the children from their new masters, "so that they do not remain in their infidelity and may be turned to the Christian faith."[184] Similarly, it was decided that black slaves from Guinea, who were perceived as having no religious status, should not be sold to Jews and Muslims, so that they, too, might be instructed in the Catholic faith.[185] The same approach is evident in the royal decree of 12 February 1502, ordering the expulsion from Castile of all male Muslims older than fourteen and of all females older than twelve.[186] Children, without the contrary influences of their families, could be raised as true Christians.

Once a Muslim accepted baptism, the king took care to see to it that the convert was well treated and that he or she did not feel in any way burdened by the new faith. In a litigation between Caterina, the daughter of a convert, and the Gaçenis, a Mudejar family of Tortosa, over the inheritance left to Caterina by her Muslim grandmother, the local bailiff had ruled in favor of Caterina. When the Gaçenis tried to appeal the decision, Fernando rejected their appeal on the grounds of its tardiness, but added that Caterina ought to remain in possession of the inheritance "lest she feel injury from the reception of baptism."[187]

Fernando was truly enthusiastic for the voluntary conversion of all his Mudejar subjects. The willing acceptance of baptism by the entire aljama of Teruel (Aragon) in 1502 filled the king with joy and high hopes.

After relating how all the Castilian Mudejars "converted to our holy Catholic faith out of free will," Fernando continued:

> it seems to us that they have done the same in the city of Teruel, that marvelously, by the grace of the Holy Spirit, there all the Moors of that aljama have converted . . . may it please God that all the others that remain in our kingdoms do the same . . . from this we would receive much consolation.[188]

Although Fernando did not employ coercion with the Crown's other Muslim communities in the pursuit of wish fulfillment, the alleged freedom with which the Mudejars of Castile and Teruel converted demands scrutiny. The conditions for emigration offered to Castilian Muslims by the Monarchs—the abandonment of their children and Egypt as practically their only destination—makes one wonder whether they had any other choice but to accept baptism. The precise circumstances which led to the conversion of Teruel's aljama are unknown, but, given Teruel's proximity to Castile and the great anxiety that the rebellions and conversions in Granada and Castile must have caused them, it may be surmised that Teruel's Muslims accepted baptism under considerable psychological duress. Still, in an age when Muslims and Jews who opted for the baptismal chrism instead of the blade of a sword were judged by theologians to have acted out of free will, Fernando's definition of freedom was perhaps more reasonable than many.[189]

It is worthwhile to consider briefly the conversion of the Muslims of Granada and Castile, in order to raise a few points regarding the contrasting views of Fernando and Isabel on the methods of conversion. Although Fernando and Isabel ruled jointly, the final responsibility for policy in Castile and Granada fell on Isabel's shoulders. The same can be asserted for Fernando with respect to Aragon. While the Monarchs differed on the use of coercion in conversion, they seem to have agreed on the measures to be implemented in treating the problem of neoconverts, either Jewish or Muslim.

The surrender treaties reached between the Monarchs and the conquered Granadans were quite similar to the Mudejar treaties of the twelfth and thirteenth centuries. Even the efforts of Hernando de Talavera, the first archbishop of Granada, to proselytize the Muslims of Granada had their precedents in the activities of the Mendicant Orders in Valencia in the wake of that kingdom's conquest.[190] That until 1499 the Monarchs had no intention of breaking the treaties is indicated by their permission to Portugal's expelled Mudejars to settle in Granada and Castile in 1497. However, by autumn 1499, it seems that the Monarchs, particularly Isabel, had grown impatient with Talavera's policy of gradual conversion. Desirous of some results, a pretext was found for sending Cardinal Cisneros to Granada, namely, that Cisneros, acting with the powers of an Inquisitor, was to return to the fold of the Church the *elches*, Christians who had converted to Islam. This in itself was a breach of the capitulations, but Cisneros went further, not only pressuring the *elches* to convert but also proceeding against their children. Consequently, the Muslims of the Albaicín quarter of Granada exploded into rebellion.[191]

Fernando expressed disapproval of Cisneros's methods, noting that one might have expected as much from a man "who never saw Moors, or knew them."[192] Isabel's silence suggests that she had few objections, and her approval seems to have overruled her husband's misgivings. In any case, the methods of Isabel and Cisneros were employed, so that the Muslims of Granada had to submit to baptism in order to be pardoned for their rebellion. While revolts were breaking out in the Alpujarras, once the Muslims there had heard of the treatment of their brethren in Granada, the Monarchs still did not envision the conversion of the entire kingdom. Letters were sent assuring the Mudejars of Ronda and Málaga that they would not be forced to become Christians. Yet, all the while, Cisneros was writing in terms of baptizing all Muslims. It is clear that the Monarchs' great error, if Isabel even considered it as such, was to send Cisneros to Granada, for he set in motion a train of events that was extremely difficult to stop. As successive rebellions were quelled in the Alpujarras and elsewhere in the kingdom (1500–1501), and baptism continued to be offered as a condition of pardon, along with the incentive of a partial remission of taxes, it became increasingly clear to the Monarchs that the bulk of the Muslim population was becoming Christian.[193]

In effect, a Morisco problem was in the making. López and Acién suggest that the Monarchs' final decision to "Christianize" the entire kingdom was financially motivated and came after the papal concession to the Monarchs of two-thirds of the tithes to be paid to the Church by all New Christians (bull of 22 March 1500).[194] Although this was probably influential in the timing of the Monarchs' decision, the most telling factor was the fear of Morisco–Muslim contact and all the danger that implied for the Catholic faith. The Monarchs expressed this concern in their instructions for Cisneros and the governor, the Count of Tendilla, just after the rebellion in the Albaicín:

> it seems to us that those who convert should not be around the Moors for the necessity that they have of being instructed in the things of our faith . . . they [Cisneros and Tendilla] should write to us if it appears that it ought to be provided that they [the converts] not live among the Moors.[195]

Prevention of the contamination of the recent converts by Islam prompted the royal proclamation of 20 July 1501, forbidding all Muslims to enter the, by now, Christian kingdom of Granada, "under pain of death and of loss of all their property." Fernando and Isabel made clear their desire "that the said conversion remain for always in the said newly converted, so that they might be good Christians." Only the threat of extreme penalties could ensure that the neophytes would "not have any cause to err in the things of our holy faith by communicating with the said Moors, who could come from other parts to this said kingdom."[196]

By September 1501 the Monarchs had decided that the Mudejars of Castile must also accept baptism or abandon the peninsula. They ordered the *corregidor* of Córdoba not to pressure the Mudejars to convert, but to inform them that if they remained Muslims, they would have to leave the kingdom.[197] Finally, on 12 February 1502 the order was issued that all Muslims must depart from Castile. In the order an explicit connection is made between the earlier Converso–Jew dilemma and the potential for a similar Morisco–Muslim problem:

> Considering. . . that since the major cause of the subversion of many Christians that has been seen in these our kingdoms was their participation and communication with the Jews, that since there is much danger in the communication of the said Moors of our kingdom with the newly converted and they [the Moors] will be a cause that the said newly converted may be drawn and induced to leave our faith and to return to their original errors . . . as already by experience has been seen in some in this kingdom and outside of it, if the principal cause is removed, that is, to expel the said Moors from these our kingdoms and lordships, and because it is better to prevent with the remedy than to wait to punish the errors after they are made and committed . . . it is right that they be expelled.[198]

In the final analysis, the protection of the faith of the neoconverts was the determining factor in the Monarchs' steps to "Christianize" Granada completely and to present the Castilian Mudejars with the choice of baptism or expulsion. Once a large number of Muslims in Granada had been converted, the threat to the health of the entire Christian body was too great if the New Christians were allowed any contact with the contagion of Islam. That much the Monarchs had learned from the Jews and the Conversos.

That the Mudejars of Valencia did not meet the same fate as their coreligionists in Castile was due to a number of factors, the most obvious of which was the absence of a large group of Muslim converts to Christianity in Fernando's dominions. The absence of a Morisco problem in Valencia had much to do with the king's opposition to forced conversion and his stand against those who were proposing baptism of the Mudejars from 1500 to 1503. Fernando's forthright position in his own realms contrasts markedly with his wavering disapproval in Isabel's Castile. Moreover, in Valencia the conversion of the Mudejars could have been carried out only in the face of fierce opposition from the nobility. Throughout the years 1500–1503 the military estate warned Fernando of the dire consequences a forced conversion would have: the ruination of the economy and a bloody Mudejar insurrection. At the Cortes of Zaragoza (1502) and at the Corts of Barcelona (1503) and Monzón (1510) Fernando had to promise that he would not convert the Mudejars of the Crown of Aragon.[199] The Mudejars of Castile lacked any substantial support. Numbering only 17,000 to 20,000 persons and located largely in urban *morerías*, Castile's Muslims had no great lords willing to plead their case before the queen. On the contrary, the Castilian municipal governments eagerly enforced the Monarchs' orders (1480) for the placement of Mudejars in separate *morerías*, and they had to be instructed to prevent Christian violence against the Mudejars during the rebellions of the Alpujarras.[200]

There is almost no comparison between the situations in Valencia and Granada. In Valencia Muslims and Christians had been coexisting for well over two centuries, and, although there were problems, society remained cohesive. Valencia's Christians and Muslims had long ago experienced the initial shock of having to inhabit the same kingdom. As for Granada, one is hard pressed to speak of a single society; rather, it was more a case of two societies that had glowered at each other across the Granadan frontier being forced together by virtue of Granada's conquest. The Castilians, moved by crusading zeal and characterized by a religious extremism fed by the anti-Jewish and anti-Converso hysteria of the previous century, had little regard for the privileges granted to the subject Muslims in the surrender treaties. When they were thrust into close quarters with the Muslims, the latter were frequently dispossessed of their lands and otherwise abused. The Muslims' resentment of the conquerors was thus enhanced. Perhaps it was only the small number of settlers (40,000 by 1498, in comparison with 250,000 to 300,000 Muslims) that forestalled the explosive Muslim rebellion that Cisneros and the Monarchs managed to provoke.[201]

Those historians who see in the marriage of Fernando and Isabel the creation of a unified Spain, or who see the Monarchs as having aimed at directing the destiny of one Spanish state, may well assert that the New Christians of Castile and Granada still could have been influenced by the Muslims of the Crown of Aragon and, therefore, may ask why the Monarchs did not convert the latter in order to prevent this eventuality. The answer lies in the fact that Fernando alone ruled in Aragon, and that Aragon and Castile still had sufficiently distinct societies and governments to allow for the cordoning off of Aragon from Castile, so that Fernando's Mudejars could not enter Isabel's realms. The same interpretive framework can be employed to explain the extension of the Spanish Inquisition from Castile into Aragon. Fernando established the Inquisition in his realms because, like Castile, they, too, were plagued by the heresy of judaizing Conversos; he did not do so because he and Isabel were utilizing the Inquisition as a tool to control their Spanish state. It was reason of faith, not reason of state, that crossed state boundaries and brought the Inquisition to Aragon.

Fernando's Mudejar policy was a subtle one, comprising a number of variables that he dexterously balanced, one against the other. Mudejarism was fostered in order to increase the population of and the taxes paid by royal aljamas, while the protection afforded Mudejars by the Crown was of an ambivalent sort, compensating Muslims for the injuries perpetrated on them without providing an effective deterrent through punishment of the offenders.

Mudejar economic activity was encouraged, while their social interaction with Christians was discouraged. The Mudejars' practice of Islam was sanctioned and their forced conversion forbidden, but, at the same time, Islam was abhorred, baptism was welcomed, and the concept of free will in conversion at times bordered on the dubious. Fernando, in whom were combined the craftiness of the Machiavellian politician and the religious fervor of the crusader, could carry on in this manner because he considered all of the variables. Others were more single-minded, and, with respect to the religious minorities, this was the case of the Inquisitors.

The Spanish Inquisition, established to extirpate heresy from the Christian body, found it difficult to restrict itself to that task alone. The Inquisitors quickly concerned themselves with those forces threatening Christian society not only from within but also from without. Because the heresy the Inquisitors were combating was a judaizing one, the Jews themselves, the source of heresy, became the Inquisition's target. Not surprisingly, the Inquisition played a fundamental role in the expulsion of the Jews. Although before 1500 there was practically no population of converts from Islam, and therefore no threat of an "Islamizing" heresy infecting the Christian body, the Inquisitors nevertheless set their sights on the Mudejars. In the process of putting the Christian house in order the Inquisitors decided that the only way to do so effectively was to remove all nefarious influences, which meant ridding Spain of both Jews and Muslims.

Early in its history in Valencia the Inquisition displayed a tendency to exceed the bounds of its proper jurisdiction. In 1482 Juan Cristóbal de Gualbes, the Inquisitor General of Aragon, clashed with the lieutenant bailiff general of the kingdom, Berenguer Mercader. The conflict was centered on a Jewess of Murviedro, Dolçina, whom Mercader had freed from the Inquisition's jail and refused to relinquish to the Inquisitors. Mercader maintained that although the Inquisition could interrogate Jews, it could not punish them, either by imprisoning them or, as it had done in the past, by torturing them. To do so was to encroach upon royal prerogatives, which it was the duty of the bailiff general to protect. Gualbes's argument is revealing, for it indicates the Inquisition's intention to proceed against Jews and Muslims as well as heretics. The Inquisitor cited a provision of King Martin—obviously in reference to the papal Inquisition—"in which he expressly commanded . . . all his officials that they not hinder the Inquisitors in their inquisition to be made against the Jews and Moors."[202]

Seen in this light, the Inquisition's attacks against the sale to Christians of meat slaughtered by Jews or Muslims (1488) and against the Muslims' call to prayer (1506) appear more sinister. It seems that the Inquisitors had some sort of plan in mind, first to restrict contact between Muslims and Christians, especially in matters with religious connotations, and then to suppress all manifestations of Islam. On Mallorca in 1491 the Inquisitors, among a number of other excesses, proceeded against approximately twenty unbaptized Muslim slaves for chanting the ṣalāt, and by 1508 the Inquisitors in the kingdom of Aragon were going so far as to coerce Muslims to receive baptism.[203] Officials and noblemen in Valencia, Mallorca, and Aragon complained that the Inquisitors were violating local laws and argued that they had no business meddling in these matters.

The Mudejars themselves were not slow to understand the Inquisition's intentions, and so began to fear that institution more than any other. In 1502, after news of the conversion of Castile's Mudejars reached them, Valencia's Muslims were gripped by a fear that they were next in line and that the Inquisition planned to proceed against them, as Muslims. This fear was based on the Inquisition's seizure of two Muslims, who, the Inquisitors maintained, were incarcerated for having dissuaded and threatened other Muslims receiving baptism. Significantly, these Muslims were being baptized in the palace of the Inquisition.[204] It mattered little to the Inquisitors that neither criminal procedure against Muslims nor proselytizing Muslims fell within the realm of their duties. In their campaign against the religious minorities the Inquisitors used every opportunity to further their goal of an entirely Christian society.

It is worth repeating that the Crown of Aragon's Mudejars were neither converted nor expelled during Fernando's reign. Nevertheless, it was Fernando who loosed the Inquisition on Valencian society. The king's view on all the Inquisition's activities is difficult to pinpoint. On the question of the Muslim and Jewish butcher shops he seems to have agreed with the Inquisitors; regarding other matters he was silent. However, on one issue—the use of force in religious conversion—Fernando did speak his mind loudly and clearly. Consistent with his stance in Valencia during the years 1500–1503, in 1508 he sharply rebuked the Inquisitors of Aragon for attempting to force Mudejars to convert, reminding them that only voluntary conversion through conviction is pleasing to God.[205] Although Fernando and Isabel were able to control the Inquisition, it was not long before it took on a life of its own, an effective and insidious apparatus, feeding and feeding off of Spain's religious passions. However durable the Muslim–Christian modus vivendi in Valencia was, there were certainly a number of Christians who concurred with the Inquisition in its drive toward religious uniformity. The Inquisition's presence only served to augment the ever-present hostility toward the Muslim. This is not to suggest that the anti-Muslim violence of the *Germanías* was in any way Inquisitorially inspired; the cause of that violence was far more complex. It is only to raise the question of how long Valencia's Muslim–Christian *convivencia* could have withstood the assaults of the Inquisition, an institution that allowed no room for ideological alternatives and made the question of religious identity an obsession. The tradition of Mudejarism that Fernando so vigorously upheld was probably partly undermined by an institution of his own creation.

2   The War against Islam and the Muslims at Home

From the broad perspective of the shifting balance of power in the Mediterranean, the foreign policy of Fernando and Isabel seems an unrelenting struggle with the enemies of the Catholic faith. The newly united Spanish kingdoms faced the threat of the Ottoman Turks to Aragon's Italian possessions while pursuing the conquest of the sultanate of Granada (1482–1492) and subsequently carrying the crusade beyond the Straits of Gibraltar. This international confrontation with Islam appears the logical concomitant of an internal policy that resulted in the expulsion of the Jews and the conversion of the Muslims of Granada and Castile. The imposition of religious uniformity at home coupled with Spain's aggression against Islam abroad marks the era of the Catholic Monarchs as the beginning of the polarization of the Mediterranean into Christian and Islamic blocs, which, in the midsixteenth century, would be led by Hapsburg Spain and the Ottoman Empire.

In this view, which emphasizes the conflictive character of the Christian–Muslim interface, Fernando's fostering of the Crown of Aragon's Mudejar communities appears to be a vestigial medieval policy at odds with his larger political and religious designs. Looking toward Lepanto and the fate of the Moriscos, Fernando's Muslim subjects seem nothing more than historical anomalies destined to be crushed in the collision of opposing Mediterranean powers.[1]

However, the Mudejars of the Crown of Aragon cannot be so easily thrust aside as the victims of an unremitting and indiscriminate assault by the Catholic Monarchs on Muslims and Jews alike. Fernando's Mudejar policy was far more nuanced and complex. Therefore, our interest here is to analyze how the wars waged against Islam affected Fernando's perception of and policy toward his Muslim subjects in the kingdom of Valencia, and how the Mudejars themselves responded to the intensification of the perennial conflict between Christianity and Islam. The focus on the kingdom of Valencia implies a recognition of the essential diversity existing within a Spain newly formed by the union of the Crowns of Aragon and Castile. That this union gave the impression that the Mediterranean states were now aligned on a strictly ideological basis—Christendom led by Catholic Spain against the Ottoman Turks and the Maghriban sultanates—and also allowed for a fuller expression of Castile's peninsular hegemony should not lead to the assumption that Aragon was always a pliant and willing partner in Castilian enterprises or that the lives of its peoples were suddenly redirected along routes laid out by Castile. On the contrary, the divergent interests of the two Crowns help to explain the apparent contradiction between Fernando's foreign policy and his Mudejar policy within the territories of the Crown of Aragon. Castile, the dominant partner in the union, provided the impetus, the zeal, and the majority of the manpower for the crusades against Granada and North Africa. To the degree that battling with Islam reflected Aragon's interests, it owed less to a crusading spirit than to a perceived need to advance and protect its political and commercial hegemony in the western Mediterranean against the threats of an expanding Ottoman empire and increasingly troublesome Maghriban corsairs. Otherwise, still vital in the lands of the Crown of Aragon were the traditions of Mediterranean frontier life which admitted the necessity of minority enclaves and impelled Catalan and Valencian to the Maghrib and Granada for trade.

The crusades and the forced conversion of Muslims in Granada and Castile were viewed from within the kingdom of Valencia in a light different from the one that illumined the vision of Castilian contemporaries. For the Castilian the conquest of Granada was the fulfillment of a long-held ambition, an ambition Valencian Christians had not shared since Castile's acquisition of Murcia (1304), which formed a buffer between Valencia and Granada. The conversions in Granada and Castile were more consonant with a Castilian drive toward religious uniformity than with a general Spanish obsession. While the difference between Castile and Aragon on this score should not be overemphasized, it is nevertheless worth noting that the campaign against the Conversos and the establishment of a national Inquisition had their most vociferous exponents in Castile. In contrast, Catalans, Aragonese, and Valencians resisted the intrusion of the Holy Office into their homelands.[2] Likewise, the majority of Valencians viewed with dismay the Mudejar policy enforced by the Monarchs in Granada and Castile, perceiving in it an unwanted challenge to their own social traditions. Throughout the period of Fernando's reign Valencia's Muslims and Christians continued to act in accordance with accustomed economic and social patterns. There was no reason to suppose that the 250-year-old Muslim–Christian modus vivendi would not weather the storm created by another clash of faiths on an international scale. An analysis of the evolution of events in Valencia demonstrates that there were alternatives to the rueful course of action pursued in Isabel's kingdoms. Valencia's Mudejarism was not an anachronism, nor was the final conversion of the kingdom's Muslims in 1525 an inevitability. At each step along the road toward religious uniformity in Spain there was room for reconsideration and redirection. That Fernando was able to encourage Mudejarism within Valencia while crusading against Islam substantiates this point.

This does not mean that as he engaged in a protracted struggle with Islamic powers Fernando was oblivious to the potential menace lurking in the kingdom of Valencia with its 30 percent Muslim population. There, Muslim–Christian *convivencia* had succeeded, but it did so in spite of certain problems, perhaps the most serious of which was the persistent danger that the Mudejars formed a fifth column. Past manifestations of Mudejar allegiance to the Crown afforded Fernando little cause for comfort, for it was a history marked by rebellion and ambivalent loyalty. Moreover, earlier anti-Muslim violence on the part of Christians suspicious of Mudejar intentions suggested a possible threat to the public order.

The conquest of the kingdom of Valencia had scarcely been completed when the Mudejars rose in revolt in the late 1240s, and then repeatedly in the 1250s, 1260s, and 1270s, the latter effort with the aid of Moroccan and Granadan allies.[3] The terrible anti-Muslim social riots of 1275–1276, although not demonstratively a direct response to the Mudejar revolts, owed their origin to an atmosphere of heightened tension.[4] Even after more than a century of Crown rule, the majority of Valencian Mudejars chose to defect to the enemy during Pedro IV's war with Castile, in contrast to the behavior of their more acculturated coreligionists in Aragon. Other abortive uprisings followed in 1359 and 1364. The messianic pretensions of Cilim, a Mudejar of Antella, inspired the first of these, while the particularly difficult conditions caused by the war with Castile were at the root of the latter.[5]

During the fourteenth century Christian violence occurred sporadically in assaults on the *morerías* of Játiva and Murviedro in 1288 and 1299, of Valencia in 1309, of Crevillente in 1385, and of Játiva and Elda in 1386. The intervention of royal and seigneurial officials quelled other potential outbreaks or at least prevented the violent actions of individual Christians from developing into mob violence. Maria Teresa Ferrer i Mallol points out that such attacks on Mudejars tended to coincide with periods of war with the sultanate of Granada or with rumors of possible Granadan attacks. Suspicions that Mudejars were spiriting Christians away to the slave markets of Granada and the Maghrib also sparked Christian hostility. While Christian anxiety must have abated somewhat in the fifteenth century as Granadan and Maghriban power and the Mudejars' demographic weight all diminished, there occurred, nonetheless, attacks on the *morería* of Elda in 1428 and on that of Valencia in 1455.[6] This last outbreak is especially instructive—as it must have been for Fernando—for the role played by the fear of Muslim aggression in the generation of Christian hostility. In 1451 the participation of the Naṣrid sultan in the factional strife of the Murcian nobility and the rumors of the massing of a Granadan army for a post-Ramadan campaign moved the jurates of Valencia to advise Alfonso V of the sultan's intention to wreak carnage in the kingdom and carry off its Mudejars. Alfonso was also reminded that the Mudejars were Valencia's "public enemies," with their "ears up and lances sharpened." Although this particular crisis blew over, Granadan forays into Valencian territory continued. The persisting ambience of insecurity and mistrust, in addition to economic difficulties and the toll taken by plague, was conducive to the eruption of violence in 1455.[7] Even days after Valencia's *morería* had been sacked, the cry "the Moors are coming!" sent hundreds of armed men scrambling to the city's walls.[8] The recurrent threat of Mudejar insurrection, real or imagined, with its backlash of Christian violence was the legacy Fernando inherited.

The Ottoman Turks

As the architect of Spain's foreign policy, in which the defense of Christendom often coincided with the furthering of Aragon's Mediterranean interests, Fernando treated with an array of Islamic states ranging from Granada to the eastern Mediterranean. Of these, the expanding empire of the Ottoman Turks posed the greatest threat. During the initial years of Fernando's reign the danger seemed very grave. In 1480 the forces of Mehmet the Conqueror besieged the island of Rhodes defended by the Knights Hospitallers and, worse still, in August of that year captured the city of Otranto on the Italian mainland. Considering this a prelude to the conquest of Sicily, an Aragonese possession, of Naples, and perhaps of Rome itself, Fernando took the Hospitallers under his protection and sent them military and financial support. Spain further responded by dispatching to Italy two fleets, Castilian and Aragonese, to assist in the Christian counterattack. This aid, however, proved unnecessary as the death of Mehmet compelled a Turkish withdrawal from Otranto in September 1481.[9]

During these critical months, Spain's ascendancy over Islam in the West suddenly seemed precarious. Turkish advances rendered the sultanate of Granada more formidable and the allegiance of Fernando's Muslim subjects more uncertain. Fernando was anxious about the possibility of a Mudejar reaction to Ottoman successes. In December 1480 he wrote to his councillors and governor in Valencia and reminded them of the Turkish entry into Italy, suggesting that this Islamic threat to Christendom could have immediate and dire consequences at home. Noting the kingdom's proximity to Granada, the king fretted over the fact that it had such a large number of Muslim inhabitants who were well armed and had access to its castles and fortresses. Having had to postpone the crusade against Granada to counter the Turkish menace, Fernando determined at least to neutralize the Mudejars, lest they "make some effort in our disservice and that of our Lord God and in damage of that kingdom." He therefore commanded that all the Muslims in the kingdom be disarmed and denied access to fortresses, which included removing from office any Muslims exercising custodianship (*alcaydies*) over castles. All this was to be done so that "we may be without any fear of the said Moors."[10]

However, Fernando added that his officials should act in this matter as they deemed best, without causing any "inconvenience or scandal."[11] In effect, this meant that they could do very little. Although arms control could be effectively exercised in the royal cities and towns, where Muslims were either fined for bearing arms or granted license to do so,[12] it was unfeasible on seigneurial lands.[13] Documents from 1487 and 1502 describe the Mudejars as still armed to the teeth.[14] As for the custodianship of castles, this probably was not a problem, for there is no evidence of Mudejar *alcaydes*. The more important question is whether there was a real need for these preventive measures. At this point there does not seem to have been any Mudejar activity even suggesting insurrection. Whatever pleasure or hope Valencia's Muslims might have derived from Islam's distant progress, Turkish advances in Italy had insufficient impact on the structure of power in Valencia to have given them any illusions as to the possible success of a revolt. Accordingly, Fernando's officials seem to have thought it best to keep only a cautious eye on the Mudejars without unnecessarily upsetting them by the application of a firm hand.

Fernando was not alone in his uneasiness over the Mudejars' intentions. In February 1481, having already ordered the religious houses of Valencia to pray for divine aid against the Turks,[15] the jurates of the city of Valencia cautioned the king that necessity demanded the taking of some action regarding the great number of Muslims residing in the kingdom. For them, the Mudejars' presence was a threat to the public peace. Despite the opinion of the seigneurs of Muslim vassals, who preferred maintenance of the status quo, the jurates urged Fernando to take measures to preserve the kingdom from "irreparable ruin."[16] It is difficult to say what measures they had in mind. In any event, no further action was taken. Given the probable opposition of the barons, who were in a better position to know of the Mudejars' plans than were the more apprehensive jurates, the efficacy of any expedient would have been minimal.

The Turks continued to preoccupy Fernando throughout the 1480s. Rumors of the massing of Turkish armadas in 1484 and 1485 and the Turks' attack on Malta in 1488 moved him to strengthen Sicily's fortifications. The conflict between the Turks and Mamluk Egypt suggested to Fernando the utility of an alliance with the Mamluk sultan, Qā'it Bāy. In 1488 Spain shipped wheat to Egypt—the revenues from its sale were to help finance the war against Granada—and, after the Mamluk victory over Turkish forces, Fernando proposed further aiding the Mamluks with a naval force of fifty caravels. This understanding between Fernando and Qā'it Bāy lasted until the latter allied with the Ottoman Bayezit II in 1491.[17]

Although himself fully capable of cutting across ideological boundaries to ally with Mamluk against Ottoman, Fernando still doubted that the fealty of his own Muslim subjects was of sufficient strength to counterbalance the political implications of their religious adherence to Islam. He was prone to lend credence to even the more far-fetched stories of Mudejar anti-Christian activity. For instance, in 1480 he commanded an investigation into the matter of certain Aragonese Mudejars who had allegedly incited the Mamluk sultan to destroy Christian churches in Jerusalem.[18]

Nevertheless, Fernando can hardly be blamed for expressing concern over the information that reached him in 1487. It involved an Islamic alliance linking the Mudejars and the Turks to Granada as a reaction to the Naṣrids' desperate situation. It was reported that for the past six years the Valencian aljamas had been sending financial aid in support of the war effort of the Naṣrid sultan. For Fernando, already into his sixth year of grueling campaigning in Granada, this news must have been particularly galling. But that was not all. The Mudejars had dispatched to "the Turk" (Bayezit II) two envoys, one from Játiva, the kingdom's largest morería, and the other, a certain Pacoret, from Paterna. They were to inform Bayezit of the Catholic Monarchs' war against Granada and that if he did not send aid all would be lost. Specific suggestions were made as to how the Turks could be most effective. Bayezit was to send "his people" to Valencia, and there, and in the other Spanish kingdoms, 200,000 Muslims would rise up in their favor and bring about the "damage and destruction of the Christians." The Moors of Valencia were preparing themselves for this eventuality. It was said that each Muslim had in his home more arms than were necessary for any one person.[19]

The king's reaction was surprisingly restrained. He ordered three officials to find out if there was any truth in these rumors. Their conclusions were to be sent to Fernando in letters under closed seal, so that he himself could decide on suitable punishment for the Muslims and the *morerías* implicated.[20] Again, as in 1480, there survive neither responses to the king's queries nor record of the punishment of Mudejar rebels.

That in both cases official inquiry produced no damning evidence against the Mudejars should not suggest that Fernando dwelled in a crusader's dream world filled with phantoms of Muslim conspirators. A distinction must be made here between intention and act. According to Fernando's informants, a Mudejar uprising was contingent on the entry of Ottoman forces into Spain. That Bayezit, his hands full in the East and in Egypt, was in no position to mount an invasion of the western Mediterranean, much less of Spain, and, thus, could not lend any substance to Mudejar plans, does not exonerate the Mudejars of the intention of rebellion under propitious circumstances. It is very much within the realm of possibility that Mudejar–Ottoman contact had, in fact, been established.

By 1487 Naṣrid poetic appeals for assistance had reached both Mamluk and Ottoman courts. Also, the Egyptian chronicler Ibn Iyās records that in A.H. 892 (A.D. 1486–1487) Naṣrid ambassadors arrived in Cairo requesting that Qā'it Bay send an army against the Spanish Christians. Qā'it Bāy responded with a message to Fernando, warning him that if he did not halt his attacks on Granada, reprisals would be inflicted on the clergy of Jerusalem and Christians would be denied access to the holy places. Bayezit, his interest aroused by the Naṣrid appeal, dispatched the privateer Kemal Reis to the western Mediterranean on a mission of reconnaissance. Reis is thought to have made direct contact with Granadan Muslims somewhere along Spain's southeastern coast. He and his Ottoman corsairs based themselves in Bougie and Bône and on the island of Jirba, and from there conducted raids on Christian coasts and shipping. Reis was active in the area until 1495, when he was recalled to Istanbul by Bayezit.[21]

Fernando's response to reports of a Mudejar embassy to the Turks (23 April 1487) after the arrival of the Naṣrid ambassadors and poetry in the Mamluk and Ottoman courts, and probably not long after Kemal Reis sailed into western Mediterranean waters, gives to these reports a ring of truth.[22] Their veracity is supported further by their specific identification of the two Mudejar envoys. Fernando's informants had emphasized three points: (1) Mudejar financial aid to Granada; (2) a Mudejar appeal to the Ottomans that Granada was desperately in need of help against the Christian onslaught; and (3) Mudejar assurances of their rising in tandem with an Ottoman invasion. The central factor was the Mudejar preoccupation with Granada's fate. It was more than coincidental that the Mudejar embassy was sent within a year of the Naṣrids' decision to take diplomatic initiatives in the hope of alleviating their grave situation. Communication between Valencian and Granadan Muslims was frequent, as they were closely linked by ties of kinship and commerce[23] and often crossed each other's national borders with or without official license.[24] Both groups realized that the Turks were Granada's only hope and acted accordingly. It is certainly possible that Mudejar envoys in conjunction with Granadan Muslims met with Kemal Reis somewhere along Spain's southeastern coast, perhaps near Almería, a city with which Valencian Muslims had close relations.[25] In this scenario "the Turk" with whom the Mudejars made contact would have been Kemal Reis, not Bayezit II. An alternative to an Iberian rendezvous was a Maghriban one, perhaps at Reis's base in Bougie, which was more accessible than Istanbul. The Mudejars were certainly in touch with Ottoman corsairs by 1502.[26] Earlier contacts, while there was still some hope for the Naṣrids, do not seem improbable.

After this episode the spectre of a Mudejar–Ottoman conspiracy ceased to haunt Fernando. Once Granada was conquered the threat of a Turkish invasion in relief of the Naṣrids was removed, and with it the possibility of an Ottoman-inspired Mudejar insurrection.

Granada

For Spanish Christians the Ottoman Turks were a relatively new arrival in the Mediterranean arena of religion and politics. Their main theater of operations lying in the East, the Turks were an unfamiliar foe whose aggressive expansion filled the Spanish with dread, each Turkish conquest conjuring up images of atrocity and horror.[27] It is not surprising that this "Turkophobia" sparked rumors of a Mudejar revolt in the Ottomans' favor. In contrast, the Spanish were well acquainted with the Muslims of Granada. For centuries the rulers of Granada, the Maghrib, Castile, and Aragon had engaged in a bewildering complexity of alliances as a means of maintaining an uneasy balance of power. The permeable Granadan frontier had seen the regular passage of both raiding parties and merchants. In Granada there lay little of mystery and even less to fear. The union of Castile and Aragon deprived the Naṣrids of the surest means of ensuring their state's survival, the ability to play off one Christian kingdom against the other.[28] Cognizant of the fact that the Naṣrids were on the defensive, Fernando did not trouble himself over the possibility of an invasion from Granada with an attendant Mudejar rising. This scenario was more characteristic of thirteenth-century than of late fifteenth-century conditions. Only when an Ottoman offensive threatened to overtake western Europe, thereby enhancing the offensive capacity of western Islam, did Fernando give serious consideration to the implications of the Mudejars' ambivalent loyalty. Otherwise, Mudejar dissidence and shadowy allegiance to Granada was little more than one of the accustomed nuisances of frontier life, a thorn in the side perhaps, but not a threat to the state.

The initial years of Fernando's reign were characterized by a continuation of the traditional contacts between Granada and the Crown of Aragon. Until the crusade began in earnest, Valencian merchants, both Christian and Muslim, plied the short-distance maritime trade between the ports of Valencia and Almería. As late as October 1482, the bailiff general and the jurates of Valencia were requesting that the *qā'id* (*alcayt*) of Almería treat Valencian merchants with favor.[29] Having recently concluded a pact with the *qā'id* of Almería and the sultan of Granada, the jurates of Valencia corresponded with Almerian officials and with the sultan himself regarding the affairs of Valencian merchants. In one case, the jurates sought the release of the merchant Perot Miquel, whom the Almerian authorities had unjustly arrested on account of the debts of another Christian merchant.[30] Mudejars from various *morerías* continued the trade with Almería that had been monopolized by the Valencian merchant families Ripoll, Bellvis, Xupio, Benxarnit, and Razbayda until the sack of Valencia's *morería* in 1455. Other Mudejars travelled there to collect the inheritances of deceased relatives or to study Arabic.[31] Likewise, business drew to Valencia Granadan Muslims such as Abdalla Çalema of Almería, who returned to Valencia, his former home, as an agent of Almería's *qā'id* and to settle accounts with his own creditors.[32] The outbreak of war understandably necessitated the restriction of movement between Granada and Valencia, thereby disrupting the flow of trade.

While Muslim and Christian merchants resided comfortably in each other's cities under official protection, both sides engaged in the desultory frontier warfare of the lightning raid and the taking of booty and captives. Although the kingdom of Valencia was not contiguous with the sultanate of Granada, Muslim raiders found that the intervening kingdom of Murcia, mountainous and sparsely populated, provided little impediment to their incursions.[33] On account of their relatively exposed position, Orihuela, Elche, and Alicante had formed, in 1399, a *Hermandad* (Brotherhood) with the Mudejar aljamas of the area. Because the Mudejars were known to act as spies for the Granadan *almugavers* (raiders), one clause of the charter of the *Hermandad* demanded that the aljamas pay the ransom of any Christian captured by the Muslims. The Christians were to do the same for any captive Mudejar whom the neighboring Castilians might carry off. The *Hermandad* had dissolved by 1407, so that the Catholic Monarchs found themselves confronted with the same frontier problem. Thus, in 1483 Isabel was compelled to command that action be taken against those Mudejars of Murcia who were bearing arms and abetting Granadan enemies by hiding them in their homes.[34]

The Granadan Muslims who were able to infiltrate Murcia encountered little hindrance to their entry into Valencia. In September 1481, Fernando felt obliged to act decisively on the matter. He deplored the fact that Muslims were secretly entering the kingdom from Granada and perpetrating many crimes against the persons and property of Christians travelling on the kingdom's roads. The king was aware of Mudejar collusion with the enemy, pointing out that the *almugavers* were making themselves inconspicuous in the kingdom's large *morerías* by mixing in with and thereby increasing their populations. Fernando sought to remedy the problem by more tightly controlling the kingdom's roads. Any Muslim seen traveling by unaccustomed routes was to be seized and brought before the bailiff general for judgment. Fernando was particularly interested in the prosecution of the guides (*adelils*), presumably Mudejars, captured in the company of enemy Muslims. They were to be handed over to royal officials and punished in exemplary fashion.[35] These measures would affect only those Mudejars clearly working with the *almugavers* as spies and guides. Entire *morerías*, the majority of whose inhabitants probably turned a blind eye to the comings and goings of the Granadan visitors, would escape chastisement. Two years later the kingdom still had its share of Granadan infiltrators. Consequently, Fernando reissued the above orders.[36]

It may be that this state of affairs was partly responsible for the royal proclamation made in the city of Valencia in 1481. So that they might be easily distinguished from the Christians, the Jews and Muslims were to wear special symbols—blue garments, beards, and tonsures in the case of the latter.[37] In 1486 Fernando explicitly cited the Mudejars' failure to wear symbols as being a factor which enabled them, incognito, to assault and kidnap Christians. However, the addition of Muslim sexual relations with Christian women to the list of resultant evils suggests that social issues were at least as compelling in the issuance of the royal proclamation.[38] Royal officials, then, had to contend with two forms of

Muslim dissimulation: the incognito *almugaver* mixed in with the Mudejar population, and the Muslim in Christian attire concealing his religious affiliation. Detection and capture of *almugavers* and Mudejar spies would have been extremely difficult.

Nevertheless, there were some successes. In 1480 there were still pending from 1475 cases of Valencian Muslims accused of the crime of *collera*, the kidnapping of Christians for sale as slaves in Islamic countries.[39] Mudejars of Nompot, near Alicante, and Aspe were arrested for the same crime.[40] *Almugavers* captured in Murcia and in an area as far north as the Vall de Uxó were to be interrogated about their mode of operation and the accessories to their crimes.[41] Enhanced travel restrictions proved effective. Mudejars traveling on the prohibited backroad linking Tibi to Cocentaina were seized.[42] Others who had journeyed to Granada without royal license were caught and punished with enslavement.[43] There was surprisingly little arbitrary seizure of Mudejars by royal officials, which excess Fernando's road controls might well have provoked. In any case, the forays of *almugavers* with the collusion of Mudejar colleagues seem to have ceased after 1483. This was due to the escalation of the war against Granada, which forced the Naṣrids into a defensive posture. Also, the war brought more stringent border controls, so that Murcian Muslims could enter the kingdom only through the city of Orihuela.[44] Therefore, the war that erected a barrier to commercial traffic also shielded Valencia from the depredations of Granadan *almugavers*.

During the decade-long crusade against Granada Fernando does not seem to have viewed the Mudejars as a serious military problem. Strategies were not adapted for the eventuality of a Mudejar rising in Granada's favor, nor were preventive measures taken beyond the investigation of rumors. It is true that after the taking of Alhama, in an effort to raise subsidies for the war from the estates of Valencia, the king warned various nobles and prelates that on account of its large Muslim population and its proximity to Granada the kingdom could be in some danger were Granada not conquered.[45] However, Fernando probably should not be taken too seriously here. Such a warning was a bargaining ploy, not an honest assessment of the real possibilities of a Naṣrid counteroffensive. It is possible that at this early stage of the war (January, 1483) Fernando still had the Ottoman threat at the back of his mind. Indeed, it was only with respect to the Turks that Fernando had even suggested the impracticable disarming of all Mudejars. The Naṣrids lacked the Turks' offensive capabilities and appeared weak before the combined power of Aragon and Castile. Fernando could afford to be confident that Christian dominance in Valencia would circumscribe Mudejar disloyalty to the few who intrigued with *almugavers* and corsairs. The royal confidence was well founded, for not a Mudejar sword was unsheathed in defense of the beleaguered Naṣrid sultanate.

If reluctant to draw their swords, it may be that the Mudejars were more willing to empty their purses in support of the Naṣrids. In December 1486, it was reported that all the *morerías* of the kingdom, seigneurial as well as royal, were providing the sultan with annual subsidies equaling the value of the hides of all the animals they had slaughtered, probably during the *ᶜīd al-kabīr*, the festival commemorating the sacrifice of Abraham.[46] Five months later the report was more detailed. Apart from their embassy to the Turks, the Mudejars had been sending financial support to the Naṣrids since 1481. In each *morería* the *faqīh* was charged with the responsibility of collecting funds from every Muslim. In addition to proffering financial aid, the Mudejars were doing what they could to turn toward the sultan the favor of the Divine. The *faqīh*s were leading their congregations in a prayer that beseeched God to exalt the sultan of Granada and to destroy the Catholic Monarch and his hosts, along with "other ignorant words of blasphemy that offend the ears." The king, exasperated, ordered investigation and, if necessary, punishment. As for the results, the documents are silent.[47]

It seems reasonable that in lieu of military activity the Muslims of Valencia would have resorted to the collection of funds to assist the monarch of the last Islamic state on Spanish soil. A subject minority, the Mudejars derived moral and spiritual sustenance from the existence of that remnant of al-Andalus to which they were bound by both religion and kinship. José Hinojosa Montalvo suggests that the Naṣrid sultan exercised a spiritual leadership over the Valencian Muslims, noting that in 1455 the sultan had expressed his concern about the welfare of the Mudejars by sending to the Valencian authorities a strong protest over the sack of the city's *morería*.[48] It is possible that the Mudejars invoked the name of the reigning Naṣrid in their Friday prayers. They might have taken it a bit further by praying for his victory over Fernando's armies. Their effort to make contact with the Turks in the Naṣrids' behalf, if true, is another indication of their deep attachment to the Granadan sultanate. Still, beyond the inaudible sinking of Muslim hearts, the fall of Granada had no further reverberations in Mudejar Valencia.

The exigencies of the war against Granada did not drastically alter Fernando's Mudejar policy. So long as the Mudejars displayed their obedience by paying taxes and refraining from anti-Christian violence on a large scale, Fernando felt free to pursue a relatively "liberal" wartime policy. Given the size of Valencia's Muslim population, their well-known contacts with Granada, and the Ottoman danger, a policy of cruel repression would not have been exceptional. Two factors probably dissuaded Fernando from resorting to harsh and hasty expedients. One was the very size of the Muslim population, which cautioned him against an oppression that might have provoked a rebellion more quickly than the feelings aroused by the war itself. The other was his assumption that the nobles could control their own Muslim vassals, and his realization that they would likely oppose any extreme departure from the traditional Mudejar policy. Thus, Fernando exercised discretion and restraint in response to the reports of Mudejar insurgency. A reading of the documentation indicates that the conduct of the war did not significantly disturb Mudejar communities in their local economic and social pursuits.

The war had its greatest impact on the Mudejars' freedom of travel. Royal control of Mudejar movement was nothing new, however. Alfonso V had established in 1418 that Muslims living in areas north of the Jijona River could not travel south of the Jijona without the permission of the bailiff general. This measure was meant to prevent their passage into Granada and Castile.[49] Although economic fluctuations must be taken into account, since the majority of Mudejars traveled south for commercial reasons, an examination of the number of travel licenses granted each year can be helpful in determining the effects of the war.[50]

Licenses for Travel South of the Jijona River

1479:	29	1491:	70
1480:	25	1492:	55 (42 may go to Granada)
1481:	38	1493:	57 (25 may go to Granada)
1482:	34	1494:	22 (13 may go to Granada)
1483:	26	1495:	12 (3 may go to Granada)
1484:	30	1496:	9 (2 may go to Granada)
1485:	18	1497:	5
1486:	22	1498:	8 (8 may go to Granada)
1487:	17	1499:	13 (12 may go to Granada)
1488:	19	1500:	2 (2 may go to Granada)
1489:	13	1501:	2 (Castilian Mudejars)
1490:	6	1502:	1

The decrease in the number of licenses granted during the war years 1485 through 1490, although only moderate until 1489 and 1490, reflects a more stringent wartime policy. In 1491, once Almería and Baza had fallen and the capture of Granada seemed certain, almost twice as many licenses were granted as in the busiest prewar year of 1481. This spurt of activity indicates a Mudejar reaction to the bailiff general's relaxation of the previous stringency. This high level continued in 1492 and 1493, except now Mudejars could travel to Castile and Granada as well as beyond the Jijona River. Postwar population shifts stimulated by Fernando's policy (see below) account for much of this movement. The marked decrease in the number of licenses granted after 1494 can perhaps be attributed to a gradual cordoning off of the former sultanate as an aid to Talavera's missionary efforts. The mere trickle from 1500 through 1502 was due to the revolts in the Alpujarras and to the subsequent conversions of the Muslims of Granada, Murcia, and Castile.[51] From this it can be ascertained that royal policy in Valencia was precautionary and mildly restrictive rather than unduly repressive. Except for the itinerant retail merchants, most Mudejars would not have found such restrictions especially burdensome.

Fernando's postwar policy was an affirmation of his belief in the continuing viability of Mudejarism. Satisfied that Valencian society had survived the shocks of the Granadan campaigns and the worst of the Ottoman threat without major incident, he saw no problem in encouraging the settlement of Granadan Muslims in Valencia. After all, as the "royal treasure" the Mudejars were a valuable asset to which the Granadans were merely an addition. Muslims from Vera, Almería, and Granada were settled in a number of Valencian localities.[52] Valencian Muslims with relatives in Granada were allowed to retrieve them for relocation in Valencia.[53] Even those Granadans who had first opted for the Maghriban sites of Oran and Tunis were given a second chance to become royal vassals in Fernando's kingdom.[54] For both conqueror and conquered the lure of material benefits outweighed the ideal of life in a land of religious uniformity.

Another aspect of this postconquest "liberalization" was the issuance of licenses for travel to and from the new kingdom of Granada. Freed Muslim slaves who had chosen to remain in Valencia were permitted to return home to Granada to visit relatives and to take care of personal affairs.[55] Some Mudejars took advantage of the opportunity to enjoy the splendor of Granada's Islamic culture. A Muslim from the Vall de Uxó went there to study Islamic law.[56] This state of affairs was to last only a few years, after which time Fernando's more balanced approach was thwarted by the extremism of Isabel and Cardinal Cisneros.

The Maghrib

The papal concession of indulgences for a crusade against North Africa and Spain's subsequent conquests along the southern Mediterranean littoral—Melilla (1497), Mers-el-Kebir (1505), Peñón de Vélez (1507), Oran (1509), and Algiers, Bougie, and Tunis (1510)—suggest a confrontation between Christianity and Islam so sharp as to have again thrown the question of Mudejar allegiance into relief. However, because the crusade was more apparent than real, particularly with respect to the Crown of Aragon, and because the Mudejars themselves had played a role during the previous centuries of Catalan–Maghriban relations, Mudejar contacts with Maghriban Muslims presented no more of a problem than those they maintained with Granada.

The key to understanding Fernando's relative lack of distress over the Mudejar–Maghriban connection, which could have compounded the difficulties presented by the rumored Ottoman–Naṣrid–Mudejar conspiracy, lies in the political circumstances of his Maghriban adversaries. Rent by internal divisiveness, with each sultan's power base urban-centered and dependent on shifting alliances with the Berber tribesmen controlling the countryside, the Maghriban sultanates were incapable of presenting a united front to the Spanish, much less of mounting an offensive. They lacked the military organization and the gunpowder technology to offer effective resistance. Even if they had been anxious to place themselves under the protective wing of the Ottomans, the latter were in no position to shore up the defenses of western Islam until they defeated the Mamluks in 1517. Indicative of the debility of the Maghriban states is the fact that during the war against Granada they remained largely on the sidelines.[57]

It would be difficult and perhaps overly artificial to disentangle Fernando's crusading fervor from the geopolitical and commercial motives behind the expansion into North Africa. Still, it seems that in his formulation of a Maghriban policy worldly considerations were more weighty. The conquest of Granada itself compelled the Spanish to gain a foothold in the Maghrib. Without the Naṣrid buffer state Spain's southern coastlines were susceptible to the raids of Maghriban corsairs, whose forces were substantially augmented by Granadan refugees desirous of vengeance on the Christian conquerors. The corsairs' depredations coupled with the restiveness of the subject Granadan population threatened the survival of the new kingdom and advised the taking of strategic points along the North African coast, from which the sea lanes could be better controlled. The lure of African gold made sites such as Melilla, a terminus of the Saharan caravan routes, more attractive. Strategic considerations guided the Spanish endeavor to establish dominion over the island of Jirba, which, along with Malta, would have allowed for the control of the seas between Sicily and Tunisia. The Crown of Aragon's wider Mediterranean interests, which, when the French advanced into Naples, diverted Fernando from the African crusade, seem to have dictated the ultimate course of his Maghriban policy. The invasion and settlement of the African interior were favored by Cardinal Cisneros, an embodiment of the crusading spirit who funded and personally led the expedition against Oran. The Cardinal's aspirations were more akin to those of Queen Isabel, whose dying wish was for the continuation of "the conquest of Africa and the war for the faith against the Moors." Fernando, however, preoccupied with Italian affairs, was unwilling to put forth the resources such an enterprise would have required. The logical conclusion to the crusade against the Moors as suggested by the Granadan experience, namely, Christian settlement and conversion of the indigenous population, was not attempted. Rather, Fernando was content to maintain a string of coastal garrisons, or *presidios*, designed to protect the coasts and commerce of Spain and Italy against Maghriban attacks, and hopefully to establish control over the Maghriban commercial networks. The outcome of Fernando's African crusade was determined as much by the desire to establish Spanish hegemony in the western Mediterranean as by a zeal to subjugate the infidel.[58]

The crusades against Granada and Africa, both largely Castilian enterprises, did not radically change the main contours of Valencia's relations with the Maghrib. Throughout the fifteenth century Valencians engaged in commerce there. The volume of this commercial traffic, never great, seems to have diminished somewhat at the end of the century, owing to the Maghrib's internal strife and to the Castilian offensive. The trade was usually carried by Christian ships, Valencian, Venetian, or Genoese. Imports included animal hides, wax, luxury items such as ostrich plumes, and, of course, African gold. The exports most in demand in the Maghrib were textiles and illegal articles of trade, such as arms, iron, sulfur, and alum. In the latter half of the century 56 percent of this trade was with Ḥafṣid Tunisia. This accorded well with Fernando's promotion of the sale of Sicilian wheat there.[59]

Maghriban merchants, the majority from Tunis and Oran, were frequent visitors to Valencia. Usually arriving on the Venetian galleys that regularly traveled the route between the Maghrib and Valencia, these merchants were granted royal license to conduct their business in the kingdom for periods of one year or more.[60]

The waters of the Mediterranean which allowed for the establishment of commercial ties between Christendom and Africa also provided the corsair with an ample field of action. Although corsairs were certainly capable of criminal acts against their coreligionists, Mediterranean piracy was, nevertheless, an essential element of the larger struggle between Christianity and Islam. Neither officially sanctioned nor ideologically inspired, piracy was no less cruel to its victims than crusade or war. It constantly threatened to undo the friendship fostered by commerce. But like commerce, piracy was profitable to Christian and Muslim alike, reaping rewards in booty and slaves. Christian merchants easily made the transition to piracy when it suited their interests. They victimized Muslims plying the Maghriban coastal trade and even those making the pilgrimage to Mecca.[61] On land Muslims were no safer. They were stolen away from their homes and sold into slavery.[62] In response to the complaints of the sultan of Tunis, Fernando had to admonish Christian merchants to cease the kidnapping of Muslims who entered their ships to inspect their wares.[63]

Perhaps because of their overall military weakness, the Maghriban sultanates often resorted to privateering as a means of inflicting damage on the increasingly aggressive Iberian powers. The Catalan, Balearic, and Valencian coastlines were constantly plagued by Maghriban corsairs. With respect to Valencia, this piratical activity seems to have increased in the latter third of the fifteenth century.[64] Indeed, the correspondence between the jurates of Valencia, Murviedro, and Cullera is filled with reports of the sightings of Maghriban galleys. Not only did Muslim corsairs wreak havoc on Valencia's coastal shipping, they also made daring forays onto the mainland. The objective was always the taking of booty and Christian captives. For instance, corsairs from Bougie set upon a galley transporting wheat to Gandía, killing two Christians and capturing another,[65] while in another case, ten Christian fishermen were borne off.[66] There is an interesting exchange of letters between the bailiff general and the jurates of Castellón de la Plana regarding the strategy to be employed against Muslim raiders ensconced on a nearby island. The jurates, whose plan was to move against the corsairs whose signal fires they had spotted, wanted to be guaranteed full rights to any Muslim they were taking the trouble to capture. On this point the bailiff general concurred, but he suggested laying an ambush for the entire raiding party instead of nabbing only a few scouts.[67] Given such harrowing conditions, efforts had to be made to improve the system of coastal vigilance and defense, particularly at Oropesa in the north and at Guardamar in the south.[68] Ships were manned and armed to patrol Valencia's coastline.[69] Although these measures had some efficacy, resulting in the capture of Maghriban corsairs,[70] Muslim galleys still slipped through. The situation, which probably worsened after 1492, when the corsairs found many new Granadan recruits,[71] became especially critical in 1502 and 1503.[72]

The sequel to the piratical episodes was the ransoming of captives. In Valencian society this was a matter of great concern, for it was always feared that Christian prisoners would be induced to renege on the Catholic faith. The Order of Mercedarians remained active in the redemption of captives,[73] and some towns, such as Biar, had special funds reserved for this purpose.[74] While families worked to ransom loved ones and lords their vassals,[75] the king did what he could to lend a hand. In 1489 Fernando instructed his ambassador to Tunis to congratulate the new sultan on his accession, to promise him support against his uncle

ruling Tripoli, and to demand the release of all the Christians imprisoned in Tunis, or at least of those of high rank.[76] In another case,
the proceeds from the estate of a condemned Converso were granted
to a man from Elche trying to ransom his son held in Bougie.[77]

Inhabiting a kingdom marked by the comings and goings of Maghriban merchants, slaves, and corsairs ensured that Valencia's Muslims
were bound to the Maghrib by much more than an abstract religious and
cultural affinity. A concrete Mudejar–Maghriban connection was further
sustained by the officially sanctioned travel of Mudejars to Maghriban
ports, especially Tunis, but also Oran, Algiers, and One. Allowed to
remain there for one year, they traded, visited relatives and collected
the inheritances of those deceased, studied Arabic, made pilgrimages
(most likely to North African shrines instead of Mecca, given the limitations of time), or simply enjoyed a bit of tourism.[78]

Mudejars had kinfolk in the Maghrib as a result of two complementary patterns of minor population movement. On one hand,
Mudejars were sometimes permitted to emigrate to North Africa,
although never in great numbers.[79] On the other hand, Maghriban prisoners of war—either victims of Christian piracy or pirates themselves—
who had been ransomed by Mudejar aljamas sometimes preferred
permanent residence in Valencia to a return to their birthplaces.[80] Thus,
Valencian and Maghriban might trade places, the difference lying more
in the religion of their respective suzerains than in the circumstances of
their community life. The settlement of Granadan Muslims in Valencia
after 1489 further complicated the picture, so that within the Christian
kingdom itself the Mudejar might rub shoulders with a variegated
throng of Muslims. Some sense of this is conveyed in the confessions of
the Malagan Muslim Caçim Abdalla before the tribunal of the bailiff
general. Caçim had journeyed from Segorbe to the city of Valencia in
the company of two Mudejars, from Cocentaina and Oliva. While in
Valencia he met Mahomat Arayz of Oran, whom he questioned about
employment opportunities in the area. Having no luck finding employment, the two turned to petty theft, which landed them in the bailiff's
court.[81]

The ease with which contact could be established between Muslims of
various origins must have increased the potential for Mudejar involvement in anti-Christian activity. Captive Maghriban corsairs and recently
conquered Granadans, embittered over their own fate, might have inspired Mudejars to take up their cause.[82] The corsairs valued the Mudejars for their knowledge of the kingdom's coastline and interior. If
the latter were willing, the corsairs could establish a network of spies
and guides to facilitate their infiltration of Valencian territory. Plans
for piratical raids could be made and messages sent with Mudejars and

with Maghriban merchants and ransomed captives crossing to North Africa.

To the good fortune of the kingdom the majority of its Mudejars seem to have declined to risk participation in such subversive action. Still, the corsairs were able to find volunteers. Some of the aforementioned Muslims accused of the crime of *collera* could have been acting in concert with either Granadan or Maghriban raiders. The documents are not always clear on this point.[83] There is no doubt about the guilt of the Mudejar of Cocentaina, who was captured by the people of Alcudiola when they beat off the attack of 100 corsairs from Oran.[84] One captive corsair told how his party was guided from Guardamar inland to Rojales by a Mudejar of Albatera.[85] It is also possible that when the corsairs left behind their own spies, the latter were hidden by Mudejar communities.[86] Even more striking is the information received by the jurates of Valencia, that Bablaguer, a Mudejar of Oliva, was piloting a corsair squadron of six ships sailing out of Oran.[87]

According to the bailiff general, the Mudejars of the coastal towns were the most troublesome. Those possessing fishing boats would, under the pretense of fishing, lead to the kingdom's shores the galleys of corsairs intent on capturing Christians. These "fishermen" would also help Muslim slaves to escape in their boats. Because his own prohibitions against the Muslim ownership of fishing boats had not been obeyed, the bailiff requested that Fernando apply the force of royal authority. He suggested that the king enact the same prohibition, with the addition that if Muslims had to fish they must do so in Christian boats. Violators should be punished with slavery and their lords penalized as well.[88] Yet it seems that Fernando did not follow the bailiff's recommendations.

The absence of energetic royal action to curb such Mudejar activity was probably due to the fact that it was not a widespread phenomenon. Even taking into account the difficulty of its detection, the few instances in which the royal authorities actually discovered Mudejars plotting with Maghriban enemies seem to indicate this. Indeed, in 1502, in their effort to persuade the king that Valencia's Muslims ought not to be converted, the nobles argued that in the past, when they were not afraid of being forcibly baptized, the Mudejars often advised Christians of the coming of corsairs.[89] Although the nobles were clearly acting out of self-interest, their argument likely held a considerable amount of truth, for if the Mudejars often associated with corsairs, they would not have been so highly valued as vassals. In 1503, the lords of Benidorm, Polop, and Calpe—all coastal towns—beseeched Fernando to permit the safe and unpenalized return of their Muslim vassals who had fled to the Maghrib during the disturbances of 1502. They maintained that while in Africa their vassals did not capture Christians, but picked up information regarding "the damage that the Moors from beyond would like to do." Fernando, impressed, complied with their request.[90] Thus, the intelligence network between Muslims of opposite Mediterranean shores could work both ways, sometimes to the kingdom's benefit.

The fact that Fernando did not govern his Muslim subjects with an iron hand does not mean he threw all caution to the winds. Just as the war against Granada had necessitated some restriction of Mudejar movement to the southern zone of the kingdom, it also resulted in the cessation of Muslim travel between Valencia and the Maghrib. The bailiff general's alternating stringency and liberality in the granting of licenses for travel abroad to Mudejars roughly parallels the pattern of the bestowal of licenses for internal travel. After 1484 no licenses were granted, but in 1491 the restriction was gradually lifted. As for the commercial activity of Maghriban merchants in Valencia, it reasserted itself in 1486, and, while not evident in 1487 and 1488, rose markedly in 1489 and continued until 1500.[91] Interestingly, this commerce was curtailed at the time of the Muslim revolts in the Alpujarras (1500–1501), but not after the declaration of a crusade against Africa in 1494. Fernando and his bailiff general were guided primarily by a sustained interest in the kingdom's economic welfare. They did not wish to curb the trade carried by Valencian and Maghriban Muslims any more than was absolutely necessary.

The formulation of policy on Mudejar emigration to the Maghrib, although apparently of great relevance to the kingdom's security, was also dictated by the economic interests of the most powerful sectors of Valencian society. While the king might make temporary monetary gains by permitting the emigration of those Mudejars able to pay the required duties,[92] the Mudejars' long-term value to the purses of the monarch and the secular and ecclesiastical lords ensured that they were conceded the privilege of emigration only rarely, if at all. If royal and seigneurial reluctance to open the doors to Mudejar emigration had been based on a fear that their erstwhile vassals might return in the guise of enemy corsairs and soldiers, then they would not have allowed them to travel to the Maghrib for temporary visits, for, if the Mudejars so wished, a year's sojourn in Africa could become a permanent change of residence.[93] The permeability of the Mediterranean frontier, a condition created by the policies of both Christian and Muslim rulers, offered the Mudejars numerous opportunities to cause trouble. Emigration would not have made a substantial difference in this potential. At any rate, there is little evidence from Fernando's reign that Valencia's Muslims were clamoring for permission to emigrate.[94] Only during the years of crisis after 1500 did this become the case.

The Mudejars

Considering the question of Mudejar loyalty in more general terms, it seems reasonable to posit that many of Valencia's Muslims harbored sentiments of allegiance to the wider Islamic world. Such sentiments made them potential insurgents against the government of the Christian state in which they resided. The course of action followed by the Mudejars was guided by their assessment of the realities of the distribution of power among Christian and Islamic polities in the West, by the habits of thought and action resulting from more than two centuries of coexistence with Christians, and by Iberian and Maghriban traditions of self-interested political alliance which often cut across religious boundaries.

The history of Mudejar rebellion in the kingdom of Valencia is a useful indicator of how the Mudejars evaluated their own position. The rebellions progressively decreased in both incidence and ferocity over the centuries. In the thirteenth century they were numerous and threatened the new kingdom's survival; in the fourteenth century they were few and ineffective; and in the fifteenth century there were no incidents, save for the minor disturbances caused by the messianic preaching of a Muslim claiming to be sent by God.[95] There are three explanations for this trend. First, Christian settlement gradually but decisively shifted the population ratio, so that if in the thirteenth century Christians had been awash in a sea of Muslims, by Fernando's reign Muslims constituted only 30 percent of Valencia's population. The sheer numerical weight of the Christians and the increasing solidification of the structures of Christian authority brought home to the Mudejars the futility of rebellion. Second, as Christian power made itself more apparent within the kingdom, the debility of the states of western Islam offered to the Mudejars little prospect of succor in the event of their rising. By Fernando's reign the tables had turned to such an extent that, far from expecting aid from the Naṣrid sultan, the Mudejars had to take up collections on his behalf. Third, it seems that the longer the Mudejars endured their state of subjection to Christian lordship, the more tolerable that burden became. The bitterness, resentment, and fear felt by the conquered for the conqueror gradually gave way to acceptance and familiarity. As Valencia's society evolved, with Muslim–Christian interaction at its core, the original relationship of colonialist Christian conqueror to vanquished Muslim subject was transformed into the more tolerable, albeit highly imperfect, one of social majority to minority. The conditions that had made the Muslim bristle in the thirteenth century were accepted with greater equanimity in the fifteenth century.

Under these conditions the Mudejars weighed their options. It is significant that the question of Mudejar rebellion was raised only with reference to the Ottoman Turks. Ottoman victories in the East raised a faint glimmer of hope that Granada might be saved and Islamic rule reestablished in Valencia. Thus they offered the Turks their support in the unlikely event of an invasion of Spain. Long shot that this was, the Mudejar–Ottoman conspiracy probably never went beyond an exchange of encouraging words between Mudejar envoys and the corsair Kemal Reis.

An understanding of political and military reality determined the Mudejar reaction to the crusade against Granada. Because the Naṣrids were besieged throughout the war, it was clear that a Mudejar revolt would not meet with any reciprocal Naṣrid action. That they begged the Turks to relieve Granada is indicative of the Mudejars' realization that alone they could do very little to turn the tide of military events. Financial aid, as an expression of their identification with Iberia's last Muslim suzerain, was the only alternative. In the end, the fall of Granada was accepted with resignation.

The assistance given to Granadan *almugavers* and Maghriban corsairs by the few Mudejar extremists—a label applicable to those who were bold enough to translate into action their discontent with Christian authority—was an accustomed feature of frontier life. The quasi-institutional framework for the redemption of captives existing on both sides of the Mediterranean was prepared to deal with the eventuality of the raid. The reluctance of the king to police his Muslim subjects and his willingness to settle still more Muslims in Valencia after 1489 attest to the fact that the extremists' activities were but an irritant insufficiently widespread to elicit a change in traditional Mudejar policy. For the majority of Mudejars, aware of the extremists in their midst, the necessities of survival and the benefits accruing from assiduous labor outweighed the meager gains to be had from spying for pirates. Indeed, abstinence from such rebelliousness ensured that the king would continue his protection of their freedom to trade and pursue family business, which redounded to their material benefit. In political terms, frontier raiding was not about to alter the structures of power long in place. Few Mudejars were willing to jeopardize their physical and economic security for the limited rewards of insurgence.

This is not to suggest that the Mudejars were insensitive to the plight of their fellows. On the contrary, they displayed considerable commitment and sense of responsibility for their Muslim brethren, but they did so in areas where they could be most effective. Rather than making war, they aided prisoners of war; and rather than vainly rebelling against their Christian lords, they acted on behalf of the victims of oppression. Mudejars helped Muslim prisoners break out of seigneurial jails;[96] they spirited away from brothels Muslim women forced into a life of prostitution,[97] and at times they violently resisted the efforts of royal officials to punish members of their communities.[98]

Most impressive was Mudejar assistance to Muslim slaves and captives. The aljamas often aided and harbored runaway slaves. A number of documents mentioning the whereabouts of runaways sound a similar note: the runaways traveling through and hiding in the *morerías* of the kingdom.[99] This suggests that some sort of network was organized between the *morerías* for the purpose of abetting escaped slaves. Although details are lacking as to the degree of communication between the aljamas and the manner in which they marshaled their human and material resources on behalf of the runaways, the records do shed some light. For example, Muslims of the *morería* of Valencia participated in the jailbreak of a Muslim slave.[100] Another aljama received a female runaway and married her off to one of its members.[101] Muslims of Denia provided fugitives with a seaworthy boat and provisions for making the journey to North Africa.[102] Owing to such covert activities, the royal authorities recognized by 1493 that they had a real runaway problem on their hands.[103] Nine years later they threatened a general investigation of all the *morerías* in the kingdom. The Mudejars disingenuously countered with the argument that although individual Mudejars might have aided runaways, this did not necessarily implicate entire Mudejar communities.[104]

In a more licit fashion Mudejar aljamas also ransomed or purchased Muslim captives, sometimes directly off the auction block. The aljamas became especially active in this regard in 1488 and 1489, when 385 Muslim prisoners from recently conquered Málaga were brought to Valencia for sale.[105] For example, in one large sale the aljama of Valencia purchased nineteen Malagan captives, all at least sixty years of age. Apparently, the Mudejars wished to prevent these elders from suffering the indignity and hardship of slavery.[106] Many of these ransomed captives stayed in Valencia permanently and were able to reimburse the aljamas with the alms they begged from individual Mudejars. Almsgiving, a religious duty for all Muslims, thus acquired a special significance. As one Mudejar explained it: "among Moors of the present kingdom such is the practice . . . that when they encounter a captive who is begging for the love of God they give [alms] to him."[107] Through aiding enslaved Muslims, both foreign and Valencian, the Mudejars met the claims made on them by membership in an international Islamic community without rashly inciting the wrath of a Christian king whose power they could not hope to challenge.

Despite all that has been said about the possibilities of Mudejar disloyalty, it should not be assumed that all or even most of Fernando's Muslim subjects understood contemporary events in terms of Muslim–

Christian confrontation, or that each one contemplated what might be done for the cause of Islam. Beneath all the rhetoric of crusade lay the weighty determinant of self-interest. In explaining the defection of Valencia's Mudejars to Castile during the midfourteenth-century wars, John Boswell emphasizes the history of "self-interested and shifting patterns of loyalty among both the Christian and Muslim populations of the area . . . abandoning one Muslim lord for another in the twelfth century or a Muslim for a Christian in the thirteenth."[108] Similar circumstances obtained in the fifteenth century. Fernando, therefore, could astutely play off one Granadan faction against the other. Maghriban cities readily accepted Fernando as their suzerain in return for protection against Muslim enemies.[109] It is hardly surprising that Fernando's wars against Islamic states did not provoke massive Mudejar defection when a fragmented and divisive Maghrib or a declining Granada were the alternatives to Valencia. Even within Valencia the Muslims expended as much energy in internecine quarreling and family feuding as they did in cooperative defiance of Christian authority.[110]

Some sense of the Mediterranean kaleidoscope of interests and loyalties, material, political, and religious, may be gleaned from a consideration of the careers of a few Granadan and Valencian Muslims. Caçim of Granada came to the kingdom of Valencia after the conquest and settled in Paterna. After some years he decided to emigrate to Oran, and once there he joined a company of corsairs. He returned to Valencia intent on capturing Christians, but unfortunately was himself taken prisoner.[111] Çayde, a potter from Málaga, was captured along with his family en route to the Maghrib. He confessed that "by the will of God they wished to travel to the land of the Moors in order to die as Moors."[112] Not all emigrés found that life in the Maghrib was to their liking (not to mention the ransomed Maghriban captives who chose to remain in Valencia). One Muslim from Baza who went to Africa "to seek adventure" returned to Valencia in order to become a Christian.[113] Another from Málaga endeavored to return to Granada "after not liking the said land [North Africa]."[114] Among the Valencian Muslims returning home after the panicked flight to the Maghrib in 1502 was Azmet Aniza of Alcudiola. He longed for Valencia, "because in that land [Africa] he did not have what [was necessary] to live."[115] Stated bluntly, some Muslims, so long as they could practice Islam, preferred eating in Valencia to starvation in an Islamic land. Pragmatism, survival instinct, striking the best deal possible with one's lord, and the Valencian Muslim's deep attachment to the land of the *Sharq al-Andalus*— these factors weighed more heavily in the balance than ideology for many of Fernando's Muslim subjects, both old and new.

The Christian Populace

Perhaps most difficult to gauge is the extent to which popular Christian hostility against Valencia's Muslim population was aroused by the king's almost constant espousal of the crusade against Islam. Whereas royal strategy and Mudejar response can to a certain extent be interpreted as having resulted from an assessment of political reality and opportunity, an understanding of popular Christian attitudes toward the religious minorities is more elusive, mainly because they were so often rooted in stereotype, imagined wrong, and irrational fear. The material success of a few individuals could earn for an entire minority group the animus of those Christians resenting the economic advancement of their social inferiors. Violence might be perpetrated for reason of crusade or for alleged minority complicity in the spreading of plague, reasons that often masked more base economic and personal motives. The violence initiated by the few could easily spark a social riot involving mass participation. Popular attitudes and their behavioral manifestations were unpredictable, volatile, and at times uncontrollable.

The state of affairs during Fernando's reign seemed propitious for an eruption of anti-Muslim violence. For those Christians who had not experienced the loss of a loved one to Maghriban and Turkish enemies the licensed begging for ransom money by the victims and their relatives brought them face to face with the results of Muslim aggression and cruelty. Seeking alms and recounting their tales of woe, these victims disseminated the seeds of fear and hatred. There were the casualties from the eastern front. The son of a Greek count, having lost his hand in battle against the Turks, came to Spain to raise the ransom for his mother and two sisters.[116] A Hungarian, who had to ransom his father within two years on pain of the latter's conversion to Islam, was allowed to beg for alms not only in Christian parishes but also in the kingdom's *morerías*.[117] Islam, in some way, would pay. Closer to home, the Valencian brothers Redo told how when captives in Tunis "they proposed to lose life, even if they should be afflicted with injuries, labors, and tortures, rather than deny the name of Christ."[118] Bernat Selles of Oropesa bewailed the plight of his two daughters, aged eight and two, whom corsairs had borne off, "because their tender age is so much in danger of denying the faith of our Redeemer."[119] It would not have been unusual if such aggrieved Christians had labeled the Mudejars as somehow responsible.

In addition to the tension evoked by the insecurity of Mediterranean frontier life, there was the preaching of the crusade, first against Granada, then against North Africa, and finally against the Turks.[120] Whatever Fernando's political intentions were and for whatever ends he employed the crusading funds, the frequent preaching of crusade indulgences must have given to the populace the impression of an almost constant mobilization for holy war. Fernando had definite ideas as to how he wanted the crusade to be preached and what sort of atmosphere was to be created:

> you [the governor] should work and see to it that the see and the twelve parishes of that city [Valencia] present themselves with their banners, drums, and trumpets, and with their procession in form, and the bearer [of the bull] whom the particular parish will present should take the cross in his hand on the pulpit before the people and should perform all the acts and things most suitable for drawing the people to devotion and to take the bulls of the holy crusade.[121]

A similar order was issued with respect to all the cities and towns.[122] Moreover, each royal victory in Granada was celebrated by the chanting of "Te Deum" in the cathedral of Valencia and by a procession in honor of the Virgin Mary.[123]

Preaching a crusade against Islam in a kingdom with numerous Muslim communities presented obvious difficulties. Preachers would have to exercise considerable discretion so as not to implicate the Mudejars in their anti-Muslim harangues. The preacher's audience would have to distinguish between their Muslim enemies and their Muslim neighbors. Yet, how muddy the waters must have been when Mudejars were suspected of collusion with Valencia's Muslim foes. Understandably, some overly zealous preachers were unable or unwilling to make any distinctions. In 1457, in the aftermath of the violence of 1455, a Dominican friar in Valencia preached the persecution of the Mudejars. As punishment, the Order's provincial prior removed him from the city.[124] As a prelude to the Germanías' attacks on Muslims in 1521, a Franciscan of Játiva, with crucifix in hand, cried "Long live the faith of Christ and war to the Sarracens!"[125]

Fernando was well aware of the trouble that could be caused from the pulpit. In 1482 he instructed the archbishop of Zaragoza to make sure that the sermons preached in the churches of his see were not such that would incite the people against the local Muslims and Jews.[126] In 1496 he had to reprimand the preacher of the African crusade in Zaragoza for inflaming the souls of his Christian audience against the local Muslims, so that, without reason, its members would wish to maltreat them. Fernando advised the preacher, "it seems to us you could preach your bulls without speaking of the Moors [of Zaragoza presumably]."[127]

Surprisingly, there were no similar royal commands to preachers in

Valencia, the kingdom where the preaching of the crusade had the greatest potential for provoking violence. However, the kingdom's nobility did complain that the Inquisitors were agitating in the see of Valencia against the Christians' eating of meat slaughtered by Muslims and Jews. This had more to do with the eradication of heresy than the crusade.[128] The mobilization for the crusade does not seem to have inspired in Valencia an unleashing of Christian hostility against the Mudejar population. Preachers and populace managed to perceive the difference between domestic and foreign Muslims. That this was so is indicated by the fact that when Muslims were assaulted the victims were Maghriban, not Valencian. In 1496 and again in 1497 it was necessary to proclaim publicly "that no one should dare to maltreat the Moors of Barbary [North Africa]."[129] It was more than coincidental that this violence occurred during the years of the preaching of the African crusade. In commanding that Maghriban merchants be treated benignly and that violent energies be reserved for corsairs and Maghriban armies Fernando was perhaps asking too much of his subjects.

Even though royal authority managed to persuade Christians to restrain their aggressive proclivities, the protracted struggle with Islam still dimmed their view of the Mudejars. One of the ordinances of Valencia's guild of cordmakers expresses the sentiment that all Muslims are the implacable foes of Christianity and that in the event of war the Mudejars are the natural allies of their Maghriban brethren. In justification of the exclusion of all Muslims from the guild and the practice of their trade, the officers of the guild argued that the Mudejars

> with cunning and crafty ways . . . work to learn and wish to know how to make all those things that are for the exercise of war in order to be able to fight with and make war against the Christians, and thus they try among other things to learn the trade of cordmaker and to know how to make crossbow string, which string it is prohibited to transport to the land of the Moors.[130]

This ordinance, approved by the king in January, 1497—the year of the capture of Melilla—makes sense in the context of the crusade against Africa. Still, economic motives must be regarded as partly responsible for the exaggeration of Mudejar ill will. The guild was ensuring that Muslim cordmakers would not encroach on its monopoly, which included a thriving trade with the Muslims of the Vall de Uxó, who specialized in the fabrication of hemp sandals.[131]

One can only surmise why Christian resentment and suspicion of the Mudejars, always evident among certain elements of the populace, were translated into extreme violence in 1455 and 1521, but not during Fernando's reign. Certainly, a measure of good fortune and official vigilance were responsible for preventing the realization of the potential for spontaneous violence. That such potential existed is illustrated by an incident that occurred on Corpus Christi Day, 1491, in the capital. While the throng of Christians and Muslims watched the processions, a Mudejar seized the opportunity to murder his Muslim enemy. Many Christians, believing that a Christian was the victim, grabbed their arms with the intention of moving against the Moors. Only the timely intervention of municipal officials prevented a riot.[132] This was, however, an isolated incident.

Because so much of Fernando's reign was enveloped in an atmosphere of holy war, which naturally underlined the Mudejars' essential dissidence, the absence of organized or widespread anti-Mudejar violence suggests that the ideological and military confrontation between Christianity and Islam was, in itself, not the decisive factor in the engendering of social violence. That confrontation was not decisive because, however much it was enhanced by the Catholic Monarchs, it was nothing new. The Granadan *almugaver*, the Maghriban corsair, and the seditious Mudejar were all familiar figures, as were the Maghriban merchant and the docile Mudejar farmer and artisan. While the former group threatened to render Muslim–Christian coexistence impossible, the latter made it workable. The centuries of experience along the Mediterranean frontier that had gradually tamed the rebellious Mudejars had also taught the Christians to make the economically essential distinction between Muslim friend and Muslim foe.

Because the crusades against Granada and Africa were primarily Castilian enterprises, it may be that their promotion in Valencia received only a lukewarm response. Certainly, a number of Christians paid little heed to the calls for crusade and followed the dictates of self-interest. The victims of Christian piracy were frequently other Christians.[133] Christian merchants pledged a twelve-year-old Christian boy as collateral in their dealings with Maghriban Muslim and Jewish merchants.[134] Christians illicitly transported arms to Maghriban Muslims and to the Turks,[135] and they piloted the fleets of Maghriban corsairs through Christian waters.[136] If Christians could deal with the Muslim enemy in this way, small wonder that the quiescent Muslims at home were left unharmed.

More decisive than the long-standing Islamic–Christian conflict in sparking the flames of violence against the Mudejars were acute social and economic problems, the reverberations of which were felt throughout society. The latent hostility between Christian and Muslim could explode into violence in times of great distress. Social struggle and reform gave way to religious conflict and forced baptisms. As members of

Valencian society the Mudejars occupied particular socioeconomic niches that linked them by bonds of interest to specific Christian social groups. When economic stress placed the latter in conflict with other Christian groups, not only were the Mudejars affected by virtue of their special alliances, they were also singled out on account of their religious difference.

Although historians have not precisely explained the causation of the attack on the *morería* of Valencia in 1455, it seems that considerable economic distress in combination with the Naṣrid threat created the necessary conditions. Plague had hit Valencia in 1450, claiming 11,000 lives in the capital alone. In 1455 drought and a rise in prices added to the calamity. The initiators of the violence were those who would have been most affected by economic dislocations: "vagabonds, apprentices of artisans as men foreign to the city, of poor and minor condition." As might be expected, the rioters looted the Muslims' homes.[137]

The anti-Muslim action of the *Germanías* (1521) occurred at a time when social tensions had reached their peak after years of increasing economic hardship. The demographic recovery of the kingdom since the 1490s had not sparked economic growth; instead, productivity in the industrial and agrarian sectors had diminished, causing in the second decade of the sixteenth century an inflation of the prices of basic food-stuffs which especially burdened poorer artisans and farmers. The *Germanías*, "brotherhoods" consisting primarily of artisans who rose in revolt in 1519, initially sought only to reform the existing social and political system; but they rapidly radicalized and soon were striving to overturn that system. The victims of the *Germanías'* revolution were to be the privileged classes—the urban oligarchs and especially the nobility—those deemed most responsible for an oppressive fiscal and judicial administration and who had abused their privileges to the detriment of the lower classes.[138]

The place held by the anti-Muslim violence in the evolution of the revolutionary movement shows that its primary cause was neither the fear of a Mudejar fifth column nor religious antagonism. In September 1519, Carlos I permitted the artisans of Valencia to arm themselves for purposes of defense against the threatening Turkish corsairs, in effect giving the *Germanías'* movement a legal foundation. This Turkish threat did not move the *Germanías* to take violent action against the Mudejars, even if some Christians might have looked askance at them. Indeed, the *Germanías*, moderate at first, did not even broach the Mudejar question until the summer of 1521, when the movement was "in full revolutionary radicalism." The murder and forced baptism of the Mudejars seem to have had little, if anything, to do with the menace of Valencia's Islamic enemies. This violence, however, had much to do with the *Germa-*

nías' desire to damage their main enemies within the kingdom, the seigneurs. Because Mudejar vassals farmed the land and provided revenue for many a Valencian noble, indeed often paying more taxes than their Christian counterparts, killing or converting the Muslims, the *Germanías* reasoned, would deliver a crippling blow to the nobility. Not surprisingly, the *Germanías*' determination in this regard became particularly marked after their battles with seigneurial armies in which many Mudejars served. Attacks on royal *morerías* occurred only after the *Germanías* had vented their wrath on seigneurial Muslims.[139] The radical *Germanías*' statement of their intentions "to raise souls to heaven and to put money in our purses" points to economic resentment as another factor moving them to the perpetration of violence. Their principal victims in areas of royal jurisdiction were the wealthier Muslims of the irrigated zones who were competing with Christians for free lands.[140] In sum, the attacks of the *Germanías* on the Mudejars were precipitated by economic and social forces distinct from the fundamental religious antagonism. Violence erupted when the network of social and economic relations, which normally helped to allay the ideological tension between Christian and Muslim, was itself radically distorted, thereby bringing that tension to the fore.

Years of Crisis: 1500–1503

The rumblings of change and the origins of crisis for Valencia's Mudejars issued neither from the crusades against Islam nor from within Valencian society itself, but from Granada and Castile, where Queen Isabel and Cardinal Cisneros pursued a harsh and injudicious Mudejar policy that resulted in the elimination of Mudejarism.

It has been recounted how problems began in Granada in late 1499 when the patient and benevolent archbishop Talavera was superseded by the immoderate Cisneros with his brand of conversion by coercion. There followed the revolt in Granada's Albaicín (December 1499), rebellions in the Alpujarras, the region of Almería, and the Sierra Bermeja (1500–1501), the pacification and conversion of the kingdom of Granada's Muslims (by May 1501), and, finally, the expulsion or baptism of the Mudejars of Castile (12 February 1502). It is worthwhile to recall the difficult conditions for emigration offered to the Castilian Mudejars. They were allowed to emigrate only to Egypt. The lands of the Crown of Aragon and those of Maghriban and Ottoman enemies were declared off-limits. Also, male children of less than fifteen years and females of less than thirteen were to be left behind, presumably for a thorough

Catholic indoctrination. As in past centuries, the indigenous labor force remained, but this time under the illusion of religious uniformity.[141]

If Fernando had thought his own kingdoms could remain immune to the tragedy of conflict and conversion transpiring in Granada, he was grievously mistaken. It took little time for news and rumors about these momentous events to reach Valencia. Only two months after the Alpujarras had risen in revolt, the jurates of Valencia reported to Fernando (29 February 1500) that on account of these incidents certain persons of ill will were propagating rumors to the effect that all the Muslims in Valencia were to become Christians, either voluntarily or by compulsion. These rumors had reached the ears of the Mudejars who, fearing for their personal safety, were trading and traveling as little as possible. The jurates, who in the wake of Ottoman victories had asked the king to take measures against the Mudejars, were now requesting that he take action against those murmuring of the Mudejars' conversion.[142]

The jurates do not identify the rumor-mongers. Undoubtedly, there were Christians in Valencia—Inquisitors, lower clergy, those resentful of Mudejar economic success—who approved of Cisneros's methods and were hoping to see a similar Mudejar policy instituted in their kingdom. Also, there might have been concern that the revolts in the Alpujarras and around Almería would inspire insurrection among Valencia's Muslims. In this light, the raids of Maghriban corsairs on Valencian and Andalusian coasts would have acquired more sinister implications. Perhaps the rumor-mongers reasoned that baptismal waters would erase the Mudejars' affiliations with Muslims outside of the kingdom.

Fernando wasted little time in responding to the jurates' plea. On 5 March 1500 he issued orders to the officials in those areas of the kingdom with large Muslim populations—Valencia, Játiva, Alcira, Castellón de la Plana, Villarreal, Oliva, Gandía, Valldigna, Murviedro, and the Vall de Uxó—and repeated the jurates' reports, but in more detail. The king labeled those promoting violence against the Mudejars as "malevolent persons . . . moved . . . by some sinister and grave intentions." Hence, they had disseminated the false rumor "that it would be and is our [Fernando's] intention and will to reduce by force to the holy faith and Christian religion all the Moors of the said kingdom [Valencia]." Fernando had little use for such propagandists, seeing them less as misguided religious zealots than as troublemakers who desired "to move all the people against the said Moors and to seek occasions to riot and rise against them." Not surprisingly, the Mudejars "fearing these novelties . . . refuse to leave their communities to conduct either business or commerce."[143] Fernando insisted that such rumors were not only detrimental to the entire kingdom, but also were contrary to his own intentions. Although events in Granada had suggested otherwise, the king declared the principle that "our holy Catholic faith in the conversion of the infidels admits neither violence nor any force but [only] complete freedom and devotion." Those who continued to say the contrary were to be punished. All the *morerías* of the kingdom, both royal and seigneurial, were to be placed under royal protection and no one was to dare inflict physical or verbal abuse on the Muslims. Anyone disturbing the Muslims in their peaceful existence was to suffer penalties beyond those demanded by the *Furs*, commensurate with the violation of a royal safeguard.[144]

The subsequent cycle of rebellion and conversion or emigration in Granada and Castile, culminating in the decree of 12 February 1502, detracted from the efficacy of these commands and kept tongues wagging. By September 1501, the rumors had spread to Catalonia, compelling Fernando to issue the same orders to officials there.[145] On 20 February 1502, the orders had to be reiterated in Valencia.[146]

Royal correspondence with the bailiff general of Valencia between March and June 1501, regarding the emigration of Mudejars through the port of Valencia, reflects the evolution of royal policy during these crucial months. On 8 March 1501 Fernando reprimanded the bailiff for permitting the emigration to North Africa of Muslims from Aragon, Catalonia, and other areas, when he had expressly forbidden the emigration of all Muslims from any of his kingdoms.[147] The bailiff responded with surprise to this new order, arguing that he had given licenses only to Muslims of Castile and Navarre, not to those of Valencia, whose emigration he knew had been prohibited in the Corts of 1488.[148] Although the bailiff promised obedience to royal wishes, he was again reprimanded (24 April 1501) for licensing the emigration of Catalan and Aragonese Mudejars.[149] At this point Fernando must have felt some uncertainty regarding the complete pacification of Granada and the final formulation of a Mudejar policy for Granada and Castile. His primary concern was to maintain order and to prevent the mass flight of Spain's Mudejars to the Maghrib. Satisfied that the port of Valencia had been effectively sealed off, the king was still compelled to command officials in Valencia and Catalonia to stop Valencia's panicked Mudejars from embarking on boats in the area of Tortosa.[150]

Once sure that the rebellions in Granada had been definitely quashed, Fernando modified the emigration policy. On 25 May 1501 he allowed for the emigration of all Mudejars of the Crown of Aragon, so long as they paid the usual passage duties. However, this did not apply to Castilian Mudejars, regarding whose passage the bailiff general would have to confer with the king, "so that according to the time we can command you what will most fulfill our service."[151] Fernando and

Isabel were probably already considering the conversion of Castile's Mudejars and so wished to curtail their movements. The lifting of restrictions on the Mudejars of his own kingdoms was perhaps intended as a display of good faith to assuage their anxiety. Only twenty-five Aragonese Mudejars took advantage of the opportunity.[152] Although there are no records of the emigration of Valencian Muslims, the nobles were complaining in September that many Muslims were doing so with license of the bailiff general.[153] Fernando's permission of this emigration was a breach of the prohibitive legislation passed in the Corts of 1488. In any case, by February 1502, the final "Christianization" of Castile necessitated that Valencia's door to the Maghrib again be slammed shut.

No one in the kingdom of Valencia had greater sensitivity to the pulse of Mudejar life than the noblemen on whose estates the majority of Mudejars were vassals.[154] They saw firsthand the Mudejar reaction to the Monarchs' Castilian policies. If Valencia's Muslims had been uneasy on account of the fate of their recently conquered fellows in Granada, the conversion of Castile's Mudejars, who had lived under Christian rule for as long a time as themselves, brought them to the verge of panic. On 12 April 1502, the military estate of Valencia informed Fernando of this in no uncertain terms.

Two things were kindling fear in the Mudejars' souls. First, the proclamation that all Muslims of Castile must either convert or emigrate led them to believe that the king would also compel them to convert "per indirectum." Valencia's Muslims had no illusions about the supposed freedom of choice offered by the Monarchs to the Castilians, and were aware of the difficult conditions attached to their emigration ("they have to become Christians or they have to leave the kingdom [Castile] in a certain manner and under certain conditions contained in the said proclamation"). They understood the Monarchs' method of conversion by indirect coercion—that is, anything short of dragging Muslims to the baptismal font—which, although it might satisfy Catholic theologians, would mean for them, as Muslims, an unwilling submission in the most trying of circumstances. The prohibition against Muslims entering and trading in Castile further aroused the Mudejars' suspicions.[155]

Second, the Mudejars believed that the Inquisition was going to proceed against them for having dissuaded Muslims from conversion and for having claimed that Islam is a better religion than Christianity. The Inquisitors' imprisonment of two Muslims led them to think that a general Inquisition of all Muslims was being planned. The Mudejars were "beside themselves with fear," because it was true that they all defended their religion, and that in their mosques the *faqīh*s preached the merits of Islam and warned that Christianity leads to damnation. They reasoned that this would provide the Inquisitors with sufficient excuse to punish them, and that, in order to escape the Inquisition's unendurable penalties, they would either have to convert or flee.[156] From the Jews' experience the Mudejars had learned the lesson of the connection between conversion, Inquisition, and the horrors of the auto-da-fé.

The lords of the military and ecclesiastical estates had already warned the Inquisitors of the great damage the kingdom would suffer if, by their actions, they provoked a Mudejar revolt. In reply, the Inquisitors had assured them that the Mudejars' fears were unfounded and that they had imprisoned the two Muslims only because the latter had come to the palace of the Inquisition in order to dissuade and threaten other Muslims who were there to be baptized. The lords were planning to circulate the Inquisitors' response among the Muslims so as to assuage their fears on at least that score.[157]

For the complete restoration of calm the nobles deemed that royal intervention was essential, and they advanced weighty arguments to prompt it. They reminded the king that the Mudejars constituted the economic foundation of the kingdom and that, were they forced to abandon it, the economy would crumble. The churches, the knights, the urban *rentier* class, and the artisans would all be grievously affected. Given the interdependence of the economy's components, "[when] some are destroyed, all are destroyed." Already the Muslims were so distraught that they no longer wished to work and ceased paying rents to their lords. Instead, they were hiding their movable goods in mountain caches and selling what they could of their remaining property.[158]

Worse still, the present state of affairs was driving the Mudejars to the brink of violent reaction. The nobles, who in previous years had been much less concerned than either the king or Valencia's jurates about possible Mudejar collusion with Muslim enemies, were now raising the specter of Mudejar insurrection. They warned that there were more than 22,000 households of Muslims in the kingdom, who were well armed, had an intelligence network, and lived near impregnable mountain fastnesses. Because the Mudejars were so apprehensive that conversion might be forced on them, any untoward movement on the king's part could result in the deaths of Christians and Muslims and in the destruction of much property, all redounding to the irreparable damage of the kingdom. At this point the nobles maintained that the Mudejars, who had once warned Christians of the approach of Maghriban corsairs, would now welcome them. Notice of the sighting of at least seventeen corsair galleys made this argument more pointed. Although the nobles had an obvious interest in exaggerating the peril in which the kingdom might be placed, the Mudejars' desperation was real enough.

Indeed, the Mudejars had boats hidden along the coast, and it was suspected that they were using them to escape to Africa. Already more than thirty Muslims had fled from Polop, while the lord Bernat de Almunia found that he was losing vassals each day. If the king did not do something to put the Muslims' fears to rest it would be almost impossible to prevent their departure.[159]

The nobles' communication to Fernando of 24 May 1502 reveals that the king had, in fact, ordered the viceroy, his sister Juana, the Queen of Naples, to take measures, but that the nobles were not at all pleased with the royal provisions. Fernando had intended to freeze Mudejar movement: Mudejars were not to change their vassalage; they were not to sell their possessions; and they were not to have boats or go near the sea, all under penalty of enslavement. The nobles felt that such provisions would do anything but inspire confidence among the Muslims, who would perceive them as preliminary to their forced conversion. Therefore, they had convinced the viceroy to delay their public proclamation. Again the nobles insisted that Fernando interdict all interference by the Inquisitors in the affairs of Muslims. The king must give assurances that Castilian Mudejar policy would not have a Valencian sequel.[160]

By July the situation still had not improved. On the contrary, the imprudent actions of the viceroy had served only to enhance the Mudejars' fears. At the instance of one of her servants, a certain Micer Julio, whose slave had run away, Queen Juana was conducting an investigation of the Mudejars' assistance to runaways. Throughout the month of June citations were affixed to the doors of the mosques of each *morería*, commanding the aljamas to send representatives to appear before the viceroy to answer the charges. The Mudejars feared that those aljamas found guilty would be offered the choice of conversion or expulsion. The citations had so terrorized the Muslims that when one was posted in Altea the entire Muslim population of 170 climbed into Turkish ships and fled the place within two days. The barony of Callosa lost twenty-five vassals in the same way. Representatives of all three estates were moved to confer with the viceroy, and they persuaded her to revoke the citations. Then they turned to the king and requested that he put a halt to all such procedures.[161] Nevertheless, throughout the summer and fall of 1502 Mudejars persisted in their attempts to flee Valencia. A number of them were captured at the coast before they could board boats and sail to Africa.[162]

During these panic-filled months there came to the fore the Mudejars' contacts with Maghriban corsairs and their Ottoman allies operating out of Maghriban ports. Muslim piratical activity noticeably increased in 1502 and 1503. Valencia's coasts were so harried that in April 1502, the capital and other coastal towns established a warning system that utilized smoke signals to advise not only of the enemy's approach but also of the size of his fleet.[163] Ships were outfitted to patrol the coastline.[164] Moreover, it appears that the corsairs grew bolder and that the size of their raiding parties increased. Almoradi and Benidorm were attacked by forces of more than 100 and 180 Muslims, respectively.[165] The corsairs' greatest success occurred in August 1503, when a party of more than 600 burned Cullera and captured at least 200 of its inhabitants.[166]

This increase in the Maghriban and Turkish corsairs' determination to inflict damage on Christian Spain was probably related to the peninsular developments of 1501 and 1502. The conquest of Granada in 1492 had already filled the corsairs' ranks with bitter Granadan Muslims. The revolts of the Alpujarras and the Monarchs' harsh policy in Granada likely would have done the same.[167] During these years Valencia's Mudejars maintained communication with the port cities of the Maghrib. Thus, when the corsairs set sail to plunder and terrorize Valencia's coasts they also had in mind assisting the kingdom's Muslims.

It seems that the Mudejars and the corsairs had prearranged plans for the escape from Valencia of those Mudejars fleeing the threat of forced baptism. Preparations might have been made as early as 1500, when the rumors of the Mudejars' forced conversion were first propagated. In any case, it is clear that when the corsairs arrived, the Mudejars were waiting for them on the shore. In May 1502 it was reported that corsairs had arrived near Corbera and that Mudejars of the coastal areas were boarding their ships.[168] In July the jurates of Valencia were more explicit, saying that Muslim galleys were arriving "with the intelligence that they have from some Moors of the present kingdom" and were carrying off many Mudejars to the Maghrib. Most recently, Muslims from Valldigna and from Piles had departed in this manner.[169] When news reached Valencia of the massing of a combined Turko-Maghriban fleet of eighteen ships in Bougie and Algiers, three reasons for the expedition were advanced: to capture ships returning from the Levant; to take booty and Christian captives on the Valencian coast; and to pick up those Muslims wishing to depart the kingdom for fear of forced baptism.[170] The ultimate destination of this particular fleet is unknown, but what is more certain is the flight of an undetermined number of Mudejars from Valencia, and many of them in the ships of Maghriban and Ottoman corsairs.

It is significant that in this desperate situation the Mudejars chose flight instead of armed rebellion. On one hand, it reflects the Mudejars' sense of impotence before Christian power in Valencia. On the other hand, the willingness to abandon their homes and possessions shows that for the Mudejars the freedom to practice Islam outweighed all other considerations. When forced to convert in 1525, the Mudejars of

the Sierra de Espadán would resort to armed resistance.[171] Nevertheless, in 1503 Fernando managed to restore some calm by assuring all
parties in the Corts of Barcelona and in the Cortes of Zaragoza that the
Mudejars could continue to live as Muslims in the lands of the Crown
of Aragon.[172] Consequently, a number of Mudejar refugees returned
home from the Maghrib.[173] As long as they could practice Islam, these
Valencian Muslims preferred to do so in Valencia. Other Mudejars,
however, were less convinced by royal assurances and thought that they
could see the handwriting on the wall, the good intentions of the king
notwithstanding. Thus, as late as July 1504, the bailiff general was still
expressing concern that some Mudejars were secretly leaving for North
Africa in hidden boats and persuading others to join them.[174]

The continuing anxiety of those Mudejars who refused to believe
that royal promises alone could protect them most likely was evoked by
the unabated circulation of rumors that the Mudejars were, indeed, to
be baptized or expelled. Once this idea had been planted in the minds of
some Christians, it could not be easily eradicated. Consequently, in the
Cortes of Monzón (1510) Fernando again had to promise that the Mudejars would remain unmolested. Likewise, in 1517 Carlos I was compelled to issue a proclamation denying any intention on his part of expelling the Muslims of Valencia and Aragon.[175] As long as order was
maintained, the promises of Fernando and Carlos were kept. But
when the revolt of the *Germanías* threw Valencian society into a turmoil
and created the conditions for radical social change, the enemies of the
Mudejars, perhaps inspired by the example of Cisneros in Granada
twenty years earlier, made the Mudejars' worst fears a reality.

The international clash between Christianity and Islam did not have
in Valencia an impact sufficient to unravel the resilient fabric of
Muslim–Christian coexistence. The Mudejars did not express their
identification with Islam by rebelling against their crusading king; nor
did that king harshly oppress his Muslim subjects while warring with
Islamic states. The occasional Mudejar collusion with Muslim enemies
was borne as a customary feature of frontier life, an insignificant
annoyance in comparison with the economic benefits accruing from the
Mudejar presence.

The survival of Mudejarism in Valencia during the years of crusade
owed much to the outlook and determination of Fernando. The king's
reply to the warning of Qā'it Bāy in 1489 affords further insight into his
stance on the question of minority enclaves. As we recall, the Mamluk
sultan had threatened to persecute Jerusalem's Christian clergy if the
Monarchs did not halt their attacks on Granada. Fernando responded
by explaining that the war against Granada was not so much a religious

war as a politically justifiable reconquest of lands taken from the Spanish Christians by the Muslims more than 700 years ago. He also noted that the Christian offensive had been provoked by the continual depredations of Granadan Muslims on Spanish Christians. To clinch his argument Fernando reminded the Mamluk of Spain's long tradition of Mudejarism in which Muslim subjects were guaranteed the freedom to practice Islam and the protection of their persons and property. If Granada's Muslims chose to remain in Spain, they would be accorded the same treatment.[176] In essence, Fernando was arguing that Christian conquest neither precluded Muslim–Christian coexistence nor demanded religious uniformity. In light of the later conversions in Granada and Castile, Fernando's reply appears the height of cynicism. However, Fernando's Mudejar policy in the lands of the Crown of Aragon thrusts into relief the difference between his approach and that of his wife Isabel, and suggests that his reply was, in fact, sincere. In Fernando's mind the tradition of Mudejarism was still one worth maintaining.

A key factor in explaining why Valencia's Christians and Muslims did not rise up against each other in response to the promotion of crusade is that, for them, Christian–Muslim conflict, on either the local or the international scale, was not anything new. Ever present in the social formula of *convivencia* itself was the element of ideological antagonism, which was either mitigated or aggravated by economic and social factors. Indeed, economic and social distress, which tended to thrust religious differences into relief, was usually most responsible for the eruption of violence. More novel than war with Islam was the harnessing of Aragon to the Castilian juggernaut, which, while it allowed for the final conquest of Granada, also unleashed forces within Valencia that threatened its tradition of Mudejarism. Although the union of the two Crowns set the stage for Spain's imperial achievements, it redirected the destinies of its constituent societies in sometimes tragic ways.

3   Mudejar Officialdom and Economic Life

Mudejar life was given shape by two divergent behavioral tendencies, one toward exclusiveness and the other toward integration, at least on an economic basis, into the larger Valencian society. Exclusiveness was to some extent necessary for cultural survival. As members of a minority community of believers in a religiously plural society controlled by the adherents of an inimical faith, the Mudejars desired to prevent the corruption of their religious beliefs and the erosion of their cultural values by excessive contact with non-Muslims. Mudejar exclusiveness was made possible by the communal autonomy that Aragonese kings had vouchsafed to individual Mudejar communities. The institutional expression of this autonomy was the corporate aljama. Under its guidance, and within the confines of the urban *morería* or rural village, the Muslims carried on their religious observances and community and family life. Yet mosque, hearth, and *morería* form only one part of the picture, for the demands of the workplace and the marketplace drew the Muslims out of their segregated existence for more frequent and diverse contact with their Christian neighbors. In the thirteenth century and through much of the fourteenth century, when from 80 to 50 percent of the kingdom's population was composed of Muslims, the Mudejars had been able to live in greater economic isolation, less frequently requiring Christian services or access to Christian markets. However, in the course of the fifteenth century important changes occurred that made such economic aloofness unfeasible. First, a significant demographic shift, which left only 30 percent of the kingdom's population Muslim, saw Christian settlement extend further into the countryside and placed the reins of the kingdom's economy more firmly in Christian hands. The demographic tables had turned such that in field, workshop, and market-place the Mudejars could scarcely avoid intermittent if not daily contact with Christians. Furthermore, the Valencian economy itself developed significantly in the fifteenth century. Far more integrated and effectively articulated than ever before, the economy was driven by and centered on the commerce and industry of the capital. Having superseded Barcelona as the Crown of Aragon's chief city, Valencia dominated the kingdom, drawing to its markets and workshops the agricultural and pastoral products of lesser towns and rural villages, and distributing throughout the kingdom goods imported from abroad or those manufactured by its own artisans. It may be argued that the Mudejars were, after all, mere serfs tied to the lands of their exacting lords, and, therefore, had little to do with the kingdom's economic expansion beyond assiduously toiling on their small plots and delivering to the seigneurs the lion's share of the harvests. However, as will be seen in the course of this chapter, Mudejar economic life was far more diversified, and they participated fully in the Valencian economy. Although few took part in the lucrative Mediterranean trade and few lived in the capital, Fernando's Muslim subjects played a crucial role in that all-important interaction between town market and rural hinterland and in the retail commerce linking the towns to Valencia itself. The Mudejars' integration into the economic life of the kingdom might have served to ameliorate somewhat the general state of Muslim–Christian relations. To be sure, the seigneurs were not alone in benefiting from the Muslims' labor and in therefore having a reason to view their presence benignly. Christian artisans and merchants also interacted with the Mudejars in a manner that may be described as symbiotic.

There were, nonetheless, recognized limitations to the extent of both Mudejar integration and exclusiveness. While it is true that Muslims and Christians often cooperated in an economic context and that such cooperation not infrequently evolved into forms of social comradeship, it must be emphasized that the Mudejars' integration into the kingdom's economic life did not result in the complete breakdown of social barriers between them and Christians. Neither Christians nor Muslims were willing to abandon the religious beliefs and social customs that differentiated them socially. It was not simply a question of social segregation imposed from above; it was, more importantly, a matter of the members of each group willingly exercising restraint in their social relations with one another. Marital and sexual taboos were especially effective in this regard, as were, to a lesser extent, the Muslims' dietary laws, especially the proscription against the drinking of alcoholic beverages. Still, even if Mudejar assimilation and social equality were neither desired nor even contemplated by either group as realistic goals, tranquility, prosperity, and friendship were sought by Muslims and Christians, and sometimes attained.

In economic terms, Mudejar exclusiveness was impractical and would have resulted in their impoverishment. Even from an institutional perspective, the autonomy of the Mudejar aljama was limited. Although the aljama is sometimes equated with the Christian urban *universitas*—as was done by the king and his officials, who often referred to the aljama as "the university or aljama of the Moors"[1]—because it was governed by a group of officials whose functions were analogous to those of the Christian justice and jurates, it nevertheless had no existence independent of the Crown, as did the *universitas*. Essentially creatures of the Crown, the aljamas at the outset of each new reign had to ask the king to confirm their most basic rights and privileges. The aljama's officials were able to exercise their authority in important areas of community life—religious observance, administration of community and mosque properties, and adjudication of certain types of litigation—but all important decisions affecting the aljama as a whole had to be approved by the king or lord. The Mudejars felt the limitations on their autonomy most markedly in fiscal and judicial affairs. For instance, they were not able to borrow funds without royal consent. Needless to say, the aljamas could not defy the Crown, as the *universitates* could and sometimes did in the Corts. The aljama's utter dependence on royal benevolence, and the ease with which the king could drastically alter its financial situation or its institutional structure must be kept in mind, lest the powers of aljama officials be exaggerated.[2] Aljama officials were administrators, judges, and religious savants; they were not governors, legislators, or formulators of public policy.

Mudejar Officials

The chief Muslim official under the Crown of Aragon was the *qāḍī* general, or royal *qāḍī*, whose authority extended over the Mudejars of all Crown lands—the kingdoms of Valencia and Aragon, and the principality of Catalonia. The *qāḍī* general's function was primarily judicial, and he had appellate jurisdiction over all Islamic courts. While there is ample evidence of the *qāḍī* general's judicial activity within the kingdom of Valencia, there is little to suggest that he exercised his authority outside of Valencia, except perhaps in Tortosa (Catalonia).[3]

In the fourteenth century the *qāḍī* general had also held a large number of other offices in Borja and Huesca in Aragon, and in Játiva and Valencia. Because these posts were of necessity held in absentia (the *qāḍī* general at this time resided in Zaragoza), this situation gave rise to abuses and to conflicts between the *qāḍī* general and his appointed substitutes.[4] The problem seems to have been largely rectified by the time of Fernando's reign, during which the *qāḍī* general held only one other office in absentia, that of *qāḍī* and scribe of the aljama of Tortosa. To this office Mahomat Bellvis, the *qāḍī* general, appointed as his substitutes Mahomat Çaragoçi during the reign of Juan II, and Sabat Abaig at the outset of Fernando's reign. Bellvis demanded only that his substitutes recognize his appellate jurisdiction.[5] Bellvis and Abaig seem to have had no jurisdictional disputes. That the *qāḍī* general also functioned as *qāḍī* of the city of Valencia is readily explained by the fact that he resided in its *morería*. The substantial reduction of the capital's Muslim population since 1455 rendered the duties of this position less burdensome, which, in any case, he shared with a lieutenant *qāḍī*.[6]

The letters of appointment of the *qāḍī* general allude to the office's scribal function: "alcadi scriva general."[7] It may be inferred that as scribe the *qāḍī* general corresponded in Arabic with the officials of various aljamas, informing them of the decisions or executive orders of the king and bailiff general. Mahomat Bellvis was also appointed as interpreter, or *torçimany*, for the bailiff general. His task here was to interrogate the Maghriban and Granadan captives brought into the port of Valencia, in order to determine whether they were captured legitimately under conditions of war ("justi belli"). If so, the captives could then be sold as slaves.[8] The *qāḍī* general was the prime intermediary between the king and his Muslim subjects. He had a hand in most Mudejar affairs that concerned the Crown, such as determining the Crown's share of Muslim inheritances or arbitrating the explosive disputes between feuding Muslim families.[9]

The *qāḍī* general was paid an annual salary of 200s, in addition to a fee for services in each case requiring his intervention.[10] However, for the Bellvis family, which held the office of *qāḍī* general throughout Fernando's reign, such remuneration did not, as will be explained, constitute the main source of their wealth.

The *qāḍī* general was appointed by the king, and the office was a lifetime appointment. Mahomat Bellvis, who had been appointed *qāḍī* general in 1458 upon the death of his father Ali, was granted the prerogative to choose one of his sons to succeed him in office.[11] In 1484 Mahomat on his deathbed chose his eldest son, Ali, as his successor.[12] Ali held the post until at least 1501. The Bellvis family continued to monopolize the *qāḍī* generalship until the mass conversions in 1525. The Bellvis were indeed a dynasty of sorts, for members of this illustrious Mudejar family, or at least an Aragonese branch of it, had served the Crown in this capacity since the midfourteenth century.[13]

In each aljama the preeminent official was the *qāḍī*. Because Islamic law encompassed both religious and secular affairs, the *qāḍī*'s role as judge lent him great moral and political authority. Under his purview fell civil and criminal litigation, family matters, such as marriage, divorce, and the guardianship of orphans, and the administration of mosque properties. The *qāḍī* also had a notarial function in the drawing up of marriage contracts and wills. The *qāḍī* of Játiva was paid a salary of 60s annually. While there is no indication that the *qāḍī*s of smaller aljamas were given a salary by the Crown, it is probable that they were remunerated by the courts for their various juridical services. Perhaps more important than the material benefits derived from the office was the great esteem the *qāḍī* commanded in the Mudejar community. The continuity and vitality of Islam under the Crown of Aragon was in great measure due to the persistence of this institution.[14]

The kings of Aragon well understood the essential role of the *qāḍī*. From the time of the conquest through the fifteenth century most of the royal provisions regulating the government of Muslim aljamas call for the creation of a *qāḍī*. However, over the course of centuries important changes had taken place. In the thirteenth century Jaime I had promised nearly every conquered Muslim city the right to elect its own *qāḍī*; yet by the midfourteenth century royal officials were themselves appointing the *qāḍī*s of most royal aljamas. This gave rise to flagrant abuses: the appointment of royal favorites ignorant of Islamic law as *qāḍī*s, and, worse still, the appointment of Christians to the office.[15] By the late fifteenth century the most galling of these irregularities had been corrected. Under Fernando no Christian occupied the post of *qāḍī*, nor did the king bestow the office on unlettered favorites. The Bellvis were certainly well suited for the office of *qāḍī* general. Fernando took care to appoint as *qāḍī*s candidates deemed suitable by the aljama. Indeed, his appointment of Çahat Valenti as *qāḍī* of Játiva seems to have been little more than the confirmation of a unanimous choice made jointly by the aljama and the local bailiff.[16] Although no royal aljama seems to have regained fully the right to choose its own qāḍī, the absence of complaints on the part of aljamas regarding the inadequacy of *qāḍī*s indicates that the bailiffs made their choices only after consultation with the leading men of the aljamas.[17]

Not every royal and seigneurial aljama had its own *qāḍī*. The small size of some Mudejar communities, such as Castellón de Játiva, made the presence of a *qāḍī* an unnecessary luxury. The residents of such communities were able to bring their cases before the *qāḍī*'s court located in a larger town in the vicinity. For instance, Muslims of Castellón de Játiva fell under the jurisdiction of the *qāḍī* of Játiva,[18] as did the residents of seigneurial aljamas in the area, like Sumacárcel.[19] Because of the large amount of business the *qāḍī* of Játiva had to handle, he had an assistant called the sub-*qāḍī* (or *sotsalcayt*).[20] In accordance with the decree of Alfonso III, many seigneurial aljamas must have had their own *qāḍī*s.[21] In the documentation there are references to *qāḍī*s in Paterna, Alcocer, Gandía, Aspe, Elda, and other places.[22]

It is arguable that in the kingdom of Valencia the *faqīh*, or jurisconsult, played a role equal in importance to that of the *qāḍī*. *Faqīh*s seem to have been ubiquitous in the kingdom. Their function as notaries and as legal advisors, formally in the *qāḍī*'s court, or informally in the community at large, supplemented that of the more institutionalized *qāḍī*. But by virtue of their teaching in Mudejar schools and their preaching in the mosques, the influence of the *faqīh*s was perhaps more far-reaching than that of the *qāḍī*s. They gave shape and Islamic meaning to Mudejar daily life in even the most isolated rural villages. Only rarely did the royal authorities recognize these vital functionaries. It seems that the *faqīh*s of most royal aljamas were not royal appointees, but that individual aljamas chose them on the basis of their piety and legal knowledge.[23] When the *faqīh* of the aljama of Valencia died, the king followed the lead of the aljama, which took special care to choose a new *faqīh* of sufficient erudition.[24] Because the Crown did not pay a salary to the *faqīh*s, the aljamas assumed the responsibility themselves and supported them with the rents from mosque properties.[25] It is not certain that the *faqīh*s attained the same degree of importance in Aragon and Catalonia, although they are evident in a number of Aragonese aljamas. It may be that the higher level of Arabo-Islamic culture in Valencia and the greater access of the Valencian Mudejars to the centers of Islamic learning in Tunis and Almería allowed for the greater proliferation of *culamā'* (learned men) in the southern kingdom.[26]

Because the *amīn* is referred to in the documentation far more than any other aljama official, one is left with the impression that he was the paramount official in the aljama. From the perspective of the royal and seigneurial bureaucrats, this was certainly the case. Whereas the *qāḍī* and *faqīh* were most responsible for the moral and spiritual well-being of the aljama, the *amīn* acted as the principal intermediary between the aljama and the fiscal machinery of the Crown and nobility.[27] The letters of appointment for the *amīn*s of royal aljamas describe their duties as "holding, collecting, maintaining, and defending the rights and regalian taxes of the lord king, just as the other *amīn*s of the said *morería* were accustomed to do in times past."[28] The *amīn* was the aljama's financial officer and was responsible for the collection of royal and seigneurial taxes from the residents of the *morería*. He kept the accounts of the aljama, apparently in Arabic, and turned over the account books to the royal or seigneurial bailiff at the end of each fiscal year.[29] When new

Muslim vassals of the Crown wished to settle accounts with their former lords, the bailiff general often wrote to the local *amīn*, asking him to cooperate in the matter. The extant Arabic correspondence of various fifteenth-century *amīns* shows that it was the *amīn* whom the royal bailiffs notified when they wished to collect outstanding debts or taxes from the Muslims of a particular aljama. Also, the *amīn* usually represented his aljama in any litigation concerning its finances.[30]

Because the *amīns* were responsible for transferring the revenues exacted from the aljamas to royal or seigneurial coffers, they were usually appointed by the royal bailiffs, although some aljamas had the privilege of choosing their *amīn*.[31] Some *amīns* held their office for life, while others served for a term of a few years.[32] Most seem to have received a salary from the receipts of their office.

Although his role as tax collector might have earned for the *amīn* the resentment of other members of the aljama, his close relations with the royal bailiff or with his lord, and his executive power in fiscal affairs and in cases of debt gave him considerable influence in the community. The nobility, even more so than the Crown, placed considerable trust in the *amīns*, whose authority was consequently greater on seigneurial lands than in royal *morerías*. On seigneurial lands many *amīns* seem to have acquired a police function and were responsible for maintaining order. For instance, when a Muslim of Cárcer wounded a vassal of Alberique, it was the *amīn* of Alberique who chased after and captured the assailant.[33] Most *amīns* responded fittingly to the trust of their lords and viewed the interests of the aljama and its lord as their own. The *amīns* were usually in the forefront of the resistance to royal officials sent to confiscate the property of indebted lords and aljamas. When a royal porter was sent to collect the crops and revenues of Castellnou in order to liquidate the 140-pound pension owed by its lord, the *amīn* hid the crops in the local castle and refused to permit the porter to enter.[34] However, some *amīns* proved to be unreliable and unworthy of their lord's confidence. Ali Sardi illicitly abandoned the lordship of Bétera and took the account books with him.[35] Also, the señora of Gaibiel blamed the *amīn* and *adelantats* for heading the "conspiracy" which resulted in the departure of all her Muslim vassals.[36] Given the influence and the authority placed in the hands of the *amīns*, it is not surprising that it was an office which many Mudejars sought to hold.[37]

Closely associated with the *amīn* were the *adelantats*, or jurates, whose role, since the thirteenth century, had come increasingly to resemble that of the Christian jurates of the *universitas*. When creating the new aljama of Castellón de Játiva, Fernando decreed that it should have jurates, whom he described as "rectors and administrators."[38] Most aljamas had two *adelantats*, although a large aljama like Játiva might have as many as four.[39] The *adelantats* were elected annually by the aljama. According to the electoral system that seems to have prevailed in most royal aljamas, the *adelantats* for the coming year were chosen by the aljama's councillors (see below) and the current *adelantats*.[40] In some Aragonese aljamas the system was different and corresponded to the local Christian method of *insaculación*, in which aljama officials were chosen from among those candidates whose names had been placed in a sack (sometimes by the Crown or local authorities).[41] In Valencia Christian officials seldom interfered in the aljamas' elections, although Fernando was once compelled to intervene when the bailiff of Játiva attempted to appoint *adelantats* more obedient to his wishes.[42]

Because the *adelantats* were elected, they were more representative of the community's interests than the appointed *amīn*. The *adelantats* probably worked with the *amīn* to apportion taxes among the aljama's members in a judicious manner. Of course, the *adelantats*' powers as popular representatives were limited, for ultimately they had no choice but to acquiesce in royal and seigneurial wishes. As pointed out above, the aljama could make few decisions of any import, so that the *adelantats* lacked the legislative power of Christian jurates. Nevertheless, as administrators and representatives of the aljama, the *adelantats* were active in representing their aljama in litigation, in voicing complaints to the Crown, in leasing the utilities of the *morería*, and in sharing with the *amīn* leadership in matters of community defense (on seigneurial lands).[43] Documents describing the actions of Mudejar communities often note the participation of the *amīn* and *adelantats*, sometimes joined by *qāḍī* or *faqīh*.[44] Even though the *adelantats* did not receive any remuneration for their services, the office seems to have carried with it a certain amount of prestige, which made its possession desirable in the eyes of some Mudejars.[45] Unlike the fourteenth century, when elected *adelantats* had to be threatened with heavy fines lest they avoid the duties of their office,[46] the Mudejars of fifteenth-century Valencia seem to have been willing enough to serve. It was only in Aragon that a Muslim pleaded that he not be forced to hold the office if elected. Perhaps the disastrous financial situation of most Aragonese aljamas caused the Muslims to view any office associated with tax collection as particularly distasteful.[47]

Some aljamas had a larger council, which was elected by the aljama and was likely composed of the heads of leading families. The councillors (the aljama of Valencia had ten) jointly made all major decisions affecting the aljama.[48] The *adelantats* chosen by them were, therefore, representatives of the council and executors of the council's wishes. When the aljama of Játiva struggled with the local bailiff over the annual *servicio* that the latter claimed the aljama was obliged to grant to him, the aljama claimed that the *servicio* had been given to the bailiff gratuitously by "some jurates of the *morería*," but that it "was not solemnly decided upon in the council of the aljama."[49] The aljama "in council" had, in fact, resolved that the bailiff should receive nothing at all. The consensus of the councillors appears to have been weightier than the opinion of any one official in the determination of aljama policy.

Beyond the core of *qāḍī*, *faqīh*, *amīn*, *adelantats*, and council, there were some auxiliary officials mentioned only rarely in the documentation. Some aljamas, such as Játiva, Orihuela, Monforte, and Alcoy, had a *çalmedina* (*ṣāḥib al-madīnah*). This official seems to have had an executive function, assisting in the execution of the commands of the aljama's council and its *qāḍī*. He also had a hand in maintaining order in the *morería* through the appointment of police to apprehend malefactors and through control of the *morería*'s jail.[50] In Játiva he was custodian of the keys to the *morería* and the supervisor of its market.[51] The aljamas of Játiva and Valencia also had a *clavari*, or treasurer.[52] To these officials may be added others, such as scribes, messengers, porters, and ritual slaughterers.[53]

Wealth and Power in the Aljama

Previous historians have suggested that Mudejar aljamas were governed by plutocracies.[54] However, for reason of either lack of documentation or different focus of study, historians have done little in the way of identifying these elite families and correlating their civil service to their possession of wealth. The resources at our disposal for doing so are limited. For instance, information on the landholdings of these families is lacking. Fortunately, the tax records of royal towns provide enough data on Mudejar officials and their farming of fiscal revenues to allow for the drawing of some tentative conclusions.

The leading Mudejar family in the kingdom was the Bellvis family, in whom the combination of wealth and power is especially evident. Although the *qāḍī* general received a modest annual salary of 200s, the emoluments accruing from all of his juridical services must have been substantial. Still, the main source of income for the Bellvis family was international commerce. They had been active in the trade with Almería since at least 1417. By Fernando's reign their business interests had taken them further afield.[55] Mahomat Bellvis, and his sons Ali, Yahye, and Çahat, a spice merchant, conducted commercial negotiations in Italy, Tunis, and Alexandria, as well as in Almería. The preeminence of the Bellvis family in the capital's aljama is further indicated by the fact that one of its members normally served as *adelantat* or councillor in addition to holding the office of local *qāḍī*.[56]

Another prominent member of Valencia's aljama was its *faqīh*, Abdurrazmen Mascor. The *faqīh* himself was a landowner,[57] but his brother Çahat was involved in commerce with Almería, where he traveled with Abdurrazmen's black slave Mobarrich.[58] The residence of other members of the Mascor family in Almería must have facilitated Çahat's trading there.[59] Evidence of the *faqīh*'s substantial wealth is the 1500s settlement that his heirs paid to the bailiff general so that the Crown would not confiscate the part of the estate the *faqīh* had bequeathed to his son (most likely worth far more than 1500s), who had abandoned it when he emigrated to the Maghrib.[60] The *faqīh* had also willed property to his widow, brother, and two sisters.[61]

Turning to Játiva, the dominant family of the aljama there, at least until 1496, was that of its *qāḍī*s, Yuçeff and Ubaydal Alçamba. Yuçeff served as *qāḍī* perhaps until 1490, when Ubaydal (his son?) succeeded him and remained in office until 1496.[62] Their monopoly of the local Islamic judiciary was complete, for Yuçeff's brother, Yahye, was the aljama's sub-*qāḍī* until his emigration to the Maghrib in 1485.[63] Yahye's son Yuçeff next fulfilled the duties of the sub-*qāḍī* until his death in 1494.[64] No doubt the Alçambas were men of considerable erudition, and their attachment to Islam was demonstrated by the emigration of at least one of them to the *dār al-Islām* (lands of Islam; Islamdom).[65] The family also seems to have possessed some wealth. Although information on the Alçambas' properties is lacking, Yuçeff Alçamba's brother, Axer (both are referred to as "Benyaye"), was the lessee of the *morería*'s butcher shop in 1478 and 1490 (and perhaps during the intervening years, the records of which are lost), for which he paid rents of 1000s and 1200s.[66] In 1484 Yahye Alçamba was charged with the collection of royal revenues in the entire city of Játiva.[67] Another indication of the Alçambas' prestige, not surprising for the *qāḍī*s of the kingdom's largest *morería*, was the marriage of the daughter of Yahye Alçamba, the sub-*qāḍī*, to the son of Mahomat Bellvis, the *qāḍī* general.[68] By marrying among themselves the Mudejar aristocrats—if they can be described as such—maintained or enhanced their status and affluence.

The aljama of Játiva took some care in finding a suitable replacement for Ubaydal Alçamba as *qāḍī*. It, along with the local bailiff, chose Çahat Valenti, who had already proved his ability as the *qāḍī* of the seigneury of Alcocer. By this time (1496) Çahat had probably accumulated substantial capital. In 1480 he and his son journeyed to Almería to sell merchandise valuing 6000s.[69]

After the demise of Yuçeff Alçamba (1494), Abdurasmen Mangay was appointed sub-*qāḍī*. Abdurasmen was a person of some estimation in the community, which had already elected him *adelantat* in 1492.[70] His family, although perhaps not rich, was not without means. In 1485 Abdurasmen had been licensed to travel with his servant Yuçeff to the southern region of the kingdom on business.[71] It seems that many of Abdurasmen's relatives were artisans, for from 1490 onward a number of them—Çahat, Mahomat, Ali, Coayat—appear as lessees of some of the *morería*'s workshops and utilities, such as the soap factory, for 160s to 220s, the olive press, for 30s to 60s, and so on.[72] However, during Abdurasmen's tenure of office the resources at the Mangays' disposal seem to have increased. In 1495 Abdurasmen himself leased the butcher shop for 1600s,[73] and in subsequent years other members of the family rented the more lucrative utilities, like the butcher shop—rented jointly by Ali Mangay and Abdalla Lirida, a former *adelantat*, in 1496—and the ovens.[74] The experience of the Mangays suggests that the holding of an important office was beneficial for family fortunes, perhaps because it earned them the favor of and influence with the royal authorities.

In the aljama of Alcira one of the most notable families was the Paziar family. They served as its *amīn*s from the outset of Fernando's reign until at least 1503.[75] At the time of the expulsion of the Moriscos a wealthy landowner named Paziar was the *amīn* for Alcira's Moriscos.[76] Mahomat Paziar, appointed in 1479, replaced Çahat Trilli, a saddler, who after his term of office continued to rent the saddle workshop.[77] The Paziars, however, possessed far greater wealth than did their predecessor. Just after his appointment Mahomat purchased the *morería*'s fonduk, in order to provide his newlywed son Çahat with a "genteel house."[78] Before being appointed *amīn* himself in 1493, Çahat kept busy by investing family money in leases of the butcher shop and in farms of the town's agricultural tithes.[79] During his father's declining years, 1488–1493, Çahat was the de facto *amīn*.[80] Çahat's investments seem to have reaped profits, for in 1491 he was able to farm the sales tax on meat for the huge sum of 10,800s.[81] By 1501 Azmet Paziar, probably Çahat's son, was renting the butcher shop in partnership with a Christian, Jacme Barbera.[82] Because the *amīn*s were cogs in the Crown's fiscal machinery, they were well situated to turn to their own advantage the Crown's tax farms and utilities. Some officials, like the Paziars, were more astute in this respect than others, such as Çahat Trilli.

In the aljama of Castellón de la Plana none of the families seem to have had as firm a grip on the reins of power as did the Alçambas in Játiva or the Paziars in Alcira. Leadership in the aljama was hotly contested and the office of *amīn* changed hands among the feuding families almost every year (in contrast to Alcira, where the *amīn* was appointed for life). Almost all of the *amīn*s had served on the aljama's council of ten, which had the thankless task of choosing the two *adelantats*, one from each of the feuding factions.[83] There is evidence about the financial status of only one of these families, the Bocayos. Thomas Glick has identified an Asmet Bocaxo (or Bocayo), a carter by trade whose family owned a substantial amount of land in the parish of St. Nicolas. Asmet himself, who possessed at least eight *fanecates* of irrigated *huerta* land, is known to us through the fines he incurred for irrigation infractions.[84] Another family member, Sat Bocayo, was active in selling and purchasing land, most of it unirrigated vineyard.[85] Given the close ties between Mudejar agnates, the *amīn* Yuçeff Bocayo probably had some share in his family's landed wealth.[86]

There is less information on the officials of seigneurial aljamas. María del Carmen Barceló Torres has identified a prominent family of *qāḍīs* in Benaguacil, the Benamirs, who held this office throughout the fifteenth century. The prestige of this family was later manifested in the person of the Morisco noble, Don Cosme de Abenamir.[87] Barceló Torres also points out that some seigneurial *amīns*, who, as has been suggested, had greater authority than royal *amīns*, enjoyed certain privileges and were exempted by their lords from paying rents for their land.[88] In this way the seigneurial *amīns* acquired influence and slowly accumulated wealth, a tendency accentuated in the case that the office passed from father to son.

An extremely interesting case is that of Ali Gehini, the *amīn* of La Foyeta (near Alberique). On Ali's death 10,000s to 12,000s were found hidden in the walls of his house. Muslims who knew Ali described him as a rich and powerful man, as rich as any knight in the kingdom. Ali had many servants in his house, and his two sons led a life of leisure, passing their time with companions in taverns. It appears that the prime source of Ali's wealth was his store, where he sold woolen cloth and other items.[89]

It is doubtful that many other officials of seigneurial aljamas were able to accumulate as much wealth as Ali Gehini. However, some farmed the taxes of the estates of their lords, from which they must have earned some profits. For example, Yuçeff Castelli, the *amīn* of Fraga, and Joan de Calatayu, a resident of Cocentaina, jointly farmed the taxes of Fraga for an annual payment of 175 pounds.[90] The *faqīh* of Buñol and the *qāḍī* of Chiva traveled to Valencia to confer with the lord of Carlet concerning the farming of the agricultural tithes.[91] Although the lords were perhaps more likely to farm out their taxes to aljama officials in whom they had confidence, they also did so to other Mudejars with sufficient means. Mudejar tax-farmers are evident on a number of seigneuries, such as Areñol, Bechí, and Picasent.[92]

All this having been said, one probably should not go so far as to regard this Mudejar civil service elite as a distinct social class, lording it over the mass of poorer Muslim farmers and artisans. First, considering Valencia's plural society in its entirety, it is apparent that every Mudejar, no matter how affluent or influential within his own aljama, was, by virtue of his religious affiliation, the social inferior of even the most miserable Christian.[93] The Mudejar official's recognition of this fundamental social reality conditioned his view of himself vis-à-vis the other members of his aljama; it had a leveling effect, limiting his social aspirations and enhancing his sense of sameness with his fellow Muslims on the basis of a shared ethnic identity. Confronted with a socially superior Christian majority, the Mudejar official's cultural identification with the minority community was a factor in his social outlook just as compelling as his level of affluence or his administrative position.

Even when viewing the aljama turned in on itself it is difficult to perceive a clear-cut social hierarchy. True, one might describe Mudejar upper, middle, and lower classes on the basis of relative affluence, but this differential economic status was not translated into sharp social stratification. Mudejar officials for the most part originated from the undistinguished mass of farmers and artisans. For instance, Abdurasmen Mangay, the sub-*qāḍī* of Játiva, was a scion of a family of artisans, as was Çahat Trilli, the *amīn* of Alcira before the Paziars. The Bocayos of Castellón de la Plana owned a substantial amount of land, but were, nonetheless, a family of carters and farmers. And Ali Gehini, that rich and powerful *amīn* of La Foyeta, was really little more than a successful shopkeeper. True, many of these officials perhaps owned more land, were more successful in their trades, or invested their money more wisely than others; still, they were by and large from the same socioeconomic background as their poorer fellows. Moreover, it is uncertain whether enough of these civil service families retained their positions long enough to have constituted a distinct upper class or an aristocracy with common class interests. The Paziars of Alcira, for instance, seem to have been newcomers to the office of *amīn* in 1479. The Alçambas of Játiva seem to have died out or emigrated by 1496. The Mascors did not maintain their prominence in Valencia's aljama after the *faqīh* Abdurrazmen's death. The class structure of Mudejar aljamas, such as it existed, was characterized more by fluidity of movement up and down the socioeconomic scale than by immutability of status.

The primary focus of the Mudejar's social allegiance was not to a particular class, but to his family, normally an extended family or lineage group bound together by the solidarity between agnates. Dissension within the aljama was expressed in feuding between families and not in class struggle. Indeed, the intensity of Mudejar feuding, essentially a contest for material wealth and status, derived from the very absence of marked social categorization. Mudejar families could un-abashedly challenge one another and jockey for status because within the aljama there was minimal class consciousness. The social organiza-tion of the aljama is better viewed as a horizontal alignment of compet-ing lineage groups, some richer than others, than as a vertical hierarchy of social classes. One family, or several, might achieve dominance over the others for any number of reasons—the successful prosecution of a feud, the accumulation of considerable material wealth, or the control of local office—but such dominance was often only ephemeral and was not predetermined by birth.[94]

Notwithstanding the affluence of some families, the religious elites, the qāḍīs and the faqīhs, constituted the most influential group in Mude-jar society. As a group their economic backgrounds were diverse: the qāḍīs tended to be richer and had more influence with the Christian authorities, while the faqīhs were often poor and were supported by the community. Their erudition and piety lent them great prestige and, be-cause of their diversity of background, their influence was pervasive and was felt by all socioeconomic groups. Their moral authority counter-balanced the influence of those whose status was based on affluence and the holding of office alone.[95]

Even if among the Mudejars the variant degrees of wealth did not result in the formation of correlative social classes, it is still important to understand that there indeed was such variation. Some Mudejar farm-ers, craftsmen, and merchants prospered, while others were abysmally poor. Because the historiography on the sixteenth-century Moriscos tends to overshadow that concerning the Mudejars, it may be unduly assumed that the economic conditions of the Mudejars in the fifteenth century were just the same as those of the Moriscos. Following the logic of this assumption, the Mudejars would have been almost exclusively servile small farmers tied to the lands of their lords. Yet, one must con-sider how larger structural changes affected the Mudejars' economic position in the fifteenth century. As has been suggested in chapter 1, the kingdom's underpopulation in the fifteenth century and the need of the towns and the landed nobility for Mudejar labor afforded the Mudejars considerable opportunity for economic advancement. That Mudejars frequently seized such opportunities is evinced in their change of vassal-age and socioeconomic mobility. As for the sixteenth century, there were two factors behind the change in the Muslims' economic situation. The first was ideological. After the forced baptism of the Mudejars in 1525, many abandoned the towns and fled to seigneurial lands. In order to continue their Islamic practices and to escape the scrutiny of eccle-siastical authorities, the Moriscos had little choice but to submit fully to the will of their lords, now their protectors. Furthermore, although Moriscos continued to work as muleteers and carters, numerous restrictions were placed on Morisco travel and, most important, they were forbidden to change vassalage. The Moriscos lived under conditions of economic restraint which the Mudejars of the previous century had not experienced. The second factor was demographic and economic. In the sixteenth century, especially during the latter half, Valencia, like almost all of Europe, experienced a huge growth in population and an attendant rise in prices. Consequently, even if the Moriscos could change vassalage, there was much less of a demand for their labor and they had far less bargaining power with their lords. The rise of prices had a devastating effect on the seigneurial economy, since fixed rents were substantially devalued. The seigneurs perforce raised rents when they could and oppressed their Morisco vassals still further. By the time of the expulsion (1609) the Moriscos were probably, in economic terms, far more depressed and less diversified than their late fifteenth-century forebears.[96]

Before entering upon an examination of Mudejar economic life it will be useful to cite a few examples of rich and poor Mudejars, in order to provide some sense of the spectrum of Mudejar economic status. Several figures have already been encountered who may be described as well-to-do, such as Çahat Paziar and Ali Gehini. It is worthwhile to recall Fernando's concern that Muslims were dressing in a manner that made them indistinguishable from Christians. The problem was not just that the Mudejars were not wearing their special blue garb, but that they were dressing sumptuously, in "silk doublets and fine clothing."[97] In 1493 the king refused permission to emigrate to "a rich Moor of Játiva."[98] Another failed attempt at emigration brings to light Abdulmalich Roget, a Mudejar originally from Huesca who had resided in Valencia for a number of years. When the bailiff general hindered Abdulmalich from embarking on a caravel at Tortosa, the caravel's patron sailed off with the Muslim's goods: "many sacks of merchandise, clothing, furniture, gold, silver, and pearl, which clothing and merchandise are worth more than 350 gold ducats."[99] It is not unusual to encounter Muslims offering their gold jewelry as collateral in commercial transactions.[100] The licenses issued to Mudejars for travel to the southern region of the kingdom for commerce or other business reveal that twenty-six of these merchants, carters, and artisans had Muslim servants (moços) attending them.[101]

These servants were not the most indigent Mudejars. There were the orphans, divorcées, and widows who resorted to prostitution in order to survive.[102] There was a substantial body of mendicants—as many as 200 begging licenses were issued in one year—who wandered throughout the kingdom begging alms from their brethren "for the love of God."[103] And, of course, the number of slaves was large. Many of these were prisoners of war from Granada and the Maghrib, and others were enslaved as punishment for capital crimes.[104] But more to the point are those Mudejars who were enslaved because they could not pay their debts or seigneurial dues. Such slaves are ample testimony to the fact that a number of Mudejars eked out the most meager of livings, existing on that fine line between subsistence and starvation. For example, Azmet Çalema of Daimuz, who owed his lord 98 pounds for wheat, rents, and seigneurial dues, was forced to hand over his eighteen-year-old daughter in debtor's servitude to a Genoese merchant, a creditor of his lord. Two months later Azmet's situation had not improved, for his twelve-year-old daughter was next sent into the service of the Genoese. The case of Azmet Çalema was not so unusual.[105]

Economic Life

Affluent or indigent, most Mudejars passed their lives engaged in one of the following activities: farming, tending livestock, manufacturing, or retail merchandising. Not infrequently these occupations overlapped. Many an artisan farmed land or traveled about selling his wares, while farmers often raised livestock. A detailed consideration of these economic pursuits will reveal much about the Mudejars' daily life and how they adapted to changing economic conditions. It will also provide insights into how Muslims and Christians in Valencia were able to coexist and interact fruitfully, despite glaring ideological differences. Both the king and the nobility favored the continued presence of the Mudejars for their agrarian and commercial activities. But the stability of Valencia's Muslim–Christian *convivencia* hinged on far more than the interests of the Christian aristocracy; it involved the Mudejars' constant interchange with Christian merchants, humble artisans, and farmers. If the aristocracy and the Mudejars stood in relation to each other as lord and exploited vassal, Muslim and Christian artisans, merchants, and farmers dealt with one another on a more or less equal footing, their economic activities being complementary as often as they were competitive. Such mundane concerns were decisive when rapprochement on a theological basis remained unattainable. Tolerance was a product of material life, not a religious or political ideal.

Agriculture

In fifteenth-century Valencia, as in the rest of preindustrial Europe, the great majority of Muslims and Christians were farmers. In a purely occupational sense, the Mudejars were not much different from their

Almohad ancestors. What had changed markedly since the Christian conquest was the nature of the Muslims' proprietary rights over the lands they farmed. During the thirteenth century most Mudejars retained the status they had before the conquest, that of free proprietors, only now paying their taxes to a Christian king or lord.[106] By the mid-fourteenth century, however, after Christian power had been consolidated, Boswell found that "the untidy remnants of the 'free' Mudejar population were swept aside into one category or another of feudal servitude."[107] By Fernando's reign this state of affairs had not altered, for all Mudejars were either vassals of the king in royal *morerías* or vassals of lay and ecclesiastical lords, normally holding their lands in enfiteusis from these lords.

Nevertheless, extreme care must be taken in discussing the Mudejars' "feudal servitude." The Mudejar's vassalage to a particular lord, beyond the fundamental obligation of the vassal to render certain rents and services to his lord in exchange for land and protection, may connote an exceedingly unfavorable situation in which the Mudejar and his progeny were irredeemably tied to their plot of land on the seigneury. Such immobility under the heavy burden of seigneurial demands, while certainly the lot of many Mudejars in the late fifteenth century, was more characteristic of fourteenth-century (at least until midcentury) and sixteenth-century conditions. As has been pointed out, the Mudejars during Fernando's reign were hardly immobilized. With the kingdom underpopulated outside of the capital, there was a great demand for their labor and many changed vassalage in the quest for more favorable conditions. The Muslims' greater opportunity and mobility, in what appears to have been a general state of flux, are reflected in the documentation concerning Mudejar land tenure. Although the royal documentation is spotty—and here, local studies would be extremely useful—there is perceptible a pattern of individual Muslims holding lands around any number of towns and villages, both royal and seigneurial. The salient point regarding the Mudejar's feudal servitude is that his bond of vassalage to a particular lord and his residence on that lord's estate did not preclude his renting lands in other localities. Thus, the Mudejar, while having only one seigneur, might have any number of landlords and a corresponding variety of rents and obligations.

Most Mudejar properties, like those of most Christians, were held in enfiteusis. According to this arrangement, the owner of the property— not necessarily the Mudejar's seigneur—ceded usufruct of it to the Mudejar tenant in return for an annual rent paid in either cash or kind. While the landlord retained eminent domain over the land, the Muslim farmer was, for all intents and purposes, its real owner. As long as he paid his rents and in no other way violated the terms of the enfiteutic contract, he could pass on the land to his heirs or alienate it to whomever he wished.[108] Usually, the landlord had the rights of *fadiga* and *lluisme*. The *fadiga* was the right of priority by which the landlord himself could buy back the land from the tenant in the case that the latter wished to sell it. When the tenant sold the land to a third party, the landlord collected from the former the *lluisme*, usually 10 percent of the sale price.[109] The new tenant then held the property from the landlord under the same conditions as the vendor. When Mahomat Metli, a vassal in the *morería* of Valencia, purchased "certain land" in Cuart (in the *huerta* of Valencia) from Joan Esthelo for 54 pounds 15s, the land was described as "held under the direct lordship [i.e., domain] of the Reverend *majoral* of the said place of Cuart at a rent of 14s to be paid each year on the feast of All Saints and with *lluisme* and *fadiga* and every other full enfiteutic right."[110]

Most landlords of Mudejar tenants were, of course, the seigneurs of the places where the properties were located—king, noblemen, and prelates. However, most Mudejar lands located within the districts of royal towns were rented from ecclesiastical institutions and not from the Crown. In Alcira the local Augustinian community, secular clergymen, and the monastery of Valldigna all figure among the Muslims' landlords.[111] Valencia's *faqīh*, Abdurrazmen Mascor, rented land in the city's *huerta* from Pasqual Yvanyes, a priest beneficed in the local see.[112] Also, many Muslims of royal *morerías* rented their homes by enfiteutic contract from the Crown, Christian citizens, or local clergy. The nuns of the convent of Santa Clara were prominent as the landlords of many houses in the *morería* of Valencia.[113]

Rents varied according to the size of the property, whether it was located in an irrigated or a dry zone, and the type of crop planted on it. Irrigated land was more valuable than dry, and vineyards and mulberry orchards, for instance, were dearer than land planted with carob trees.[114] Most rents seem to have been paid in cash, although even within the same seigneury the type of payment demanded by the landlord might vary for different parcels of land. For instance, of the properties of Fuçey Zignell held in enfiteusis from the abbot of Valldigna, most had monetary rents. However, Fuçey was obliged to render to the abbot one-third of the produce from his carob orchards and one-ninth of the produce from a piece of *huerta* land planted with cereals.[115]

One also finds Mudejars involved in sharecropping arrangements of a more temporary nature. Mahomat, Juçef, and Azmet Perromalo, vassals in the *morería* of Murviedro, cultivated the lands of an *alquería* (hamlet) located within the town's district and owned by Joan Sparça, a local resident. Sparça had advanced money to the Perromalos, presumably for the purchase of seed and tools. In return the Muslims—

described as *migers*—were to give to Sparça one-half of the harvest and olive oil produced therefrom.[116] *Alqueries* owned by canons of Játiva were also tilled by Mudejars, perhaps under similar sharecropping arrangements.[117]

It was not unusual for Muslims to possess allodial lands, and it is probable that the phenomenon of free Muslim proprietorship increased during the fifteenth century. Barceló Torres suggests that as a result of Crown efforts from the beginning of the century to attract Mudejars to royal towns, Mudejars cultivated lands in the marginal zones of the towns that they then held as allods.[118] The data collected by Tomas Peris Albentosa on the property of Mudejars within the municipal district of Alcira (1512) shows that a substantial portion of it was allodial (e.g., 51.9 percent in the zone of Almunia).[119] Peris's qualification of his findings with the conjecture that rented lands tended to be the best lands fits well with Barceló's thesis of Mudejars reclaiming lands in the towns' marginal zones. If the allodial properties of such enterprising Mudejars were not the most valuable, they nevertheless could be quite substantial. Mahomat Algazel of Alcira, for instance, owned a jovate and a half (i.e., 54 *fanecates*; 1 *fanecate* = 831 square meters) of land planted with olive trees ("olivar tua franqua").[120] Although the allodial holdings of the Muslims of Alcira might have been exceptional, considering the impressive growth of the town's aljama,[121] free Muslim proprietors turn up elsewhere. For example, a number of Muslims of Micleta with allods in the seigneuries of Albalat and Altea are described as holding the lands "as lords . . . and thus they have the said possession [of the land] titled with the said domain."[122] Ali Alami and Azmet Almoli of Alcocer each purchased sixteen *fanecates* of land, more or less, located within the limits of the struggling town of Castellón de Játiva. They, too, were "lords" of their properties, and the previous owner of all 32 *fanecates* was another Muslim.[123]

There is general agreement among historians that the Mudejars were gradually pushed out of the kingdom's rich irrigated *huertas* into zones of dry farming.[124] The dichotomy between irrigated and dry land largely paralleled that between royal and seigneurial land, so that the Mudejars, for the most part seigneurial vassals, were primarily dry farmers from the midfourteenth century onward. This description is most applicable to the *huertas* of Castellón de la Plana and Valencia, although there is evidence of Muslim property around Cuart in the capital's *huerta*.[125] Irrigation farming by Mudejars is more evident in the *huertas* of other towns, such as Villarreal, where Muslim tenants from the Vall de Uxó and Artana paid the *sequiatge* (canal maintenance tax), or Orihuela, where three Muslim and two Christian villages were settled around the Quartal irrigation canal.[126] Mudejars inhabiting towns with larger Muslim populations tended to hold a more substantial share of irrigated land. This was particularly the case at Játiva, where, for instance, Azmet Bugeig possessed an irrigated parcel planted with olive and carob trees and grapevines, and Gandía, where Muslims grew sugar cane in the *huerta*.[127] Alcira also had its Muslim irrigation farmers, like Çaat Hualit.[128]

It should not be thought that seigneurial lands were exclusively dry farming areas. A number of seigneuries benefited from irrigation, although their systems were less developed than those of the urban centers. Seigneuries located near a royal town often channeled water into their own lands from the town's main canal. Thus, the town's *sequier* (irrigation officer) could fine seigneurial vassals who misappropriated or wasted water. Mudejars of Torres Torres and Alcocer were penalized by the *sequiers* of Murviedro and Alcira, respectively.[129] Precious commodity that water was, the question of access to it occasioned a number of clashes between lords and vassals of adjacent seigneuries. The viceroy was forced to reprimand the bailiff, *alcayt*, and *amīns* of the Foya de Llombay for restricting the flow of water through the canal, thereby endangering the millet and corn crops of Alginet.[130] The Muslims of Les Benexides complained that their lands were on the point of ruination because the lord of Alcantera had somehow obstructed the irrigation canal that ran from the Sallent River through Alcantera.[131]

Glick points out that irrigation generally was not used for growing exotic plants, but to increase the yield of ordinary crops.[132] In conformity with the general pattern of Mediterranean agriculture, the triad of cereals, olives, and vineyard was prevalent in Valencia. Although chronically deficient in wheat production, the majority of the land, particularly *huerta* land, was devoted to the cultivation of cereals, primarily wheat, but rice and barley were also important. Vineyard and olive trees were grown mainly in dry farming areas, though they were irrigated as well. Important secondary crops were sugarcane, carob, and figs. Industrial plants were also grown: flax, for the fabrication of linen, and mulberry trees, for the growing local silk industry.[133]

It appears that most Mudejars cultivated only small amounts of land, whether rented or allodial. For a more precise understanding of Mudejar material life it would be helpful to know just how small their properties were. Unfortunately, the royal documentation is not especially useful for answering this question. Even the descriptions of individual parcels of land have only a limited value, for, owing to the dispersed and patchwork pattern of Valencian land tenure—a couple of *fanecates* of vineyard here, a few planted with wheat there—one cannot be certain that the parcel under consideration was in fact the full extent of the Muslim's landed property. Fortunately, there is one local study of

Mudejar land tenure, that of Peris Albentosa on Alcira, to provide some guidelines. In 1512 65.7 percent of Alcira's Muslims held a small quantity of property (1 to 25 *fanecates*), 29.7 percent a middling quantity (25 to 75 *fanecates*), and only 4.5 percent a large quantity (more than 75 *fanecates*). Regarding the number of parcels of land held, 34.2 percent of the Muslims possessed only one parcel, 13.5 percent two parcels, 27.9 percent from three to five parcels, 19.8 percent from six to ten parcels, and 4.5 percent more than ten parcels.[134] However, certain qualifications must be made about even this data. First, one cannot necessarily correlate the extent of a Mudejar's landed property to his level of wealth. This especially applies to the residents of an urban *morería* like Alcira, many of whom were artisans. It may well be that a number of smallholders were artisans for whom agriculture was merely a subsidiary activity.

Second, Peris's study treats only those properties located within the limits of Alcira's district. Yet, as has been pointed out, Mudejars frequently rented lands outside of their place of residence. Sources other than those explored by Peris show that Muslims of Alcira had properties in Corbera, Alberique, and Turís.[135] Thus, not even a detailed local study can fully answer the question of how much land was actually held by the individual Mudejar.

Nevertheless, the pattern of Muslims renting property both from their seigneurs and from landlords in other localities is significant in itself. It seems to have been characteristic of the land tenure of many Mudejars, not only the most affluent. Numerous examples of this pattern can be found in the documentation (table 2), and the fact that such cases almost always involve the complaints of either the distant landlord or the absentee Muslim tenant suggests that it was widespread, noted by the officials only when problems arose.[136]

The lands held by Mudejars outside of their place of residence were usually located on a seigneury or within the district of a town close to the place of residence. To a certain extent this parallels the movement of those Muslims who became vassals in royal towns: most originated from neighboring seigneuries, with the exception of those who settled in the *morería* of Valencia. The localization of the Mudejars' additional properties was logical enough. If the absentee tenant intended to cultivate the land himself, it was necessary that he be able to reach it within a few hours. Even if the tenant sublet his land to Muslim sharecroppers, it was still preferable to be close enough to ensure that the land was being properly attended to and that he was receiving his share of the harvest. Considering the not infrequent attempts of landlords to hinder the absentee tenants in the collection of their harvests, vigilance on the part of the latter was all the more necessary.[137]

Table 2.   Mudejars Holding Property outside Their Place of Residence

Document	Residence	Location of land
ARV: B1159: 248r (1 Oct. 1489)	Valencia	Vall de Uxó
ARV: B1160: 532v–533r (22 Sept. 1492)	Valencia	Castellnou
ARV: B1160: 578v (19 Dec. 1492)	Valencia	Ribarroja
ARV: B1160: 635r–v (12 March 1493)	Valencia	Pedralba
ARV: B1162: 367r (Nov. 1502)	Valencia	Mislata
ARV: B1222: IV 18v–19r (20 Feb. 1498)	Valencia	Tabernes de Valldigna
ARV: B325: 10r–v (25 Feb. 1494)	Valencia	Valldigna
ARV: C137: 193v–194v (4 Feb. 1496)	Alcira	Corbera
ARV: B1156: 804r (1 July 1480)	Alcira	Foya de Llombay
ARV: B1158: 75v–76v (2 Sept. 1485)	Alcira	Turís
ARV: B1159: 3r (March 1488)	Alcira	Alberique
ARV: B1160: 412v–413r (1 March 1492)	Alberique	Alcira
ARV: B1158: 170v–172r (13 Dec. 1485)	Játiva	Valldigna
ARV: B1222: IV 15v (9 Feb. 1498)	Játiva	Beniarjó
ARV: B1156: 806r–807r (7 July 1480)	Alcocer	Castellón de Játiva
ARV: G2359: M.15: 33r–35r (1481)	Alcocer	Castellón de Játiva
ARV: B1159: 10r (2 April 1488)	Castellón de Játiva	Alcocer
ARV: C154: 132r–v (13 June 1498)	Villarreal	Chova
ARV: B1160: 917r–v (7 Oct. 1494)	Villarreal	Vall d'Artana
ARV: B1160: 917v–918r (7 Oct. 1494)	Villarreal	Villavella
ARV: B1157: 161v (9 Jan. 1482)	Bechí	Villarreal
ARV: B1161: 578v–579r (18 Feb. 1499)	Castellón de la Plana	Mascarell

Table 2.   (cont.)

Document	Residence	Location of land
ACA: C3641: 8v–9r (31 Jan. 1484)	Castellón de la Plana	Cirat
ARV: C148: 167v–169r (24 April 1493)	Algimia	Torres Torres
ARV: G2359: M.15: 25r–v (1481)	Torres Torres	Segorbe
ARV: B1161: 439r (23 Aug. 1497)	Benaguacil	Murviedro
ARV: G2351: M.11: 27r–v (21 May 1479)	Segorbe	Murviedro
ARV: G2357: M.37 19r–20r (1480)	Petrés	Murviedro
ARV: C151: 47v^a–46r^b (20 Oct. 1496)	Gilet	Albalat, Segart
ARV: G2355: M.20: 21r–23r (1480)	Algar (Callosa)	Altea, Albalat
ARV: G2356: M.25: 33r–35r (1480)	Micleta	Altea, Albalat
ARV: G2357: M.38: 18r–21r (1480)	Callosa, Micleta, Algar	Altea
ARV: C310: 36v–37v (2 Jan. 1496)	Albatera	Callosa
ARV: C139: 65v–66v (30 April 1495)	Aspe, Novelda, Monforte	Agost
ARV: C245: 97r–98r (15 July 1490)	Cocentaina (?)	District of Alicante
ACA: C3647: 98v–99r (21 July 1490)	Elda	Agost
ARV: C139: 77v–78v (20 May 1495)	Gandía	Benipeixcar, Beniopa
ARV: C148: 75r–v (14 April 1492)	Triega	Argilita
ARV: C317: 26v (13 Nov. 1496)	Jérica	Fuentes
ARV: G2352: M.21: 9r–v (1479)	Chelva	Alpont
ARV: G2359: M.11: 1r–4v (1481)	Mislata	Picasent
ARV: G2371: 301r–v (1484)	Eslida	Nules
ARV: G2372: 446r–447v (1484)	Antella	Rafalet de Antella

Mudejars, especially seigneurial vassals, had a good reason for purchasing or leasing land outside of their place of residence instead of simply doing so at home: the obligations of tenants to their landlords were lighter than those of vassals, particularly Muslim vassals, to their lords. When landlords attempted to exact from their tenants the same taxes that their vassals were liable to pay, the tenants would object that they were liable for only those taxes "the other landholders (*terratinents*) are accustomed to pay."[138] The obligations of tenants varied somewhat from place to place. All tenants, of course, paid the annual rent on their land. They were also obliged to pay the *peyta* (property tax) and the tithes collected from all landholders by royal, ecclesiastical, or seigneurial officials.[139] There are a few more specific references to arrangements between landlords and tenants. In one case the landlord would collect from his Muslim tenants all the raisins they had grown, and after selling them would retain for himself the amount owed to him as rent, returning the remainder of the proceeds to his tenants.[140] Muslims of Elda renting land in Agost were obliged to render to their landlord the *terratge*, that is, a certain portion of their harvest.[141]

Still, such taxes were lighter than the various obligations incumbent on vassals. Vassals were obliged to use the royal or seigneurial utilities and to pay fees for their use. Had the tenants been compelled to grind their wheat in the landlord's mill or to press their olives in his press, they would have had to repeat the payment of a tax they were already paying to their own lord. Moreover, there was a wide variety of other taxes and services for which vassals were liable: a gift of two chickens each year, a certain amount of honey, spinning flax, laboring on the lord's land, the *cena, morabatí*, and other taxes, and, beyond the rent and tithe, a further portion of the harvest.[142] Therefore, the Mudejars who rented lands outside of their own seigneury were able to retain for themselves more of the produce from these lands than they could from the lands they held from their own lord.

That such a state of affairs should have arisen was due to the underpopulation and chronic labor shortage in the kingdom. King, nobles, and prelates all needed more hands to work their fields, preferably new vassals, but if not, then new absentee tenants. Chapter 1 described how Fernando and the barons competed for the vassalage of Mudejars, and how some royal towns, such as Alcoy and Castellón de Játiva, their populations decimated by pestilence, were in desperate need of new inhabitants. The straitened circumstances of some lords whose estates were underpopulated and uncultivated are well illustrated by the example of the seigneury of Terrateig in the Vall de Albaida. Its lords, Don Pedro Dixer and his wife Dona Johana, were compelled to lease the place to Francesch Vilana, a citizen of Valencia residing on the barony of Castellón de Rugat, and Adam Alactar, a Muslim of Castellón, for six years at an annual rent of 3200s. Much of the property in Terrateig had been abandoned, and Vilana and Alactar had their work cut out for them. Later, when Don Pedro violated their agreement and attempted to drive the lessees out of Terrateig, it was described how "they [Vilana and Alactar] have diligently worked to have vassals and landholders [*moros vassalls* are mentioned earlier in the document] in the said place, loaning them wheat, barley . . . and other grains for the purpose of sowing and cultivating . . . in a manner that the said place and area may be increased and improved." The diligence of the lessees indeed paid off, which explains Don Pedro's rather timely breach of contract: "the said place and area being so much increased and prospering that it has been a long time since there has been seen in the said place and area such a great planting of all manner of grains . . . as a result of the said work and industry and expenses of the said plaintiffs [Vilana and Alactar]."[143]

Clearly, land was available, and astute lords and enterprising townsmen investing in the land were willing to offer favorable conditions to prospective vassals and tenants to see that it was farmed. It was a buyer's or tenant's market and prices and rents were probably reasonable (one may recall how the Christians of Alcoy desired the settlement of Mudejars so that land values would increase). There is no lack of evidence of Mudejars buying land. For example, Çaat Hualit purchased from Galçeran Gombau some allodial land in Alcira's *huerta* worth 70 pounds, adding to the at least five *fanecates* he held in enfiteusis in the Almunia.[144] Significantly, some of the property that Muslims rented from the Crown in Alcira had been "abandoned land" (*terra derrenclida*).[145] Again, the picture comes to mind of a regional economy struggling to recover and expand through the reclamation, repopulation, and cultivation of abandoned land.

The purchase of land by Mudejars, their ability to change vassalage, and their possession of land in diverse localities reflects an improvement in their material conditions during the course of the fifteenth century. However, one author has suggested that the Mudejars' holding of land outside of their place of residence attests to their need to obtain a surplus of crops in order to pay seigneurial rents and dues; in other words, it is evidence of their material difficulties.[146] It is undeniable that the burden of seigneurial dues weighed heavily on many vassals, and that it ground some into a state of abject poverty which they could not escape. To this the enslavement of insolvent Mudejar vassals is dramatic testimony. Also, the fact that a number of lords and their aljamas were in financial straits, weighed down by outstanding pensions (*censals*), casts a shadow over any picture of increasing Mudejar prosperity.[147] Nevertheless, that Mudejars were able, for whatever reason, to purchase and cultivate more land, either at home or in other places, indicates an improvement in their situation. Even if the resultant surplus was used only to meet the demands of the lord—and this often was not the case, for there is evidence of Muslims selling their surplus crops in urban markets[148]—this was still far better than not being able to pay at all. Moreover, many of the Mudejars who held property in diverse places did so as a consequence of having changed vassalage. Since dissolving the bonds of vassalage required the settling of accounts with one's lord, the absentee land tenure of such Muslims is indicative of at least their solvency, if not their prosperity.

Truly impoverished Muslims would have been unable to purchase or lease additional land. Therefore, one can infer that there were two classes (at least) of Mudejar proprietors: a class of growing affluence able to invest in new land, change vassalage with the hope of obtaining better conditions, or both; and a class devoted to subsistence agriculture, rendered immobile by poverty and hardly making ends meet.

An example from the more prosperous class is Fuçey Zignell, a Muslim from Valldigna who later became a royal vassal in the *morería* of Valencia. Fuçey and his sons appear most frequently in the documents as retail merchants trading in the capital. At the same time, Fuçey continued to hold in Valldigna land planted with flax, mulberry and carob trees, and wheat.[149] This combination of retail merchandising, or manufacturing, with agrarian pursuits was not uncommon, and further explains why seigneurial Muslims moved to royal towns: urban life was more conducive to entrepreneurship and economic diversification.

The activities of the Mudejar underclass do not emerge as clearly. That a Fuçey Zignell could be a merchant in Valencia while renting lands in Valldigna raises an interesting question: who tilled the lands of Fuçey and of others like him? It has been conjectured with good reason that the kingdom's wealthier Muslims often sublet their properties, especially those located outside of their place of residence, to poorer coreligionists.[150] Perhaps sharecropping arrangements were common in these circumstances. In addition, there probably was a substantial body of Mudejar day laborers who subsisted by working the lands of their more fortunate fellows. There is an interesting incidental reference to "certain Sarracens plowing or otherwise laboring on a certain field of Abrahim Juçefi."[151] Because Christian officials were concerned mainly with the contracts between Christian landlords and Muslim tenants, and not with the arrangements worked out among the Muslims themselves, there is little other solid evidence about these sharecroppers and day laborers.

It is difficult to know what portion of the Mudejar population constituted this lower stratum and what portion had the means to leave their land in another's care. In the latter one should not see an upper class of great wealth, but more of a prospering middle class. Given the considerable evidence of a number of Mudejars augmenting their landholdings or striking out on new commercial ventures, it may be inferred that this middle class was of some size and was perhaps growing. The anti-Muslim violence of the *Germanías*, ideological motives notwithstanding, may well have been in part an expression of Christian resentment against the members of this class.[152]

Livestock-raising

Sheep-raising in the kingdom of Valencia never attained the importance that it long held in Castile, where, through the shepherds' association of the *Mesta*, much of the economy was organized around it and the export of wool. Nevertheless, pastoral activity was an important adjunct to agriculture. Livestock, primarily sheep and goats, were raised for self-consumption as well as for the market. Meat, especially lamb, was a basic component of the Valencian diet, as were cheese and milk. Wool production was geared to both the domestic textile industry and export. The hides of goats and, to a lesser degree, cattle were sold to urban tanners for the manufacture of leather. Farmers utilized manure to increase crop yields; however, given the prevalence of irrigation in Valencia, this factor in agricultural production was less significant there than elsewhere.[153]

Although the Mudejars were active in raising livestock, the extent of their pastoral pursuits was by no means extraordinary. The amount of livestock possessed by the kingdom's Muslims was roughly commensurate with their proportion of the population. Of the 931,743 head of livestock counted in the census of 1510, 28.5 percent were owned by Muslims and 61.5 percent by Christians.[154]

Most Mudejar pastoral activity took place on seigneurial lands in the mountains bordering the alluvial plains. Muslim shepherds living in the lowlands engaged in seasonal transhumance, driving their flocks up to the mountains for the summer months. Three Muslim brothers of Alcácer explained how they took their 300 head of sheep and goats to the mountains "according to the custom and practice each year of the animals that are in the present kingdom." Unfortunately, this year (1480) armed horsemen waylaid them and stole their flock.[155] Livestock was also grazed in the pastures surrounding the *huertas*. A Muslim of Albatera was permitted to graze his animals in the *huerta* of Orihuela.[156] Grazing rights to unclaimed wasteland were not clearly defined, and this sometimes caused problems. When the citizens of Alcira created a new pasture that extended to the limits of the seigneury of Masalaves, they unwittingly included in it lands allegedly held by Muslim vassals of Masalaves who had been grazing their own livestock there.[157]

Mudejars owned livestock collectively as well as individually. Any number of families from a particular village might pool their resources for the purchase of livestock. For instance, six Muslims of Ribarroja bought animals from a merchant of Cuenca for 1654s.[158] Whereas the livestock possessed by an individual family of limited means might be sufficient for only its own consumption, such jointly owned flocks allowed for more extensive breeding and for the production of enough wool and hides for sale on the market.

There were individual Mudejars who owned substantial flocks. Mahomat Alazrach of Benegida owned 1,100 head, and Çahat Ageg of Alcira had a flock of 500 goats.[159] The owners of large numbers of sheep or goats were not necessarily shepherds by occupation; for them the livestock might have represented a form of capital investment. However, it seems that there were professional Mudejar shepherds who for some form of remuneration attended to large flocks comprising the animals of a number of proprietors. Ali Barrazi, a shepherd from Alasquer, related how he and Abrahim Xativi of Alcira looked after the 380 goats of Ageg b. Çahat Ageg and those owned by Xativi, while Xativi's son tended the sixty newborn goats.[160] The shepherds were able to ascertain to whom each animal belonged by the symbol with which each owner marked his animals. In this manner Ali Barrazi recognized another ten of Ageg's goats running in the flock of a certain Mofferig. Itinerant as they were, the shepherds sometimes acted as middlemen, selling the livestock on behalf of the owners to buyers in various towns and villages.[161]

There was a lively commerce in livestock between the towns and the satellite rural villages involving both Muslims and Christians. This is reflected in the activities of Mahomat Ageig of Alcira, who leased the butcher shop of the local *morería* (1473) and who, therefore, was obliged to provide a quantity of meat sufficient for the needs of the Muslim population. Ageig turned to the stockmen in the region of Alcira, purchasing forty-five sheep and fifteen goats from a Muslim of Cortes, more than 100 sheep from Bernat Cathala, a merchant of Alcudia, and still more sheep from Mahomat Vizcaya of Masalaves.[162] The demand for meat, particularly in the towns, made livestock-raising a profitable pursuit for Christian and Muslim alike.

However, it was the commercial and industrial demand for wool and hides that gave pastoral activity its particular market orientation. Christian merchants in the capital seeking wool, either for export to Italy or for sale to local textile manufacturers, often contracted with Mudejar stockmen for the delivery of a certain amount of wool each year. The quantities of wool involved seem to have ranged between ten and twenty *arrobes* (one *arroba* = 10.4 kilograms, or twenty-six pounds) annually. Usually the merchant would pay the Muslim the accustomed price for the wool during the winter months, and the stockman would deliver the wool to the merchant after the spring shearing. The merchant Pere d'Aragon contracted with Muslims of Alasquer and Masalalí (Valldigna) for eighteen and twelve *arrobes*, respectively,[163] while the brothers Açia and Ali Çelim of Chelva had a similar contract with the merchant Anthoni Albert of Valencia.[164]

Goat and cow hides were always needed for the manufacture of leather and for the industries dependent on the availability of leather, such as shoemaking. Muslim vassals of the Foya de Buñol were active in supplying artisans in the capital with hides. Francesch Martí, a tanner, paid Amet Caçim and Abrahim Ale 20 pounds for "all the hides of goats, both male and female, that they slaughter in 1488." Interestingly, a Muslim shoemaker of Valencia seems to have acted as an intermediary between the tanner and the stockmen.[165]

Many Mudejars owned horses, mules, and donkeys, all valuable as draft animals and for transportation. Muslim carters and itinerant merchants, familiar figures on the Valencian scene, were always in need of such animals. They frequently purchased or rented horses and mules from Muslims and Christians.[166] Conversely, a number of Mudejars were in a position to sell or lease their livestock to Christians. Ali Çequien of Benaguacil sold mules to five Christians of Liria and three of Castellnou for a total price of 181 pounds 5s.[167]

Beekeeping, chicken-raising, and fishing also figure among the Mudejars' economic activities. Seigneurial Muslims usually had to render two chickens to their lord each year, and on some seigneuries lords exacted a quantity of honey from their vassals.[168] Some Muslims owned apiaries, while others leased them from the Crown or from private individuals. The honey thus produced was sold in its pure form or as confections.[169]

Fishing did not hold a prominent place among Mudejar occupations. Still, for Muslims living in coastal villages it was a subsidiary economic pursuit, and throughout the kingdom fish was an important dietary supplement.[170] Mudejars owned fishing boats, for which reason they were sometimes suspected of aiding Maghriban corsairs, and there are records of Muslim fishermen purchasing fishing line.[171] Muslims who rented lands in the coastal seigneuries of Altea and Albalat had the right to fish in the rivers and the sea, since the waters were common to all tenants.[172] By the midsixteenth century fishing ceased to be a Muslim pursuit because, for security reasons, the authorities prohibited the Moriscos from inhabiting villages near the coast.

Industry

Mudejar artisans engaged in a wide variety of industrial activities. While most evident in urban centers, where they produced for a large local or sometimes a kingdom-wide market, Mudejar artisans were also active on seigneurial lands,[173] although here their manufacturing was intended strictly for local consumption. Notwithstanding their skills as craftsmen and the general shortage of labor in the kingdom, the Mudejars' opportunities in industry were not unlimited, for the monopolization of certain crafts by Christians guilds tended toward the exclusion of Muslim artisans.

Because Christian craft guilds were essentially religious confraternities, the membership of Muslim and Jewish artisans was problematic. The guilds justified their ordinances prohibiting the membership of non-Christians by emphasizing the religious dissidence of the latter. The ordinances of Valencia's confraternity of mattressmakers and quilt-makers, presented to the king for confirmation in 1479, are quite explicit in this regard:

> We ask and demand that it be ordained that no one who is a Moor or a Jew may practice the trade of mattress and quilt maker in the city of Valencia, nor may they [Muslims and Jews] be admitted to the examinations of the confraternity, nor may they practice the said trade as masters. The same should be [ordained] for slaves or bastard sons of slaves, so that the trade not fall to vile persons or to enemies of the Holy Faith.[174]

The guild of cappers similarly ruled "that any Moor or Jew, who are enemies of the Holy Catholic Faith, if he is not already a slave of the capper, cannot in any manner practice or work in the said trade."[175]

Other guilds, in justifying such discriminatory legislation, voiced their fears of the Mudejars as a fifth column who might reveal the Christians' technological secrets to Aragon's Islamic foes. The cord-makers reasoned that Mudejars given access to the trade might teach to Maghriban Muslims the art of making crossbow string; the carpenters claimed that Mudejars who became skilled in woodworking would aid Muslim corsairs in constructing ships (1424); and the Christian manufacturers of cuirasses, harnesses, swords, and spears all had obvious reasons for excluding Muslims from their trades (1480).[176]

Nevertheless, anxiety about Muslim or Jewish competition was weightier than ideological or political concerns in motivating the Christian guilds' exclusivity. The silkweavers of Valencia at least were more forthright in explaining why the masters of the trade could not give instruction to Muslim and Jewish apprentices: "it would be a great damage . . . to the workers of the said craft, for whom work would be lacking."[177] It was also for economic reasons that Christian guilds consistently prohibited Muslim and Jewish craftsmen from working on Sundays and Christian feast days—it would have given them an edge in productivity.[178] Yet other guilds less pressed by "infidel" competition were not adverse to the idea of Muslims and Jews being examined and approved as masters. The feltmakers of Valencia ordained that "no person of whatever law [i.e., religion] or condition can have a loom or looms if he is not already an examined master," implying that persons of all religions could become master feltmakers.[179] Nor do the guilds' professed political fears appear too convincing when one considers that although Mudejars did not manufacture cuirasses or swords, they nevertheless were active in producing shields and bucklers, and many were smiths, metalworkers, and carpenters. Even Christian carpenters employed Maghriban Muslim slaves, despite enactments to the contrary.[180] A guild's profession of religious and political concerns seems to have served mainly as a screen for the more practical aim of maintaining its monopoly of a particular trade. As for the trades in which Christian craftsmen were less interested, such concerns strangely disappeared; there was room enough for Christian, Muslim, and Jew.

Muslim and Jewish artisans responded to the exclusive legislation of Christian guilds by forming their own craft guilds. The Muslim shoemakers of the capital had a confraternity, and, according to Dolors Bramon, there were many minority guilds, all characterized by religiously exclusive membership.[181] It made perfect sense that Muslims and Jews would have wanted confraternities for the mutual support and services they provided for members. In those trades where Christian masters refused to examine Muslims and Jews, the latter would have needed an organization for maintaining standards and setting prices. The barring of Muslims and Jews from Christian guilds, therefore, did not necessarily prevent them from practicing the trades in question.

However, it should not be imagined that there existed a minority guild system—or an "authentic counter-society," as Bramon has proposed[182]—paralleling and competing with that of the Christians. The Valencian economy was far more integrated and functioned far more efficiently than such a bipartite guild system would have allowed for. In the treatment of Mudejar artisans that follows, three characteristics of the economy will emerge with clarity: (1) although Muslims and Christians practicing the same trade often competed with one another, they were also able to work cooperatively; (2) Muslims and Christians were more apt to practice different trades that complemented one another than to be rivals within the same trade (the restrictive legislation of the Christian guilds might have been little more than a confirmation of this tendency); and (3) as a consequence of the second point, Muslim and Christian artisans were as likely to sell their wares to clients of different faiths as to coreligionists. The Valencian economy was structured in a manner that left far less room for Muslim–Christian rivalry than the regulations of Christian guilds would suggest.

The documentation is most revealing about the activities of Mudejar shoemakers in the capital. They had their own guild, the ordinances of which were approved by the bailiff general in 1497.[183] The Muslim shoemakers organized themselves for their own protection and to maintain standards of craftsmanship. They were particularly anxious about those Muslims who were coming to the city and, without making themselves royal vassals, were renting workshops and houses in or near the *morería*. The problem was not so much a glut of shoes on the market as the quality of the product being marketed by these free-lance shoemakers. Valencia was an expanding city and a center of economic opportunity. Persons of diverse origins flocked there either to make their fortunes or to join the ranks of the urban proletariat. Muça Almedino, a metalworker from Calatayud (Aragon), had little difficulty finding day work with Christian cutlers and boilermakers in Valencia; even a Muslim from Málaga sought employment there.[184] Even though there were 45,000 pairs of feet to be shod in the city, the *morería's* shoemakers probably feared losing customers to the newcomers. The latter, although manufacturing an inferior product, most likely were undercutting the guild's prices. The masters of the guild complained that "the products that those [newcomers] make are neither good nor suitable, nor made with the perfection that ought to be done by good shoemakers." The masters maintained that this state of affairs could lead to the diminution of the *morería's* population (always a convincing argument with the Crown authorities), the implication being that the circulation of inferior products and the undercutting of prices would cause the guild's ruination.[185]

In order to remedy this situation the masters proclaimed with the bailiff general's concurrence that no Muslim could rent a workshop without first having been examined and approved by them. The prerequisite for certification was a three-year apprenticeship with one of the masters. Sons of shoemakers had to work with their fathers for three years, and had to be eighteen years of age and married before they could have their own shop.[186] In this way the masters could enforce quality and price controls and strengthen their own economic and social position.

Muslim and Christian shoemakers seem to have coexisted amicably enough. Aside from the Christian shoemakers demanding that their Muslim and Jewish counterparts not labor on Sundays and feast days,[187] there is little evidence of an intense Christian–Muslim competition. In fact, Christian shoemakers sometimes toiled in the homes and shops of Muslims, although it is difficult to know in what capacity they did so. Joan de Gandía and Miquel de Boro manufactured shoes in the home of Abdalla Torralbi, a linen-draper, whose sons Azmet and Çahat were shoemakers. Joan recounted that he conversed with Azmet as he worked, stopping only to go home for lunch.[188]

When in need of materials, Muslim shoemakers patronized Christian tanners and manufacturers of brass buckles (oripells). In the capital these two crafts seem to have been exclusively in the hands of Christians. The sources for the business between these Muslim and Christian artisans are spotty, inasmuch as they consist of either the bailiff general's letters of execution against those Muslims late in paying their Christian creditors—who would have been more the exception than the rule— or the Muslims' public acknowledgment of their debts. Nevertheless, the sources are revealing. They show that the working capital needed to operate industry in Valencia was provided in part by short-term credit arrangements between artisans whose crafts were complementary.[189] Thus, the Christian tanner would furnish leather to the Muslim shoemaker on credit, with the understanding that he would be paid as soon as the Muslim received payment for his finished products. The tanner's confidence that the shoemaker would, indeed, fulfill his obligation was enhanced by the fact that the members of the latter's guild were accustomed to stand as pledges for honest repayment of one another's debts. For example, when Azmet Alboruch purchased leather on credit from Jaume Caldes, Axet Carcaix stood as surety for him, liquidating Alboruch's debt to Caldes when he was unable to pay at the time agreed upon.[190] In addition to the tanner's confidence that the Muslim shoemaker's guild would not allow one of its members to default on a debt, a more fundamental mutual trust developed through frequent transactions and consequent familiarity. The sources indicate that certain Christian tanners were especially active in dealing with Muslim shoemakers. Of the sixty-one debt cases involving the shoemakers, the tanner Girart Boix appears as the creditor in twenty-one, Jaume Caldes in eight, Joan Carbonell in six, and Joan Gironella and Alfonso Delgado in three apiece.[191] A similar pattern is apparent in the transactions between the shoemakers and the Christian manufacturers of brass buckles.

Here, in the nineteen debt cases considered, Pere Ribesaltes was the creditor eight times, his relative Bernat Ribesaltes twice, and Francesch Cabanes three times.[192]

Játiva had Mudejar shoemakers and tanners, the latter renting the local tannery from the Crown.[193] Travel licenses issued by the bailiff general reveal that one of the shoemakers, Çahat Cantsevol, made periodic trips to the southern part of the kingdom in order to purchase hides, probably for the morería's tanners and shoemakers. One of Çahat's Valencian counterparts, Yuçeff Abducarim, stood as surety for him (in case he did not return), which suggests that Yuçeff had an interest in Çahat's quest for hides. And Yuçeff was not alone, for on different occasions Pedro Navarro, a Jativan merchant, and Andreu Mestre, a Valencian tanner, joined him in backing Çahat. Navarro likely intended to sell the hides retail in Játiva, while Mestre must have tanned the hides himself.[194]

Artisans were usually artisan-retailers, responsible for both manufacturing and selling their wares. Beyond selling their products from their shops or in Valencia's market, it may be that the capital's Muslim shoemakers made some attempt to distribute their shoes throughout the kingdom. When Abrahim Fato of Cárcer traveled south "to sell clothing and certain merchandise," Yuniç Tarongeta, a shoemaker of Valencia, stood as surety for him.[195] Perhaps shoes made by Yuniç and his fellows were part of the merchandise Abrahim was vending, in which case Abrahim would have received a share of the proceeds as compensation for his labor as an itinerant merchant.

Another important center for the manufacture of footwear was the Vall de Uxó. The hemp-sandal (espardenya) industry was almost completely monopolized by Mudejar espardenyers. The espardenyers carried on a brisk trade with the Christian cordmakers of the capital, from whom they purchased hemp thread on credit. The cordmakers' guild, which prohibited the practice of their trade by Muslims, had no qualms at all about doing business with Muslim espardenyers. Certain cordmakers figure prominently in these transactions. In the thirty-two debt cases of Mudejar espardenyers, Jaume Lobet was the creditor ten times, Joan de Caritat nine times, Francesch Nadal five times, and Joan Bonet twice.[196] One of the cordmakers, Joan Pérez Bou, on a few occasions pooled his resources with the espardenyers Mahomat and Suleymen Garbi in order to buy hemp from Valencian merchants. Pérez also made an interest-free loan (prestech gratios) of 63s to the Garbis.[197] The largest market for hemp sandals was the capital. It is therefore not surprising to find there a Muslim espardenyer from the Vall de Uxó renting a stall beside the fonduk, where he made and sold the sandals.[198]

Mudejars were active in the textile and clothing industry as dyers, weavers, linen-drapers, tailors, and retailers. Most royal *morerías* had their resident dyers, as did many seigneurial *morerías*, especially in Valldigna.[199] In Játiva and Murviedro Muslims rented the dyeworks from the Crown.[200] Muslim dyers from all over the kingdom came to Valencia to purchase cloth from Christian wool-dressers and drapers, and the dyes and alum necessary for the dyeing process from merchants.[201] There were some Mudejar cloth merchants, such as the aforementioned Ali Gehini, who made a fortune selling woolens. Mudejar tailors seem to have been located mainly on seigneurial lands, where they worked on the clothing of the local population. They, too, had to go to the urban centers for materials. Azmet Lopo, a tailor of Bellreguart, purchased over two meters of black cloth in Gandía.[202]

In the capital there were a number of Muslim linen-drapers. One was Abdalla Torralbi, whose varied activities were probably not typical of the other practitioners of his craft. Abdalla wove linen himself and purchased flax from farmers for that purpose (twelve *arrobes* from Pere Màcia).[203] As a retailer Abdalla not only sold his own work but also resold linen he had purchased from a variety of Christian parties—monks, feltmakers, tailors, notaries, and merchants.[204] Nor did he confine himself to the retailing of only locally woven linens. He sold especially fine linens (*olanda*) purchased from a Venetian wholesaler, as well as other types of cloth bought from local wool-dressers and wholesale drapers, and from a Florentine merchant.[205] Abdalla's retail trade seems to have been quite successful, considering the large quantities of cloth he purchased from wholesale merchants. In one instance, Abdalla bought 155 pounds 7s 11d worth of cloth from the merchant Joan Allepus, whom he repaid at a rate of 3 pounds per week.[206] Abdalla's retailing activities appear to have extended beyond the confines of the capital, for there is record of him standing as surety for Azmet Ubeyt of Valldigna, who was traveling south for commercial purposes ("per mercadejar"), perhaps with some of Abdalla's linen and cloth. He also invested in small-scale commerce with the Maghriban port of Oran.[207] Abdalla managed to finance his retail trade by borrowing money from Christians whom he repaid with annual pensions.[208]

The Mudejars of Valencia were not as prominent in the construction industry as were their fellows in Aragon. Aragonese Muslim "masters" were often hired to work on the royal *aljafería* in Zaragoza or on churches, and some were even sent down to Granada after the conquest to make repairs on the Alhambra.[209] Still, some Valencian Mudejars labored as masons and carpenters in urban and rural areas, and they were hired by the Crown to repair royal ovens, fonduks, and other public works.[210]

Mudejars seem to have played a somewhat more important role in the metalworking industries as smiths, boilermakers, and manufacturers of shields and bucklers. All carried on business with Christian merchants from whom they purchased their materials, both iron and copper.[211] Through their ability to supply the artisans with materials on credit, the merchants attained a position of dominance in industry. It enabled them to some degree to dictate the terms of production to the artisans. For example, when the merchants Dionis Miguel and Francesch Miro supplied Muslim shieldmakers with iron, the latter agreed to sell bucklers to the merchants at a set rate.[212]

Muslim saddlers are evident throughout the kingdom, and in Alcira and Játiva they leased the royal saddleworks. Játiva's Muslim residents were also involved in the fabrication of soap.[213]

Mudejars took part in Valencia's sugar industry, not only growing sugarcane but also refining it and preparing confections for sale. Some Muslims leased sugar refineries, such as Çahat Mucellem who rented a refinery from the lawyer Miguel Albert for a number of years.[214] Çahat Flori, a confectioner of Játiva, often did business with the representatives of the Cardinal in Valldigna. Çahat rented (or owned) fields in Valldigna planted with sugarcane, from which he supplied his own confectionary shop. However, Çahat also had to buy sugar from Valldigna's officials (they probably ran a refinery), to whom he later sold his own confections.[215]

This brief look at Mudejar artisans may be rounded out by mentioning Muslims who made a living as entertainers (juglars), those who fashioned musical instruments or played them, and those who worked as physicians, barbers, and surgeons.[216] Although Mudejar medical practitioners did not have the same prominence as Jewish physicians, when all else failed a Mudejar surgeon might be called in to care for Christian notables.[217] Mudejars, in turn, did not always go to their coreligionists with their medical problems. Some were treated by Christian physicians in Valencia's hospital.[218]

Muslim artisans did not restrict themselves to the activity of manufacturing one specific product. Many, as has been seen, were necessarily retailers. Most in all likelihood had some land under cultivation in the area. Some were active in more than one craft. For example, Muslim shoemakers sometimes supplemented their income by repairing pots or weaving silk.[219]

Commerce

In 1502, when rumors were circulating concerning the possible forced baptism of Valencia's Muslims, Fernando reckoned the cessation of

Mudejar commerce to be one of the most injurious consequences of the rumors: "the said Moors desist from leaving their villages and from conducting business and commerce as they were accustomed . . . which things are . . . damaging for our entire kingdom."[220] Viewed from the perspective of international trade, the king's fears appear insubstantial, for the role of the Mudejars in this sphere was minimal, not significant enough for their abandonment of commerce to have had any impact. An understanding of what Fernando meant by Mudejar "business" and "commerce" and why he deemed them crucial for the kingdom's economy requires a shift of focus from international maritime commerce, where the largest profits were to be made, to the more modest domestic, land-based trade that linked town and countryside and brought the entire kingdom within the commercial orbit of the capital.

The relationship between town and rural hinterland, which included neighboring seigneuries, was necessarily reciprocal. From the countryside the urban inhabitants received victuals and raw materials for industry. For the rural folk the town was above all a market center where they sold their agricultural surpluses and purchased manufactured goods. Yet this urban–rural division of labor was not all that precise, for townsmen often invested in and cultivated land, while rural villages had their own artisans. Nonetheless, towns could scarcely survive without the importation of foodstuffs from the countryside and the business of the inhabitants of satellite villages.

The Mudejars took part in this constant interchange between urban and rural spheres, traveling freely from their seigneurial villages to the towns with their produce. The weekly trek made by Mahomat Bolagui and his wife Madoneta from the barony of Corbera to the market of Alcira was typical of the commercial activities of many a Muslim or Christian peasant: "the said Moor and Mooress [were] travelling to the town of Alcira with their animals burdened with victuals and other things which are customarily brought every Wednesday by those residing near the said town, for on that same day each week they are accustomed to have a market."[221] Muslims from nearby Llombay also provisioned Alcira with wheat and those from Alcocer usually marketed their goods there.[222] The commercial network linking town to regional villages prevailed throughout the kingdom. Muslims of Gilet were frequent visitors to Murviedro, while Oriheula likewise opened its gates to a Mudejar carrying merchandise from Elche.[223] The marketing of crops in urban markets by Mudejar farmers indicates that a number of them were producing above the subsistence level. This was made possible in part by their purchasing and leasing of additional land both inside and outside of their place of residence, and by their reclamation of wasteland.[224]

Most Muslims, when they did not bring their crops to the nearest town market, brought them to Valencia. The capital was always in need of victuals and raw materials, and as a center of massive consumption drew to it the surplus produce of farmers and stockmen from all over the kingdom. Ali Gibi traveled there from the Foya de Buñol "with certain packs of hides and other merchandise and victuals. . . to sell."[225] Açen Açanego of Torres Torres transported 104 jugs of wine to Valencia.[226] Mudejars brought to the city a wide variety of products for sale: wheat, honey, sugar, figs, raisins, oil, wood, and so on.[227] The large number of Muslims who came to Valencia for this purpose prompted the bailiff general to restrict their vending to the city's main market: "let no Moor or Moors dare to go through the city of Valencia or through its houses or places selling flax, linen, or any other merchandise [such as] anis, sugar, caraway, . . . and other seeds but only in the market of the present city."[228] Merchants of Valencia would pay Muslim farmers in advance for the delivery of crops. For example, Mahomat Benfat of Carlet agreed to deliver to the merchant Ferrando Vilareyal 300 *arrobes* of olive oil, a considerable quantity.[229] Mudejars might act as middlemen between the farmers and Valencia's merchants. Maymol Gathneu, an oil merchant of Játiva, purchased olive oil from rural producers and delivered it to the city.[230]

While the Mudejars found the towns and the capital a ready market for their produce, urban merchants and shopkeepers could likewise count on the patronage of Muslim customers. The records reveal a lively traffic between merchants and Mudejars, especially in the capital. Credit transactions seem to have predominated. That the merchants were compelled to extend credit to the Mudejars (and to their Christian clients as well) reflects an insufficiency of cash in the hands of the latter, or, more generally, deficiencies in the supply and circulation of coinage. At the same time, it suggests that the merchants viewed the Mudejars as safe credit risks. It is difficult to know whether the Muslims normally made a down payment upon receipt of the goods, or if their credit extended to the entire cost of their purchase. Probably both types of credit arrangement were used. Sometimes the Muslim buyers left with the merchants articles of property, frequently jewelry, as collateral.[231]

Unfortunately, the records, primarily the bailiff general's letters of execution against Muslim debtors, seldom state what goods were being purchased by Mudejars. Naturally, there was much traffic in comestibles—grain, olive oil, cheese, fish, and so on.[232] Grain shortages, a chronic Mediterranean problem, caused Muslims to journey from places such as Bétera and Macastre to the capital to buy wheat.[233] In the spring of 1479 Francesch Conill sold more than 76 pounds worth of wheat to Muslims of Alicra, who were to pay him by Christmas of that year.[234] Along with food, clothing ranked among life's most basic necessities. Christian drapers, such as those with shops in Cuart, had a steady Muslim clientele.[235] Of course, Muslim artisans were always in need of materials—iron, copper, steel, alum, dyes, flax, cloth, thread, and the like—and shopkeepers were more than happy to oblige them.[236] Besides such essential articles, some Mudejars could afford to buy luxury items. Yuçeff Turis and Abdulazis Alboruch satisfied their taste for Sardinian cheeses, while other Muslims purchased spices and sugar.[237] Some preferred garb more sumptuous than that of locally woven fabrics, and so bought silks, fine linens, and cloth imported from Bruges and Brabant.[238]

In addition to these small purchases of a retail nature, Mudejars also made wholesale purchases of large quantities of goods with the intention of selling them retail. As retail merchants the Mudejars played an important role in the distribution of commodities throughout the kingdom from the centers of production and importation. Sometimes the large size of the purchases made by Muslims suggests that they were buying for their own retail businesses. Abdalla Xeyt of Castellnou had credits with Valencian merchants amounting to 171 pounds 3s 2d, and Abdalla Medalla purchased 100 pounds' worth of goods from the merchant Joan Allepus.[239] Muslim fishmongers from diverse localities bought eels, sardines, hake, and other fish directly from Christian fishermen in Sueca and Valencia.[240] Mascor Borrachet, a retailer from the Vall de Uxó, bought thirteen pounds of saffron from Gabriel Polo (an Italian?), and Amet Alami of Segorbe owed 82 pounds 16s 11d to the merchant Miguel Pérez for fifteen *arrobes* of pepper.[241] Men such as Mascor and Amet probably sold the goods thus purchased to the inhabitants in or near their own towns and villages. Muslims who made such wholesale purchases were not necessarily full-time merchants. The artisan or farmer might turn retailer if the wholesale price was right and there was the likelihood of earning a profit from retail sales. A soapmaker and a linen-draper pooled their resources to buy fifteen *quintars* (41.5 kilograms) of cheese from the merchant Gaspar Valenti.[242]

The Zignells, a large Mudejar family of Tabernes de Valldigna, devoted themselves to mercantile pursuits more fully, with one branch of the family eventually establishing itself in the capital. While holding land from the abbot of Valldigna, the Zignells were involved in commerce in the Orihuela-Alicante region since at least the beginning of Fernando's reign. Various members of the family traveled there to sell linen, mules, and other merchandise.[243] The Zignells also backed other Muslims of Valldigna journeying southward for commerce (at least that is what their standing as surety for them seems to indicate). Perhaps the latter, such as the carter Abrahim Çaffont, were the Zignells' agents, in which cases the Zignells would have furnished the merchandise and the agents their marketing skills.[244] In the 1480s the Zignells were doing business with merchants and farmers in the capital, perhaps purchasing goods and produce wholesale for retail distribution in the south.[245] By 1491 one branch of the family, consisting of Fuçey Zignell, his sons Yuçeff, Abdulazis, Mahomat, and Çahat, and their wives and children, set up commercial operations in Valencia. The city offered a considerably larger market for the enterprising retail merchant. Pere Eximenez, a wealthy innkeeper who had become Fuçey Zignell's partner, described Fuçey's (and his sons') retailing activities:

he has made and is accustomed to make many contracts, buying from merchants and from other persons many and diverse dry goods and merchandise of diverse kinds, having them to sell retail [per menut] and selling them retail both in his own house and throughout the present city to those who wish to buy.[246]

Indeed, the merchant Luis Nadal made to Fuçey and his sons "many sales of cloth from his shop . . . he sold goods to the said Moors who left pledges for the said merchandise."[247] Dionis Miguel, Francesch Miro, Berthomeu Pinos, Gaspar de Gallach, and a company of German merchants all dealt with the Zignells, selling to them in the gross Neapolitan linen, cloth, and other goods.[248] The Zignells also retailed vegetables and sugar, which Ali Zignell, Yuçeff's son, was licensed to vend in the city.[249] At the same time, the Zignells of Valldigna and Valencia continued their commercial dealings south of the Jijona River. In 1502 Yaye Zignell (Fuçey's grandson?) stood as surety for a Muslim of Alberique traveling to the Vall d'Elda to sell mules.[250] It was the backing of the innkeeper Pere Eximenez that enabled the Zignells to carry on these rather far-ranging commercial operations. Eximenez stood as pledge when the Zignells bought wholesale on credit. Whenever the proceeds from the Zignells' retail sales were insufficient for the repayment of the wholesalers, Eximenez would provide the funds that kept the Zignells' business afloat. In 1494 Eximenez paid 14,000 of the 22,000s owed by Fuçey Zignell and his sons to various creditors. When Fuçey and sons proved unable or unwilling to repay the 14,000s to Eximenez— at one point the sons had fled the city—their cousins in Valldigna, Umaymat and Yaye, came forth with 100 pounds (20,000s).[251] But this incident did not terminate the Zigne ll Eximenez partnership, for two years later Eximenez interceded with the bailiff general in the Zignells' behalf and obtained for them safe-conducts against prosecution for debt.[252]

Trading in the capital on a far more modest scale than the Zignells was the widow Xempsi Bizqueya. Her late husband Azmet had been involved in the retailing of cloth, and Xempsi followed in his footsteps somewhat, selling the second-hand clothing of affluent Christian women. The women commissioned Xempsi to sell articles of their clothing, and, after Xempsi returned the proceeds to them, they paid her a pittance for her troubles.[253] However meager her earnings, Xempsi still was able to offer to her daughter-in-law a bridewealth of two gold bracelets and a silk robe worth 21 pounds.[254] The capital also had its Muslim shopkeepers, such as Amet Mathera, a *botiguer*, and Mahomat Fandaig, a druggist.[255] Any town with a sizable Muslim community likely had a similar array of merchants.

The Mudejars did much to facilitate the flow of goods throughout the kingdom. Many worked as carters and muleteers, and were hired by merchants and artisans. Ali Borrachet, a carter of the Vall de Uxó, carried honey to a spice merchant in the capital.[256] A Murcian Jew importing goods through Valencia hired a Mudejar of Alcantera to transport them, and a Jewess employed Maymo Açen to deliver paper to a Christian printer.[257] Mudejars were sometimes commissioned as the agents of Christian entrepreneurs and were given funds *en comanda* for the purchase of certain commodities in bulk. For example, Simo Sánchez, a citizen of Valencia, gave 84 pounds 16s 8d to Açen Tintorer of Valldigna "for the purpose of buying for him [Sánchez] as much silk as the said . . . [money] can buy."[258] Açen was probably familiar with silk producers, many of whom were Muslims.

It was partly through the offices of the Mudejar carters and muleteers that Valencia's commercial network was extended to the cities and towns of the kingdom of Aragon. Ali and Azmet Ferriol of Benaguacil were active in transporting goods from Valencia to Calatayud.[259] A merchant of Zaragoza entrusted 1,200s *en comanda* to a Muslim of Segorbe, probably for the purchase of merchandise in Valencia.[260] Mudejar muleteers from Aragon and Castile complemented the activities of their Valencian cousins. Caçim of Ávila carried "packs with diverse things"[261] from Valencia to the king. Muleteers and carters could achieve some prosperity, as is evinced in the person of Azmet Bocayo, a carter of Castellón de la Plana who also had substantial landholdings.[262]

In addition to merely transporting goods, Mudejars sold them as itinerant merchants. The evidence for Mudejar mercantile activity is derived largely from the licenses granted by the bailiff general to Muslims for travel to the region south of the Jijona River, often for reasons of commerce. It may be presumed that Mudejar merchants traded in areas north of the Jijona as well, where Muslims could move freely without a license. These merchants rarely worked merely on their own account; rather, they were vending on behalf of sedentary partners who furnished the necessary goods or cash. The travel licenses reveal nothing about the details of the arrangement between the itinerant vendor and the sedentary partner. However, they do provide the names of those who acted as guarantors of the licensees, in case the latter did not return to the capital in the time specified. It seems likely that those who took the trouble to be guarantors, especially the Christians who acted in this capacity for Muslims, had some interest in the licensee's commercial venture. This is indicated in the case of Yuçeff Abducarim of Játiva, who with his son and servant traveled south "to sell pots and some other things of his trade." His guarantor was Francesch Sarria, a boilermaker (*calderer*).[263] Likewise, it may be conjectured that when March Casterellenes, a silversmith, and Alexandre Alvespi, a glassworker, acted as guarantors for Muslim merchants, their wares represented part of the merchandise to be sold by the latter.[264] Wholesale merchants such as Francesch Sparça and Pasqual Vicent were able to extend their commercial interests from the port of Valencia to Orihuela through the marketing expertise of itinerant Mudejar retailers.[265] The fact that the Mudejars had to come to the capital in order to obtain travel licenses worked to the benefit of Valencia's entrepreneurs who wished to expand the scope of their businesses beyond the city's limits. At times local bailiffs were authorized to grant licenses to Muslim merchants to facilitate the flow of goods not emanating from the capital. For instance, since "each day some Moors of the said place [Orcheta] have to go to the Vall d'Elda, Orihuela, and the town of Alicante with loads of some merchandise," the bailiff of Penáguila was empowered to grant the licenses.[266]

It has been mentioned above how Mudejar artisans and merchants, like Abdalla Torralbi, Çahat Cantsevol, and the Zignells, also backed these itinerant merchants.[267] Entire aljamas sometimes acted as guarantors for Muslim merchants, as did lords for their merchant vassals.[268] Perhaps in such cases the merchant was vending the crops and manufactures produced on the seigneury itself.

Mudejar carters, muleteers, and itinerant retail merchants had Christian counterparts. Still, the Muslims' familiarity with the rural, seigneurial areas, where many of them resided, made them especially suitable for the role of linking the commerce of the capital to that of the outlying towns and villages. Were one to pose a mercantile division of labor between Christians and Muslims, one would conclude that the former monopolized maritime commerce and wholesale trade, while the latter moved the goods of the wholesalers and distributed them throughout the kingdom through their retailing activities. No doubt the commerce in Christian hands was substantially more lucrative. Still, the retailing of the Mudejars reaped some profits and for the regional economy was no less essential. The king expressed concern about the cessation of Mudejar commerce in 1502, because the result would have been a considerably slower circulation of goods through the kingdom's commercial arteries.

Mudejar participation in international trade was of far lesser moment. There had been important mercantile families in the *morería* of Valencia during the early decades of the fifteenth century. These families—the Ripoll, Xupio, Benxarnit, and Razbayda—conducted trade with Granada and North Africa. However, as a consequence of emigration and the destruction of Valencia's *morería* in 1455, this Mudejar commercial elite had largely disappeared by the last quarter of the century.[269] The inhabitants of the *morería* subsequently focused most of their energies on manufacture and the local retail trade.

During Fernando's reign Mudejars nonetheless continued the small-scale maritime trade with Almería in the sultanate of Granada and with Tunis and Oran in North Africa. Mudejar merchants did not have ships of their own, and so traveled with their goods on Venetian, Genoese, and Valencian vessels. The volume of this commerce was not great, and the merchandise of individual merchants only occasionally had a value of more than 50 pounds.[270] Among the commodities sold by Mudejars in North Africa were silk, saffron, cloth, and metalware.[271] Whereas previous to 1455 the majority of Mudejar merchants had originated from the capital's *morería*, most now came from seigneurial lands, the exception being those who were residents of Játiva.[272] It is unlikely that these Muslims were full-time merchants; most probably represented only the interests of other members of their aljama. Some combined commercial pursuits in Islamic lands with family business and study. The war with Granada eventually terminated the trade with Almería and, combined with the later crusade against Africa, also seems to have slowed the movement of Mudejar merchants between Valencia and the Maghrib.[273]

The outstanding exception to the general decline of Mudejar maritime commerce was the mercantile activity of the *qādī* general, Mahomat Bellvis. Like other Mudejars, the Bellvis participated in the trade between Valencia, Almería, and North Africa. Sometimes Mahomat sent his sons there to conduct family business and other times agents were sent to represent Bellvis interests. However, commerce took the Bellvis much further afield, for they were also involved in the eastern Mediterranean spice trade. Mahomat's son Yahye purchased spices in Alexandria and sold them in Italy and Valencia. In one case Yahye sold spices in Naples and was given letters of exchange for repayment in Tunis. Traveling with Yahye were other members of his "company of Moors" from Valencia. Bellvis' commercial expertise seems to have attracted other Mudejars to invest in their commercial ventures, though no doubt the Bellvis were dominant in this Mudejar company.[274] It appears that the Bellvis shipped spices to Valencia on Venetian and Florentine vessels, or at least this is suggested by a litigation between Mahomat Bellvis and Dominic de Tella, a representative of Florentine ship patrons.[275] Çahat Bellvis, described in the sources as a spice merchant, must have handled the Bellvis' wholesale-retail business in Valencia. By 1498 Yahye Bellvis had emigrated to Tunis, in all likelihood to facilitate his family's commercial ventures between the Levant, Italy, the Maghrib, and Valencia.[276]

Notwithstanding the evidence of Mudejar prosperity, the great majority of the kingdom's wealth was concentrated in the hands of the Christian upper classes. Of Valencia's Muslims perhaps only the Bellvis family had attained a financial status similar to that of Christian noblemen and successful merchants. Prosperous Mudejars only rarely rose above the level of the middle class. The fact that enterprising Muslim merchants and artisans, such as the Zignells or Abdalla Torralbi, often relied on the financial backing and loans of far wealthier Christian investors and partners indicates the true locus of economic power in Valencia. The careers of Mudejar officials who farmed royal and seigneurial taxes tell much the same story, for their middling wealth was acquired mainly through their access to the fiscal machinery of the Crown and the Christian aristocracy. The inescapable fact was that the economy remained securely under Christian control, a state of affairs evident since the thirteenth century, when political conquest was followed by the wresting of economic power from Muslim hands.

4   Taxation of the Mudejars

Royal Mudejar policy balanced religious scruples with political and economic imperatives. As we have seen, rumors of royal plans for a wholesale conversion or expulsion of Valencia's Muslims elicited vehement protests and dire warnings from the nobility. Fernando's maintenance of the status quo reflected his unwillingness to embroil himself in a protracted struggle with the nobility on this issue, particularly when so many of his political concerns lay further afield in a wider Mediterranean arena. It is useful to recall the persuasive arguments against conversion or expulsion offered by the magnates. Of one contention, the specter of a bloody Mudejar insurrection, we have already discussed the implications and plausibility. What concerns us presently is the other argument, that an expulsion of the Muslims, or a flight en masse provoked by the threat of forced baptism, would entail the economic ruination of the entire kingdom, not just of the nobility. The nobles pointed out that the kingdom's economy was all of a piece and that the Mudejars could not be extracted without the entire edifice crumbling. Since Mudejar labor was essential for agricultural productivity, urban markets would stagnate without the steady input of Mudejar produce from the rural hinterlands. The disaster that Mudejar emigration implied for seigneurial lands suggested equally severe consequences for the growing *rentier* class, comprising townsmen, clergymen, and lesser noblemen, whose incomes depended on the payment of annuities (*pensions de censals*) by the barons and seigneurial aljamas to whom they had loaned considerable sums. In short, the Mudejars were integral to the kingdom's economic prosperity. The fortunes of nobleman, cleric, and bur-

143

gher were all linked, some more directly than others, to the Mudejars' fate. An expulsion of the Mudejars could not have been achieved without a fundamental restructuring of the economic relations between lord and peasant, town and country, and debtor and creditor.

Viewed from the throne, the Mudejars' economic importance had two aspects. First and foremost, the Mudejar presence redounded to the prosperity of the kingdom as a whole. A sound Valencian economy boded well for royal finances, since the Valencian Corts and the capital itself, the motor of the kingdom's economy, could then afford to grant to the Crown more substantial *servicios* and loans. The fifteenth century, often touted as Valencia's golden age, saw a steady increase in the Valencian contribution to the Crown treasury, most marked during the reign of Fernando II.[1]

Second, the king profited from the direct taxation of Mudejar vassals residing in royal *morerías*. We have seen how the king and his officials struggled with the nobility in their endeavor to attract Muslims to royal aljamas. This effort was exerted in order to improve the economies of underpopulated royal towns and augment the number of taxpayers providing revenue for the royal treasury. Nevertheless, in comparison with the Mudejar contribution to the general economic health of the kingdom and, therefore, indirectly, to the funds the kingdom was able to proffer to the king, the weight of the small body of Mudejar taxpayers in the balance of the Crown's budget was not great.

As a consequence of demographic and political change, the number of Mudejar taxpayers and their significance for royal finances had steadily declined since the latter half of the fourteenth century. By Fernando's reign the Mudejars represented only 30 percent of the kingdom's total population. Furthermore, because of the continued alienation of royal lands to the nobility, the proportion of that 30 percent living in royal *morerías* had diminished as well. During the reign of Juan II the heavily Muslim-populated Sierra de Eslida and Vall de Uxó had been awarded to the Infante Enrique.[2] Thus perhaps only 10 percent of the kingdom's Muslim population, and therefore a mere 3 percent of the combined Muslim-Christian total, had Fernando as their direct overlord. The remaining 90 percent of the Mudejar population paid their taxes to their noble and clerical lords. Only a few of the extraordinary taxes, such as the *maridatge*, were paid to the Crown by seigneurial and royal vassals alike. While it is understandable why Fernando would have wanted to increase the number of Mudejars owing vassalage to himself, at the same time it is clear that the feasibility of royal enterprises hardly hinged on taxes paid by royal Muslim vassals.

In the kingdom of Valencia the capital city was the most important source of royal revenue. With a population of approximately 45,000 (perhaps one-sixth of the kingdom's total) and as a center of commerce and finance, Valencia was the focus of the king's attention. Fernando's control of the municipal government allowed him to exact more than 8 million *maravedis* in "loans." Even taking into account this substantial sum, the fact remains that Castile still contributed far more than the lands of the Crown of Aragon to royal enterprises, even those involving the expansion of Aragon's Mediterranean empire.[3] In an inverted pyramid describing fiscal contributions to the Crown it would seem that royal Muslim vassals occupied the lowest level.

Unfortunately, we are unable to calculate the percentage of Crown revenues composed of Mudejar taxes. Juan II's bureaucratic decentralization, by which the royal archives of Valencia, Aragon proper, and Catalonia, all previously housed in Barcelona, were subsequently maintained in the respective capital cities of Valencia, Zaragoza, and Barcelona, and the vicissitudes of time and war, particularly the destruction of much of Aragon's royal archives during the Napoleonic war, have resulted in the loss of virtually all Aragonese tax records and in the survival of precious few for the aljamas of Catalonia. Even for the kingdom of Valencia alone our information is incomplete. While we possess tax data for the aljamas of some towns—Alcira, Játiva, Castellón de la Plana, and Murviedro—for certain years, information on the taxation of other royal aljamas is lacking. Moreover, in the records of a number of taxes paid by both Muslims and Christians, especially the taxes on agriculture and commerce, the scribes did not distinguish the religious affiliation of the taxpayers. These lacunae in our sources impede us from making as thorough and complete a study of royal taxation of the Mudejars as the outstanding analysis done by Boswell on the fourteenth-century Mudejars. Of course, in the fourteenth century the proportion of the population represented by Muslims was considerably larger, fewer Muslim aljamas had been alienated to the nobility, and the Aragonese kings did not have the extensive financial resources of Castile at their disposal. All of these factors raised the taxation of royal Mudejars to a far more important place in royal fiscal considerations in the fourteenth century than it would have during Fernando's reign.[4]

Nevertheless, whatever significance Mudejar taxes had in the larger scheme of Crown finances, taxation itself was a factor of great import in the lives of individual Mudejars and their aljamas. Taxation necessarily limited the material well-being of Mudejar families and was a decisive determinant in their changing vassalage from one lord to another. The Mudejars' obligation to pay taxes to either king or lord defined and structured much of their relationship with the Christian authorities. The myriad reasons for which the Christian king or lord could demand taxes and fees from Muslim vassals—in areas as diverse as oven rentals and prostitution licenses—meant that the Christian fiscal machinery impinged on almost every aspect of Muslim life. While the Mudejar aljamas enjoyed communal autonomy, it was an autonomy circumscribed by the tentacles of a Christian bureaucracy organized for tax collection. Therefore, a description of the various taxes that burdened the Mudejars should further our understanding of Mudejar life and its intimate relation to Christian authority.

Although a discussion of royal taxation involves only a small part of the Mudejar population, it should be noted that seigneurial Muslims bore a similar tax burden and saw their relation with their lord patterned along similar fiscal lines. That the rivalry between the king and the nobility over Mudejar vassals centered largely on the question of fiscal benefits suggests a similarity in the attitudes of the rivals toward their taxpaying vassals.

The Besant Tax

Each Muslim household paid a tax known as the *besant*, a tribute symbolic of their subject and inferior status in a Christian society. In this way it was similar to the *jizyah*, or poll tax, paid by the *dhimmī*s in Islamic societies, though the *jizyah* differed in that it fell on every male beyond the age of puberty. While the *besant* continued to be collected from the Mudejars of the kingdom of Valencia in the fifteenth century, its collection seems to have fallen into abeyance in Aragon and Catalonia.[5]

The *besant* was not an especially burdensome levy; each household paid 3s 4d annually. The Muslims of Castellón de la Plana paid a higher *besant* of 4s, the explanation for this probably lying in that aljama's later foundation.[6] The aljama of Valencia, still suffering from the effects of the sack of 1455, was exempted from payment of the *besant*. Temporary exemption was also offered as an inducement to new vassals in the *morería* of Játiva.[7] Impoverished Mudejars were perforce excused from payment. In the large aljamas of Játiva and Alcira (table 3) the number of Muslims not paying ranged from 5 to 15 percent of the total population in any given year.[8] Although the Crown might be lenient with individual Muslims, the remission was only temporary. Once he had sufficient funds, the Muslim in arrears had to satisfy all outstanding *besants* (table 4). It followed that the Muslim dissolving his bonds of vassalage to the king had to discharge his *besants* before departure to seigneurial lands.[9]

Table 3.   Alcira (ARV: MR 942–959)

	Butcher shop	Saddleworks	Rents on houses and land	*Besant*	*Peyta*
1479	400s	120s		270s	
1480	403s 4d	120s		276s 8d	
1481	403s 4d	120s	104s 6d	257s	
1482	403s 4d	120s	104s 6d	193s 4d (incomplete)	100s
1488	440s	120s	97s 6d	306s 8d	100s
1489	540s	76s		336s 8d	100s
1490	540s	164s	104s 6d	344s 8d	
1491	540s	120s	104s 6d	350s	100s
1492	633s 4d	120s	86s 6d	373s 4d	100s
1493	633s 4d	120s	104s 6d	323s 4d	100s
1494	633s 4d	120s	104s 6d	327s 8d	100s
1495	666s 8d	120s	104s 6d	183s 4d (incomplete)	100s
1496	666s 8d	120s	104s 6d	280s	100s
1497		120s	104s 6d	286s 8d	
1498	866s 8d	120s	104s 6d	310s	200s
1499	866s 8d	120s	104s 6d	306s 8d	100s
1500	866s 8d	120s	104s 6d	310s	100s
1501	833s 4d	120s	91s 6d	310s	100s
1502	833s 4d	120s	91s 6d	310s	100s

Table 4.   Alcira (ARV: MR 942–959)

Inheritances	*Besants* in arrears
128s—Yaye Gini (1489)	119s (1489)
480s—Fumeyt Mosqueret (1490)	46s 8d (1491)
169s 3d—Ayet Rocayz (1491)	10s (1492)
140s—Hayet Moxentech (1493)	10s (1493)
148s—Ayoça, wife of Fumeyt (1495)	13s 4d (1494)
240s—Fotaya Alazrach and Açot Axer (1502)	30s (1495)
	10s (1496)
	36s (1497)
	56s 8d (1498)
	30s (1499)
	20s (1500)

Table 5.   Alcira: Lessees (ARV: MR 942–959)

Butcher shop	Saddleworks
Çahat Capo and Çahat Galliç (1479)	Çahat Trilli (1479)
Çahat Paziar (1480–1482)	Abdulazis Crespi and Çahat Trilli et al. (1480–1482)
Pere Olmedes (1489–1491)	Abdulazis Crespi (1488)
Alamany Casalils (1492–1494)	Abdulazis Crespi and Çahat Trilli et al. (1489–1491)
Lorens Garcia (1495–1496)	Çahat Trilli (1492–1502)
Padon Paziar (1498–1500)	
Jacme Barbera and Azmet Paziar (1501–1502)	

The varied patterns of vassalage, land tenure, and residence complicated the collection of the *besant* (see tables 5–10). A number of Muslims, while royal vassals in specific aljamas, continued to live in or later changed their residence to seigneurial lands. Fortunately for the aljamas' finances, the *besant* was assessed only on individual households, so that the aljama was not made to compensate for the unpaid *besants* of absentee vassals. The responsibility of collecting from these vassals thus fell to the local bailiffs, who seem to have carried out this task efficiently. Muslims dwelling in the lordships of Alcocer, Alberique, Catadau, and Valldigna are recorded as having paid the *besant* to the bailiff of Alcira. Likewise, the bailiff of Murviedro collected from royal vassals resident in Algimia.[10]

Also linked to the Mudejars' status of a conquered and dissident minority was the requirement that they have a royal license to bear arms, beg for alms, and practice prostitution. The fees charged by the Crown for these licenses figured as only a minor source of royal revenue, and, although not especially high, must have proved burdensome to mendicants. It is probable that such licenses, as well as those granted to Mudejars for travel and emigration, were more important as a means of controlling the movement and activities of the Muslim population. Chapter 2 discussed how suspicions about a Mudejar fifth column prompted the king to recommend stricter control of Mudejar arms-bearing and to curtail the granting of travel licenses. Because most mendicants and many prostitutes were itinerant, the demand that they bear licenses allowed for some surveillance of transient Muslims.[11] It is not surprising that the bailiff general expressed the most concern about unlicensed Muslim beggars and prostitutes during the years 1499–1503, when revolts in Granada and the resultant Mudejar fears and attempted

Table 6. Castellón de la Plana (ARV: MR 2469–2491)

	Besant		Rents on land and mills		Butcher shop of Muslims and Jews (until 1492)		Inheritances
1479–1481	112s/year	1482–1485	2s/year	1479–1503	1s 6d/year		
1482–1489	120s/year	1487–1489	14s/year				
1490–1491	108s/year	1490–1499	20s/year			1490	110s
1492	116s	1500	34s			1501	50s
1493	108s	1501	20s				
1494	112s						
1495–1496	120s/year						
1497–1498	128s/year						
1499	164s						
1500	192s						
1501	172s						
1502	188s						
1503	180s						

Table 7.   Murviedro (ARV: MR 4016–4034)

	Besant (+ morabatí)	Butcher shop	Dyeworks	Rents on land
1483	86s 8d	7s	50s	4s 6d
1484	66s 8d	7s	50s	4s 6d
1486	60s	7s	50s	4s 6d
1487	46s 8d	7s	50s	4s 6d
1488	53s 4d	7s	50s	4s 6d
1489	53s 4d	7s	50s	4s 6d
1491	66s 8d	7s		4s 6d
1492	66s 8d	7s	50s	4s 6d
1493	66s 8d	7s	50s	4s 6d
1494	60s	7s	50s	10s 3d
1495	33s 4d	7s	50s	18s
1496	33s 4d	7s	50s	18s
1497	73s 4d	7s	50s	18s
1498	140s	7s	50s	18s
1499	140s	7s	50s	18s
1500	140s	7s	50s	18s
1501	140s	7s	50s	18s
1502	140s	7s	50s	10s 3d

Table 8.   Játiva (ARV: MR 3052–3062)

	Paper mill	Large oven	Small oven	Pasture	Prostitution Tax	Mealles	Bath
1478	15s	480s	360s	260s	120s	300s	640s
1490	10s	700s	480s	200s	100s	390s	1,100s
1494	18s	740s	720s	300s	160s	330s	1,000s
1495	16s	740s	720s	300s	150s	210s	1,000s
1496	16s	800s	820s	300s	150s	200s	1,000s
1497	20s	700s	700s	300s	120s	210s	900s
1498	16s	600s	600s	350s	190s	200s	850s
1500	16s	600s	500s	260s	190s	160s	920s
1501	13s	600s	460s	260s	190s	160s	800s
1502	14s	440s	400s	260s	240s	300s	1,000s

Table 9.   *Játiva (ARV: MR 3052–3062)*

	Butcher shops	Market	Soap factory	Dye-works	Saddle-works	Inheri-tances	Cena
1478	500s	1,060s	200s	90s		400s	600s
1490	600s	1,400s	220s	90s	120s	400s	600s
1494	650s	1,500s	160s	90s	120s	400s	600s
1495	800s	1,645s 4d	160s	90s	120s	400s	600s
1496	800s	1,645s 4d	160s	90s	120s	400s	600s
1497	900s	1,645s	160s	90s	120s		
1498	1,000s	2,000s	160s	90s	120s	400s	600s
1500	1,550s	1,800s	160s	90s	120s	400s	600s
1501	1,550s	1,600s	160s	90s	300s	400s	600s
1502	1,550s	1,900s	160s	90s	400s	400s	600s

Table 10.   *Játiva (ARV: MR 3052–3062)*

	Besant	Olive press	Tannery	Fonduk	Annual payment
1478	1,363s 7d	60s	10s		416s 8d
1490	1,193s 10d	60s	10s		416s 8d
1494	1,150s 6d	30s	10s	99s	416s 8d
1495	1,173s 10d	30s	10s	147s 2d	416s 8d
1496	1,173s 10d	30s	10s	183s 4d	416s 8d
1497		30s	10s	30s	416s 8d
1498	1,133s 10d	30s	10s	30s	416s 8d
1500	1,093s 10d	30s	10s	30s	416s 8d
1501		30s	10s	15s	416s 8d
1502	1,070s 6d	30s	10s		416s 8d

flight created a potentially explosive state of affairs.[12] Like the *besant*, these licenses were more important for what they signified—in this case, a restriction of the Muslims' freedom of movement and a basic royal mistrust of Mudejar intentions—than for the revenue they brought to the king.

Public Utilities

The royal monopoly of utilities providing vital community services assured the Crown a steady flow of annual income. The Crown controlled butcher shops (*carnicerías*), ovens, mills, baths, taverns, and a variety of other services, such as tanneries and dyeworks. Generally, the local bailiffs rented out these utilities in public auction to the highest bidder, Christian, Muslim, or Jew. The lessee gave the Crown a fixed annual rent derived from what he earned from control of the utility. The rental of these utilities in public auction meant that the rents were subject to fluctuations consonant with the realities of the marketplace and the prevailing prices of commodities.

Few utilities were specifically linked to Muslim communities as such. The size of an aljama and the clauses of its foundation charter determined whether it need have, for instance, its own special oven. To take another example, the prevalence of Muslim artisans in certain crafts, such as saddlemaking or dyeing, resulted in the consistent Muslim rental of the local saddleworks and dyeworks, which were perhaps also attached to the *morerías*. However, on account of Islamic and Jewish dietary laws, quite similar in many details, it was necessary for Muslims and Jews to have their own butcher shops. It seems that every Mudejar community had this privilege, which, as Burns points out, may be equated with an extension of religious privileges. In Castellón de la Plana the Muslims shared a butcher shop with the Jews.[13]

Despite the religious complications implied in the rental of a Muslim butcher shop to a Christian, it was an established practice and seems to have raised no complaint from Mudejar leaders. In Alcira and Játiva Christians and Muslims alternated in their rental of the Muslim butcheries, depending on who could offer the highest bid.[14] The butcher shop of the new *morería* of Castellón de Játiva was the one exception to the usual rental arrangements. There Fernando conceded to Joan Bleda, already the concessionaire of the Christian butcheries, the Muslim butchery perpetually and in enfiteusis, at an annual rent of one *morabatí*. In any case, whoever the lessee or concessionaire, the butcher who actually slaughtered the meat had to be a Muslim. Thus, in the terms of the concession of the Muslim butcher shop to Joan Bleda it was stipulated "let its butcher be a Sarracen and not a Christian."[15] Presumably the lessees either sublet the butcheries to Muslim butchers or paid them a salary. Unfortunately, the documentation, concerned mainly with the rents accruing to the royal treasury, reveals next to nothing on Muslim butchers and their arrangements with the lessees. One glimpse is offered in the plea of Joan Lopiç, a merchant and lessee of the Muslim butcher shop of Játiva, to whom the Muslim butcher, al-Ayeret, owed 262s 6d for the sheep slaughtered in the butcher shop.[16] Apparently the lessee had furnished the animals necessary for the aljama's consumption, and the butcher, who slaughtered and sold the meat, was expected to reimburse the lessee from the proceeds. The absence of Mudejar grievances on this score suggests that Muslim butchers consistently functioned as the all-important intermediaries between lessees and Muslim consumers.

Crown supervision extended beyond rental of the butcher shop to ensuring that the abattoir was provisioned with sufficient livestock—sheep, goats, and beef cattle—to meet the demands of local consumption. Crown pasture land was therefore allotted for grazing the flocks of the royal butcheries; these flocks were exempted from payment of the *herbatge*, a tax on the use of Crown pastures.[17] The Crown sometimes stipulated precisely how many head of livestock the lessee ought to provide. In Castellón de Játiva the Christian butcher shop was to be furnished with 250 head, and the Muslim butcher shop with 150, although Joan Bleda, the concessionaire, later complained that the bailiff was forcing him to have slaughtered for the Muslims an excessive amount of meat, much of which was left to rot in the summer sun.[18] One clause of the lease of Joan Sancho stated that if he did not provide sufficient livestock for Játiva's Muslim butcher shop the Muslims could slaughter meat in the Crown abattoir for themselves.[19] Neither royal provisions nor leases specify the sale price of meat, nor do they suggest that Muslims were charged more for their meat. Lessees were admonished only to sell the meat at "accustomed prices," which were set more by the local market than by royal guidelines.[20] There is no evidence indicating that lessees engaged in any price speculation regarded by aljamas as immoderate or burdensome.

Apart from the renting of butcheries, the Crown also collected a sales tax on each pound of meat, known as the *sisa del carn* (*sisas* were also imposed on bread, wine, and other essential commodities). Information from Gandía (1492) indicates that the *sisa* paid there was 1s per pound of billy-goat and ram, 9d per pound of she-goat and ewe, and 4s 6d per pound of beef.[21] The rates of the sales tax in Murviedro (1483) were only half as high as those paid in Gandía.[22] The explanation for the difference in *sisa* rates lies in the Crown's concession of the right to collect the *sises* to many municipal governments, which were then able to establish the local rates. The aljama of Játiva paid the bailiff to farm out the sales tax collected in its butcher shop and market.[23] Leaving the collection of the sales tax in the hands of municipal governments created problems, for at times the jurates arbitrarily raised the sales tax rates, prompting resistance from lords with lands within the general limits of Gandía and from the aljama of Murviedro.[24] In Castellón de la Plana the jurates were not allowed to exact the *sisa* from the local Muslims, which induced them to prohibit Christians from purchasing meat in the Muslim butcher shop where they could escape the sales tax.[25]

Because the butcheries provided such an essential commodity, they were lucrative utilities. The almost unique restriction of their services to the members of a particular aljama rendered the butcheries a highly appropriate and efficient means of aiding an aljama in financial straits, without affecting the rest of the local economy. Since 1376 the aljama of Valencia had enjoyed the privilege of renting its own butcher shop and retaining the proceeds from the rental to defray its own expenses. Such revenue was so crucial to the aljama's finances after 1455 that when the guild of Christian butchers attempted to place restrictions on the Muslim butcher shop's sale of meat, the aljama pleaded that it did not have any "other substance or property with which to pay the royal taxes and rents that it is ordinarily obliged to pay."[26] The aljama of Daroca (Aragon) benefited from a like royal concession, and it was allowed to retain the sales tax collected in its butcher shop as well.[27] The Crown met the aljama of Játiva halfway: the lessee paid half the butchery rent to the Crown and half to the aljama's treasurer.[28]

Some Muslims tried to evade the Crown's close supervision of the sale of meat by slaughtering meat outside of the Muslim butcheries, sometimes in Christian butcheries, and then selling it at more competitive prices. Mahomat Paziar, Alcira's amīn, whose son was renting the butcher shop, and the aljama of Daroca both complained about the losses they were sustaining from the activities of these "free-lance" butchers.[29]

Another important royal monopoly related specifically to the Mudejars was the institution of the alfondech or fonduk. Described in the documentation as a "hospitium maurorum," and located within the confines of the morería, the fonduk functioned as an inn for Muslim travelers and merchants, and, almost invariably, as a center for Muslim prostitution. As suggested in chapter 1, the fonduk was an adjunct to a royal policy of social segregation. That a fonduk was created in the fledgling morería of Castellón de Játiva suggests that all other royal morerías had one.[30] However, perhaps only the fonduk in Valencia bore any resemblance to the thirteenth-century institution described by Burns as "at once a public inn, goods depository, mail drop, center for any notarial or customs services, and exhibit hall . . . it could elaborate into a home-away-from-home."[31] The continued success of Valencia's fonduk lay in the capital's preeminent role in the kingdom, and in the entire Crown of Aragon, as a center of domestic and international commerce, and as the arrival and embarkation point of the Venetian galleys that carried Maghriban merchants and their cargoes. The small size of Valencia's aljama should not blind one to the fact that through the city there traversed a large transient Muslim population, Valencian and foreigner, slave and free. The fonduk was leased for terms of two to four years, with the annual rent steadily increasing from 1,000s (1479–1483) to

3,000s (1498–1502). Only in 1490, on account of a plague that discouraged Muslims and Jews from traveling to the capital, did the fonduk suffer.[32] Still, the lodging of Muslims in other hostels was a consistent problem, and Diego de Soria, the lessee in 1490, complained that the bailiff general was protecting an innkeeper who had Mudejars from Arevalo (Castile) as guests.[33] Seigneurial Muslims were exempted, at least temporarily, from the necessity of lodging in the royal fonduk.[34]

Allied to the leasing of Valencia's fonduk, and likewise sustained by the large number of Muslims visiting the capital, was the rental of an office unique to the capital, that of the *basto* (i.e., "baton," symbolic of the possession of the office and its policing function) or guard of the bailiwick of the *morería*. This office, rented to Joan de Vich (1481–1488) and to his son Joan after his death, had little to do with the normal duties of a local bailiff, which in Valencia were incumbent on the resident bailiff general. Rather, the *basto* exercised a supervisory and policing function in the *morería*. He managed the royal tavern and bordello, regulated the practice of prostitution in the *morería*, and collected the required tax (*dret de tarquena*) from the Muslim prostitutes or their pimps. He also saw to it that Muslims did not bear arms in the *morería*, travel at night without a lamp, gamble, drink wine outside the royal tavern, or dress in excessive finery, all infractions being punishable by fine.[35] The *basto* and the lessee of the fonduk, or *alfondeguer*, likely worked closely together, since the guests of the fonduk might well have indulged in the pleasures of the tavern and bordello.

In the other royal towns the offices of the *alfondeguer* and *basto* were combined in the person of the former. Wine, if it was drunk anywhere in the *morerías*, was most likely served in the fonduks. In Zaragoza the fonduk also housed the *morería*'s jail, and the *alfondeguer* served as its jailer.[36] Gambling seems to have been forbidden throughout the kingdom, so that the fonduks were freed of this vice. The prominence royal leases give to prostitution as a source of income for the fonduks' concessionaires indicates that most fonduks were quasi-bordellos where the *alfondeguers* were responsible for collecting the *tarquena* from the prostitutes. In contrast to its firm stand against gambling, the Crown seems to have concluded that prostitution could be more effectively regulated than eradicated, and, as was so often the case, regulation translated into fiscal profits. Every Muslim prostitute in the kingdom had to purchase from the bailiff general for 18s a license to ply her trade.[37]

The fonduks of Alcira and Játiva brought little revenue to the Crown. In 1479 a member of the important Mudejar family of Paziar purchased the building housing the fonduk of Alcira so that he could provide a "genteel home" for his newlywed son. The bailiff and aljama concurred on this, feeling that Paziar's remodeling of the house would help to beautify the *morería*. The resultant problem was that another house for the permanent establishment of a fonduk could not be found, inasmuch as none of the local Muslims were interested in selling. It seems that for most of Fernando's reign Alcira's *morería* lacked a fonduk, although occasionally individuals were paid for the use of their home for this purpose.[38]

Játiva's fonduk was in a state of considerable disrepair, and desultory efforts were made to refurbish it, even constructing special rooms for the prostitutes. Although Muslim saddlers rented a part of the fonduk as a shop, few were willing to rent it for its intended purpose. The royal prohibition against gambling seems to have taken all life out of the place, and the tax records state that the prohibition was, indeed, the cause for the reluctance of potential lessees. Even when lessees were found, the fonduk, because it attracted so much lowlife, did more harm than good. In 1495 the aljama complained that Christian youths were sneaking into the fonduk through a window and spending the night in the *morería*. Worse still, the wife of the Christian lessee was traipsing about "dishonestly dressed" and tempting Muslim youths.[39] Perhaps the aljamas of Játiva and Alcira reasoned that they were well rid of such riffraff as were associated with the fonduks; Muslim visitors could easily be lodged in someone's home.

Public baths, necessary for ritual ablutions and purification and essential as centers of social intercourse, were fixtures in the life of most medieval Muslim communities. Islamic Valencian towns had been no exception, and presumably most Mudejar aljamas continued to support baths, however modest or elaborate. By Fernando's reign Mudejar baths had ceased to be a source of Crown income. Probably the Crown had ceded to each aljama control over its own bath. As in the case of the butcher shops, such concessions would have aided the aljamas in attaining or maintaining solvency. The Mudejar bath of Játiva, however, was an exception and remained a Crown monopoly. Because the aljama of Játiva was by far the largest in the kingdom, the revenues accruing from its Mudejar taxes and from the rental of its *morería* utilities were substantial when those from many smaller aljamas were negligible. Consequently, the Crown was loath to alienate its monopoly over any of the utilities servicing the aljama of Játiva. Játiva's Mudejar bath was always leased to Muslims at an annual rent ranging from 640s to 1,100s.[40] On the question of whether Jews might use the Muslim baths, Fernando vacillated. First, in 1488, he commanded that the Muslim aljama must permit the Jews to have access to the baths, otherwise royal rents would decrease. Two years later he changed his mind and forbade such contact between Jews and Muslims in the baths, deeming it "pernicious," as he perhaps viewed the exposure of anyone to Judaism at this juncture.[41]

In terms of the pervasiveness of the royal monopoly, the situation of Mudejar ovens was similar to that of the baths. In the kingdom of Valencia only the two ovens of the *morería* of Játiva—the *forn maior* (large oven) and the *forn menor* (small oven)—were leased by the Crown, and for considerable rents.[42] Inasmuch as communal ovens served individual neighborhoods, it seems likely that most other *morerías* had their own ovens, although, unlike the Jews with their baking of matzoh, Muslim baking had no ritual significance. Just as the Christians of Mislata baked their bread in the Muslims' oven, it may be that smaller aljamas made use of Christian ovens. In 1496 two of Murviedro's ovens were rented by Muslims.[43] In Catalonia, the *morerías* of Tortosa and Lérida both had ovens, the rent from the former going toward the support of the local castle.[44]

The Crown also had a monopoly over mills, essential appurtenances to agricultural and industrial life. Mudejars were allowed to grind their wheat and barley wherever they wished. Apparently, Fernando had followed the bailiff general's advice and discarded his plan to construct in Játiva one royal mill that all of the aljama's Muslims would have to use. In every town Mudejars were active as lessees of royal mills.[45] The *morería* of Játiva had its own olive mill or press (*almacera*) which was rented from the Crown and served the needs of Muslims bringing in their produce from nearby olive orchards. The Mudejars of Játiva continued to participate in the local paper industry, and a paper mill was leased to them.[46]

The activity of Mudejar artisans in certain local crafts and industries allowed the Crown to maintain a monopoly over certain workshops probably located within or adjacent to the *morerías*. In Alcira Muslim saddlers rented the saddleworks from the Crown, as did Muslim dyers the dyeworks of Murviedro. Játiva's *morería* had a much larger industrial complex, its Muslims renting saddleworks, dyeworks, a tannery, and a workshop devoted to the fabrication of soap.[47] Whatever success the king had in augmenting the populations of his *morerías* might have enhanced Mudejar participation in local industries monopolized by the Crown, thereby fueling the local economy and perhaps raising the rents of industrial workshops.

On account of its large size, the *morería* of Játiva had its own marketplace or *suq* (Catalan *açoch*), and, unlike the other royal *morerías*, its own *mustaçaff (or çalmedina)*, who served as inspector of the market and of its weights and measures. Municipal officials, however, challenged the aljama's right to appoint its own *mustaçaff*. In any case, Játiva's aljama was unique in leasing from the Crown its market as well as the weights-and-measures service (*pes e açoch*). The lessees were individual Mudejars and the rent was understandably steep, ranging from 1,060s to 2,000s per year.[48]

Table 11. *Játiva: Some Lessees (ARV: MR 3052–3062)*

	Large oven	Small oven	Bath	Market	Butcher shops	Pasture	Soap factory
1478	Mahomat Dondon	Ali Badahuy	Çat Cathala	Ali Cominxi	Axir Benyaye	Faraig Alfaqul	Ali Aro et al.
1490	Yaye Peus	Abdalla Mucaddar	Ali Badahuy	Omeyet Ferruç	Axir Benyaye	Axer Benyaye	Çaat Mangay
1494	Ali Catralli	Çaat Mucaddar	Ali Badahuy	Çaat Comixi	Juan Lopiç	Mahomat Recuti	Çaat Mangay
1495	Yuçeff Redona	Cuayet Amit	Ali Badahuy	Mahomat Tagari	Abdurasmen Mangay	Ali Aro	Çaat Mangay
1496	Çaat Çuqussi	Soayet Anqitet	Ali Badahuy	Mahomat Tagari	Ali Mangay and Abdalla Lirida	Luis Costa	Çaat Mangay
1497	Mahomat Tagari	Çahat Amit	Ali Badahuy	Mahomat Tagari	Mahomat Mangay and Abdalla Lirida	Mahomat Mangay	Mahomat Xep and Coayat Mangay
1498	Çahat Abib	Çahat Mangay	Ali Badahuy	Mahomat Tagari	Mahomat Mangay	Francesch de Gallano	Mahomat Xep and Cohayet Mangay
1500	Çahat Abib and Ali Catralli	Abdalla Mucaddar	Abdalla Tagari	Ali Metany	Franci Crespi	Çahat Abib	Mahomat Xep and Cohayet Mangay
1501	Joan Puteda	Çahat Abib	Abdalla Tagari	Ali Metany	Francesch Crespi	Çahat Porri	Mahomat Xep and Cohayet Mangay
1502	Azmet Mangay and Ayet Maymo	Çale Cocussi and Çahat Mangay	Çahat Abib	Çahat Comrexi	Perot Real	Joanot Sans	Coayat Mangay

The rents of some Crown utilities, particularly those in Játiva, increased markedly, although not necessarily consistently, over the course of Fernando's reign. The raising of rents was stimulated by the leasing of utilities to the highest bidder. In Játiva the Crown offered further incentive by, in effect, sharing the increased profits with the lessee, who was remunerated with a percentage—approximately 10 to 15 percent—of the difference between the current rent and that of the previous year.[49] The lessee's bid was likely based on an informed prediction of the size of the clientele having recourse to the utility's services and of the fee that could be charged to the consumer for use of those services. Increases in the size of local populations would have encouraged higher bids.

Besides acting as consumers and lessees (e.g., table 11), Mudejars played another important role with respect to Crown utilities by providing the skilled labor necessary for their maintenance or improvement. In some cases the lessees themselves effected the improvements, as did the saddlers renting the saddleworks of Alcira.[50] It was more usually the case that Muslim carpenters and masons maintained the serviceability of royal ovens, baths, fonduks, mills, and official market scales. Unskilled labor was also needed for the procurement and transport of materials, such as wood, sand, and stone.[51] Thus, around the Crown utilities, providing essential services to the Mudejar populace and needed revenue to the king, there developed a community of interests, involving king, lessee, consumer, and laborer. (See tables 12–14 for further listings of Crown revenue.)

The king also exercised direct lordship over certain houses and lands in royal towns that were rented to Mudejars. The rents received from Mudejar lessees were negligible, ranging from 2s to 5s per year for a house, and from 2s to 12s per year for land. In Alcira, which had the largest number of Mudejars leasing homes and land from the Crown, the aggregate of rents never amounted to more than 104s 6d in any one year.[52] Muslim lessees were allowed to sell the rented property to either Muslim or Christian buyers, although there was a sales tax, called the *lluisme*, collected from the vendor, which amounted to 10 percent of the sale price. The *lluisme* was paid by both Muslim and Christian vendors.[53]

Cena, Peyta, Tithes, and Other Taxes

Muslims, Christians, and Jews each year paid regular taxes known as *cena* and *peyta*. The *cena* originated as a feudal duty of hospitality paid by each town on the visit of the itinerant royal court, and was more

Table 12.   Valencia (ARV: MR 89–110)

	Payment of aljama	*Basto* of the *morería*	Fonduk
1478	500s	248s	
1480	500s	116s 6d	849s 1d
1481		81s	1,123s 10d
1482	500s	113s 6d	817s
1483			
1484			706s 8d
1485			
1486	500s	121s	
1487	500s		1,555s 5d
1488			
1489	500s	618s	2,132s 1d
1490	500s	206s	1,132s 1d
1491	500s	206s	2,132s 1d
1492	500s	206s	1,648s
1493	500s	206s	
1494	500s	206s	
1495	500s	206s	
1496			2,060s
1497	500s	206s	2,060s
1498	500s		1,948s 8d
1499			1,366s 8d
1500	500s	355s 8d	1,284s 6d
1501			1,009s
1502	500s	105s 8d	1,135s 6d

properly known as the *cena de presencia*. When the court became more stationary a *cena de absencia* was levied, which evolved into a fixed annual tribute, termed variously as *cena de absencia, cena reyal*, or simply *cena*. The aljama of Játiva paid a *cena* of 600s per year. The tax lists for the aljama of Alcira have no entry for the *cena*, but occasionally the *peyta* entry is written as *peyta e cena* or just *cena*, which, if not merely a scribal error, suggests that the aljama's *peyta* payment comprised both *peyta* and *cena*. Before 1455 the aljama of Valencia had paid 100s per year for the *cena*. Regarding the other aljamas in the kingdom, the scribes included their *cena* contributions with those of the Christians in the account books.[54]

In the kingdom of Aragon and Catalonia Fernando was avid to collect the *cena*, particularly in Catalonia, where, as a result of the civil war, the *cena* had not been paid during the years 1461–1479. All previous

Table 13.   Onda (ARV: MR 4273–4284)

	Licenses for begging	Licenses for prostitution	Licenses for arms-bearing	Inheritances
1478	4s 9d	12s		304s
1480	4s 3d	2s	3s 6d	
1481	5s 11d	13s		
1482	3s 9d	2s	1s 7d	
1483	2s 6d			
1484	1s 6d	8s 9d		24s
1485	3s	2d	11d	
1486				460s
1487	2s 2d	6d	1s	50s 8d
1488	9d	2s 6d	—	145s
1490	2s 9d	1s 6d	1s 9d	1,170s 4d (plague year)
1491				90s
1492	9s 9d			246s 5d
1493	19s 8d			285s 4d
1494	9s 1d	13s		34s 4d
1495	13s 2d	15s 6d		
1496	11s 3d	1s 10d		50s 2d
1497	15s 2d		15s	
1498	8s 6d	3s 6d		111s 6d
1499	9s 9d		6s	
1500	4s 6d		7s 6d	100s
1501	8s 6d			
1502	2s 6d			

remissions conceded by Juan II were nullified, despite the objections of the Catalan Muslim and Jewish aljamas.[55] The Aragonese and Catalans were also obliged to pay separately the *cena de primogenito*, which Fernando collected on behalf of the princes Juan and Miguel. The annual *cena* rate for most Muslim aljamas of Aragon-Catalonia (the Jews' rates were usually higher) was 33s 4d, although the Muslims of Tortosa paid twice as much.[56]

It is extremely difficult to pinpoint exactly what was meant by the term *peyta*. Leopoldo Piles Ros maintains that in the kingdom of Valencia the *peyta* was an annual levy on all property-holders which included the *cena del rey o primogenito*, and was applicable toward the payment of the salaries of royal justices, jurates, and other officials, and toward the defraying of other royal expenses. This view is substantiated by the complaint made by the lord of Gilet "on account of some *peytes* that the

Table 14.   Bailiff General (ARV: MR 89–110)

	Licenses for alms-begging	Licenses for prostitution
1478	660s	36s
1480	570s	36s
1481	600s	18s
1482	736s	36s
1483	440s	18s
1484	470s	18s
1485	180s	
1486	660s	
1487		
1488	960s	18s
1489	2,010s	18s
1490	1,630s	36s
1491	1,700s	18s
1492	1,600s	18s
1493	830s	72s
1497	730s	36s
1500	370s	18s
1502	1,160s	72s

jurates and *universitas* of the said town of Murviedro are violently attempting to impose on certain lands possessed by some Sarracen vassals of the said noble."[57] It also helps to explain why the scribes at times recorded the aljama of Alcira's payment of the *peyta* as including the *cena*. Indeed, in Valencia the *cena* is only infrequently mentioned as a separate tax and usually seems to have been regarded as a part of the more amorphous *peyta*. The Mudejars of most royal towns paid their *peyta* along with the local Christians. Thus, the Muslims of Onda were described as paying all the "*peytes* and contributions" that the Christians of the town were accustomed to pay, while the charter founding the new aljama of Castellón de Játiva obliged it to contribute along with the Christians to the payment of the "*peytes, sises*, and other impositions."[58] Before 1455 the aljama of Valencia had paid an annual *peyta* of 250s, whereas during Fernando's reign only the aljama of Alcira paid its 100s *peyta* separately from the Christians. The singularity of this arrangement was conducive to conflict between Alcira's jurates and the aljama, for the jurates insisted on trying to collect the *peyta* from the aljama as was the practice in other towns.[59]

In Aragon-Catalonia the *peyta* had a somewhat different significance. There, as Macho y Ortega suggests, the *peyta* became by the fifteenth century a lump-sum substitute for the payment of a wide array of taxes. The high annual *peyta* rates burdening the Arago-Catalan aljamas support this interpretation. The aljama of Tortosa was obliged to pay a *peyta* of 160 pounds (3,200s), while those of Borja and Daroca had to pay 3,000s and 700s, respectively.[60] Given the precarious financial state of these aljamas, it is difficult to see how they could have paid any other taxes beyond these *peytes*, which alone were almost insupportable.

Another regular tax, less burdensome than the *cena* and *peyta*, was the *morabatí*. This tax, granted to Jaime I (1266) in exchange for a royal promise never to tamper with the coinage, had a set rate of one *morabatí* (7s) and was to be collected every seventh year from each household, of whatever faith, owning property worth fifteen or more *morabatins*. Like the *peyta*, it was, in effect, a form of property tax. By the fourteenth century it was not collected at regular seven-year intervals, but often more frequently. However, during Fernando's reign greater regularity in collection was established; the *morabatí* was exacted every six years, in 1481, 1487, 1493, and 1499. In Aragon the *morabatí* was collected only in the region of Huesca.[61]

A fairly lucrative source of revenue for the king was the share he received from the inheritances of royal Mudejar vassals. The records neither state explicitly what percentage of the deceased's property normally constituted the Crown's share nor note the total value of the property, from which the portion accruing to the Crown could be calculated. In fact, the Crown bureaucracy dealt with cases of Mudejar inheritance on an ad hoc basis, the royal portion being exacted without fail for a variety of reasons, and not only from those Muslims who died intestate and without legitimate heirs. Rubrics such as the one found in the records of the bailiff of Onda—"Revenues from [the inheritances of] the Moors and Mooresses who died without heirs, of which part goes to the lord king"—are misleading. Mahomat Hubaydal of Onda had to render to the Crown and to the Order of Montesa, which exercised lordship over Onda, 92s 10d from the inheritance left to him by his father.[62] After the death of Abdurrazmen Mascor, the *faqīh* of Valencia, the bailiff general noted that the "king has succeeded to a certain portion of the said inheritance of the said *faqīh*," and then went on to instruct the procurator of the Vall de Uxó to allow the wife, brother, and two sisters of Mascor to collect the property left by the deceased in the valley.[63] Indeed, the taking of a royal share from the estates of deceased Mudejars was so established a practice that the aljama of Játiva simply paid an annual inheritance tax of 400s, in lieu of Crown interference in every inheritance case.[64]

Nevertheless, within the limitations of a system in which the fiscal demands of an overarching Christian bureaucracy meshed with the

Mudejar administration of civil affairs in accordance with the Shariah, the Islamic laws of inheritance were largely respected. For instance, so long as they were royal vassals, the siblings and other relatives of the Mudejar who died intestate and childless were allowed to divide the inheritance among themselves (subtracting, of course, the royal share), as the Qur'ān required. Operative, in effect, was a two-tiered process. At one level the royal *qāḍī* adjudicated the division of the inheritance between the legitimate heirs as the will of the deceased and the Shariah demanded. This entailed the resolution of any attendant complications or litigation, such as ensuring that Mudejar widows were put in possession of their bridewealth before their husband's property was divided. In one case the *qāḍī* had to effect a compromise between the brother and the husband of a deceased woman before the king could receive his portion of the inheritance.[65] The royal *qāḍī*'s participation, noted by the scribes in the records of almost every inheritance case, was crucial for two reasons. First, the *qāḍī* guaranteed that the Shariah was observed, thereby allaying potential Mudejar grievances that the Crown was excessively encroaching upon their legal autonomy. As a key figure in the kingdom's bureaucracy working closely with the bailiff general, the *qāḍī* could enlist the executive power of the latter to ensure that Mudejar wills were properly executed. With the counsel of the lieutenant *qāḍī*, the lieutenant bailiff general instructed the bailiff of Murviedro to protect the rights of the sisters Fatima and Mariem to a carob orchard bequeathed to them by their father, Mahomat Nayna.[66] Second, while upholding the Shariah, the *qāḍī* also had the king's interests in mind, so that both royal Muslim heirs and the king received their due. When the *faqīh* of Petrés ruled on the division of the property left by a Mudejar woman of Murviedro, it was deemed detrimental to the royal revenues and to the *qāḍī*'s prerogatives, for a seigneurial *faqīh* was not about to trouble himself over whether the Crown received its portion.[67]

Some marginal notes of the scribe of the *Maestre Racional* are quite revealing as to the complexity of procedure in Mudejar inheritance cases, involving first the Islamic–Arabic execution of the will and then the Christian–Romance collection and recording of the Crown's share. Clearly, the *qāḍī* was the pivotal figure, attending to both Mudejar and Crown interests. The scribe begins by stating that the figures he is recording were taken from a Romance translation of an Arabic "act of the inventory of the property and adjudication of the said inheritance carried out by the said *qāḍī*." He then carefully notes the share of the inheritance to be collected by the Crown:

> certain deductions having been made, there remain for division from the
> value of the property 255 pounds 5s, of which the part that pertains to the

lord king—that is, the portion of the brother of the said Fatima [the deceased] who is not a vassal of the lord king—is only 28 pounds 7s 2d, since all the rest pertains to Abdalla Perpiu—one third by legacy—and to the husband, and to the mother, and to the sister of the said Fatima.[68]

These marginalia also show one of the ways by which the Crown, on the second level of inheritance procedure, could come into possession of a sometimes substantial portion of the inheritance, that is, when the heir of a royal vassal was himself not a royal vassal. This contradicted a provision of Pedro IV (1337), which allowed children and relatives who were seigneurial vassals to inherit the property of royal Mudejar vassals, and vice versa. However, this provision seems to have had little practical effect, or at best for only a short time, since by 1363 Pedro himself no longer observed it.[69] Certainly by the fifteenth century the general rule was that only royal vassals could succeed to the property of royal vassals. This helped to maintain the integrity of the royal patrimony. Therefore, the sister-in-law of Mahomat Fandaig, a seigneurial vassal, was denied access to the property of her deceased sister, a royal vassal in Valencia.[70] Actually, with respect to the aljama of Valencia, the Crown had taken matters one step further: only royal vassals residing in the city had inheritance rights. Çahat Alatar forfeited his portion of his dead brother's property to the king because he lived outside of the city.[71]

The obverse of the Crown's exacting supervision of the inheritances of its own vassals was its, and its vassals', forfeiture of any claims to the estates of seigneurial Muslims. Valencian patterns of land tenure could, however, complicate matters somewhat. For instance, when the bailiff of Villarreal notified the bailiff general that a seigneurial Muslim of Bechí, who had died intestate and childless, happened to have property in Villarreal, he was ordered to confiscate the property on behalf of the king.[72]

The Crown demanded its due from even the most meager inheritances. Two Muslim widowers of Castellón de la Plana each paid 50s from the estates of their wives, who, it seems, had left them next to nothing.[73] However exacting, even avid, royal bureaucrats were in their administration of Mudejar estates, their actions drew no protests from Mudejars. No doubt the scrupulousness of the $q\bar{a}d\bar{\imath}$ in handling inheritances within the framework of the Shariah softened the impact of Christian bureaucratic intrusions in a sensitive area of family law. Moreover, Fernando's reign was no different in this respect from those of his predecessors. It may be that Játiva's aljama fared best. By paying a simple inheritance tax its members were irritated less by a grasping Christian bureaucracy, and, given the size of its population, 400s per year was probably cheaper in the long term.[74]

Through an array of tariffs, tolls, and taxes the Crown was able to derive revenue from the commercial, agricultural, and pastoral activities of Muslim and Christian alike. These taxes were not too burdensome, for the king did not wish to depress the economy by discouraging the enterprise of his subjects. Many of these tariffs and tolls were collected at the kingdom's borders, on royal roads, and in the markets of royal towns, and were, therefore, paid by both royal and seigneurial vassals, whose marketing of crops, pasturing of flocks, and peddling often took them beyond the confines of their respective hamlets and towns.

The *peatge* was a transit duty on commercial use of the roads, collected in each locality from "all the persons who enter, pass through, or sell livestock and other merchandise."[75] For instance, Muslims of Ribarroja bringing goats into the kingdom from Castile had to pay the *peatge*,[76] as did the vassals of barons who herded their livestock into the district of Játiva, although only once per year and not every time their flocks crossed over into royal lands.[77] It was not unusual for certain baronies and their vassals to have *franquesa*, or exemption, from the payment of the *peatge* and similar tolls. Barons were often moved to complain when collectors of the *peatge* exacted tolls from their exempt vassals.[78] During Fernando's reign additional exemptions were conceded only to certain Muslims of the *morería* of Valencia, probably as a means of aiding individual members of a financially prostrate aljama. In contrast, Fernando denied exemptions to Granadan Muslims settling in communities where the financial situation was less dire.[79]

Other taxes affecting merchants and shepherds were the *lleuda*, a tariff imposed on goods imported into major towns and cities; the *quema*, a tariff on goods imported from Castile; the *portatge*, a bridge toll; the *herbatge*, a grazing fee collected for the use of certain pastures; and the *montatge*, a sheepwalk toll. Some Mudejars were involved in the royal collection machinery, such as Amet Samaris, who was appointed custodian of the *quema* in the district of Aspe.[80]

The Crown exercised a monopoly over the production and sale of salt. Some Valencians found royal control over access to this essential commodity particularly irksome, and so attempted to obtain it fraudulently or elsewhere. The lessees of the royal saltworks of Játiva were often immersed in litigation with those they accused of procuring salt fraudulently, among whom were Muslims of Antella and the Vall de Serra.[81] In 1503 the bailiff general considered it a special problem that Mudejars "use other salt [*sal estranya*] that is not from the monopolies of the lord king."[82] Nevertheless, at the same time Muslims labored in salt production on behalf of the king, and also turn up as agents for Játiva's saltworks.[83]

Muslims and Christians holding lands in territories under the direct lordship of the king all had to pay the *terç de delme*, that is, one-third of one-tenth (i.e., 3.33 percent) of their produce of whatever sort. The *terç de delme* originated in the crusader's patronage right by which King Jaime I had retained for the Crown one-third of the ecclesiastical tithe, leaving the other two-thirds to the Church. As was the case with most other taxes, the *terçes de delme* were farmed out under contract to the highest bidder. In Alcira Mudejars were prominent as lessees of the *terçes* of local collectories (or tax-collection districts).[84]

Regarding the other two-thirds of the tithe owed to the Church, the situation was somewhat more complex. Theoretically, Mudejars were not liable to pay ecclesiastical tithes and first-fruits for lands that had always been held by Muslims; the obligation was incumbent only on those lands that Muslims had acquired from Christians. It seems, however, that by the late fifteenth century most, if not all, Mudejars farming on royal land were paying tithes. A royal order treating the city of Valencia with its district and *huerta* states quite clearly that all persons "of whatever law [i.e., religion], status, or condition" must give one-third of the tithe to the Crown and the other two-thirds to the episcopal official.[85] Implicit in the complaint of the bishop and chapter of Cartagena, that Muslims and Christians of Agost were evading payment of the tithe by threshing their wheat outside of Agost where the tithe collector could not find them, is the assumption that farmers of both faiths normally paid tithes. Royal proclamations against such tithe evasion were to be posted throughout the diocese of Cartagena.[86] It is understandable how Mudejar liability to pay tithes had become the norm. Considering the not infrequent sale of Christian land to Muslims, and the Muslims' ability to change vassalage, which often entailed the purchase or rental of new land, the amount of property held by Muslims since time immemorial must have steadily diminished. Most seigneurial Muslims probably paid the tithe only indirectly, the lord making the direct payment from the rents he received from his vassals. Litigation surrounding Valencian Mudejar liability to tithes is, in contrast to the thirteenth and fourteenth centuries, conspicuously absent.[87]

Quite different from the apparent normalcy prevailing in Valencia, in the kingdom of Aragon the tithe question continued to create considerable tension between the Church and the Mudejars and their royal and seigneurial lords. The bishop and chapter of Tarazona were most aggressive in the campaign to exact tithes from Mudejars. In 1479 they reached an agreement with the lord and aljama of Conchiellos, whereby the Muslims cultivating lands in the *huerta* and mountains of Tarazona, and in Conchiellos itself, would pay tithes and first-fruits; as for those lands immemorially Muslim (*moriegas*), the lord would pay their tithes.[88] Later, the chapter was engaged in a tithe litigation with the aljamas of Torrellas and Santa Cruz.[89] The most difficult suit pitted the chapter against the aljama of Borja. The chapter complained to the king in 1489 that Borja's Muslims refused to pay their tithes "and this not only for their properties which were from Moors, but even for those which have been of Christians and have come to them." The canons argued that by virtue of provisions of Queen María and of a papal bull they had the right to collect these tithes, but that the aljama had enlisted the support of the Justice of Aragon against them. Eleven years later the suit was still unresolved, and Fernando had to reprimand sharply the bishop and the chapter for decreeing an interdict in Borja against the local Muslims.[90] Even more serious was the attempt of the archbishop of Zaragoza to obtain from the pope a bull authorizing the Aragonese clergy to collect tithes from the Muslim vassals of all barons. Fernando felt compelled to foil the archbishop's plan. It was probably a desire to avoid provoking an already uncooperative Aragonese nobility that moved the king to act decisively.[91]

Extraordinary Taxes and Aljama Finance

In the realm of regular taxation royal policy was only mildly discriminatory against the Mudejars. Muslims and Christians both paid for the use of utilities, and both were liable to the annual *peyta* and *cena* and the commercial tariffs and agricultural tithes. That Muslim and Christian taxpayers are often indistinguishable in royal account books, and that Muslims participated freely in the collection machinery as lessees of utilities and tithe collectories indicates a rough parity of Muslim and Christian before the fiscal bureaucracy. The annual payment of the *besant* singled out the Muslims, although the tax had greater significance as a symbol of the Mudejars' subject status than as a source of royal revenue. The share of Mudejar inheritances demanded by the Crown was another expression of its ultimate authority over a conquered population and its property.

The extent of the religious minorities' fiscal servitude to the Crown becomes clear only upon consideration of the extraordinary taxes that burdened them. Fernando's descriptions of the Mudejars as "our coffers" and "servants of our chamber" were not empty rhetoric but were firmly rooted in the king's understanding that he could freely impose new taxes—*servicios graciosos* or *donativos*—on his Muslim (and Jewish) subjects with or without their consent. Whereas the local laws of his individual kingdoms limited the demands Fernando could make on his Christian subjects, and the representative Cortes at times rejected these demands outright, there were not institutional restraints on his taxation of the Mudejars. That the Muslims' very raison d'être in a Christian society was founded on their economic usefulness had as its logical conclusion a royal policy that would seek from them maximum fiscal benefits. Long-term fiscal considerations, however, advised against rapacity in the short term, for a consistent and reliable income from the aljamas was the preferable state of affairs. Nevertheless, political and economic urgencies sometimes resulted in a less cautionary policy, with the consequence that aljamas were financially devastated by extraordinary royal exactions. Aljamas were often forced to borrow funds in order to meet the Crown's demands, and this, combined with subsequent interest payments and regular taxes, could cripple an aljama's finances, leaving it in a state of indebtedness for years at a time. Aljamas that were not deep "in the red" struggled to maintain solvency. The wealth of individual Mudejars notwithstanding, the financial troubles of Muslim communities were symptomatic of their corporate dependence on the needs of the royal treasury.[92]

Fernando's numerous military campaigns and foreign adventures were a constant drain on the resources of the royal treasury, and it was necessary to tap all available sources of funds. The royal Muslim aljamas of the kingdom of Valencia were, of course, called on to contribute what they could, although they were burdened less frequently by royal *servicios* than were the aljamas of Aragon. Considering the greater prosperity of the kingdom of Valencia and the greater financial stability of its Muslim aljamas, the heavier taxation of the Aragonese aljamas seems a bit illogical. However, the determinant of royal fiscal policy vis-à-vis the Mudejars was not so much what the aljamas could give—as for what they would give, they had little choice— as what the Christians and their Cortes were able and willing to concede. It seems that the number of extraordinary taxes exacted from the aljamas of a particular kingdom related inversely to the amount of funds provided by the Christians of that kingdom. In other words, what Fernando could not procure from the kingdom as a whole he tried to compensate for with *servicios* imposed on royal aljamas. The kingdom of Valencia, particularly its capital city, granted to the king a number of generous "aids," whereas the kingdom of Aragon, less wealthy than Valencia, exceedingly parochial in its interests, and highly uncooperative, gave much less toward royal enterprises, conceding funds only for the campaigns to recover Roussillon, and for those in Navarre and, belatedly, in North Africa (1510).[93]

One extraordinary tax collected from all of Fernando's subjects, Muslim, Christian, and Jew, in all of his kingdoms was the *maridatge*, used to defray the expenses of the weddings of the king's children. The *maridatge* was imposed four times, on the occasion of the marriages of the Infantas Isabel (1491), Juana (1496), María (1500), and Caterina (1502). The amount of *maridatge* collected from each community was determined by the number of its households and its wealth. Judging by the *maridatges* paid by Muslim aljamas in Valencia on the occasion of the marriage of Juan II's daughter Elionor (1477), the *maridatge* could be quite burdensome. At that time the aljama of Játiva contributed 4000s, that of Alcira 220s, and a large seigneurial aljama like that of Bétera 550s.[94] The imposition of the *maridatge* was capable of disrupting an aljama's precarious financial affairs. Thus, in 1502 the aljama of Castellón de la Plana was compelled to take out a loan in order to do its part for the weddings of María and Caterina.[95]

Apart from the *maridatges* the Valencian aljamas were obliged to contribute other *servicios*. Still pending from the previous reign was a *servicio* of 40,000s which the military estate had promised Juan II in 1463. Fernando ordered that this sum be collected from the nobles and from the *universitates* and aljamas of their Christian and Muslim vassals.[96] In 1482 the Muslim aljamas were asked to make a donation (*donatiu*) of 15,041s on the occasion of Queen Isabel's entry into the kingdom. The sums paid by certain aljamas were 3,900s by that of Paterna, 260s by that of Castellón de la Plana, 650s by that of Monforte, and 91s by that of Murviedro.[97] In 1485, when the king needed further funding to press his campaign against Granada, he turned to his Muslim and Jewish vassals. The Jews of Murviedro and the Muslim aljamas, particularly that of Játiva, on account of its size and relative wealth, were to give to the king as large a *servicio* as they could afford.[98] The convoking of the Corts in Orihuela in 1488 occasioned another *servicio* to which the entire kingdom was liable. The aljama of Alcira alone was required to pay 40 pounds.[99]

For the kingdom of Aragon the list of *servicios* demanded of its Muslim and Jewish aljamas was considerably longer, although, as we shall see below, the resources at their disposal to pay them were, in the case of the Muslims, decidedly less. In 1481 all Muslim and Jewish aljamas were asked to provide a *servicio* of an unspecified sum.[100] In 1484 all royal Muslims were expected to contribute as much as they could spare to the king's effort to capture Roussillon.[101] Furthermore, from 1484 through 1487 the Jews and Muslims were paying "some quantities" for the Granadan campaigns,[102] when, in contrast, the Cortes of Aragon refused to provide aid for a royal enterprise so far beyond the kingdom's frontiers. In 1494 and 1495 the Mudejars were asked to pay still more *servicios* in amounts potentially devastating for aljama finances. The king sought 8,000s from the aljama of Zaragoza and 6,000s from that of

Borja, although these sums perforce were reduced to 6,000s and 5,400s, respectively.[103]

On two occasions Fernando displayed a definite canniness in the tack he took when demanding *servicios* from the Mudejars. In Aragon in 1484 and again in Valencia in 1485, instead of requesting lump sums from each aljama, the king ordered his officials to obtain from individual Muslims *servicios* consonant with their personal wealth.[104] Because aljamas normally divided *servicio* payments equally, the inability of impoverished Muslim families to contribute reduced the *servicio* the aljama could offer, even if the aggregate wealth of aljama members could well support the full *servicio* requested. By taxing Muslims on an individual basis Fernando spared the poor, many of whom would not have paid in any case, and exacted from the wealthier families as much as possible and likely much more than these families would have otherwise contributed. Consequently, the king probably received via individual assessment a larger total *servicio*. Furthermore, by approaching Muslim families individually, much of the wrangling and quarreling that plagued aljamas in their own internal tax collection was avoided. When the collection of lump *servicios* was left to aljama officials some Muslims were emboldened to avoid payment, claiming that they possessed a royal exemption, or, conversely, aljama officials might create tension by taxing certain families in excess.[105] However, individual Muslim families were less likely to evade the royal bureaucracy, and, since with individual assessment the equal apportionment of *servicio* contributions per household was rendered inoperative, wealthier Muslims who found themselves being more heavily taxed than their poorer fellows could not cry foul.

Although the account books do not reveal how much of the *servicios* requested were actually deposited in the royal treasury, it is probable that the king usually received from his Muslim subjects the desired sums. At times Fernando was quite insistent, indicating to his officials that the Muslims should be compelled to pay if they did not do so voluntarily.[106] When preoccupied with pressing international concerns, the king was not likely to pay much heed to the grievances of his Muslim subjects.

The apparently harsh and unrelenting attitude of the king when demanding extraordinary *servicios*, induced by the pressing needs of the moment, such as the campaigns in Roussillon and Granada, was by necessity tempered with the application of more far-sighted and benign measures. As Boswell has demonstrated for the reign of Pedro IV, the Crown's judicious granting of remissions and deferments of tax payments was essential in alleviating an aljama's sometimes insupportable tax load, in effect striking a balance between its needs and those of the aljama.[107]

Although it was preferable to receive from the king a remission or a deferment, the aljamas had a means of raising capital in order to pay taxes: they could, with the permission of the king, borrow money through the sale of annuities, or *pensions de censals*. The creditor purchasing the *censal* delivered a sum of capital to the aljama at an annual interest rate of 6.6 to 10 percent, and, in return, the aljama paid annual pensions to the creditor (*censalista*) until the price of the *censal* was paid off. Normally, as part of the *censal* contract, the aljamas, and their individual members, had to mortgage their property. Default of the payment of a pension resulted in the confiscation and sale of an aljama's property. In the fifteenth century the *censal* was an instrument of credit of central importance in the financing of the debts of cities, aljamas, and individuals, especially the nobility. Belenguer Cebrià has shown how Fernando wreaked havoc on the city of Valencia's finances: by exacting such large "loans" from the city, he forced the municipality to sell increasing numbers of pensions, which created an unwieldy public debt.[108] On a much smaller scale, Fernando's permission to his aljamas to sell pensions, although providing them with ready capital to make tax payments, in the long run sometimes encumbered them with crushing public debts and made the *rentier* or *censalista* class a Mudejar nemesis.

For the most part Valencia's royal aljamas managed to pay their taxes, both ordinary and extraordinary, without having to sell pensions or to ask the king for remissions. However, that this was not always the case suggests that some aljamas, even when meeting fiscal demands, did so only with difficulty. As has been mentioned, the additional burden of the *maridatges* for the Infantas María and Caterina compelled the aljama of Castellón de la Plana to sell a *censal* in order to raise 870s.[109] Extraordinary taxes also put the aljama of Alcira into financial straits, causing it to take on a *censal* of 600s, probably to pay the *maridatge* of the Infanta Juana, and two years later another *censal* of 800s in order to make the contribution occasioned by the convocation of the Corts (1488). In addition, Fernando allowed the aljama to defer its payment of the *peyta* in 1497 and again in 1503. In both cases the aljama was able to pay its outstanding *peyta* the following year, which indicates that its financial troubles were not especially grave.[110]

The poverty of the aljama of Valencia, which had only partially recovered from the destruction of the *morería* in 1455, was atypical. The reduction of the aljama's taxes to an annual lump sum of 25 pounds (500s) was alone insufficient to cure its financial ills. In 1481 and in 1483 Fernando remitted the aljama's annual payment, on account of "the poverty that is in it." These remissions, combined with the orders of

Juan II and Fernando that the aljama's creditors (*censalistas*) reduce the debts burdening it, enabled the aljama to attain sufficient stability to pay its lump tax from 1484 through 1503.[111] The king further aided the aljama by commanding Christians who had purchased property within the *morería* to pay the property taxes for which the Muslims were liable, and by obstructing the effort of the butchers' guild to impose restrictions on the Muslim butcher shop, inasmuch as the aljama derived essential revenue from the sale of meat.[112]

Royal regulation of Mudejar finances extended beyond the level of the corporate aljama to that of the individual Muslim family. The king's intervention in the financial affairs of Muslim families consisted of granting them licenses to sell annuities (table 15). The licenses stipulated the maximum sum of money that could be borrowed through the *censal*, and these sums ranged from as little as 10 pounds to as much as 75 pounds. The Mudejars invested the funds mainly in the purchase of land and homes or in home improvements. It was expected that the debts thus incurred would be liquidated within four years. The Mudejars granted such licenses by Fernando's bailiff general were all royal vassals in the *morerías* of Valencia and Alcira. Such financial paternalism on the part of the Crown ultimately worked in favor of its own treasury. By ensuring that Mudejar vassals borrowed and invested money wisely, at the same time often bettering the physical plant of the royal *morerías*, the king hoped to foster their prosperity and, indirectly, that of the aljamas. Wealthier aljamas, of course, meant that the king would have a more reliable source of *servicios*.[113]

The much graver financial situation of many Aragonese and Catalan aljamas presented a greater test to royal benevolence. The Aragonese aljamas, it seems, had never fully recovered from the effects of the fourteenth-century wars between Aragon and Castile, and throughout the fifteenth century were often on the verge of ruin. Catalonia's Muslims probably suffered during the wars that ravaged the province during Juan II's reign. Neither Aragon nor Catalonia could boast of an economic growth such as Valencia enjoyed from which the Mudejars might have benefited. At the outset of his reign Fernando was faced with the prospect of taxing Muslim communities whose resources were already dwindling. His initial zeal to recover revenues relinquished by his father was quickly dampened. For instance, in 1480 Fernando annulled Juan II's partial reduction of the *peyta ordinaria* paid by Borja's aljama (from 3,000s to 2,000s), but in the following year, after having permitted the aljama to sell a *censal* of 15,000s in order to pay its diverse debts, he realized his error and extended the reduction of the aljama's *peyta* obligation until 1498.[114] Indeed, the king responded to the aljamas' complaints of poverty and declining population with a fiscal policy

Table 15. *Licenses to Muslims to Sell* Censals

Document	Date	Name	Amount	Reason
ARV: B1157: 367v–368r	9/1/1483	Azmet Albanne, alias Bizquey, and wife Xemçi of Valencia	30 pounds	To pay off 20 pounds owed on house in the *morería*
ARV: B1160: 309v–310r	12/10/1491	Yuçeff Bizquey and wife Xemçi of Valencia	30 pounds	To pay off debts, especially 80 pounds owed to Marti Dordya
ARV: B1160: 314v–315r	22/10/1491	Abrahim Burguet and wife Mariem of Valencia	10 pounds 10s	To pay off debts
ARV: B1160: 332v–333r	7/11/1491	Various Muslims of the *morería* of Valencia	12 pounds 10s	To pay customs duties of three Muslims arriving on Venetian galleys
ARV: B1160: 387r	7/1/1492	Çahat Bellvis, Mahomat Çalema, et al. of Valencia	63 pounds	Necessities
ARV: B1160: 412v–413r	1/3/1492	Çahat Faraix, guardian of the heirs of Maymo Jaheni, and Maymo's widow of Alberique	75 pounds	For necessities of the heirs and widow
ARV: B1160: 443r–v	18/5/1492	Mahomat Algazel of Alcira	20 pounds	Necessities
ARV: B1160: 566r–v	24/11/1492	Azmet Toledano and Abdulazis Pulelo of Elda	70 pounds	For settlement made with Don Pero Maça de Licana
ARV: B1160: 719r	3/8/1493	Açen Gini and Çahat Gualit of Alcira	12 pounds	Necessities
ARV: B1160: 943v–944r	20/22/1494	Xemçi Bizquey, widow of Valencia	20 pounds	To pay off debts

Reference	Date	Name	Amount	Purpose
ARV: B1161: 41v–42r	26/2/1495	Azmet Xeyt of Valencia	20 pounds	To be invested in a house in the morería
ARV: B1161: 92r–v	1/7/1495	Juçef Groyo of Valencia	12 pounds	To pay 10 pounds owed for a house in the morería
ARV: B1161: 95r	13/7/1495	Nuza Xugeta of Valencia	20 pounds	For house in the morería
ARV: B1161: 101v–102r	4/8/1495	Abdalla Mochli and wife Nexma of Valencia	15 pounds	To pay debts owed for land located in Cuart
ARV: B1161: 336r–v	7/12/1496	Çaat Hualit and Çaat Dinar of Alcira	33 pounds	To pay debts owed for land in huerta of Alcira
ARV: B1161: 435v–436r	8/8/1497	Çaat Hualit of Alcira	15 pounds	To pay pensions owed to notary
ARV: B1161: 443r–v	6/9/1497	Ali Maloxa of Alcira	12 pounds	To pay debt owed for land
ARV: B1161: 443v–444r	6/9/1497	Çuleymen b. Abdalla of Valencia	30 pounds	For work on his house in the morería
ARV: B1161: 451r–452r	13/9/1497	Abdalla Murçi of Valencia	30 pounds	For work on his house in the morería
ARV: B1161: 495v–496r	27/3/1498	Mahomat Alguazel of Alcira	60 pounds	For the price of animals
ARV: B1161: 508r–v	13/10/1498	Nuza of Valencia	15 pounds	For work on her house in the morería
ARV: B1161: 580r–v	20/2/1499	Çahat Perpir and wife Axa of Valencia	20 pounds	For a door and other necessities of their house
ARV: B1161: 587r–v	9/3/1499	Azmet Cortoni of Alcira	45 pounds	To pay debts owed for olive grove
ARV: B1161: 644r–v	12/8/1499	Çahat Hualit of Alcira	20 pounds	Necessities
ARV: B1161: 674r–v	1/10/1499	Abrahim lo Prom and wife Fotoix, Ali Malequi and wife Fatima of Alcira	20 pounds	Not specified

Table 15. (cont.)

Document	Date	Name	Amount	Reason
ARV: B1161: 700v–701r	14/11/1499	Abdalla Torralbi and wife Fatima of Valencia	21 pounds	Urgent necessities
ARV: B1162: 60r–v	23/6/1500	Abdalla Torralbi and wife Fatima of Valencia	60 pounds	To pay off 60 pounds owed for a house
ARV: B1162: 91r–v	18/9/1500	Abdalla Torralbi and wife Fatima of Valencia	10 pounds 10s	To pay off debts owed to merchant
ARV: B1162: 115v–116r	28/11/1500	Fuçey Mandarani and wife Axa of Alcira	30 pounds	To pay for houses purchased
ARV: B1162: 174r–v	23/2/1501	Ali Malequi of Alcira	30 pounds	Necessities
ARV: B1162: 269r–v	8/10/1501	Abraym Murçi of Valencia	30 pounds	To pay pension owed to a Christian silversmith

marked largely by realism and restraint. The numerous demands of extraordinary *servicios* from the aljamas were balanced by remissions of the payment of regular taxes. During the years 1480–1485 and 1490–1495 (the documentation is unclear about 1485–1490) Fernando exempted Huesca's Muslims from paying their *peyta* of 1,450s; and later he ordered an investigation of the extent of the aljama's population decline and of its poverty so as to ascertain whether its taxes needed to be further reduced.[115] Fernando maintained throughout his reign Juan II's reduction of the Tortosa aljama's *peyta* obligation from 160 pounds to a mere 50 pounds.[116] Daroca's Muslims were granted a twenty-year remission of their annual *peyta* payment.[117] Even with a lighter regular tax load, some aljamas still insisted that the *servicios* were onerous and had to be reduced. The aljama of Huesca sought a reduction of its *maridatge* obligation, and the aljamas of Zaragoza and Borja were conceded reductions of their 1495 *servicios*.[118] The king took additional measures to ameliorate the situation of aljama finances. He allowed the Mudejars of Albarracín to open their own store for the sale of staples and to use the profits for defraying communal expenses.[119] The aljama of Darcoa was similarly permitted to turn to its own account the proceeds from the *sisa* on meat and butchery rental.[120] Fernando made sure that Muslim masons of Zaragoza were paid proper wages for their labors on the royal *aljafería*, so that the resources of the aljama for sustaining its tax burden were not depleted.[121]

Royal taxation formed only one part, albeit the most important part, of the Mudejars' financial dilemma. The necessity of raising capital induced the aljamas to sell annuities, which, while in the short-term providing them with immediate funds, in the long term compounded their debt problems. Scarcely possessing the financial resources to pay royal taxes, much less to pay annual pensions to *censalistas*, aljamas were compelled to sell more annuities just to make other pension payments. Consequently, the public debt of Aragonese and Catalan aljamas spiraled, often becoming quite unmanageable. Much of the responsibility for this state of affairs must be placed on the shoulders of Fernando and his predecessors, since the Mudejars could not sell pensions without royal license. The remission or reduction of taxes, therefore, solved only part of the problem; the Mudejars still had to deal with the *censalistas* waiting to foreclose on their mortgages.

Fernando dealt with the problem of the *censals* weighing on Mudejar aljamas in two ways. First, he permitted the aljamas to sell more pensions, a not especially prudent course of action. The aljama of Albarracín sold a *censal* of 4,000s in order to pay other pensions, and the aljama of Zaragoza sold a *censal* of 6,800s for the same purpose.[122] The public debt of Borja's aljama mounted ruinously: in 1480 it sold a *censal* of

15,000s to liquidate diverse debts; in 1496 it took on another *censal* of 80,000s in order to pay other pensions; and in the same year the king permitted it to sell a *censal* of 4,000s so that it could meet its *sisa* obligations.[123] The second approach was to order the creditors harrying the aljamas to reduce the pensions owed them, that is, to renegotiate the aljamas' debts. In this manner Fernando provided temporary relief to the aljamas of Albarracín, Teruel, Huesca, and Tortosa.[124] However, there were limits to the losses the creditors were willing to sustain, and, inasmuch as the aljamas were bound by contract to pay the pensions, Fernando could only briefly delay the inevitable. Thus, although the king was able to shield Albarracín's Muslims from the *censalistas* in 1484, by 1488 he had little choice but to allow for the foreclosure on their mortgaged property.[125] Nor should it be imagined that Fernando was the staunch defender of Mudejars against grasping creditors, for in the case of pensions owed by aljamas to Conversos condemned by the Inquisition he did not act in the aljamas' best interests. Here Fernando had an ideal opportunity to assist struggling aljamas significantly by simply waiving the pensions payable to the condemned. Instead, he rewarded a royal servant with the pensions owed to a Converso by the aljama of Teruel, and, after a six-year deferment, allowed the Inquisition to collect from the aljama of Huesca a pension owed to one of its victims.[126]

The king's exercise of some moderation in his fiscal policy did not achieve the reinvigoration of the finances of the Aragonese and Catalan aljamas. Given the desperate situation in which some aljamas entered Fernando's reign, it is unlikely that anything less than complete and long-term remission of regular taxes and *servicios* would have been a suitable remedy. In both Tortosa and Teruel, despite royal efforts to provide relief, Muslims were selling their property and leaving the *morerías* because they lacked the means to meet their tax obligations. Fernando responded by having all Muslim property sequestered and inventoried so as to ensure that at least some royal taxes would be paid.[127] At best, by alternating tax remissions and reductions with the exaction of needed *servicios*, Fernando enabled the aljamas to make some contribution to the royal treasury while maintaining a precarious financial existence.

Fernando's treatment of the Mudejars of Aragon-Catalonia did not differ significantly from his handling of his Muslim vassals in Valencia. In both cases royal fiscal policy was characterized by a limiting of the Crown's voracity to demands that the aljamas could reasonably afford to meet. Aragonese and Catalan aljamas suffered more as a result of factors largely extrinsic to royal policy; their difficulties in supporting their tax burdens stemmed primarily from their integration in local economies that still had not recovered from the traumas of the fourteenth and fifteenth centuries. If the Valencian Mudejars' share in their kingdom's greater prosperity allowed them to bear royal taxes with more ease, the king was no less keen to exact his due from the Muslim servants of his Valencian treasury.

Seigneurial Aljamas

Unfortunately, there are no seigneurial account books similar to those of the royal bailiffs from which a detailed study of seigneurial taxation of the Mudejars might be made. The few *cartas pueblas* studied by Miguel Gual Camarena provide some information on the various taxes demanded from Muslims who resided on seigneurial lands, but reveal nothing about the ability of the Muslims to pay them. Blanket generalizations regarding a seigneurial fiscal regime cannot be offered, since the situation seems to have varied from one barony to another. Still, on the basis of the *cartas pueblas* a few general comments are possible.[128]

To a large extent the seigneurial fiscal regime was quite similar to that of the Crown. Like royal vassals, seigneurial vassals were obliged to use the public utilities and workshops—ovens, mills, taverns, ironworks, saddleworks, and the like—owned by their lord, and they, too, had to pay a fee for the privilege. They were likewise liable for the rents of their homes and land, the tithe (*terç de delme*), and property taxes (*peyta* [or *almagram*, as it was sometimes called on seigneurial lands]). However, there seems to be little doubt that seigneurial vassals bore a heavier tax burden. In addition to the annual rent on their land, they were also obliged to give their lord a certain percentage of their harvest (these percentages varied from seigneury to seigneury), and sometimes a certain number of chickens or a certain amount of honey each year. On some baronies vassals were required to sell agricultural and pastoral products to their lord at a price lower than the market price.

In most cases it seems that the lords exacted more from their Muslim vassals than from the Christians (in contrast to royal towns, where taxation was relatively equitable). Thus, in his efforts to attract Mudejars to his new *morería* in Ayora Don Rodrigo de Mendoza promised the Muslims that he would "not demand from them any tax other than those the Christians are obliged to pay."[129] And in 1526 the recently converted Moriscos specifically requested of Carlos I "that they not be pressed to pay more or less [taxes] than the Christians."[130] Sometimes the Mudejars had to give the lord a higher percentage of their harvest, but usually their heavier tax burden consisted of the *sofras*, a series of personal services they owed to their lord. Such services might include working in the lord's vineyards and *huerta*, provisioning the lord's house with wood and charcoal, transporting crops to the lord, maintenance and repair of the lord's utilities, and weaving linen and silk for the lord. The Mudejars were paid a low daily wage for their labors.[131] That most Mudejars chose to remain on seigneurial lands despite an option to move to royal *morerías* suggests that the Mudejars had other noneconomic reasons for doing so, and that perhaps life there was not as difficult as the preceding list of taxes and services would indicate. In the previous chapter it was pointed out that some seigneurial Muslims were able to prosper, in part through pursuing a strategy of renting or purchasing land outside of their seigneuries, where they were not liable for the heavy seigneurial dues. In the sixteenth century the Moriscos living on seigneurial lands probably felt their lord's exactions much more keenly, since prevailing conditions deprived them of the options available to their fifteenth-century predecessors.

The picture of relative financial stability that has been drawn regarding the royal aljamas of the kingdom of Valencia cannot easily be extended to include their seigneurial counterparts. There is evidence that a number of seigneurial aljamas had financial difficulties, which in part derived from the insolvency of their lords. This royal–seigneurial dichotomy mirrors that which seems to have existed between the prosperity of the capital and perhaps of other towns and the economic stagnation of at least some rural areas. While agrarian productivity seems to have declined between 1410 and 1518, textile production and commerce in the capital experienced growth until the final decades of the fifteenth century. The agrarian decline was a consequence of the plagues that swept over the kingdom throughout the fifteenth century (1411, 1428, 1439, 1450, 1459, 1475, 1478, 1489, 1508, 1519) and left many areas seriously underpopulated. Although urban areas also suffered greatly from the plagues, their populations, or at least that of the capital, were replenished by immigration from Castile.[132] Such conditions, although allowing individual Muslim and Christian farmers to take more land under cultivation and thereby prosper, were detrimental to the finances of the landed nobility and the corporate *universitates* and aljamas of their Christian and Muslim vassals.

The reduction in the amount of land being farmed resulted in decreasing revenues for the nobility. Lords could not easily increase the productivity of their estates, for even when their enterprising vassals tilled idle land they tended to do so in areas outside of the seigneury. Furthermore, the progressive substitution of rents in kind for rents in cash seems to have stimulated greater expenditure on the part of the nobility, who found, however, that their diminishing monetary income was insufficient to support the lifestyle to which they had grown accustomed. Thus many nobles entered into a state of indebtedness and raised more money through the sale of pensions to prosperous urban merchants or to other lords who possessed the funds to invest. Seigneurial aljamas and *universitates* were implicated in the lords' debts, because when the lords sold pensions they normally mortgaged their properties and the rents they received from their vassals as security for the payment of the pensions. Consequently, if a lord defaulted on his pension payment, the creditor could initiate executions against the property and rents of the lord's vassals. Or, in what amounted to the same thing, as a lord's monetary resources dwindled he might compel his *universitates* and aljamas to take on ("cargasen") the responsibility of the pension payment themselves. In both cases, either through the lord's default or through formal assumption of the responsibility of payment, the vassals found themselves paying their rents to their lord's creditors. The creditors in effect replaced the lord as rent collector.[133]

As long as the pensions owed by the lord did not exceed the amount of rent the lord normally received the vassals could tolerate the demands of the creditors, for it made little difference whether the creditor or the lord's tax farmer collected the rent. However, when the rents proved insufficient to liquidate outstanding pensions, the vassals were then faced with the attempts of the creditors to confiscate and auction off the properties and possessions remaining to them, as a corporation or as individuals, after tax payment. For those vassals who barely met the fiscal demands of their lords, additional exactions on the part of the creditors might prove disastrous.

The aljamas and *universitates* of Benaguacil, Paterna, and la Pobla (collectively called the *antich patrimoni*), whose lord was the Infante Enrique, were burdened with numerous pension obligations that, Fernando admitted, had been taken on by his royal predecessors and other lords (e.g., the 1,480s annual pension sold by the Count de Luna to a knight).[134] Because the rents were insufficient to meet all the pension payments, Fernando took measures to excuse the aljamas and *universitates* from all superfluous payments and expenses, and therefore relieved them of the responsibility of paying the 500s salary of the advocate of the *antich patrimoni*.[135] However, that such a measure would have provided only minimal relief is clear from subsequent claims against the Infante and his vassals by the Count of Oliva (1495), the Count of Trivento (1501), and Joan Ferrando, a lawyer (1502), for 5,107s, 8,400s, and 166s 8d, respectively.[136]

The powerful Duke de Cardona and his aljamas—Benicanena, Beniopa, Alcarea Nova, Benipeixcar, and el Real, all located in the *huerta* of Gandía, and those of the valleys of Guadalest and Confrides and the town of Ondara—were constantly engaged in legal battles with their creditors over outstanding pensions. One document from 1486 lists no less than nineteen creditors, among whom were noblemen, urban citizens, and the Hospital of Holy Innocents in Valencia.[137] For instance, at least 180s were owed to Dona Yolant de Aragon, 8,000s to the knight Françi Crespi de Valldaura, and 500s to Luis de Vilanova.[138] It seems that during the period covered by this study only a few of these debt cases were resolved. The Duke de Cardona would argue that excessive executions against the property of his vassals would cause them to abandon their lands.[139] Or if the king actually commanded that executions be made, the Duke would see to it that they were carried out moderately and according to strict guidelines he himself had set.[140] The success of the Duke and his aljamas in evading their creditors may be attributed to the fact that the Duke was, as the knight Françi Crespi complained in frustration, a "potent person."[141]

The Infante Enrique and the Duke de Cardona certainly were not alone in endangering the financial stability of their aljamas and *universitates* through their own excessive borrowing. One also finds creditors harrying the Count of Cocentaina and his vassals in the town of Elda, or the lords and aljamas of Dos Aguas, Alacuás, and Novelda.[142] It is difficult to determine from the debt litigation just how much of a threat was posed to the solvency of seigneurial aljamas by having to satisfy their lords' creditors. Presumably, some lords had the good sense not to overextend themselves to the point that their debts could not be covered by the rents they received from their vassals. The aljamas of such lords would not have been placed in any jeopardy. However, other lords were not so concerned about maintaining a balanced budget. They eventually were forced to plead with their creditors to renegotiate their pension payments, for they feared that execution against their vassals' mortgaged property—beyond the normal rent payments—would force the vassals to flee and settle elsewhere. And these fears were not exaggerated in some cases. Many Muslim vassals abandoned the seigneuries of Dos Aguas and Olocau rather than endure the confiscation of their goods by their lords' creditors.[143] In such cases the lords and the remaining vassals were left in even direr straits, for with fewer vassals less land could be cultivated, and with the consequent smaller harvests there would be even less revenue available for satisfying the creditors. And, as has been seen, new vassals were difficult to come by.

However, the financial difficulties experienced by some seigneurial aljamas cannot always be attributed to the imprudent spending of their lords, for many aljamas sold pensions to raise money on their own account. An aljama might need to borrow money for any number of reasons, such as purchasing grain after a poor harvest or a flood, or buying materials for repairing the local irrigation system.[144] Apparently, aljamas had been borrowing money in this fashion since the late four-teenth century. Thus Francesch Vilar, a priest beneficed in the church of Santa María del Mar in Barcelona, sued the aljamas of the Vall de Uxó for 81 pounds 10s in outstanding pensions. This pension had been sold by the aljamas in 1383 to a citizen of Barcelona, Arnau Alos, who sub-sequently bequeathed it to the church of Santa María.[145] The same al-jamas also owed 216s 8d in pensions to the heirs of one Bartholomeu Ros.[146] The aljama of Elda sold numerous pensions in its own behalf, distinct from those which had been sold by their lord, the Count of Cocentaina. In 1497 the aljama concluded an agreement with eighteen of its creditors, among whom were noblemen, merchants, and clergy-men, including the cardinal-bishop and chapter of Zaragoza and the monastery of Poblet. Realizing that the aljama's goods and rents were sufficient for little more than to pay the salaries of the officials sent to confiscate them for the payment of outstanding pensions, the creditors decided to stay the order of execution and renegotiate the aljama's debt, so that the aljama would be left with some means of paying future pensions.[147] Other aljamas involved in suits with their creditors were those of Ribarroja, Villamarchante, and Mislata, although none of these seems to have had debt burdens like that of the aljama of Elda.[148]

It is probably wise to refrain from making any general conclusions as to the widespread financial difficulties of seigneurial aljamas. The evi-dence is too scanty and scattered, and it is not at all clear from the documents that the creditors' claims were always valid and acted upon or that the aljamas were unable to pay the pensions. In any case, it is certain from the study of Eugenio Císcar Pallarés that the problem of seigneurial insolvency was far more serious in the latter half of the six-teenth century. At that time considerable inflation devalued the lords' cash rents (prices were, in contrast, relatively stable in the late fifteenth century) to such an extent that not even the huge population increase— 50.9 percent between 1563 and 1609—and the consequent growth in agrarian production could close the gap between expenses and income and relieve the lords' financial troubles. The situation of the vassals also worsened. Unable to change vassalage because of an overabundance of labor, and left with less land to farm owing to the progressive subdivi-sion of family properties, they were hard-pressed to meet the increasing fiscal demands of their lords.[149] Therefore, a more modest conclusion may be offered: during Fernando's reign there are evident signs of the later crisis of the seigneurial regime.

5   Mudejars and the Administration of Justice

The question of law and the judicial process is a troublesome one for the historian of the Mudejars. Owing to the nature of the extant documentation—virtually all in Latin or Romance and treating the concerns of the Crown and its officials—our view of the juridical state of affairs is necessarily one-sided. The extreme paucity, or almost complete lack, of Arabic documentation obscures the working of the kingdom's Islamic courts and the extent to which Islamic law governed Mudejar life.[1] Fortunately, the documents provide enough references to the activities of Muslim judges and jurists and to sentencing by specifically Islamic penalties to allow for a piecing together of some elements of the puzzle. The laws of the kingdom regulating the judicial process for Christians, Muslims, and Jews—found in the *Furs* and the *Aureum opus*—also offer some rough guidelines. However, it must be emphasized that the practical administration of justice often differed significantly from the theoretical strictures set forth in the law codes. By the late fifteenth century, if not earlier, Christian and Muslim judges and jurisprudents seem in somewhat of an ad hoc fashion to have arrived at a juridical modus vivendi, in which Muslim and Christian officials recognized one another's exclusive spheres of jurisdiction, but at the same time were able to work cooperatively at those points where the two legal systems meshed.

Islamic and Christian Legal Systems: Autonomy and Convergence

For the medieval Muslim the law, or Shariah, was of essential importance, the very foundation of religious identity. The Shariah derived from two sources: the Qur'ān, God's revelation; and the *Sunnah*, the statements and deeds of the Prophet Muḥammad, preserved in the *hadīth*, orally transmitted statements by and about the Prophet eventually written down by legal scholars. Encompassing both the religious and the secular, and Shariah guided religious practice, set forth moral values, and created a framework for private and, theoretically at least, public life. The Christian authorities had long recognized the Muslim and Jewish minorities' legal identities, often referring to them as adherents of distinct "laws" instead of different religious beliefs. Royal enactments applicable to subjects of all three faiths were therefore often addressed to persons "of whatever law or status."[2]

As stipulated in the thirteenth-century treaties between Jaime I and the conquered Muslims of Valencia, the latter were granted legal autonomy and the ability to administer justice according to *çuna* and *xara* (*Sunnah*, here probably meaning the Muslims' local customary law, and Shariah).[3] Pedro IV confirmed this basic Mudejar right, commanding that all cases between Muslims, both civil (see tables 16 and 17) and criminal, were to be judged according to the Shariah (1337).[4] Of course, if Islamic law were to remain in force among the Mudejars, the Islamic courts had to be maintained and manned by Muslim judges, or *qāḍī*s. Alfonso IV provided for the establishment of a sufficient number of *qāḍī*s in royal towns and on those seigneuries where the lords had criminal jurisdiction over their vassals (1329). Furthermore, Alfonso permitted the *qāḍī*s to delegate their powers to substitutes competent to administer justice in their absence.[5] The measures taken by the jurates of Alcoy, and approved by Juan II, for the creation of a new *morería* there (1468) attest to the continuing importance of Mudejar *qāḍī*s:

> let there be made or created a *qāḍī* in the said *morería*, who may judge and have the power and faculty to judge the litigations arising between the said Moors, who will live in the said *morería*, according to *Sunnah* and Shariah, just as is accustomed among Moors of other *morerías* of the said kingdom.[6]

At the pinnacle of Valencia's Islamic judiciary was the *qāḍī* general, or royal *qāḍī*. During the years covered by this study this post was held by various members of the Bellvís family—Mahomat until 1484, and Ali from 1484 until at least 1501—who resided in the capital. Along with a

Table 16. Civil Cases between Muslims of Valencia

Document	Date	Presiding official[a]	Subject of litigation
ARV: C 131: 61v–62r	18 April 1483	Lieutenant bailiff of Játiva; local *qāḍī* (1), bailiff general, *qāḍī* general (2), bailiff general, lieutenant *qāḍī* general (3)	Sum of money
ARV: C 134: 107r–v	26 Jan. 1488	Lieutenant bailiff of Castellón (local *qāḍī*?) according to Shariah	Various civil and criminal litigations between Muslims of Castellón
ARV: C 139: 75v–76r	19 May 1495	Lieutenant of bailiff general in Segorbe and J.D. of Valencia	"Controversia" between Muslims of Geldo and aljama of Segorbe
ARV: C 148: 104v–105r	23 Nov. 1492	Royal audience (viceroy) and J.D	Muslim of Petrés vs. Muslim and Christian lord re. sale of lands
ARV: B 1156: 370r–v	6 Feb. 1479	Bailiff of Burriana	Unpaid debt, recalcitrant debtor
ARV: B 1156: 664r–v	14 Dec. 1479	Bailiff of Alcira (?)	"Questio" between Muslims of Llombay and Muslims of Alcira
ARV: B 1156: 856v	14 Sept. 1480	*Qāḍī* general and lieutenant *qāḍī* general	Inheritance
ARV: B 1157: 255v–256r	4 June 1482	Bailiff of Játiva	Possession and restitution of *jubbah* (long outer garment; robe)
ARV: B 1157: 308r–v	11 Sept. 1482	Bailiff of Játiva; local *qāḍī* (1), bailiff general, *qāḍī* general (2)	Unspecified

ARV: B 1157: 311v, 314v, 366v, 377v, 378r	20 Sept. 1482–5 Feb. 1483	Bailiff of Játiva; local *qāḍī* (1), bailiff general, *qāḍī* general (2), bailiff of Játiva, local *qāḍī* and other *qāḍī* and *faqīhs* (3)	Sum of money
ARV: B 1157: 344r–v	3 Dec. 1482	Bailiff general	Possession and restitution of *jubbah*
ARV: B 1157: 392r	7 March 1483	Bailiff and lieutenant bailiff of Játiva, local *qāḍī*	Inheritance
ARV: B 1158: 264r	24 July 1486	Bailiff of Játiva	Planting and location of mulberry trees
ARV: B 1159: 120v–121r	28 Aug. 1488	Bailiff general	Alleged debt for purchases of cloth
ARV: B 1160: 361v–362r	5 Dec. 1491	Bailiff general	Ownership and theft of goats
ARV: B 1160: 631r–v	20 Feb. 1493	Bailiff general and Justice of Valldigna	Debt of 69 pounds
ARV: B 1161: 263r	16 April 1493	Bailiff general	Unspecified

Table 17. Civil Cases between Muslims of Aragon-Catalonia

Document	Date	Presiding official	Subject of litigation
ACA: C 3562: 26r, 42r–v	28 Dec. 1479– 20 May 1480	Governor of Aragon	Aljama of Tarazona vs. aljama of Tortoles re. payment of *peche (peyta)*
ACA: C 3562: 145v	27 Feb. 1484	Bailiff of Tudela	Inheritance
ACA: C 3523: 104r–v	12 March 1481	?(1) J.D. of Lérida and *faqih* of Lérida (2)	Unspecified; one litigant is the *qāḍī* of Lérida
ACA: C 3571: 21r	15 May 1492	Official of royal chancery (1), new official of royal chancery and Muslim "maestros" (*faqīhs?*) (2), another official of royal chancery (3)	Opening of window of house of Muslim prejudicial to Muslim of neighboring house—in Zaragoza
ACA: C 3637: 82v–83r	2 Aug. 1481	*Merino* of Zaragoza (and local *qāḍī?*) according to Islamic law	Inheritance, between father and husband of deceased woman
ACA: C 3647: 60v–61r	15 Feb. 1490	Lieutenant of bailiff general of Aragon	Attempt of Muslim wife to annul marriage; husband objects
ACA: C 3647: 112v–113r	30 Jan. 1491	King	Between coguardians of four girls re. marriage of their wards
ACA: C 3648: 219r–220r	15 Oct. 1491	Delegate of lieutenant general of Aragon, vice-chancellor	Woman attempts to escape marriage contracted with her cousin
ACA: C 3560: 156r–v	5 Oct. 1492	Lieutenant of bailiff general of Aragon (and *qāḍī?*) according to Islamic law	Women dispute terms of guardianship of male cousin over them
ACA: C 3651: 117v–118r	30 Nov. 1493	Lieutenant bailiff general and receiver general of Aragon	Debt pending from loan
ACA: C 3665: 141v	2 Sept. 1489	Lieutenant bailiff general of Aragon (and *qāḍī?*), according to Islamic law	Brothers vs. aljama of Huesca re. unfair taxation

variety of other duties, the *qāḍī* general exercised appellate jurisdiction over the kingdom's Islamic courts. Beyond his court, the Mudejar dissatisfied with the decision of a local *qāḍī* could have recourse only to the bailiff general or the king.[7]

Although in the thirteenth century accusations against Muslims by Christians were heard in Islamic courts,[8] by Fernando's reign it was established procedure to try all cases between Muslims and Christians (see table 18) in Christian courts according to the *Furs*.[9] Confining our present discussion to those cases involving only Muslims, it appears that even they were frequently adjudicated in Christian courts. This was far truer of criminal than of civil litigation. This state of affairs may be explained in part by the legislation of Jaime II, which provided that the bailiff general was to have ultimate jurisdiction over all criminal and civil cases between Muslims resident on royal and ecclesiastical lands (1298). The governor general was later granted a similar jurisdiction over the cases of seigneurial Muslims. The *qāḍīs* were still supposed to have primary jurisdiction in these cases.[10]

However, by the midfourteenth century the intervention of Christian magistrates in Mudejar litigation was far more frequent than the occasional ruling by bailiff or governor warranted by Jaime II's legislation. Boswell found that Christians were constantly meddling in the Muslims' judicial proceedings. Between 1355 and 1365 89 percent of all cases involving only Muslims were heard by Christian judges, and often were decided according to Christian and not Islamic law. Put in an advantageous bargaining position by the fortunes of Pedro IV's war with Castile, a number of the kingdom's aljamas were able to wrest from the king guarantees that henceforth they would be judged according to the Shariah.[11]

The picture derived from the documentation of Fernando's reign contrasts strikingly with the Mudejars' juridical woes in the midfourteenth century. There was only one complaint about Christian interference in Muslim cases, and this was voiced by the aljama of Valencia. The aljama began by recalling the allegedly long-established judicial procedures: "for the past great while by ancient custom and practice observed without contradiction in all the present kingdom of Valencia the cases and litigations which involve Moor against Moor, both civil and criminal, were decided according to *Sunnah* and Shariah." Now, however, the aljama complained, "sometimes obstacles and impediments are placed so that such litigations are not judged or decided in the aforesaid form," which was manifestly prejudicial to the Muslims of Valencia's *morería*. The king responded with the command that "all the litigations, both civil and criminal, involving Moor against Moor should be determined according to *Sunnah* and Shariah." Anyone violating this

Table 18. Decisions in Cases between Muslims and Christians

Document	Date	Presiding official	Subject of litigation	Decisions in favor of/against
ARV: C127: 121r–v	20 Oct. 1480	Bailiff general	Unspecified	Muslim or Murviedro/wife of nobleman
ARV: C128: 52r	11 Sept. 1480	Viceroy	Pensions owed	Noblewoman/Muslims of Gandía
ARV: C129: 87r–v	2 June 1481	?	Unspecified	Muslim of Játiva/Christian of Játiva
ARV: C130: 77r–v	1 Oct. 1481	Bailiff general	Unspecified	Priest/Muslim of Benaguacil
ARV: C131: 105r–v	1 July 1483	Governor	Pensions owed	Noblewoman/Muslims of Beniareda
ARV: C131: 166r–v	25 Oct. 1483	Lieutenant bailiff of Játiva	Unspecified	Muslim/lord of Genovés
ARV: C131: 168r	15 Nov. 1483	Lieutenant bailiff general	Unspecified	Christian of Játiva/Muslim of Játiva
ARV: C131: 179r–v	15 Dec. 1483	Bailiff of Játiva	Right of female vassal to marry	Muslim vassals/lord of Genovés
ARV: C132: 215v	1 Nov. 1485	Bailiff general	Unspecified	Christians/Muslims
ARV: C133: 174v–175r	7 May 1486	?	Freedom of slave(?)	Converted slave/master: canon of Orihuela
ARV: C134: 23r–v	25 Nov. 1486	Bailiff of Játiva	Unspecified	Muslim of Játiva/priest of Mogente
ARV: C134: 67v–68r	17 April 1487	Bailiff of Játiva	Unspecified	Notary of Játiva/Muslims of Játiva
ARV: C134: 150r–v	31 March 1488	Viceroy	Unspecified	Christian of Játiva/Muslim woman
ARV: C135: 60r–v	24 April 1488	Civil justice of Valencia	Unspecified	Muslim of Manises/miller of Valencia
ARV: C136: 110r	1 Aug. 1491	Bailiff general and royal council	Unspecified	Former Muslim vassals/lord of Alberique

ARV reference	Date	Official	Crimes	Parties
ARV: C136: 192v–193r	26 April 1493	Governor	Crimes	Christian lord/Muslim
ARV: C138: 290v–291r	1499	Governor	Unspecified	Aljama of Mislata/Christian of Valencia
ARV: C139: 196v–197r	8 Feb. 1496	Governor	Unspecified	Aljama of Ondara/Christian
ARV: C140: 46r–v	23 July 1499	Bailiff of Orihuela	Unspecified	Lord of Cox/Muslims of Aspe
ARV: C140: 136r–v	30 Jan. 1500	Governor	Unspecified	Muslim of Valldigna/notary of Valencia
ARV: C140: 224v–225v	7 Oct. 1500	Judge appointed by king	Unspecified	Aljama of Aspe/Christians
ARV: C142: 81r	2 May 1502	Governor	Unspecified	Christian of Moncofa/Muslim of Vall de Uxó
ARV: C148: 11r–v	2 June 1492	Viceroy	Unspecified	Muslim vassal of Sellent/lord of Sellent
ARV: C148: 19v–20r	18 June 1492	Bailiff of Alicante	Unspecified	Muslim/Christian of Alicante
ARV: C148: 92v	19 Oct. 1492	Governor	Unspecified	Muslim of Albatera/canon of Cartagena
ARV: C148: 153r–154r	1493	Governor	Money owed by Muslim	Christian widow/Muslim of Valldigna
ARV: C148: 156r–v	14 March 1493	Bailiff of Játiva	Unspecified	Muslim of Játiva/Christian of Játiva
ARV: C151: 46v[a]–47r[b]	20 Oct. 1496	Viceroy	Fruits from certain lands	Former Muslim vassals/lord of Albalat
ARV: C151: 62r–63r	10 Dec. 1496	Bailiff of Játiva	Unspecified	Christian laborer/Muslim
ARV: C151: 75r–v	7 Jan. 1497	Royal audience	Rents owed	Rent collectors of Corbera/Muslims of Alcira with lands in Corbera
ARV: C151: 150v–151r	18 April 1497	Viceroy and J.D.	Money owed on purchase of sheep	Christian of Puzol/Muslims of Petrés
ARV: C156: 107r	14 Dec. 1501	Justice of Játiva	Unspecified	Knight of Játiva/Muslim woman

Table 18. *(cont.)*

Document	Date	Presiding official	Subject of litigation	Decisions in favor of/against
ARV: C156: 108r–109r	11 Dec. 1501	Viceroy	Unspecified	Christian/Muslim
ARV: C303: 78v–79v	12 Oct. 1499	Bailiff of Játiva	Unspecified	Muslim/knight of Játiva
ARV: C304: 141r–v	12 Dec. 1480	Bailiff general	Unspecified	Muslim of Murviedro/noblewoman
ARV: B1157: 637v–639r	25 May 1484	Bailiff general	Assault by Muslim	Christian/Muslim of Oliva
ARV: B1160: 750r–751r	4 Dec. 1493	Bailiff general	Rents allegedly owed	Former vassal/lord of Benimuslem
ARV: B1431: 394v ff.	14 Feb. 1494	Bailiff general	Money owed for goods purchased	Hosteler of Valencia/Muslim family of local merchants
ARV: B1431: 421v ff.	14 May 1494	Bailiff general	Money owed for purchase of linen	Merchant of Valencia/Muslims of Valencia
ACA: C 3636: 73r–v	18 Jan. 1481	Bailiff general	Unspecified	Muslim/Christian
ACA: C 3639: 12v–13r	30 Nov. 1481	Bailiff general	Crime	Muslim/Christian
ACA: C 3652: 43r–v	23 May 1494	J.D.	Unspecified	Muslim of Valencia/notary

order was to pay the heavy fine of 1,000 gold florins.[12] As is evident from Boswell's study, the aljama exaggerated the supposedly ideal conditions of earlier days, for there certainly had been frequent and excessive "contradiction" of the "ancient custom."

At any rate, the articulation of only one complaint does not mean that elsewhere Christian officials remained aloof from all Mudejar litigation. On the contrary, they were often active in the conclusion of such cases. The point of contrast between the midfourteenth century and Fernando's reign is not that in the latter period Christian intervention was lacking; rather, it is that in the late fifteenth century the Mudejars for the most part did not perceive such Christian involvement as interference or as a violation of their privileges. The exception, the aggrieved aljama of Valencia, may be explained by the greatly reduced population of the *morería* (since 1455) and the burgeoning Christian population of the city, perhaps more apt to interfere in Muslim affairs than previously.

It is difficult to explain this contrast, or to trace a clear line of development from the midfourteenth to the late fifteenth century. Boswell's concluding remarks on the judicial process provide a useful point of departure. He argues that even though Christian officials frequently violated the judicial autonomy that had been promised to the Mudejars in the thirteenth century, "the system of interlocking justice prevailing under the Crown of Aragon in the fourteenth century may represent a successful departure from the general pattern of institutional separation between Christians and Muslims." This system ultimately satisfied the needs of the greater part of both communities.[13] Indeed, at the root of the Mudejars' acceptance of the judicial status quo was likely a progressive accommodation between the Islamic and Christian legal systems. Such accommodation paralleled and contributed to the Mudejars' increasing sufferance of Christian rule reflected in their relative political quiescence under Fernando. In other words, Valencia's Muslims became more accustomed to the participation of Christian magistrates in their judicial affairs and more willing to plead their suits before Christian courts.

One must also take into account the chronological focus of Boswell's study, which covers the years of the war between Castile and Aragon (1355–1366). The upheaval and disorder of these years likely afforded unscrupulous Christian officials an unusual freedom to abuse Mudejars and to usurp their judicial prerogatives. Perhaps the restoration of order and Valencia's greater stability in the fifteenth century were less propitious for the blatant violation of Mudejar privileges. In any case, the Mudejar grievances expressed to Fernando were scarcely concerned with infringements on their judicial autonomy. Given the active role still played by Valencia's Islamic judiciary and the persisting importance of the Shariah among the Mudejars, it may be supposed that many of the fourteenth-century abuses had been corrected. Islamic justice continued to be administered in Valencia, and the posts of *qāḍī* and *faqīh* were not mere sinecures apportioned among the king's Muslim favorites. This being the case, it is necessary to establish in what areas the Islamic courts still had exclusive jurisdiction, in which types of cases the jurisdictions of Islamic and Christian courts overlapped, and in such cases of jurisdictional convergence, how Muslim and Christian magistrates divided their juridical labors.

Almost all criminal cases between Muslims were tried before Christian tribunals: royal and ecclesiastical vassals in the courts of the bailiff general or local bailiffs, seigneurial vassals of lords with only civil jurisdiction in the court of the governor, and seigneurial vassals of lords with criminal jurisdiction in the court of the lord and his justice.[14] However, this did not thereby exclude the *qāḍī*s and Islamic law from the judicial process. Burns describes how in the thirteenth century the exercise of criminal justice by Mudejar courts was placed under the supervision of royal bailiffs. Gradually, as it came to be viewed as a function of the bailiff's court effected with the assistance of Muslim jurists, the nature of the court was transformed.[15] Thus, by 1329 Alfonso IV could command that on royal lands and seigneurial lands with criminal jurisdiction the Christian magistrates "ought to exercise [their] jurisdiction and inflict penalties with the counsel of Sarracen judges, commonly called *qāḍī*s."[16] In those cases requiring a *qāḍī*'s participation, which were, of course, judged according to Islamic law, the *qāḍī*'s role necessarily would have been central, not merely advisory. Documentary references to the "counsel of the *qāḍī*" are misleading and ought not to obscure the fact that Islamic justice was being administered, even if under the auspices of a Christian court. In such cases the presiding Christian official served to ensure that the *qāḍī*'s sentence was duly executed, for Muslims were not permitted to administer capital or corporal punishment themselves. He also saw to it that the proceeds from any monetary fines imposed were delivered to royal or seigneurial treasuries.

For our purposes there are two categories of criminal cases to be considered: those in which a *qāḍī* intervened and which were decided according to Islamic law, and those which were handled only by Christian judges according to the *Furs*. An understanding of the development of judicial institutions in Islamic lands will help to clarify how Mudejar criminal cases were apportioned among the Islamic and Christian courts.

In Islamic lands there was a practical distinction between those criminal offenses for which God had defined a punishment—known as *hadd* offenses—which fell under the jurisdiction of the *qāḍī*'s Shariah court, and those concerning which neither the Qur'ān nor the *Sunnah* made explicit provisions, and which, therefore, were handled either by the police (*shurṭah*) in their judicial capacity or by the court of complaints (*mazālim*) of the ruler. Outside of the *hadd* offenses, the Muslim ruler had discretionary powers to determine, for the public good, what constituted an offense and the punishment it merited.[17]

The *hadd* offenses, for which there were divinely ordained penalties, were illicit sexual relations—premarital sex and adultery—slanderous accusations of unchastity, theft, wine drinking, and armed robbery.[18] Mudejar *qāḍī*s, as the dispensers of Shariah justice, probably would have been most insistent on retaining their competence in such cases. This is precisely what the documentation indicates. Almost all of the criminal cases that mention the activity of a *qāḍī* concern *hadd* offenses, particularly illicit sexual relations and theft. The Shariah prescribed harsh penalties for these crimes. The penalty for adultery was death by stoning, and that for the sexual misconduct of an unmarried woman was one hundred lashes. In such cases the intervention of a Mudejar judge is usually explicitly indicated in the documents, and if not, it may be presumed by the invoking of Shariah penalties. For instance, the lord of Gilet, "with the counsel of our [royal] *qāḍī* Bellvis," sentenced his adulterous vassals, Mahomat Vaquer and Marien Tagormia, "that according to *Sunnah* and Shariah they should be overwhelmed by stones [unto death]."[19] Mahomat Bayrini of Onda paid to the bailiff a fine of 100s in lieu of the twenty-five lashes his unwed daughter was to receive "because she was found in a room with a Christian of the said town and was judged by the *qāḍī* of Villarreal with the license of the *qāḍī* de Bellvis [*qāḍī* general]."[20] Corporal and capital punishments were normally commuted either to the payment of a fine, or, more often, to enslavement to the king or lord. Despite the show of mercy here, royal and seigneurial justice was nevertheless cruelly exploitative. These royal and seigneurial slaves were later sold to the highest bidder, the payments going to the coffers of the king or lord.[21]

Although some cases of Mudejar theft were judged by Christian officials alone according to the *Furs*,[22] most involved a *qāḍī*'s counsel and Shariah penalties, either the amputation of the right hand or flogging. As with adultery, the sentences were often commuted to a monetary fine or enslavement. The accounts of the bailiff of Játiva record the receipt of 600s from Çuleymen Alahuy "because he was condemned to have his hand amputated for having stolen, along with others, a large pot from the hostal . . . for which sentence was given by the *qāḍī* by *Sun-*

nah and Shariah."[23] Two Muslim thieves, from Málaga and Oran, were made royal slaves after the *qāḍī* general passed sentence. Ironically, the Muslim from Oran had just recently been manumitted.[24]

Another case of theft from Játiva sheds further light on the place of Islamic law in such cases. Ali Yalle of Benillup appeared before the bailiff of Játiva and denounced Yuçeff and Çatdon Zam Zam, who lived in the area of Játiva, for having stolen goods from his home. Two days later the royal prosecutor intervened in the case, to which Yuçeff Zam Zam objected, maintaining that the case must be decided according to the Shariah, inasmuch as it was "Moor against Moor," and citing a provision of Pedro IV to that effect. The bailiff agreed with Yuçeff, recalling a recent precedent in which the bailiff general had ruled on another case of Muslim theft in concurrence with Pedro IV's provision. However, just as the bailiff began to try the case as Yuçeff requested— presumably with the counsel of the *qāḍī*—the bailiff general ruled that since the royal prosecutor had already initiated proceedings the case should be decided by the *Furs*. Most likely the bailiff general was attempting to obviate additional legal expenses. In the end, because Yuçeff Zam Zam refused to relent, the case was brought before the bailiff general's tribunal.[25]

The prosecution of those Mudejar criminals for whose offenses there were no prescribed Shariah penalties does not seem to have required the participation of a *qāḍī*. The great majority of such crimes that appear in the documentation are homicides and other acts of violence. The Muslim perpetrators of such acts were tried in the courts of the royal and seigneurial magistrates whose task it was to maintain the public order— bailiffs, governors, and seigneurial justices. Furthermore, since murderers seldom remained at the scene of the crime, it was necessary to bring into play the kingdom-wide network of royal officials to apprehend them. Mudejar judges did not have such manpower at their disposal. Thus, when a Muslim of Valldigna, sentenced by the local justice for the murder of another Muslim, fled from the valley, the viceroy ordered royal officials to hunt him down.[26] In another case, a royal constable was commanded to bring to justice fifteen Muslims who had broken into the home of a Muslim widow, abusing her and her daughter.[27] Mudejar judges seem to have been content to allow their Christian counterparts to proceed in such cases howsoever the *Furs* required.

While royal and seigneurial justice in Valencia certainly differed from that administered by Muslim rulers, it is nevertheless worth noting by way of comparison that it was also the non-Shariah courts of the latter that meted out punishment for homicide and other such disturbances of the public peace. Originally, homicide had been more a matter of private justice, as allowed for by the Qur'ānic maxim of just retaliation (*qisas*). However, it eventually became a public concern, at which point justice in such cases was administered by the courts of the police (*shurṭah*).²⁸ As will be seen in chapter 6, local bailiffs not only punished Mudejar murderers but also supervised settlements between the victim's family and the murderer through the latter's payment of compensation, or blood money. In a sense, the local bailiffs were asserting their public authority to encourage feuding Muslims to reach a private settlement. The Crown, of course, received its share of the compensation payments.²⁹ It appears, then, that Mudejar judges participated in those criminal cases which in Islamic lands pertained to the jurisdiction of the Shariah courts, while they left in the hands of royal and seigneurial officials those cases over which the jurisdiction of the *qāḍī*'s court had been superseded by that of the *shurṭah* or *maẓālim* courts of Muslim rulers.

The amount of civil litigation between Muslims that comes to light in the documentation, and therefore somehow involved the Christian courts, is relatively small in comparison with the far greater number of civil and criminal cases between Muslims and Christians, and the criminal cases involving only Muslims. The obvious explanation is that the majority of Mudejar civil suits were heard in the Islamic courts and, consequently, did not come to the attention of Christian officials. Royal provisions, while granting to Christian judges considerable leeway to preside over Muslim criminal cases, are much less ambiguous in their position that in civil litigation between Muslims the court of first instance should be that of the *qāḍī*. In 1337 Pedro IV ruled that the bailiff general was to have jurisdiction over the criminal cases of the Muslims of Valencia's *morería*, but that their civil cases were to be handled by the *qāḍī* of the *morería*.³⁰ It is doubtful that the small number of Mudejar civil cases referred to in the Christian documents is an accurate indication of either the amount or the variety of cases tried by the Islamic courts. The high degree of violent conflict in Mudejar society (see chap. 6) hints at a wide range of civil litigation involving only Muslims. It is probable that most Mudejars preferred to settle their differences peacefully in the forum of the *qāḍī*'s court or through the arbitration of the ubiquitous *faqīh*s.

A handful of Muslim civil suits never came before a *qāḍī*'s court and were treated by the Christian courts alone. Usually there was good reason for this. Legal controversies pitting one Muslim aljama against another were best resolved by the laws of the kingdom. The claim of some Muslims of Geldo against the aljama of Segorbe was judged by the lieutenant bailiff general in Segorbe, though with the counsel of a doctor of law, whose opinions were meant to counterbalance any bias the lieutenant bailiff, a resident of Segorbe, might have in the aljama's favor.³¹

In some instances lords identified their Muslim vassals' interests so strongly with their own that lawsuits that originally might have been solely between Muslims soon involved a lord as one of the claimants, and so found their way into the Christian courts. This seems to have occurred when the knight Gracian de Monsorin took up the cause of his Muslim vassal in her dispute with Çahat Piten of Petrés concerning the ownership of land. Of course, the loss of the land might have affected Monsorin, the probable real owner of the land, as much as it would have his vassal, who rented the land from him.[32]

Muslims most often pleaded before Christian courts against their fellows in order to set in motion the executive machinery of the royal bureaucracy against recalcitrant debtors and those who lived at a distance from them. Mudejars sought the king's justice for its relative efficiency and coercive power. Even the decisions of the *qāḍī* general carried little weight without the backing of the bailiff general to enforce them. For example, when Abraym Xativi fled from Alcira with the 500 goats at issue between himself and Çahat Ageg, Çahat prompted the bailiff general to have his officials find Abraym and the flock.[33] When Mahomat Roget took his sister's robe (*aljuba*; Arabic *jubbah*) and gave it as security to a Jew of Murviedro, Mahomat's father and sister requested that the bailiff see to the robe's return, since it had not been Mahomat's to give away.[34] Fuçey Zignell of Valencia was informed by the bailiff that his property in Valldigna would be sold if he did not pay to his relatives in Tabernes the money he owed "for the causes and reasons contained in a Moorish letter and/or obligation."[35]

Two other civil cases indicate that Mudejars found the *Furs* to have applicability in questions concerning commercial transactions and property rights. One case concerned an alleged debt owed by the purchaser of some cloth.[36] In the other, the plaintiff, Yuçeff Rodona, demanded that the mulberry trees of Azmet Beniale be removed from his land. It is significant that Yuçeff based his claim on the "constitution of Játiva."[37] Through the conduct of commerce and the exchange of property with Christians as well as with Muslims, the Mudejars of necessity acquainted themselves with the details of the *Furs* and local customary law as they applied to their particular transactions. Still, it is unlikely that in such matters there would have been much substantial difference between the *Furs* and Islamic law as it was administered by Mudejar judges. The Mudejars' wide-ranging economic activities made it unfeasible for them to operate, even among themselves, by a different code of commercial law. Moreover, since so few of these commercial cases were judged in Christian courts, one must presume that the *qāḍī*s had adapted their legal practices to meet the needs of a situation in which the regional economy was regulated by a framework of Christian law. Even in Islamic lands it was in the area of commercial law that the Shariah had proven most malleable and Muslim jurists most innovative.[38]

In those civil cases decided by Islamic law but involving Christian magistrates there was a clear division of labor: the *qāḍī* passed judgment and the Christian official saw to the execution of the *qāḍī*'s sentence. This can be seen in the judicial disputes over inheritance. In one case, the lieutenant of the *qāḍī* general ruled that two Muslim sisters should receive a carob orchard allegedly bequeathed to them by their father. The bailiff of Murviedro was then ordered to put them in secure possession of the land.[39] Also revealing is the litigation "over certain inheritances," which aligned a Muslim vassal of Cárcer and a resident of Játiva's *morería* against some other Muslims of the *morería*. The bailiff general's order to the lieutenant bailiff of Játiva is couched in terms that obscure the *qāḍī*'s essential judicial function: "do justice in the said matter with counsel of the *qāḍī* of the lord king in that *morería*." The bailiff general's concluding remarks indicate, however, that it was the *qāḍī* who handed down the decision in the case: "And if the said *qāḍī* [of Játiva] is considered suspect [i.e., biased] by one of the said parties, you [the lieutenant bailiff] should determine whether the said suspicions are to be admitted, and in such case that they have to be admitted you should administer prompt and expeditious justice with the counsel of another *qāḍī* unsuspected by the said parties."[40] The royal official's function was primarily supervisory and executive.

As the above case indicates, the royal official's role was nonetheless of great importance. The presence of royal authority encouraged the equitable administration of justice by the *qāḍī*. Furthermore, the royal official could be turned to as a board of appeal, at which point the case was ushered through the appropriate channels of the royal bureaucracy to the tribunal of the *qāḍī* general and bailiff general. Thus, when Çaat Siquuti appealed the sentence of the *qāḍī* of Játiva (literally, of the lieutenant bailiff with counsel of the *qāḍī*), the case was sent on to the *qāḍī* general for a final ruling. When Çaat argued that the *qāḍī* general, due to family connections with the *qāḍī* of Játiva, was predisposed to confirm the sentence, the king commanded the bailiff general to re-examine the case, this time with the counsel of the lieutenant of the *qāḍī* general, a neutral party.[41]

The guidance and supervision of the royal bailiffs were crucial for the conclusion of another extremely complex litigation. The case between Azmet Xerica, the vassal of a canon of Játiva, and the Muslim vassal of the lord Lançol de Lançol, was initially ruled on by the *qāḍī* of Játiva in favor of Azmet. Lançol then brought to the bailiff of Játiva the letter of another *qāḍī* that demanded the revocation of the first *qāḍī*'s sentence. Perplexed, the bailiff turned to the bailiff general. The latter, along with the *qāḍī* general, decided that if the second *qāḍī*'s revocatory letter was based on the testimonies of new or reinterrogated witnesses, then the first sentence should stand (this decision was based on a recent precedent in which the *qāḍī* general had counseled the bailiff general that witnesses could not be reinterrogated once sentence had been given); however, if there was a just cause for appeal without the introduction of new testimonies, then the bailiff of Játiva, counseled by the local *qāḍī* and *faqīh*, was to consider the appeal.[42] More than two months later the case was still unresolved. The bailiff was now ordered to attempt to bring the parties to a settlement, but, failing that, he was to hear the opinions of the *qāḍī* and *faqīh*s Lançol had introduced into the case and to render judgment, again with the counsel of Játiva's *qāḍī* and *faqīh*. Finally, the bailiff general, seconded by the *qāḍī* general and his lieutenants, one being the *faqīh* of Valencia, ordered that the sentence (of the *qāḍī* of Játiva?) be executed.[43]

The procedure through which Muslim magistrates judged cases between Muslims under the auspices of the bailiff's court is referred to in the documents as "the Moorish process." The Muslim officials involved were remunerated for their juridical labors. After having collected a 5,000s fine from Muslim thieves of Játiva, who had been judged according to the Shariah, the bailiff of Játiva was commanded, by way of general principle, that "if some Moorish process will be made by the *çalmedina* or the *qāḍī* of the said *morería* see to it that they are paid for the writing of the said Moorish process according to their labors."[44] Anxious to keep court costs at a manageable level, the Crown frowned on the unnecessary intervention of royal officials in the cases of Muslims. Thus, when the royal prosecutor meddled in a case under the consideration of the *qāḍī* general, the bailiff general expressed his disapproval in this manner: "I stand amazed that the process which was made against that [Muslim] is Moorish and that the prosecutors and the notary [nevertheless] are asking for a salary."[45] The prosecutor had no business interfering in a case not being judged according to the *Furs*.

One can only surmise the kinds of cases treated by Valencia's Islamic judiciary without any Christian intervention. It is probable that much of this litigation was in the area of family law, which, in the words of Noel Coulson, was "generally administered in accordance with strict Shariah doctrine . . . because [it] . . . was regarded as a particularly vital and integral part of the scheme of religious duties."[46] As indicated above, *qāḍī*s were often called on to resolve any problems associated with the execution of Mudejar wills. Evidence from Aragon, where, owing to their greater degree of acculturation, Muslims were probably more willing to plead their lawsuits before the Christian authorities, suggests that problems stemming from marriage—divorce or breach of contract—

and guardianship of minors also came before the *qāḍī*'s court.[47] In Valencia *qāḍī*s were instrumental in the drawing up of marriage contracts.[48] In attending to such matters Mudejar judges were probably much less flexible in their interpretation and application of the law than they were in the area of commercial litigation.

Beside the formal judgeship of the *qāḍī*, one must also take into account the juridical activity of the *faqīh*, or jurist. In Valencia's Mudejar communities the jurists were accorded great status, largely on account of their knowledge of the law. In fact, in 1526 the newly converted Moriscos stated that the *faqīh*s devoted their lives to the study of jurisprudence.[49] They utilized their knowledge in two ways, formally, in the *qāḍī*'s court, and, informally, in the community at large. Regarding their formal function, the detailed discussion (see above) of the case involving the participation of the *qāḍī* of Játiva, a second *qāḍī*, and finally the *qāḍī* general shows that each *qāḍī* was attended by at least one *faqīh*. In other words, the jurists acted as advisors to the judges in the Islamic courts. According to Māliki law, the school of law long dominant in both Spain and North Africa, the *qāḍī* was required to consult jurisprudents before passing judgment. The Mudejar *faqīh*'s formal role may be viewed as a survival of the institutionalization of the *qāḍī*'s council (*shūrā*) in al-Andalus.[50]

Equally, if not more important, was the *faqīh*'s role as an informal arbitrator in the Mudejar community. There is evidence of jurists, outside of court, executing wills, offering legal advice to parties involved in litigation, and counseling couples with marital problems.[51] The *faqīh*s played a role, analogous to that of the Maghriban *muftī*s, who offered their legal opinions (*fatwā*) either verbally or in writing to both the populace and the *qāḍī*s when requested.[52] The importance ascribed by historians of Islamic law to the *muftī*s in bridging the gap between the strict orthodoxy of the Shariah and the changing necessities of daily life seems applicable to the position of the *faqīh*s in Valencia. In their adjustment to life as a minority in a Christian society, Valencia's Muslims needed guidance from those possessed of a legal acumen sufficient to interpret and modify the substance of the Shariah as the exigencies of their situation required, while preserving the law's spirit. The dearth of documentary evidence about the *faqīh*s is due probably as much to their informal and largely verbal adjudication as to the almost complete loss of Arabic documentation.

In sum, Muslims and Christians appear to have arrived at a system of sharing judicial responsibilities in cases involving only Muslims, which both minority and majority found satisfactory. The Islamic courts, manned by *qāḍī*s and their *faqīh* advisors, handled the *hadd* criminal offenses and handed down decisions according to the Shariah in a large portion of the civil cases coming before them, especially those in the realm of family law and to a lesser degree those concerning commerce and property. Royal and seigneurial magistrates helped to ensure the execution of the decisions of Mudejar judges, and administered the king's justice to those Muslims who, by their violent acts, were a threat to the common good. Meanwhile, the *faqīhs*, scattered throughout the Mudejar population, met the legal needs of many Muslims. Owing to their good offices it may be that many of the disputes between Mudejars never reached the courts as litigation.

Muslims in Christian Courts: Jurisdictional Conflict

The foregoing account lends the impression that the judicial system of the kingdom of Valencia ran smoothly and efficiently with hardly a snag. This was for the most part true to the extent that in cases between Muslims the Muslim and Christian judiciaries were content with their respective spheres of jurisdiction and with the division of juridical labor when collaboration was necessary. However, regarding those cases over which the Christian courts had exclusive jurisdiction, namely, the Mudejars' non-*ḥadd* crimes and litigation between Muslim and Christian, this impression bears little relation to the reality of late medieval Valencia. The administration of justice to Mudejars, and apparently to Christians as well, was fraught with obstacles created by the strife between those officials who presided over the kingdom's various tribunals. The main problem was that royal, municipal, and seigneurial officials were unwilling to recognize the boundaries of their respective jurisdictions. While at times jurisdictional conflict arose from an official's honest mistake and erroneous interpretation of the law, most often it was the result of a willful trespassing on the jurisdictions of others. Such official bickering affected Muslim plaintiffs and defendants, although the resultant confusion might work to the benefit of the latter.

Three types of jurisdictional conflict are apparent in the documentation: (1) the bailiff general and the local bailiffs against the governor general and his lieutenants; (2) the local bailiffs against the municipal justices; and (3) lords and seigneurial officials against royal and municipal officials. The royal towns found this dissension to be so troublesome that in the Cortes of Monzón (1510) their representatives complained to the king that "many times it happens in your city and kingdom of Valencia contention and difference over jurisdiction between the governor and bailiff, and their surrogates and lieutenants, and the justices of the royal towns of the said kingdom." No specific mention was made of the cases involving Muslims.[53] The clash of antagonistic officials in such cases, therefore, was only part of a more widespread phenomenon.

It was long established that the bailiff general and the local bailiffs were to have jurisdiction over those Muslims living on royal and ecclesiastical lands. Since the fourteenth century the local bailiffs, though subordinate to the bailiff general, had acquired greater power to administer justice to the inhabitants of the local *morerías*.[54] It was not so much that the bailiff general's powers had been reduced as that the increasing complexity of administration necessitated the more frequent delegation of his authority to local representatives of the Crown. This tendency was especially marked in Játiva, where, owing to the very large population of its *morería*, close Crown supervision was essential. For the most part, the bailiff of Játiva and the bailiff general were able to attend to their respective duties without stepping on one another's toes. However, royal directives were occasionally issued to ensure that this cooperation continued. In 1405 King Martin had ordained that "the local bailiff of Játiva should have no power concerning the cases of Sarracens pending before the bailiff general."[55] Fernando was more concerned with hindering the flow of cases in the opposite direction, and so commanded the bailiff general that he should, as little as possible, issue pardons to or make settlements with those Muslims whom the bailiff of Játiva had already sentenced.[56] In both cases the idea was to prevent redundancy and additional legal expenses.

Quite unlike the relative ease with which any tension between the bailiff general and local bailiffs was smoothed over was the great difficulty in resolving the discord between the bailiffs and the governors (i.e., the different regional governors and their lieutenants). The governor was supposed to have jurisdiction over only those seigneurial Muslims whose lords did not exercise criminal jurisdiction on their lands. However, the governors were not satisfied with this limited judicial competence. They frequently interfered in the cases of Muslims that properly belonged to a bailiff's jurisdiction. Simply stated, their motives were financial; they wished to divert more cases to their courts in order to collect for themselves and their subordinates the proceeds from monetary fines and settlements. Of course, the bailiffs, as the guardians of the royal patrimony, were equally determined to defend their jurisdictions and thereby, as they often claimed, "the rights and revenues of the lord king."[57]

Játiva and its region were the main judicial battleground between the bailiffs and the governors. Logically, the royal town with the largest *morería* drew the highest degree of gubernatorial interference. For this reason, among others, Fernando confirmed, at the request of the aljama of Játiva, the privileges that Alfonso V and Juan II had granted to it.

Among the privileges was that placing Játiva's Muslims under the exclusive jurisdiction of the bailiff general and the bailiff of Játiva.[58] This confirmation of privileges, however, had minimal impact.

Early in Fernando's reign the bailiff of Játiva, Joan Dezpuig, and the lieutenant governor beyond the Júcar River, Francesch de Malferit, were at loggerheads. After Dezpuig's lieutenant imprisoned a Muslim criminal, Malferit's men proceeded to pardon the Muslim. Dezpuig responded by issuing a proclamation that called for the revocation of all pardons and safe-conducts previously granted to Muslims and Jews. Malferit next attempted to prevent the public crier from making the proclamation. Failing that, Malferit had the Muslim in question arraigned before his court and reached a settlement with him. According to Dezpuig, Malferit had forced the royal prosecutors to cooperate in the matter. At Dezpuig's request, the bailiff general sent off an angry letter to Malferit, reminding him that in such cases pertaining to the jurisdiction of the bailiff only the king could interfere. Moreover, he required the prosecutors to denounce Muslims before the bailiff and no one else. The case, therefore, was to revert to Dezpuig's court.[59] The bailiff general's words were not heeded for long. By 1487 Fernando was compelled to reprimand the governor general for pardoning Christian and Muslim criminals of the district of Játiva, thereby giving others "boldness to live evilly."[60]

The bailiff of the new *morería* of nearby Castellón de Játiva, given jurisdiction over the Muslims like other local bailiffs, seems to have felt especially beset by the judicial encroachments of the lieutenant governor. In 1482 Fernando was informed that the bailiff and the local Muslims "dreaded" being called before the court of the lieutenant governor. The king responded by remitting all cases involving the bailiff and Muslims of Castellón to a citizen and a jurist of Játiva for consideration.[61] Eventually, the jurisdiction of the bailiff of Castellón de Játiva was incorporated within that of the bailiff of Játiva.[62]

Despite the seemingly incessant bickering, differences were resolved and justice administered. The account books of the bailiff of Játiva reveal that the bailiff and the lieutenant governor many times extricated themselves from these judicial quagmires by simply splitting the proceeds from individual cases. For instance, of the 150s fine paid by the chicken thief Mahomat Melich, the bailiff received 75s and the lieutenant governor the other 75s.[63]

It should not be thought that the governors were always in the wrong. Of the two arguments between the bailiff of Játiva and the governor concerning the prosecution of Muslims for sexual relations with Christian women, the king decided one in favor of the governor.[64] Furthermore, the resolution of other jurisdictional disputes hinged on such legal hairsplitting that it is difficult to know whose interpretation of the law was correct. For instance, in March 1482 the bailiff general reprimanded the lieutenant governor for having tried a Muslim of the seigneury of Manuel for the murder of another Muslim of the same place. Since Manuel was located within the limits of the district of Játiva, a royal town, and since its lord did not possess criminal jurisdiction, the bailiff general maintained that the case belonged to his jurisdiction. The lieutenant governor agreed that, yes, Manuel was located within the district of Játiva, but countered by citing a ruling of the jurist Domingo Masco (21 July 1457), according to which the governor was to have jurisdiction over all seigneurial Muslims inhabiting lordships "within the boundaries [i.e., the surrounding districts] of the royal cities and towns where the lord king has criminal jurisdiction."[65] In his reply the bailiff general corrected the lieutenant governor's reading of Masco's decision, stating that the governor, indeed, had jurisdiction over seigneurial Muslims, "but only if the said towns, castles, and hamlets and places are not located within the boundaries [i.e., district] of some royal city or town."[66]

Here, however, the bailiff general was wrong, and he probably knew it; for just four months prior (December 1481) to this dispute with the lieutenant governor, the king had made a decision on precisely this question of law in the governor's favor, even citing the opinions of Domingo Masco as authoritative support.[67] A royal letter of July 1483 seems finally to have disabused the bailiff of his pretensions on this point.[68]

The bailiffs and governors also managed to come into conflict over another closely related fine legal point, that is, whether or not royal bailiffs had jurisdiction over seigneurial Muslims who committed crimes in royal towns (as distinct from the wider districts of towns) or on royal roads. In February 1481 the king answered this question in the affirmative: "the Moors of the barons [who are] delinquent in the royal cities, towns, or roads, even those who live on royal lands, both [vassals] of knights and of citizens, are totally under the forum and jurisdiction of the said bailiff general and local bailiffs."[69] Fernando reiterated this position the following year.[70] The governors, however, true to form, did not abide by the substance of these decisions. There are two possible explanations: either confusion and legal misinterpretation, or a determination to encroach on the bailiff's jurisdiction, whatever the decisions of the usually absent king. The latter seems most likely, since until at least 1489 the governors frequently interfered in the judicial procedures of local bailiffs against seigneurial Muslims who had committed crimes in the royal towns. For example, the lieutenant governor challenged the jurisdiction of the bailiff of Villajoyosa over a Muslim of the lordship of

Finestrat who had assaulted a Christian of Villajoyosa.[71] The governor of la Plana meddled in similar fashion when Muslims of the seigneury of Nules were cited to appear before the bailiff of Burriana for crimes committed in Burriana.[72] In sum, legal misinterpretation, a disregard for the law even when properly understood, and a desire to extend authority and thereby to increase revenues all contributed to the almost constant strife between the offices of the bailiff and the governor.

The governor general and his lieutenants were not the only nemeses of the bailiff general and the local bailiffs. The municipal justices also were prone to impugn the jurisdiction of the bailiffs over the king's Muslim and Jewish vassals. This was part of a more general tendency displayed by municipal governments, which encouraged the settlement of Mudejars in their towns only to attempt to secure for themselves an inordinate portion of the resultant increased revenues properly belonging to the Crown. In some towns the justices seem to have had as allies the royal prosecutors. In a letter to the Crown prosecutors of Játiva Fernando expressed a clear understanding of the financial motives prompting them to accuse Muslims before the courts of either the local justice or the lieutenant governor: "so that you might more easily conclude settlements with those Moors and Jews and secure a larger part of the settlements."[73]

While one might ascribe gubernatorial interference partly to a misinterpretation of the law, it is far more difficult to give municipal justices such benefit of doubt. The law was unequivocal with respect to the exclusive jurisdiction of the local bailiffs in cases involving Muslims or Jews: "by the laws and privileges of that kingdom of Valencia . . . all cases of Sarracens and Jews, both civil and criminal, should be brought personally before the bailiff of that city or town under whose jurisdiction were committed the aforesaid offenses and cases." At best, local criminal justices had a role in the execution of sentences against Muslims condemned to death or to the mutilation of a limb.[74] Nevertheless, the bailiff general often was compelled to remind municipal justices and jurates that they had no right to try Muslims or make executions against their property. For instance, he rebuked the justice and jurates of Liria not only for initiating procedure against Muslims for their crimes, but also for releasing them after the bailiff had arrested them.[75] There is only one case in which a municipal justice voiced anything close to a legitimate reason for proceeding against a Muslim. The justice of Játiva, who had confiscated the arms and other possessions of Muslims as securities for the fines they incurred for gambling, maintained that he had done so because the Muslims had been found playing dice with Christians. Had it been a question of only Muslims gambling, the justice argued, he would not have penalized them.[76]

The lords of Mudejar vassals were at the center of much jurisdictional squabbling. Seigneurial judicial competence varied from place to place. Some lords were entitled only to civil jurisdiction over their vassals, while others, especially the powerful magnates like the Duke of Gandía, were empowered to exercise criminal jurisdiction as well.[77] The king might grant full jurisdiction to a lord as a reward for services rendered. When Fernando ceded to his vice-chancellor, Joan Pages, lordship over Pobla Tornesa, Benicacim, and Montornés, he stipulated "You and yours can force, punish, and castigate them [Sarracenos] as your and their vassals, and you can exercise over them criminal and civil and all jurisdiction."[78] Some lords with criminal jurisdiction were nevertheless restricted in their ability to administer capital or severe corporal punishment. Thus, Bernat Sorrell, the lord of Geldo, at first allowed the lieutenant bailiff of Segorbe (Geldo was located within the "general boundaries" of Segorbe, where the Duke of Segorbe had supreme jurisdiction) to proceed against his Muslim vassal, guilty of assault. However, after the victim recovered the case was remitted to Sorrell, because now the assailant no longer deserved capital punishment.[79]

Lords prized and jealously guarded their judicial prerogatives for the revenues accruing to them from monetary penalties. They bitterly resented the intervention of royal and municipal officials in the business of their seigneurial courts, although this occurred often enough. There were a number of quarrels between the Cardinal of Valencia, who was the lord of Valldigna, and the bailiff general. They arose because the Muslims of Valldigna were in the habit of appealing the decisions of the justice of Valldigna to the bailiff general. In fact, the Muslims had recourse to the bailiff general so frequently that the king appointed a special assessor specifically for assisting the bailiff in handling their appeals.[80] While this practice was perfectly licit, inasmuch as the bailiff general was the final court of appeal for any Muslim in the kingdom, the officials of Valldigna still complained that the bailiff general, under the pretext of his appellate jurisdiction, was attempting to make his the court of first instance in the Muslims' cases. The king, therefore, cautioned the bailiff to interfere as little as possible.[81] At times Valldigna's officials refused outright to release arrested Muslims into the bailiff's hands.[82] In the case of two wandering Muslims who had committed theft in Játiva, the Cardinal's men summarily hanged them, despite the fact that their appeal was pending in the court of the lieutenant bailiff general.[83]

Lords vied with royal magistrates for judicial authority throughout the kingdom. Turning south, one finds the bailiff general and the governor disputing the jurisdiction over a Muslim murderer of Albatera, only to hear the lord of Albatera chime in that both were wrong and that

the Muslim ought to be arraigned before his court.[84] Further north near
the capital, the bailiff general and the criminal justice of Valencia
attempted to arrest a Muslim vassal of Catarroja who had carnal relations with a Christian prostitute. Joan Canoguera, Catarroja's seigneur,
argued that he had purchased jurisdiction over the place from Juan II
for 75 pounds, and, therefore, the royal officials had no right to interfere. Even after the bailiff general bought back the jurisdiction from
Canoguera, the latter shrewdly asserted that he could still rule on this
case because the crime had been perpetrated before he gave up his jurisdiction. In the end, the case was remitted to the royal council and then
to the governor for sentencing.[85]

The discord between seigneurs and town officials over judicial questions may be seen as a component of a more general social tension between urban and rural areas. The lord of Alberique complained about
the initiatives of Játiva's prosecutors against his vassals and other Muslims implicated in violence on his seigneury.[86] Officials of Gandía
antagonized the lord of Jaraco for much the same reason.[87]

The Mudejars' change of vassalage, which exacerbated the fiscal
rivalry between the nobility and the Crown and the royal towns, also
caused considerable jurisdictional turmoil. This is reflected in the objection of the military estate to a privilege that Castellón de la Plana had
obtained from the king. The privilege gave to the lieutenant governor of
la Plana competence in all cases concerning crimes which had been committed by new Muslim vassals of Castellón when they were still seigneurial vassals. The nobles argued that by virtue of their criminal jurisdiction their former vassals were still liable to answer to them for their
previous crimes.[88]

The lords' objection is understandable, for it seems that Mudejars
took advantage of the Crown's avidity for new vassals in order to avoid
the penalties of seigneurial courts. Thus, when Manuel Lançol, the lord
of Gilet, was in the midst of passing judgment against Mahomat Hube-
quer, apparently his vassal, the prosecutor of Murviedro, stopped the
proceedings by claiming that the Muslim was a royal vassal.[89] Don Enrique de Rocasfull, the lord of Albatera, was similarly hamstrung in the
administration of justice to a Muslim vassal, who, much to his surprise,
had changed vassalage.[90] In such cases royal and municipal officials
either knowingly abetted the Muslims in their evasion of seigneurial justice or were simply hoodwinked. Royal vassals less frequently enlisted
seigneurial support to frustrate Crown magistrates. However, it occasionally happened, as when the officials of the seigneury of Carlet protected their "new" vassal, Mahomat Ametler of Alcira, who had
already been sentenced to enslavement to the king.[91]

From the aforementioned complaint of the royal towns in the Cortes of Monzón (1510) it appears that during Fernando's reign jurisdictional controversy was never completely resolved. This is further evinced in the aggression of the *Germanías*, especially those of Játiva, Alcira, and Murviedro, against the surrounding lordships, for the question of jurisdiction was one of the many points of contention between the seigneurs and the urban citizenry. Judicially, as in other respects, the Mudejars were in the vortex of a larger socioeconomic conflict, the explosion of which would prove catastrophic for them. In the meantime, so long as order reigned, justice was administered, but not without intermittent starts and stops.

Muslims in Christian Courts: Judicial Procedure

Despite the more than occasional jurisdictional disputes, Muslim plaintiffs undauntedly continued to appear before Christian courts to plead their suits against both Muslims and Christians. Such disputes, which originated more in the magistrates' acquisitiveness than in a widespread disrespect for the law, were probably far more vexing for the contending judges than for Muslim plaintiffs and defendants. Once bailiffs, governors, and justices settled their differences and the legal machinery of the court was set in motion, Mudejars could be confident that the due process of law would be respected and justice done. Relative to the bulk of litigation found in the documentation Mudejar complaints of immoderate or illegal procedure by the Christian courts are very few. To some degree the propensity of rival judges to stray beyond their proper jurisdictions and their willingness, for fiscal reasons, to hear the cases of most anyone served as a crude system of checks and balances. The governor's or the seigneurial justice's knowledge that Muslims could always have recourse to the bailiff general, or, conversely, the local bailiff's awareness that the governor or municipal justice would avail themselves of any opportunity to intervene must have curbed excesses in court and encouraged fairness on all sides simply as a means of avoiding the interference of rival courts. More important, neither the king nor the lords were prepared to permit their appointed judges to abuse their vassals in court. In the competition between the Crown and the nobility for Muslim vassals it was perhaps as important to guarantee the Mudejars fair treatment in court as to offer them tax breaks. The prevailing conditions, which were so conducive to this rivalry, afforded the Mudejars room to maneuver, manifested in their change of vassalage and their judicial appeals to higher or rival courts. Since royal authority and the subjects' contentment were largely predicated on the ability of the king to provide justice, blatant injustice to Mudejars in the courts, both royal and seigneurial, was usually corrected by the king and his bailiff general.

The legal mechanisms for the handling of the cases of Muslims in Christian courts were well established by the reign of Fernando. Muslims appeared in court as both plaintiffs and defendants in litigations with Christians, and it was not unusual for them and Christians to file suit as coplaintiffs or to be arraigned as codefendants.[92] Once in court and removed from jurisdictional controversy, cases concerning Muslims presented few procedural dilemmas. Christian magistrates were not perplexed by the prospect of having to hear the pleas of Muslim plaintiffs or receive the testimonies of Muslim witnesses. Nor did the Mudejars find the chamber of a Christian tribunal to be unfamiliar or intimidating territory. On the contrary, the conduct of Mudejars in the various trials often reflects a familiarity with the legal system and a facility in skirting its pitfalls. Far from being victimized by coteries of Christian judges and lawyers, the Muslims were sometimes able to manipulate the system to their own advantage. This was a necessary and positive form of acculturation.

In Christian courts Muslims and Jews took oaths proper to their own religions. While Christians swore on the Gospels, and the Jews, according to the *Furs*, on the Ten Commandments, the Muslims swore on the Qur'ān.[93] In the trial records the Muslims are usually described as having "made an oath. . . to our Lord God and to the *qiblah* of Muḥammad, turning the face toward midday and saying the words that Moors are accustomed to swear."[94]

Trials followed a standard procedure, the length of which varied according to the complexity of the case and the gravity of the crime. (For instance, cases of homicide usually required the laborious interrogation of witnesses, which was often unnecessary in many minor civil suits.) In their most extended format, usually in criminal cases, trials were conducted as follows: (1) the prosecutor presented the accusations, which were sometimes followed by further and more detailed accusations of the plaintiff; (2) the court received any confessions the defendant wished to make; (3) the defense counsel and/or the defendant responded to the specifics of the prosecution's accusations; (4) the testimonies of the witnesses for the prosecution were presented; (5) the testimonies of the witnesses for the defense were presented; (6) the above witnesses were cross-examined by the defense and the prosecution, which sometimes included the depositions of new witnesses intended to impugn the testimonies of previous witnesses; and (7) the presiding judge rendered judgment and passed sentence.[95] Even in cases of what were deemed the most execrable of crimes, restraint was exercised and due process scrupulously observed. When word reached the bailiff general that a Muslim had forced a Christian boy of Sueca to commit sodomy with him, he sent a notary to Sueca to receive "information of the said case and detestable crime and judicial confessions from the said Moor and . . . the account of the said boy."[96]

The same respect for proper procedure was displayed in cases of Muslim violence against Christians. Mahomat Ayub, accused of the murder of a Christian of Teruel, was able to have removed from the panel of judges treating the case a lawyer whom he thought to be prejudiced against him.[97] Ali Ubequer, who had wounded a Christian of Murviedro, delayed the bailiff's procedure against him through clever legal maneuvering.[98] When Alfonso Mendo dropped the assault charges he had leveled at Çahat Salamo, all legal action was duly ceased.[99]

Christian procurators (*procuradors*), usually notaries given power of attorney, frequently represented Muslims in court. The Christian procurator might also act as a Muslim's defense counsel, and some notaries seem to have been court-appointed public defenders. There is no evidence suggesting that the procurators were in any way negligent in the causes of their Muslim clients. For the notaries such dereliction of duty probably would have resulted in an undesired loss of clientele.[100]

Muslims were in no way restricted from bringing charges against Christians. Thus, when the widow Axa Christelli was unable to appear in court to make the requisite formal accusations against the knight Gaspar de Monsorin and his squire for the murder of her son, the viceroy obliged her by sending an official to Algimia to record her accusations and to seize the accused for trial.[101]

A somewhat thornier issue was that concerning witnesses in cases between Muslims and Christians. The *Furs* had originally provided that in such cases witnesses from the religious group of the defendant were required to prove the defendant's guilt. In other words, a Christian filing suit against a Muslim needed the testimony of at least one Muslim as proof. In 1301 Jaime II significantly modified the law to the detriment of the Mudejars by admitting the testimonies of two reputable Christians as sufficient proof against a Muslim.[102] It is difficult to perceive how the law was translated into practice on this question. In some cases when witnesses are mentioned their faith is not identified, or when witnesses are identified there are enough Muslim and Christian witnesses produced by both sides to preclude any quibbling on the grounds of the specific question treated by the *Furs*. Perhaps most telling is the notable absence of any queries concerning the admissability of witnesses, Muslim or Christian. Muslims do not seem to have been in any way limited as to the witnesses they might produce in their own behalf, as long as the witnesses were reputable and honest persons. Indeed, at a Muslim's request court notaries were sent out to record the testimonies of the witnesses specified. When Seydi Melvix, acting as procurator for other Granadan Muslims (new settlers in Valencia?) in a litigation with the bailiff general beyond the Jijona River, wished to bring forth witnesses "to prove certain clauses," a notary of Orihuela was dispatched to examine the witnesses and record their depositions.[103] Muslims could also use Arabic documents as legitimate evidence in Valencia's courts.[104] Suits between Muslims and Jews did not create any special problems.[105] Even in cases in which Muslims were not implicated, their testimonies as witnesses were acceptable. In order to defend himself and his town of Ondara against the royal prosecutor, Don Joan de Cardona produced a long list of Muslim and Christian witnesses who were to be duly interrogated.[106]

Another potential source of problems in cases between Muslims and Christians was the question of by which law, Christian or Islamic, a Christian judge should sentence a guilty Muslim. Jaime II quashed any possible Christian complaints that convicted Muslims were being punished too leniently when sentenced according to the Shariah by ruling that, for any crimes committed by Muslims against Christians, the Muslims were to be sentenced by the law that demanded the heaviest penalty.[107] This was to the manifest disadvantage of the Mudejars. However, it seems that during Fernando's reign all Muslims culpable for crimes against Christians were penalized in accordance with the *Furs*.[108]

Occasionally Muslims were pardoned for their crimes, although this was by no means a frequent occurrence.[109] Far more usual was the Crown's granting of safe-conducts (*guiatges*) against prosecution and arrest to accused or convicted Muslims. The king or the bailiff general determined the length of time during which such safe-conducts were valid. The safe-conducts protected Muslim debtors who needed more time to settle accounts with their creditors. Procedure against Muslims for more serious crimes, such as theft or homicide, was likewise halted until they could gather the funds necessary for the payment of fines and settlements.[110] Also, the courts sometimes released Muslims on bail. Those who posted bail were called *caplleuators*. Both Muslims and Christians acted as *caplleuators* for Muslim defendants. It was understood that the Muslim would return to court for trial when the presiding magistrate requested. Failure to appear resulted in execution against the property of the *caplleuators*, who were held responsible for the defendant's absence.[111]

Royal authorities sometimes employed torture as a means of extracting confessions from Muslim criminals. Although Muslims were theoretically exempt from torture in the kingdom of Aragon, such was not the case in Valencia.[112] Still, the courts resorted to torture only rarely, and almost always in cases of crimes against the state. An *amīn* of Alcudia

was tortured for having counterfeited money.[113] Other Mudejars implicated in the crimes of Maghriban Muslims suffered the same fate.[114] The
bailiff general's court tortured a Tunisian Muslim accused of abetting
runaway slaves, but he nevertheless remained close-mouthed.[115] However, the mere threat of torture was sufficient to make Ubaydal Allepus
of Bétera confess to the murder of another Muslim.[116]

In general, Muslims received equitable treatment in the Christian
courts. The king and the bailiff general sought to promote fairness in the
kingdom's judicial system by correcting the blatant favoritism of magistrates either through replacing them or through balancing their partial-
ity with the opinions of disinterested doctors of law. Also, attempts
were made to neutralize the influence of powerful persons on local
judges. Owing to the system of appeals, both Muslims and Christians
could have their cases reconsidered by superior judges. If this sometimes lengthened the judicial process excessively, it nevertheless
guaranteed that in most cases justice was fairly administered.

Muslims relied on the solicitude of the Crown to prevent injustice.
When Abrahim Alaxera was involved in a property dispute with the
knight Perot Sanç he turned to the viceroy, "inasmuch as the said mos-
sen Perot Sanç is a knight and principal person in that city [Játiva] and
the said Moor [Abrahim] is a simple and defenseless person." At Abrahim's request, a doctor of law from Valencia was added to the case to
counterbalance Sanç's influence.[117] In a similar instance, the viceroy
ordered another knight of Játiva to appear before the royal audience, so
that his suit with a Muslim woman might be decided justly. The knight
had employed threats to hinder the woman's procurator from defending
her, and had thereby obtained from the justice of Játiva two judgments
in his own favor.[118]

The litigants' expectation that the courts would render judgment im-
partially, and that the Crown would do its best to ensure that this was
so, inspired them to scrutinize closely the motives of the presiding
judges and jurists. Consequently, Muslims and Christians often based
their appeals to higher courts on the allegation that such and such local
magistrate or jurist was "suspect," that is, that he favored the opposing
party. Mudejars resorted to this legal ploy many times, but, one sus-
pects, not always with complete sincerity. The king and bailiff general
usually obliged them by removing the "suspect" magistrate from the
case. When the king appointed Pere Prats of Orihuela to hear a canon's
appeal of a sentence passed against him and in favor of his converted
slave, Carmesina ("de genere sarracenorum"), the latter impugned the
honesty of Prats, arguing that he was a relative of the canon. Prats was
replaced forthwith.[119]

The Crown's willingness to respond to such allegations and to satisfy the aggrieved parties could lead to the removal of numerous judges and lawyers before justice was finally administered. After Fernando responded to the appeal of a noblewoman, who maintained that the bailiff general's assessor was "suspect," by replacing the assessor with two doctors of law, the opposing party, a Muslim of Murviedro, countered by claiming that the two lawyers were biased. The king was forced to find two more lawyers.[120] Still more confusing was the litigation between Dona Lorença de Loriz and certain Muslims of Gandía concerning pensions allegedly owed by the latter. After numerous appeals and before a panel of three jurists was finally appointed to render a conclusive judgment on the case, the Muslims had challenged the impartiality of two jurists—one of them the governor's assessor, who, they argued, did not like to revoke judgments he had already pronounced—and Dona Lorença, that of three others.[121]

After two centuries of being increasingly drawn into the sphere of the Christian legal system, the Mudejars had acquired an essential understanding of how it functioned. They knew what limitations there were on the powers of magistrates, what kind of evidence was decisive for the conclusion of a case, and what channels they had to go through to have their appeals heard by superior courts. Thus, some Muslims of Bechí made an appeal to the bailiff general, maintaining that they had been denounced before the bailiff of Villarreal without legitimate evidence and then needlessly harassed and molested by the same bailiff. The king supported the Muslims, voiding the bailiff of Villarreal's initiatives and ordering the bailiff general to rule on the case.[122] Abdalla Xax of Castellnou, involved in a litigation with a creditor, a merchant of Valencia, displayed an ability to operate effectively in the Christian courts. He successfully demanded that the merchant's account books be examined as evidence by the court. He also managed to have the justice of Segorbe intervene in the case, although the justice was later removed because, as was alleged, he showed Abdalla excessive favor.[123]

The Mudejars utilized their grasp of the complexities of the legal system not only to defend themselves against the malfeasance of the Christian judiciary but also, through cunning and deceptive legal maneuvers, to evade the magistrates' issuance and execution of sentences against them. In particular, they turned to their own advantage the officials' propensity to trespass on the jurisdictions of others and the slowness, or sometimes lack, of communication between the different levels of the kingdom's judicial hierarchy. This is evinced in the case of Ali Gombau. Ali, a vassal of Joan de Vallterra and tax farmer for his lord in Areñol, had been judicially condemned by his lord for the debts he owed him. Ali then fled from Areñol to the court of the viceroy, who had never heard Vallterra's side of the story. Ali claimed that he was a royal vassal and prompted the viceroy to proceed against other vassals of Areñol for the rents purportedly owed to him. By means of such chicanery Ali was able for a time to take the legal offensive against Vallterra.[124]

Other Muslims took advantage of the bailiff general's willingness to hear their appeals in order to escape the punishment of local bailiffs. Through the telling of half-truths, such as the claim that their safe-conducts had been violated, they managed to convince the bailiff general to stay the execution of local bailiffs against them.[125] Some Muslims actually procured safe-conducts from unwitting or pliant officials in order to delay procedure indefinitely.[126]

Even the king, having no previous knowledge of a case, could be duped. A Muslim adulteress of Gilet, who had already been sentenced and enslaved by her lord, was able, by concealing the facts of the case, to move the king to appoint the bailiff of Murviedro to consider her appeal. However, when the king learned of the truth of the matter, he revoked the bailiff's commission.[127]

The Mudejars can hardly be blamed for availing themselves of every possible legal protection, even if at times dishonestly. The protection afforded the Muslims by the king and the nobility, usually self-interested, did not deter townsmen and barons from committing crimes against them. The law was the Mudejars' refuge, a flimsy but sometimes effective barrier of defense necessary for a minority in so many ways at the mercy of the whims of the majority.

The king and his watchdog, the bailiff general, were anxious to guarantee the Mudejars the security of a fair hearing in the kingdom's courts. They were willing to hear almost any Mudejar appeal and were quick to reprimand any magistrate who strayed from the proper judicial procedures. The problem here, as in other cases of abuse of Muslims, was that reprimands and corrections were not followed by penalization of the offending official. For instance, Joan de Vich, an official of the lord of Albalat, hanged a Muslim for certain crimes, even though he had received an order from the governor forbidding such action. Vich, at first sentenced to death in absentia, was later pardoned by the king.[128] At most, unscrupulous officials were commanded to release the Muslim in question to a superior court and to appear themselves to explain their actions. The lieutenant governor south of the Júcar River was summoned before the viceroy to explain why he had harassed Abrahim Menne and denied to him the right of appeal.[129] The bailiff general issued similar subpoenas to the officials of Valldigna, who had imprisoned and tortured a Muslim of Simat without having passed a legitimate judgment against him,[130] and who later illicitly imprisoned a royal vassal for not having paid the tax on wheat to the abbot.[131]

Still, even though the offending officials were not punished, the Muslims eventually received a fair hearing in court. Moreover, such occurrences were far more the exception than the rule. It must be stressed that, in general, the Muslims were not at a disadvantage in the Christian courts. In the cases between Muslims and Christians for which we know the results (see table 18) it appears that on the whole the Muslims might have fared better than their Christian opponents. Although almost all of these decisions were mentioned by the scribes only because they were in the process of being appealed, the initial decisions of the judges nevertheless provide us with a useful and roughly accurate picture of how the Mudejars fared in the Christian legal system. Of the forty-two cases considered, twenty-three, or 54 percent, were initially decided in favor of the Muslim party. This rough parity of Muslims before the law explains why they were not greatly troubled by the prospect of appearing in Christian courts. The gradual erosion of the Mudejars' judicial autonomy was a largely painless process resulting from the diminution of their demographic weight in Valencia and from their increasing integration, although not assimilation, into the society and economy of the kingdom. It correlated with an acculturative process through which the Mudejars acquired the practical know-how essential for holding their own in the Christian courts while, at the same time, retaining for their own Shariah courts the administration of justice in those matters most meaningful for their religious identity.

Muslim–Christian Litigation: A View of Valencian Society

The interpretation of a given litigation, or a number of them, poses problems for the historian. Because lawsuits and complaints comprised a large part of the affairs handled by the Crown authorities, the less contentious and routine occurrences of daily life have been lost from view. It is all too easy for historians to amplify the significance of the evidence at their disposal, to find in a series of commercial lawsuits a widespread economic problem, or to see in a homicide the eruption of class and ethnic violence. Some litigations, like many of those associated with commerce and property, were random events arising haphazardly from the daily social and economic interchange of a society. They had no repercussions beyond the lives of the individuals whom they immediately concerned and no connection with others of their kind. Other judicial disputes, while not of great import as isolated events, when linked to others of their type formed a larger pattern. In the aggregate they could affect a large part of society and were expressions or harbingers of serious tensions. Here we will briefly discuss the various types of litigation between Muslims and Christians as a means of providing a view of some facets of Christian–Muslim relations in Valencia. Care will be taken to distinguish between the litigation as a random event and the litigation as part of a larger social problem.

Quite a few cases involved Christian lords and Muslim vassals as allies. This can be accounted for by the symbiotic relationship between lords and vassals, and their mutual concern for seigneurial properties and finances. Lords sometimes took a special interest in the lawsuits of their Muslim vassals. When the governor passed sentence against a Muslim vassal of the Duke of Segorbe in her litigation with a Christian, the Duke "on account of his certain interest felt vexed and prejudiced," and therefore appealed to the king.[132] Lords and vassals also appeared in court as coplaintiffs or codefendants in disputes with adjacent seigneuries over irrigation, livestock, and boundaries. The resultant armed clashes might lead to arraignment for more serious charges. The noble Luis Ladro and "some *almugavers* and some Sarracens" were denounced before the royal audience for having set fire to Relleu.[133]

Seigneurs and their aljamas most often banded together against their creditors, the *censalistas*, who sued in court for the payment of the pensions owed them. As the financial situation of many seigneuries worsened, the lords and aljamas became more evasive and their creditors, many of them urban folk, ever more insistent. The debtor–creditor relationship between the landed nobility and the town citizens contributed to the tension between the two social groups. This tension expressed itself in other court battles concerning the right of municipal governments to collect taxes from the vassals of neighboring seigneuries or to penalize lords and vassals for improper use of the irrigation systems.[134] Cases such as these, by themselves not of great moment, cumulatively provided some of the tinder for the conflagration of the revolt of the *Germanías*.

Yet, the symbiosis between lords and Muslim vassals was a delicate one, easily upset when their interests diverged. Most suits pitting lord against vassal arose from any action on the part of the vassal that threatened to diminish the revenues received by the lord. The bailiff of Játiva ruled on a case in which the lord of Genovés disputed the right of a female vassal to marry another Muslim, probably from another seigneury.[135] That the lord feared his vassal's change of residence and the consequent loss of seigneurial dues is suggested by another case in which the lord of Argelita resisted the attempt of a Muslim of Triega to sell the property owned by his wife in Argelita.[136] Apparently lords preferred that their female vassals marry local boys. The lord's fiscal concerns led to the leveling of charges at those vassals who defaulted on their rent payments, especially those who abandoned the seigneury without settling accounts. For instance, the lord of Alberique sought from the king the prosecution of his former *amīn* who was still indebted to him for the purchase of some wheat.[137] The tendency of insolvent vassals to seek refuge in other seigneuries, the lords of which were often happy to receive them, complicated matters further. Thus, Joan Miralles, lord of Beniala, asked the viceroy to proceed against his debtor vassals whom the lord Ramon Pujades was protecting.[138] Already familiar to us is the large body of litigation between seigneurs and their former vassals residing either in royal *morerías* or on the lands of other lords. Most of this litigation concerned the lords' resistance to the efforts of their erstwhile vassals to cultivate and collect the harvest from the lands they continued to rent on their seigneuries.[139]

While the lawsuits that aligned lords and vassals against creditors, townsmen, and other seigneuries attest to grave tensions straining the kingdom's socioeconomic structure, those between individual Muslims and Christians arising from commercial transactions reflect another reality equally important, but far less dire. Such cases, usually involving the claims of unpaid vendors against indebted buyers, reveal some of the few difficulties encountered by Muslims and Christians in the wide-ranging trade between them in land, livestock, agricultural produce, and a variety of manufactured goods. There is nothing in this type of litigation indicating widespread Muslim–Christian animosity on the basis of economic competition. Commercial claims were not made by or against Muslims on religious grounds; they were not a divisive force in Valencian society. Rather, they are fragmentary evidence of the regular economic interaction between Muslims and Christians, which, because it was normally unencumbered by legal problems, never aroused the interest of the royal bureaucracy.[140]

A consideration of the crimes that Muslims committed against Christians does not reveal a special pattern of Mudejar criminal activity. Muslims were accused of theft, vandalism, gambling, defrauding the lessee of the royal saltworks, tax evasion, and the possession of false money.[141] However, Mudejars were by no means notorious for such crimes, for Christians committed them as well. Nor is there an easily perceptible link between Mudejar criminality and their relatively oppressed status. The victims of Mudejar crimes seem to have been more often Muslims than Christians. Mudejar actions to correct perceived injustices were directed against their official and seigneurial oppressors and not against the Christian populace as a whole. Any causal relationship that might have existed between poverty—a social ill which did not especially afflict the Mudejars as a group—and crime, particularly theft, would have applied as much to Christians as to Muslims.

Turning to cases of homicide and assault involving Muslims and Christians, these do not point toward any dramatic trends in social violence. It is important to distinguish between the random violence occurring for any number of reasons in the context of distinct personal relationships and the systematic violence of the mob directed against a specific social group. Regarding the latter type, although it had occurred as recently as 1455, in the form of the attack on Valencia's *morería*, and would occur again in 1521, when the *Germanías* murdered or forcibly baptized thousands of Mudejars, it did not happen during the reign of Fernando.

Random violence, however, was not unknown. Yet, lest one think that Mudejars were always the victims of Christian hoodlums, it is worth noting that there were eight cases in which Muslims were the perpetrators of assault and homicide. In four of these cases the violence seems to have arisen from personal disputes. For instance, Hubaydal Baçanet wounded Luys Lançol in the face and hand.[142] In Játiva Coayat Çarahi, a *juglar*, and some Muslim companions threw Rodrigo Castanyeda into an irrigation ditch and tried to injure him further.[143] At times individual Muslims reacted violently to official pressure. This seems to have been the case with Azen Satmer, who struck the justice of Manises in the face.[144] In three cases Mudejar violence was linked to the conflict between seigneuries, or between seigneuries and towns. As part of the recurrent troubles between the lordship of Gilet and the town of Murviedro, Ali Ubequer of Gilet and Domingo de la Lança of Murviedro had a brawl during which the latter was wounded.[145] One case of feuding between seigneuries saw unidentified Muslims raid the home of the lord of Náquera and mortally wound one of his vassals.[146] Some of the less sanguinary crimes of Mudejar vassals also fit into the broader picture of seigneurial feuding. For example, a Muslim of Cox was accused of breaking into the home of the lord of Albatera. Characteristically, his lord refused to cooperate in the judicial procedure against him.[147] The lord of Dos Aguas brought charges against Muslim vassals of Resalany and the Vall de Tous for having descended upon his lands and released Muslim prisoners from his jail.[148]

The murder of Muslims by Christians conforms to the picture already sketched of powerful Christians, mostly knights and noblemen, abusing the vassals of their rivals as a means of indirectly injuring them. A Mudejar woman complained to the king that the noble Pere de Montagut and his squires had killed her son.[149] Two Muslims of Játiva also turned to Fernando when a local lord imprisoned a fellow Muslim, as a result of which the latter died, apparently of epilepsy.[150] Although in both cases the king ordered the initiation of legal procedure, it is unlikely that the murderers, in these cases or others, were ever punished. A constable was fined for the murder of a Muslim slave, but only so that the slave's master could be reimbursed for his lost property.[151] Reprehensible as such violence was, it is nevertheless significant that its perpetrators were largely restricted to the ranks of unscrupulous nobles and officials, men who acted for calculated political and economic motives. Violence against Muslims was not for the most part inspired by religious fanaticism, and the large majority of the Christian populace did not engage in it. In fact, Muslims sometimes joined Christians, their fellow vassals, in attacking Muslims of rival seigneuries.[152] Moreover, Christian violence against Muslims was greatly exceeded in terms of both ferocity and frequency by that between Mudejars. To explain all Christian violence against Muslims as a manifestation of religious animosity is too simplistic. True, Christians displayed greater temerity in their acts against Mudejars because the latter were Muslims; nevertheless, their actions had a firm political and economic foundation related to the complex tensions and rivalries in Valencian society. And, as we have seen, the Mudejars were not always ones to take such abuse lying down.

Legal Oppression

A perusal of the judicial disputes between Muslims and Christians does not disclose the infliction of gross injustices on the Mudejars by the kingdom's courts. On the contrary, such litigation shows that the laws of the kingdom were for the Mudejars more often a source of protection against Christian aggressors than an oppressive burden. To discover the true legal oppression of the Mudejars, one must look beyond their lawsuits with Christians to the cases in which they were penalized for the violation of laws that applied almost exclusively to them. Mudejars were arraigned, tried, and harshly punished for acts that the authorities viewed as crimes only because they had been committed by Muslims, believers of an "inferior" religion that also constituted a political threat. The same body of laws that often protected the Mudejars from the aggression and abuse of Christians also brought home to them with brutal clarity their socioreligious inferiority and political subjection in a Christian kingdom.

One area in which the laws of the kingdom weighed heavily against the Mudejars was that of sexual relations between Muslims and Christians. Boswell has convincingly described how these laws established a sexual and religious double standard that facilitated the sexual exploitation of Muslim women by Christian men.[153] Still, it is a point worth belaboring, especially since the situation in some respects seems to have deteriorated by the late fifteenth century.

The *Furs* provided that in the case of a Muslim man sleeping with a Christian woman, both parties were to be burned alive. In the case of a Christian man sleeping with a Muslim woman, however, the man received no punishment whatsoever, while the woman was punished according to Islamic law for fornication or adultery (unless she was a licensed prostitute), which meant either flogging or death by stoning.[154] The Islamic penalties were invariably commuted to enslavement. Thus, as Boswell concludes, "those members of the society with no power, i.e., Muslims and women, were penalized for unions which were permissible for members with power, i.e., Christian men."[155]

The severity of the prescribed penalties did not deter Muslims and Christians from such liaisons. The abundance of Christian and Muslim prostitutes in the kingdom made deterrence extremely difficult. In fact, in the large majority of illicit unions between Muslim men and Christian women the women were prostitutes. The law, however, made no distinctions with respect to the status and profession of the Christian woman, so that Muslims were punished for sexual relations with Christian prostitutes as well as with Christian wives and daughters. In one case Muslims were actually sentenced to be burned alive for having availed themselves of the services of a Christian prostitute, although probably because some coercion was involved.[156] Still, in most cases the criminal proceedings against Muslim males for sexual crimes did not result in a death sentence. Neither the king nor the nobility could afford to lose the services of Muslim vassals in this way. Thus, some guilty Muslims were heavily fined. Abrahim Murçi was fined 400s for having merely solicited a Christian woman (prostitute?),[157] while Azmet Mufferix paid the hefty fine of 1,000s for having slept with a prostitute.[158] Those who lacked the resources to pay such fines were probably enslaved. In this way the lord still retained the services of his vassal, or at least cashed in on the sale of the slave.

It is difficult to know whether or not Christian women were punished for these liaisons. It seems that legal procedure was initiated against Catherine, the wife of Christofol Pujol, for her affair with Ayet Capo.[159]

There were very few instances of sexual relations between Christian men and Muslim women who were not prostitutes or slaves. Cases like that of the Muslim girl of Liria who ran off with her Christian lover, Jaume Ricarder, converted to Christianity, and set up house with him, were a rarity (the girl's father accused Ricarder of abducting his daughter).[160] The jealousy with which Mudejar fathers guarded the chastity of their daughters—against other Muslims, and certainly all the more against Christians—precluded such liaisons.

The sexual exploitation of Muslim women is most evident in the authorities' promotion of Muslim prostitution, which went hand in hand with the flagrant interference of Christians in the private lives of Muslims. The motives of all Christians involved—king, lords, and owners of female Muslim slaves—were blatantly economic. The Crown's legal stance on the question of Muslim prostitution set the tone for all related abuses: Muslim women could practice prostitution only with a license purchased from the Crown; all unlicensed prostitutes were to be penalized with enslavement to the Crown. On a number of occasions the bailiff general dispatched deputies to arrest all unlicensed prostitutes, who, the bailiff noted, were plying their trade "in great damage and detriment of the rights and revenues of the. . . lord king."[161] Once arrested, these women were sold into slavery for the profit of the Crown. Their new masters often put them out as prostitutes and retained the earnings of the women for themselves, despite the laws prohibiting such practices.[162] Thus, these enslaved prostitutes were forced to commit for another's profit the same acts for which they had originally incurred punishment.

Realizing that revenues were to be had from the promotion and regulation of Muslim prostitution, royal and seigneurial authorities sought new recruits from among the condemned in the Islamic courts. There the authorities commuted to slavery the Islamic penalties to which the qāḍī had sentenced Mudejar adulteresses. Many of these slaves were probably put to work in the royal brothels. If the aljamas did not object to Christian interference in this sensitive area, it was because the rigid sexual mores of the Mudejars relegated adulterers and fornicators to the status of social and family outcasts. The enslavement of these women to the Crown was, the Mudejars realized, by no means a merciful act, but a form of execution more gradual than stoning, albeit no less symbolic of their social death in the eyes of the Muslim community.

However, Christian interference in the Muslims' private lives became excessively predatory. Christians hovered about like vultures waiting to feed off the sexual transgressions and social miseries of Muslims. They acquired a knowledge of Mudejar laws and customs to suit their own purposes. This would explain the bizarre case in which Manuel Lançol, the lord of Gilet, accused a Muslim couple of Murviedro of living in sin, of not being legally married according to Islamic law. Although the qāḍī general found that Lançol's accusations were justified, this hardly excuses such prying into Mudejar family matters. What Lançol hoped to gain is unclear; perhaps he bore a grudge against the couple for having moved from Gilet to become royal vassals in Murviedro.[163] It is, in any case, difficult to imagine a disinterested Christian concern with Muslim morality.

By the latter half of Fernando's reign the bailiff general was going so far as to order his subordinates to seek out and apprehend Muslim men and women who had committed adultery. Significantly, this order was contained in the same letter that demanded the arrest of all unlicensed prostitutes.[164] Together, the two formed a cruel and relentless strategy in which the sexual exploitation of Mudejar women for the financial gain of the Christian authorities is patent: all Muslim adulteresses were to be arrested, punished, and reduced to enslaved prostitution; and all prostitutes were to be licensed, taxed, and regulated by the Crown. The case of Axa of Villamarchante, a widow and mother of three, attests graphically to this policy. While in Valencia, Axa met Çale Duraydach from the Vall de Uxó. He took her to a hostel and there they slept together. As they lay together, a royal constable burst into their room and demanded to know whether they had committed "adultery" (really fornication, since she was a widow). Axa confessed to her "crime" and so was brought before the tribunal of the bailiff general. The bailiff and the qāḍī general sentenced her to death by stoning, which sentence, of course, resulted in her enslavement to the Crown.[165] Of Axa we know no more, but an educated guess as to her fate could be posed. It is, in any case, clear that the basis for this systematic and humiliating exploitation of Muslim women was the law that allowed Christian men to enjoy the sexual favors of Muslim women with impunity. There stemmed from this law a growing assumption on the part of the governing classes of the kingdom that their political authority and professed religious superiority over the Mudejars gave them the moral authority to judge Muslim sexual misconduct by standards far more rigorous than those which they applied to members of their own faith. Ironically, this assumption was associated with their increasing understanding of the Mudejars themselves and of the rigidity of their sexual mores. Sadly, they could think only of exploiting that understanding for their own profit.

There also existed a body of laws that may be described as policing measures, laws facilitating the scrutiny of Mudejar activities and movements. The political and fiscal concerns of the king and the nobility led them to restrict the Mudejars' freedom of movement, because they were a dissident, but economically valuable, minority. It was thought that some Mudejars harbored political allegiance to Islamic states and perhaps wished to emigrate there. Thus, Mudejars needed royal licenses to travel to Granada or the Maghrib, or even to the southern part of the kingdom. Usually they were prohibited from emigrating to Islamic lands. Even wandering Muslim mendicants were required to have licenses to beg from their coreligionists. Those who were caught traveling or begging for alms without these licenses were punished, and usually harshly. Most unlicensed mendicants were enslaved to the Crown and then sold to the highest bidder.[166] The ease with which Mudejars could be enslaved for such infractions forcefully emphasized their subject status and the very real limitations on their freedom. The phenomenon of Muslim slavery itself resulted in a number of cases in which Muslims were accused of abetting runaway slaves.[167] The Mudejars' aid to runaway slaves is striking testimony to their acute awareness of just how precarious their position was; they were prepared for the eventuality of the loss of freedom.

In addition, there was the series of laws that required of the Mudejars obeisance to a faith so inimical to their own. Although it is unlikely that Muslims were actually forced to kneel in the street as Christian processions passed by, and although Muslims and Christians frequently associated and socialized in manners deemed inappropriate by the Crown and the Church, the very existence of such laws reminded the Mudejars of Christianity's present superiority over Islam. And, indeed, Muslims were fined for such indiscretions as swearing in the name of the Christian God.[168] Furthermore, as long as the laws were on the books, there always hung over the Mudejars' heads the possibility that these laws would all be enforced in their full rigor. This is exactly what the Inquisitors and their backers desired.

Even if some Mudejars prospered in Valencia and had no intention of leaving, the knowledge that they could not depart if they so wished, that their movements were restricted and subject to the scrutiny of royal officials, that they were, in effect, prisoners in their own land, all this must have constituted a form of psychological oppression and alienation just as painful as more blatant forms of physical abuse. The law for the Mudejars was, like so many other aspects of their existence, a double-edged sword, both protective and oppressive; it afforded them justice within the framework of a politicoreligious system which was in a number of ways essentially unjust.

6 Conflict and Solidarity in Mudejar Society

The activity of the industrious Mudejar at practically all levels of the economy, and the quotidian mingling of Muslim and Christian in field, workshop, and marketplace provided the foundation of—and the most effective adhesive reinforcing—the structure of Valencia's plural society. A common preoccupation with cultivation and harvest, manufacture and profit fostered among Muslims and Christians a certain homogeneity in outlook and understanding and opened the door to more meaningful social interaction, however hesitant and limited. It is, nevertheless, clear that Valencia's plural social structure was imperfectly articulated and fragile, and that the cement of economic relations was ultimately an unequal match to the solvent of overt religious antagonism. Thus, in 1502 when the Mudejars were faced with the threat of forced conversion in Valencia, many chose flight to the Maghrib with its detrimental material consequences, and a century later, after the abject failure of a policy meant to persuade the Moriscos to become true Christians, the Crown decided that the economic repercussions of the Moriscos' expulsion could be more easily endured than the risks of Morisco dissidence.[1] Both episodes are indicative of the tenacious adherence of Valencia's Muslims to Islam, and this adherence reflects a religious and social reality far more compelling than the material life they shared with Christians. The aim of this chapter will be to provide some understanding of that reality and to explain how the Mudejars maintained both their identity as Muslims and a group cohesiveness while living in a Christian world. It will be suggested that Mudejar self-perception and group-perception were founded not only on religious belief per se, but also on the perpetuation of a social world the organization and mores of which were distinct from those of Valencian Christians. Indeed, it is perhaps more accurate to view the Mudejars as forming a distinct subsociety separated from the larger Christian society by patterns of intragroup social and cultural behavior, but intersecting with that Christian society in a number of ways not without telling acculturative impact.

The Acculturative Challenge

However durable Mudejar society might have been, it had nevertheless experienced considerable acculturative change. Prior to analyzing late-fifteenth-century Mudejar society, it will be useful to outline briefly some of the more significant of these changes, brought about both subtly by the Muslims' informal interaction with the Christian populace, and forcefully by the formal imposition of Christian authority on an Islamic society.

Valencia's Muslims underwent their most radical cultural adjustment in the half-century immediately following the Christian conquest. During that time the Islamic society was essentially decapitated, losing its political and cultural elites to emigration and in failed rebellions. Islamic government and the public application of the Shariah were rudely shunted aside by a Christian colonial administration with its own body of law, the *Furs*.[2] Even the autonomous and corporate aljama, vouchsafed to the Muslims by their Christian overlord, had no Islamic antecedent, compelling the Muslim *adelantats* to administer their communities in a foreign manner analogous to that of the Christian jurates in their corporate *universitas*.[3] As has been indicated, the Christian bureaucracy, particularly when functioning as a tax-collecting mechanism, intruded on most areas of Mudejar life, so that in even so intimate a family affair as inheritance strict observance of the Shariah had to be modified in compliance with the king's demands. Furthermore, the Muslim by necessity had to learn to function in a Christian as well as Islamic legal system. Although this was to be expected for cases involving both Christian and Muslim parties, the fact that some Muslim litigants pursued civil suits with coreligionists in Christian courts is indicative of an acculturative process potentially damaging to the internal harmony of Mudejar communities.

Also important were the more gradual processes of Christian urbanization and seigneurialization, which, coupled with the decreasing size of the Muslim population (from an overwhelming majority in the thirteenth century to 30 percent of the kingdom's total by the midfifteenth century), altered the very appearance of the kingdom, as churches replaced mosques and Muslims retreated from the urban centers to the countryside. Although the rhythms of agricultural and pastoral life remained largely unchanged, Christian control of the economy, especially of the larger domestic and international markets, meant that Muslim farmers, artisans, and retail merchants were dependent on Christians for marketing their produce, selling their manufactured goods, and purchasing raw materials and bulk goods. Mudejar dependence was further manifested in their vassalage to Christian lords and their loss of ultimate control over their land.[4] Outside of the walls of his own home or mosque, the Mudejar could hardly avoid coming to grips with the Christian presence, and having to do so on Christian terms.

The greatest threat to the integrity of the Mudejars' Islamic culture and Muslim identity lay in the cities and towns, where the populations were overwhelmingly Christian. There the expressions of Christian religiosity were most pervasive and most aggressive, while conversely the public observance of Islam was all the more restricted. The best example of this tendency is the anti-Muslim and anti-Jewish preaching of the Inquisitors from the pulpits of Valencia and Cartagena. Another urban danger, particularly in the capital, was the volatility of the Christian mob. Although the evocation of despair fed on fear might have been an efficacious proselytizing tool with some Muslims, it is arguable that the demagoguery of Inquisitors and like-minded clerics and Christian mob violence would have been more likely to repel Muslims from Christianity and to inspire among them a reactionary zeal in their commitment to Islam.[5] The cities posed another threat perhaps more serious than Christian aggression, namely, the possibility of friendly and leisurely contact with Christians and their religion. Adherents of both faiths congregated in city taverns and fonduks, passing their leisure time gambling together, drinking together, and sleeping together.[6] For the Muslim such activities meant a violation of the precepts of his own faith, and signaled his entry into a gray area of cultural amorphousness, where, if his Muslim identity was not overtly challenged, there nevertheless resulted a weakening of his own sense of distinctiveness. That Mudejars flocked to Valencia to enjoy with their Christian friends the spectacle of the Corpus Christi Day processions has a similar significance:[7] it does not mean that these Muslims were on the road to baptism; rather, it indicates that they had acquired non-Islamic cultural accoutrements and forms of behavior born of a long-term exposure to Christian society.

A useful index of acculturation is the extent of Mudejar bilingualism. Burns, in unison with Fuster and Barceló Torres, concludes that in the thirteenth century the Muslim masses were unilingual Arabic-speakers.[8] For midfourteenth-century Valencia Boswell points to only a minimal change in this pattern: "the vast majority of the Mudéjares did not speak the language of the dominant culture." This was in contrast to the kingdom of Aragon, where the Mudejars spoke Romance but had for the most part lost the ability to function in Arabic.[9] It is thought that throughout the fifteenth and sixteenth centuries this state of affairs remained more or less unchanged. In support of this view historians note the Moriscos' obdurate use of Arabic as their language of daily parlance and the systematic effort of the Christian authorities (from 1565) to discourage the teaching and use of Arabic. Of particular significance is the agreement reached between the Moriscos and Carlos I in 1526, in which the Moriscos maintained that "the greater part of the Moorish men and almost all of the women do not know how to speak *aljamia* (Romance)." Moreover, the Moriscos stated that they would need forty years in which to learn Romance (Carlos I allowed them only ten).[10] The evidence is impressive, and that both the Mudejars and the Moriscos spoke and read Arabic seems indisputable (see below); however, their avowed unilingualism is open to debate. I would argue for a more extensive Mudejar bilingualism, although with Romance spoken with an imperfect accent and syntax. Given the Moriscos' insincere conversion and their anxiety to forestall thorough catechization in the Catholic faith and Inquisitorial inquiries, their presentation of their linguistic status in the negotiations with Carlos I might have been somewhat disingenuous, a device meant to discourage zealous Romance-speaking clergymen. Clearly, in asking for a forty-year period of grace the Moriscos were playing for time. In the years between 1526 and 1609 there very well might have ensued a decreasing bilingualism. As the Moriscos further withdrew from the cities, their contact with the Christian world would have decreased, while, in a reactionary manner, their desire to avoid Christian culture and to cultivate their own cultural distinctiveness—in effect, to freeze the acculturative process—would have intensified. Just as the Christian authorities realized that the Arabic language had to be removed as an impediment to the effective "Christianization" of the Moriscos,[11] it is equally possible the Moriscos understood that by inculcating their children in the Arabic language, the sacred language of the Qur'ān, and by forbidding them any education in Romance they were strengthening their fidelity to Islam. In sum, the Moriscos' linguistic status is not necessarily an accurate indicator of that of their Mudejar predecessors.

The records of cases tried in the court of the bailiff general, in which Muslims appear as litigants and witnesses, are suggestive of a significant Mudejar bilingualism. Normally, if a Muslim witness was in need of an interpreter, a role usually fulfilled by the royal *qāḍī*, the latter's participation in the case was explicitly indicated. For instance, Nuzeya, a Muslim prostitute from Oliva, confessed with "Ali Bellvis, *qāḍī*, intervening."[12] More explicitly, one defendant, Ubaydal Allepus of Bétera, is described as *"mal algemiat* (i.e., he speaks Romance poorly) . . . he does not understand algemia," but his interpreter, the *amīn* Açen Amet, was a "Moor *molt algemiat* and a person who understands *la algemia* very well."[13] Yet it is striking that the large majority of the Mudejars appearing in these trial records did not require an interpreter. While it is not surprising that the Muslims of urban *morerías* spoke Romance, given their constant mixing with the Christian populace, or that the *amīn* of a rural aljama had mastered enough Romance to act as intermediary between the aljama and its lord, it is impressive that many Mudejars from rural areas could testify in Romance. Some examples are Açen Muça of Serra,[14] Homar b. Perellos of Benaguacil,[15] Ubaydal Suleymen of Mirambell,[16] Maymo ben Çabit of Manises,[17] and Abdulcarim of Oliva,[18] among others. Equally significant are the testimonies of Christians about their seemingly routine verbal exchanges with Muslims. Ursula, the daughter of the innkeeper Joan Jeroni, testified how Alasdrach and Abdalla Sinube of Buñol, and Ali Alcayet of Chiva, "were speaking Arabic (*alguaravia*) with the said captive Moor," whom they had allegedly helped to escape, and how later, after returning from a meeting with the lord of Carlet, "they requested [from her] a good room for sleeping."[19] Miguel de la Serra, a tailor of Valencia, remembered that on Corpus Christi Day Muslim youths from Chiva had come to his house, eaten there, and then invited him and others to accompany them to the festivities.[20] The odyssey of Angela de Vanya, a prostitute from Cuenca plying her trade in Onda, is revealing. She was first approached by Hadal, a Muslim from Benigazlo (Vall de Uxó), but did not know he was a Muslim, because he spoke "in the Valencian tongue and very suavely and not showing any sign of knowing the Moorish tongue." Hadal compelled Angela to go with him to Tales, a Muslim village (*loch de moros*), and brought her to the house of Mahomat Cotalla. There, as the frightened Angela sat weeping in the Cotallas' kitchen, Mahomat and his wife assured her that she would not be harmed.[21] Although these trial records afford only a glimpse at a small cross section of Mudejar life, they do show an erosion of linguistic barriers since the fourteenth century. The increasing size of the Christian population and the variety and frequency of its economic dealings with the Mudejars must have necessitated the latter's acquisition of at least enough Romance to carry on day-to-day affairs. It is unrealistic to assume that Muslim and Christian artisans, farmers, and merchants all had interpreters at their disposal for conducting their mundane but essential business. The documentation does not indicate that this was so. If the Mudejars assiduously cultivated an Arabic culture, there is still no reason to assume that at this point in time, before the mass conversions, they had any reason for a self-conscious refusal to communicate in Romance. Demography and economy advised otherwise, and linguistic adaptation proceeded apace.

It should not be thought that such acculturation of the Mudejars to Romance-Christian culture as did take place was necessarily a negative or a degenerative process, or a process the flow of which was only unidirectional,[22] although it is likely that the recessive but resilient culture of the Mudejar minority had experienced greater modification from its continual contact with a dynamic and expanding Christian majority. Rather, such acculturation was inevitable, an evolutionary process of adaptation necessary for the social and economic viability of a society that juxtaposed the proponents of mutually hostile ideologies. Even if the behavior of some Mudejars seemed almost to flout Islamic convention, this did not signal a reorientation of their fundamental religious beliefs. (If anything, it attests to a kind of secularization, in which beliefs were not so much altered as ignored.) In a medieval plural society, where identity was finally defined by religious affiliation, cultural erosion and unorthodox conduct were not evidence of Mudejar assimilation into Christian society. Such assimilation—the lessening of social distance, as opposed to acculturation, the lessening of cultural distance[23]—could be achieved only through religious conversion, that is, through a fundamental change of identity. Therefore, in order to grasp the degree to which Mudejar society was truly threatened by absorption into the Christian body, one must broach the question of the extent of Mudejar conversion to Christianity.

Unlike the thirteenth century, with its mendicant preachers, schools of Arabic, and refined techniques of polemic, the result of which had been the conversion of a considerable number of Muslims,[24] the Valencia of the Catholic Monarchs saw no organized ecclesiastical campaign of proselytizing. After recovering from the trauma of the conquest, a factor that probably accounted for much of the Dominicans' early success, the Mudejars had regrouped, and so effectively that the Valencian Church seems to have made little or no further headway in the fourteenth century. This caused the Dominican preacher Vicent Ferrer to lament the inactivity of the clergy in missionary work (1413).[25] The stimulus of Ferrer's zeal led to the establishment of an Arabic school in Valencia during the reign of Alfonso V (ca. 1424), but it seems to have quickly faded into oblivion.[26] As we have seen in chapters 1 and 2, although King Fernando cautiously welcomed the baptism of individual Mudejars, he did not promote conversion on a mass scale. The lords of the kingdom, both ecclesiastical and secular, staunchly opposed any attempts to proselytize their vassals, since they could not wring as much rent out of Christian vassals.[27]

There were compelling social reasons for not converting. The convert, it seems, entered a sort of "no-man's land," being a full member of neither Christian nor Muslim society. If anything, owing to the strong ties of blood uniting Mudejar families (see below), converts tended to associate more with their Muslim relatives than with Christians. The convert Miguel Crestia was implicated along with his Muslim brother Ubaydal Allepus in the murder of another Muslim.[28] A *tornadizo* of Cocentaina came to the aid of a Muslim relative, a runaway slave from Córdoba.[29] Of course, Mudejars did not regard the conversion of their fellows favorably. Thus, the Inquisition arrested two Muslims who boldly and vociferously attempted to dissuade some Muslims from receiving baptism.[30] Moreover, the convert put in jeopardy whatever inheritances he hoped to receive from Muslim relations. However, it seems that the Crown was no longer confiscating the estates of deceased converts, as had once been the case. Therefore, the potential convert was not burdened by the fear of depriving his descendants of their inheritances.[31]

Even so, Christian society did not welcome the convert with open arms. In previous centuries Christians had insulted converts by calling them "dogs," "renegades," and the like.[32] Given the lukewarm reception of the judeo-conversos by Old Christians and the beginning of an obsession with the purity of Christian blood, it is highly unlikely that the situation would have improved. The murder of Mudejar converts by Old Christians supports this supposition.[33]

Nevertheless, a small number of Muslims chose to convert. The large majority of the proselytes were slaves who had the most to gain from conversion. Slaves with Jewish or Muslim masters had to be manumitted after their baptism, for infidels could not own Christian slaves. One Muslim woman preferred conversion to four years of servitude to a Jew.[34] For slaves with Christian masters, the situation was less clear-cut. The law provided that the slave should be freed only if he converted with the consent of his master. Therefore, the decision to manumit the baptized slave was solely the master's. Some masters granted their Christian slaves freedom, but most did not. Business sense usually prevailed over religious scruples.[35] Runaway slaves sometimes converted so as to conceal their fugitive status. When the Muslim slave Fatima fled from Valencia into Aragon, she became Elinor de Vellasquo. From there she journeyed to Barcelona and to Mallorca, where she was apprehended.[36]

There were some sincere free converts. The best known of these was the son of a *faqīh* of Játiva, who received baptism in 1487, became a priest, and preached to the Muslims of Granada and Aragon. Under the name of "Juan Andres" he translated into Aragonese the Qur'ān and the "seven books of the *Sunnah*."[37] Of the few other Valencian converts who appear in the documentation, we know nothing more than their name or place of residence, or sometimes both.[38] Conversion among the Aragonese and Catalan Mudejars seems to have been equally infrequent. In an extremely bizarre incident, a Muslim woman of Albarracín converted just fifteen days after her wedding and then endeavored to retrieve her bridewealth from her Muslim husband.[39] Perhaps conversion was a way of escaping an unhappy arranged marriage, although divorce might have been easier.

Mudejar conversion, then, was not unknown, but it amounted to, at best, a few drops in the font. The large majority had no intention of abandoning Islam.

Mudejar Feuding and Social Structure

A discussion of Mudejar acculturation and religious conversion has served to clarify certain aspects of Muslim–Christian interaction and its impact on the minority culture. It has, however, revealed little about the Mudejar subsociety itself when it did not somehow mesh with the public life of the Christian kingdom. Posing a dichotomy between Valencia's Muslim and Christian societies may appear somewhat artificial, since both groups, after all, lived and labored together in the same kingdom. But occupying the same physical space does not necessitate the rigid conformity of all inhabitants to one all-encompassing social system with its prescribed modes of behavior. Even when dwelling in urban *morerías* amid large concentrations of Christian population, the Mudejars were enmeshed in distinct networks of social relations articulated in accordance with the moral and material demands of their families.

As to the precise nature of Mudejar social structure, the documentation affords us only precious glimpses. Of course, the Christian bureaucrats had little intrinsic interest in the internal life of the king's Muslim communities. What they have left are details that for them were incidental to their fiscal and administrative concerns, bits and pieces that in the aggregate form a coherent, albeit by no means complete, picture.

An exploration of the royal records for patterns of Mudejar behavior and the social structures underlying them reveals a high incidence of intracommunal violence, greatly exceeding the occurrence of violent conflict between Muslims and Christians (although probably not that between Christians). The discovery of 120 Crown-sponsored truces between antagonistic Mudejar families, not to mention the large number of assaults and murders, suggests that the family feud occupied a central place in Mudejar social life.[40] The Mudejars' internecine violence indicates that their subsociety was still vital, and represents their channeling of energy inward into prescribed forms of behavior and association that had social meaning for them alone. In order to comprehend the origins of such feuding and the historical significance of this phenomenon, it will be necessary first to discuss the Berber and Arab settlement of the Valencian region and its structural implications, and then to describe the structure of the Arabo-Berber family, particularly its Mudejar variant.

Historians differ as to the precise chronology and nature of the Muslim settlement of the Valencian region (*Sharq al-Andalus*). Guichard argues in favor of an early (eighth through ninth century) Berberization of the area, but noting that from the eleventh century onward the Berbers were so Arabized that they pretended an affiliation to prestigious Arab tribes, conveniently forgetting their Berber origins.[41] Barceló Torres disputes Guichard's use of toponyms as evidence for early Berber settlement, suggesting that these Berber place names originated in later waves of Berber immigration under al-Ḥakam II (961–976) and al-Manṣūr (978–1002), or perhaps during the conquests of the Almoravids and the Almohads.[42] Míkel de Epalza has made important contributions regarding the religious status of Valencia's indigenous population following the Muslim conquest. Taking account of new evidence showing only a limited Christianization of pre-Islamic Valencia, he proposes a rapid mass conversion to Islam (in contrast to Bulliet's model of a more gradual conversion), a trend that was intensified in the tenth and eleventh centuries with a Cordoban-controlled campaign of politicoreligious indoctrination intended to stave off a Fatimid Shīʿī threat to Sunnī al-Andalus. The result was that the *Sharq al-Andalus* became perhaps the most highly Islamized and Arabized region in the peninsula.[43] From the above it may be said that on the eve of the Christian conquest the Valencian region was Islamized and Arabized with a greater or lesser portion of the population being possessed of Berber roots. Moreover, it is likely that the region was settled on a tribal pattern, in which individual villages were peopled by particular clans. For our purposes, whether these clans were Berber, Arab, or Arabized Berber is not important, inasmuch as Arabs and Berbers had and, indeed, still have, very similar forms of social organization.[44]

The social and political consequences of Arab and Berber settlement, and of Islamization and Arabization have been set forth by Guichard. He convincingly repudiates the views of Sánchez Albornoz and likeminded historians who argue in favor of the assimilation of the Muslim conquerors to the social norms of the indigenous population. According to Guichard, not only did the religion and literate culture of the conquerors become predominant in al-Andalus, but Arabo-Berber tribal structures prevailed as well. In terms of social organization, this meant that the Arabs and Berbers were members of agnatic, patrilineal groups in which endogamous marriage was preferred so as to maintain the cohesion, wealth, and power of the lineage. These agnatic groups were embedded in a segmentary social system characterized by the balanced opposition between the increasingly inclusive segments of elementary family, lineage, clan, and tribe. This system allowed for both atomization, when segments of equal size competed within the tribe or clan, and amalgamation, when the various segments of a tribe formed a unified front in opposition to an enemy tribe. Thus, tribal in-fighting, most notably between the confederations of Mudarī and Yemenī Arabs, marked the political history of al-Andalus well into the tenth century. The intermarriage of Arabs and Berbers with women of the native population—the offspring would have been Muslims and full members of their father's lineage—and the clientage of *muwalladūn*, the descendants of converts to Islam, to particular tribes allowed for the retention of tribal structures.[45]

By the eleventh century tribalism had played itself out as the dominant factor in the political life of al-Andalus. In addition to the political centralization and pacification achieved by ᶜAbd al-Raḥmān III, Guichard emphasizes the processes of sedentarization and urbanization, which hindered segmentation, the dynamic of tribal organization. David Wasserstein argues that an "Andalusian identity" had supplanted tribalism, any politically significant elements of which were destroyed by the military reforms of al-Manṣūr, which had dissolved the tribally based *jund* units. Glick suggests an additional factor—the explosion of conversion to Islam in the midtenth century (according to the Bulliet model) saw the Arabs and Berbers being numerically swamped by neo-Muslims for whom tribal issues were not a major concern.[46] However, if Epalza's thesis of an earlier and more intense Islamization of the Valencian region is correct, it may be that Arabo-Berber structures had taken deeper roots there. This may explain the particular vitality of Arabo-Berber social structures among Valencia's Mudejars.

In any case, the decline of tribalism as a political force, or the dissolution of the tribal unit as a form of social organization, need not have resulted in the lapse of the more elementary segments of agnatic family and lineage as significant structures. In fact, among the Muslims of Naṣrid Granada, and even among the Moriscos of postconquest Granada, agnatic solidarity (ᶜaṣabīyah) continued to be a potent social force.[47]

It is one thing to remark on the survival of agnatic solidarity in an Islamic polity, or in a recently conquered one like Granada; it is quite another matter to assert that Arabo-Berber social attitudes and structures, at the level of family and lineage, remained largely intact in

Valencia some 250 years after the submission of that region to western Christian domination. The defeat and emigration of Muslim military elites in the thirteenth century had eliminated whatever political significance still remained to either the tribe or clan. Since the government was Christian and denied Muslims access to political power, it is difficult to see what sociopolitical role and aims even the smaller solidarities of family and lineage would have had. Furthermore, progressive Mudejar emigration to Granada or the Maghrib, coupled with the internal migration and fragmentation brought about by seigneurial alteration of rural settlement patterns, must have severely strained or severed the ties binding some Muslim lineages together, in effect, fostering a more radical segmentation.

Still, at the same time, the conquerors' granting of communal and legal autonomy to the Mudejars was probably conducive to the retention of preconquest structures, or at least to the alleviation of the pressures for fragmentation. As will be seen below, the various official posts of the corporate aljama, however much they were distortions of their Islamic antecedents, became sources of prestige and power within the Mudejar community, prizes over which rival families deemed it worthwhile to feud. Also, Māliki law, according to which the Mudejars regulated their daily lives, seemed to justify the perpetuation of feuding relations by its provision for either retaliation or the payment of blood money (*diyah*) in cases of homicide and assault.[48]

Aside from the persisting legal and institutional supports for traditional patterns of social relations, it is important to emphasize the peculiar resilience and structural coherence of medieval Islamic society at its lower levels, despite the frequent and sometimes traumatic political upheavals in its upper reaches.[49] In the Valencian case, this resilience derived from the ability of the larger solidarities of an Arabo-Berber society to segment without disturbing the primary social structures. Thus, if a family were broken up—say, through the emigration of one of two brothers to the Maghrib—the sons of the remaining brother could create a new agnatic solidarity composed of themselves, their father, and their own male children, even though their position would be weakened through the loss of their paternal uncle's support. In other words, so long as traditional attitudes were not eroded, preconquest structures could be perpetuated merely through biological reproduction. If 250 years seems an incredibly long time for such structures to have endured, it was also more than enough time for them to have reemerged and solidified. Since Mudejar political life was reduced to the confines of the local *morería* or village there was no impetus for the amalgamation of clans or tribes; family and lineage, however, remained important.

That lineage long continued to be a special concern of Valencian Muslims is evinced in the claims of a Morisco family in 1567 to have descended from al-Manṣūr and Valencia's Muslim rulers.[50] *ʿAṣabīyah* in Valencia was buttressed through the practice of endogamy, that is, through parallel cousin marriage with the daughter of the paternal uncle (*bint al-ʿamm*). The negotiations of the newly converted Moriscos with Carlos I in 1526 leave little doubt that this type of marriage had been the preferred one among the Mudejars:

> inasmuch as among the Moors today there are many marriages concluded between close relations in a degree prohibited by the Christian law and permitted by the Moorish law, which law permits marriage to the degree of that between cousins-germane—the children of two brothers inclusive—should the said marriages begin to be disturbed, and to prohibit those marriages which could be made from today henceforth, would result in the greatest damage and disturbance among the said Moors.

The Moriscos then requested that Carlos intercede with the papal legate and persuade him to grant a dispensation for the endogamous marriages consummated before the mass conversions.[51]

Our documentation is less useful on this matter. Normally, only the name (*ism*) of the wife is given—as Fatima, wife of so and so—without ascription to her lineage (*nisbah*). This was in keeping with the far greater importance given to patrilineal descent, whereby the offspring of the marriage pertained to the lineage of the father. Of course, in the instance of marriage with the *bint al-ʿamm*, the husband and wife would have the same *nisbah*. In a few rare cases the documentation shows unequivocally the marriage of parallel cousins. In Alcira, Fotoix bint (daughter of) Mahomat Xativi was the betrothed of Ali ibn (son of) Abrahim Xativi.[52] Two cases from Aragon (where the practice of endogamy is all the more impressive, given the greater acculturation of Aragonese Mudejars) suggest that although the right of the male cousin to the hand of the *bint al-ʿamm* was recognized, the prospective brides were sometimes less than enthusiastic about their fate. For five years there was pending in the courts of the kingdom a decision on the litigation between a reluctant bride, Fatima bint Mahomat Margnan of Huesca, and her cousin, Ybraym ibn Mofferiz Margnan, concerning the marriage that Ybraym and his father "were claiming" to contract with her.[53] Fatima bint Jayel de Gali of Zaragoza asked for a divorce from her cousin, Faraig ibn Juçe de Gali, on the grounds that he had maltreated her. Faraig maintained that his mother-in-law had put Fatima up to it and pleaded before the king that his wife be restored to him.[54] Questions of marital harmony aside, there were compelling reasons for the practice of endogamy. The marriage of paternal cousins enhanced the solidarity of the lineage by linking the interests of brothers and their children, and giving the bride's kin more control over the bridegroom. They could then present a more powerful front to rival lineages. Moreover, the reproductive power of the daughter was retained within the lineage; more children, particularly more sons, increased prestige, power, and economic potential.[55] The economic angle was crucial. Since among the Mudejars daughters were able to inherit from their fathers, the exogamous marriage of a daughter implied the loss of property by her lineage.[56] True, the groom had to render a specified bridewealth (*ṣadāq*, Catalan *accidach*) to his intended, but, because that was paid to and retained by the bride, her family did not profit from it. In some instances wives left their husbands and took their bridewealth home with them, or when couples separated the wives demanded their bridewealth, but it is highly unlikely that families planned for such eventualities.[57]

While endogamy was preferred, exogamous marriage was not at all unusual. Demography militated against every person being able to wed his or her cousin. More important, exogamy served to define relationships between various lineages. Marriage ties created a community of interest, mitigated conflict between families, and stabilized community life.[58] That Mudejars regarded such affinal connections as determinants of conduct is demonstrated in the judicial appeal of Çaat Siquuti. The lieutenant bailiff of Játiva, with the counsel of the local *qāḍī*, Yuçeff Alçamba, had passed sentence against Çaat, which sentence was then upheld by the bailiff general, with the counsel of Mahomat Bellvis, the *qāḍī* general. Çaat complained that the final ruling had gone against him because the two *qāḍī*s "are joined by a certain affinity, that the son of the said *qāḍī* Bellvis had married the niece of the aforesaid Yuçeff Alçamba, daughter of Yahye Alçamba his brother."[59] In another case, Mahomat Perpir, when he fled to the Maghrib in 1501, was recorded as having Abdalla Murçi and Yuçeff Zignell as brothers-in-law. In 1499 he had reached a truce with Azmet Murçi, a relation of Abdalla, and in 1500 had done the same with Yuçeff Zignell.[60] It may be that affinal ties had helped to close the rift separating the Perpirs from the Murçis and the Zignells, or perhaps in the end they proved insufficient and Mahomat had reasons other than the fear of forced baptism for taking refuge in the Maghrib.

Since endogamous marriage was practiced, and the bonds between agnates thereby strengthened, it should follow that agnates acted jointly in the conduct of feuding relations. This is precisely the state of affairs encountered in the documentation. In a number of cases the perpetrators of violence were two or more agnates. Homaymat and Çuleymen Montani of Alacuás, with accomplices, shot and killed with a crossbow another Muslim vassal of the seigneury.[61] Ali Orfayçi and his brother Mahomat Çaffahi of Alcira burst into the house of Pedro Delgado and wounded Juçeff Bolaix with two lacerations.[62] On different occasions Muslims of Valldigna were wounded by Mahomat and Abdalla Giber,[63] and by Çat and Ali Bolarif.[64] Mahomat Malich had the misfortune somehow to incur the wrath of Ali and Mahomat Guayna of Artesa.[65] Clearly ᶜaṣabīyah was crucial for providing the strength in numbers that allowed for such aggression.

At the same time, the readiness to resort to violence, combined with the support of sons, brothers, uncles, and cousins, tended to discourage the violent initiatives or retaliation of rivals. The threat posed by the enemy's group solidarity determined the very nature of much of the violence that occurred. Assault and murder were often committed under the cover of night; ambushes were laid and enemies attacked at unexpected moments; and victims were often alone and outnumbered by their assailants who struck in tandem with agnates or other—perhaps affinal—accomplices.[66] We have mentioned elsewhere Juçeff Cabot of Játiva who returned to Valldigna, where, one evening, with henchmen, he did away with an enemy in his own home.[67] Abdalla Çentido and Fuçey Ylel dispatched Azmet Gradano with a dagger-thrust to the throat as he was leaving his father's house in Mirambell.[68] Mahomat Flori of Játiva was fined 110s, in lieu of eighty lashes, "because he had hidden in his house certain Moors [relatives] from Gandía and from the Vall d'Alfandech [Valldigna] for the purpose of killing Gabix, Moor of the said morería."[69] Mahomat Chiquet of Alcira even resorted to arson, attempting to burn down the house of the Arrayço family.[70] Only rarely were attempts made on the lives of more than one member of a family at the same time, and in such cases the elements of surprise, darkness of night, and superiority in arms are apparent. The brothers Çahat and Amet Pachando were the victims of a ferocious nocturnal assault in Liria by Caet Natjar and Abraym Rabaça of Bétera. Natjar practically cut off Çahat's head with his sword, while Rabaça seriously wounded Amet with a poisoned crossbow dart.[71]

As ᶜaṣabīyah was predicated on the responsibility of each agnate to uphold the honor of his family, an attack on one member of the group demanded of the others reprisal against the offender or his agnates. Failure to fulfill this responsibility resulted in the family's loss of honor and in a decrease in its prestige and power in the community. Thus violence elicited a violent response, setting in motion a potentially endless sequence of aggressive acts characteristic of the feud.[72]

The understanding of family members involved in feuds that violence would inevitably ensue and vengeance be exacted prompted Muslims of Oliva, Carlet, Játiva, the Vall de Uxó, and Valencia to apply for licenses to bear arms for the purpose of self-defense against their "enemies."[73] Yuçeff Albanne's application hinged on the presumption that because Abrahim Corumbell had already wounded his brother he was next in line.[74]

A consideration of the feud between the Murçi and the Torralbi families of the *morería* of Valencia demonstrates the centrality of agnatic solidarity in the prosecution of a feud. We first encounter the brothers Azmet and Çahat Torralbi receiving from the bailiff general arms-bearing licenses (20 March 1503). Because Çahat had denounced Azmet Murçi before the bailiff's court (for a reason unknown to us), he believed he needed to be armed so that he would not be "damaged by the said Azmet Murçi *or by another relative of his*" (italics mine). Azmet Torralbi, sharing responsibility for his brother's legal actions, whether he liked it or not, felt equally threatened. Such was the expectation of Murçi vengeance that the Torralbis were licensed to bear arms not only for self-defense but also for the defense of "one other companion who will go in your company."[75] Clearly, it was inadvisable for a man embroiled in a Mudejar feud to walk alone.

Less than three months later the Torralbis took the offensive and, putting his licensed arms to good use, Azmet Torralbi severely wounded Abrahim Murçi. The precise relation of Abrahim to Azmet Murçi is unknown, although it seems most likely that they were brothers. In any case, they had the same enemies. Both Abrahim and Azmet had concluded truces with Mahomat Perpir and Ali Perpir, and both had fallen out with even the same agnate, Ubaydal Murçi, perhaps their cousin.[76] Abrahim had also made Azmet's dispute with the Torralbis his own. Nusa, Abrahim's wife, maintained that Azmet and Çahat Torralbi, and their father Abdalla, all bore a grudge against her husband for no reason, and that Çahat and Abdalla prompted Azmet and planned with him the attack on Abrahim. She also asserted that as early as the previous January (1503) Çahat Torralbi had shown much bravado toward her husband and an intention to kill him.[77]

The testimonies of other witnesses contradicted some of Nusa's charges. First, it seems that Abrahim Murçi was not entirely blameless. Abrahim was said to have a "foul mouth," and many thought that "because of his tongue the said Azmet Torralbi has wounded him."[78] Abrahim had indeed gone about stating that Azmet was a fool and deserved to be treated as such.[79] Second, it seems that Çahat and Abdalla Torralbi had not urged on Azmet or planned the crime with him; rather, the attack was more of a spontaneous act on Azmet's part.[80] In fact, Abdalla Torralbi had attempted to mollify his son's animosity toward Abrahim, urging Azmet to make peace with him. On the very day of the assault, Abdalla confronted Abrahim, demanding to know why he was deliberately antagonizing his son. Abrahim retorted that he did not have to answer to Abdalla, then wheeled and strode off.[81]

Abrahim's inability to hold his tongue proved calamitous, for when Azmet vented his wrath against him, he showed little mercy. Azmet slashed Abrahim about the head and arms with his sword, and, when Abrahim fled into the home of Gil Sanchiz, he followed him there and cut off his right foot.[82] According to the painter Gabriel Gosalbo, it was his own intervention that prevented the affair from escalating into a bloodbath. With a lance he barred the way into Abdalla Torralbi's house against those (Abrahim's relatives, perhaps) who spoke of entering to slit the throats of Abdalla's daughters. Later, he met Çahat Torralbi and advised him to avoid the area of his father's house, lest he fall victim to Murçi revenge.[83]

In another case, the brothers Ali and Azmet Thorruc of Millena killed Azmet Araye of Benilloba on account of some disagreement. Consequently, Azmet's brothers, Mahomat and Çahat Araye—their father was an eighty-year-old invalid—recruited some neighbors in Benilloba and proceeded to Millena, where they took their revenge, slaying Azmet Thorruc.[84]

Açen Muça of Serra was similarly motivated by a desire to vindicate the murder of his half-brother Azmet Gradano ("jermans de mare," a blood tie not as strong as that between sons of the same father) by Abdalla Çentido. For four years he had restrained himself, but on Corpus Christi Day, 1491, he stabbed Abdalla to death as he sat watching the processions in Valencia.[85] Earlier that day, Yuçeff Ada had asked Abdalla about the state of his relations with Açen Muça, and, upon learning that the two were still feuding, admonished Abdalla to be careful.[86] The feud, then, seems to have been a matter of (Mudejar) public knowledge. This makes perfect sense, for the honor and status of a family rested on public evaluation and approval. This approval could best be attained through the display of solidarity and the willingness of the agnates to fulfill their responsibilities to the group, that is, through the family conducting itself properly in a feud.

A number of victimized Mudejar families, either too weak in numbers or too law-abiding to retaliate against their enemies in kind, or perhaps exceedingly confident in the efficacy of royal and seigneurial justice, beseeched their Christian overlords to mete out the punishment due for assault or homicide. The parents of the murdered Azmet Zichnel of Valldigna, "although they have the ability and it would be permitted to them to kill with impunity Juçef Cuyta, the killer," turned first to the criminal justice of Valldigna, a seigneury, and then, once Juçef had fled the valley, to the Crown "to have him fittingly punished and chastized through the measures and means of that [justice]."[87]

It is due to this type of legal recourse to the Christian authorities that much of the information concerning Mudejar violence turns up in the documentation.

The records of the kingdom's fiscal auditor (*Maestre Racional*) indicate that royal officials, and probably their seigneurial counterparts as well, acted as mediators between feuding Mudejar families. The result of a bailiff's intervention in a dispute appears in the records as the payment of a monetary settlement (*composicio*) by the offending Muslim or his family to the bailiff. Of course, payment to the Christian official provided little compensation for the victim and his family. It is probably safe to assert, therefore, that either the bailiff and the victim divided the settlement or the victim received a separate settlement equal to that received by the bailiff, who, in either case, would have presided over the entire transaction. This conjecture is substantiated in some cases by scribal notations that state that the victim "admitted" or agreed to the settlement.[88] In the eyes of the victim and his family, the settlement would have appeared a form of blood money releasing them from the obligation, although not necessarily from the desire, to retaliate violently.

A more effective means of maintaining the public peace was in the hands of the bailiff general, namely, the official "peace and truce," supposed to last for 101 years, or its permanent variant, the "final peace."[89] Although many of these officially sponsored truces involved Muslims of the *morería* of Valencia, for keeping order was most difficult in the capital, many others bound Muslims from all over the kingdom. The truces highlight the importance of agnatic solidarity by emphasizing that each party swearing to abide by the truce was representing himself and his "relatives, friends, and defenders." In some cases entire families were present at the conclusion of the truce. Unfortunately, only in rare instances do the documents state the causes for the mutual hostility necessitating a formal truce. When given, the causes usually are acts of violence.[90] The texts of the truces are written according to standard format, in which steep monetary fines are emphasized as the deterrent to any resumption of the feud.

For example, in a truce dated 31 March 1489 we find various members of the Capo family of Alcira, standing "for themselves, friends, relations, and defenders," and Abdalla Pollet, his son Mahomat, Azmet Biari, Çahat Biari and his son Caleth, and Çapdon Eça, all of the same *morería*, pledging "a good peace and truce between them, to last for 101 years, concerning whatever debates, quarrels, rumors, ill-will, and wounds that might have existed between them until the present day." By virtue of an oath sworn "with hands and with mouth" in the presence of Joan Aduart, royal constable and vicar of the bailiff general, " 'to our

Lord God and to the *qiblah* of Muḥammad' the face turned toward mid-day, according to the *Sunnah* and the Shariah of the Sarracens," both parties promised that "there will not be done nor caused to be done nor arranged nor attempted, neither openly nor secretly, neither directly nor indirectly, any evil or damage on the persons or goods of them [the other party]." For any violation of the truce, the Crown would penalize the offending family with a fine of 500 florins—100 florins to the injured party and 400 florins to the royal treasury.[91]

It is not difficult to understand why the royal authorities expended such effort to curb the Mudejars' feuding propensities.[92] The death of vassals, the destruction of property, and the disruption of economic activity, all of which resulted from feuding, had the most negative im-plications for the state of the royal treasury. Moreover, the control of social violence and the efficient administration of justice were essential components of the effective exercise of royal authority. Stated more simply, public order had to be maintained. Feuds not only affected indi-vidual families but also at times threatened to engulf entire *morerías* in tumultuous and bloody disorder. Three royal aljamas were seen to be tottering on the edge of such calamity. In Valencia, the feud between the Roget and the Bizquey families had become so serious that they and "their fathers and mothers" had to be banished from the *morería*.[93] In Alcira, the bailiff believed the aforementioned truce between the Capo and Biari families to be necessary in order to "pacify the said *morería* and to put the [*morería*] in repose."[94] The bailiff general urged the bailiff of Castellón de la Plana to do something to resolve the conflict between the Bocayos and their rivals "for the benefit and repose of that *morería*, which today . . . is on the road to destruction."[95]

While official intervention prevented the growth of widespread vio-lence within *morerías*, it is less certain that the truces between families always had their intended durability. Social anthropologies have ob-served in Mediterranean and Middle Eastern societies where the feud is a central element in social relations the ultimate inefficacy of truces and various forms of compensation as means of permanently extin-guishing a feud. Rather, despite the fact that hostilities cease for varying lengths of time, feuds tend to be perpetual in nature.[96] The Valencian evidence does not contradict these conclusions. Azmet Coxet of Paterna was to be apprehended "for breaking the peace and truce."[97] Although Azmet Aixbir and Çaat Borrabe had concluded a truce, Azmet later seized the opportunity to attack Çaat.[98] One also encounters the repeti-tion of truces between the same families, such as the Murçis and the Perpirs, or the Bizqueys and the Rogets. Even if different members or combinations of members of the families appear in successive truces, this hardly masks the fact of the continuing and potentially explosive state of animosity existing between them.[99]

It should not be thought, however, that without the intervention of royal and seigneurial officials Mudejar society would have destroyed itself through unabated internecine violence. The Mudejars had their own mechanisms for achieving a cessation of hostilities, a state of affairs necessary if routine social and economic life were to continue.

A settlement arrived at through the efforts of Muslim jurists preceded some of the truces established through the office of the bailiff general. When the powerful Paziar family of Alcira and the Getdi family of Picasent concluded an official "peace and truce" after the killing of Abdalla Getdi, the Paziars came with a "*carta morischa* (Arabic letter) received from Ali Bellvis, son of Mahomat Bellvis, *qāḍī* of the lord king," while the Getdis had an Arabic letter from their local *faqīh*.[100] In other cases Muslims abandoned legal initiatives against enemies, having come to an understanding with them by their own methods and for their own reasons.

In the feud between the Araye and Thorruc families, rather than pursuing the prosecution of Mahomat and Çahat Araye in the governor's court, the Thorrucs dropped the charges against them, after having "established peace with all [their] adversaries."[101] It may be inferred that the Thorrucs realized that the capital punishment of the Araye brothers, even if executed through proper legal procedure, would have served only to provoke the perpetration of retaliatory violence by the Araye and their friends in Benilloba. Each family had already lost a son; with the score even, an uneasy truce seemed wiser than more killing and the disruption of the activities of those still alive. When the wife of the murdered Ali Dabbau, his sister, and the guardian of his children, Azmet Pulpul (apparently not an agnate of Ali), dropped charges against the killer, Çaat Melich, the reasons for their doing so were even more pressing than those motivating the Thorrucs.[102] Here, the surviving members of the victim's family, two women and young children, were incapable of either exacting revenge themselves or defending themselves against later retaliation should they press prosecution through the bailiff's court. This evidence suggests that what moved Mudejars to accept compensation or blood money instead of physical retribution, or to make peace with the enemy, however temporary that peace might be, was not so much the threat of censure by the Christian authorities as the fear of triggering further violence, of reactivating the feud in its most destructive form. In other words, the most effective deterrent to feuding was the feud itself. Rival families eyed each other warily and exercised restraint, committing violent acts sporadically in an often calculated manner. It was to no one's interest to give violence free rein.

The plethora of official truces between rival Mudejar families, the numerous acts of violence in which agnates were implicated, and the importance of vengeance as a motive for such violence all indicate that the feud was so pervasive as to constitute a primary determinant of Mudejar social relations. Jacob Black-Michaud, whose conclusions are based on the studies of various Mediterranean and Middle Eastern feuding societies, goes so far as to state that "feud can be regarded as a social system per se."[103] While it is not our intention to discuss the validity of this conclusion, nor, for that matter, to attempt to fit Mudejar feuding within the framework of an anthropological model, it is crucial to emphasize a viewpoint on which most observers of feuding societies would seem to agree, namely, that feuding is better viewed as a social process than as a social aberration. If this is the case, then there must have been something other than the necessity to respond to a previous act of violence behind much of the Mudejar violence we have observed, a stake, or stakes, worth the risk of initiating a feud. These stakes were wealth and power. Among Mudejar farmers and artisans wealth was attained through the acquisition of land and through the control of a limited market for manufactured goods. Power, or local influence, rested on the prestige and status afforded by the possession of wealth and by the defeat of rivals in the competition for it. The agnates who constituted the feuding group also functioned as an economic unit, holding land jointly and practicing the same crafts, so that mutual material concerns strengthened agnatic solidarity. Mudejar feuding, then, may be interpreted as a consequence of the competition for material wealth and local status, and as a process determining the allocation of these scarce commodities, thereby stratifying individual communities.

The official truces, which sometimes indicate the professions of the subscribing parties, strongly suggest that economic competition was at the root of much Mudejar discord. In a number of cases both of the feuding parties were practitioners of the same craft, producing for the same limited market. Conflict occurred between Muslim blacksmiths, shieldmakers, and shoemakers in Valencia, between Muslim fishermen in Oliva, and between hemp sandalmakers in the Vall de Uxó.[104] The competition seems to have been most intense among Valencia's Mudejar shoemakers. The feuding Bizquey and Roget families, whom the authorities had to expel from the morería, both practiced shoemaking. The Bizqueys also concluded truces with other enemy shoemakers, namely, Çatdon Caeli, the brothers Abrahim and Çalema Cabero, Çilim Maymo, and Çahat Perpir with his nephews Ali and Mahomat Perpir.[105] The Perpirs themselves clashed with shoemakers other than the Bizqueys: Çahat Carcaix, Azmet Murçi, Ali Maguarell, and Çaat Abducarim.[106] In the feud which resulted in the wounding of Abrahim Murci, a shieldmaker, by Azmet Torralbi, a shoemaker, it is interesting that the Torralbis seem to have first come into conflict, not with Abrahim, but with Azmet Murçi, a shoemaker (see above).

However, in many other feuds the parties were not of the same profession, in which cases one cannot delineate so precisely the clash of competing economic interests. The ties and common interests created through exogamous marriage or simple friendship complicated intracommunal relations considerably, so that families came into conflict who, had they been guided by economic concerns alone, otherwise might not have. Thus, one encounters truces like the one concluded between the shoemakers Ali Perpir of Valencia and Azmet Naixe of Mislata, on one side, and Ali Maguarell and Çaat Abducarim, shoemakers, and Azmet Claret, a linen salesman, all of Valencia, on the other side. The documentation does not reveal what, other than shoemaking, brought together Perpir and Naixe, Muslims from different families and locales, or why a linen salesman was involved in the feud at all.[107]

The frequent and varied business transactions between Mudejars of all walks of life, and matters associated with the complex pattern of land tenure, in which Muslim artisans also were concerned, provided ample opportunity for the sparking of controversy and mutual hostility. For instance, Çale Magarell had Çaat Feçi imprisoned for money Çaat owed him for the purchase of a donkey.[108] In Játiva, Yuçeff Redona complained that Azmet Beniale had planted mulberry trees on his land and demanded that they be uprooted.[109] Muslims of Valldigna went to court over the alleged sale of cloth,[110] while Muslims of Alcira disputed the ownership of goats.[111]

Material interests fueled the fires of dissension even within families. For instance, Ali Gehini, a wealthy *amīn* of la Foyeta, was so afraid of being robbed by his own sons, disreputable characters who frequented taverns, that he hid his money in the walls of his house.[112] Mahomat Negral had the justice of Valldigna sell his brother Abducalem's mule for debts Abducalem owed him on account of the justice's earlier sale of Mahomat's field for debts that had really been Abducalem's.[113] Unfortunately, because most Mudejar civil litigation was handled in Islamic courts, the records of which do not survive, our information on Mudejar disputes over land or other commodities is extremely limited. Consequently, direct correlations cannot be made between such disputes and the occurrence of violence and feuding. Considering the extent of feuding between Muslims of the same profession reflected in the truces and the few instances of Mudejar property litigation encountered, it can be

cautiously postulated that much of Mudejar feuding had its roots in conflicting economic interests.

The feuding that threatened to destroy the *morería* of Castellón de la
Plana was the violent manifestation of a struggle for political power.
The struggle centered on the control of the two posts of *adelantat* and
pitted Abdulazis and his son Yuçeff Bocayo against a faction headed by
Çale Arroçen and Ubequer Faraig, which also included Caet Fando,
Yuçeff Salio, Ali Gordo, and Ali Gerret. Shortly before 19 April 1487
the Bocayos informed the bailiff general of a fight that had broken out
between Yuçeff Bocayo and Ali Gerret.[114] Within weeks matters took a
more serious turn: two Christians and some unidentified Muslims entered the Bocayos' home and wounded Yuçeff in the arm and hand,
cutting off his finger. Investigation revealed that this was not random
violence, but that the two Christian assailants had been hired by Çale
Arroçen and Ubequer Faraig to do the dirty work.[115] At this point the
bailiff general had Ali Bellvis, the *qāḍī* general, intervene. Bellvis managed to persuade the Bocayos and their rivals to agree to a power-
sharing arrangement. According to this arrangement, the ten councillors of the aljama, among whom were members of both feuding factions, and the *adelantats* from the previous year would elect the *amīn*
and the two *adelantats*. Most important, it was stipulated that "in any
year either Ubequer Faraig or Çale Arroçen is elected as jurate [*adelantat*] that in such case let there be elected as jurate one of the said
Bocayos, either the father or the son."[116] That the two posts of *adelantat*
were so hotly contested was probably due to the *adelantats'* function as
advisors to the *amīn* in the apportionment and collection of taxes. This
is suggested by the fact that Ali Bellvis also inspected the aljama's
account books to ensure that the *amīn* had justly confiscated certain
goods of the Bocayos and Yuçeff Pollina, presumably for reason of unpaid taxes.[117] The Bocayos, then, had a clear material interest in being
elected as one of the *adelantats*. Eventually (August 1488), the authorities established a formal truce between the two factions; however, by
1492 Yuçeff Bocayo was again complaining about wounds inflicted by
his former antagonists (it is not clear that these were new wounds). [118]
There is no further evidence indicating that the feuds in other Mudejar
communities were similarly motivated, and the aljama of Castellón, in
which the office of *amīn* changed hands annually, may well have been
more politically unstable. Still, given that all the communities had more
or less the same political structure with officials executing the same functions, it may not be too far-fetched to infer a more general phenomenon
of feuding as being in part a contest for local political power, the exercise of which could influence individual rates of taxation. Even families
secure in their possession of official posts, like the Paziars, the *amīn*s of

Alcira, were involved in feuding, which suggests that the holding of office was not the sole basis of power among the Mudejars.

Intimately linked to the competition for economic and political power as a source of feuding was a punctilious concern for honor. The Mudejar conception of honor differed somewhat from that of western Christians. For the latter, honor was attached to social rank and varied according to the possession of wealth and title. For the Mudejars, honor had the same significance at all socioeconomic levels and was the possession of the family, to be augmented or lost.[119] This may help to explain the apparently unusual phenomenon of Mudejar shoemakers and the like fighting over points of honor.

As suggested above, family honor could be maintained and increased only through the agnates' fulfillment of their responsibilities to each other. Inasmuch as the family constituted an economic unit jockeying for its share of wealth and influence in the community, its performance in that contest reflected on its honor. However, a family without honor was by virtue of its loss of face excluded from participation in that same contest. Honor, then, was a prerequisite for the attainment of status and power in the community. Because in economic terms Mudejar society was relatively homogenous, being composed largely of small farmers and artisans and lacking an established aristocracy, the possession of honor, achieved through a family's action in accordance with the dictates of agnatic solidarity, was probably as great a determinant of local status as real wealth.[120]

This helps to explain why so much of the violence committed by Mudejars seems to have been in defense of family or personal honor. Although economic competition might have inspired the incidents leading families or individuals to believe that their honor had been somehow sullied, it was not considered to have been in itself a sufficient cause for violence. Questions of purely economic concern were settled licitly in court; questions of honor were settled extralegally in the forum of the community. Of course, the settlement of a question of honor through violence to some extent also resolved the economic question, inasmuch as the competition was then either temporarily or permanently eliminated. Thus, in the feud between the Torralbis and the Murçis, which seems to have originated in the clash between shoemakers—Azmet Murçi against Azmet and Çahat Torralbi—Azmet Torralbi inflicted violence on Abrahim Murçi, a shieldmaker, because Abrahim had ridiculed him and thereby stained his honor. It is worth recalling that many in the *morería* recognized that Abrahim had incurred Azmet's wrath because of his loose tongue.

Another incident involving Muslims of Bétera shows the Mudejars' extreme sensitivity where their honor was concerned. Ubaydal Allepus and his convert brother Miguel Crestia went to a hamlet near Bétera where they intended to mow grass with a sickle that a Christian hosteler had given them. There, a Muslim named Raboça accused the two brothers of having stolen the sickle from him. Apparently, Ubaydal and Miguel felt they had been defamed and their honor challenged, for they immediately tried to strike Raboça. Raboça then called for his brother-in-law, Amet Biari, at which point a brawl ensued that resulted in Amet's death. Although Ubaydal denied any previous acquaintance with Amet Biari, the latter's widow claimed that Ubaydal had harbored ill will against her husband.[121] Perhaps Ubaydal's spontaneous violence in defense of his honor was the culmination of a long-standing controversy with Biari's family.

Because honor was essentially a social value, the possession of which depended on the community's evaluation of the conduct of an individual and his family, acts that entailed a challenge to or a defense of honor had a meaning recognized and understood by the entire community. Violence begot violence because social norms demanded that vengeance be exacted if honor was to be maintained. Thus, in the aforementioned stabbing of Abdalla Çentido by Açen Muça, Abdalla's friends expected that Açen would be seeking revenge. Açen, it seems, was a somewhat reluctant avenger, but he felt compelled to act when Abdalla passed by him in the street three times making insulting gestures and faces calculated to shame him publicly.[122]

If the childrearing methods of Axa, the wife of Abdalla Murçi, are any indication of a widespread phenomenon, then Mudejar children were from an early age socialized in the ways of violent initiative and riposte in the pursuit of honor. When her nine-year-old son came home weeping after having been hit by the son of Alfona, Axa deemed that he had been shamed. She upbraided the boy for not striking back, and she demanded retaliation: "Look, when he [the son of Alfona] passes, hit him with a rock." If this were not enough, she even nagged at her husband and servant: "If you do not strike either the husband or the wife [the Alfonas] I will not consider you men. If you do not do it, go to the devil!"[123]

A consideration of the position of women in Mudejar society confirms the continued importance of Arabo-Berber attitudes and social structures. To some extent women were pawns manipulated by their male relatives in the politics of marital alliance. Ideally, a woman was kept within the lineage through endogamous marriage, so that her lineage benefited from her reproductive power. However, if exogamous marriage were unavoidable, it was better and more honorable to receive than to give a woman in marriage. Families that had to give away their daughters in marriage did so to those families with whom alliance would prove most useful in the local scheme of feuding relations. Although the woman in an exogamous marriage lived with her husband's lineage, she still maintained important connections with her father's family. In fact, her behavior, particularly her sexual conduct, affected the honor of her father's family, not that of her husband.[124] This ambivalent position of the woman, bearing children for her husband's family while being responsible for the honor of her father's family, is reflected in a number of ways in the documentation.

First, because the children of a marriage belonged to the husband's family, Mudejar widows lost custody of their children, who were given into the hands of male guardians, presumably the agnates of the deceased husbands. The strategy here was to ensure that the children, along with the inheritances their fathers had bequeathed to them, continued to adhere to the father's family when their mother remarried. This explains why Fotayma resided in Sot with her new husband, Amet Albaytar, while her daughter Axa lived with two guardians in Cuart, the home of her deceased husband.[125] Apparently, the only way a widow could continue to play a significant role in the lives of her children was either not to remarry, or to do so only to a man of the same town.

The wife's continued close ties with her father's family divided her allegiance and seem to have contributed to the instability of some exogamous marriages. This is indicated by the fact that when a Mudejar wife separated from her husband she usually returned to the home of her father. When Suçey, the wife of Abrahim Çuleymen of the morería of Valencia, went to her father's home in Petrés to attend her brother's wedding, she never returned, "her father, mother, and brother detaining her and not allowing her to come in the power of her husband."[126] Çoltana departed with her father from the seigneury of Castell de Castells without license of the lord, even though her husband was still living there.[127] When Ali Mançor changed vassalage from Benimuslem to Castellón de Játiva, his wife refused to accompany him and demanded the payment of her bridewealth. The bailiff of Játiva did not quite comprehend what was happening and asserted, as a Christian might, "the wife has to follow the husband wherever he would wish to go . . . and to live."[128] Probably her confidence in and attachment to her agnates allowed this woman such freedom of choice.

Although the father's household offered a haven to a woman in case of an unhappy marriage, it also harbored the harshest judges of her sexual misbehavior. An adulterous woman's shameful behavior affected mainly the honor of her father's lineage; that of the husband's remained largely unstained. Therefore, it was the responsibility of the woman's agnates to punish her. In some traditional Arabo-Berber societies the agnates were expected to kill her, and Islamic law required that adulterers be stoned to death.[129] The Valencian documentation records a surprisingly large number of cases of Mudejar adultery, in which the Islamic death penalty was normally commuted by the Christian authorities to enslavement to the king. This indicates not that Muslims involved themselves in adulterous affairs any more than did Christians, but that because the honor of the father's lineage was involved in the case of an adulterous wife—and those prosecuted were almost all women—her agnates were themselves especially eager to prosecute her so as to erase their own shame. Since royal law would not permit the agnates to dispose of the woman themselves, they had to go through the proper legal channels. Unfortunately, the documents do not reveal who brought the adulteresses before the *qāḍī*'s court (the criminal penalty itself had to be executed by the local Christian authority), but, all else being consistent, the agnates, not the husbands, seem the most likely candidates.[130]

The social origins of Mudejar prostitutes further substantiate the importance of the woman's relation to her agnatic group, for the position of such women seems to have derived precisely from their having lacked the support of their agnates. Fotayma was an orphaned maidservant maltreated by her Muslim master. She ran off with a male servant who subsequently became her procurer.[131] Mariem had left her husband, but, because her mother was forcing her to return to him, she departed from Alacuás for the brothel of Valencia.[132] Nuzeya of Oliva had also separated from her husband, and since her parents were dead she, too, was compelled to earn a living in the brothel.[133] Xuxa left her husband in Villamarchante for a lover who later became her procurer. Having committed adultery, she could not hope for forgiveness from her father's family.[134] Adulterous women and prostitutes were the outcasts of Mudejar society.

If fathers were preoccupied with the sexual conduct of their married daughters, so much more were they anxious to defend the chastity of their unmarried ones. The violation of a daughter's chastity, committed with the consent of the daughter or not, constituted an assault on the family's honor. Daughters could not bring honor to a family; they could only bring shame through sexual impropriety. Thus, Aragonese Mudejars conducting business in Zaragoza brought their daughters with them and kept them secluded in the fonduk so that they would not be "maltreated" or spoiled for marriage.[135] The Mudejars' concern to guard their daughters' chastity in defense of family honor may be explained as a reaction to an unusual phenomenon encountered in the documentation, namely, the abduction of women. In pre-Islamic Arab society, and also to some extent among Arabs in Islamic times, women were abducted in order to shame the victimized family. The honor of the abductor's family was at the same time increased.[136] Mudejars in royal and seigneurial *morerías* also seem to have employed abduction as a tactic to disgrace their enemies. Although in some cases abduction might have been, in fact, only an elopement,[137] which still would have shamed the father who could not control his daughter, in other cases the participation of more than one man in the abduction indicates a deliberate intention to dishonor the woman's family. Mahomat and Omeymet Maixquarn of Valldigna paid a 340s settlement to the bailiff of Játiva "for having kidnapped Çayma, Mooress, daughter of the *amīn* of the place of Manuel."[138] The knight Miguel Çetina was sent to the Vall de Villalonga to search for the daughter ("mora donzella") of a Muslim of Millena who had been abducted by Muslims of Cocentaina.[139] The fate of the abducted women is unknown, but it is likely that abduction lessened their prospects for a good marriage.

The passive role of women (outside of the home at least) in the maintenance or loss of family honor was linked to the economic and local political considerations underlying much of Mudejar feuding. The primary factor at stake was the woman's reproductive power. Children, particularly sons, increased a family's economic potential, and the family with many sons and strong *ʿaṣabīyah* was a force to be reckoned with in the community. Thus endogamous marriage was preferred to keep offspring within the lineage, while if exogamous marriage was necessary, it was preferable to receive the woman of another family. The widow lost control of her own children to her late husband's family for the same reasons. Adulterous unions were frowned upon because the bastard offspring did not belong to any lineage and were of no help to anyone. Prostitutes, bereft of honor and family ties, existed on the margin of Mudejar feuding society.

Above the level of family or lineage the most important solidarity among the Mudejars was that formed by the rural village or urban *morería*. During the era of Islamic rule such solidarity had greater force owing to the settlement of particular localities by individual clans (thus the prevalence of "Beni" in Valencian toponyms).[140] The dissipation of larger tribe or clan solidarities and the post-Christian conquest seigneurialization of the countryside significantly modified the basis of local identity. The Mudejar no longer identified himself as the member of a particular clan, but as the vassal of a particular lord. Seigneurial control of a rural community meant that the lord's interests largely determined those of his vassals. So long as Muslim vassals stayed put, their lords tended to defend them, but not without a large degree of self-interest (see chaps. 1 and 2). The vassals themselves acted as a unit, and appear in the documentation as the aljama of a particular place of which a particular nobleman is lord. The community of interest between vassals, and between vassals and their lords, was necessitated by economic pragmatism and a scarcity of resources. Labor, water, arable land, and livestock were all in short supply. Efficient exploitation of available resources demanded communal cooperation, and retention of these resources required collective action for purposes of communal defense. Endogamous marriage, creating large extended families, and exogamous marriage, binding different families together, both would have served to reinforce the community's unity of purpose.

One manifestation of the ability of Mudejar communities to overcome their internal differences and present a united front to their antagonists was their aggressive and joint defiance of the authorities, particularly of those sent to their villages to make arrests or to confiscate goods. When a royal constable and other officials arrived in Callosa, where they were to collect 19,666s 8d from the Muslims for pensions owed, they discovered that the Muslims had hidden their goods in places nearby. As they were returning with the goods from one of these places, the Muslims ambushed them with a barrage of stones.[141] Officials sent to Matet to arrest two Muslims, fugitive vassals from Gaibiel, had even less luck: "there was made a great resistance by the Moors of the said place, not only breaking open the prisons where the said constable had put one arrested Moor and carrying him away, moreover, they inflicted on the said constable many blows with swords on the staff and one on the arm by which they wounded him." Three years later the *amīn* and *adelantats* of Matet were still refusing to cooperate in the matter.[142] Muslim vassals of Alcocer possessing lands in the *huerta* of Castellón de Játiva together cleverly constructed hidden threshing floors near the river, so that they could quickly send threshed wheat downstream without paying their agricultural taxes. When the tax collector later confiscated a horse as a pledge for the unpaid taxes, two Muslims with a lance convinced him to let the horse go.[143]

More numerous than the instances of resistance to royal officials were the clashes between vassals of various seigneuries. Neighboring villages were frequently at odds over boundaries, possession of land, distribution of irrigation water, and other such matters that affected the livelihood of their residents. Conflict of interests issued in the courts as litigation, but not infrequently took on the more sinister aspects of theft and violence. Animosity between lords also soured relations between their vassals. It is often unclear whether the actions of vassals against communities nearby were perpetrated with the consent and direction of their lord or whether the vassals took action of their own accord. For the most part one can probably presume a concurrence between lords and

vassals in such affairs, inasmuch as any gains or losses sustained by the
vassals were also felt by the lord.

A brief description of the difficulties and hostility faced by the vassals
of some seigneuries should provide some sense of the necessity for communal cooperation and a minimal degree of cohesion. The Muslims of
Llombay's marketing of their wheat in Alcira seems to have threatened
the interests of some Muslims of the town's *morería*. Litigation ensued
between them, and the bailiff of Alcira confiscated the wheat and pack
animals of Yuçeff Carroff of Llombay.[144] A decade later eight Muslims
of Llombay murdered a rival of Alcira just outside the walls of the town,
which suggests a long-term dispute.[145] Llombay's bailiff and Muslims
also rustled livestock from the pastures of neighboring Carlet, for which
crime the residents of Carlet planned to enter Llombay and take
action.[146] The vassals of Carlet had already been involved in a more
serious dispute with Alcudia, which had resulted from the feud between
their respective lords, Gaspar de Castellvi and Pere de Montagut. The
latter and two henchmen killed Silim Bono of Carlet and wounded his
son. Muslims and Christians of Carlet retaliated by wounding a Christian miller and killing a farmer in Alcudia. The feud was finally resolved
when Montagut married Castellvi's daughter.[147] Some conflicts were
more one-sided. The attack of the brothers Ferrer with their squires and
Muslim vassals so terrorized the Muslim residents of Faldeta that they
deserted the place.[148]

Perhaps the most frequent cause of strife was a community's mis-
appropriation of irrigation water, which placed in jeopardy the crops of
other communities in the vicinity. The lord of Alginet complained that
his village was "perishing" because the officials, including the *amīn*s,
of the Foya de Llombay were not allowing the water to flow as
accustomed.[149] The consequences of such disputes could prove dire,
such as the one between Antella and Sumacárcel over "a bridge or a
duct of an irrigation canal," which provoked Muslim and Christian vassals of Antella to kill Çahat Torraboni of the rival village.[150]

At the local level Mudejar society displays two conflicting tendencies:
on one hand, fragmentation, as manifested in the feuding relations between rival family or lineage groups; and, on the other hand, a reflexive
solidarity necessitated by the struggle between communities over the
possession of scarce natural resources. The former tendency was rooted
in traditional Arabo-Berber modes of social organization. The sources
of the latter tendency are more complex, for the importance of seigneurial rivalry and the role of Christian vassals in the strife between communities disallows a description of local solidarity as a purely Mudejar
phenomenon. Nevertheless, it is evident that the Muslims inhabiting
individual villages were able to unite when the livelihood of the entire

community was threatened, even if at the behest of their lord and in conjunction with their Christian neighbors. That such was the case perhaps can be explained in part by the ability of Arabo-Berber segmentary societies to amalgamate when necessary, as well as to atomize.

Considerable space has been devoted to a discussion of Mudejar social structure and to an analysis of Mudejar feuding relations not only to provide some insight into life within the *morería* below the surface of the Muslim–Christian interface but also to make a point crucial to the understanding of the remarkable tenacity with which the Mudejars and, later, the Moriscos adhered to Islam despite considerable pressures, both informal and formal, to the contrary. The point is that for the Mudejars religious conversion involved much more than a change in their religious beliefs, a change radical enough in itself; it demanded a fundamental alteration of their social attitudes and social organization. The Mudejars were shielded from the allure of Christianity not only by their profession of a faith as exclusive as Christianity but also by the vitality and structure of their subsociety, which was founded on social practices and assumptions distinct from those of their Christian neighbors. While Mudejar feuding in its outward bloody manifestations did not differ from Christian feuding, the social significance Muslims ascribed to it and the family structures and system of values on which it was based were distinct. The feud as a process of status determination was group-specific, functioning in its very intensity to reinforce traditional attitudes and structures. Moreover, religious belief and social practice were largely coterminous, so that the Mudejars' distinct social customs were as much a sign of their "Moorishness" as was their belief in the oneness of God and the prophethood of Muḥammad. For instance, conversion to Christianity would have meant a prohibition of the practice of endogamous marriage (between first cousins), a custom sanctioned by the Prophet and essential for the maintenance of their Arabo-Berber social structures.[151] The frequent and often friendly meeting of Muslim and Christian on the neutral ground of marketplace or tavern no more resulted in a merging of their different forms of social organization than it did in religious syncretism. Indeed, Mudejar social behavior, particularly the marked propensity for feuding—or at least the style and dynamic of that feuding—was sufficiently different so as to evoke comment from among the Christians. Francesch Centelles, a shoemaker well acquainted with the Muslims of Valencia's *morería*, when asked to testify in court about the character of Abrahim Murçi, responded in a manner that suggests that the feuding Mudejar had become a stereotype: "he is a man who seeks fights and quarrels, like any other Moor."[152]

Muslim Solidarity

It seems clear that the Mudejars' distinctively Arabo-Berber mode of social organization helped to shore up their cultural boundaries against the acculturative attrition of an overwhelming Christian presence. These boundaries preserved the essential element of their ethnic identity, the profession of Islam. Although social mores and behavior were intimately bound up with and were to a large extent the product of religious belief, nevertheless, they in themselves were insufficient to perpetuate the religious faith of the social group. The decision of Mudejars to flee the kingdom in 1502–1503 instead of abandoning Islam was the expression of an intensity of faith that transcended the more amorphous "Moorish" cultural identity engendered by repetitive social practice. It is necessary, therefore, to comprehend how the Mudejars actively instilled and fostered their Islamic faith and identity.

An essential element buttressing the faith of individual Muslims was the sense of belonging to a larger community of believers, the *ummah*. Whatever the situation of the *ummah*'s individual component polities, even those long since subjugated to Christian powers, membership in the *ummah* served to distinguish them from all non-Muslims. Unfortunately, the Muslims' adherence to a common faith did not preclude divisiveness within the *ummah*. Since the fall of the Umayyads in the eighth century the Islamic world had been rent by factionalism, and, as has been seen, this was no less true of the Mudejars. However, making allowances for human imperfection and the not unusual inconsistency between religious precept and social practice, that the Mudejars frequently embroiled themselves in feuds, despite the fact that Muḥammad had inveighed against such fratricidal strife among Muslims, does not mean that they had lost their sense of Muslim identity, particularly their collective identity vis-à-vis the Christian world. On the contrary, there were a number of instances in which the Mudejars appear to have acted as a collectivity or were perceived by the Christian authorities to have been such. Let us recall how the nobility advised Fernando against the forced conversion of Valencia's Muslims (1502), noting that "they have their communications with each other," and that any untoward royal initiatives would provoke a violent mass Mudejar reaction. The Mudejars also seem to have been united in a common concern for the embattled sultan of Granada, as was manifested in their taking up collections on his behalf, praying in their mosques for his victory, and negotiating with the Ottoman Turks to come to his rescue. Likewise, the aid provided to runaway slaves by the Mudejars—not just by one community but by any number of *morerías* in which the fugitives hid on their way to freedom—demonstrates their ability to act together as Muslims for the benefit of other Muslims.[153]

Mudejar group-consciousness may be seen as the sum of each Muslim's perception of the fundamental difference between himself and his Christian neighbor, and of each Muslim's participation in the life of an autonomous community juridically framed by the Shariah, a corpus of law at once religious and secular. This aggregate awareness of individual Mudejars, however, seems in itself insufficient to have counterbalanced the animosity between feuding families and competing communities, or to have allowed for the Mudejars' alleged network of "communications" and their ability to act as almost a single political entity. One must seek a more concrete pattern of relations transversing the cleavages between agnatic lineages and rival neighboring communities.

The role of exogamous marriage in binding families together and the factor of intercommunal strife in promoting solidarity among the inhabitants of any one village has been discussed. The apparent impediment of intercommunal conflict to a larger, kingdom-wide Muslim solidarity presents a greater problem. Mudejar economic activity, establishing contacts between Muslims of all walks of life from a variety of localities, would have been a key factor in circumventing, or at least lessening, the rivalry between communities. It must be emphasized that while the Mudejars were vassals of particular royal or seigneurial *morerías*, their economic activities were not circumscribed by the boundaries of any one place. This was especially true of itinerant retail merchants, whose vending took them from the northern to the southern reaches of the kingdom. Since by the nature of their work they were more or less unattached to any particular local interest, these merchants would have served as an appropriate medium for relaying information from one community to another, tying together the separate worlds of distinct aljamas.[154]

Another group whose activities were equally unhampered by specifically local concerns were the licensed mendicants, who traveled throughout the kingdom begging alms from their Muslim brethren. Since charity was one of the Five Pillars of Islam, these itinerant mendicants provided an opportunity for pious Muslims to express their religiosity in a manner unrelated to the secular aims of the family and community. Both the giver and the receiver of alms participated in a transaction that emphasized exclusively their obligations as members of an Islamic community, not those stemming from kinship or from residence in a particular place.[155]

The economic interplay between town and countryside made the kingdom's urban centers sites for the meeting and mingling of Muslims from various rural villages. Mudejars traveled to town to market produce, to purchase the manufactures of local artisans, or to pass their leisure time in the taverns or fonduk. The large Christian populations of the towns would have induced Muslims from out-of-town to congregate with their coreligionists before turning to Christians for comradeship. If towns like Játiva, Alcira, Castellón de la Plana, and Villarreal attracted Muslims from surrounding hamlets, the capital city gathered in Muslims from all over the kingdom—indeed, from all over the peninsula. Valencia, a veritable teeming metropolis, served as a "melting-pot" for the kingdom's Mudejars. This is indicated in the documentation by the frequent appearance of non-local Muslims working, purchasing, and pursuing litigation in the capital.[156] Furthermore, new vassals in Valencia's *morería* originated from seigneuries of a wide geographic range, whereas those swearing vassalage to the king in towns such as Játiva or Alcira came from seigneuries nearby.[157] Change of vassalage in itself accentuated two other trends that created links between Muslims of different communities. First, many Muslims who changed vassalage still continued to hold and cultivate land in their former seigneuries, either themselves or through local sharecroppers. This further complicated the already complex Valencian pattern of land tenure, which saw farmers and artisans renting small parcels of land in a variety of places, not just in their place of residence.[158] Mudejars with economic interests in diverse localities likely would have had friends and contacts of equally diverse origins. Thus land tenure itself sometimes cut across the lines of economic competition contingent upon strictly local affiliations. Second, change of vassalage caused the fragmentation of local lineage groups as nuclear families left their agnates behind when they settled elsewhere. Given the importance of *ᶜaṣabīyah* in Mudejar society, agnates living in different places were probably still bound by kinship. In addition to these intercommunal agnatic links, there also occurred exogamous marriages between families of different towns, such as the one uniting the niece of Játiva's *qāḍī* to the son of Valencia's *qāḍī*. Therefore, kinship, both agnatic and affinal, created a network of interests that would have mitigated the intensity of the rivalry between communities for economic reasons alone.[159]

The individual Mudejar's sense of belonging to a kingdom-wide Muslim community and the ritual expression of his commitment to Islam coalesced in the act of pilgrimage to the mosque of Atzeneta in the Vall de Guadalest. This mosque housed the sepulcher of the Sufi mystic Abū Aḥmad Jaᶜfar b. Sīd-bono al-Khuzāᶜī (d. 1227). From the thirteenth century until 1570, when King Felipe II had the mosque of Atzeneta destroyed, the tomb of this saint attracted Muslim pilgrims from all over the kingdom of Valencia, and sometimes from Aragon, Catalonia, Granada, and the Maghrib as well. Ecclesiastical views, expressed at the

Council of Vienne in 1311, that such Muslim pilgrimages were an affront to the Christian community, combined with royal misgivings about large numbers of Muslims of diverse origins gathering each year at the shrine of Atzeneta by 1379 resulted in Crown attempts to prohibit this pilgrimage. The royal authorities, however, were unsuccessful, for throughout the fifteenth century and much of the sixteenth century Valencian Muslims continued in "semiclandestine" fashion to journey to the tomb of Sīd-bono. This annual act of Islamic devotion thus became for the individual Mudejar a statement of resistance to Christian authority, a politically dangerous affirmation of identity with the other participants in the pilgrimage.[160]

As evinced by the Mudejars' awareness of the events occurring in the wider Islamic world, especially in Granada and the Maghrib, and by their political activities in conjunction with Granadan, Maghriban, and Ottoman Turkish Muslims, their understanding of what constituted the community of believers extended far beyond the borders of the kingdom. Recognition of this much larger community alleviated their sense of isolation and hopelessness, and strengthened their own Muslim identity, particularly when the large majority of that community was governed by Muslim rulers, some of whom, like the Ottoman sultan, were extremely powerful. As was pointed out in chapter 2, concrete family and commercial connections underlay the Mudejars' politicoreligious identification with the dār al-Islām. As a consequence of previous Mudejar emigration to Granada and the Maghrib, Valencian Muslims had family branches in Islamic lands. On account of these kinship ties, Mudejars traveled to Almería, Tunis, and Oran for the purpose of collecting the inheritances left them by deceased relatives, or, like Ali Fotoffa of Bétera, in order to visit those still alive.[161] A Muslim family of Cocentaina journeyed to Granada to attend a family wedding,[162] while a widow of the morería of Valencia married a Granadan Muslim and then departed with him to North Africa.[163] Like this marriage, there were other instances of recent emigration that forged new links of kinship between Valencia and the Maghrib. The sub-qāḍī of Játiva decided to spend his retirement in the Maghrib, while his son stayed behind in Játiva and succeeded him in office.[164] Yahye Bellvis, the brother of the qāḍī general, moved to Tunis and continued to benefit from his commercial connections in Valencia.[165] It was precisely such ties of kinship that facilitated Fernando's settlement of Granadan Muslims in Valencia after the conquest. Thus, Mahomat Fuçey of Bellreguart was licensed to travel to Almería "in order to fetch some relations that he has in the city."[166] Reciprocal commercial interests strengthened Mudejar affinity for Granada and the Maghrib. Mudejars journeyed to Almería and Tunis to sell their merchandise, while Maghriban merchants came to Valencia on business.[167] The royal licenses that permitted these merchants to reside in the kingdom for a year or more created ample opportunity for contact with Mudejars. Religion, kinship, and commerce all bound the Mudejar inextricably to the *dār al-Islām*. It is doubtful that the Mudejars' Muslim identity and group consciousness would have fared as well had they been isolated.

Relative isolation of a different sort actually abetted the Mudejars in their preservation of an Islamic culture. Historians have puzzled over the fact that despite royal efforts to attract Muslims to urban royal *morerías*, where the tax burden was lighter, the large majority nevertheless preferred to remain on seigneurial lands.[168] The Mudejars' choice of residence is best interpreted as having had a religiocultural foundation, rather than an economic one. Life in the largely Christian cities posed obvious threats to the integrity of Mudejar Islamic culture. Either militant Catholics were endeavoring to eradicate all signs of Islam—calling for the destruction of minarets, prohibiting the call to prayer, and the like—or the pleasantries of city life were insidiously weakening the Muslims' resolve to live in accordance with the Shariah. That pious Muslims were sensitive to the latter threat is evinced in the complaint of the aljama of Játiva regarding the nocturnal activities of Christian youths in the *morería* and the deleterious effect that the "dishonest dress" of the *alfondeguer*'s wife might be having on Muslim youths.[169]

In contrast, life in seigneurial villages afforded the Mudejars a refuge from an aggressive and expanding Christian presence. In these villages Muslims sometimes composed the majority of the population, and their freedom and comfort in religious observance were correspondingly greater. The lords seem to have had few qualms about the public manifestations of Islamic worship. For instance, they allowed their Muslim vassals to make the call to prayer with a horn and perhaps vocally, whereas it was prohibited in the cities.[170] During the time of the Moriscos, the seigneurs were infamous for permitting their ostensibly Christian vassals to practice Islam and for protecting them from the Inquisition.[171] The Mudejars also seem to have benefited from their lords' religious tolerance, even if at a price. For most Mudejars the religious freedom thus secured was sufficient compensation for the heavier burden of seigneurial dues.

Not surprisingly, the centers of Islamic learning in Valencia, such as they existed, were for the most part located in rural villages, not in urban *morerías*. Of the twenty-five Mudejars who journeyed to Almería, Tunis, Oran, and Granada for the purpose of studying the Arabic language and Islamic law (see table 19), only five came from urban *morerías*—four from Játiva and one from Castellón. The others all came from seigneurial lands—Ondara, Cuartell, Artana, Mascarell, Valldig-

Table 19.   Valencian Muslims Studying Abroad (ARV: C 707)

Date	Student	Origin	Destination
10/1/1480	Mahomat Abenferis	Cuartell	Tunis
12/1/1480	Cuayet Batora	Ondara	Tunis
12/1/1480	Çahat Tarbani	Valldigna	Tunis
14/1/1480	Yuçeff Exerri	la Llosa	Tunis
17/4/1480	Amet Alfaqui b. Yuçeff Alfaqui	Mascarell	Almería
19/4/1480	Çahat Galip	Játiva	Almería
21/4/1480	Ali de Medina	Castile	Almería
26/4/1480	Yuçeff Nocola	Artana	Almería
26/4/1480	Çahat Alluix	Mascarell	Almería
28/4/1480	Mahomat Tagari	Artana	Almería
28/4/1480	Alet Benhamet Benaheza	Artana	Almería
28/4/1480	Mahomat Purri	Játiva	Almería
28/4/1480	Maymo Sonaydach	Artana	Almería
9/5/1481	Abrahim Marnhan	Játiva	Tunis
9/5/1481	Ali Lenlu	Játiva	Tunis
21/5/1481	Çilim Polo	la Llosa	Tunis
21/5/1481	Azmet Axer	Benilloba	Tunis
21/5/1481	Mahomat Chorrut	Benilloba	Tunis
21/5/1481	Ali Ezbala	Castellón	Tunis
2/6/1481	Abdalla Camarell	Carlet	Tunis
24/10/1481	Fuçey Maçot	Vall de Uxó	Tunis
10/11/1481	Ali Mila	Beniopa	Tunis
10/11/1481	Amet Açen	Matet	Tunis
25/6/1484	Çahat Abducarim	Oliva	Oran
26/3/1493 (B 1160: 646v–647r)	Fotaya Çot	Vall de Uxó	Granada

na, Benilloba, the Vall de Uxó, and so on.[172] Barceló Torres, intimating the cultural inferiority of the urban morerías, notes that of the 270 Mudejar and Morisco Arabic documents she has found, only nine were drawn up in the morería of Valencia.[173] It is indicative of this state of affairs that Çahat Coret of the Foya de Buñol, who "applied himself diligently to Agarene letters," was appointed faqīh of Valencia, after the aljama had failed to find anyone in the morería sufficiently learned to fill the post.[174]

It appears, then, that the Mudejars' Muslim identity was nurtured both through the unobstructed public worship of Islam, a freedom they secured by their choice of residence, and through the maintenance of and participation in a literate Arabic culture. Clearly, the latter was needed to sustain the former. Even a minimal level of popular religious awareness necessitated the mediation of learned men (ᶜulamā') who could read and interpret the Qur'ān for the faithful (the Arabic dialect spoken by Mudejars was different from the classical language of the Qur'ān). Beyond that, men conversant in jurisprudence (fiqh) and all that entailed—a knowledge of the Qur'ān and of the customs of Muḥammad and his companions (Sunnah) as set down in the traditions (hadīth)—were needed to administer justice in the Islamic courts, either as qāḍī or as faqīh, and to see to it that the community lived as much as possible within the framework of the Shariah. Taking into account the Mudejars' situation as a minority enclave composed primarily of farmers and artisans, the grooming of even a small group of ᶜulamā' required a determined and sustained effort. Mudejar acquisition of the necessary cultic and legal knowledge was in itself a considerable achievement. The social and intellectual environment was unpropitious for the creation of original scholarly works.

Arabic instruction given to Mudejar children in local schools perpetuated this rudimentary but essential Arabic culture. The thirteenth-century capitulations had granted the basic privilege of maintaining schools to the Mudejars.[175] The Muslims inhabiting the new morería of Orihuela (formed in 1446, but lasting only until 1451) were allowed "to have a schoolmaster." The morería of Valencia also had a school, at least until 1455.[176] Documentation from Fernando's reign contains references to schools operating in Ondara, Oliva,[177] and Valldigna.[178] Perhaps Çahat Coret of the Foya de Buñol began his studies of "Agarene letters" in his hometown. Since the Mudejars were able to give at least an elementary Arabic education to their children in Valencia, one may infer that the Mudejars who took the trouble to travel to Granada or North Africa for study did so not merely "to learn to read and write Moorish," as the travel licenses state, but to pursue more advanced studies, particularly in jurisprudence. Tunis and Almería were both well equipped to meet the academic needs of the aspiring Mudejar faqīh.[179]

It is difficult to know whether there were schools for more advanced studies in Valencia, although it seems that the Mudejars possessed a sufficient amount of learned Arabic works to have allowed for at least the informal meeting of erudite ᶜulamā' with students eager to learn. Juan Andres, the convert from Játiva, recounted that his father, a faqīh, had taught him jurisprudence.[180] Barceló Torres's search for the bits of Arabic literature surviving in Valencia reveals that fifteenth-century Mudejars had access to Qur'āns, hadīth literature, devotional works, and legal works.[181] Also, in 1450 a *faqīh* of Paterna brought back from Cairo a treatise on trigonometry, in which the use of an astronomical instrument is explained.[182] The most impressive information on Mudejar higher learning comes, surprisingly, from the kingdom of Aragon. The letter of a student to a *faqīh* in Belchite reveals the existence of a *madrasah* (school) in Zaragoza as late as 1494. There the student in question studied theology, and medicine from the *Qānūn* of Ibn Sīnā (Avicenna).[183] Considering that such a school still functioned in Aragon, where the Muslims' fluency in Arabic was much less than that of their brethren in Valencia—although perhaps not as minimal as was once thought[184]—it would seem that similar centers of advanced study must have existed in Valencia as well. It is doubtful that every Valencian *faqīh* had the opportunity to travel to Islamic lands for study; some were probably purely local products. Moreover, there were Mudejar physicians and surgeons in Valencia, and these professions required a certain amount of learning, perhaps in the classical Arabic medical texts. Juçeff Alatar, a surgeon of Valencia, was granted a royal license to practice after administering to a Christian knight and passing the examination given by a Christian "master in medicine."[185]

The Mudejars frequently utilized their Arabic literacy in a far more mundane fashion in the writing of letters and contracts for official and private business. The extant Arabic documentation contains records of tax payment, and letters to and from local *amīn*s concerning the collection of taxes and debts from Muslim vassals or judicial procedure against them.[186] Much of this correspondence was between *amīn*s and royal bailiffs, which indicates the functioning and interpenetration of two levels of bureaucracy: the all-encompassing royal Romance-Latin administration and the local Mudejar Arabic administration manned by *amīn*s, *qāḍī*s, and *faqīh*s. It has already been demonstrated how the two bureaucracies interrelated in the matter of the Crown's taxation of Mudejar inheritances (chap. 4). The Christian authorities' recognition of Arabic documents as valid evidence in litigation and as contractually binding in business transactions, even those between Muslims and Christians, gave Arabic an "official" status in the kingdom of Valencia.[187] For instance, when passing sentence in favor of Fatima Bisquey, who claimed that she owned half of a house given to her as bridewealth (*ṣadāq*) by her husband, against the opposing claimant, the merchant Berthomeu Pinos, the bailiff general pointed out that the decisive evidence was "an act of *acidach* (*ṣadāq*) and/or marriage contract—exhibited in the trial on behalf of the said Fatima—received by the *qāḍī* and/or *faqīh* Mahomat ben Abdulaziz Alcari on the date of 11 March 892 of the Moorish calendar."[188] Muslims bound themselves to pay debts to Christian creditors by acknowledging their debts in Arabic documents. In an Arabic document written in his own hand, Ubaydal Donzell confessed, "I, Ubaydal Donzell, recognize that I owe to you, Manuel Bou, eighteen and one-half pounds, which are for spices and alum."[189]

The cultivation of Arabic for higher intellectual pursuits—Qur'ānic study, *fiqh*, medicine, and so on—for the drawing up of legal instruments of various sorts—marriage contracts, letters of debt, and tax records—and for daily parlance lent the Mudejars a common ethnic identity and group consciousness on the basis of language alone. Their knowledge of Arabic allowed them to participate in the intellectual life of the wider Islamic world, just as their understanding of Romance enabled them to function more efficiently in Valencia's Christian society. The Mudejars' use of Romance, however, was far more occasional, employed only when they desired or needed to communicate with Christians. Otherwise, Arabic was an effective social and intellectual barrier between Valencia's Muslim and Christian communities. Indeed, the Mudejars' use of Arabic sometimes aroused Christian suspicions. When Muslim slaves escaped from their masters, any Mudejar who had been seen speaking with the slave in Arabic was considered a prime suspect as an accessory to the crime.[190] The Christians assumed that the Mudejars' choice of language defined their sympathies and guided their actions as persuasively as did their religious faith. There was much truth in this assumption. Since Arabic was the language of the Qur'ān, literally the word of God dictated to Muḥammad, its use by the Mudejars had a special spiritual significance, and therefore contributed to their perception of themselves as Muslims. The veneration of the Arabic language itself explains the Aragonese and Castilian Mudejars' and Moriscos' writing of *aljamiado* literature (Romance written in Arabic script) as a means of strengthening their Muslim identity. It also explains why the Christian authorities decided to prohibit the Valencian Moriscos' teaching of Arabic to their children as a means of effecting their true conversion to Christianity.[191]

Social structure, language, communal and judicial autonomy, ties of kinship and commerce within Valencia and with their coreligionists in the *dār al-Islām*—all contributed to the Mudejars' distinct religioethnic identity and to their perception of themselves as a single body united in stark cultural opposition to Christian society. Still, the body required animation and direction, a sense of purpose particularly Islamic. This was provided by the *faqīh*s. They functioned in the Mudejar social body as spiritual cadres, infusing its individual communal cells with a commitment to Islam and, by virtue of their grounding in a common intellectual tradition and world view, binding those cells together in a unity of religious purpose. As the local fonts of religious and legal knowledge, the

jurists were eminently suited for this task. By offering their legal opinions and resolving disputes on the basis of the Shariah, they ensured that
it remained the lofty standard against which Mudejars evaluated their
own conduct and by which they endeavored to regulate their lives.

The plea of the newly converted Moriscos in their negotiations with
Carlos I in 1526 reflects the great esteem in which the *faqīh*s were held
by the kingdom's Muslim populace. The Moriscos informed the king
that in the days before the conversions, "when the call to prayer was
made in the mosques," the Muslims of the kingdom used the rents from
those properties bequeathed by the pious to the mosques to pay the
salary of the *faqīh*s, "who have consumed their whole life in studying
and knowing the Moorish law and have not been concerned with other
offices." The Moriscos went on to request that a portion of the rents
pertaining to the new Morisco churches, formerly mosques, continue to
be reserved for the support of the baptized jurists.[192] The Morisco
*faqīh*s—and they are still referred to as *alfaqin*s in the sixteenth-century
documentation—continued throughout the sixteenth century to form
the core of Morisco resistance to the official Christian program of religious and social assimilation.[193]

The aforementioned Morisco request reveals important information
about the Mudejar jurists. It is clear that they devoted their entire lives
to the study of Islamic law and, presumably, of its foundations, the
Qur'ān and the *Sunnah*. Because the study of the jurists ensured the
continuity of Islam as a living religious and intellectual tradition, the
Mudejars deemed it an essential activity, so essential that they used the
pious endowments (*waqf*) bequeathed by the faithful to the mosques to
support the jurists. Furthermore, the jurists were supported in such a
way that they would not need to bother themselves with any labor other
than that properly religious and legal. It is important to note that in
Islam there were neither priests nor an ecclesiastical hierarchy for whom
financial support was institutionalized, as was the case with the Catholic
Church. The Mudejars' support of the *faqīh*s was made possible by the
will of the community, a local adaptation to a situation in which Islam
had long been deprived of public primacy.

Despite the *faqīh*'s key role in the life of the Mudejar community, the
documentation provides, unfortunately, very little information about
him. The reason for this is that the *faqīh*'s sphere of activity—the mosque, the *madrasah*, the Islamic court—was very rarely impinged on by
the Christian world. Matters concerning Muslims alone and not affecting the public life of the kingdom had no importance for the king and his
officials. As a result, it is the *amīn*, the fiscal and juridical intermediary
between Muslim and Christian worlds, who appears most often in the

documentation. The activities of the *faqīh* held as little interest for the Christians as did the Muslims' theological views.

The primary role of the *faqīh* was that of jurisconsult, acting either as counsellor or as arbitrator in litigations between Muslims. Ageg b. Çaat Ageg of Alcira paid 10s to the *faqīh* of Villalonga for having counseled him in his dispute with Abraym Xativi.[194] A *faqīh* of Ondara traveled to Ribarroja in order to "treat with and reconcile a Moor and a Mooress, husband and wife, who wanted to separate."[195] The *faqīh* also taught in the local school, a task for which his years of study had well prepared him.[196]

Also, as the Moriscos stated in 1526, the *faqīh*s "were serving in the mosques," undoubtedly as preachers. Regarding the content of their sermons, the only information comes indirectly from the allusions made by the nobility when, in 1502, they beseeched Fernando not to convert their Muslim vassals. It seems reasonable to assert that the sermons of the jurists comprised primarily instruction in the basic tenets and precepts of Islam and positive exhortation to conduct oneself accordingly. As a consequence of their teaching, the lords stated, "among them [the Mudejars] each one defends the said sect [of Islam] and has worked and works [to the end] that the Moor may be a good Moor."[197] More interesting is a type of sermon more negative in tone, which constituted a defense of Islam through a disparagement of Christianity. The nobles offered an illuminating explanation of why the Mudejars were "beside themselves" with fear that the Inquisition would proceed against them all:

> they [the Mudejars] say that . . . none of them could be excused [from prosecution by the Inquisition] because publicly they have had and have in the present kingdom their mosques and their *faqīh*s, who publicly admonish them that the sect of Mahomat is better than the law of the Christians and that all [Christians] end in this damnation.[198]

By emphasizing the threat of eternal damnation, the jurists hoped to discourage potential Muslim apostates who might be toying with the idea of baptism for worldly reasons. This kind of preaching may be interpreted as a reaction to the pressures exerted by an increasingly militant Spanish Church and to the threatening pervasiveness of Christian culture. The tragic end of the Spanish Jews and Conversos, and the incipient movements of the Inquisition against Islam, could hardly have failed to impress upon the *faqīh*s the necessity of a defensive anti-Christian posture.

The contemporary struggle between Christian and Islamic states did not fail to influence the direction of the *faqīhs'* activism. The jurists understood what implications the conquest of Granada might have for the future of Islam in the Iberian peninsula, in terms of both the morale of the Mudejar populace and the Mudejars' treatment by the Catholic Monarchs. Consequently, the jurists' activity, particularly their preaching, took on a markedly political tone. It was they who collected in the *morerías* funds for the aid of the beleaguered Naṣrid sultan. Moreover, the king was informed:

> the said Moors and the *faqīhs* of the said *morerías* since the time of this enterprise [the war against Granada] have ordered a certain prayer and they make that [prayer] continually in their hours [of prayer], [the prayer] containing, in effect, that God should exalt the said king of Granada and that He should destroy us [King Fernando] and all our people.[199]

While the efforts of Mudejar jurists could hardly have altered the course of political events, they nevertheless succeeded admirably in strengthening the commitment of their congregations to Islam. This commitment is evinced in the very low rate of Mudejar apostasy. One document offers a rare glimpse of Mudejar sensitivity in matters of faith, an area of life where Christian interference was not easily endured. When royal officials made the mistake of entering a mosque in Ondara in order to apprehend a condemned Muslim criminal, the reaction of the congregation was one of violent indignation. "The Moors, *amīns*, jurates [*adelantats*], and all the people" hurled "stones and . . . the tiles from the roofing, and with lances and crossbows wishing and working to damage you [the lieutenant governor] and your ministers, made a great resistance against you, perturbing you and preventing the capture of the one convicted."[200]

The success of the *faqīhs* in overcoming intracommunal and intercommunal factionalism and imparting to each community a sense of commitment to the common cause of Islam was furthered by two factors: the communication between those possessed of religious and legal knowledge, and the foundation of the jurists' status on terms different from those which determined the prestige of other community members. Even though each *faqīh* belonged to a particular community, the *faqīhs* did not exist in a state of intellectual isolation, instructing their congregations and offering legal opinions without consideration of the opinions and perhaps greater knowledge of their learned fellows in other places. On the contrary, their role as the transmitters of a common tradition and their very similar intellectual formation—all having been educated in Granada, the Maghrib, and Valencia—facilitated consultation among the learned and, indeed, advised it, if they were to maintain a consistent orthodox standard. The activities of the *faqīh* Abdalla, originally a captive from Tripoli, suggest a network of communication and consultation among the Muslim judges and jurists of the kingdom. While in Valencia, Abdalla met the *faqīh* of Manises, and they discussed Islamic law. The latter then invited him to dinner in Manises. He was also a friend of the *qāḍī* of Benaguacil and lodged in his home. In Ribarroja Abdalla acted as marriage counselor to an unhappy couple. He taught school in Ondara, Oliva, and other places, and while in Oliva he conferred with the *faqīh* and "read in the said *morería*." More interesting still, he and the *faqīh* of Paterna exchanged Arabic books.[201] Abdalla's career was probably somewhat more peripatetic than that of most jurists, since he had to wander about collecting alms to repay the aljama of Ondara for having ransomed him. Nevertheless, Abdalla was able to "go among the *faqīh*s of the present kingdom begging for the love of God," because there were established channels of communication among the learned, and because he himself was "a man of knowledge."[202]

The career of Abdalla also demonstrates that the Mudejars on the whole respected and heeded the opinions of learned and holy men. Abdalla was known by Muslims throughout the kingdom and was reputed to lead the life of a saint.[203] The *qāḍī* of Játiva, the kingdom's largest *morería*, related why he and the aljama wished to make Abdalla their jurist. Abdalla, the *qāḍī* pointed out, "is a very good Moor and . . . leader of prayers [*oracioner*]," so much so that after the death of the former *faqīh* of Játiva, Abdalla, owing to his "good fame, life, and knowledge," was the unanimous choice to succeed him.[204]

Clearly, the prestige of Abdalla, a foreigner and technically a slave, and of men like him in the eyes of the Mudejar community, rested neither on wealth nor on family backing; rather, their status and influence, both local and, in the case of Abdalla, kingdom-wide, derived from their knowledge of religious and legal tradition and from the holiness of their lives. This is suggested in two other cases mentioned above: the intervention of a *faqīh* from Villalonga as legal counselor in a litigation between Muslims in distant Alcira, and the appointment of a Muslim of the Foya de Buñol as *faqīh* of Valencia on the basis of his diligent studies alone. Put in another way, the jurists were able to rise above the petty feuding between Mudejar families and villages because their way of life, financially supported by the community, removed them from the competition for honor, wealth, and political power. Their opinion was heeded because they were nonpartisan and had no stakes in that competition. It is probable that the jurists were able to attenuate the intensity of local feuding by acting as legal counselors and arbitrators between disputants. Their preaching was persuasive because it was an expression of the knowledge and piety that so few possessed. The jurists were able to appeal to the Mudejars as Muslims on a level of consciousness unrelated to mundane local concerns. Because the jurists themselves had a scholarly network of sorts and a certain consensus of opinion regarding the Mudejar community's needs, they preached a similar message. Their message, that of Muslim resistance to Christian assimilative pressure, had efficacy and resonance because, on one hand, they themselves were dispersed throughout the kingdom's Muslim population, local products closely tied to their people, while on the other hand, they possessed vital knowledge that raised them above the mass of Mudejars in an overarching network of religious leadership.[205]

For reasons beyond the control of Valencia's *faqīhs*, the Muslims of the kingdom were to spend their final years in the peninsula as unwilling Christians. As has been seen, the chain of events that led to the Mudejars' conversion began with the fall of Granada. This signal and seemingly conclusive event in the long and bloody peninsular struggle between Islam and Christianity had an unforeseen and somewhat ironic consequence. For the Mudejars of Valencia it resulted in a cultural windfall that would help them in the difficult days ahead.

When Fernando settled conquered Granadan Muslims in Valencia and promoted the sale of Maghriban and Granadan prisoners of war within the kingdom, he was not only helping himself by increasing royal revenues but also unconsciously contributing to the Mudejars' Muslim identity and group solidarity. The influx of numerous Muslim captives—hundreds from Málaga alone—elicited from the Mudejars considerable cooperative effort on behalf of their Muslim fellows. Mudejar communities collectively ransomed Muslims and, in a seemingly organized fashion, provided assistance to runaway slaves. More important still was the type of Muslim brought into the kingdom through Christian conquest and piracy. These Muslim captives and settlers, unaccustomed to Christian rule and little affected by the acculturative impact of long-term coexistence with Christians, were in all likelihood more steadfast in their commitment to their ancestral faith. Among the new arrivals were men of learning. There were physicians from Granada, jurists and readers of the Qur'ān from both Granada and the Maghrib, and a Sufi mystic from the Maghrib.[206] True, it is not known what became of these men, although the career of the *faqīh* Abdalla of Tripoli, a captive known throughout the kingdom for his learning and piety, is, if not typical, suggestive. In this regard, a puzzling but interesting comment was made by some Christians about Abdalla. When the Christian hostess of a hostel and some Muslims lodging there introduced Abdalla to some Christian guests as a *faqīh*, the Christians remarked, apparently in jest, "he is black and he could be a *faqīh*."[207] Given the similarity between Iberian Muslims and Christians in terms of skin color, the reference to Abdalla's darker coloration as if it were part of a widespread stereotype of Valencia's *faqīh*s hints at a perhaps more general phenomenon of Mudejar religious leaders with Maghriban origins. In any case, the social organization of Mudejar society would have facilitated the integration of Granadan and Maghriban Muslims, both erudite men and less extraordinary folk. Thus, Mudejar society was strangely reinvigorated as a result of the Monarchs' war against Islam. While the conquest of Granada ushered in the tragedy of the Moriscos, it also ensured that the Christian authorities of Valencia would have more formidable opponents in their struggle to eradicate Islam from the kingdom. Islam survived in Valencia not as a fossilized remnant of thirteenth-century Almohad glory, but as a resilient and adaptive society, steeled by its social structure and inspired by its *faqīh*s.

Conclusion

The historian studying the religious minorities of Christian Spain during the reign of Fernando and Isabel can hardly escape a sense of impending doom and a tendency to comb the documentation for indications of royal plans to eliminate them, through either baptism or expulsion. The Catholic Monarchs' crusades against the sultanates of Granada and North Africa, or further afield against the Ottoman Turks, provide even more reason for pessimism regarding the position of the Mudejars in the late fifteenth century.

Yet the study of Fernando's policy toward the Muslim subjects of the Crown of Aragon, particularly toward those in the kingdom of Valencia, has produced conclusions that defy our expectations. For Fernando had no intention of removing the Islamic presence from his kingdoms, and it seems that at least on this score he and his wife were not of one mind. In the kingdom of Valencia (and presumably in Aragon and Catalonia as well), where Fernando alone ruled, the king made a considerable effort to augment the population of royal *morerías* by drawing Muslim vassals away from seigneurial lands, by constructing new *morerías*, or by settling Muslims from the conquered sultanate of Granada in Valencia. The Catholic Monarch saw no need to change in any way the centuries-old tradition of Mudejarism, and was most concerned to ensure that the Crown received as great a share as was possible of the economic benefits accruing from the Mudejars' labor and enterprise.

Nor did the international confrontation with Islamic states divert Fernando from this traditional policy. It is true that the forays of the Ottoman Turks on and around the Italian peninsula caused the king to look somewhat askance at his Muslim subjects, and it is equally true that those same subjects sometimes collaborated with Maghriban corsairs and Granadan *almugavers* or attempted to aid the Naṣrids in their struggle for survival against the Spanish Christian onslaught. Nevertheless, royal fears were not great enough, nor were Mudejar subversive activities serious enough to undermine the tradition of Mudejarism. Indeed, the position of the Mudejars as a fifth column, whether grounded in reality or fabricated from paranoia, was integral to that tradition and a factor with which Fernando and his predecessors were willing to contend.

The popular Christian view of the Mudejars did not differ substantially from that of the king, for although the crusade against Islam was constantly preached throughout Fernando's reign, the Christian masses did not rise up in violence against the local Moors. If anything, Fernando deemed that many of his Christian subjects mingled with the Mudejars all too closely and freely. While the king preferred that the Mudejars contribute to the kingdom's economy but remain socially segregated, his Christian subjects were unable or unwilling to make such strict distinctions between economic activity and social life. It was above all the daily interaction between Muslim and Christian in the workplace and the marketplace that lent stability to Muslim–Christian *convivencia* in Valencia, and allowed for the breakdown of some, although by no means all, of the social barriers between them.

It must be emphasized that the economic foundation of *convivencia* consisted of far more than a desire on the part of the Crown and the nobility to retain Muslim serfs for purposes of taxation. Rather, Christian farmers, artisans, and merchants also had good reason to view favorably the Muslims, with whom they worked, traded, and became commercial partners. Furthermore, the Mudejars themselves were able to profit from this economic activity. Far from being oppressed and immobile serfs, many Mudejars were able to take advantage of the more favorable conditions of the fifteenth century. They changed vassalage with the aim of achieving better working and living conditions; they bought, leased, or reclaimed additional land; and they struck out on new commercial ventures. The Mudejars partook of the relative prosperity that the kingdom of Valencia enjoyed in the fifteenth century.

Nevertheless, beneath the apparent normalcy and continuity of tradition signs of change and a movement toward explosive conflict are evident. By Fernando's reign the towns and the rural nobility were well entrenched in their bitter rivalries over boundaries, irrigation rights, and court jurisdictions. Not infrequently the Mudejars found themselves unwillingly at the center of these disputes. Because they were so highly valued as vassals, the Mudejars were often victimized by their lord's antagonists, and because they were Muslims the Mudejars' oppressors were not inhibited by conscience and only minimally by law. However, this oppression stemmed from the political and economic strategies of the nobility and the municipal authorities; it was not an expression of widespread hostility against the Mudejars. It took the social revolution of the *Germanías* (1519–1522), when the animosity between barons and town citizens was most furiously expressed, to bring the latent anti-Muslim sentiments of the Christian populace to the fore. And this did not occur until two years after the revolt had erupted. The anti-Muslim violence of the *Germanías*, like that of the Christian mob who had assaulted the *morería* of Valencia in 1455, was an expression of both religious hostility and economic resentment. The difference between 1455 and 1521 was that in the former instance the violence was more limited, order was quickly restored, and *convivencia* was able to persist, much as it always had, with a potentiality for ethnic violence. In the latter case, although the royal forces restored order through the crushing of the *Germanías*, *convivencia* was no longer possible, for the *Germanías* had taken an irrevocable step: they had forcibly baptized thousands of Mudejars. Now royal policy—that of Carlos I—was dictated by theological considerations, not by tradition or economic pragmatism. Baptism, the theologians had ruled, was ineffaceable, and, lest the faith of the new converts be corrupted by Islam, all Muslims had to choose between conversion and exile.

Of course, the emperor Carlos was merely following the example of his grandparents, Fernando and Isabel, whose decisions to expel the Jews and to convert the Muslims of Granada and Castile were founded on the same inescapable logic. And this was the sad irony of Fernando's Mudejar policy, for despite his determination to uphold Mudejarism in the lands of the Crown of Aragon, he had set a dangerous precedent by acquiescing in his wife's treatment of the Mudejars of her own kingdoms. Notwithstanding the institutional and cultural distinctiveness of Aragon, Fernando's Christian subjects could not remain unaffected by what had transpired in Granada and Castile between 1499 and 1502. Thus they began to murmur about converting or expelling their own Mudejars, and this murmuring continued until the revolt of the *Germanías*. Moreover, Fernando by his own actions—not merely through his inaction in Castile—had unintentionally strengthened the resolve of these Christians who felt that Castilian Mudejar policy should have a sequel in Aragon. For through his determination to establish the Inquisition in his own kingdoms at whatever cost in order to eradicate the judaizing heresy, Fernando had demonstrated quite clearly not that the Catholic faith was to be used as a tool to unify the Spanish state—which his subjects only dimly recognized—but that religious unity, or rather the purity of the faith, was an end in itself. Unfortunately, many of Fernando's Christian subjects could not make the fine distinction that their king made between protecting the faith of new converts by converting or expelling their former coreligionists, and protecting all Christians by ridding Christian society of the Islamic and Jewish presence once and for all. Even though Fernando's intention was undoubtedly the former, the goal of the Inquisitors, whom he himself had set loose in his kingdoms, was patently the latter. Mudejarism in the Crown of Aragon expired both despite and because of Fernando's policy.

Yet Islam was to outlive the Mudejars for another century in Spain and then would be carried out of the peninsula by the Moriscos when they were finally expelled in 1609. Islam endured among the Mudejars and the Moriscos not through fervor of religious belief alone, but also through their perpetuation of a distinct social world, structurally coherent and of great vitality. Social structures and mores, family life—even feuding—an Arabic culture, and religious belief all lent the Mudejars a sense of distinctiveness, tradition, and pride which the baptismal waters could not erase. Fernando, Isabel, Cardinal Cisneros, and the Inquisitors were all tragically mistaken in supposing that the true conversion of the Muslim minorities was simply a theological problem. Only the lonely figure of Hernando de Talavera, the first archbishop of Granada, sensed how intimately cultural form and social practice were linked to religious belief. Only his sensitive approach to proselytizing the Muslims by meeting them halfway on their own cultural ground had any chance of success. Because the Spanish Church chose the path of Cisneros, the competition between the Catholic clergy and the Muslim *faqīh*s for the souls of Mudejars and Moriscos had a foregone conclusion.

Abbreviations

ACA: Archivo de la Corona de Aragón
ARV: Archivo del Reino de Valencia
AMV: Archivo Municipal de Valencia
  C: Cancillería Real
  B: Bailía General
MR: Maestre Racional
  G: Gobernación
  g^3: Cartas Missivas

Notes

Introduction

1. See Américo Castro, *España en su historia: cristianos, moros, y judíos* (Barcelona, 1983, second edition), pp. 200–209; idem, *The Spaniards. An Introduction to Their History*, Willard F. King and Selma Margaretten, trans. (Berkeley, 1971), p. 584, where *convivencia* is translated as a "living-togetherness."

2. Cited by Claude Cahen, "Dhimma," in *Encyclopaedia of Islam* (Leiden, 1960, second edition), II: 227. On this question, see also Antoine Fattal, *Le statut légal des non-musulmans en pays d'Islam* (Beirut, 1958).

3. Robert I. Burns, *Muslims, Christians, and Jews in the Crusader Kingdom of Valencia* (Cambridge, 1984), p. 59.

4. Thomas F. Glick, *Islamic and Christian Spain in the Early Middle Ages* (Princeton, 1979), pp. 168–169.

5. Miguel Gual Camarena, "Mudéjares valencianos, aportaciones para su estudio," *Saitabi* 7 (1949): 165–199; idem, "Los mudéjares valencianos en la época del Magnánimo," *IV Congreso de Historia de la Corona de Aragón* I (1959): 467–494; Leopoldo Piles, "La situación social de los moros de realengo en la Valencia del siglo XV," *Estudios de Historia Social de España* 1 (1949): 225–274; Francisco Macho y Ortega, "Condición social de los mudéjares aragoneses (siglo XV)," *Memorias de la facultad de filosofía y letras de la Universidad de Zaragoza* I (1923): 137–319; and Miguel Angel Ladero Quesada, *Los Mudéjares de Castilla en tiempos de Isabel I* (Valladolid, 1969).

6. Stephen H. Haliczer, "The Castilian Urban Patriciate and the Jewish Expulsions of 1480–92," *American Historical Review* 78 (1973): 35–58; Henry Kamen, *The Spanish Inquisition* (London, 1965), p. 7; idem, *Inquisition and Society in Spain in the Sixteenth and Seventeenth Centuries* (Bloomington, 1985), pp. 14–15, where Kamen abandons his earlier views; Tarsicio de Azcona,

Isabel la Católica: estudio crítico de su vida y su reinado (Madrid, 1964), pp. 641–643; and Maurice Kriegel, "La prise d'une décision: l'expulsion des juifs d'Espagne," *Revue Historique* 260 (1978): 49–90.

7. Tulio Halperin Donghi, *Un conflicto nacional: moriscos y cristianos viejos en Valencia* (Valencia, 1980); Henri Lapeyre, *Géographie de l'Espagne morisque* (Paris, 1959); Joan Regla, *Estudios sobre los moriscos* (Barcelona, 1974); Louis Cardaillac, *Morisques et Chrétiens: un affrontement polémique (1492–1640)* (Paris, 1977). Most recently, Dolors Bramon, *Contra moros i jueus* (Valencia, 1981) and María del Carmen Barceló Torres, *Minorías islámicas en el país valenciano: historia y dialecto* (Valencia, 1984) have produced valuable syntheses that treat both the Mudejars and the Moriscos. However, both authors display a tendency to leap all too easily from the Mudejars to the Moriscos without considering the social and economic, as well as religious, changes involved. The reign of Fernando II is a notable gap in the these works.

8. Robert I. Burns, *Islam under the Crusaders: Colonial Survival in the Thirteenth-Century Kingdom of Valencia* (Princeton, 1973); John Boswell, *The Royal Treasure: Muslim Communities under the Crown of Aragon in the Fourteenth Century* (New Haven, 1977).

9. Thomas F. Glick and Oriol Pi-Sunyer, "Acculturation as an Explanatory Concept in Spanish History," *Comparative Studies in Society and History* 11 (1969): 136–154; Glick, *Islamic and Christian Spain*; and Pierre Guichard, *Structures sociales "orientales" et "occidentales" dans l'Espagne musulmane* (Paris, 1977).

Chapter One:
Fernando II and the Mudejars

1. Andrés Bernáldez, *Memorias del reinado de los Reyes Católicos*, J. de M. Carriazo and M. Gómez-Moreno, eds. (Madrid, 1962), p. 107

2. A recent example is Joseph Pérez et al., *Historia de España*, Vol. V: *La frustración de un imperio (1469–1714)*, Manuel Tuñon de Lara, ed. (Barcelona, 1982), pp. 155–162.

3. J. N. Hillgarth, *The Spanish Kingdoms*, Vol. II: *Castilian Hegemony (1410–1516)*, (Oxford, 1978), pp. 349–532, emphasizes the importance of tradition in the Monarchs' formulation of policy.

4. Kriegel, "L'expulsion des juifs."

5. For the conversion of the Muslims of Granada and Castile, see Ladero Quesada, *Mudéjares de Castilla*, pp. 69–82, and Hillgarth, *Spanish Kingdoms*, II: 470–483. On the Mudejars and Moriscos under Carlos, see Ricardo García Cárcel, *Orígenes de la Inquisición Española: el tribunal de Valencia, 1478–1530* (Barcelona, 1976), pp. 98–101, 116–132, and the still useful Pascual Boronat y Barrachina, *Los moriscos españoles y su expulsión* (Valencia, 1901), 1: 121–169.

6. José María Lacarra, "Introducción al estudio de los mudéjares aragoneses," in *I Simposio Internacional de Mudejarismo* (Madrid-Teruel, 1981),

pp. 17–28; Macho y Ortega, "Mudéjares aragoneses," pp. 165–174; Burns, *Islam under the Crusaders*, pp. 117–138; Boswell, *Royal Treasure*; Bramon, *Contra moros i jueus*, pp. 68–91; Barceló Torres, *Minorías*, pp. 51–105; and Pierre Guichard et al., *Nuestra Historia*, vol. 3 (Valencia, 1980), pp. 13–108. Robert I. Burns, "Immigrants from Islam: The Crusaders' Use of Muslims as Settlers in Thirteenth Century Spain," *American Historical Review* 80 (1975): 21–42, demonstrates the economic importance of the Muslim population for the Christian conquerors.

7. The percentages of Mudejar population I have offered here are only approximations. For the Mudejars of Valencia, Barceló Torres, *Minorías*, pp. 64–70, traces the steady decline of their population. Utilizing the census of 1510, she arrives at a figure of 13, 056 Mudejar households out of 55, 631 households, or 23.4 percent of the population. However, she does not reveal how she arrived at such a figure. The census data given by Ricardo García Cárcel, "El censo de 1510 y la población valenciana de la primera mitad del siglo XVI," *Saitabi* 26 (1976): 171–188, indicates that usually no distinction was made between Muslim and Christian households, which leads one to question Barceló's precise figure. In 1502 the military estate estimated that the kingdom had a Muslim population of at least 22,000 households—ARV (Archivo del Reino de Valencia): C (Cancillería Real) 650: 242v—or 39.5 percent of the total population (55,631 households), which, although it seems a bit exaggerated, suggests that Barceló's estimate is too low. Lapeyre, *Géographie*, pp. 20–21, estimates a Morisco population in 1565 of 19,000 households, or 29 percent of the total. He also notes (pp. 29–30) that the emigration of a number of Muslims after the conversion of 1526 prevented a marked increase in the Morisco population by 1565. My own estimate of 30 percent, or approximately 17,000 Muslim households, is a rough compromise between the excessively high and low estimates of the military estate and Barceló. It also allows for a minimal increase in Muslim population to the level suggested by Lapeyre for 1565. The estimates for the Mudejars of Aragon and Catalonia come from Lapeyre, *Géographie*, pp. 96–99, and A. Domínguez Ortiz and B. Vincent, *Historia de los moriscos* (Madrid, 1978), p. 77.

8. On the supremacy of royal authority vis-à-vis the Mudejars, see Macho y Ortega, "Mudéjares aragoneses," pp. 165–174, and Boswell, *Royal Treasure*, pp. 30–31. ACA (Archivo de la Corona de Aragón): C 3567: 151v (8 February 1496): "Queriendo que aquellos por ser coffres nuestros no sean vexados"; ACA: C 3644: 147r (19 February 1489): "la dicha aliama que es nuestro patrimonio y cofre nuestro"; and ARV: C 134: 21r (23 November 1468): "quoniam sarraceni dicte aliame servi sunt camere nostre."

9. Jaume Vicens i Vives, *Ferran II i la ciutat de Barcelona*, 3 vols. (Barcelona, 1936–1937), esp. I: 365–424; García Cárcel, *Inquisición*, pp. 37–82; and Ernest Belenguer Cebrià, *València en la crisi del segle XV* (Barcelona, 1976).

10. Belenguer Cebrià, *València*, pp. 19–21. ARV: C 650: 251r–252v (6 July 1502): the viceroy chooses perhaps the worst time possible to conduct a general investigation of Mudejar aid to runaway slaves. See chap. 2.

11. Leopoldo Piles Ros, *Estudio documental sobre el Bayle General de*

Valencia, su autoridad y jurisdicción (Valencia, 1970), pp. 35–48. ARV: B (Bailía General) 1157: 388r–389r (1 March 1483) is a good example of the king's reliance on the bailiff general's advice. See text below.

12. The appointment of local bailiffs and their duties with respect to Muslim aljamas are found in ARV: C 307: 97v–99r, for Játiva; ARV: C 423: 64v–65v, and ARV: B 1156: 826r–827v, for Castellón de Játiva; and ARV: C 424: 35r–v, for the *morería* of Valencia.

13. ARV: C 141: 100v–101r; ARV C 127: 98v; ACA: C 3605: 31r–v; and ACA: C 3647: 53v–54r are examples of the governor acting as a royal deputy in Mudejar affairs. Piles Ros, *Bayle General*, pp. 114–115, discusses the conflict of interests between the governor and the bailiff general. The governor's jurisdiction over cases involving Mudejars will be discussed in chap. 5.

14. ARV: C 141: 100v–101r (5 November 1500).

15. ACA: C 3571: 85r–v (20 June 1493).

16. ACA: C 3647: 53v–54r (5 February 1490).

17. ACA: C 3605: 31r (8 July 1479) to Don Noffre de Rocasfull. ACA: C 3605: 31r–v is Fernando's command to the governor of Orihuela.

18. ACA: C 3638: 153r–v (27 December 1481).

19. ACA: C 3653: 1v–2r (23 October 1495).

20. ARV: C 304: 171r–173r (21 February 1481).

21. ARV: B 1157: 180v–181v (15 December 1481). ACA: C 3637: 135r–v (12 December 1481)—Fernando concedes to the aljama Valencia all privileges, immunities, and prerogatives his predecessors had granted to the aljamas of Játiva, Alcira, and Gandía.

22. ACA: C 3650: 255v–259r (19 February 1496).

23. ACA: C 3644: 82r–83r (21 February 1488).

24. ACA: C 3571: 23v–24r (30 August 1492).

25. ARV: C 128: 169v–170v (21 February 1481).

26. ARV: C 127: 98r–v (6 April 1480); ARV: C 128: 117v–118r (2 January 1481); and ARV: C 131: 102v–104r (3 July 1483).

27. Piles, "Moros de realengo," pp. 144–145, and Gual Camarena, "Mudéjares valencianos," p. 471, suggest a movement of Mudejars from seigneurial to royal lands because conditions were better in the latter. María del Carmen Barceló Torres, "La morería de Valencia en el reinado de Juan II," *Saitabi* 30 (1980): 53–71, shows that Juan II was able to reconstruct Valencia's *morería* after the sack of 1455. Maria Teresa Ferrer i Mallol, *La frontera amb l'Islam en el segle XIV: cristians i sarraïns al País Valencià* (Barcelona, 1988), p. 15, notes royal attempts to restore or create new *morerías* in the fourteenth century. Burns, "Immigrants from Islam," discusses the earlier use of foreign Muslims as settlers.

28. *Furs e ordinations fetes per los gloriosos reys de Aragó als regnicols del regne de València*, Lambert Palmart, ed. (Valencia, 1482): King Martin, Rubric VI: 184r—"De sarracenis qui sine comptare se faciunt vassallos alterius"; King Juan II, Rubric XV: 239v–240r: "De sarrahins." *Aureum opus regalium privilegorium civitatis et regni Valentie* (1515): Alfonso V, 196v–197r: "De sarracenis baronum volentibus mutare eorum domicilia ad loca domini regis." On

the military obligations of Mudejar vassals in the thirteenth and fourteenth centuries, see Burns, *Islam under the Crusaders*, pp. 289–290 and chap. XII, passim; Boswell, *Royal Treasure*, pp. 171–193; and Ferrer i Mallol, *Frontera*, pp. 33–35. Mudejars, however, did serve in the seigneurial armies against the *Germanías*, although these were extraordinary circumstances; see Ricardo García Cárcel, *Las Germanías de Valencia* (Barcelona, 1981), pp. 122–125, and Eulàlia Duran, *Les Germanies als Països Catalans* (Barcelona, 1982), pp. 180–196.

29. ARV: B 1158: 270v–271r: (14 August 1486). While there is much evidence of this kind, Jacqueline Guiral-Hadziiossif in her fine study, *Valence: port méditerranéen au XVe siècle (1410–1525)* (Paris, 1986), pp. 338–341, nonetheless maintains that fifteenth-century seigneurial Muslims were immobilized by their lords.

30. Gual Camarena, "Aportaciones," pp. 171–174; Piles, "Moros de realengo," pp. 244–245. Barceló Torres, *Minorías*, p. 52, challenges this view.

31. ARV: C 128: 8v–9v (30 May 1480).

32. ACA: C 3610: 124v (2 December 1492). ACA: C 3571: 172r–v(15 November 1494) disscusses the new arrangement for assessing the taxes to be paid by the Muslims of Borja's lower (i. e., original) *morería* and its upper (i. e., former *judería*) *morería*.

33. ACA: C 3568: 3v–4v (2 July 1490).

34. ACA: C 3608: 167v (13 February 1484).

35. ARV: B 1157: 388r–389r (1 March 1483).

36. ARV: B 1160: 687v–688r (1 July 1493). ARV: C 129: 118r–v (5 July 1481) concerns the case of Muslim vassals of the lordship of Gaibiel, who "fugam comiserunt" (committed flight) by moving to the *morería* of Jérica without settling accounts with the señora of Gaibiel.

37. ARV: C 138: 72v–73v, 74r–75r (21 December 1496), and 113r–v (25 August 1497).

38. *Cortes del Reinado de Fernando el Catolico*, Ernest Belenguer Cebrià, ed. (Valencia, 1972), pp. 5–6.

39. ARV: C 650: 64r–v (15 October 1490), for Sellent, 80v–81r (22 August 1492), for Cuart, and 81v–82r (25 September 1492), for Turís.

40. ARV: C 129: 142v–143v (13 September 1481).

41. ACA: C 3655: 15v–16v (23 May 1499).

42. ACA: C 3610: 53r–v (12 July 1490). On the efforts of towns to attract Mudejar residents, see text below for Castellón de la Plana and Alcoy.

43. ARV: C 311: 44r–46v (16 September 1499), for Castellón de la Plana; and ACA: C 3650: 255v–259r (19 February 1496), for Alcoy.

44. ARV: B 1161: 123v–124r (14 September 1495).

45. ARV: B 1158: 75v–76v (2 September 1485).

46. ARV: C 148: 61r–62r (13 August 1492).

47. ARV: C 148: 61v (see above)—"Reservant nos maior deliberacio axi sobre la residencia personal per part vostra pretesa contra lo dit moro." ARV: B 1160: 635r–v (12 May 1493). The lord of Pedralba uses the same argument against Muslims wishing to become royal vassals in Valencia.

48. ARV: B 1162: 367r (undated and incomplete).

49. ARV: B 1161: 508v–509r (17 October 1498) and 578v–579r (18 February 1499).

50. ARV: B 1160: 917r–v (7 October 1494).

51. On tensions between the towns and the nobility, see García Cácel, *Germanías*, pp. 56, 186–188. ARV: B 1161: 671r–v (28 September 1499). ARV: C 140: 82v–83v (16 September 1499) concerns the same case.

52. ARV: C 311: 44r–46v (16 September 1499).

53. ACA: C 3568: 3v–4v (1 July 1490).

54. ARV: C 650: 102v–103r (5 July 1493).

55. For instance, ARV: C 135: 194v–196r (19 April 1490). The knight Luis Joan filed suit against the Cardinal of Valencia because he thought the prelate had received homage from two Muslim vassals still indebted to him. It turned out that the Muslims had become royal vassals in Játiva.

56. ACA: C 3568: 5v–6r (2 July 1490).

57. ARV: C 304: 144v–145v (11 December 1480).

58. García Cárcel, *Germanías*, pp. 46–47; Antoni Furió and Ferran Garcia, "Dificultats agràries en la formació i consolidació del feudalisme al País Valencià," in *La formació i expansió del feudalisme català*, J. Portella i Comas, ed. (special volume of *Estudi General*, issue nos. 5–6, Girona, 1985–1986), pp. 306–307; Ramón Ferrer Navarro, "La Plana: su estructura demográfica en el siglo XV," *Cuadernos de Historia* 5 (1975): 67–91; Fernando Arroyo Ilera, "Estructura demográfica de Segorbe y su comarca en el siglo XV," *Hispania: Revista Española de Historia* 112 (1969): 295–313.

59. ACA: C 3650: 255v–259r (19 February 1496)—Fernando's confirmation of Juan II's measures (1468).

60. ARV: C 304: 88v–90r (19 July 1480).

61. ARV: C 304: 88v–90r. ARV: C 305: 39v–40r (7 December 1481), and ARV: C 306: 77v–79v (26 March 1484) discuss details regarding the Muslims' *carnicería* (butcher shop).

62. ARV: B 1156: 826v–827v (19 July 1480); and ARV: C 423: 64v–65v (19 July 1480). *Furs de Valencia*, Germà Colon and Arcadi Garcia, eds., (Barcelona, 1970), I: 221; Llibre I: Rubrica III: 90 (1488). Fernando dissolves the office of bailiff of Castellón de Játiva and places the *morería* under the jurisdiction of the bailiff of Játiva.

63. ARV: C 304: 89v.

64. ARV: C 304: 144r–v (13 December 1480).

65. ARV: B 1159: 10r (2 April 1488).

66. ARV: B 1160: 745r–v (5 October 1493); 761v–762v (24 October 1493); and 780r–781r (4 December 1493).

67. ARV: B 1157: 115v–117v (26 September 1481). ARV: C 130: 113v–114r (10 December 1481). Fernando prohibits interference of the lieutenant governor in the affairs of the aljama of Castellón de Játiva, when Caldes and the aljama express their fear of his actions against them.

68. Gual Camarena, "Mudéjares valencianos," pp. 472–494, on the sack of the *morería*; Barceló Torres, "Morería de Valencia," and José Hinojosa Montalvo, "Las relaciones entre los reinos de Valencia y Granada durante la primera

mitad del siglo XV," in *Estudios de Historia de Valencia* (Valencia, 1978), pp. 111–116. See also Guiral-Hadziiossif, *Valence*, pp. 341–345.

69. These conclusions are based on licenses for travel abroad granted to Muslims found in ARV: C 707: 786v–918v.

70. ARV: B 1156: 343v–344v (4 October 1478)—Juan II's order that the aljama's creditors reduce the debts owed them; ARV: B 1158: 534r–v (6 February 1488)—Fernando confirms the said reduction of the aljama's debts and the aljama's payment of only an annual sum of 25 pounds. ARV: C 305: 65v–66r (15 December 1481), and ACA: C 3637: 135r–v (12 December 1481) are other confirmations of the aljama's privileges.

71. Barceló Torres, "Morería de Valencia," pp. 54–55.

72. Registers ARV: B 1220–1223 contain documentation on Muslims swearing homage to the king in the *morería* of Valencia.

73. ACA: C 3566: 66r–v (24 March 1488)—Fernando licenses Çelim Alturmici of Almería and his family to enter his realms; Çelim is leaving Almería "por temor que ha tenido del Rey del dicho Reyno de Granada e de los moros de la dicha ciudat." ACA: C 3566: 159r (2 February 1489)—a similar license for Muslims from Baza.

74. ACA: C 3664: 294r–295r (23 September 1488).

75. See chap. 2 nn. 52–53.

76. See chap. 2 n. 54.

77. See chap. 2 nn. 52–53.

78. ARV: C 596: 91r (28 September 1491)—Játiva and Alcira; ARV: B 1160: 447v (25 May 1492)—Valencia; ARV: B 1160: 572r–v (29 November 1492)—Calatayud; ARV: B 1159: 156r–v (24 January 1489)—Alcira and Játiva; ARV: B 1160: 41v (5 March 1491)—Valencia; ARV: B 1160: 376v (23 December 1491)—Valencia.

79. ARV: B 1160: 18v (28 January 1491)—Vall de Uxó; ARV: B 1160: 354v–355r (26 November 1491)—Manises; ARV: B 1160: 424r (31 March 1492)—Novelda; ARV: B 1160: 424v (2 April 1492)—Valldigna; ARV: B 1160: 581r (24 December 1492)—Elche; ARV: B 1160: 634v–635r (12 March 1493)—Bétera; and ARV: B 1161: 320v–321r (30 September 1496)—Foya de Buñol. See chap. 2 n. 55.

80. ARV: C 148: 214r–v (4 September 1493).

81. ARV: C 596: 64v (24 October 1489). Ladero Quesada, *Mudéjares de Castilla*, pp. 159–161, document no. 45: a safe-conduct to Granadan Muslims going to settle on the lands of the Cardinal Pedro González de Mendoza in the kingdom of Valencia.

82. ARV: C 596: 65r–v (24 November 1489).

83. ACA: C 3665: 216v (30 April 1490).

84. ACA: C 3610: 178r (21 March 1493). ARV: C 596: 119r–v (27 February 1493), and 121v (21 March 1493) treat the same question.

85. Ladero Quesada, *Mudéjares de Castilla*, pp. 222–224, document no. 80: Granadan Muslims returning to Granada from North Africa are to be made royal captives, owing to the problem of coastal security.

86. ARV: B 1160: 519v (21 August 1492), in reference to previous practices.

87. Emilia Salvador, "Sobre la emigración mudéjar a Berbería. El tránsito legal a través del puerto de Valencia durante el primer cuarto del siglo XVI," *Estudis* 4 (1975): 39–45; *Cortes*, Belenguer Cebrià, ed., pp. 6, 70. See also Maria Teresa Ferrer i Mallol, *Els sarraïns de la Corona catalano-aragonesa en el segle XIV: segregació i discriminació* (Barcelona, 1987), pp. 150–183, who traces royal emigration policy until 1407 and shows that Pedro IV, despite the enactment of 1370 and the resistance of the nobility, still continued to grant emigration licenses to Mudejars.

88. ARV: C 659: 479r–480r (16 April 1479). Fernando confirms Juan II's restoration of this right to the bailiff general. See also Guiral-Hadziiossif, *Valence*, p. 341, who notes that between 1421 and 1431 the bailiff general issued 118 emigration licenses, but suggests that such licensing promoted the establishment of "bridgeheads of overseas commerce" in North Africa.

89. ARV: C 307: 117v–118r (14 December 1486).

90. ARV: C 307: 116v–117v (14 December 1486)—Fernando reprimands the justice and jurates of Alicante for allowing Muslims to emigrate from their port in violation of the bailiff general's prerogatives; and ARV: MR 4570: 8r–12v (1486) records the issuing of 44 licenses for Mudejar emigration by the bailiff general "beyond the River Jijona."

91. ARV: C 650: 85r (11 December 1492).

92. ARV: B 1160: 351r–352r (22 November 1491). The bailiff general instructs his *algutzir* to expedite the embarcation of Maghriban Jews and Muslims on Venetian galleys in Tortosa; he is also to see to it that all Muslims of Valencia, Castile, or Granada who board the galleys pay their passage duties to the Crown.

93. Salvador, "Emigración," pp. 47–60.

94. ACA: C 3649: 252r–253r (5 January 1492).

95. ACA: C 3610: 191v (7 May 1493).

96. See chap. 2.

97. Pedro López Elum, "La población de la morería de Játiva (1493)," in *Estudios de Historia de Valencia* (Valencia, 1978), pp. 161–162, notes that of 382 Muslim households only 341 paid the *besant*. ARV: MR 4030: 6r (1498)—Murviedro's *besant* list notes a Muslim who moved out of his father's house to form his own household.

98. Some examples are ARV: B 1160: 194r–v (15 April 1491)—Amet Uçey and his son Yuçeff move from Gestaglar to Liria; ARV: C 154: 132r–v (13 June 1498)—Çuleymen Obecar and family move from Chova to Villarreal; and ARV: B 1160: 532v–533r (22 September 1492)—Ali and Yuçeff Perrello move from Castellnou to Valencia. For more on this, see my doctoral dissertation, "Between *Convivencia* and Crusade: The Muslim Minority of the Kingdom of Valencia during the Reign of Fernando 'el Católico'" (University of Toronto, 1987), tables 1 and 2, pp. 100–103.

99. Piles, "Moros de realengo," pp. 239–245; and Macho y Ortega, "Mudéjares aragoneses," pp. 165–174.

100. Boswell, *Royal Treasure*, pp. 324–326, makes an important distinction between *issue* and *problem*, noting that although certain of the Mudejars' dis-

advantages were, for them, not *issues*, they were nevertheless *problems* that vitally affected them.

101. ACA: C 3609: 106v (16 February 1486)—"Item, per quant alguns barons stan circumvehins a les dites viles reals los quals nos es dit fan moltes vexacions als poblats de aquelles."

102. ARV: C 135: 183v–184v (29 March 1490).

103. ARV: C 311: 143v–144v (17 October 1500).

104. ARV: C 130: 129v–130r (29 December 1482). AMV: (Archivo Municipal de Valencia): g³ (Cartas Missivas) 29: 116r–v (31 March 1479), and 160r (4 September 1479) concern complaints of lords that the *jurats* of Gandía are wrongly collecting the *peyta* from their vassals. ACA: C 3521: 21r–22r (30 August 1479)—the *jurats* of Tortosa try to collect taxes from the Muslims of nearby Benifallet.

105. *Furs e ordinations*, Palmart, ed.: King Martin, Rubric III, 180r: "Si juheu o sarrahi o altre infeel nafrara alcun crestia acordadament no defenentse, ordenam que muyra sens tot remey. E sil nafrara en cas de baralla pach les penes dobles en fur contengudes contra aquells qui nafren alcu." The Mudejar could defend himself against a Christian only at great legal risk to himself.

106. ARV: C 148: 108r–v (28 November 1492).

107. ARV: C 139: 249r–v (30 March 1497). ARV: C 317: 26v (13 November 1492)—the baron of Ayodar imprisons Çilim and Jael Roig, royal vassals in Jérica, and tries to extort feudal dues from them.

108. ARV: B 1161: 80r–v (23 May 1495).

109. ARV: B 1161: 570r (5 February 1499).

110. ARV: B 1156: 819v–820r (21 July 1480).

111. ARV: B 1162: 59v (13 June 1500).

112. ARV: B 1157: 93v–94v (22 August 1481).

113. ACA: C 3605: 135v (13 April 1482).

114. This conclusion is based on a reading of the relevant documentation. Christian offenders are almost never punished for crimes against Muslims.

115. ARV: B 1157: 212r–v (18 March 1482), and 388r–389r (1 March 1483).

116. ARV: C 596: 105v (20 February 1492); and ACA: C 3667: 267r–v (20 February 1492).

117. ARV: B 1160: 665r–v (18 May 1493).

118. ARV: B 1161: 569v–570r (4 February 1499).

119. ACA: C 3521: 51r–v (13 September 1479). The Christian officials of Tortosa are forcing local Muslims to stand guard in Tortosa's castle and are interfering in the aljama's elections.

120. ARV: C 128: 170v–172r (21 February 1481).

121. ARV: C 305: 71r.

122. ARV: C 126: 77r (13 October 1479); and ARV: C 128: 168v–169v (21 February 1481).

123. ARV: C 305: 71r.

124. ARV: B 1157: 266r–267r (28 June 1482), and 267r–v. ARV: B 1157: 426r–v (6 May 1483)—the officials of Murviedro compel the Muslims to pay exorbitant rates for the *sisa* on slaughtered meat.

125. ACA: C 3644: 147r–v (19 February 1489).

126. ACA: C 3568: 5r–v (2 July 1490).

127. ACA: C 3606: 79r–80r (8 February 1483). Fevollet seems to have worked in the Muslims' interests. ACA: C 3609: 106v (16 February 1486) finds Fevollet intervening to protect a Muslim of Játiva against the harassment of a Christian, Noffre Fillach.

128. ARV: B 1157: 556r–557r (6 February 1484).

129. ARV: C 135: 183r–v (29 March 1490).

130. ARV: C 137: 147r–148r (5 August 1494).

131. ACA: C 3665: 18v–19v (23 November 1486).

132. ARV: C 139: 94r–v (6 July 1495)—Dezpuig pleads his case, blaming Fevollet for advising the aljama not to pay him the 13 pounds 11s and asserting that the payment of the said quantity was established by orders of Alfonso V and Juan II. ARV: C 139: 174r–175r (9 January 1496)—the aljama counters with the argument that the kings had made no such provisons, adding "per quant lo dit balle ha mudat sa habitacio continua a Valencia que no esta james en Xativa e . . . no tendria raho . . . pera demanar dit present pux no habita en la dita ciutat de Xativa ni assestex per la dita moreria en cosa alguna." ARV: C 140: 151r–v, 159v–160v (11 April 1500), and 179v–180r (29 May 1500)—the litigation continues and the positions of both parties are restated, and the rulings of various jurists are appealed by both parties. ARV: B 1158: 444r–v (26 June 1487) also deals with the case. One must also take into account the plague that hit Játiva in 1490 when considering the aljama's population decline.

133. ACA: C 3567: 98r (20 April 1494).

134. ACA: C 3607: 189r–v (30 July 1495).

135. ARV: C 132: 194r–195r (18 January 1485).

136. Vicens i Vives, *Barcelona*, I: 365–424, esp. p. 418, where Fernando concludes that "el servei de Deu havia de sobreposarse a tota altra classe de consideracions." Belenguer Cebrià, *València*, pp. 158–166, emphasizes that in Fernando's mind spiritual concerns outweighed all other considerations, economic or legal; and see García Cárcel, *Inquisición*, pp. 37–82.

137. Burns, *Islam under the Crusaders*, pp. 201–203 and chap. IX, passim; Boswell, *Royal Treasure*, pp. 261–267; and Ferrer i Mallol, *Els sarraïns*, pp. 85–87.

138. ARV: C 650: 337v (23 April 1506): "puix la sglesia los [moros] tollera els permet tenir mesquites e refer aquelles com solament los prohebeixqua ferne de noves."

139. ARV: C 304: 88v–90r, the document that concerns the founding of the *morería* of Castellón de Játiva, makes no mention of a mosque; however, ACA: C 3650: 255v–259r specifically mentions a mosque for Juan II's new *morería* in Alcoy. Barceló Torres, *Minorías*, pp. 95–96, notes that not every Mudejar community had its own mosque. ACA: C 3650: 171v (16 February 1493): Fernando orders the investigation into the matter of the mosque of Castellón de Játiva.

140. ACA: C 3669: 129r (10 August 1498).

141. ARV: C 311: 24v–26r (31 July 1499); ARV: C 140: 49r–v (31 July 1499), 116r–117r (9 November 1499); and ARV: C 141: 4v–5r (18 November 1499).

142. See Cahen, *Encyclopaedia of Islam* (2 ed.), I: 187–188, on the *adhān*. Boswell, *Royal Treasure*, pp. 261–267; and Ferrer i Mallol, *Els sarraïns*, pp. 87–95. *Furs e ordinations*, Palmart, ed.: King Martin, Rubric XLVI: 178v–179r: "De sarrahins que la çala no sia cridada publicament," and King Alfonso, Rubric XXI: 221v: "De la çala." *Aureum opus*, 62r–v (Jaime II): "Quod in nullis locis invocetur seu proclametur per sarracenos alta voce çalla sub pena ultimi supplitii," and 67r (Jaime II): "Mandatur baiulo quod puniat sarracenos clamantes çabaçala."

143. García Cárcel, *Inquisición*, p. 117.

144. ARV: C 650: 336v–338v (24 April 1506).

145. *Aureum opus*, 183v–184r (Alfonso V): "Contra sarracenum blasfemantem de domino deo et beata virgine maria." ARV: MR (Maestre Racional) 948: 12r concerns the case of Ali Castellano, who "jura les parts insanes de nostre Senyor Deu"; and ARV: B 1157: 342r–v (26 November 1482) concerns a similar case.

146. *Aureum opus*, 56v–57r (Jaime II): "Et quod judei et sarraceni dum corpus Christi portant per civitatem teneantur genuaflectere vel se occultare sub pena ibi aposita." *Furs*, Colon and Garcia, eds., II: 81–82: Llibre I: Rubrica VIII: II: "Juheus ne serrahins no . . . obren en los dies de les festes publicament dintre la ciutat ne de fora en alcuna part del regne de Valencia." See also Ferrer i Mallol, *Els sarraïns*, pp. 100–101.

147. ACA: C 3648: 58r–59r (18 September 1492). ACA: C 3565: 62r (8 May 1486) contains Fernando's previous command.

148. With respect to Ayora, n.141. The Christians of the town made no objections to the Marqués's construction of a *morería* and mosque there. In Alcoy the Christians themselves asked for the new *morería* and mosque—see n.59.

149. ACA: C 3576: 145r–v (19 September 1498).

150. ARV: C 304: 89r (19 July 1480)—"deputamus locum ibidem ubi serraceni . . . habitare possint . . . extra versus locum depopulatum inter christianos se non inmiscendo"; and 144r (13 December 1480). On the question of separate Muslim quarters in the fourteenth century, see Ferrer i Mallol, *Els sarraïns*, pp. 1–7.

151. ARV: C 305: 71r–v. Here Fernando was clearly disregarding previous royal legislation found in the *Aureum opus*, 240r (Martin I): "Quod nullus christianus possit habitare seu suum domicilium tenere intra clausuras morerie Valentie."

152. ARV: C 3565: 62r (8 May 1486); and ACA: C 3648: 58r–59r (18 September 1492).

153. ARV: B 1157: 266r–267v (28 June 1482).

154. ARV: C 650: 3r–4r (7 April 1488), and 56v (6 April 1489).

155. ACA: C 3667: 265v (25 February 1492).

156. Boswell, *Royal Treasure*, pp. 330–332, and Ferrer i Mallol, *Els sarraïns*, pp. 41–60. ACA: C 3605: 149v (22 May 1482).

157. ARV: MR 92: 321r (23 January 1482)—payment to the public crier for the "crida Reyal per la dita ciutat e lochs acostumats de aquella per los senyals que los juheus e moros deven portar segons los furs e ordinacions Reyals per

que entre les crestians sien coneguts." ACA: C 3665: 20v–21r (5 December 1486).

158. For example, ARV: C 126: 40v–41v (11 September 1479); ARV: C 135: 102r (26 July 1488); ARV: C 140: 256v (7 January 1501); and ARV: C 308: 87v–88r (26 July 1488).

159. ACA: C 3567: 151r–v (8 February 1496).

160. ARV: B 123: 30v–31r (1488) contains a provision restricting the richness of Muslim clothing within the *morería* of Valencia, but no mention is made of special distinctive blue garb or of other *senyals*. García Cárcel, *Inquisición*, p. 100: in 1521 the Consell of Valencia was deliberating whether the Mudejars must "vaguen senaliats."

161. *Aureum opus*, 216r–v (Fernando II) and 230r–232r (Fernando II).

162. ARV: C 310: 167v (23 January 1498).

163. ARV: B 1156: 511v–512r. See also Ferrer i Mallol, *Els sarraïns*, pp. 12–14.

164. Boswell, *Royal Treasure*, pp. 70–72. ARV: B 123: 30r–v (1488).

165. ARV: B 123: 31r–v (1488).

166. ARV: B 123: 142r–v (1493). ARV: B 123: 263r–v (1499) is a reiteration of this provision.

167. ARV: B 123: 108r–109v (1492), 149r–150v (1494), 189r–191r (1496), 214v–215v (1498), and 286r–v (1502) contain the same command.

168. ARV: B 123: 108r–109v.

169. ARV: B 123: 108r–109v emphasizes the "gran dan e prejuhi als drets e regalies del dit molt alt Senyor Rey" that would result were Muslims to lodge in any inns other than the royal fonduk.

170. The documentation found in ARV: B 123 shows that these prohibitions had to be proclaimed every two years. While the regularity of these prohibitions can be attributed to the fact that the bailiwick and the fonduk of the *morería* were farmed out every two years, it still points to a persistent problem.

171. ARV: B 1433 (16 June 1503)—Ysabel Sanchez (406v), Lorens Garcia (412r), Isabel Lop (413v), Francesch Centelles (416r), Anthon Bernat (417r), Gil Sanxiz (420v), Joan de Gandia (422v), and Miguel de Boro (425v) all testify to the "bona fama e vida" of the Torralbis, a Mudejar family.

172. See chap. 3.

173. ARV: B 1431: 385r (14 June 1493).

174. ARV: B 1431: 278v–280r (6 February 1493)—the confessions of Alasdrach and Ali Alcayet.

175. ARV: B 1431: 92v–93r (10 June 1491)—"[Serra] era grandissim amich com a germa del dit Ubaydal Çentido e es grandissim amich de la germana del dit Ubaydal."

176. ARV: B 1431: 89v–90r (8 June 1491)—the testimony of Domingo Roda; and 92v—the defense challenges Domingo's testimony.

177. ARV: B 1431: 90v–91v (9 June 1491)—Bernat Canon and Johan de Bolea testify how they went to the processions with Abdalla Çentido and other Muslims.

178. Haim Beinart, "The Converso Community in 15th Century Spain," in *The Sephardi Heritage*, R. D. Barnett, ed., (London, 1971), I: 425–456, pro-

vides a fine discussion of the controversy surrounding the Conversos, although his comments on the Inquisition and the Spanish State should be read with caution. See also Angus MacKay, "Popular Movements and Pogroms in Fifteenth-Century Castile," *Past and Present* 55 (1972): 33–67; idem, "The Hispanic-*Converso* Predicament," *Transactions of the Royal Historical Society*, 5th series, 35 (1985): 159–179; and Kriegel, "L'expulsion des juifs."

179. ACA: C 3612: 84r–v (18 March 1498).

180. Haim Beinart, *Records of the Trails of the Spanish Inquisition in Ciudad Real*, 4 vols. (Jerusalem, 1974–1983). A reading of these records gives one a good sense of Converso lifestyle and religiosity.

181. ACA: C 3567: 152r (8 February 1496).

182. See chap. 2 nn. 143–144.

183. ACA: C 3568: 71r (22 November 1493).

184. ARV: B 1161: 122v–123r (12 September 1495).

185. ARV: B 1220: V 5v–6r.

186. Ladero Quesada, *Mudéjares de Castilla*, pp. 320–323, document no. 148.

187. ACA: C 3636: 54v–55r (2 January 1481). ACA: C 3523: 126v also treats this litigation.

188. ACA: C 3670: 24v–25r (11 April 1502).

189. García Cárcel, *Inquisición*, pp. 116–121, discusses the intellectual acrobatics of clergymen on the question of the validity of the forced conversion of the Mudejars by the *Germanías*; see also, Boronat y Barrachina, *Moriscos*, I: 131–144. On the forced baptism of Jews, see Yitzhak Baer, *A History of the Jews in Christian Spain*, Louis Schoffman, trans. (Philadelphia, 1966), II: 95–110.

190. Robert I. Burns, "Christian–Muslim Confrontation: The Thirteenth-Century Dream of Conversion," in *Muslims, Christians, and Jews in the Crusader Kingdom of Valencia* (Cambridge, 1984), pp. 80–108.

191. Ladero Quesada, *Mudéjares de Castilla*, pp. 69–82; Hillgarth, *Spanish Kingdoms*, II: 470–483.

192. Ladero Quesada, *Mudéjares de Castilla*, p. 228, document no. 84: "Despues que supe la forma que alla se tenia no pense menos de lo que veo . . . . Porque del arzobispo de Toledo, que nunca vio moros, ni los conocio, no me maravillo."

193. Ladero Quesada, *Mudéjares de Castilla*, pp. 237, 240–241, document nos. 90 and 93: the royal assurances to the Mudejars of Ronda and Málaga; and pp. 228–229, 235–239, 244, and 250, document nos. 85, 88, 89, 91, 96, and 99: Cisneros's letters to the chapter of the church of Toledo giving his view of events.

194. José-Enrique López de Coca Castañer and Manuel Acién Almansa, "Los Mudéjares del obispado de Málaga (1485–1501)," in *Actas del I Simposio Internacional de Mudejarismo* (Madrid-Teruel, 1981), pp. 339–341.

195. Ladero Quesada, *Mudéjares de Castilla*, pp. 230–232, document no. 86.

196. Ladero Quesada, *Mudéjares de Castilla*, pp. 307–309, document no. 139.

197. Ladero Quesada, *Mudéjares de Castilla*, pp. 315–316, document no. 144.

198. Ladero Quesada, *Mudéjares de Castilla*, pp. 320–324, document no. 148.

199. See chap. 2.

200. Miguel Angel Ladero Quesada, "Datos demográficos sobre los musulmanes de Granada y Castilla en el siglo XV," *Anuario de Estudios Medievales* 8 (1972–1973): 481–490; idem, "Los Mudéjares de Castilla en la Baja Edad Media," in *Actas del I Simposio Internacional de Mudejarismo* (Madrid-Teruel, 1981), 349–390; and idem, *Mudéjares de Castilla*, pp. 90–94, 99–100, 124–125, 241–242, and 245–246, document nos. 3, 4, 5, 9, 25, 94, and 97.

201. López de Coca Castañer and Acién Almansa, "Mudéjares del obispado de Málaga," pp. 323–339; and Miguel Angel Ladero Quesada, "La repoblación del Reino de Granada anterior a 1500," *Hispania* 28 (1968): 489–563.

202. ARV: B 1157: 322r–324v (16 October 1482).

203. ACA: C 3666: 48r (7 April 1491), for Mallorca; on the Inquisition's activities in Aragon, Henry Charles Lea, *A History of the Inquisition of Spain* (New York, 1906), 1: 294.

204. See chap. 2. n. 157.

205. Lea, *Inquisition*, I: 294.

Chapter Two:
The War against Islam and the Muslims at Home

1. Discussions of Fernando's foreign policy have not given enough attention to his internal policy as an indication of his motives and priorities. It seems to me that there would have been some consistency between the two. The view that Fernando was motivated solely by a desire to crusade against Islam, presented by José M. Doussinague, *La política internacional de Fernando el Católico* (Madrid, 1944), does not jibe with Fernando's consistent encouragement of Mudejarism in the lands of the Crown of Aragon. Andrew C. Hess's *The Forgotten Frontier: A History of the Sixteenth-Century Ibero-African Frontier* (Chicago, 1978) emphasizes the increasing separation of Christian and Islamic civilizations along the Ibero-African frontier as a result of the conflict between Hapsburg Spain and the Ottoman empire. Because the focus is on the conflictive character of the Christian—Muslim interface, the vitality of religioethnic pluralism under Fernando's Crown of Aragon is lost from view, as are the possible alternatives to Castilian Mudejar policy and the resultant Morisco problem. Hillgarth, *Spanish Kingdom*, II: 534–584, presents a more balanced view of Fernando's Mediterranean policy, in which confrontation with Islamic powers and the furthering of Aragon's Mediterranean interests often coincide.

2. Vicens i Vives, *Barcelona*, I: 365–424; J. Angel Sesma Muñoz, *El establecimiento de la Inquisición en Aragón (1484–1486): documentos para su estudio* (Zaragoza, 1987?), pp. 10–24; and García Cárcel, *Inquisición*, pp. 47–82.

3. Burns, *Islam under the Crusaders*, pp. 37–45.

4. Robert I. Burns, "Social Riots on the Christian–Moslem Frontier: Thirteenth Century Valencia," *American Historical Review* 66 (1961): 378–400, esp. 398.

5. Boswell, *Royal Treasure*, pp. 372–400; Ferrer i Mallol, *Frontera*, pp. 41–43.

6. Gual Camarena, "Mudéjares valencianos," pp. 473–474; see also Ferrer i 'Mallol, *Frontera*, pp. 21–29, who demonstrates that official intervention prevented anti-Mudejar violence in 1316, 1331, 1369, and 1391 in the wake of anti-Jewish pogroms and 1397–1399 when the Christians were organizing for a crusade against North Africa.

7. Hinojosa Montalvo, "Relaciones," pp. 101–103. The disturbances caused in the *morerías* by a Muslim of Alcala claiming to have been sent by God might have added to the atmosphere of tension; see Piles Ros, *Bayle General*, p. 299, document no. 819.

8. Gual Camarena, "Mudéjares valencianos," p. 479.

9. Luis Suárez Fernández, *Política internacional de Isabel la Católica* (Valladolid, 1965), I: 249–255; Antonio de la Torre, *Documentos sobre relaciones internacionales de los Reyes Católicos* (Barcelona, 1949), I: 408–411, 444–445; and Doussinague, *Política*, pp. 45–52.

10. ACA: C 3605: 87r (13 December 1480).

11. ACA: C 3605: 87r.

12. ARV: B 1156: 874r–v (12 October 1480) and ARV: B 1157: 265v–266r (27 June 1482) are examples of licenses for bearing arms granted to Muslims. ARV: B 1160: 270r (16 August 1491)—the justice of Onda confiscates Muslims' arms.

13. AMV: g^3 29: 247v–248r (15 February 1481). While informing Fernando of their own concern about the Mudejars' intentions in the wake of Turkish successes, the jurates of Valencia noted that the seigneurs would prefer to maintain the status quo instead of taking action against the Mudejars.

14. ACA: C 3665: 72r (23 April 1487)—"cascun moro segons se diu te en sa casa armes sobrades moltes mes de les que cascu d'ells ha mester." ARV: C 650: 242r–243v (12 April 1502).

15. AMV: g^3 29: 231r–v (6 September 1480).

16. AMV: g^3 29: 247v–248r (15 February 1481).

17. Suárez Fernández, *Política*, II: 13–15, 52–55, 144–149; and La Torre, *Documentos*, II: 565–567, 569–570; III: 547–553.

18. ACA: C 3606: 107r (11 February 1480).

19. ACA: C 3665: 72r (23 April 1487).

20. ACA: C 3665: 72r.

21. Rachel Arié, *L'Espagne musulmane au temps des Naṣrides (1232–1492)* (Paris, 1973), pp. 172–174, discusses the Naṣrid embassy to the Mamluk court; Suárez Fernández, *Política*, II: 149, treats Qā'it Bāy's warning to Fernando; and Doussinague, *Política*, pp. 515–517, transcribes Fernando's letter to the king of Naples in response to the Mamluk warning. Hess, *Frontier*, pp.60–61, 228, gives an account of the mission of Kemal Reis in response to the Naṣrid appeal. ARV: C 137: 192r–193r (29 October 1494), which concerns the capture of Christians of

Biar by Turkish galleys operating out of Bône, confirms the Ottoman presence in peninsular waters. For a later and more serious manifestation of the connection between Spanish Muslims and Ottomans, see Andrew Hess, "The Moriscos: An Ottoman Fifth Column in Sixteenth-Century Spain," *American Historical Review* 74 (1969): 1–25.

22. Although Arié, *L'Espagne musulmane*, p. 173, conjectures that Muḥammad XII (Boabdil), in power in Granada after 29 April 1487, was responsible for sending the ambassador to Cairo, I would suggest that al-Zaghal took this diplomatic initiative. This would allow for the arrival of the Naṣrid ambassador in Cairo in later 1486, since the Islamic year 892 A. H. is equivalent to A. D. 1486–1487. If the poetic appeal to the Ottoman court had any relation to the embassy to Cairo, and if Mudejar envoys had established contact with Kemal Reis before 23 April 1487, then an earlier date makes more sense. Of course, there need not have been a precise temporal conjunction between the appeals to Cairo and Istanbul.

23. Hinojosa Montalvo, "Relaciones," pp. 111–128, treats Valencia's commerce with Granada and Mudejar participation. ARV: C 707 contains licenses for travel to Almería granted to Mudejars; examples are 789v–790r (17 May 1479), and 889v–890r (30 June 1481) for commerce and 786v–787r (12 May 1479) and 891v–892r (5 July 1481) for family affairs.

24. ARV: C 305: 210r–v (30 June 1483), and ARV: B 1157: 590r (11 March 1484) are cases of Mudejars who traveled to the sultanate of Granada without license. They were all punished with the penalty of enslavement.

25. ARV: B 1159: 9v (27 March 1488)—license to Mahomat Fuçey of Bellreguart to go to Almería for one year "per traure alguns parents que te en la ciutat e per alguns fets e negocis quey ha a fer." See also n. 23.

26. See the discussion of "Years of Crisis: 1500–1503" in this chapter.

27. Some sense of the fear inspired by the Turks can be had from a reading of contemporary chroniclers, such as Bernáldez, *Memorias*, pp. 103–107; or Hernando del Pulgar, *Crónica de los señores Reyes Católicos*, Benito Monfort, ed. (Valencia, 1780), pp. 172–173.

28. See, for example, Charles Emmanuel Dufourcq, *L'Espagne catalane et le Maghrib aux XIIIe et XIVe siècles* (Paris, 1966); and Hinojosa Montalvo, "Relaciones," pp. 91–106.

29. ARV: B 1157: 327r–v (23 October 1482) and AMV: g³ 30: 114r–v (24 October 1482).

30. AMV: g³ 29: 179r–180r (9 December 1479), 182v–183v (20 January 1480) and 183v–186r (21 January 1480) deal with the problems of Perot Miquel in Almería; and 209r (5 May 1480) notes that the Miquel affair was satisfactorily resolved, and that the sultan of Granada owes money to the heirs of a Christian merchant.

31. Hinojosa Montalvo, "Relaciones," pp. 111–116; Guiral-Hadziiossif, *Valence*, pp. 341–345; and see n. 23 for commerce and family business. ARV: C 707: 820r–v (19 April 1480) is a license to Çahat Galip of Játiva to go to Almería "per saber scriure e legir lo morisch." Between 12 May 1479 and 5 July 1481, forty-six licenses for travel to Almería were granted to Mudejars.

32. ARV: B 1156: 735r–v (15 May 1480). ARV: B 1156: 704r–v (30 Decem-

ber 1479)—license to remain in the kingdom for one year is granted to Ali from Granada and his black servant Caet.

33. ACA: C 3633: 57r–v (25 February 1479) and ARV: C 302: 47v–48r (14 June 1479) are cases of Christians of Orihuela captured by Muslim *almugavers* from Vera.

34. Ferrer i Mallol, *Frontera*, pp. 196–222, discusses the earlier, short-lived *Hermandades* of 1394 and 1396, as well as that of 1399. Augustin Nieto Fernández, "Hermandad entre las aljamas de moros y las villas de la governación de Orihuela en el siglo XV," in *Primer Congreso de Historia del País Valenciano* (Valencia, 1980), 2: 749–760; and Juan Torres Fontes, "La Hermandad de moros e cristianos para el rescate de cautivos," in *Actas del I Simposio Internacional de Mudejarismo* (Madrid-Teruel, 1981), 499–508. On pp. 507–508, Torres Fontes transcribes Isabel's order to the *adelantado* of the kingdom of Murcia.

35. ARV: B 1157: 119r–120r (15 September 1481). For a detailed treatment of this problem in the fourteenth century, see Ferrer i Mallol, *Frontera*, pp. 47–186. In the fourteenth century the problem was considerably more serious, owing to the greater power of the sultanate of Granada and to a larger and more restive Mudejar population.

36. ACA: C 3663: 117r–v (10 February 1483), and ARV: B 1157: 498v–500r (10 February 1483).

37. ARV: MR 92: 321r (23 January 1482).

38. ACA: C 3665: 20v–21r (5 December 1486); see chap. 1.

39. ARV: C 304 71r–v (26 May 1480).

40. ARV: C 126: 124r–v (3 March 1480), is the case of the Mudejar from Nompot; and ARV: C 131: 90v–91r (30 July 1483) concerns the case of Ali Jabbeu of Aspe, accused "de crimine intercipiendi et captivandi cristianos." Torres Fontes, "Hermandad," p. 500, notes that the Mudejars involved in this activity were usually from the *morerías* of Elche, Crevillente, Elda, Aspe, Novelda, Monóvar, Chinosa, and Petrel located in the region of Orihuela.

41. ACA: C 3605: 85v–86r (7 December 1480), for the Vall de Uxó, and 118r (28 September 1481), for Murcia.

42. ARV: B 1157: 156r (7 January 1482).

43. See n. 24.

44. ACA: C 3649: 150v–151v (6 April 1492). Once the war had ended, the commander of the Order of Santiago, lord of the Valle de Ricote in Murcia, asked that these travel restrictions on his Muslim vassals be lifted.

45. ACA: C 3606: 65v–66v (12 January 1483).

46. ACA: C 3665: 20v–21r (5 December 1486). For the Moriscos' observance of the *ʿīd al-kabīr*, see Cardaillac, *Morisques et Chrétiens*, p. 35.

47. ACA: C 3665: 72r (23 April 1487).

48. Hinojosa Montalvo, "Relaciones," pp. 103–104 and 133–134, document no. 9, for the response of the jurates of Valencia to the sultan's concerned queries.

49. Ferrer i Mallol, *Els sarraïns*, pp. 106–109, shows that the authorities imposed some restrictions on Mudejar movement south of the Jijona River during the fourteenth century; for the fifteenth century, see Piles, "Moros de

realengo," pp. 258–261. While Piles is correct in stating, "Las incidencias de la guerra de Granada repercutieron sensiblemente en los cambios de lugar y residencia de los moros valencianos," his subsequent assertion that the number of Muslims who traveled beyond the Jijona in the two or three years before the fall of Granada was greater than in previous years is inaccurate. This can be said only for the year 1491. Piles does not present statistics, nor does he suggest specific reasons for the fluctuating number of licenses granted.

50. Licenses for Mudejar travel beyond the Jijona River are found in the registers ARV: B 1156–1162.

51. Ladero Quesada, *Mudéjares de Castilla*, pp. 307–309, document no. 139 (20 July 1501), is an order prohibiting the entry of all Muslims into the kingdom of Granada; and pp. 312–314, document no. 142 (21 September 1501), describes the Muslims of Murcia as having been converted to Christianity.

52. Some examples are ARV: C 148: 178r–v (10 June 1493)—a litigation between Seydi Melvix and other Muslims from the city of Granada (probably now residing in Valencia) and the bailiff general of the kingdom "beyond the Jijona"; ARV: C 148: 214r–v (4 September 1493)—Fernando settles Muslims from the city of Granada on lands held by the bailiff general near Orihuela, and the new vassals swear to remain there for five years; ARV: C 596: 119r–v (27 February 1493)—Muslims from Almería have letters of *franquesa* exempting them from all taxes in the kingdom of Valencia; ARV: B 1160: 41v (5 March 1491)—license to travel to Almería is granted to Muslims originally from Almería now living in the city of Valencia; ARV: B 1160: 354r–355r (26 November 1491)—a Muslim of Manises, once a *faqīh* in Málaga, is granted license to go to Baza to bring a relative from there to Valencia; and ARV: B 1160: 424r (31 March 1492)—a Muslim from Málaga is to become a seigneurial vassal in Novelda. See also chap. 1.

53. ARV: B 1159: 9v (27 March 1488)—a Muslim of Bellreguart, near Gandía, is granted license to go to the city of Granada to fetch some relatives; and ARV: B 1160: 18v (28 January 1491)—a Muslim of the Vall de Uxó is granted license to go to Almería to fetch his mother and sister.

54. ARV: B 1159: 251r–252r (25 October 1489)—Muslims, originally from Vera, come from Oran to speak with Fernando regarding the settlement in Valencia of others from Vera still in Oran; ARV: B 1159: 252v–253r (25 October 1489)—Muslims, originally from Vera, come from Oran and are allowed to return to Vera; ARV: B 1159: 265v (12 November 1489)—a Muslim from Almería is granted license to go to Tunis to fetch his wife; and ARV: B 1159: 281v–282r (15 December 1489)—Muslims, originally from Vera, come from Oran to relocate in the Valle de Ricote in Murcia.

55. ARV: B 1160: 554v–555r (27 October 1492), and 555v–556r (30 October 1492)—ransomed slaves, originally from Málaga, are granted license to visit family in Málaga and Granada, whence they will return; and ARV: B 1160: 703v (23 July 1493)—a woman from Málaga, having resided in Valencia for two years, is granted license to return to Granada "per fer sos affers."

56. ARV: B 1160: 646v–647r (26 March 1493).

57. Hess, *Frontier*, pp. 11–25, contrasts the political and military weakness of the Islamic West with the strength and gunpowder technology of the unified

Castile and Aragon. See also Jamil M. Abun-Nasr, *A History of The Maghrib* (Cambridge, 1975), pp. 119–166.

58. Doussinague, *Política*, pp. 52–229, 483–493, and Fernand Braudel, "Les Espagnols et l'Afrique du Nord de 1492 a 1577," *Revue Africaine* 69 (1928): 184–233, present contrasting points of view, the latter emphasizing Fernando's more worldly motives. Taking into account Fernando's Mudejar policy in Aragon, I tend to agree with Braudel in qualifying the picture of Fernando as an indefatigable crusader painted by Doussinague. Hillgarth, *Spanish Kingdom*, II: 534–584, strikes a reasonable balance between the two viewpoints. On the problem of defending the coasts of the postconquest kingdom of Granada, see Ana María Vera Delgado, *La última frontera medieval: la defensa costera en el obispado de Málaga en tiempos de los Reyes Católicos* (Málaga, 1986).

59. Jacqueline Guiral, "Les relations commerciales du royaume de Valence avec la Berbérie au XVe siècle," *Mélanges de la Casa de Velázquez* 10 (1974): 99–131; and Suárez Fernández, *Política*, III: 28–31, IV: 24–27, and V: 73–76. Some examples of Christian commerical activity in the Maghrib are ARV: C 137: 214v–215r (7 December 1484)—Andreu Castellano, a merchant of Valencia, transports "certes robes" from Almería to the Maghrib; ARV: C 246: 4v–5r (16 March 1498)—Matheu de Cardona of Messina, Fernando's agent in Tunis, sells Sicilian wheat valuing 4,000 gold ducats; ARV: C 304: 146r–147r (13 December 1480)—a Portuguese squadron captures the caravel of the Valencian merchant Daniel Valleriola, "lo qual con su mercaderia andava a les partes de Barberia assi como siempre es acostumbrado de aquella nuestra ciutat de Valencia muchos navios ir e venir a las dichas partes de Barberia"; ARV: B 1160: 884r (10 July 1494)—Bernat Rabaça sells wine in Oran on behalf of the Valencian Noffre Puig; and ACA: C 3549: 118r–120r (1 September 1485)—the city of Valencia sends a ship laden with goods to be exchanged for needed wheat in Oran.

60. Guiral, "Relations commerciales," pp. 107–111. However, Guiral's article needs some correction. Her graph and tables on pp. 123–124 and 131 suggest that there were not any Maghriban merchants in Valencia between 1493 and 1502, when, in fact, the registers ARV: B 1160 (e.g., 915v–916r), B 1161 (e.g., 15v–16r) and B 1162 (e.g., 123v–124r) contain safe-conducts permitting one year of residence in the kingdom to Maghriban merchants. In 1500 two safe-conducts were issued, one to a Muslim from Bougie—ARV: B 1162: 123v–124r (14 December 1500)—and one, an extension of the safe-conduct to a Maghriban, originally from Málaga, who had been in the kingdom since 1495–ARV: B 1162: 3v–4v (16 January 1500). No safe-conducts for Maghriban merchants were issued in 1501.

61. Some examples are ACA: C 3610: 161r (25 February 1493)—as compensation for his goods confiscated in the Maghrib, Anthoni Johan captures Maghriban "persones de importancia"; ARV: B 194: 156r–162r (1494)—fifteen Muslims and a Jew of Bône are captured while transporting wheat to Bône; and ARV: B 195: 113r–114r (1502)—two Muslims from Fez bound for Mecca are captured by a Christian ship.

62. The registers ARV: B 194 (1494–1497) and B 195 (1502–1503), entitled "Cautivos," contain numerous examples of these victims.

63. ARV: B 1160: 937r–v, 951r–v (31 August 1494).

64. Jacqueline Guiral, "La piratería, el corso: sus provechos y ganancias en el siglo XV," in *Nuestra Historia* (Valencia, 1980), 3: 269–270; idem, *Valence*, pp. 106–110.

65. AMV: g³ 29: 182r–v (27 January 1480).

66. AMV: g³ 33: 26r (4 August 1496).

67. ARV: B 1157: 312r–v (21 September 1482) and 312v–313r (23 September 1482).

68. ACA: C 3550: 116r–118r (31 March 1488), AMV: g³ 31: 198r–v (8 February 1487), AMV g³ 33: 132v–133r (23 May 1498), 184r–185r (6 June 1499), and 214v–215r (2 March 1500) are all concerned with the construction of defenses at Oropesa. ARV: C 138: 11v–12v (6 January 1496) notes the importance of Guardamar for coastal defense, although in ARV: C 311: 201r–v (16 June 1501), Fernando points out to the governor of Orihuela that Muslims are entering the kingdom through Guardamar without resistance. The documentation also mentions other fortifications near Orihuela—ARV: C 151: 118r–119r (4 March 1497)—and at Jávea—ARV: C 303: 144v–146r (13 February 1480).

69. ARV: C 248: 15v–17v (28 December 1493); ARV: C 158: 83v–84v (6 September 1502); ARV: B 1162: 318v–319v (11 March 1502); ACA: C 3610: 126r–127v (28 December 1492); and ACA: C 3570: 60r–v (30 August 1492), 63v–64v (2 September 1492), and 71r–72r (18 September 1492).

70. ARV: B 1158: 62r–v (5 August 1485), 124r–v (17 November 1485) and ARV: B 1160: 308r (11 October 1491)—ships from Peñiscola capture Maghriban galleys at sea. ACA: C 3569: 85v–86r (3 October 1491)—Muslims are captured at sea near Tortosa; and ACA: C 3607: 88v (12 January 1495)—the same near Alicante. The efforts of the officials of coastal towns to keep each other informed about corsair movements are themselves indicative of a more effective system of coastal vigilance. See also Guiral-Hadziiossif, *Valence*, pp. 131–140.

71. Doussinague, *Política*, pp. 53–67, and Braudel, "Afrique du Nord," pp. 203–208, agree that the crusade against Africa had as one of its motives the elimination of the danger of the Maghriban corsairs, among whom the refugees from Granada proved to be Spain's bitterest enemies.

72. See the discussion under the heading "Years of Crisis: 1500–1503" in this chapter.

73. ACA: C 3563: 66r–v (3 December 1481), ACA: C 3561: 197r–198r (6 April 1496), ARV: C 131: 133v–134v (28 August 1483), ARV: C 133: 134v–136r (18 January 1486), ARV: C 304: 135v–136r (28 November 1480), ARV: C 305: 159r–v (5 September 1482), and ARV: C 596: 310r–v (3 November 1500), all deal with the Mercedarians' activities of ransoming captives in North Africa or raising funds for that purpose.

74. ARV: C 137: 192r–193r (29 October 1494). Normally, the municipal government of Biar gave the funds to the Mercedarians, but in this case the funds were given directly to a native of Biar who had to ransom himself and his son, still captive in Bône. Orihuela also had special funds set aside for ransoming Christians held captive in Granada—ARV: C 302: 47v–48r (14 June 1479).

75. For example, ARV: C 134: 135r–v (26 March 1488)—a man of Benicassim who, along with his wife, had been a prisoner of the Muslims for fifteen

years is still trying to raise the ransom money for his wife; and ARV: C 707: 915r–v (4 June 1479)—Muslim vassals of the Count of Oliva are granted license to go to Algiers to ransom the Count's Christian vassals.

76. La Torre, *Documentos*, III: 178–181, document nos. 3–6.

77. ARV: C 309: 94r–v (16 April 1493).

78. These licenses are found in ARV: C 707, for example, 789v–790r (17 May 1479) to Mahomat Monem of Mislata "per mercadejar"; 875v–876r (21 May 1481) to Amet Talio of Castellón "per veure hun germa seu"; 795v–796r (12 January 1480) to Azmet Benulini, alias Hoffri, of Valencia "per recaptar una herencia de la mare de aquell"; 793v–794r (10 January 1480) to Mahomat Abenferis of Cuartell "per apendre de letra morisch"; 917r–v (12 November 1491) to Maomat Alfaqui of Avila (Castile) "va en romeria"; and 857r–v (18 May 1481) to Çahat Alagari "per veure terra."

79. ARV: MR 4570: 8r–12r (30 September to 9 October 1486)—officials of Alicante grant license to emigrate to forty-four Muslims of Monforte, a royal *morería* near Alicante, and collect the required emigration duties. ARV: B 1158: 365r–366r (14 December 1486)—Fernando expresses concern that the said duties were not collected and that the bailiff general's prerogative of issuing emigration licenses was usurped. ARV: C 424: 33r–v (27 December 1487)— when Yuçeff b. Yahye is chosen to succed his father Yahye b. Axer as sub-*qāḍī* of Játiva, it is noted that "pater tui Axer Abenyahye [should read Yahye Abe-naxer] . . . ad terras Barberie sive Africe totaliter se transtulit perpetuo in terris illis infidelium moraturus . . . in eadem moreria remanere voluisti." In the Corts of Orihuela of 1488 all further Mudejar emigration was prohibited.

80. Some examples are ARV: B 1161: 320v–321r (30 September 1496)—Ali Tuneçi from Tunis is now living in the Foya de Buñol; ARV: B 1431: 324r–343r (10 January 1493)—the case of Azmet Çahat from Tunis, now living in Valencia; and ARV: B 1431: 344r–375r (29 October 1492)—the case of Abdalla Alfaqui from Tunis, now living in Ondara.

81. ARV: B 1431: 192r–v (18 January 1492).

82. That such vengeful Muslims were present in Valencia is suggested by the career of Caçim from Granada—ARV: B 195: 65r–v (30 April 1502).

83. ARV: C 126: 124r (3 March 1480)—"fonch detengut en preso en lo castell de Galinera Taher Alazrach moro de la dita vila vassall nostre per ço com fonch inculpat de crim de collera e donada per la dita raho sentencia."

84. ARV: C 311: 254v–255r (6 June 1502).

85. ARV: B 195: 65r–v (30 April 1502).

86. ARV: B 1162: 92r–v (22 September 1500). After attacking Calpe, Maghriban corsairs "an exit en terras algunes scoltes e adalils perque ab millor seguretat los dits moros puixen venir e tornar en les dites parts." One of these spies was captured in Ondara by the local lord, although Mudejars of Ondara were not specifically implicated in the affair.

87. AMV: g³ 33: 249r (2 April 1501).

88. ARV: C 596: 147r–v (7 June 1494).

89. ARV: C 650: 243r (12 April 1502).

90. ARV: B 1162: 428v–429r (1 April 1503).

91. See n. 60. Guiral's data, "Relations commerciales," pp. 123–124 and

131, is accurate for the years before 1493. ARV: C 707 shows that between 1484 and 1491 there were no licenses for travel to the Maghrib granted to Mudejars. There was a very slight resumption of Mudejar travel in 1491: six licenses were granted, although three were to Castilians and one to an Aragonese Mudejar. Unfortunately, there are no registers following ARV: C 707, which terminates in 1491. As Maghriban merchants continued to come to Valencia throughout the 1490s, even during the years of the crusade against Africa, there is no reason why Mudejars should not have resumed their visits to the Maghrib, particularly when one considers that the majority of the Mudejars had been traveling to Tunis, a city with which Fernando maintained consistent commercial relations. ACA: C 3568: 132v–134r (15 February 1496) shows that the Mudejar Yahye Bellvis was active in the Mediterranean spice trade and had business in Alexandria, Naples, and Tunis.

92. For instance, in 1486. See n. 79.

93. Boswell, *Royal Treasure*, p. 375, notes that in 1365 the Christians of Valencia induced Pedro IV to curtail the emigration of Mudejars for fear that they might betray secrets to the Maghriban enemy. However, in the midfourteenth century the Marinid and Hafṣid states presented a greater threat to Aragon than was the case during Fernando's reign. The reasons behind the prohibition of Mudejar emigration by the Corts of 1488 were economic, that is, a seigneurial interest in keeping their lands populated with Muslim vassals.

94. Boswell, *Royal Treasure*, pp. 318–320, contrasts the desire of Valencia's Mudejars to emigrate with the relative contentment of the Mudejars of Aragon-Catalonia. He explains the latter group's behavior by their greater acclimatization to Christian rule. Certainly, another century of life in Christian Valencia would have made the Mudejars less anxious to depart.

95. Burns, *Islam under the Crusaders*, pp. 37–45; Boswell, *Royal Treasure*, pp. 372–400; and Piles Ros, *Bayle General*, p. 299, document no. 819.

96. ACA: C 3633: 79v–80r (25 February 1479), and ARV: C 139: 72v–73v (19 May 1495), discuss the attack of Muslims of Resalany on Dos Aguas to free Muslims held prisoner there. ARV: C 148: 148v–149r (12 February 1493)—a Muslim is freed by coreligionists from the jail of the seigneur of Albatera.

97. ARV: B 1160: 17v (25 January 1491)—"Dos mors la hun del loch de Mizlata l'altre de la ciutat de Xativa sen hagen portat huna sclava mora çabia del dit Don Altobello Centelles la qual sen han portat del bordell de la moreria de la dita ciutat."

98. For example, ARV: C 148: 142v–143v (25 January 1493)—the *amīn* and *adelantats* of Matet resist the efforts of the governor's officials to seize two Muslims who had fled from the place of Gaibiel.

99. ARV: C 127: 125v (27 May 1480); ARV: C 148: 30v–31r (6 July 1492), 193v–194r (17 July 1493); ARV: B 1158: 423r–v (21 May 1487); B 1159: 6r (17 March 1488); B 1160: 295v–296r (23 August 1491), 417r–v (15 March 1492), and 551r–v (22 October 1492).

100. ARV: B 1159: 339r (12 June 1490).

101. ARV: C 127: 125v; C 129: 1v–2v (23 January 1481); and C 130: 11v–12r (30 May 1481) all concern this case.

102. ARV: C 156: 200r–v (19 April 1502).

103. ARV: B 1431: 341v (26 October 1493)—while sentencing Azmet Çahat, a Muslim from Tunis accused of aiding runaways, the bailiff general notes the "moltes fuytes que de poch temps en ça se son seguides en la present ciutat e Regne"; and B 1431: 372v (31 October 1493)—the bailiff general expresses the same concern in the case of Abdalla Alfaqui, accused of the same crime.

104. ARV: C 650: 251r–253r.

105. The records of the aljamas' purchasing and ransoming of Muslim slaves are located in the registers ARV: B 217–221, especially B 219: 140v–528v for the sale of the slaves from Málaga. The register ARV: B 325 records the debts owed by various aljamas for the purchase of Muslim slaves.

106. ARV: B 219: 239r–240r (13 October 1488).

107. ARV: B 1431: 358r–v (10 December 1492)—the testimony of Maymo ben Çabit.

108. Boswell, *Royal Treasure*, p. 394.

109. For instance, Abun-Nasr, *Maghrib*, pp. 159–163; Doussinague, *Política*, p. 75, notes that Ruhama offered to surrender the city of Oran to the Monarchs on the same terms that had been offered to the Muslims of Granada.

110. It is abundantly clear from the documentation that the victims of Mudejar violence were most often Muslims, not Christians. One example is ARV: C 129: 142v–143v (13 September 1481)—Juçeff Çabot, a royal vassal in Játiva originally from Valldigna, returns to the valley and, with accomplices, murders a Muslim of Tabernes. The registers ARV: B 217–221 contain official truces established between feuding Mudejars. See chap. 6.

111. ARV: B 195: 65r–v (30 April 1502).

112. ARV: B 1433: 332r–333v (10 December 1502).

113. ARV: B 194: 58r–59v, 61r–63r (1494).

114. ARV: B 194: 244r–245v (1495). Abun-Nasr, *Maghrib*, p. 158, discusses the opinions of the theologian Aḥmad al-Wanshirisi of Fez (d. 1508), who denounced as infidels those Andalusian Muslims who opined that life in Spain was preferable to the conditions in the Maghrib. See also Leila Sabbagh, "La religion des Morisques entre deux fatwas," in *Les Morisques et leur temps*, L. Cardaillac, ed. (Paris, 1983), pp. 43–56.

115. ARV: B 1433: 615v–616r (29 August 1504).

116. ACA: C 3546: 58r–v (17 May 1480).

117. ARV: B 1156: 654v–655r (17 November 1479).

118. ARV: C 303: 38r–v (10 August 1479).

119. AMV: g³ 33: 185r–v (10 June 1499).

120. J. Goñi Gaztambide, *Historia de la bula de cruzada en España* (Vitoria, 1958), pp. 371–403, 431–436. Regarding the promotion of the crusade against Granada, ARV: C 306: 76v–77r (16 July 1484); ARV: C 245: 32r–34r (30 August 1485), 43r–v (11 January 1486); ACA: C 3549: 22r–v (5 August 1484), 180r–v (8 July 1486); ACA: C 3609: 47r–50v (November 1485), 178r–180v (January 1488); and ACA: C 3610: 63r–64r (15 September 1490). Regarding the crusade against Africa, ACA C 3601: 110r–111r (18–20 May 1495), 173r–v (7 August 1496), 175v–176v (2 September 1496), 178r–v (6 September 1496), and 183r–v (30 October 1496). Regarding the crusade against the Turks,

see ACA: C 3600: 199r–201r (10 June 1502), 205v–206v (30 June 1502), and 209v–210r (8 August 1502).

121. ARV: C 307: 39v–40r (13 May 1486).

122. ARV: C 307: 39r–v (13 May 1486).

123. For instance, AMV: g³ 30: 169v (17 May 1483).

124. Gual Camarena, "Mudéjares valencianos," p. 480.

125. Cited in Ricard Garcia Càrcel and Eduard Císcar Pallarés, *Moriscos i agermanats* (Valencia, 1974), pp. 122–123.

126. ACA: C 3605: 136r (13 April 1482). This preaching might not have been specifically related to the crusade.

127. ACA: C 3567: 152r (8 February 1496).

128. ARV: C 650: 3r–4r (7 April 1488); see also chap. 1.

129. ARV: MR 106: 245r (13 February 1496)—"publicar dos crides... el altra... que negu no gosas maltractar los moros de Barberia." ARV: MR 107: 245r (3 March 1497)—"E altra crida que nigu no fos gosat de injuriar ningun moro berberuz."

130. ARV: C 310: 119r (30 January 1497).

131. A number of the transactions between Christian *corders* of Valencia and Muslim *espardenyers* of the Vall de Uxó are documented, for instance, ARV: B 1220: III 35r (16 March 1486), where Ali Gerret confesses to owing to Francesch Nadal 53 sous for the "fil de canem" he purchased from him.

132. ARV: B 1431: 67v and 77v (3 June 1491)—the case of Açen Muça of Serra.

133. For instance, ARV: C 131: 157v–158v (19 November 1483)—a Genoese ship conducting business in Cazaza with Fernando's safeguard is robbed by pirates from Alicante.

134. ARV: C 139: 179v–181r (2 January 1496).

135. ARV: B 1157: 637v–639r (25 May 1484), and ARV: B 1158: 73v–74v (30 August 1485), treat the confiscation of arms intended for illicit sale in the Maghrib. See also the comments of Guiral, "Relations commerciales," pp. 118–121, 130. ACA: C 3566: 28r–v (8 January 1488)—a Sicilian ship captures a Turkish galley, and on board are found two Catalans and a cargo of contraband goods, mainly armaments. On the antecedents of such activity, see Robert I. Burns, "Renegades, Adventurers, and Sharp Businessmen: The Thirteenth Century Spaniard in the Cause of Islam," *Catholic Historical Review* 57 (1972): 341–366.

136. ARV: C 650: 253r–v (18 July 1502): Joan Andreu of Ibiza is reported to be piloting a corsair fleet gathering in Bougie and Algiers.

137. Hinojosa Montalvo, "Relaciones," p. 103; Garcia Càrcel and Císcar Pallarés, *Moriscos*, p. 30; Leopoldo Piles Ros, *Apuntes para la historia económico-social de Valencia durante el siglo XV* (Valencia, 1969), pp. 115–119; and Gual Camarena, "Mudéjares valencianos," pp. 472–485, esp. p. 485. For a perceptive discussion of the relationship between economic difficulties and anti-Jewish and anti-Converso violence, see MacKay, "Popular Movements and Pogroms."

138. García Cárcel, *Germanías*, pp. 39–90; idem, "Las Germanías y la crisis

de subsistencias de 1521," *Boletín de la Sociedad Castellonense de Cultura* 51 (1975): 281–315; and Duran, *Germanies* , pp. 122–128, 369–400.

139. García Cárcel, *Germanías*, pp. 96, 189; Duran, *Germanies*, pp. 180–205, 394–395, 415–416.

140. García Cárcel, *Germanías*, pp. 188–191; Garcia Càrcel and Císcar Pallarés, *Moriscos*, pp. 121–130.

141. See chap. 1.

142. AMV: g³ 33: 214r (29 February 1500).

143. ACA: C 3655: 34r–v (5 March 1500).

144. ACA: C 3655: 34r–v. ARV: MR 109: 276v (1500)—a public proclamation of the royal safeguard protecting all Muslims of the kingdom. ACA: C 3614: 53v–54r (26 March 1500)—Fernando assures the Infante Enrique that the rumors are false and that no action will be taken against the Mudejars.

145. ACA: C 3600: 176v–177r (30 September 1501).

146. ACA: C 3600: 191v–192r (20 February 1502). Salvador, "Emigración," pp. 61–63, transcribes this document, which is a reiteration of the order of 5 March 1500.

147. ARV: C 596: 325r–v (8 March 1501).

148. ARV: C 596: 328v–329r (21 March 1501).

149. ARV: B 1162: 193v (24 April 1501).

150. ARV: B 1162: 199v–200v (11 May 1501).

151. ARV: B 1162: 239r–v (25 May 1501).

152. Salvador, "Emigración," p. 56.

153. ARV: C 650: 277r (3 September 1501).

154. ARV: C 650: 248r (24 May 1502)—"nosaltres [the nobles] qui tenim clara noticia dels recels e temors que los dits moros tenen per la gran conversacio e practica que ab aquells tenim com vixcam entre aquells."

155. ARV: C 650: 240v (12 April 1502).

156. ARV: C 650: 240v–241r.

157. ARV: C 650: 241v.

158. ARV: C 650: 242r–v (12 April 1502).

159. ARV: C 650: 242v–243r.

160. ARV: C 650: 247v–248r (24 May 1502).

161. ARV: C 650: 251r–252v (6 July 1502).

162. ARV: B 1162: 316r (17 June 1502)—a Mudejar family flees Castellnou with the intention of emigrating; 326r–v (4 July)—three Muslims of Polop are captured while trying to board boats for Africa; and 349v (19 October 1502)—other Mudejars are captured and killed while attempting to escape. ARV: MR 110: 82r, 83v–84r (1502)—Mudejars are fined for attempting illegal flight.

163. AMV: g³ 33: 290v–291r (1 May 1502).

164. ARV: C 158: 83v–84v (6 September 1502); ARV: C 311: 300v–301r (20 October 1502); ARV: B 1162: 318v–319v (11 March 1502); and ARV: MR 110: 278r (1502).

165. ARV: C 311: 254v–255r (6 June 1502)—Almoradi; and AMV: g³ 34: 118r (13 April 1503)—Benidorm.

166. AMV: g³ 34: 171r–173r (30 August 1503).

167. Braudel, "Afrique du Nord," pp. 203–208.
168. AMV: g³ 34: 2v (27 May 1502).
169. AMV: g³ 34: 11r (16 July 1502).
170. ARV: C 650: 253r–v (18 July 1502).
171. Ricardo García Cárcel, "La revuelta morisca de Espadán," *Al-Andalus* (1976): 121–146.
172. *Constitucions de Cathalunya* (ACA: Camara V: XXVI/5/20): folio 30r: Cap. XV (1503): "Que los moros no sien expellits de Cathalunya." Ricardo del Arco, "Cortes aragonesas de los Reyes Católicos," *Revista de Archivos, Bibliotecas, y Museos* 60 (1954): 92.
173. ARV: B 1162: 264v–265r (20 September 1501), 320r–v (22 June 1502), 428v–429r (1 April 1503), 455r (10 June 1503); and ARV: B 1433: 615v–616r (29 August 1504).
174. ARV: B 1162: 578r (18 July 1504).
175. García Cárcel, *Germanías*, pp. 188–189, 219–220, document no. 1; idem, *Inquisición*, pp. 116–117.
176. The document containing Fernando's response is published in Doussinague, *Política*, pp. 515–517, apendice (appendix) no. 1: Fernando to the king of Naples, his intermediary in relations with Qā'it Bāy, (5 September 1489).

Chapter Three:
Mudejar Officialdom and Economic Life

1. For example, ARV: C 137: 244v (9 January 1495)—"contra lo dit loch e o universitat aljama e singulars moros vehins"; or ARV: C 138: 24v (26 January 1496)—"contra universitatem et aljamam sarracenorum loci de Chiva."
2. See the comments of Boswell, *Royal Treasure*, pp. 103–106; and concerning the limitations on aljama autonomy in fiscal and judicial affairs, see chap. 4 and chap. 5, respectively.
3. ACA: C 3545: 17v–20v (18 July 1479) and C 3522: 65v–66r (11 October 1479) concern the appointment of the qāḍī and scribe of Tortosa by the qāḍī general. See chap. 5 on the qāḍī general's judicial functions.
4. Boswell, *Royal Treasure*, pp. 47–48.
5. See n. 3.
6. Barceló Torres, "Morería de Valencia," pp. 58–59, 68–69; ARV: C 131: 61v–62r (18 April 1483): an appeal of the qāḍī general's decision is given to Ali Cunes, the lieutenant qāḍī, for consideration.
7. ARV: B 1157: 696r (1484).
8. ARV: C 423: 97v–98r and ARV: B 1157: 307r–v (both dated 22 December 1481).
9. Regarding the qāḍī general's role in determining the Crown's share of Muslim inheritances, see chap. 4, and as arbiter between feuding families, chap. 6.
10. The registers ARV: MR 93–110 record the bailiff general's payment of a

salary to the *qāḍī* general. ARV: B 1157: 637v–639r (25 May 1484)—the *qāḍī* general is paid for having received the confession of a Muslim criminal; ARV: B 1222: II 54r (24 May 1497)—Azmet Chiqala owes 42s to the *qāḍī* general "de salari de la judicatura de la herencia de sa muller."

11. ACA: C 3545: 17v–20v; and ACA: C 3635: 34v–35r (15 October 1479).

12. ARV: B 1157: 696r–698v (1484); and B 1157: 724v–726r (30 August 1484) is a confirmation of Ali's appointment.

13. ARV: B 1433: 160r (2 October 1501)—Ali Bellvis appears as *qāḍī;* Barceló Torres, *Minorías*, pp. 61–62; and Boswell, *Royal Treasure*, p. 48, concerning the Bellvis family in the fourteenth century.

14. Boswell, *Royal Treasure*, pp. 77–79. The registers ARV: MR 3052–3062 record the payment of a salary to the *qāḍī* of Játiva; see chap. 5 for the various juridical activities of the *qāḍī* .

15. See Burns, *Islam under the Crusaders*, pp. 231–233, for the thirteenth century; and for the fifteenth century, Augustín Nieto Fernández, "La morería de Orihuela en el siglo XV," in *Primer Congreso de Historia del País Valenciano* (Valencia, 1980), 2: 765; Gual Camarena, "Aportaciones," p. 176, for the new aljama of Monforte (1459); and ACA: C 3650: 255v–259r (19 February 1496), concerning the new aljama of Alcoy (created in 1468). See Boswell, *Royal Treasure*, pp. 79–87, for fourteenth-century abuses.

16. ARV: C 310: 26v–28r (January 1496).

17. The royal orders creating aljamas in Monforte and Alcoy (see. n. 15) give the bailiff general "beyond the Jijona River" and the local bailiff, respectively, the prerogative of appointing the local *qāḍī* . The aljama of Borja (Aragon) seems to have been the one exception in that it could elect its *qāḍī*—ACA: C 3656: 174v–175v (20 April 1505).

18. This may be inferred from the fact that when Fernando created the aljama of Castellón he did not provide for the appointment of a *qāḍī*—ARV: C 304: 88v–90r (19 July 1480).

19. Vicente Pons Alós, *El Fondo Crespí de Valldaura en el Archivo Condal de Orgaz (1249–1548)* (Valencia, 1982), pp. 219–221, 226, document nos. 281, 284, 288, and 305.

20. ARV: C 423: 86r–87v (14 March 1481), C 424: 8r–10r (7 April 1485), and 84r–85r (30 July 1494) are all appointments of the sub-*qāḍī*s of Játiva.

21. *Aureum opus*, 81r.

22. ARV: C 139: 95v–97r (9 July 1495)—Elda; ARV: B 1158: 159v–164r (23 January 1486)—Gandía; ARV: B 1431: 384r (14 June 1493)—Alcocer; ARV: C 129: 98v–99v (6 July 1481)—Apse; and ARV: B 1431: 384v (29 October 1492)—Paterna.

23. On the *faqīh*s, see chaps. 5 and 6.

24. ACA: C 3568: 40v–42r (15 April 1493).

25. ARV: B 1158: 413v–414v (9 May 1493) notes that the salary of the *faqīh* of Castellón de la Plana derives from the rents of the properties of the local mosque; see also chap. 6.

26. Macho y Ortega, "Mudéjares aragoneses," does not ascribe any importance to the *faqīh*s; however, from his appendix of documents—for example, document no. 68, p. 285—it is apparent that many Aragonese aljamas in fact

had *faqīh*s. On the scholarly connections between Valencian Mudejars and Almería and Tunis, see chap. 6 and table 19.

27. Boswell, *Royal Treasure*, pp. 88–89, corrects the views of Francisco A. Roca Traver, "Un siglo de vida mudéjar en la Valencia medieval (1238–1338)," *Estudios de Edad Media de la Corona de Aragón* V (1952): 13–14, and Macho y Ortega, "Mudéjares aragoneses," pp. 155–157, who were led to believe that the *amīn* was the real power in the aljama.

28. For example, the appointment of Çahat Paziar as *amīn* of Alcira, ARV: C 309: 171r–172v (11 September 1493).

29. Some examples are ARV: C 134: 141r–v (11 April 1488)—the *amīn* of Bétera leaves the seigneury and takes the account books with him; and ARV: C 158: 32r–33r (5 July 1502)—the *amīn*s of Albaida are involved in rent collection.

30. Barceló Torres, *Minorías*, pp. 221–376, for the Arabic documentation; ARV: B 1156: 804r (1 July 1480)—the bailiff general contacts the *amīn* of the Foya de Buñol regarding a new royal vassal who wishes to settle accounts; ARV: C 154: 132r–v (13 June 1498)—the *amīn* of Chova is involved in settling accounts with a former vassal; and ARV: C 140: 80r–v (28 September 1499)— action is to be taken against the *amīn*s and elders of the aljamas of Segorbe and the Vall de Almonezir regarding pensions owed by them.

31. ARV: C 304: 74r–75v (6 July 1480)—appointment of the *amīn* of Alcira; ARV: C 309: 300r–301r (9 January 1496)—appointment of the *amīn* of Játiva; ARV: C 304: 88v–90r (19 July 1480)—the aljama of Castellón de Játiva may elect its *amīn*; and ACA: C 3650: 255v–259r—the aljama of Alcoy may elect its *amīn*.

32. The *amīn*s of Alcira were appointed for life, while those of Castellón de la Plana rarely served for more than a year at a time. The aljama of Valencia was unusual is not having an *amīn*, for the post had been abolished in 1337 by royal decree; see Boswell, *Royal Treasure*, pp. 88–89.

33. ARV: C 151: 41r–v (22 September 1496).

34. ARV: C 129: 119r–v (2 August 1481); and ARV: C 148: 142v–143v (25 January 1493)—the *amīn* and *adelantats* of Matet resist execution on aljama property.

35. ARV: C 134: 141r–v (11 April 1488).

36. ARV: C 130: 15r–16r (9 June 1481).

37. At least this was the case in the aljama of Castellón de la Plana; see further discussion of the struggle for aljama office in Castellón in this chapter and in chap. 6.

38. ARV: C 304: 88v–90r—"juratos sive rectores et administratores et alios officiales ad regimen dicte aljame necessarios."

39. ARV: B 1158: 413v–414v—the aljama of Castellón de la Plana has two *adelantats*, as does that of Valencia (Barceló Torres, "Morería de Valencia," p. 58). ACA: C 3665: 18v–20r (23 November 1486)—Fernando confirms the privilege of the aljama of Játiva to elect its four *adelantats*.

40. Barceló Torres, "Morería de Valencia," p. 58; and ARV: B 1158: 413v–414v.

41. ACA: C 3567: 98r (20 April 1494)—election via *insaculación* in the aljama of Zaragoza; and ACA: C 3571: 204r (12 February 1496)—the same for

the aljama of Huesca. However, the aljama of Zaragoza was forced to complain when the archbishop insisted on placing in the sacks the names of candidates who were not residents of the *morería*—ACA: C 3571: 162v–163r (18 August 1494).

42. See chap. 1 n. 131. The aljama of Tortosa also complained about the local *alcayd* (Christian official) hindering its elections—ACA: C 3521: 51r–v (13 September 1479).

43. Some examples are ARV: C 141: 122v–123r (31 January 1500)—the *adelantats* of the aljama of Valencia lease the *carnicería* to a Christian butcher; ARV: C 148: 132v–134r (11 January 1493)—Muslim jurates represent Benaguacil in a litigation; and for the importance of community defense on seigneurial lands, see chap. 6.

44. ARV: B 1158: 159v–164r (23 January 1486)—the *qāḍī, amīn,* and *adelantats* of the aljama of Gandía swear fealty to their new lord; ARV: B 1160: 477r (8 June 1492)—the *qāḍī,* sub-*qāḍī,* and *adelantats* of the aljama of Játiva recognize the newly appointed bailiff; and ARV: C 130: 15r–16r (9 June 1481)—the *amīn* and *adelantats* of Gaibiel are seen as responsible for the departure of Muslim vassals from the seigneury.

45. See chap. 6 for a discussion of violent conflict in the aljama of Castellón de la Plana over the posts of *adelantat.*

46. Boswell, *Royal Treasure,* p. 73.

47. ACA: C 3571: 204r (12 February 1496)—Fernando commands that the aljama of Huesca should not force Junez Burro to hold office if elected. On the financial difficulties of Aragonese aljamas, see chap. 4.

48. Barceló Torres, "Morería de Valencia," p. 58; and ARV: B 1158: 413v–414v concerning the councillors of the aljama of Castellón de la Plana. See Macho y Ortega, "Mudéjares aragoneses," pp. 159–160, regarding the function of aljama councillors in Aragon.

49. ARV: C 140: 159v–160r (11 April 1500); and ARV: C 139: 174r–175r (9 January 1496).

50. Burns, *Islam under the Crusaders,* pp. 235–236; Gual Camarena, "Aportaciones," p. 177; and Boswell, *Royal Treasure,* pp. 87–88. ARV: B 1160: 851v–853v (2 June 1494)—the appointment of the *çalmedina* of the aljama of Játiva, which unfortunately reveals little about his function.

51. ARV: B 1157: 556r–557r (6 February 1484).

52. ARV: C 306: 126v–128v (22 December 1484) and ARV: B 1157: 556r–557r for Játiva; and Barceló Torres, "Morería de Valencia," pp. 58–59. Macho y Ortega, "Mudéjares aragoneses," p. 160, for the *clavari* in Aragonese aljamas.

53. Barceló Torres, *Minorías,* p. 55.

54. Boswell, *Royal Treasure,* pp. 43–49, 104; and Barceló Torres, *Minorías,* p. 57.

55. Hinojosa Montalvo, "Relaciones," p. 114, on the Bellvis' commercial activities in the early fifteenth century; Guiral-Hadziiossif, *Valence,* p. 344; and on Bellvis commerce during Fernando's reign, see discussion of Mudejar commercial activity in this chapter.

56. ARV: B 1433: 160r (2 October 1501)—Çahat Bellvis is one of the *ade-*

lantats, while Ali Bellvis is *qāḍī*.

57. ARV: B 1159: 248r (1 October 1489).
58. ARV: C 707: 815r–817r (17 April 1480).
59. See chap. 1 n.74, where members of the *faqīh*'s family move from Almería and resettle in Valencia.
60. ARV: MR 99: 174r (1489).
61. ARV: B 1159: 248r
62. ARV: C 131: 61v–62r (18 April 1483); ARV: C 310: 26v–28r (9 January 1496); and ARV: MR 3052–3062.
63. ARV: C 424: 8r–10r (7 April 1485).
64. ARV: C 424: 8r–10r and 84r–85r (30 July 1494).
65. ARV: C 424: 8r–10r.
66. ARV: MR 3052: 6r (1478); and MR 3053: 6v (1490). Axer also rented the *debea* (pasture ?) in 1490 for 200s—MR 3053: 6r.
67. ARV: C 423: 86r–87r (14 March 1481).
68. ARV: C 131: 61v–62r. Also, ARV: B 1157: 636r–637v (26 May 1484)—Yuçeff Alçamba and Çahat travel together to the southern part of the kingdom for "affairs."
69. ARV: C 310: 26v–28r; and ARV: C 707: 848r–v (11 May 1480) for Çahat's commerce with Almería.
70. ARV: B 1160: 477r (8 June 1492).
71. ARV: B 1158: 60v–61r (29 July 1485).
72. ARV: MR 3053–3062 (1490–1502); and see chap. 4, table 11 for lessees of the soap factory (*çabonería*).
73. ARV: MR 3055: 5r (1495).
74. ARV: MR 3056–3062 (1496–1502); and see chap. 4, table 11 for the lessees of the ovens and the butcher shop. Another Játiva family that combined civil service with investment in Crown utilities were the Tagaris. In 1490 Mahomat was the aljama's *çalmedina*, in which office his relative Abdalla followed him in 1494–1495 and in 1498–1502 (ARV: MR 3053–3062). Mahomat, who as *çalmedina* had supervised the *morería*'s market, went on to lease the market in 1495–1498 for rents as high as 2,000s (ARV: MR 3055–3058). Abdalla, although lacking the financial wherewithal of Mahomat, had enough money to rent the *morería*'s baths in 1500 and 1501 for 920s and 800s (ARV: MR 3060–3061). See also chap. 4, tables 8, 9, and 11.
75. ARV: C 304: 74r–75r (6 July 1480); ARV: C 309: 171r–172v (11 September 1493).
76. Halperin Donghi, *Conflicto*, pp. 86–87.
77. ARV: MR 942–959 (1479–1502); and chap. 4, table 5.
78. ARV: B 1156: 595v–596r (18 September 1479).
79. For example, ARV: MR 945: 16r (1489)—Çahat farms the tithes of the districts of Alquerencia and St. Bernat for 2880s and 1820s, respectively.
80. ARV: C 309: 171r–172v.
81. ARV: B 1160: 244v–245r (17 June 1491).
82. ARV: MR 958: 1v (1501); and MR 959: 1v (1502).
83. The *amīn*s of Castellón's aljama were Ubequer Faraig (1483, 1493, 1495), Yuçeff Bocayo (1489), Yuçeff Polina (1492, 1496), Juçeff Calio (1482), and his

son (?) Jabar (1497), Eça Mascor (1499), Fando (1500), Çahat Bendariff (1501), and Ozmen Rubeyt (1502, 1503)—ARV: MR 2469–2490.

84. Thomas F. Glick, *Irrigation and Society in Medieval Valencia* (Cambridge, Mass., 1970), pp. 61–64; and ARV: B 1159: 48r (19 May 1488) concerns Azmet Bocayo, *traginer* (carter).

85. ARV: MR 2478: 6r (1490)—Sat Bocayo purchases four *fanecates* from Pere Moncet; MR 2479: 4r (1491)—6s are paid by Sat for rent on six *fanecates* of land, four of which "solia esser vinya"; and MR 2483: 7r (1495)—10s *lluisme* is collected from Azmet Bocayo for the sale of land to another Muslim for 100s.

86. See chap. 6 for a discussion of the Bocayos' political role in Castellón.

87. Barceló Torres, *Minorías*, pp. 61–62; and Halperin Donghi, *Conflicto*, p. 89.

88. Barceló Torres, *Minorías*, p. 57.

89. ARV: B 1431: 542v–550v (5 November 1493)—especially the testimonies of Abraym Alfat, the *amīn* of Alberique (544r–546r); Mahomat Lopo of La Foyeta (546v–548r); Mahomat ben Lup of Alberique (548v–549r); and Azmet Toraybi of Resalany (549r–550r).

90. ARV: G (Gobernación) 2396: 269r–v, 284r–285r (24 April 1493).

91. ARV: B 1431: 278v–280r (6 February 1493)—the testimonies of Alfaqui Alasdrach of Buñol and Ali Alcayet of Chiva.

92. ARV: C 138: 72v–73v (1 December 1496)—Areñol; ARV: C 140: 82v–83v (13 September 1499)—Bechí; and ARV: B 325: 58r–v (26 January 1495). Other examples are ARV: C 154: 66r–67r (7 February 1498), regarding a Mudejar *arrendador* of the rents of the Vall de Alcalá and the Vall de Gallinera; and ARV: C 156: 85r–86r (17 November 1501), concerning Ali Çequien, "arrendador dels drets e rendes pertanyents al receptor del antich patrimoni [i.e., Benaguacil, Paterna, and La Pobla]."

93. Thomas F. Glick, "The Ethnic Systems of Premodern Spain," *Comparative Studies in Sociology* 1 (1978): 157–171, views the system of ethnic stratification in late medieval Aragon as a paternalistic one, in which a horizontal bar between the higher ethnic group, the Christians, and the lower ethnic group, the Muslims, precludes the upward social mobility of the latter. Also, see Boswell's qualifications of Glick's conclusions in *Royal Treasure*, pp. 22–23.

94. See chap. 6 for a detailed treatment of Mudejar social structures and feuding.

95. Burns, *Islam under the Crusaders*, pp. 401–413, regarding the elite of wealth and the coordinating elite of religious erudites in Almohad and postconquest Valencia; and Ira M. Lapidus, *Muslim Cities in the Later Middle Ages*, (Cambridge, 1984), pp. 130–142, on the role of the ᶜulamā'.

96. That the newly converted Muslims fled from the urban areas is indicated in Tomas V. Peris Albentosa, "La estructura de la propiedad agricola en la morería de Alzira (1508–1579), "*Qüestions Valencianes* 1 (1979): 54–55; and Garcia Càrcel and Císcar Pallarés, *Moriscos*, p. 37, regarding Játiva. See Halperin Donghi, *Conflicto*, pp. 15–45 and 79–95, for sixteenth-century economic conditions, and pp. 58–69, for relations between Moriscos and their lords; also Eugenio Císcar Pallarés, *Tierra y señorio en el País Valenciano (1570–1620)* (Valencia, 1977), pp. 88–134, regarding the response of the seigneurs to their

worsening financial situation; and James Casey, *The Kingdom of Valencia in the Seventeenth Century* (Cambridge, 1979), p. 33, for the importance of Morisco muleteers. Although Furió and Garcia, "Dificultats agràries," pp. 300–303, see great difficulties burdening Valencian farmers in the late fifteenth century, I would nonetheless argue that the economic position of the Mudejars in the fifteenth century was better than that of the Moriscos in the sixteenth century, and that some Mudejars formed part of the "capa de grans emfiteutes enriquits" and "llauradors benestants" they describe.

97. ACA: C 3665: 20v–21r (December 1486).

98. ACA: C 3610: 191v (7 May 1493).

99. ARV: C 156: 111r–112r (15 December 1501).

100. For example, ARV: B 1159: 99r–v (5 July 1488); and ARV: C 137: 144r–145v (2 August 1494).

101. Registers ARV: B 1156–1162. ARV: B 1160: 249v–250v (24 June 1491)—Abrahim Alahuy, a shoemaker, complains when his maidservant Fotayma runs off with another Muslim.

102. See chaps. 5 and 6 for more details on Muslim prostitutes.

103. See ARV: MR 89–110, for the licenses issued to Mudejar mendicants; and ARV: B 1431: 344r–375r (29 October 1492)—the case of Abdalla Alfaqui, in which Muslim witnesses discuss begging "per amor de Deu."

104. See chap. 5 for the judicial enslavement of Mudejars.

105. ARV: B 1162: 331v, 333r (1 August 1502), and 349r (15 October 1502).

106. Robert I. Burns, "Muslim–Christian Conflict and Contact: Mudejar Methodology," in *Muslims, Christians, and Jews in the Crusader Kingdom of Valencia: Societies in Symbiosis* (Cambridge, 1984), pp. 39–49.

107. Boswell, *Royal Treasure*, pp. 41–42.

108. Antoni Furió, *Camperols del País Valencià: Sueca, una comunitat rural a la tardor de l'Edat Mitjana* (Valencia, 1982), pp. 106–119; and Císcar Pallarés, *Tierra y señorio*, pp. 76–77.

109. For example, ARV: MR 959: 6r (1502). The Crown collects 8s for *lluisme* from Pere Soriano, who sold a "troç de terra . . . tengut sots directa senyoria del Senyor Rey" to Mahomat Nuçayre for 80s.

110. ARV: B 1161: 101v–102r (4 August 1495).

111. Peris Albentosa. "Propiedad agricola," pp. 89–91.

112. ARV: B 1162: 365v (14 November 1502).

113. For example, ARV: B 1161: 92r–v (1 July 1495).

114. Peris Albentosa, "Propiedad agricola," pp. 76–85; and Concepción Domingo Pérez, "La agricultura de Castellón de la Plana, 1468," *Saitabi* 27 (1977): 223–233.

115. ARV: B 325: 10r–12v (9 April 1494).

116. ARV: C 151: 74r–v (7 January 1497). Hamet Perromalo also leased one of the town's ovens for 115s–ARV: MR 4028: 1r–v (1496).

117. For example, ARV: C 131: 61v–62r, where Azmet Xarica is the vassal of Ausias Rotla, a canon of Játiva.

118. Barceló Torres, *Minorías*, p. 81. Furió and Garcia, "Dificultats agràries," p. 297, point out the existence of a significant amount of allodial land in the districts of royal towns and cities.

119. Peris Albentosa, "Propiedad agricola," pp. 91–92.

120. ARV: B 1160: 443r–v (18 May 1492).

121. See chap. 1 n. 35.

122. ARV: G 2356: Manus 25: 33r (1480).

123. ARV: G 2359: Manus 15: 33r–v (1481).

124. Burns, "Mudejar methodology," p. 49; Glick, *Irrigation*, pp. 231–232; and Barceló Torres, *Minorías*, pp. 80–81.

125. See nn. 110, 112.

126. Barceló Torres, *Minorías*, pp. 262–263, document nos. 76–77, concerning the payment of the *sequiatge*; and ACA: C 3650: 220v–221r (26 October 1493) for the irrigation communities near Orihuela. Maria Teresa Ferrer i Mallol, *Les aljames sarraïnes de la governació d'Oriola* (Barcelona, 1988), pp. 95–99, discusses Mudejar irrigation agriculture in the southern region of the kingdom.

127. ARV: B 1156: 882v–883r (18 November 1480)—Játiva; and ARV: C 148: 131v–132v (9 January 1493)—Gandía.

128. ARV: B 1161: 336r–v (7 December 1496). ACA: C 3655: 88r–v (13 October 1501) mentions Muslims with lands in Alcira's "orta del cent" in the context of irrigation matters.

129. ARV: C 148: 167v–169r (24 April 1493)—Torres Torres; and ARV: B 1157: 734v–735r (13 October 1484)—Alcocer.

130. ARV: C 148: 213v (4 September 1493).

131. ARV: G 2356: Manus 26: 46r–v (13 September 1480). Other examples of seigneurial lands where irrigation agriculture was practiced are ARV: C 148: 190r–191r (9 July 1493)—Benaguacil, Pedralba, Ribarroja; ARV: C 135: 183v–184v (29 March 1490)—Alberique and Alcocer; ARV: C 310: 149r–150r (17 October 1497)—Callosa; and ARV: B 325: 495r–496r (16 May 1501)—Valldigna.

132. Glick, *Irrigation*, pp. 26–27.

133. Furió, *Camperols*, pp. 74–83; Peris Albentosa, "Propiedad agricola," pp. 76–85; Domingo Pérez, "Agricultura," pp. 226–231; and Barceló Torres, *Minorías*, pp. 83–84. See also my doctoral dissertation, "Between *Convivencia* and Crusade," pp. 266–268, for a table listing crops raised by Mudejars on royal and seigneurial lands.

134. Peris Albentosa, "Propiedad agricola," pp. 58–75.

135. ARV: C 139: 193v–194v (4 February 1496), and ARV: C 151: 75r–v (7 January 1497)—Corbera; ARV: B 1159: 3r (March 1488)—Alberique; and ARV: B 1158: 75v–76v (2 September 1485)—Turís.

136. See table 2, this chapter.

137. See chap. 1 for a discussion of the difficulties caused by the seigneurs in this regard.

138. Some examples are ARV: C 317: 26v (13 November 1492), concerning Muslim vassals of Jérica with "heretats" in Fuentes; and ARV: B 1161: 578v–579r (18 February 1499)—a Muslim vassal of Castellón de la Plana with land in Mascarell "seria anat a la dita baronia per coltivar les terres que alli te com a terratinent . . . pagant los drets que com a terratinents se deven pagar."

139. ARV: C 317: 26v—"peyta"; and ARV: B 1156: 806r–807r (7 July

1480)—"delmes," i. e., tithes.

140. ARV: C 306: 69r–70r (11 May 1484).

141. ACA: C 3647: 98r–99r (21 July 1490). In what seems to have been a more unusual arrangement, Mudejar tenants in the district of the town of Segorbe paid *murs e valls*, as well as the *peyta*—ARV: G 2359: Manus 15: 25r–v (1481).

142. Gual Camarena, "Aportaciones," pp. 181–199.

143. ARV: G 2355: Manus 14: 15r–v (1480).

144. ARV: B 1161: 336r–v (7 December 1496), and 435v–436r (8 August 1497). Other examples of purchases are ARV: B 1157: 344v–345v (27 November 1482); ARV: G 2351: Manus 11: 27r–v (21 May 1479); ARV G 2359: Manus 15: 33r–v (1481); ARV: G 2372: 446r–447v (1484). Antoni Furió, "El País Valencià de l'Edat Mitjana a la Modernitat (segles XIII–XVI)," in *Història de l'Economia Valenciana* (Valencia, 1983), p. 52, notes "l'aparició d'unes capes d'emfiteutes enriquits (a les terres de senyoriu) o de camperols lliures (a les terres i hortes reial), que basaren el creixement agricola dels camps explotats."

145. For example, ARV: MR 943: 7v (1481). Ayet Naçayr and Mahomat Bençarco pay 12s and 6s, respectively, for the rent of "terra derrenclida."

146. Barceló Torres, *Minorías*, p. 84.

147. See chap. 4 for a discussion of the finances of the seigneurs and their aljamas.

148. See the discussion of Mudejar commercial activity in this chapter. Ferrer i Mallol, *Les aljames*, pp. 108–109, asserts that in the gubernatorial district of Oriheula during the fourteenth century Mudejar farmers were producing sufficient surplus to allow for the sale of produce in Alicante and in Castile.

149. See n. 115.

150. Císcar Pallarés, *Tierra y señorio*, p. 299; Barceló Torres, *Minorías*, p. 83.

151. ARV: C 310: 85r (8 July 1496)—"quosdam sarracenos arantes seu alias laborantes in quodam agro Abraham Juçefi." Furió and Garcia, "Dificultats agràries," pp. 301–302, note that many Christians worked as day laborers on the lands of wealthier farmers in order to supplement the produce from their own family parcels.

152. García Cárcel, *Germanías*, p. 190.

153. Ricardo García Cárcel, "La ganadería valenciana en el siglo XVI," *Saitabi* 27 (1977): 97–100; Glick, *Irrigation*, p. 26.

154. García Cárcel, "Ganadería," pp. 80–97; but see Barceló Torres's correction of García's computations—*Minorias*, p. 78.

155. ARV: G 2357: Manus 37 (2d): 32v–33r (27 May 1480). ACA: C 3649: 77v–78r (29 February 1492) mentions Muslims of Alcira taking their flocks up to the mountains. Also, see Barceló Torres, *Minorías*, p. 80.

156. ARV: C 151: 174v–175r (18 May 1497); and ARV: B 1156: 628v–629r (18 October 1479)—the complaint of a Christian of Alcira that local Muslims were grazing their livestock in his oak grove.

157. ARV: G 2351: Manus 13: 4r–5r (4 June 1479); and ARV: B 1157: 30v (11 April 1481)—the lord of Chella complains when the *peatger* of Enguera collects the *peatge* from his Muslim vassals grazing their animals in the district of Enguera.

158. ARV: C 131: 25v (23 December 1482); and C 134: 139r–140r (9 April 1488), regarding the same case. Other examples are ARV: C 151: 150v–151r (18 April 1497)—Muslims of Petrés owe 120 pounds to a Christian of Puzol for sheep purchased; and C 156: 146r–v (26 January 1502)—Muslims of Benifayó and Santa Coloma buy "bestiar" from a Christian of Salzadella.

159. García Cárcel, "Ganadería," p. 96, concerning Mahomat Alazrach; ARV: B 1160: 361v–362r (5 December 1491) for Çahat Ageg; and B 1160: 780r–781r (4 December 1493) concerns a Muslim of Castellón de Játiva, formerly of Benimuslem, who owns at least 100 sheep. Çahat Tabernaxi of Mascarell—ARV: C 148: 169v–170r (18 May 1493)—and Mahomat Tuniçi of Mislata—ARV: B 1220: II 19v (23 October 1486)—purchased 300 and 100 head of sheep, respectively, each one probably augmenting his already sizable flock. ARV: B 1223: III 37r–40r (1502)—Muslims of Alcira buy 97 goats from a Christian of Teulada and subsequently sell some of the goats to other Muslims of Alcira.

160. ARV: B 1431: 387v–388r (8 July 1493)—the testimony of Ali Barrazi.

161. ARV: B 1431: 388r—Ali testifies that he sold some of Abrahim Xativi's goats.

162. ARV: B 1432: 192v (27 October 1484)—Mahomat allegedly borrowed 33 pounds from the bailiff of Alcira in order to buy the sheep and goats from the Muslim of Cortes; 201r (15 April 1486)—Bernat Aymerich testifies that Mahomat bought sheep from Vizcaya when he was *alcayt* of Masalaves; and 203r–v (18 April)—the testimony of Bernat Cathala. ARV: C 151: 174v–175r (18 May 1497)—a Muslim of Albatera sells sheep to a Muslim of Callosa and a Christian of Orihuela.

163. ARV: B 323: 410r (30 September 1480)—Alasquer, and 411r (same date)—Masalalí; other instances involve Muslims from Paterna (B 323: 365v [22 June 1480]), Ribarroja (B 323: 434r [2 May 1481]), and the Vall de Uxó (B 323: 480r [4 September 1481]).

164. ARV: G 2372: 400r–405r (23 February 1484)—the testimonies of Joan Annayar (404r–v), Amet Chompar (404v), and Ali Pagonti, the *amīn* (405r), all residents of Chelva, concerning the Çelims' delivery of the wool and some cheese to Albert's agent.

165. ARV: B 324: 50r–v (22 June 1489); and ARV: G 2358: Manus 43: 18r (1480)—a Muslim of the Foya de Buñol is robbed while bringing hides and other goods to Valencia.

166. Some examples are ARV: B 1220: III 31v (7 March 1486)—Ali Alazdrach of Beniopa confesses to owing to Johan Ferrer, a farmer of Rafol de Valldigna, 52s for the rent of a mule; B 1220: III 40r (6 April 1486)—Çaat Abducamet of Játiva owes 60s to Johan Allepus, merchant of Valencia, for the price of an ass; B 1220: V 30r (6 November 1486)—Mahomat Miller of Picasent owes 125s to Johan Gombau of Valencia for the price of a mule; B 1220: VI 13r (14 February 1487)—Mahomat Martorell of Játiva owes 70s to Çahat Durdura of Játiva for the price of a horse.

167. ARV: B 324: 366r–368v (14 June 1492)—Castellnou; and 370r–379v (16 June)—Liria. ARV: B 1223: III unnumbered folios between 22v and 23r (4 February 1502)—the complaint of a Muslim of Eslida who rented a donkey to a Christian squire who then sold it to someone else.

168. Gual Camarena, "Aportaciones," pp. 186–199; Barceló Torres, *Minorías*, p. 88.

169. ARV: B 1158: 75v–76v (2 September 1485)—a Muslim of Alcira is to be allowed to go to Turís to get his beehives and other property; B 1157: 487r–v (4 September 1483)—Muslims of the Vall de Uxó rent beehives from the Crown in Burriana; ARV: B 1220: IV 39r (26 June 1486)—Ali Vizquey, a shoemaker, owes 6s 7d to the merchant Jacme Pironat for the rent of an apiary; B 1222: I 19r, 20v–24v (26 September 1496)—"Capal moro" brings honey into the capital; and for the activities of Çahat Flori, a confectioner of Játiva, see n. 215 below.

170. García Cárcel, "Ganadería," pp. 98–100.

171. ARV: C 596: 147r–v (7 June 1494) concerning the subversive activities of Mudejar fishermen (and see chap. 2); ARV: B 1156: 359v (January 1479), B 1158: 237r (5 June 1486), and B 1162: 192r–v (24 April 1501) all record the money owed by Muslims for the purchases of fishing line.

172. ARV: G 2356: Manus 25: 33r–v (1480); and Barceló Torres, *Minorías*, p. 77, mentions the sixteenth-century prohibitions.

173. For example, ARV: C 305: 140v–141r (23 May 1482). A Muslim smith, a new vassal in Crevillente, is pardoned from prosecution for a crime at the request of his new lord (the implication being that the lord valued his skills as a smith).

174. ARV: C 126: 53v (8 October 1479).

175. ARV: C 308: 172r (15 March 1490).

176. ARV: C 310: 116v–119v (30 January 1497)—the ordinances of the cordmakers' guild (see chap. 2 for the text of the prohibition); Broman, *Contra moros i jueus*, p. 111, and Piles, *Apuntes*, p. 95, for the carpenters' guild; and Bramon, *Contra moros i jueus*, p. 112, for the makers of swords, cuirasses, and so on.

177. Cited in Bramon, *Contra moros i jueus*, pp. 110–111.

178. ARV: G 2392: 87r (1491)—the shoemakers' guild of Valencia prohibits laboring on feast days and Sundays; and ACA: C 3655: 168v–172v (28 March 1503)—the shoemakers' guild of Calatayud makes a similar ruling.

179. ACA: C 3635: 85r–89r (13 October 1479). The confraternity of tailors and shoemakers of Lérida (Catalonia) similarly ruled that every tailor and shoemaker, "Christian, Jew, or Moor," had to be examined by a master before practicing these crafts—ACA: C 3550: 97v–98v (14 February 1488).

180. ARV: B 1431: 333v–335r (24 January 1493). Ali, the slave of Vicent Calamocha, a carpenter of Valencia, testifies regarding how he was approached by Azmet Çahat of Tunis (accused of facilitating the escape of runaway slaves) while he was working on the house of Domingo Vines.

181. Bramon, *Contra moros i jueus*, p. 109; and regarding the shoemakers' guild, see below, nn. 183, 185–186.

182. Bramon, *Contra moros i jueus*, p. 109.

183. ARV: B 1222: III 14r–15r (5 December 1497).

184. ARV: B 1431: 531v–536r (20 May 1495)—the testimonies of Johan Bramon, boilermaker, Anthoni Comos, boilermaker, Baltasar Collado, cutler, and Christofol de Monserrat, boilermaker (all regarding Muça Almedina, ac-

cused of having stolen various things from the fonduk); and B 1431: 192r–v (19 January 1492)—the confession of Caçim Abdalla, accused of theft.

185. ARV: B 1222: III 14r.

186. ARV: B 1222: III 14v–15v. It is apparent from the feuding between Mudejar artisans, including shoemakers, that they regarded their economic competitors with deadly seriousness; see chap. 6 for a detailed discussion of this problem.

187. See n. 178.

188. ARV: B 1433: 422r–v (16 July 1503)—the testimony of Joan de Gandía; and 424v–425v (24 July)—the testimony of Miquel de Boro.

189. The sources in question are the registers ARV: B 323 (1479–1484), 324 (1489–1492), and 325 (1494–1500), entitled *Executions*; and ARV: B 1220 (1485–1487), 1222 (1496–1500), and 1223 (1501–1502), entitled *Manaments y Empares*. On the importance of credit for medieval industry, see, for example, Sylvia Thrupp, "Medieval Industry, 1000–1500," in *The Fontana Economic History of Europe: The Middle Ages*, Carlo M. Cipolla, ed. (Glasgow, 1981), pp. 244–249; and Maryanne Kowaleski, "Local Markets and Merchants in Late Fourteenth-Century Exeter," (Ph.D. diss., University of Toronto, 1982), pp. 176–178; or on the role of credit in the marketplace in general, Kathryn L. Reyerson, *Business, Banking and Finance in Medieval Montpellier* (Toronto, 1985), pp. 40–60.

190. ARV: B 323: 327r (22 November 1489).

191. ARV: B 323–325, and B 1220, 1222–1223. Kowaleski, "Markets and Merchants," pp. 176–178, points out the importance of regular commercial dealings and credit arrangements for supporting social and personal relationships between the parties involved.

192. ARV: B 323–325, and B 1220, 1222–1223.

193. ARV: MR 3052–3062; and see chap. 4, table 10, for the revenues received by the Crown from the leasing of the tannery (*adobería*).

194. ARV: B 1156: 836v–837v (8 August 1480)—Yuçeff Abducarim stands as surety; B 1157: 69r–70r (7 July 1481)—Abducarim and Pedro Navarro stand as surety; B 1157: 163r–v (25 January 1482)—Abducarim and Andreu Mestre stand as surety; and B 1158: 525r–v (18 January 1488)—Abducarim and Mestre again.

195. ARV: B1158: 333r–v (22 December 1486).

196. ARV: B 323–325, and B 1220, 1222–1223.

197. ARV: B 325: 471r (22 October 1499), 515r–v (16 January 1500)—Pérez and the Garbis buy hemp; and B 325: 570r–v (13 October 1500)—the loan. Sometimes the *espardenyers* bypassed the cordmakers and purchased hemp directly from the producers. ARV: B 1223: III 13r–v (8 January 1502), and 16r (18 January)—Çahat and Suhey Cotera purchase large quantities of hemp from Christian farmers.

198. ARV: B 1431: 529r–v (20 May 1495)—the testimony of Suleymen Alguarbi.

199. ARV: B 323: 446r (6 June 1481)—Abrahim Xeyt, dyer of Valencia; B 324: 217r (25 February 1491)—Çahat and Ali Baelel, dyers of Valldigna; B 325: 37r (10 August 1494)—Abducalem Margarit, dyer of Alcira; and ARV:

B 1162: 185v–186v (15 March 1501)—Acent, dyer of Valldigna.

200. ARV: MR 3052–3062, and chap. 4, table 9, for the dyeworks of Játiva (*tintorería*); and MR 4016–4034, and chap. 4, table 7, for the dyeworks of Murviedro.

201. ACA: C 3636: 54r–v (2 January 1481)—Muslims of Gandía owe money to a merchant of Valencia for dyes purchased; ARV: B 323: 446r (6 June 1481)—Abrahim Xeyt, dyer, buys cloth from a Christian wool-dresser; ARV: B 1222: II 46v–47r (5 May 1497)—a Muslim dyer of Valldigna buys cloth from a merchant; and B 1222: VII 23r (1 June 1500)—Galip Cindi of the Vall de Almonezir owes 7 pounds to the merchant Johan Abello for alum purchased.

202. ARV: B 324: 39r (20 May 1489)—Maymo Embravi, tailor of Cuart in the Vall de Sego; B 324: 61r–v (27 July 1489)—Maymo Bençebit, tailor of Manises; ARV: B 1159: 375r–v (14 September 1490)—Azmet Artanet, tailor of Valldigna; and ARV: G 2412: 161r–v (1501), concerning Azmet Lopo.

203. Some examples of other linen drapers and weavers in Valencia are ARV: B 323: 609r (19 April 1482)—Yuçeff Turis, *lençer*, and B 324: 14r–v (17 February 1489)—Mahomat Coret, *texidor de lli*; and ARV: B 1222: IV 43r (16 May 1498) for Abdalla's purchase of flax.

204. ARV: B 325: 172r (14 December 1495)—Abdalla owes 63s to a notary for linen purchased; ARV: B 1222: I 38r (27 October 1496)—Abdalla owes 18s to a carpenter for "hun drap de lenç"; B 1222: II 70v (11 July 1497)—Abdalla owes 24s to a monk of Valldigna for "cert lenç"; II 103v–104r (9 October 1497)—Abdalla owes 22 pounds 5s 6d to Pere Luca, a tailor, "de preu de cert lenç"; and B 1222: VII 41r (30 July 1500)—Abdalla owes 25s 3d to Vicent Borrel, a feltmaker, for linen purchased.

205. ARV: B 325: 14r–v (27 February 1494)—Abdalla owes 77 pounds to Pere Aymar, a wool-dresser (*perayre*), for cloth purchased; ARV: B 1222: V 34v (20 March 1499)—Abdalla owes 6 pounds 10s to the Venetian merchant Luis Mascelli for "una peca de olanda," twenty-eight *alnes* (one *alne* = approximately one meter) in length; B 1222: VI 37r (14 October 1499)—Abdalla owes 7 pounds to the Florentine merchant Eran Girart "de certa teleria."

206. ARV: B 323: 375r (28 August 1480) for Abdalla's debt to Allepus. Other debts of Abdalla also attest to the large volume of his retail trade: B 324: 197r–v (11 November 1491)—164 pounds owed to the merchants Dionis Miguel and Francesch Miro, and B 324: 205r–v (24 January 1491)—200 pounds owed to the heirs of J. Allepus.

207. ARV: B 1158: 357v–358r (6 February 1487)—Abdalla acts as guarantor for Azmet Ubeyt; and ARV: C 707: 909r–v (26 April 1484)—Abdalla acts as guarantor for Yuçeff Albanne of Valencia, who is traveling to Oran with "seda e altres mercaderia valents L lliures."

208. ARV: B 325: 332r–v (9 June 1498)—Abdalla owes 6 pounds 10s in pensions from the quantity of money he borrowed from J. Duart (by selling a *censal* to him).

209. ACA: C 3567: 4v (2 May 1488) and C 3571: 34v–35r (5 October 1492) concern the payment of Muslim craftsmen working on the royal *aljafería* in Zaragoza; C 3571: 219r (8 August 1496) concerns Muslim "maestros" working

on a church in Zaragoza; and C 3571: 11v–12r (13 March 1492)—Muslims of
Zaragoza are sent to Granada to work on the Alhambra just after the conquest.

210. ARV: B 1431: 544r–v (28 November 1494)—Cuayet Ginnuenhi, mason
of Alasquer; ARV: B 1160: 915v–916r (3 October 1494)—a Muslim mason of
Manises; ARV: B 323: 351r (23 August 1480)—Azmet de la Almunia, mason of
Valencia; B 323: 358r (5 June 1480)—Yuçeff Tutilli, carpenter of Valencia; and
see chap. 4, regarding the work of Mudejar artisans on royal utilities.

211. ARV: B 323: 464r–v (19 July 1481)—Azmet Caeli, boilermaker
(calderer) of Valencia; B 323: 723r (24 July 1483)—Mahomat and Ali Longo,
smiths (ferrers) of Valencia, owe 6 pounds to the smith Bernat de Medina for
bellows purchased; ARV: B 1222: IV 10r (24 January 1498)—a Muslim shieldmaker (broquerer) buys iron needed for making shields ("fulla dels broquers");
and B 1223: I 7v (15 April 1501)—Caet Tatany, a smith of Benaguacil, owes 42s
8d to the merchant Bernat Fillol for "certa ferra" purchased.

212. ARV: B 324: 365r (8 June 1492); and see the comments of Thrupp,
"Industry," pp. 245–246, concerning the role of merchants in the organization
of production.

213. Some examples of Mudejar saddlers are ARV: B 1431: 528r (25 May
1495)—Ali Mudarra, a saddler from the Vall de Uxó residing in Valencia; B
1433: 107r–v (13 October 1501)—Çahat and Amet Pachando of Segorbe working as saddlers in Liria; ARV: B 325: 309r (24 January 1498)—Çahat Catala and
son Açen, saddlers of Valencia; see chap. 4, tables 3 and 9 regarding the leasing
of Crown saddleworks in Alcira and Játiva; and chap. 4, table 9, for the leasing
of the Crown soap factory.

214. ARV: G 2360: Manus 29: 17r (1481).

215. ARV: B 1158: 170v–172r (23 December 1485). The Floris were also
involved in commerce: B 1157: 262r–v (20 June 1482)—Mahomat Flori and his
servant travel to the Orihuela-Alicante area "ab mercaderies," and Çahat and
Yuçeff Flori act as his guarantors.

216. ARV: B 1223: III 50v (28 April 1502)—Ali Alfona, "violer" of Valencia; ARV: B 1160: 502r–v (August 1492)—a Mudejar trumpeter (trompeta) of
Valencia; B 1162: 320r–v (22 June 1502)—Catdon Algodar, "moro jutglar" of
Llauri; ARV: MR 3062: 152r (1502)—a Muslim juglar of Játiva; ARV: B 324:
158r–v (7 August 1490)—a Mudejar barber of Picasent; B 1220: I 13v (2 July
1485)—Mahomat Burgi, barber of Petrés; and B 1220: IV 7r (26 April 1486)—
"lo alfaqui Xeyt metge de Xativa."

217. ACA: C 3640: 77v–78v (26 January 1484). A Mudejar surgeon of
Valencia is licensed by the Crown to practice after he cures a Christian
nobleman.

218. ARV: B 1222: II 75v (28 July 1497)—Mahomat Perpir owes 10s 6d to
"mestre Jacme Quexaler per certa cura que ha fet a una moratella de la moreria
de Valencia"; B 1222: V 6r (12 January 1499)—Çahat Catala owes 30s to Anthoni Not, surgeon, for "lo curar que ha fet una naffra feta en la ma de Abdolaziz Catala . . . cosingerma del dit Çahat Catala"; and B 1223: 4v (31 March
1501)—physicians of the royal hospital of Valencia attend to a Muslim.

219. ARV: B 1220: 7r (9 June 1485)—Yuniç Tarongeta, a shoemaker, fixes

"huna caldera chica" for a Christian woman; and B 1222: VII 39r (27 July 1500)—Mahomat Perpir buys from a Christian farmer "certa fulla. . . per obs de fer seda."

220. ACA: C 3655: 34r–v (5 March 1500); and see chap. 2.

221. ARV: G 2352: Manus 23: 4r–v (20 November 1479).

222. ARV: B 1156: 668r–v (14 December 1479)—Muslims of Llombay selling wheat in Alcira; and ACA: C 3647: 87v–88r (7 July 1489), concerning the Muslim of Alcocer with "mercibus."

223. ARV: C 154: 102v–103v (3 April 1498)—officials of Murviedro seize Muslims of Gilet who are there to "comerciar e negociar"; and ACA: C 3648: 252r–v (24 December 1491), concerning the Muslim bringing "mercaderias" from Elche to Orihuela.

224. ARV: B 1157: 354v–355r (10 December 1482)—Çahat Boamir of Benisanó travels to Orihuela with his servant to sell rice, a crop usually cultivated on undesirable land at the edge of marshes.

225. ARV: G 2358: Manus 43: 18r (1480); and ARV: C 245: 87v–88v (19 February 1489) refers to "crestian e moro vassalls. . . portant victualles a la dita ciutat."

226. ARV: B 1222: IV 35r (9 April 1498).

227. ARV: B 1220: VI 18r^b (19 March 1487)—Abrahim Valenti of Gandía brings oil to Valencia; B 1220: VI 25v–26v (3 December 1487)—Yuçeff Macana of Castellnou brings honey to Valencia; B 1222: I 19r, 20v–24v (26 September 1496)—the records of the collectors of the *peatge* record Muslims bringing into the city sugar, honey, wheat, oil, raisins, and figs; and B 1222: VII 70r–v (November 1500)—Muslims from Bétera sell wood in Valencia.

228. ARV: B 1222: IV 33r (27 March 1498).

229. ARV: B 325: 192r–v (21 April 1496).

230. ARV: B 1161: 441r (29 August 1497).

231. For example, ARV: C 154: 64v–65r (31 January 1498) presents a list of Muslims from Oliva, Gandía, Novelda, Aspe, Petrés, and other places who owe money to the Valencian merchant Dionis Roig. The large majority of the evidence for credit transactions between Valencia's merchants and Mudejars is in the registers ARV: B 323–325.

232. For example, ARV: B 1220: III 22r (13 February 1486)—a Muslim of Alberique owes 34s 6d to the merchant Pere Orçaffa for "certs formatges" bought.

233. ARV: B 325: 113r (3 August 1495)—Macastre, and 479r (6 November 1499)—Bétera.

234. ARV: B 325: 516r–517v (23 January 1500).

235. For example, ARV: B 1222: II 45r (26 April 1497)—Azmet Perpir owes 6 pounds 11s to Jacme Eximeno, "botiguer e o draper. . . de preu de drap." Cloth might also be procured from more unlikely sources, such as the innkeeper Anthoni Angelo—ARV: B 1220: IV 25v (6 June 1486).

236. For example, ARV: B 1222: II 46v (5 May 1497)—Çaat Requin of Játiva owes 14 pounds to the German merchant Noffre Ompis for copper purchased.

237. ARV: B 323: 609r (19 April 1482)—Sardinian cheese; ARV: B 1220:

III 10v (11 January 1486)—Yuçeff Alaboti of Segorbe owes six pounds to Pere Pomar, "botiguer de drogueria," for spices purchased.

238. ARV: B 323: 740r (9 September 1483)—various Muslims of Valencia owe 36 pounds to Perot Plener, merchant, for "teles de Brabant" purchased; and ARV: B 1222: VII 5v (10 December 1499)—Ali Gragiti of Benaguacil owes 63s to the merchant Johan Celma "de preu de ceda."

239. ARV: B 323: 255r–v (30 June 1479), and 309r–v (20 October 1479)—Abdalla Xeyt; and ARV: B 1220: VI 40v (September 1487)—Abdalla Medalla.

240. For example, ARV: B 1161: 491v (21 March 1498)—a Muslim of Segorbe purchases 2,000 eels from a fisherman of Sueca, and 78v (20 May 1495)—a Muslim of Benaguacil purchases 25 "millere" of fish from a fisherman of Sueca.

241. ARV: B 1220: VI 31v (9 May 1487), and VII 8r (9 June 1487)—Mascor Borrachet; and B 1220: I 7v (13 June 1495)—Amet Alami.

242. ARV: B 323: 746r (25 September 1483); and ARV: B 1222: VI 38r (19 October 1499)—a Muslim farmer of Valldigna purchases thirty-one meters of fine linen from a citizen of Valencia.

243. On Zignell lands in Valldigna, see ARV: B 325: 10r–12v. Licenses to various members of the Zignell family to travel south: ARV: B 1156: 512v–513r (20 July 1479), 649v–650v (29 October 1479); B 1157: 136v–137v (5 November 1481); B 1158: 396r–398v (28 March 1487); B 1159: 11r–12r (10 April 1488), and 127r–v (13 September 1488).

244. Cases of the Zignells backing other merchants: ARV: B 1157: 89v–90v (21 August 1481), 91r–92r (21 August 1481)—Abrahim Çafont, 92r–93r (22 August 1481), 292v–293v (9 August 1482)—Abrahim Çaffont, 293v–294v (9 August), 473r–v (20 August 1483), 474r–v (20 August); B 1159: 153r–v (10 January 1489), and 168v–169r (13 February 1489).

245. Cases of Zignell debts to merchants and farmers in the captial before 1490: ARV: B 323: 357r (29 May 1480), 765r (20 November 1483); B 324: 19r (11 March 1489), 78r (14 September 1489), and 122r (1 December 1489); and ARV: B 1158: 411r–412r (17 April 1487), and 425r–v (22 May 1487)—Zignells are granted safe-conducts against prosecution for debts.

246. ARV: B 1431: 395r (14 February 1494).

247. ARV: B 1431: 410v–411v.

248. Some examples of Zignell wholesale purchases: ARV: B 324: 295r (2 February 1491)—the Zignells owe 221 pounds 14s 9d to a company of German merchants; B 324: 389r (25 June 1492)—the Zignells owe 73 pounds 6s 6d to the merchants Dionis Miguel and Francesch Miro; ARV: B 1222: VI 47r (2 December 1499)—A. Zignell owes 10 pounds 10s to J. Uguet for "teleries" bought; ARV: B 1160: 734r–v (10 September 1493)—the Zignell brothers owe 40 pounds to the citizen Gaspar de Gallach for flax purchased; and ARV: C 139: 194v–195r (8 February 1496)—the Zignell brothers owe 50 pounds to Berthomeu Pinos, merchant, for Neapolitan linen purchased.

249. ARV: B 1431: 415r–v (25 February 1494)—the testimony of Amet Mathera, *botiguer* of Valencia; and ARV: B 1222: I 42r (12 November 1496)—Ali Zignell is licensed to sell sugar of whatever nature throughout the city.

250. ARV: B 1162: 312r–v (9 June 1502).

251. ARV: B 1431: 406v–407v (20 February 1494)—Dionis Miguel, merchant, testifies that Eximenez stood as surety for the Zignells when the latter purchased goods from him; 408r–v—Guillem Gualderi, a German merchant, testifies that Eximenez once paid him 5,000s in behalf of the Zignells. B 1431: 394v–421r, is the case of Eximenez against the Zignells, who owed him 14,000s. ARV: B 325: 41r–v (30 September 1494), concerns the 100 pounds to be paid by Umaymat and Yaye to Eximenez.

252. ARV: B 1161: 280v (3 June 1496).

253. ARV: B 323: 394r (16 September 1480)—Azmet and Xempsi purchase 111 pounds' worth of cloth from the merchant Joan Allepus. For Xempsi's selling of second-hand clothing, see B 323: 809r (26 May 1484); ARV: B 1220: VI 33r (10 May 1487), 35v (22 May); B 1222: V 34r (18 March 1499), 40r–41v (April 1499), VI 14r (10 July 1499), and VII 9v (17 December 1499).

254. ARV: B 1223: I 15v (5 May 1501).

255. ARV: B 1431: 412r–v—Mahomat Fandaig, and 415r–v—Amet Mathera (both dated 25 February 1494).

256. ARV: B 1222: V 19v (6 February 1499).

257. ARV: C 135: 175r–v (12 March 1490)—Murcian Jew; and ARV: B 1220: III 34r^b (March 1486)—Maymo Açen.

258. ARV: B 1222: I 31v (14 May 1497).

259. ARV: B 1220: V 3r (16 August 1486)—Ali Ferriol; and VIII 23r (9 August 1487)—Azmet Ferriol.

260. ARV: C 148: 206v–207r (13 August 1493).

261. ARV: B 1158: 332v (22 December 1486).

262. See nn. 84–85.

263. ARV: B 1159: 2r–v (10 March 1488).

264. The cases in which March Casterellenes acted as guarantor are: ARV: B 1156: 854r–855r, 855r–856r (both dated 5 September 1480); B 1157: 120r–121v, 121–122r (both dated 28 September 1481); and B 1158: 306r–v (10 November 1486). B 1157: 743r–v (26 October 1484)—Alexandre Alvespi.

265. ARV: B 1157: 130v–131v (17 October 1481), 252v–253r, and 253v–254r (21 May 1482)—Francesch Sparça; and B 1159: 319r–v (27 October 1491)—Pasqual Vicent.

266. ARV: B 1157: 339r–v (14 November 1482); and B 1162: 27v (March 1500) is a reiteration of this authorization.

267. Another example of a Mudejar guarantor-partner is Çahat Hamis, a merchant of Játiva. ARV: B 1157: 38r–39r (4 May 1481)—Çahat acts as guarantor for another merchant of Játiva, Ali Haro; and 47v–48r (5 June 1481)—Çahat backs Abdalla Fuçey of Játiva.

268. ARV: B 1156: 534v–536r (11 August 1479)—the amīn, jurats, and castellan of Ribarroja act as guarantors for Azmet Homar and Yuçeff Ageix of Ribarroja; and B 1156: 662v–663v (7 December 1479)—Gaspar de Castellvi, lord of Carlet, acts as guarantor for his vassal, Ali Bocoro.

269. Hinojosa Montalvo, "Relaciones," pp. 113–116; Barceló Torres, Minorías, p. 76; and Guiral-Hadziiossif, Valence, pp. 340–344.

270. This information may be found in the register ARV: C 707. Some ex-

ceptions are 813v–814r (17 April 1480)—Abrahim Annache, Abrahim's servant, and Helel Fumeyt of Cárcer travel to Almería with merchandise valuing 100 pounds; or 824r–v (24 April 1480)—Mahomat Boayadar of Carlet brings 200 pounds' worth of merchandise to Almería.

271. ARV: C 707.

272. Hinojosa Montalvo, "Relaciones," pp. 113–116; ARV: C 707.

273. See chap. 2.

274. For the travels of the Bellvis or their agents to North Africa and Almería, see ARV: C 707: 845r–v (2 May 1480), 846r–v (same date), 881v–882r (24 May 1481), 885v–886r (29 May 1481), and 890v–891r (3 July 1481). ACA: C 3568: 132v–134r (15 February 1496) concerns the mercantile activities of Yahye Bellvis; and ARV: C 596: 236r (15 March 1498) concerns the voyage of Yahye Bellvis, brother of the qāḍī general, to Naples on the Venetian galleys "por recuperacion de ciertos dineros que en Napoles son devidos."

275. ARV: C 126: 102r–v (28 January 1480); and C 127: 85v–86r (2 March 1480). The case was to be adjudicated by the Consuls of the Sea.

276. ARV: B 1161: 474v–475r (19 February 1498)—Yahye is granted a license to stay in Valencia for one year.

Chapter Four:
Taxation of the Mudejars

1. Belenguer Cebrià, *València*; and Franciso Sevillano Colom, "Las empresas nacionales de los Reyes Católicos y la aportación económica de la ciudad de Valencia," *Hispania* 57 (1954): 511–623.

2. On Mudejar demography, see chap. 1 n. 7; also Peregrin-Luis Llorens, "Los sarracenos de la Sierra de Eslida y Vall d'Uxó a fines del siglo XV," *Boletín de la Sociedad Castellonense de Cultura* 43 (1967): 56–60.

3. Belenguer Cebrià, *València*, pp. 43–46; Hillgarth, *Spanish Kingdoms*, II; 379–381, 503–505, 513–515. For an important revision of the previously high estimates of the population of the capital, see Augustín Rubio Vela, "Sobre la población de Valencia en el cuatrocientos (Nota demográfica)," *Boletín de la Sociedad Castellonense de Cultura* 56 (1980): 158–170.

4. Boswell, *Royal Treasure*, chap. V, passim.

5. Claude Cahen, "Djizya," *Encyclopaedia of Islam* (second edition), II: 559–562; and Robert I. Burns, *Medieval Colonialism: Postcrusade Exploitation of Islamic Valencia* (Princeton, 1975), pp. 79–85. Winfried Küchler, "Besteuerung der Juden und Mauren in den Ländern der Krone Aragons während des 15. Jahrhunderts," *Gesammelte Aufsätze zur Kulturgeschichte Spaniens* 24 (1968): 228, 231, erroneously asserts that neither Muslims nor Jews paid a special tax, a surprising conclusion since much of his study is based on documentation from the Archivo del Reino de Valencia. Boswell, *Royal Treasure*, p. 197, incorrectly defines the *besant* as a "small property tax," although it is unclear to which part of the Crown of Aragon the author is referring. Macho y Ortega, "Mudéjares aragoneses," p. 181, notes that the *besant* was collected in Aragon only very rarely.

6. Data on the *besants* and other taxes collected from royal aljamas are found in ARV: MR registers 942 to 962 for Alcira; 2469–2491 for Castellón de la Plana; 3052 to 3062 for Játiva and Castellón de Játiva; 4016 to 4034 for Murviedro; and 4567 to 4573 for Monforte. ARV: MR 4031: 6r (1499)—the *besant* is collected from Çat Susen b. Amet Susen even though he is still living in his father's house, because Çat is married and it is thought that he should have his own house. The aljama of Castellón de la Plana was not founded until the early fifteenth century; see Arcadio García Sanz, "Mudéjares y moriscos en Castellón," *Boletín de la Sociedad Castellonense de Cultura* 28 (1952): 103–110.

7. On Valencia, see ARV: B 1158: 534r–v (6 February 1488) and on Játiva, ACA: C 3568: 3v–4v (2 July 1490), and see chap. 1.

8. López Elum, "Morería de Játiva," pp. 161–162, shows that only 341 out of 382 households paid the *besant* in 1493. ARV: MR 3053: 6r–7r—in 1490 of the 356 Muslim households in Játiva 15 did not pay the *besant*; and MR 3055: 6r—in 1495, 36 out of 353 households did not pay. Data for Alcira shows that, for instance, in 1497 (ARV: MR 954: 12r) 17 out of 103 households did not pay the *besant*, while in 1498, 19 out of 110 households did not pay (MR 955: 12r).

9. For example, ARV: MR 945: 4r (1489)—Abdalla Albarder of Alcira pays 10s for the *besant* of 1489 and the *besants* outstanding from the previous two years. MR 953: 12r (1496)—Mahomat Xafra pays 6s 8d for outstanding *besants* after he "se desavassallas del Senyor Rey."

10. ARV: MR 945: 17v–18r (1489)—Çahat Valenti and Abdolazis Arnoni of Alberique, Ali Haquim, Fuçey Moçarrif, Azmet Almigi, Yuçef Tagari, and Azmet Jayar of Alcocer, and Çahat Manahen of Catadau all pay the *besant*. MR 948: 11r (1491)—Azmet Zichnell of Valldigna pays. MR 4030: 6r (1498)—Fat Acavejo, Soberch, and Mahomat and Abraym Calet of Algimia pay *besants* to the bailiff of Murviedro.

11. Küchler, "Besteuerung," pp. 246–248; and Boswell, *Royal Treasure*, pp. 269–271, discusses the security threat thought to have been posed by Muslim mendicants in the fourteenth century. For the proceeds from the licenses for alms-begging and prostitution collected by the bailiff general, see table 14 (this chapter). The bailiff of Onda also collected fees from Mudejars for licenses to bear arms, beg, and practice prostitution; see ARV: MR registers 4273–4284, and table 13 (this chapter).

12. ARV: B 1161: 689r–v (22 October 1499), B 1162: 409v–410r (11 February 1503), and B 1162: 578r (18 July 1504) all concern the problem of Muslims practicing prostitution, begging, and traveling to North Africa without licenses.

13. Burns, *Colonialism*, p. 43. For the shared Muslim-Jewish *carnicería* of Castellón, see ARV: MR registers 2469–2491. Of course, after the expulsion of the Jews in 1492 the Muslims had the *carnicería* to themselves.

14. For the lessees of the Muslim *carnicería* of Alcira, see ARV: MR: 942–962, and table 5 (this chapter); and for those of the Muslim *carnicería* of Játiva, see ARV: MR 3052–3062 and table 11 (this chapter).

15. ARV: C 306: 77v–79v (26 March 1484).

16. ARV: B 1161: 273r–v (13 May 1496).

17. ARV: C 305: 39v–40r (7 December 1481); C 306: 77v–79v (26 March

1484); C 134: 128r–129r (24 March 1488) deal with the Muslim *carnicería* of Castellón de Játiva and its provisioning with livestock; and ACA: C 3644: 82r–83r (21 February 1488) treats the Muslim *carnicería* of Daroca and the right of its livestock to graze in surrounding pastures.

18. ARV: C 307: 87r–v (8 November 1486). ACA: C 3667: 265v (25 February 1492)—after prohibiting the Muslim butcher shop of Alcira from selling meat to Christians, Fernando decides that its lessee does not need to supply it with as many sheep as before.

19. ARV: C 306: 126v–128v (22 December 1484).

20. ARV: C 306: 126v–128v—"Item es concordat que lo dit Joan Sancho arrendador puxa tallar e talle en les dites taules de la dita carniceria durant lo temps del dit arrendament carns de molts, cabra, cabro, ovella, bon vedell, cabrits, e qualsevulla altra carn. . . als fors e preus acostumats." In contrast, see Boswell, *Royal Treasure*, p. 96.

21. ARV: C 148: 108r–v (28 November 1492).

22. ARV: B 1157: 426r–v (6 May 1483).

23. ACA: C 3665: 19v (November 1486).

24. For Gandía, ARV: C 148: 108r–v; and for Murviedro, ARV: B 1157: 426r–v. ARV: C 306: 159r–v (29 March 1485)—two "administratores" are appointed in Murviedro to hear cases arising over the question of *sises* and other taxes involving Christian, Muslim, and Jew.

25. ARV: B 1157: 266r–267v (28 June 1482).

26. Burns, *Colonialism*, p. 48. ARV: C 141: 122v–123r (31 January 1500)—the aljama of Valencia leases its *carnicería* to a Christian butcher; see ARV: C 305: 71r–72r (15 December 1481), for the aljama's plea.

27. ACA: C 3632: 160r–161r (27 July 1479); and ACA: C 3644: 82r–83r.

28. ARV: C 306: 126v–128v; and ARV: MR 3052–3062.

29. For Alcira, ARV: B 1157: 42r–v (18 May 1481); and for Daroca ACA: C 3644: 82r–83r.

30. ACA: 3636: 201v–203v (5 April 1481).

31. Burns, *Colonialism*, p. 64.

32. ARV: MR 89–110; and ARV: B 122–123 (*Arrendamientos*). ACA: C 3568: 51v–52r (23 May 1493) discusses the effect of the plague of 1490 on the rent of the fonduk.

33. ARV: B 123 contains repeated prohibitions against Muslims lodging in inns other than the royal fonduk; see chap. 1 nn. 164–170. ARV: C 596: 76v–77r (16 October 1490) is the complaint of the lessee of the fonduk.

34. ARV: B 123: 108r–109v (1492).

35. ARV: MR 89–110 and B 122–123 list the rents received from the *basto*; and ARV: B 123: 30r–v (1488) lists the duties of the *basto* in the *morería*. B 123: 132r–v (21 May 1493)—the *comissari* of the bailiff general and the lessee of the *basto* go to the bordello of the *morería* and inform the prostitutes of the new lease; the prostitutes promise to pay the accustomed *drets* to the *basto*.

36. ACA: C 3654: 89v–90v (10 September 1497).

37. On prohibitions against gambling, see chap. 1 nn. 161–163. See ACA: C 3654: 89v–90v for Zaragoza, ACA: C 3636: 201v–203v for Castellón de Játiva,

and ARV: C 306: 160r–161v (29 July 1484) for Játiva—all note that prostitution will bring significant revenue to the royal fonduks. On licenses to prostitutes, see n. 11 (above) and table 14.

38. ARV: B 1156: 595v–596r (18 September 1479); ARV: MR 951: 19v (1494)—Ali Vermell is paid 50s for the use of his house as the royal fonduk.

39. ARV: MR 3056: 16v (1496)—payment of Muslim carpenters for work done on the royal fonduk and its "cambres per star les çabies"; MR 3054: 5v (1494)—Maffomat Cathala, saddler, rents the "palau e cambra del alfondech . . . per tenir albardes y alla e altres coses necessaries de llur offici"; MR 3060: 6v (1500)—"com lo dit alfondech no sia stat arrendat en lo present any . . . per no esser hi trobat arrendador per causa com no's comporta tenir joch"; and MR 3055: 5v (1495) contains the aljama's complaint about the Christian youths and the Christian temptress.

40. Burns, *Colonialism*, pp. 57–63; see table 8 (this chapter) for the rents received from the Mudejar baths of Játiva. Maestre Racional registers for Valencia and Alcira sometimes include the Mudejar baths in the lists of Crown rents, but without any entries for rents received; this suggests that the Crown had leased these baths in the recent past.

41. ARV: C 135: 36v–37v (27 March 1488); and ACA: C 3568: 4v (25 June 1490).

42. See table 8.

43. For the Muslim oven of Mislata, see ARV: C 127: 98r–v (6 April 1490), and chap. 1 n. 26; and ARV: MR 4028: 1r–v (1496)—Hamet Perromalo rents the "forn de la porta nova" for 115s, and Ali Ubequer of Gilet rents the "forns del Raquo" for 320s.

44. For Tortosa, see ACA: C 3521: 81r–v (12 December 1479); C 3522: 46r–v; and C 3561: 37v–38r; and for Lérida, ACA: C 3615: 83v–84v (9 April 1482).

45. Some examples are ARV: MR 2478: 6v (1490)—Ali Alborroc of Burriol rents the mill "del Romeral" for 14s from the bailiff of Castellón de la Plana; MR 3053: 5r–v (1490)—the Muslim Borgunyo rents a mill near Játiva for 2s, and 10r–Ali Jaffer of Játiva sells a "moli fariner" leased from the Crown to a Muslim of Alfarrazi.

46. For the rents received from the *almacera* and the *marcham de paper*, see tables 8 and 10.

47. For the rents received from the Mudejar *obradors dels albardaners* of Alcira, see table 3; for the rents received from the Mudejar *tintorería* of Murviedro, see table 7; and for the rents received from the Mudejar *obradors dels albardaners*, *tintorería*, *çabonería*, and *adobería* of Játiva, see tables 9 and 10.

48. For the rents received from the *pes e açoch* of the *morería* of Játiva, see table 9. *Furs e ordinations* Palmart, ed.: King Jaime II, Capitulo X, 137v: "Que los jueus e los moros no tinguen mustaçaff propri." ARV: C 128: 169v–170v (21 February 1481).

49. ARV: MR 3052–3062; for example, MR 3055: 14v (1495)—Yuçeff Redona is paid 7s 7d for raising the rent of the *forn maior* from 600s to 740s, Cuayat Amit is paid 21s for raising the rent of the *forn menor* from 600s to 820s, and

Mahomat Tagari is paid 21s for raising the rent of the *pes e açoch* from 1500s to 1635s.

50. ARV: MR 943: 26v[b] (1482)—46s are paid to Çahat Trilli and other Muslims renting the *obradors dels albardaners* "per raho de les obres per aquells fetes."

51. Some examples are ARV: MR 3053: 17v (1490)—Ali Pego, carpenter of Játiva, is paid 96s 6d for his labors on the Mudejar bath; MR 3055: 15v–16r (1495)—Muslim carpenters and masons of Játiva are paid various sums for their labors on the bath, fonduk, and stall of the *pes reyal*; MR 4023 (Murviedro): "Llibre de la obra dels forns del Raquo, porta nova e de la Plaçeta de la vila de Murvedre feta en lo any MCCCCLXXXX" (folios unnumbered)—various Muslims are paid for their labors, especially in transporting materials to the workplace; and MR 4029: 11r (1497)—Ali Redondo is paid 10s for work done on royal mills.

52. Some examples are ARV: MR 946: 10r–v (1490)—Çahat Gomeri paid a rent of 3s 6d for houses, Açen b. Abdalla Grini 3s 6d for houses, Ayet Rocahiz 5s for houses and 12s for vacant land, Mahomat Bonzarqua 6s for vacant land, Çahat Trilli 3s for houses, the heirs of Mahomat Boamir 7s for houses, Hamet Mosqueret 6s for two houses, Ayet el Castellano 12s for houses, Mahomat Bugui 2s for a "corral," Çilim and Çahat Cheo 12s for land, Azmet Yaye 7s for land, Mahomat Paziar 12s 6d for houses, and Ali, Yaye, and Çahat Grini 13s for land; and MR 2479: 4r (1491)—Saat Bocayo pays 2s to the bailiff of Castellón de la Plana for the rent of two *fanecates* of land, and 4s for another four *fanecates* that used to be a vineyard.

53. Some examples are ARV: MR 2478: 16r (1490)—6s are received from Mahomat Tagari for the *lluisme* on land he sold to Pere Macanet for 60s; MR 2483: 7r (1495)—10s are received from Azmet Bocayo for the *lluisme* on land he sold to Abdulazis Mascor for 100s; MR 3060: 15r (1500)—428s are received from Azmet and Ali Arbuix of Bellus for the *lluisme* on a mill sold to Bernat Matheu of Beniganim for 4,280s (the mill was being rented from the Crown).

54. Küchler, "Besteuerung," p. 242; Burns, *Colonialism*, pp. 173–176; and Piles Ros, *Apuntes*, p. 27. For Játiva, ARV: MR 3052–3062, and for Alcira, MR 942–960.

55. ACA: C 3599: 10v–11r (25 September 1479); ACA: C 3634: 10r–11r (20 September 1479); and ACA: C 3547: 121r–v (14 March 1481).

56. Macho y Ortega, "Mudéjares aragoneses," p. 184; and ACA: MR 2356 for the *cena* rates of Aragonese and Catalan aljamas.

57. Piles Ros, *Apuntes*, p. 35; and ARV: C 139: 249r–v (30 March 1497).

58. For Onda, ARV: C 307: 14v (9 April 1485); and for Castellón de Játiva, ARV: C 304: 88v–90r (19 July 1480). Piles Ros, *Bayle general*, p. 88, notes that not all towns paid the *cena* "sino algunas determinadas que figuran en las cuentas de la Baylia."

59. For Valencia, see Küchler, "Besteuerung," p. 242; for the attempts of the jurates of Alcira to collect the *peyta* from the aljama, see chap. 1 nn. 115–116; and, in contrast, ARV: C 148: 97r–v (17 September 1492) implies that the Muslims of Játiva paid the *peytes* and *sises* with the Christians of the city.

60. Macho y Ortega, "Mudéjares aragoneses," pp. 181–182; for Tortosa, ACA: C 3570: 153r (20 February 1493); for Borja, ACA: C 3562: 66v (20 February 1481), and C 3564: 150v–151v (15 October 1498); and for Daroca, ACA: C 3632: 158v–159v (3 August 1479).

61. Earl J. Hamilton, *Money, Prices, and Wages in Valencia, Aragon, and Navarre, 1351–1500* (Cambridge, Mass., 1936), pp. 9, 84; Burns, *Colonialism*, pp. 150–153; Boswell, *Royal Treasure*, pp. 196, 199–200; Macho y Ortega, "Mudéjares aragoneses," pp. 186, 203; and ARV: MR 10877–10880 contain the data on the collection of the *morabatí*. The aljama of Murviedro had a unique arrangement; each of its households paid an annual *morabatí* of 3s 4d that was collected along with the *besant*. It would seem that here the term *morabatí* had lost its original meaning.

62. Piles, "Moros de realengo," pp. 271–272, concludes that the king took a part of every Mudejar inheritance. ARV: MR 4273: 23r (1484)—"Rebudes dels moros e mores qui moren sens hereus del qual ne ve part al S. Rey"; and MR 4274: 3r (1492)—the inheritance of Mahomat Hubaydal.

63. ARV: B 1159: 248r (1 October 1489).

64. ARV: MR 3052–3062. Nevertheless, in one case—MR 3061: 9v (1501)—the bailiff collected 100s from the inheritance left by a Muslim woman of the *morería*. Many of the MR registers of the royal towns contain records of the sums exacted by the local bailiffs from Mudejar inheritances.

65. Boswell, *Royal Treasure*, pp. 278–280, discusses the controversy surrounding the question of the inheritances of Mudejars dying intestate and without heirs. ARV: MR 4273: 43r (1491)—the royal *qāḍī* gives the wife of the deceased, Açen b. Mahomat Alfaqui, her bridewealth (*accidach*, from the Arabic *ṣadāq*), and does the same for the mother of the deceased siblings Çilim and Nuza Patri; and MR 959: 4r (1502)—the royal *qāḍī* helps to effect a compromise between Fotaya Alazarch, the husband of the deceased, and Açot Axer, her brother.

66. ARV: B 1156: 856v (14 September 1480).

67. ARV: B 1157: 106r (4 September 1481).

68. ARV: MR 89: 225r (1478).

69. *Aureum opus*, (Pedro IV) 103v–104r; and Boswell, *Royal Treasure*, pp. 283–284.

70. ARV: MR 107: 63r (1497).

71. ARV: MR 107: 63v (1497).

72. ARV: B 1157: 161v (9 January 1482).

73. ARV: MR 2478: 8r (1490); and MR 2489: 7v (1501).

74. Given the population of Játiva's aljama, each Muslim family would have had to contribute less than 2s per year to meet the 400s inheritance tax. Since the heirs to an estate might pay as little as 50s to the Crown or as much as 480s—ARV: MR 951: 5r (1494), division of the inheritance of Fumeyt Mosqueret of Alcira—the amount of inheritance tax paid by each Muslim family of Játiva was negligible, even over the long term.

75. ARV: C 148: 97r (17 September 1492). Burns, *Colonialism*, pp. 86–88; and Piles Ros, *Apuntes*, p. 26.

76. ARV: B 1161: 386r (30 March 1497); and B 1161: 662r (4 September

1499)—the *peatger* of the Foya de Buñol complains that two Muslims are avoiding payment of the *peatge* with "fraus e decepcions"; the accused are to appear before the bailiff general to explain their conduct.

77. ARV: C 148: 97r–v (17 September 1492)—the lords of Genovés, Señera, and Alboy object when Játiva's *peatger* confiscates from their Muslim vassals securities (*penyores*) for the payment of the *peatge* in addition to the one annual payment.

78. ARV: B 1157: 30v (11 April 1481)—the *peatger* of Játiva collects the *peatge* from Muslim vassals of Chella, allegedly "franchs" from payment; and B 1157: 341v (22 November 1482)—a similar case involving the *jurados* of Albarracín and Muslim vassals of the lord of Olocau.

79. ARV: C 624: 168v–173v (1477–1516). In contrast, see chap. 1 n. 84.

80. Burns, *Colonialism*, pp. 85–96; and Piles Ros, *Apuntes*, pp. 26–27. The aljama of Játiva might have rented its own pasture from the Crown, listed in the MR registers as the *debea* (= *devea* = *defessa*). ARV: B 1158: 19r (19 April 1485)—the appointment of Amet Samaris.

81. For litigations with the Muslims of Antella, see ARV: B 1156: 391v (5 March 1479) and B 1156: 838r–839r (4 August 1480); and for those with Muslims of the Vall de Serra, see ARV: B 1158: 475r (7 September 1487). ARV: B 1157: 412r–v (17 April 1481)—an order of the bailiff general that Muslims in the area of Játiva must use salt from the royal *gabelle* on pain of captivity.

82. ARV: B 1162: 409v–410r (11 February 1503).

83. ARV: B 1157: 126r–128r (10 October 1495)—Muslims of Játiva are described as "factors de la sal per lo gabellot"; B 1161: 127r–128r (22 September 1495).

84. Burns, *Colonialism*, pp. 190–198; Piles Ros, *Apuntes*, p. 25. Examples of Muslim lessees of the *terçes de delme* in Alcira are ARV: MR 945: 16r (1489)— Çahat Paziar rents "lo terç de delme appellat de Alquerrencia e orta dels cent" for 2880s and the "terç de delme appellat de Sent Bernat" for 1820s; and MR 954: 2v–3r, 4r (1497)—Muslim lessees of the *terçes de delme* "de carnatge," "de la ortalica," and "de Guadaçuar." ARV: B 1156: 806r–807r (7 July 1480)— Muslims of Alcocer holding lands in the *huerta* of Castellón de Játiva try to avoid paying the *terç de delme* on the wheat harvested on those lands.

85. ARV: C 308: 7v–11v (14 April 1488).

86. ARV: C 139: 65v–66v (30 April 1495).

87. Burns, *Colonialism*, pp. 190–198; Boswell, *Royal Treasure*, pp. 200–202.

88. Macho y Ortega, "Mudéjares aragoneses," pp. 284–285, document no. 67.

89. ACA: C 3571: 225v (14 September 1496).

90. ACA: C 3646: 227v–228r (27 September 1489). ACA: C 3669: 186v–187v (16 March 1500)—a series of letters from the king to the bishop and chapter of Tarazona, and to the royal vice-chancellor and fiscal advocate.

91. ACA: C 3607: 189r–v (30 July 1495).

92. Küchler, "Besteuerung," pp. 230–235, 241–242, concludes that it was in its extraordinary taxes that the Crown discriminated most markedly between Christians and religious minorities, to the great disadvantage of the latter.

93. José Angel Sesma Muñoz, *La Diputación del Reino de Aragón en la época*

de Fernando II (Zaragoza, 1977), pp. 319–322, 142–143; idem, "Instituciones parlamentarias del Reino de Aragón en el tránsito de la Edad Moderna," in *Aragón en la Edad Media* (Zaragoza, 1981), IV: 226–234; and Fernando Solano Costa, "Estudios sobre la historia de Aragón durante la Edad Moderna," *Cuadernos de Historia: Anexos de la revista "Hispania"* 1 (1967): 154–158.

94. ARV: MR 94: 197r–202v lists the *maridatges* received in 1478 for the marriage of Doña Elionor, the illegitimate daughter of Juan II, to the Count of Lirin. ARV: MR 9052: 110r–113r, 124v–126r, 137v–138r, and 143r–v are documents concerning the *maridatge* for Fernando's daughters.

95. ARV: C 318: 38v–39v (29 July 1502). ACA: MR 2571, 2576–2578, show that in Catalonia smaller aljamas, such as Vinebre and Miravet, paid 8s per household, while Tortosa's larger aljama paid 17s per household.

96. ARV: C 302: 148r–v (11 October 1479).

97. ARV: B 1157: 200v–201r (4 March 1482) concerns the aljama of Paterna; and ACA: C 3615: 74v (28 December 1482).

98. ACA: C 3613: 126v–127r (7 February 1485).

99. ARV: B 1161: 434v–435r (21 July 1497).

100. ACA: C 3615: 62v –63r (18 May 1481).

101. ACA: C 3608: 171v–172r (20 February 1484).

102. ACA: C 3655: 55r–v (12 March 1501).

103. For Zaragoza, see ACA: C 3616: 228v (4 January 1495); and for Borja, ACA: C 3666: 104r (13 September 1495).

104. For Aragon, see ACA: C 3608: 171v–172r; and for Valencia, ACA: C 3613: 126v–127r.

105. ACA: C 3665: 141v (2 September 1489)—Muslim brothers of Huesca complain that the *amīn* and *adelantados* are forcing them to pay more taxes than they ought; ACA: C 3633: 82r (9 January 1492)—Muslims of Albarracín, father and son, are granted *franquesa* from payment of the *peyta*. Boswell, *Royal Treasure*, pp. 210–217, discusses the efforts of individual Muslims to escape paying taxes and the problem of the exemption in aljama finances.

106. ACA: C 3608: 171v–172r and C 3613: 126v–127r.

107. Boswell, *Royal Treasure*, p. 225–242.

108. Belenguer Cebrià, *València*.

109. ARV: C 318: 38v–39v (29 July 1502).

110. ARV: B 1161: 83v (4 June 1495); B 1161: 434v–435r; and for the deferred *peyta* payments of the aljama of Alcira, ARV: MR 954: 4v (1497); MR 955: 4v (1498)—200s is received for the years 1497 and 1498; MR 960: 3v (1503)—the *peyta* is deferred "per donar algunt conport al dita aljama," and MR 962: 9r (1504)—200s is received for the years 1503 and 1504.

111. ARV: B 1156: 343v–344r (2 January 1479); B 1158: 534r–v (6 February 1488); and MR 92: 19r (1481), and MR 94: 24r (1493)—500s tax deferred "per la pobresa que's en aquella."

112. ARV: C 305: 71r–72r (15 December 1481).

113. See table 15.

114. Macho y Ortega, "Mudéjares aragoneses," pp. 168–169; ACA: C 3605: 83v (22 October 1480); ACA: C 3562: 60r–61r (9 December 1480)—license to

the aljama of Borja to sell a *censal* of 15,000s; and ACA: C 3562: 66v (20 February 1481).

115. ACA: C 3663: 178v (4 April 1486); ACA: C 3607: 279v (8 November 1496), and ACA: C 3612: 81r–v (24 February 1498).

116. ACA: C 3570: 153r (20 February 1493).

117. ACA: C 3632: 158v–159v (3 August 1479).

118. For Huesca, see ACA: C 3576: 46v (21 April 1497); for Zaragoza, ACA: C 3616: 228v; and for Borja, ACA: C 3666: 104r.

119. ACA: C 3644: 147r–v (19 February 1484).

120. ACA: C 3632: 160r–161r (27 July 1479); and ACA: C 3644: 82r–83r (21 February 1488).

121. ACA: C 3650: 51r–v (18 May 1492).

122. ACA: C 3632: 166v–167v (18 August 1479)—the aljama of Albarracín is licensed to sell alone a *censal* of 4,000s or along with the Jewish aljama a *censal* of 8,000s; and for Zaragoza, ACA: C 3567: 151r (8 February 1496)—the Castilian version of the license, and C 3567: 152v–153r (6 February 1496)—the Latin version.

123. ACA: C 3562: 60r–61r—the 15,000s *censal*; ACA: C 3571: 209r–v (24 March 1496)—the 80,000s *censal*; and ACA: C 3576: 64v (27 October 1497)—the 4,000s *censal*.

124. For Albarracín, see ACA: C 3640: 102v–103v (3 April 1484); for Teruel, ACA: C 3571: 25r (30 August 1492); for Huesca, ACA: C 3567: 60v–61v (31 October 1492) and 62r–v (28 October 1492); and for Tortosa, ACA: C 3631: 2r–3v (28 January 1493)—the aljama is made to pay only a portion of the pensions it owes to a priest.

125. ACA: C 3644: 90v–91v (7 February 1488); ACA: C 3644: 58v (27 February 1488); and ACA: C 3649: 18r–v (17 February 1492)—all call for the confiscation of the Muslims' property in order to pay the pensions.

126. For Teruel, see ACA: C 3644: 55r–57v (27 February 1488); and for Huesca, ACA: C 3567: 60v–61v, 62r–v.

127. For Tortosa, see ACA: C 3601: 47r–48r (9 July 1493), and especially ACA: C 3600: 100r–101v (11 April 1500); and for Teruel, ACA: C 3571: 131r–133r (24 December 1493).

128. Gual Camarena, "Aportaciones," pp. 181–199. For a detailed discussion of the taxes paid by seigneurial aljamas in the gubernatorial district of Orihuela during the fourteenth century, see Ferrer i Mallol, *Les aljames*, pp. 123–180.

129. ARV: C 311: 24v–26r (31 July 1499).

130. Boronat y Barrachina, *Moriscos*, I: 426, document no. 5.

131. Gual Camarena, "Aportaciones," pp. 181–183, 198–199; Císcar Pallarés, *Tierra y señorio*, pp. 88–113.

132. Garcia Càrcel and Císcar Pallarés, *Moriscos*, pp. 53–56; Duran, *Germanies*, pp. 122–128; and Guiral-Hadziiossif, *Valence*, pp. 9–43, 479–484.

133. Garcia Càrcel and Císcar Pallarés, *Moriscos*, pp. 57–58; Císcar Pallarés, *Tierra y señorio*, pp. 114–121.

134. ARV: C 303: 121v–124r (15 December 1479).

135. ARV: C 306: 158r–159r (15 April 1484).

136. ARV: C 139: 99r–100r (9 July 1495)—the Count of Oliva; ARV: C 156: 85r–86r (17 November 1501)—the Count of Trivento; and ARV: C 158: 34r–35r (28 June 1502).

137. ARV: C 306: 176r–180r (9 May 1486).

138. ARV: C 156: 122v–123v (20 December 1501)—Dona Yolant; ARV: C 158: 48v–50r (21 July 1502); and ARV: C 131: 74r–v (28 April 1483)—Luis de Vilanova.

139. ARV: C 131: 74r–v.

140. ARV: C 136: 163r–v (15 February 1493).

141. ARV: C 158: 48v–50r.

142. ARV: C 139: 95v–97r (9 July 1495)—Count of Cocentaina and Elda; ARV: C 137: 244r–245r (9 January 1495) and C 139: 130v–131v (2 September 1495)—Dos Aguas; C 137: 261r–v (31 January 1495) and C 139: 62v–63r (15 May 1495)—Alacuás; C 148: 23v–24r (20 June 1492), 171v–172r (25 May 1493) and C 151: 45r–v (8 October 1496), and 173r–174r (18 May 1497)—Novelda.

143. ARV: C 137: 244r–245r—Dos Aguas; and ARV: C 156: 102v–103r (4 December 1501)—Olocau.

144. Barceló Torres, *Minorías*, p. 89.

145. ARV: C 309: 125v–129r (11 July 1493).

146. ARV: C 141: 204v–205r (23 September 1502).

147. ARV: C 153: 28v–30v (27 May 1497). Other documents concerning the debts of the aljama of Elda are ARV: C 137: 20v–21r (6 September 1493) and C 148: 182v–183r (25 June 1493).

148. ARV: C 137: 212v–213r (24 November 1494)—Ribarroja; ARV: C 141: 182v (1 September 1501) and 226r–v (6 March 1503)—Villamarchante; and ARV: C 138: 290v–291r (26 October 1499) and C 309: 187r–188v (20 August 1493)—Mislata.

149. Císcar Pallarés, *Tierra y señorio*, pp. 122–134. Furió and Garcia, "Dificultats agràries," p. 297, remark that even though peasants were not subject to a juridical servitude, a form of economic servitude could develop, whereby peasants were immobilized by debt. Such economic servitude no doubt increased during the sixteenth century.

Chapter Five:
Mudejars and the
Administration of Justice

1. The surviving Arabic documentation can be found in Barceló Torres, *Minorías*, pp. 220–376.

2. Boswell, *Royal Treasure*, p. 131. For example, ARV: C 308: 7v–11v (11 April 1488)—a royal order concerning the collection of tithes in the *huerta* of Valencia is directed to all persons "de qualsevol ley o condicio."

3. Burns, *Islam under the Crusaders*, pp. 124–138.

4. *Aureum opus*, 103v.

5. *Aureum opus*, 81r.

6. ACA: C 3650: 256v (19 February 1496). The *carta puebla* of Monforte (1459) also stipulated that a *qāḍī* would be appointed for the *morería* of the town; see Gual Camarena, "Aportaciones," p. 176.

7. The *qāḍī* general's appellate jurisdiction is seen in ACA: C 3545: 17v–20v (18 July 1479), where the *qāḍī* general delegates his judicial authority to Mahomat Çaragoçi, the *qāḍī* of Tortosa. Çaragoçi is given full judicial authority with the condition that the *qāḍī* general retains the right to hear any appeals of Çaragoçi's judicial decisions. This appellate jurisdiction can also be seen in the cases discussed later in this chapter.

8. Burns, *Islam under the Crusaders*, p. 264.

9. I have not encountered in the documentation any cases between Muslims and Christians being tried in Islamic courts. The one exception, ARV: B 1158: 147r (14 January 1486), concerns a property litigation between a Christian knight, apparently the son of a convert from Islam ("Luys Tallada olim Zaycaran"), and a Muslim of Játiva, in which the local *qāḍī* was involved.

10. *Aureum opus*, 40v; and *Furs*, Colon and Garcia, eds., I: 208: Llibre I: Rubrica III: 65.

11. Boswell, *Royal Treasure*, pp. 109, 131, 364–369.

12. ARV: C 305: 71r–v (15 December 1481).

13. Boswell, *Royal Treasure*, p. 148.

14. *Aureum opus*, 40v, 102v; *Furs*, Colon and Garcia, eds. I: 208: Llibre I: Rubrica III: 65. Boswell, *Royal Treasure*, pp. 143–144, notes that Pedro IV's ruling that the *qāḍī* general should be the sole judge in criminal cases involving only Muslims did not have much practical effect.

15. Burns, *Islam under the Crusaders*, p. 263.

16. *Aureum opus*, 81r.

17. Émile Tyan, *Histoire de l'organisation judiciaire en pays d'Islam* (Leiden, 1960), pp. 433–451, 566–571; N. J. Coulson, *A History of Islamic Law* (Edinburgh, 1964), pp. 120–134.

18. Tyan, *Organisation judiciaire*, pp. 566–569.

19. ARV: C 132: 108r–v (3 August 1484).

20. ARV: MR 4276: 1r (1494). Pons Alós, *Fondo Crespí*, pp. 198, 219–221, lists instances in which the lord of Sumacárcel accepts as slaves adulterous Muslim vassals who had been condemned to death by stoning by the *qāḍī* of Játiva. *Aureum opus*, 236r: "Sarracenis dicti regni concedimus cum presenti quod si aliqua sarracena habens coniugem seu maritum cum aliquo christiano sive judio crimen commiserit adulterii puniatur iuxta eorum çunam: et pena inde sibi debita in peccunia nullatenus convertatur." Perhaps the latter clause was no longer observed.

21. See chap. 6 n. 130.

22. For instance, ARV: MR 955: 6r (1498, Alcira).

23. ARV: MR 3054: 6v (1494).

24. ARV: B 1431: 192r–v (18 January 1492).

25. ARV: B 1158: 3r–v (21 February 1485). *Aureum opus*, 103v: Pedro IV's aforementioned provision.

26. ARV: C 317: 2v–3r (15 June 1492).

27. ARV: C 150: 3v–4v (27 September 1493).

28. Tyan, *Organisation judiciaire*, pp. 62–64; Coulson, *Islamic Law*, p. 18.
29. Chapter 6 n. 88.
30. *Aureum opus*, 102v.
31. ARV: C 139: 75v–76r (19 May 1495).
32. ARV: C 148: 104v (23 November 1492).
33. ARV: B 1160: 361v–362r (5 December 1491).
34. ARV: B 1157: 344r–v (3 December 1482). ARV: B 1157: 255v–256r (4 June 1482) is a similar case.
35. ARV: B 1160: 631r–v (1 March 1493). Some similar cases are ARV: B 1156: 370r–v (6 February 1479) and B 1161: 263r (16 April 1496).
36. ARV: B 1159: 120v–121r (28 August 1488).
37. ARV: B 1158: 264r (24 July 1486).
38. Coulson, *Islamic Law*, pp. 138–148.
39. ARV: B 1156: 856v (14 September 1480).
40. ARV: B 1157: 392r (7 March 1483).
41. ARV: C 131: 61v–62r (18 April 1483).
42. ARV: B 1157: 311v (20 September 1482); and 314v (27 September 1482). The precedent on which this decision was based is ARV: B 1157: 308r–v (11 September 1482), which seems to be the same decision of the *qāḍī* general that Çaat Siquuti appealed some months later; see above, n. 41.
43. ARV: B 1157: 351v (4 December 1482); 366v (8 January 1483)—the bailiff general orders the bailiff of Játiva to urge the *qāḍī* and *faqīh* of Játiva to give their opinions within eight days; and 377v–378r (5 February 1483) is the bailiff general's order that the sentence be executed.
44. ARV: B 1156: 552v–553r (25 August 1479).
45. ARV: B 1159: 175r–v (12 March 1489).
46. Coulson, *Islamic Law*, pp. 135, 147.
47. ACA: C 3647: 60v–61r (15 February 1490)—a Muslim of Zaragoza makes a plea to the king when his wife wishes to annul their marriage without just cause; ACA: C 3647: 112v–113r (30 January 1491)—a Muslim of Zaragoza, guardian to his four granddaughters, complains to the king when his coguardian refuses to cooperate in the marriage of two of the girls; ACA: C 3648: 219r–220r (15 October 1491)—the complaint of a Muslim of Huesca when his wife-to-be breaches contract and refuses to marry him; and ACA: C 3650; 156r–v (5 October 1492)—Aragonese Muslim sisters file suit against their male cousin regarding his guardianship over them.
48. ARV: B 1433: 134r (30 March 1501).
49. See chap. 6.
50. Tyan, *Organisation judiciaire*, pp. 219–236.
51. For more on the *faqīhs*, see chap. 6.
52. Coulson, *Islamic Law*, pp. 142–143, 148; and Robert Brunschvig, *La Berbérie orientale sous les Ḥafṣides des origines a la fin du XVe siècle* (Paris, 1947), II: 138–143, on the role of the *muftī* in the Maghrib.
53. *Furs*, Colon and Garcia, eds., III: 171: Llibre III: Rubrica V: 111.
54. Compare with the fourteenth century—Boswell, *Royal Treasure*, pp. 120–121—during which the role of the local bailiffs was far more limited.
55. *Aureum opus*, 169v.

56. ACA: C 3568: 5r (2 July 1490).

57. For example, ARV: B 1156: 670v (16 December 1479).

58. ARV: C 304: 172v (21 February 1481).

59. ARV: B 1156: 670r–v (16 December 1479); and B 1156: 669v (14 December) is the letter of the bailiff of Játiva about the public crier.

60. ACA: C 3665: 29v (4 January 1487).

61. ARV: C 423: 64v–65v (19 July 1480) describes the appointment of the bailiff of Castellón de Játiva, in which his jurisdiction over the local Muslims is defined; and ARV: C 130: 113v (10 December 1481).

62. *Furs*, Colon and Garcia, eds., I: 221: Llibre I: Rubrica III: 90: Corts of Orihuela, 1488.

63. ARV: MR 3060: 13r (1500). Other examples are MR 3056: 6v; 3058: 7v, 8v, 9r–v; and 3062: 15r.

64. ARV: C 135: 102r (26 July 1488)—Fernando decides in the bailiff's favor because the Muslims are from Játiva; and ARV: C 135: 141v–142r (9 December 1488)—Fernando decides in favor of the governor because the Muslims are from the seigneury of Annahuir. ACA: C 3645: 136v–137v (31 July 1488) and 170r–v also concern the latter case.

65. ARV: B 1157: 210r–v (14 March 1482); and 214r–215r (16 March 1482) is the lieutenant governor's reply.

66. ARV: B 1157: 217v–218r (23 March 1482).

67. ACA: C 3639: 68r–v (29 December 1481).

68. ARV: C 131: 89r–90r (29 July 1483).

69. ARV: C 129: 26r (21 February 1481).

70. ACA: C 3639: 126r–v (13 April 1482). A more detailed discussion of these jurisdictional conflicts—Meyerson, "Between *Convivencia* and Crusade," pp. 438–440—shows that the legal arguments were somewhat more complex and convoluted than I have presented them here; the sometimes confused response of the king himself to these questions served to muddy the waters further still.

71. ARV: B 1157: 206v–208r (13 March 1482)—the bailiff general reprimands the lieutenant governor; and B 1157: 211r–v (16 March 1482)—the bailiff general informs the bailiff of Villajoyosa that he has reprimanded the lieutenant governor and orders him to proceed in the case of the Muslim of Finestrat.

72. ARV: B 1158: 406r–v (21 April 1486). Other examples are ARV: B 1159: 204r–v (10 June 1489)—the lieutenant governor interferes in the procedure of the bailiff of Burriana against a Muslim who committed crimes in Villarreal; and B 1159: 232r–v (8 September 1489) and 232v–233r (12 September 1489)—the bailiff general and the lieutenant governor exchange letters on this matter.

73. ARV: C 126: 77r (13 October 1479).

74. *Aureum opus*, 52r–v; and 184v–185r (Alfonso V).

75. ARV: B 1158: 458v–459r (4 August 1487); and B 1159: 203v–204r (5 June 1489). Other examples are ARV: B 1157: 487r–v (4 September 1483)—the town officials of Burriana are reprimanded for having confiscated beehives that Muslims of the Vall de Uxó are renting in Burriana; B 1157: 225r–v (7 June 1482)—the justice and jurates of Alpont try to convince the local bailiff that he

has no jurisdiction over the local Jews and Muslims; B 1157: 342r–v—the justice of Cullera proceeds against a Mudejar for swearing; B 1160: 270r (16 August 1491)—the justice of Onda interferes in the cases of Muslims and confiscates their possessions; B 1160: 315v–316r (22 October 1491)—the lieutenant justice of Murviedro refuses to hand over to the bailiff livestock confiscated from Muslims; and ACA: C 3528: 43v–44v (15 January 1493)—the *consuls* of Tortosa confiscate the property of a local Muslim in violation of the aljama's privileges and the prerogatives of the local bailiff.

76. ARV: B 1156: 502r–503r (5 July 1479), 506v–507r (10 July), 511v–512r (23 July), and 534r (9 August) all concern this case.

77. ARV: B 1158: 159v–164r (23 January 1486).

78. ARV: C 305: 73r (9 July 1492).

79. ARV: C 148: 33v–34r (10 July 1492).

80. *Furs*, Colon and Garcia, eds., III: 129–130, 135: Llibre III: Rubrica V: 78, 83 discuss the rights of the seigneurs to the "penes e calonies" exacted from their Muslim vassals for civil and criminal offenses; this explains why they reacted so strongly to encroachments on their jurisdiction. Regarding the appeals of the Muslim vassals of Valldigna, ACA: C 3639: 121v–122r (6 April 1482); see also ARV: C 129: 142v–143v.

81. ARV: C 130: 10v–11r (1 June 1481).

82. ARV: B 1157: 93v–94v (22 August 1481). The officials of Valldigna refuse to release to a vicar of the bailiff general's court a Muslim vassal of the *morería* of Játiva.

83. ACA: C 3639: 121v–122v (6 April 1482); and ACA: C 3605: 135v (13 April 1482).

84. ARV: C 133: 89v–90v (1 September 1485); and ARV: C 302: 9r–v (20 March 1479)—the lord of Albatera and the lieutenant governor clash.

85. ARV: C 140: 256v (7 January 1501), C 141: 114v–117r (12 December 1500), 137r–138v (10 February 1501), and 153v (16 March 1501) all concern this case.

86. ARV: C 151: 41r–v (22 September 1496).

87. ARV: C 151: 31r–32r (30 August 1496). ARV: C 307: 181r–v (15 March 1488)—officials of Castielfabib and Ademuz interfere in the jurisdiction of the lord of Torre Fondonera over his thirty Muslim vassals.

88. ARV: C 650: 195v (2 September 1499).

89. ARV: B 1157: 528v (23 December 1483); and B 1159: 259r–v (31 October 1489)—the case begun in the court of the lieutenant governor against Muslim vassals of Nules is removed to the court of the bailiff when the Muslims become royal vassals in Villarreal.

90. ARV: C 148: 148v–149r (12 February 1493), and 163r–v (28 March 1493).

91. ARV: B 1159: 236r–237r (11 September 1489).

92. For example, ARV: C 137: 211r–212r (24 November 1494), C 148: 74r (September 1492), and C 156: 8v–9r (July 1501).

93. *Furs e ordinations*, Palmart, ed., 265v–266r.

94. The Muslims who appeared before the tribunal of the bailiff general as

witnesses, plaintiffs, or defendants are usually described as having sworn an oath in this manner—ARV: B 1431–1433.

95. The cases that were tried in the court of the bailiff general followed this procedure—ARV: B 1431–1433 (1491–1504). ARV: B 1159: 355r–v (4 August 1490) concerns the questioning of witnesses in behalf of both parties in a litigation between a Muslim of Mislata and a Jewess of Murviedro.

96. ARV: B 1157: 468v–469r (12 August 1483); and ARV: B 1158: 154r–v (17 January 1486)—the bailiff of Játiva receives "respostes e confessions judicials" from Muslims accused of crimes.

97. ARV: C 141: 240v–241r (26 May 1503).

98. ARV: C 141: 81v–82v (25 September 1500). After the bailiff of Murviedro passed sentence against him, Ali appealed to the bailiff general and maintained that the bailiff had proceeded against him in violation of a safe-conduct he had been given.

99. ARV: B 1157: 206v (13 March 1482).

100. For example, ARV: B 1159: 355r–v (4 August 1490)—Pere de Campos, notary, acts as procurator for Mahomat Monnen of Mislata in a litigation with a Jewish widow; ARV: C 156: 217r–v (30 April 1502)—Joan Cardona, notary of Valencia, acts as procurator for Azmet Comina; and C 302: 139v (8 August 1479)—Pere de Galbe of Oriheula acts as procurator for certain Muslim vassals of the Count of Cocentaina.

101. ARV: C 154: 168r–169r (26 September 1498).

102. *Furs*, Colon and Garcia, eds., IV: 77–78: Llibre IV: Rubrica IX: 51 (Jaime I) and 52 (Jaime II). Boswell, *Royal Treasure*, pp. 122–123; Burns, *Islam under the Crusaders*, p. 265, and Roca Traver, "Un siglo," pp. 188–189.

103. ARV: C 148: 178r–v (10 June 1493). ARV: B 1158: 170v–172r (23 December 1486)—the same was done for Çahat Flori of Játiva, involved in a lawsuit against the canon Esteve Costa.

104. See chap. 6 nn. 187–189.

105. ARV: B 1159: 183r–v (30 March 1489) and 355r–v (4 August 1490) are both litigations between Muslims and Jews and do not involve any special legal procedures or legal problems.

106. ARV: C 148: 208r–v (12 August 1493).

107. *Aureum opus*, 52r–v, 77r–v; and ARV: C 304: 38r–v (28 April 1480).

108. This conclusion is based on a reading of all cases treated in the documentation.

109. For example, ARV: C 305: 140v–141r (23 May 1482).

110. There were many safe-conducts granted. Some examples are ARV: B 1157: 672r–v (16 July 1484)—a *guiatge* is granted to Azmet Bochini and Çahat Ganim, protecting them and their possessions against prosecution for the murder of Ubaydal Hiem; B 1161: 439r (23 August 1497)—a *guiatge* is granted to a Muslim of Benaguacil so that he can go to Murviedro to sell the produce from his lands there and use the proceeds to pay off his creditors.

111. For example, ACA: C 3638: 165r (6 January 1482).

112. Boswell, *Royal Treasure*, pp. 127–128.

113. ARV: C 158: 144r–v (10 December 1502).

114. ACA: C 3667: 290r–v (13 March 1491); and ARV: B 1157: 238r–239r (14 May 1482).

115. ARV: B 1431: 338v–341r (20–26 April 1493). The accused, Azmet Çahat of Tunis, was released on bail and was not punished because the torturers could not extract any confession from him.

116. ARV: B 1432: 133r–v (11 August 1497).

117. ARV: C 156: 4v (8 July 1501).

118. ARV: C 158: 100r–101r (8 October 1502).

119. ARV: C 133: 174v–175r (7 May 1486); and 186r–v (13 May 1486).

120. ARV: C 304: 141r–v (12 December 1480).

121. ARV: C 127: 107r–v (27 April 1480); and ARV: C 129: 145r–v (15 September 1481).

122. ACA: C 3639: 58v–59r (10 December 1481); ARV: C 130: 144v (7 January 1482), and 171v–172r (8 January 1482).

123. ARV: C 132: 207v–208r (19 March 1485); and ARV: C 134: 115v–116r (12 March 1488).

124. ARV: C 138: 72v (21 December 1496); ARV: C 151: 23r–v (17 August 1496), and 36r–37r (5 September 1496).

125. ARV: B 1158: 291v–292r (28 September 1486): Çaat Amiz, accused of assault against another Muslim, goes to the bailiff general and deceives the latter ("callant nos les dites coses") into ordering the bailiff of Játiva not to proceed against him; and ARV: C 141: 81v–82v (25 September 1500).

126. ARV: C 148: 169v–170v (18 May 1493). Apariçi Noguera complained that he was unable to have procedure initiated against Çahat Tabernaxi because Çahat was "defenent se ab guiatges e molts altres diffugis."

127. ARV: C 132: 108r–v (3 August 1484).

128. ARV: C 310: 139v–140v (1 September 1497).

129. ARV: C 156: 106r–v (11 December 1501).

130. ARV: B 1158: 284v–285r (14 September 1486).

131. ARV: B 1162: 59v (13 June 1500).

132. ARV: C 142: 81r (2 May 1502).

133. ACA: C 3639: 69r–v (28 December 1482).

134. Some examples are ARV: C 130: 43r–v (14 August 1481)—the lord and aljama of Alberique are involved in a litigation with Christians of Alcira regarding the royal "çequia"; C 132: 33v–34v (6 April 1484)—the heirs of a knight of Valencia sue for the more than 25,000s in pensions owed to them by Don Hugo de Cardona and his aljamas of Beniopa, Benipeixcar, and so forth; C 139: 62v–63r (15 May 1495)—the lord and aljama of Alacuás owe pensions to the widow Yolanta Joan; C 140: 173r–v (20 May 1500)—a litigation between the jurates of Segorbe and the lord and vassals (aljama mentioned) of Navarrés regarding the taxes the jurates maintain they can collect in Navarrés; C 148: 167v–169r (24 April 1493)—the lord and Muslims of Torres Torres make a complaint against the jurates and *sequier* (overseer of the irrigation system) of Murviedo regarding the *sequier*'s confiscation of the Muslims' goods for improper use of the irrigation system.

135. ARV: C 131: 179r–v (15 December 1483).

136. ARV: C 148: 75r–v (14 September 1492).

137. ACA: C 3645: 13r–v (14 April 1488).

138. ARV: C 148: 211r–v (10 August 1493).

139. See chap. 1.

140. Some examples are ARV: C 139: 194v–195r (8 February 1496)—a Christian merchant files suit against Muslims who owe him 50 pounds for linen purchased; C 148: 169v–170r (18 May 1493)—a Christian requests procedure against a Muslim of Mascarell who owes him money for sheep purchased; C 151: 150v–151r (18 April 1497)—the Muslims and *alcayt* of Petrés are sued for the 120 pounds they owe to a Christian of Puzol for the purchase of sheep; and B 1157: 344v–345v (23 November 1482)—a Christian notary pleas that execution be made against Muslims of Játiva who owe him money for the purchase of an olive orchard.

141. Some examples are ARV: C 148: 71v (2 September 1492)—a Christian of Castellón de la Plana accuses a Muslim of the same town of stealing money from him; C 130: 144v (7 January 1482)—Muslims of Bechí are accused of burning 1,500 or more olive and carob trees near Villarreal; B 1156: (5 March 1479)—the lessee of the royal saltworks of Játiva makes accusations against Muslims of Antella; B 1156: 806r–807r (7 July 1480)—the farmers of the *delmes* (agricultural taxes) of Castellón de Játiva request that steps be taken against Muslims of Alcocer holding lands in the area of Castellón who attempt to avoid the payment of the *delmes*; and B 1158: 42r–43r (27 June 1485)—procedure is initiated against a Jew of Murviedro and a Muslim of Petrés found in possession of false money.

142. ARV: B 1157: 638v (25 May 1484).

143. ARV: MR 3062: 152 (Játiva, 1502).

144. ARV: C 140: 199v–200v (11 August 1500).

145. ARV: B 1158: 523v (14 January 1488). ACA: C 3639: 142v–143v (17 October 1502)—a guard of the *huerta* of Murviedro is killed when Muslims attack and vandalize the property of a leading Christian of the town.

146. ACA: C 3609: 71v (20 January 1486).

147. ARV: C 137: 52r–v (15 December 1493).

148. ACA: C 3633: 79v–80r (25 February 1479); and ACA: C 3640: 41v–42v (2 May 1483).

149. ARV: C 130: 158r (29 December 1482).

150. ARV: C 134: 141v–142r (11 April 1488).

151. ARV: C 304: 92v–93r (1 August 1480).

152. For example, ACA: C 3568: 121v–122r (25 September 1495)—Muslims and Christians of Antella are accused of killing a Muslim of Sumacárcel. Regarding this case and others like it, see chap. 6.

153. Boswell, *Royal Treasure*, pp. 343–353.

154. *Furs e ordinations*, Palmart, ed., Llibre IX: Rubrica II: 8–9; *Aureum opus*, 236r. Although the *Furs* provided that a Christian man and a Muslim woman caught sleeping together were both to be driven naked through the streets, it is clear that the law had been a dead letter since at least the mid-fourteenth century (see Boswell, *Royal Treasure*, p. 346 n. 70).

155. Boswell, *Royal Treasure*, p. 344.

156. ARV: B 1433: 119r–123v (1 February 1501) describes the case of Ange-

la de Vanya, a prostitute from Cuenca practicing in Onda, against various Muslims from the area.

157. ARV: MR 102: 174r (1491).

158. ARV: MR 102: 174r.

159. ARV: C 126: 40v–41v (11 September 1479).

160. ACA: C 3653: 157r–v (23 March 1498).

161. ARV: B 1161: 452r–v (16 September 1497); B 1162: 98r (22 October 1500) is another order of the same tenor. Such orders also called for the arrest of all mendicants begging without license.

162. ARV: B 1162: 7v (21 January 1500)—Ali Chanchan and other Muslims kidnap from the royal brothel of Valencia two Muslim prostitutes, slaves of the Infante Enrique and the knight Francesch Aguilo. ARV: B 1433: 57v (23 June 1491)—Mariem, a prostitute from Alasquer, testifies that she was sold to Don Altobello de Centelles, who then sent her to work as a prostitute in the royal brothel. For the prohibition against such practices by the masters of female slaves, see *Furs*, Colon and Garcia, eds., II: 85: Llibre I: Rubrica IX: 3. See also, Boswell, *Royal Treasure*, pp. 350–351.

163. ACA: C 3640: 119r–120r (8 May 1484).

164. ARV: B 1162: 409v–410r (11 February 1503).

165. ARV: B 1433: 321r–325v (31 May 1502). For more on the matter of Muslim prostitution, see my "Prostitution of Muslim Women in the Kingdom of Valencia: Religious and Sexual Discrimination in a Medieval Plural Society," in *The Medieval Mediterranean: Cross-cultural Contacts*, M. Chiat and K. Reyerson, eds. (St. Cloud, Minnesota, 1988), pp. 87–96.

166. Some examples are ARV: MR 90: 173r–v, 175r; MR 103: 172r; and MR 110: 80r.

167. For example, ARV: B 1431: 278r–286r (6 February 1493).

168. For example, ARV: B 1157: 342r–v (11 November 1482).

Chapter Six:
Conflict and Solidarity in
Mudejar Society

1. Domínguez Ortiz and Vincent, *Historia*, pp. 159–223.

2. Glick and Pi-Sunyer, "Acculturation," p. 153; and Burns, *Islam under the Crusaders*, pp. 249–264, 273–299.

3. Robert I. Burns, "Spanish Islam in Transition: Acculturative Survival and Its Price in the Christian Kingdom of Valencia, 1240–1280," in *Islam and Cultural Change in the Middle Ages*, Speros Vryonis, Jr., ed. (Wiesbaden, 1975), pp. 96–100.

4. Guichard, *Nuestra Historia*, 3:65–97.

5. On anti-Muslim preaching, see chap. 1; on Christian mob violence and on possible coercion in proselytizing of Valencian Musliums, see chap. 2.

6. See chap. 1 nn. 160–177. Also, ARV: B 1156: 502r–503r (5 July 1479) and 511v–512r (23 July 1479)—Muslims are fined for playing dice with Christians in

the tavern of Enova, near Játiva; ARV: B 1222: I 38v–39r (27 October 1496)—
Muslims are prohibited from drinking in the tavern of Liria to prevent fights and
scandals; B 1222: VII 50v (29 August 1500)—a Muslim shoemaker is fined for
"bevent a una taverna al costat del alfondech a les nou hores de la nit"; and
ACA: C 3645: 136v–137v (31 July 1488), C 3644: 209v–210r (9 August 1488)—
procedure against various Muslims of Játiva who slept with a Christian woman.
At first glance one might think that Mudejar wine-drinking is yet another sign of
their acculturation to Christian practices. However, this was not necessarily the
case, for Glick (*Islamic and Christian Spain*, p. 80) points out that as a result of
Iraqi, not Christian, influence, Andalusi jurists had declared the legality of
wine-drinking during the reign of ᶜAbd al-Raḥmān II. Hence, it is not surprising
that the documents do not record Mudejar jurists penalizing their fellows for
drinking wine, even though it was originally a *ḥadd* offense. Life in a Christian
society probably strengthened the inclination of Hispano-Muslim jurists to disregard the Qur'ānic prohibition of wine-drinking.

7. ARV: B 1431: 67r (3 June 1491)—the accusation of the wife and sisters of
Abdalla Çentido against his killer, Açen Muça: "dia de corpore christi . . . en lo
qual dia molts moros e crestians de diverses lochs del present Regne venen a
veure la dita gran festa"; and ARV: C 137: 201v–202v (18 November 1494)—
seigneurial Muslims go to the town of Murla for the festivities of San Miguel.

8. Robert I. Burns, "The Language Barrier: Bilingualism and Interchange,"
in *Muslims, Christians, and Jews* (Cambridge, 1984), pp. 172–192; Joan Fuster,
Poetas, Moriscos y Curas, Josep Palacios, trans. (Madrid, 1969), pp. 123–146;
María del Carme Barceló Torres, "La llengua àrab al País Valencià (segles VIII
al XVI)," *Arguments* (Valencia), 4 (1979): 123–149; idem, *Minorías*, pp. 121–
151.

9. Boswell, *Royal Treasure*, pp. 381–384.

10. Boronat y Barrachina, *Moriscos*, 1: 424, document no. 5.

11. Fuster, *Poetas*, pp. 142–146.

12. ARV: B 1431: 391v (3 April 1494); and, for example, B 1431: 192r (19
January 1492), describing the testimony of Caçim Abdalla of Málaga "migan-
cant Ali Bellvis moro alcadi."

13. ARV: B 1432: 128v (8 August 1497)—the confession of Ubaydal
Allepus.

14. ARV: B 1431: 65r–v (3 June 1491).

15. ARV: B 1431: 76v–77r.

16. ARV: B 1431: 80v–81r.

17. ARV: B 1431: 358r (10 December 1492).

18. ARV: B 1431: 358v–359r.

19. ARV: B 1431: 283v–284r (6 February 1493)—the testimony of Ursula.

20. ARV: B 1431: 90r (8 June 1491)—the testimony of Miguel de la Serra
in the case against Açen Muça.

21. ARV: B 1433: 119v (1 February 1501)—the accusation of Angela de
Vanya; and 120r–v for the words of the Cotallas to Angela.

22. Glick and Pi-Sunyer, "Acculturation," p. 140.

23. Glick, "Ethnic Systems," p. 169.

24. Burns, "Dream of Conversion," passim; idem, "Journey from Islam: Incipient Cultural Transition in the Conquered Kingdom of Valencia (1240–1280)," *Speculum* 35 (1960): 337–356.

25. Boswell, *Royal Treasure*, pp. 379–380; and for the lamentations of Vicent Ferrer, Fuster, *Poetas*, pp. 112–113.

26. Barceló Torres, *Minorías*, pp. 143–144.

27. In their negotiations with Carlos I in 1526, the Moriscos requested that they not be compelled to pay any more taxes than the Old Christians, now that they were Christians themselves. See Boronat y Barrachina, *Moriscos*, 1: 425–426, document no. 5.

28. ARV: B 1432: 129r (8 August 1497) and 133v (11 August)—the confessions of Ubaydal Allepus.

29. ARV: C 140: 230v–231r (21 October 1500); and ARV: C 311: 146v, concerning the same case.

30. ARV: C 650: 241v–242r (12 April 1502).

31. On the difficulties faced by converts in receiving inheritances from Muslim relations, ACA: C 3636: 54v–55r (2 January 1481)—the Muslim Gaçeni family disputes the right of the convert Caterina to collect the inheritance of her deceased Muslim grandmother and their mother; and ACA: C 3655: 115r–v (21 February 1502)—a convert of Tarazona complains that "moros que se dizen parientes del quondam padre del dicho exponiente [the convert] que fue moro" have deprived him of lands left by his father. Boswell, *Royal Treasure*, p. 378, points out that thirteenth-century legislation declared the estate of the deceased convert forfeit to the Crown. In contrast, ARV: G 2350: Manus I: 16r–17v (27 January 1479)—the rights of a Muslim family to the property of a murdered convert relation are recognized.

32. Burns, "Journey from Islam," p. 341; Boswell, *Royal Treasure*, p. 379; *Aureum opus*, 40r: Jaime II prohibits Christians from calling converts "renegat vel tornadiç vel alio verbo consimili deshonestando eum."

33. ARV: G 2350: Manus I: 16r–17v (27 January 1479)—two Christians are accused of murdering a Muslim convert; and ARV: B 217: 185v–186r (11 January 1480)—Muslims of Villamarchante and Pedralba make a truce with Christians of Cuart who killed their son and brother, a convert.

34. *Furs*, Colon and Garcia, eds., II: 81: Llibre I: Rubrica VIII: 1. ARV: B 1220: VIII 14r–v (July 1487); and ARV: B 1159: 312r–v (23 January 1490)—a black female Muslim slave who received baptism is freed.

35. *Furs e ordinations*, Palmart, ed., Llibre V: Rubrica I: 40v (Jaime I). Vicenta Cortes, *La esclavitud en Valencia durante el reinado de los Reyes Católicos* (Valencia, 1964), p. 136. ARV: C 156: 202v–203r (21 April 1502)—"causa libertatis" between a baptized Muslim slave and his master; ARV: B 1157: 713r–v (2 September 1482)—a baptized Muslim slave runs away from his Christian master; B 1158: 423r–v (21 May 1488)—two slaves, one baptized and one Muslim, run away from their Christian master; in contrast, B 1160: 819v–820r (2 April 1494)—a slave from Granada was manumitted "apres feyt crestia."

36. ARV: B 1157: 381v (17 February 1483).

37. Francisco Pons Boïgues, "Retazos moriscos," *El archivo* 3 (1889): 131–134.

38. ARV: C 140: 230v–231v (21 October 1500)—"tornadizo" of Cocentaina; ARV: B 1160: 820r–v (2 April 1494)—a Maghriban Muslim comes to Valencia to convert; B 1162: 103v–104r (5 November 1500)—a new convert of Ondara; and ARV: B 1432: 129r—the convert Miguel Crestia.

39. ACA: C 3649: 10r–v (14 February 1492).

40. That feuding violence among Christians was a persistent problem in late medieval and early modern Valencia is apparent in the comments of Furió and Garcia, "Dificultats agràries," p. 303 n.44, and Casey, *Kingdom of Valencia*, pp. 206–222. The truces are contained in the registers ARV: B 217–221 (1479–1500). In contrast to the 120 truces between Muslims, there were only 21 made between Muslims and Christians.

41. Pierre Guichard, "Le peuplement de la région de Valence aux deux premiers siècles de la domination musulmane," *Mélanges de la Casa de Velázquez* 5 (1969): 103–158.

42. Barceló Torres, *Minorías*, pp. 133–136.

43. Míkel de Epalza, "Notas sobre el lingüista Ibn Sidah y la historia de Denia y su región en el siglo XI," *Revista de instituto de estudios alicantinos* 33 (1981): 163–166; Míkel de Epalza and Enrique Llobregat, " Hubo mozárabes en tierras valencianas? Proceso de islamización del Levante de la Peninsula (Sharq al-Andalus)," *Revista del Instituto de Estudios Alicantinos*, 36 (1982): 7–31; Burns, *Muslims, Christians, and Jews*, pp. 4–5, 178–179. Richard W. Bulliet, *Conversion to Islam in the Medieval Period: An Essay in Quantitative History* (Cambridge, Mass., 1979), pp. 114–127.

44. For instance, see the studies collected in Ernest Gellner and Charles Micaud, eds., *Arabs and Berbers* (Lexington, Mass., 1972).

45. Guichard, *Structures*. Also, see the comments of Glick, *Islamic and Christian Spain*, pp. 137–146; on segmentary societies, David M. Hart, "The Tribe in Modern Morocco: Two Case Studies," in *Arabs and Berbers*, Gellner and Micaud, eds., pp. 25–58; idem, "Segmentary Systems and the Role of 'Five Fifths' in Tribal Morocco," in *Islam in Tribal Societies from the Atlas to the Indus*, Akbar S. Ahmed and David M. Hart, eds., pp. 66–105. There is a vast literature, mainly by social anthropologists, on the sociopolitical organization of Arabs and Berbers. Throughout this chapter I will cite only those sources I have found to be especially useful. Much of this literature is synthesized by Guichard and by Jacob Black-Michaud, *Feuding Societies* (Oxford, 1975), and can be found in their extensive bibliographies.

46. Guichard, *Structures*, pp. 213–214, 242, 290; David Wasserstein, *The Rise and Fall of the Party-Kings: Politics and Society in Islamic Spain 1002–1086* (Princeton, 1985), pp. 163–189; Glick, *Islamic and Christian Spain*, p. 141.

47. Julio Caro Baroja, *Los Moriscos del Reino de Granada* (Madrid, 1976), pp. 65–80; Bernard Vincent, "Les éléments de solidarité au sein de la minorité morisque," in *Le concepte de classe dans l'analyse des sociétés méditerranéennes XVIe–XXe siècles* (Nice, 1978), pp. 91–100. This contradicts the views of the fourteenth-century historian-sociologist Ibn Khaldūn, *The Muqaddimah: An Introduction to History*, Franz Rosenthal, trans. (London, 1958), 1: 252–269, that sedentarization results in the loss of ʿaṣabīyah. He was correct regarding tribal solidarity, but not regarding family and lineage solidarity.

48. F. H. Ruxton, *Māliki Law, Being a Summary from the French Translations of the "Mukhtasar" of Sīdī Khalīl* (Westport, Conn., 1980 [London, 1916]), pp. 311–321.

49. For instance, Lapidus, *Muslim Cities*, pp. 79–142.

50. Caro Baroja, *Moriscos*, p. 77.

51. Boronat y Barrachina, *Moriscos*, 1: 424, document no. 5.

52. ARV: B 1157: 94r (22 August 1481).

53. ACA: C 3648: 219r–v (15 October 1491); C 3650: 156v–157r (5 October 1492); C 3652: 1r (29 October 1495)—Ybraym and his father still "pretendian" to make the marriage with Fatima; and C 3653: 239v–240r (16 July 1496). ACA: C 3665: 141v (2 September 1489) finds the brothers Mofferiz and Mahomat Margnan jointly protesting against excessive taxation.

54. ACA: C 3647: 60v–61r (15 February 1490). On divorce in Islamic law, see John L. Esposito, *Women in Muslim Family Law* (Syracuse, 1982), pp. 28–38, especially p. 35; and Ruxton, *Māliki Law*, pp. 91–92, 97, 105–108.

55. Guichard, *Structures*, pp. 27–36, 59–64; Robert F. Murphy and Leonard Kasdan, "The Structure of Parallel Cousin Marriage," *American Anthropologist* 61 (1959): 17–29; Reuben Levy, *The Social Structure of Islam* (Cambridge, 1957), p. 102; Raphael Patai, *The Arab Mind* (New York, 1983), pp. 92–93, 226–227; Joseph Ginat, *Women in Muslim Rural Society* (New Brunswick, N.J., 1982), pp. 77–82; and Jack Goody, *The Development of the Family and Marriage in Europe* (Cambridge, 1983), pp. 31–32.

56. Esposito, *Muslim Family Law*, pp. 39–46. Levy, *Social Structure*, pp. 245–246, and Ginat, *Women*, p. 79, note that in many Muslim societies women did not inherit. ARV: B 1156: 856v (14 September 1480)—two Muslim daughters inherit a carob orchard from their father.

57. On bridewealth, or dower as it is sometimes called, see Esposito, *Muslim Family Law*, pp. 24–26; Ruxton, *Māliki Law*, pp. 91–92, 106–109, 111; Goody, *Family and Marriage*, pp. 19–21, 243, 261; and Levy, *Social Structure*, pp. 95–96. ARV: B 1160: 780r–781r (4 December 1493), B 1221: VI 35r (19 May 1487), B 323: 519r–520v (18 October 1481), and ACA: C 3649: 10r–v (14 February 1492) are all examples of Muslim women claiming their bridewealth either after separation or divorce or in order to prevent their husband's creditors from confiscating it.

58. Guichard, *Structures*, pp. 41–45; Patai, *Arab Mind*, p. 226; Murphy and Kasdan, "Marriage," pp. 24–28; Ginat, *Women*, pp. 90–91; and Donald P. Cole, "Alliance and Descent in the Middle East and the 'Problem' of Patrilateral Parallel Cousin Marriage," in *Islam in Tribal Societies from the Atlas to the Indus*, A. S. Ahmed and D. M. Hart, eds. (London and Boston, 1984), pp. 179, 181–182.

59. ARV: C 131: 61v (18 April 1483).

60. ARV: B 1433: 136v (1501)—Abdalla Murçi and Yuçeff Zignell are referred to as the "cunyats" of Mahomat Perpir; ARV: B 221: 566v (7 December 1499)—"pau final" between Mahomat Perpir and Azmet Murçi; and B 221: 696v (17 August 1500)—"pau final" between Mahomat Perpir and Yuçeff Zignell.

61. ARV: B 1432: 361r–363v (23 November 1500).
62. ARV: MR 89: 181r–v (1479). Ali Orfayçi pays a 600s *composicio* for the crime.
63. ARV: MR 957: 6r (Alcira 1500). Mahomat and Abdalla Giber pay a fee of 8s "per un guiatge [against legal prosecution] a aquells atorgat per haver nafrat a Xixoni moro de la dita vall."
64. ARV: MR 959: 4v (Alcira 1502). Çat and Ali Bolarif pay a fee of 6s "per hun guiatge que li's fonch atorgat . . . per benefici de pau per certes nafres que avien perpetrades en la dita vall."
65. ARV: MR 4282: 1v (Onda 1500). Ali and Mahomat Guayna pay a 100s *composicio* "per certes nafres que feren en la persona de Mahomat Malich."
66. ARV: C 128: 182v–183r (15 March 1481)—"quod Abdalla Cumaynet seracenus habitator olim dicti loci de Benipescar diabolica persuasione dictus nocturno temore necem in personam cuiusdam alterius seraceni Mahomet Carner vocati habitatories etiam dicti loci de Benipescar perpetravit"; ACA: C 3653: 241v (19 July 1496)—Ybraym de Arrondi and Mahoma Cotin assert that while they were peacefully strolling down the street in Zaragoza they were assaulted by Yuçe Calan, whom, in self-defense, they mortally wounded by striking him on the nose with a stone; ARV: MR 951: 4r (Alcira 1494)—Mahomat Cheoquar and Selemica are fined "per esser exits al camin de Alberich [a] Ali Coxoxet e altres moros e havent nafrat aquell"; MR 957: 6v (Alcira 1500)—Mahomat Xalamci, Galip Xarch, and Çilim Guardar pay 30s "per un guiatge a ells atorgat . . . per ells haver mort a Alasdrach moro"; MR 3055: 7r (Játiva 1495)—150s *composicio* from Obaydal Reyes "per quant aquell e altres moros foren denunciats per la mort de Çaat Abdulazis," and 240s *composicio* from Mahomat Alban of Corbera and Azmet Fondell of Pintor "per esser entrats en la moreria de Xativa e haver naffrat de una coltellada en lo cap a Mariem alias Cuqua viuda mora"; MR 3056: 6v (Játiva 1496)—300s *composicio* from Ali Cayduni "per esser exits ab armes a matar Abrahim Meter carnicer anava de sa casa"; MR 3058: 13r–v (Játiva 1498)—200s *composicio* from Çahat Asis "per cert homey que en dies passats aquell feu en un moro apellat Faratget . . . de Anna e encara per altra mort que fonch denunciat per un altre moro apellat Ali Fino . . . de Chella ensemps ab altres moros"; MR 3060: 13r (Játiva 1500)—Abrahim Anova and other Moors are denounced "per que en lo cami real li [Mahomat Nocayre] dispararen una ballesta," and 13v—900s *composicio* from Abrahim Arrona and Ali Mandonet of Alcocer "denunciat ensemps ab altres moros tots del dit loch per Çahat Abbet moro del loch de Sant Joan com a pare e coninucta persona de Yuçeff Abbes de edat de XVIII anys per haver lo mort apunyalades."
67. ARV: C 129: 142v–143r (13 September 1481).
68. ARV: B 1431: 79v–81r (8 June 1491). The testimonies of Johan Olzina of Bonrepos and Ubaydal Suleymen of Mirambell describe this murder.
69. ARV: MR 3055: 6v (Játiva 1495).
70. ARV: MR 953: 11v (1496).
71. ARV: B 1433: 107v–108v (13 October 1501). The accusations of the father Abdalla Pachando describe the attack on his sons in gory detail.

72. Black-Michaud, *Feuding Societies*, pp. 63–85, emphasizes that the feud is an essentially interminable process.

73. ARV: B 1156: 547r (16 August 1479)—license to Ali Chachaz and Fuçey Sinsinet of Oliva; 874r–v (12 October 1480)—license to Abdulazis Tarongera of Carlet; B 1157: 265v–266r (27 June 1482)—license to Çahat Mayor, alias Maçot; and B 1159: 250r (15 October 1489)—license to Fat Renda of the Vall de Uxó to bear arms in Valencia. That the Renda family had enemies is attested to by a number of truces in which its members were involved: ARV: B 217: 123r (3 March 1479), 685v (7 July 1484); B 218: 26r (25 January 1485); B 219: 335r–v (3 March 1489). Fat himself concluded a truce with Mahomat and Açen Navarro of the Vall de Uxó—B 219: 383v (4 April 1489).

74. ARV: B 1159: 48v (22 May 1488). Not long after, Yuçeff and Abrahim Albanne, alias Bizquey, concluded a truce with Abrahim Colombret (Corumbell)—ARV: B 219: 49v (19 June 1488).

75. ARV: B 1162: 418r–v (20 March 1503).

76. ARV: B 217: 169v (28 September 1479)—truce between Abrahim Murçi and Mahomat Perpir; B 221: 371r (22 August 1497)—truce between Abrahim Murçi and Ubaydal Murçi; 438r (27 September 1498)—truce between Abrahim Murçi and Ali Perpir; 524v (31 May 1499)—truce between Azmet Murçi and Omaymet and Ali Perpir; 527v (27 June 1499)—truce between Azmet Murçi and Ubaydal Murçi; 547v (30 September 1499)—truce between Azmet Murçi and Mahomat Perpir and others; and 566v (7 December 1499)—truce between Azmet Murçi and Mahomat Perpir, alone at the time.

77. ARV: B 1433: 394r–426v (16 June 1503)—the case of Nusa, wife of Abrahim Murçi versus Abdalla and Azmet Torralbi; 394v–395v, 402v–404r for the accusations of Nusa against the Torralbis.

78. ARV: B 1433: 406v–407v—the testimony of Ysabel, wife of Gil Sanchiz.

79. ARV: B 1433: 415v–416v—the testimony of Francesch Centelles, shoemaker of Valencia.

80. ARV: B 1433: 406v–407v—the testimony of Ysabel, wife of Gil Sanchiz: at the time of the assault Abdalla was walking "per ciutat venent lens" and Çahat was at the tannery buying leather; 413v—Isabel, wife of Joan Lop, testifies that Abdalla and Çahat were not at home when Azmet attacked Abrahim Murçi.

81. ARV: B 1433: 415v–416v—the testimony of Francesch Centelles.

82. ARV: B 1433: 394v–395v—the accusations of Nusa; 406v–407v—the testimony of Ysabel; and 420v–421v—the testimony of Gil Sanchiz.

83. ARV: B 1433: 426r–v—the testimony of Gabriel Gosalbo.

84. ARV: C 132: 194r–v (18 January 1485).

85. ARV: B 1431: 64v–99v (3 June 1491)—the case of Mariem, the wife of Abdalla Çentido versus Açen Muça; 65r–v, 70r–v—the confessions of Açen Muça.

86. ARV: B 1431: 95v–96r—the testimony of Yuçeff Ada.

87. ARV: C 317: 2v (15 June 1492). Another example is ARV: C 148: 199r–v (3 August 1493)—the mother of the murdered Azmet Jabar denounces the killer, Lopo Vellet, before the court of the lieutenant governor.

88. ARV: MR 89: 181r–v (1479)—"com lo dit Bolaix [wounded by Ali

Orfayçi and Mahomat Caffahi; see text above, near citation of n. 62] hagues posada a vollicio fon admes a la dita composicio [600s]"; MR 952: 8r (Alcira 1495)—a 500s *composicio* is received from Abdalla Baterna "perque sen porta la filla de Açen Gemi squerrer de la dita moreria la qual apres fon sa muller fon admes a la dita composicio"; MR 3058: 13r–v (Játiva 1498)—after his payment of a 200s *composicio* (see n. 66 [above] for the details of the crime) "lo dit Asis per les parts denunciants es stat remes e feta pau ab aquells."

89. Black-Michaud, *Feuding Societies*, pp. 149–150, notes that although feuding normally occurs in the absence of centralized government, "as long as feuding is restricted to conflicts between fairly small groups of equal status and does not upset traditionally defined relations between the different strata of the society . . . the feud is perfectly consonant with centralized government." The Valencian situation substantiates this view, inasmuch as Mudejar feuding posed no threat to Christian authority or to the dominance of Christian society over the conquered and socially inferior Muslims.

90. For instance, ARV: B 221: 99v–100r (14 January 1496)—Abrahim and Mahomat Corunbell of Valencia make peace with Mahomat, Ali, and Çahat Lupe of Paterna "sobre lo coltellada e nafra per aquells [Lupes] feyta e perpetrada en lo cap del dit Mahomat Corunbell en lo dit loch de Paterna."

91. ARV: B 219: 373v–374r (31 March 1489).

92. There is no indication that the Crown consciously pursued a "divide and rule" policy, that is, encouraging Mudejar divisiveness as a means of social control. The fascinating modern study of the social anthropologist Abner Cohen, *Arab Border Villages in Israel: A Study of Continuity and Change in Social Organization* (Manchester, 1965) discusses how the Israeli authorities encouraged intravillage feuding between lineage groups (*ḥamūla*) as a means of preventing the Arabs from forming a united political front.

93. ARV: MR 93: 311v (1482); and ARV: B 217: 658r–v (15 November 1483)—a truce is concluded between the Bizquey and Roget families.

94. ARV: B 219: 374v (31 March 1489).

95. ARV: B 1158: 413r–v (5 May 1487).

96. Black-Michaud, *Feuding Societies*, pp. 86–118.

97. ARV: C 148: 210v (26 August 1493).

98. ARV: B 1433: 373r–374v (6 May 1503).

99. ARV: B 217: 599v (10 March 1483)—"pau final" between Abrahim Bizquey and Abdulmelich and Abrahim Roget; and 658r–v (15 November 1483)—"pau e treua" between Mahomat, Abrahim, and Yuçeff Bizquey and Mahomat, Abdulmelich, Mahomat and Abrahim Roget. On the various truces between the Perpirs and the Murçis, see n. 76.

100. ARV: B 217: 603v (7 March 1483).

101. ARV: C 132: 194v.

102. ARV: C 135: 183r (29 March 1480).

103. Black-Michaud, *Feuding Societies*, p. 171.

104. ARV: B 221: 263v (25 October 1496)—truce between Çale Pasunquet and Mahomat Alguarami, "ferrers" of Valencia; B 217: 690v (17 August 1484)—truce between Abdalla Çalema and Abrahim Murçi, "broquerers" of Valencia; B 221: 32v (11 April 1495)—truce between Ali Bachari of Oliva and

Yuçeff "peixcadors"; and B 219: 18r (15 January 1488)—truce between Mahomat Xoni and Abdalla Alloba, "espardenyers."

105. ARV: B 217: 599r (28 February 1483)—truce with Çatdon Caeli; B 218: 325r (20 December 1486)—in this truce Abdalla Torralbi is allied with the Bizqueys, and Ali Alarabi with the Caberos; B 221: 92v (4 January 1496)—truce with Çilim Maymo; B 221: 99v (14 January 1496)—here Çilim Maymo is allied with the Perpirs; and B 221: 413r (23 March 1498)—here the Perpirs are allied with Abdalla Chiulet and Ali Granati, a physician (metge).

106. ARV: B 217: 168v (23 September 1497)—truce with Çahat Carcaix; B 221: 524v (31 May 1499)—truce with Azmet Murçi; and B 221: 731v (16 November 1500)—here Azmet Naixe, a shoemaker of Mislata, is allied with Ali Perpir, while Maguarell and Abducarim have Azmet Claret, a linen dealer of Valencia, as an ally.

107. See n. 106.

108. ARV: B 1220: VIII 12r (16 July 1487).

109. ARV: B 1158: 264r (24 July 1486). ARV: MR 954: 6r (1497)—a similar case from Alcira in which Çahat Vinquiçi pays a 180s settlement for having chopped down Paziar family fig trees.

110. ARV: B 1159: 120v (28 August 1488).

111. ARV: B 1160: 361v–362r (5 December 1491).

112. ARV: B 1431: 545v (28 November 1494)—the testimony of Abraym Alfat, amīn of Alberique, who explains why Ali Gehini hid his money.

113. ARV: B 221: 225v (15 July 1496)—on account of this dispute, Mahomat and Abducalem had to make a truce.

114. ARV: B 1158: 403r–v (19 April 1487).

115. ARV: B 1158: 413r (5 May 1487), and 415r–v (12 May 1487).

116. ARV: B 1158: 414r–v (9 May 1497).

117. ARV: B 1158: 414r.

118. ARV: B 219: 75r (3 August 1488)—the truce; ACA: C 3650: 19r–v (15 May 1492).

119. Guichard, Structures, pp. 37–41, 91–96, 154–159; Patai, Arab Mind, pp. 90–95, 100–102, 104–106; and Goody, Family and Marriage, pp. 29–30. Registers of the Justicia Criminal of Valencia record considerable violence among Christian artisans as well, but thus far we know little about the motives of the parties involved or about the structure of the Valencian Christian family.

120. Black-Michaud, Feuding Societies, pp. 175–184.

121. ARV: B 1432: 128v–129v, 133r–134r (8–11 August 1487)—the confessions of Ubaydal Allepus; and 127r–128r—the accusations of Fuçey, the widow of Amet Biari.

122. ARV: B 1431: 73v–76r (6–7 June 1491)—the defense of Açen Muça; and 88v–89r (8 June)—confessions of Açen.

123. ARV: B 1433: 372r–385r (6 May 1503)—the testimony of Mariem, wife of Abrahim Montique; and 371r—the testimony of Mahomat Perpir.

124. Ahmed Abou-Zeid, "Honour and Shame among the Bedouins of Egypt," in Honour and Shame: The Values of Mediterranean Society, J. G. Peristiany, ed. (London, 1965), pp. 253–254, 256–257; Guichard, Structures, pp. 36–38, 41–43; Levy, Social Structure, pp. 91–94; Patai, Arab Mind, pp.

119–127; Ginat, *Women*, pp. 152, 173, 176; and Black-Michaud, *Feuding Societies*, pp. 217–225. ARV: C 132: 219v–220r (9 November 1495) shows that the wife lived with her husband's family.

125. ARV: C 126: 120r–121r (23 February 1480). ARV: B 1160: 412v–413r (1 March 1492) is a similar case; and ACA: C 3647: 112v–113r (30 January 1491) is an unusual case in which the wife's father is given partial custody of his four granddaughters after the demise of both parents. The other coguardian perhaps was an agnate of the girls' father.

126. ARV: B 1162: 497r–v (30 December 1503).

127. ARV: C 148: 125v (17 December 1492), and 137r–v (21 January 1493).

128. ARV: B 1160: 780r–781r (4 December 1493).

129. Abou-Zeid, "Honour," pp. 256–257; and Ruxton, *Māliki Law*, p. 331.

130. ARV: C 129: 1v–2r (23 January 1481)—Mariem of Beniarjó is made a slave and sold by her lord as a punishment for adultery; and ARV: C 132: 108r–v (3 August 1484)—Mahomat Vaquer and Marien Tagarinia of Gilet are convicted of adultery and made slaves. MR 942: 1v (Alcira 1480)—a Muslim woman is made a slave "per eser sen anada de poder de son marit e esser stada atrobada en adulteri"; and similar cases from Alcira: MR 950: 4r (1493), MR 958: 4r (1501), and MR 959: 4v (1502); and from Játiva: MR 3054: 7r (1494), MR 3062: 15r, 15v (1502).

131. ARV: B 1431: 55r–56v (28 June 1491).

132. ARV: B 1431: 57r–61v (23 June 1491).

133. ARV: B 1431: 391r–393r (3 April 1494).

134. ARV: B 1433: 545r–v (6 May 1504).

135. ACA: C 3567: 150v (8 February 1496). See also Ginat, *Women*, pp. 222–225; and the very interesting study of David Gilmore, *Aggression and Community: Paradoxes of Andalusian Culture* (New Haven, Conn., 1987), pp. 126–135, 144–153.

136. Abou-Zeid, "Honour," pp. 253–254; Guichard, *Structures*, pp. 41, 51, 107, 109.

137. ARV: C 148: 62v–63r (17 August 1492). Çahat Menari of Relleu takes Marien, a "moratella donzella," from her father's house, along with jewels and clothing, and then goes to Busot, where he and Marien live together.

138. ARV: MR 3056: 6v (1496). Also, MR 944: 8r (Alcira 1488)—the Capo family pays a 240s *composicio* on behalf of Azmet Capo who "era estat condemnat per haver sen portat fugitivament la filla de Chanchan moro de la dita moreria"; MR 947; 26v (1490)—Çale b. Mahomat Çale of Cocentaina is made a royal slave "perque sen porta una mora que havia nom Zehayra la qual fou condempnada a pena de apedreguar [for sexual relations with Çale?]"; and MR 952: 8r—see n. 88 (above).

139. ARV: C 151: 84r–85r (23 January 1497). As an etymological note, it is interesting that the Catalan term for a Muslim prostitute, *sabia*, has two possible Arabic sources. *Diccionari català-valencià-balear, inventari lexicogràfic i etimològic de la llengua catalana*, Antoni M. Alcover, et al. (Palma de Mallorca, 1964), 2: 776, suggests that the source is *ṣabīa*, meaning girl. I would suggest *sabīa*, meaning a captive woman, as a possible source, inasmuch as both the prostitute and the abducted or captive woman were shamed. Guichard *Struc-*

tures, p. 41, notes that *sabī* was the term used to describe the abduction of the women of rival tribes in pre-Islamic Arabia.

140. Black-Michaud, *Feuding Societies*, p. 125; Guichard, "Peuplement," pp. 131–151; and idem, *Structures*, pp. 334–341.

141. ARV: C 148: 58r (1492).

142. ACA: C 3646: 30v–31r (27 April 1489); and ARV: C 148: 142v–143v (25 January 1493).

143. ARV: B 1156: 806r–807r (7 July 1480). ACA: C 3613: 179r (17 August 1485) refers to "lo cas de la resistencia feta per los officiales e moros de la Vall d'Alfandech al sorrogat de la loctinent del governador de Xativa."

144. ARV: B 1156: 668r–v (14 December 1479).

145. ARV: C 596: 66r–v (24 November 1489). The Muslims of Alcira had disputes of an economic nature with Muslims of other localities: AMV: g³ 31: 220r–v (9 June 1487)—officials of Alcira confiscate the oil of a Muslim of Castellón at the urging of a Muslim of Alcira; and ARV: B 1161: 80r (23 May 1495)—the Muslims and lord of Corbera take the goats of a Muslim of Alcira.

146. ARV: C 310: 52v–53r (19 February 1496).

147. ACA: C 3642: 10v–11v (14 June 1486).

148. ARV: C 156: 5v (14 July 1501).

149. ARV: C 317: 36v–37r (23 August 1493). ACA: C 3645: 35r–40r (2 May 1488), ARV: C 138: 149r–150r (17 October 1497), and 228v (19 December 1498) treat an irrigation suit between the lords and aljamas of Cárcer and Alcantera; and see Glick, *Irrigation*, pp. 5–6, 68–93, on conflicts over irrigation.

150. ACA: C 3568: 121v–122r (25 September 1495). ACA: C 3650: 251r–v (19 May 1495) and C 3651: 162v (10 August 1495) treat the appeal of Maymo Borax, one of the killers.

151. James T. Monroe, "A Curious Morisco Appeal to the Ottoman Empire," *Al-Andalus*, 31 (1966): 295–300, where the Moriscos of Granada complain about being forced to abandon endogamy. See also Glick, *Islamic and Christian Spain*, pp. 141–142, who asserts that "Islam provided a framework which legitimated tribal values and gave them religious significance." Although Goody, *Family and Marriage*, pp. 6–33 (esp. 10–12), tends to play down the differences between Muslim ("Eastern") and Christian ("Western") social structures—in comparison to the more striking contrasts between the structures of sub-Saharan Africa and those of Europe and North Africa—the differences were, I believe, significant enough to give them considerable value for understanding the phenomenon of Valencian Muslim solidarity (Mudejar and Morisco) and resistance to Christianity.

152. ARV: B 1433: 415v (16 June 1503).

153. ARV: C 650: 242v (12 April 1502): "tots los moros de aquest Regne . . . tenen ses intelligencies los huns ab los altres." On the Mudejars' political activities, see chap. 2.

154. ARV: B 1156–1162 contain 533 licenses granted to Mudejars to travel to the southern half of the kingdom and to Castile and Granada for commercial and other business. See also chap. 2.

155. ARV: MR 89–110 record the granting of mendicancy licenses to Mudejars. See chap. 4, table 14. ARV: B 1431: 358v (10 December 1492)—Maymo

Çabit of Manises testifies regarding the importance of alms-giving among the Mudejars, in this case to Muslim slaves.

156. There are numerous examples of this. Some of the official truces were made between Muslims of Valencia and those of other localities: for example, ARV: B 219: 35v (19 April 1488)—truce between Açen Torraboni of Valencia and Mahomat Cotayna of Mascarell. ARV: B 1431: 529r–v (20 May 1495)— Suleymen Alguarbi, a hemp-sandal-maker from the Vall de Uxó, testifies that he had a shop beside the door of the fonduk; 528r and 530r contain the testimonies of Muslim saddlers of the Vall de Uxó who stayed at the fonduk and sold their wares in Valencia. As for litigation, those cases tried before the tribunal of the bailiff general required the presence of litigants and witnesses in the capital.

157. See chap. 1 for more details.

158. See chap. 1 and chap. 3, table 2.

159. It is arguable that such contact between Mudejars of different localities for reasons of business and kinship was equally conducive to feuding. However, if the regional economy was to function with reasonable efficiency, the initiation of feuds as a result of such contacts must have been more the exception than the rule.

160. Burns, *Islam under the Crusaders*, pp. 196–197, 417; Ferrer i Mallol, *Els sarraïns*, pp. 95–100.

161. ARV: C 707 shows that from 1479 to 1484 Muslims from the following places traveled to Almería to collect inheritances: Castellnou (786v–787r), Valldigna (788v–789r), Estivella (790v–791r), Valencia (823r–v), Fanzara (827r–v), Vall de Uxó (832r–v), Serra (835r–v), Mascarell (838r–v), Castellón de Rugat (841r–v), and Alcudia de Veo (835r–v); and to Tunis: Valencia (795v–796r), Oliva (796v–797r), Vall de Uxó (797v–798r), Beniopa (800v–801r), Valldigna (802v–804r), Gandía (809v–810r), Alcira (812v–813r), Cuartell (862v–863r), Mascarell (863v–864r), Náquera (871r–v), Rubau (882v–883r), and Callosa (913r–v). ARV: MR 2480: 8r (Castellón de la Plana, 1492) records a Muslim coming from the Maghrib to split with his brother the estate left by their father in Castellón. ARV: C 707: 901v–902r (13 November 1481)—Ali Fotoffa is granted license to go to Tunis "per veure huns parents seus que te en les dites parts." See the methodological comments of Míkel de Epalza, "Les Morisques, vus à partir des Communautés Mudéjares précédentes," in *Les Morisques et leur temps*, L. Cardaillac, ed. (Paris, 1983), pp. 36–39, who advocates viewing the Mudejars and the Moriscos as belonging to one post-Almohad western Islamic world.

162. ARV: B 1161: 440r–v (25 August 1497).

163. ARV: B 1220: VIII 52v (10 November 1487).

164. ARV: C 424: 33r–v (27 December 1487).

165. ARV: B 1161: 474v–475r (19 February 1498) is a license to Yahye Bellvis to reside in the kingdom for one year with his "mercaderies."

166. ARV: B 1159: 9v (27 March 1488).

167. See chap. 2 nn. 60, 78; and chap. 3.

168. Gual Camarena, "Aportaciones", pp. 173–174; idem, "Mudéjares valencianos," p. 471; and Piles, "Moros de realengo," pp. 244–245, note that Mudejars migrated to royal *morerías* because of the better conditions there, but

do not explain why the majority, in fact, did not migrate. Barceló Torres, *Minorías*, p. 52, points out this contradiction. ARV: C 650: 241r (12 April 1502)—the nobles remind Fernando that "fora lo cors de la vostra ciutat de Valencia en tot lo present Regne son molt mes los moros que no los crestians e molts d'ells poblats en serres, valls e montanyes."

169. ARV: MR 3055: 5v (1495).

170. See chap. 1nn. 141–144.

171. Domínguez Ortiz and Vincent, *Historia*, pp. 146–150.

172. See table 19.

173. Barceló Torres, *Minorías*, p. 52.

174. ACA: C 3568: 40v–41r (15 April 1493).

175. Burns, *Islam under the Crusaders*, pp. 198–201.

176. Nieto Fernández, "Morería de Orihuela," p. 765; Barceló Torres, *Minorías*, p. 139.

177. ARV: B 1431: 358v–359r (10 December 1492)—when asked where the *faqīh* Abdalla taught school, Abdulcarim of Oliva "dix que en Oliva e en altres lochs e en Ondara."

178. Barceló Torres, *Minorías*, p. 273, document no. 96 (16 June 1484), mentions a "maestro" in Tabernes, Ibrāhīm al-Ṭarbānī.

179. Brunschvig, *Berbérie*, 2: 352–411; and Arié, *L'Espagne musulmane*, pp. 423–462, especially p. 423, where Almería is regarded as an intellectual center inferior only to Granada and Málaga.

180. Pons Boïgues, "Retazos moriscos," pp. 131–134.

181. Barceló Torres, *Minorías*, pp. 42–43, 139–140.

182. Luis García Ballester, *Historia social de la medecina en la España de los siglos XIII al XVI*, vol. 1: *La minoría musulmana y morisca* (Madrid, 1976), p. 72. This work was translated from Arabic into Catalan in Paterna in 1456, and into Latin by Juan de Bosnia in 1463.

183. García Ballester, *Historia*, pp. 65–70; and for the Arabic text of the letter, Julián Ribera y Tarragó, "La enseñanza entre los musulmanes españoles," in *Disertaciones y opúsculos* (Madrid, 1928), I: 357–359.

184. The Arabic documents discovered by María Jesús Viguera Molíns, "Dos nuevos documentos árabes de Aragón (Jarque y Morés, 1492)," in *Aragón en la Edad Media: estudios de economía y sociedad (siglos XII al XV)* (Zaragoza, 1981), IV: 235–261, and Ana Labarta, "Reconocimiento de tutela a un mudéjar de Daroca (documento árabe de 1477)," ibid., V (Zaragoza, 1983), also advise a moderation of Boswell's view (*Royal Treasure*, pp. 381–382) that the Aragonese Mudejars had almost completely lost a knowledge of Arabic.

185. ACA: C 3640: 77v–78v (26 January 1484).

186. Barceló Torres, *Minorías*, pp. 221–323.

187. Barceló Torres, *Minorías*, pp. 136–143.

188. ARV: B 1433: 134r (30 March 1501). In the trial of Azmet Axer of Alcira, ARV: B 1431: 385r (14 June 1493), there are presented as evidence "los albarans morischs de propria ma de aquell [Ageg b. Çahat Ageg] scrits, los quals splanats per lo alcadi Real en lengua materna."

189. ARV: B 1222: I 53v (9 December 1496).

190. For instance, ARV: B 1431: 278r–286r (6 February 1493)—the trial of the *faqīh* Alasdrach and Abdalla Sinube of Buñol, and Ali Alcayet of Chiva for having allegedly aided a Muslim slave in his escape. The main evidence of the prosecution was that the defendants had spoken in Arabic to the slave.

191. Bramon, *Contra moros i jueus*, pp. 144–154; and O. Hegyi, "Minority and Restricted Uses of the Arabic Alphabet: The *Aljamiado* Phenomenon," *Journal of the American Oriental Society* 99.2 (1979): 262–267.

192. Boronat y Barrachina, *Moriscos*, 1: 424–425, document no. 5.

193. Halperin Donghi, *Conflicto*, pp. 106–111.

194. ARV: B 1431: 384r (14 June 1493).

195. ARV: B 1431: 348v (29 October 1492)—the confessions of Abdalla, *faqīh* of Ondara.

196. ARV: B 1431: 358r—the testimony of Maymo ben Çabit of Manises.

197. ARV: C 650: 243v (12 April 1502).

198. ARV: C 650: 241r.

199. ACA: C 3665: 72r (23 April 1487). See chap. 2.

200. ARV: C 248: 31v–32r (6 July 1493).

201. ARV: B 1431: 361r–v—the testimony of Mahomat Alfaqi, *faqīh* of Manises; 348v—the confession of Abdalla; 358r–359v—the testimonies of Maymo ben Çabit of Manises and Abdulcarim of Oliva; and 357v—the testimony of Ayet, *faqīh* of Paterna.

202. ARV: B 1431: 358r–v—testimony of Maymo ben Çabit: "per quant es home de sciencia va entre alfaquins del present Regne demanant per amor de Deu."

203. ARV: B 1431: 358v—"lo dit Abdalla Alfaqui es tengut . . . reputat lo qual sa vida de moro sant."

204. ARV: B 1431: 360r–v—the testimony of Axir, *qāḍī* of the *morería* of Játiva.

205. See Lapidus, *Muslim Cities*, pp. 130–144, on the role of the ʿulamā'.

206. ARV: C 148: 214r–v (4 September 1493)—a *faqīh* of Granada settles near Orihuela; ARV: B 1160: 354v–355r (26 November 1491)—a *faqīh* from Málaga becomes a vassal in Manises; ARV: B 221: 413r (23 March 1498)—Ali Granati, *metge*, is party to a truce; and ARV: B 194 (1494–1497) records the Maghriban captives brought into Valencia, among whom were Ali Alcutentini, a *faqīh* of Constantine (34r), four *faqīh*s from Bône, including Ali who "dix que lig en les mezquites lo alcora [Qur'ān]" (157r–158v), and a Muslim mystic who "feya vida ermitana que es morabit" (272r). On Sufi mysticism and "maroubtisme" in the eastern Maghrib, see Brunschvig, *Berbérie*, 2: 317–351.

207. ARV: B 1431: 348v. On the similarity in physiognomy of Valencian Muslims and Christians, see Bramon, *Contra moros i jueus*, pp. 129–132.

Glossary

adelantat: An elected administrator of a Muslim community involved in the fiscal and judicial affairs of the community as a whole; each community had from two to four such officials.

alfondeguer: The Christian lessee of the fonduk (see below) of a Muslim community.

aljama: The corporate municipal body of the Muslims; it was roughly comparable to the Christian *universitas*.

almugaver: A foreign Muslim raider, usually from the sultanate of Granada.

amīn: The chief financial official of the Muslim community and the most prominent intermediary between it and the Christian authorities.

ᶜaṣabīyah: Agnatic solidarity among the members of a Muslim lineage group.

çalmedina: A Muslim official with police and executive functions within the community.

censal: A long-term loan liquidated by the debtor through the payment of annual pensions, with interest, to the creditor.

Converso: A convert from Judaism to Christianity.

dār al-Islām: Islamic lands where Islamic law is in force.

dhimmah: A contract according protection to Christians and Jews living under Islamic rule.

dhimmī: A beneficiary of the *dhimmah*.

faqīh: A Muslim jurist, often acting as a schoolteacher and preacher in the mosque among the Muslims of Valencia.

fonduk: An inn and goods depository, often with a tavern, intended for visiting Muslims and Jews.

Furs: The law code of the kingdom of Valencia.

morería: The Muslim quarter of a city or town.

Morisco: A convert from Islam to Christianity.

Mudejar: A Muslim living under Spanish Christian rule.

qāḍī: A Muslim judge; the most important official in the aljama.

Shariah: Islamic law, based on the Qur'an and the *Sunnah*.

Sunnah: The deeds and statements of the Prophet Muhammad that acquired
normative force in Islam.

ummah: The international Islamic community.

Bibliography

Primary Sources

Archival Sources

Archivo de la Corona de Aragón: Cancillería Real registers 3521–3526, 3528, 3545–3551, 3561–3572, 3576, 3599–3601, 3605–3616, 3630–3656, 3663–3669. Maestre Racional registers 1103–1126, 1497, 1567, 2356, 2570–2571, 2576–2578, 2602.

Archivo del Reino de Valencia: Cancillería Real registers 126–142, 148, 150–151, 153–154, 156, 158, 245–246, 248, 302–311, 317–318, 412, 423–424, 468, 596, 610 (*Aureum opus*), 616 (*Furs*), 624, 633, 650, 658–659, 707. Maestre Racional registers 9052, 89–110, 942–960, 2469–2491, 3052–3062, 4016–4034, 4273–4284, 4567–4574, 10877–10880. Bailía General registers 122–123, 194–195, 217–221, 323–325, 1156–1162, 1220, 1222–1223, 1431–1433. Gobernación registers 2350–2361, 2371–2372, 2392–2399, 2409–2415.

Archivo Municipal de Valencia: Cartas Missivas registers (g³) 29–34.

Printed Sources

Aureum opus regalium privilegiorum civitatis et regni Valentie. Valencia, 1515.

Beinart, Haim, ed. *Records of the Trials of the Spanish Inquisition in Ciudad Real*, 4 vols. Jerusalem: The Israel National Academy of Social Sciences and Humanities, 1974–1985.

Bernáldez, Andrés. *Memorias del reinado de los Reyes Católicos.* J. de M. Carriazo and M. Gomez-Moreno, eds. Madrid: Real Academia de la Historia, 1962.

Cortes del Reinado de Fernando el Católico. Ernest Belenguer Cebrià, ed. Valencia: Universidad de Valencia, 1972.

Furs e ordinations fetes per los gloriosos reys de Aragó als regnicols del regne de València. Lambert Palmart, ed. Valencia, 1482.

Furs de València, 4 vols. Germà Colon and Arcadi Garcia, eds. In *Els Nostres Clàssics*, nn. 101, 105, 113, 121. Barcelona: Editorial Barcino, 1970–1983.

Ibn Khaldūn. *The Muqaddimah: An Introduction to History*, 3 vols. Franz Rosenthal, trans. London: Routledge and Kegan Paul, 1958.

Pulgar, Hernando del. *Crónica de los señores Reyes Católicos*. Valencia: Benito Monfort, ed., 1780.

Ruxton, F. H. *Māliki Law. Being a Summary from the French Translations of the "Mukhtasar" of Sīdī Khalīl*. Reprint of 1916 edition. Westport, Conn.: Hyperion Press Inc., 1980.

Torre, Antonio de la. *Documentos sobre relaciones internacionales de los Reyes Católicos*, 6 vols. Barcelona: Consejo Superior de Investigaciones Cientifícas, 1949–1966.

Secondary Sources

Abou-Zeid, Ahmed. "Honour and Shame among the Bedouins of Egypt." In *Honour and Shame: The Values of Mediterranean Society*, pp. 245–259. J. G. Peristiany, ed. London: Weidenfeld and Nicolson, 1965.

Abun-Nasr, Jamil M. *A History of the Maghrib*. Second edition. Cambridge: Cambridge University Press, 1975.

Ahmed, Akbar S., and David M. Hart, eds. *Islam in Tribal Societies from the Atlas to the Indus*. London and Boston: Routledge & Kegan Paul, 1984.

Arco, Ricardo del. "Cortes aragonesas de los Reyes Católicos." *Revista de Archivos, Bibliotecas, y Museos* 60 (1954): 77–103.

Arié, Rachel. *L'Espagne musulmane au temps de Naṣrides (1232–1492)*. Paris: Éditions E. de Boccard, 1973.

Arroyo Ilera, Fernando. "Estructura demográfica de Segorbe y su comarca en el siglo XV." *Hispania: Revista Española de Historia* 112 (1969): 287–313.

Azcona, Tarsicio de. *Isabel la Católica: estudio crítico de su vida y su reinado*. Biblioteca de Autores Cristianos. Madrid: La Editorial Católica, 1964.

Baer, Yitzhak. *A History of the Jews in Christian Spain*, 2 vols. Louis Schoffman, trans. Philadelphia: Jewish Publication Society of America, 1966.

Barceló Torres, María del Carme. "La llengua àrab al País Valencià (segles VIII al XVI)." *Arguments* (Valencia) 4 (1979): 123–149.

———. "La morería de Valencia en el reinado de Juan II." *Saitabi* 30 (1980): 53–71.

———. *Toponímia aràbica del País Valencià. Alqueries i castells*. Valencia: Diputació de València, 1982.

———. *Minorías islámicas en el país valenciano: historia y dialecto*. Valencia: Instituto Hispano-Árabe de Cultura, 1984.

Beinart, Haim. "The Converso Community in 15th Century Spain." In *The

Sephardi Heritage, I: 425–456. R. D. Barnett, ed. London: Vallentine, Mitchell, 1971.

Belenguer Cebrià, Ernest. *València en la crisi del segle XV*. Barcelona: Edicions 62 s/a., 1976.

Black-Michaud, Jacob. *Feuding Societies*. Oxford: Basil Blackwell, 1975.

Boronat y Barrachina, Pascual. *Los moriscos españoles y su expulsión*, 2 vols. Valencia: F. Vives y Mora, 1901.

Boswell, John. *The Royal Treasure: Muslim Communities under the Crown of Aragon in the Fourteenth Century*. New Haven, Conn.: Yale University Press, 1977.

Bramon, Dolors. "La reconquesta valenciana i els orígens del problema morisc." *Arguments* (Valencia) 3 (1977): 49–62.

———. *Contra moros i jueus: formació i estratègia d'unes discriminacions al País Valencià*. Valencia: Eliseu Climent, ed., 1981.

Braudel, Fernand. "Les Espagnols et l'Afrique du Nord de 1492 a 1577." *Revue Africaine* 69 (1928): 184–233, 351–410.

———. *The Mediterranean and the Mediterranean World in the Age of Philip II*, 2 vols. Siân Reynolds, trans. Second rev. edition. New York: Harper and Row, 1973.

Brunschvig, Robert. *La Berbérie orientale sous les Ḥafṣides des origines a la fin du XVe siècle*, 2 vols. Paris: Adrien-Maisonneuve, 1940–1947.

Bulliet, Richard W. *Conversion to Islam in the Medieval Period: An Essay in Quantitative History*. Cambridge, Mass.: Harvard University Press, 1979.

Burns, Robert I. "Journey from Islam: Incipient Cultural Transition in the Conquered Kingdom of Valencia (1240–1280)." *Speculum* 35 (1960): 337–356.

———. "Social riots on the Christian–Moslem Frontier: Thirteenth-Century Valencia." *American Historical Review* 66 (1961): 378–400.

———. *The Crusader Kingdom of Valencia: Reconstruction on a Thirteenth-Century Frontier*, 2 vols. Cambridge, Mass.: Harvard University Press, 1967.

———. "Renegades, Adventurers, and Sharp Businessmen: The Thirteenth-Century Spaniard in the Cause of Islam." *Catholic Historical Review* 57 (1972): 341–366.

———. *Islam under the Crusaders: Colonial Survival in the Thirteenth-Century Kingdom of Valencia*. Princeton: Princeton University Press, 1973.

———. *Medieval Colonialism: Postcrusade Exploitation of Islamic Valencia*. Princeton: Princeton University Press, 1975.

———. "Spanish Islam in Transition: Acculturative Survival and Its Price in the Christian Kingdom of Valencia." In *Islam and Cultural Change in the Middle Ages*, pp. 87–105. Speros Vryonis, Jr., ed. Wiesbaden: Otto Harrassowitz, 1975.

———. "Immigrants from Islam: The Crusaders' Use of Muslims as Settlers in Thirteenth-Century Spain." *American Historical Review* 80 (1975): 21–42.

———. *Muslims, Christians, and Jews in the Crusader Kingdom of Valencia: Societies in Symbiosis*. Cambridge: Cambridge University Press, 1984.

———. "Muslim–Christian Conflict and Contact: Mudejar Methodology." In *Muslims, Christians, and Jews in the Crusader Kingdom of Valencia: Societies in Symbiosis*, pp. 1–51. Cambridge: Cambridge University Press, 1984.

————. "Christian–Muslim Confrontation: The Thirteenth-Century Dream of Conversion." In *Muslims, Christians, and Jews in the Crusader Kingdom of Valencia: Societies in Symbiosis*, pp. 80–108. Cambridge: Cambridge University Press, 1984.

————. "The Language Barrier: Bilingualism and Interchange." In *Muslims, Christians, and Jews in the Crusader Kingdom of Valencia: Societies in Symbiosis*, pp. 172–192. Cambridge: Cambridge University Press, 1984.

Cahen, Claude. "Dhimma." *Encyclopaedia of Islam*. Second edition, II: 227. Leiden: E. J. Brill, 1960.

————. "Djizya." *Encyclopaedia of Islam*. Second edition, II: 559–562. Leiden: E. J. Brill, 1960.

Cardaillac, Louis. *Morisques et Chrétiens: un affrontement polémique (1492–1640)*. Paris: Librairie Klincksieck, 1977.

————, ed. *Les Morisques et leur temps*. Paris: Éditions du Centre National de la Recherche Scientifique, 1983.

Caro Baroja, Julio. *Los Moriscos del Reino de Granada*. Second edition. Madrid: Ediciones Istmo, 1976.

Casey, James. *The Kingdom of Valencia in the Seventeenth Century*. Cambridge: Cambridge University Press, 1979.

Castro, Américo. *España en su historia: cristianos, moros, y judíos*. Second edition. Barcelona: Editorial Crítica, 1983.

————. *The Spaniards. An Introduction to Their History*. Willard F. King and Selma Margaretten, trans. Berkeley, Los Angeles, London: University of California Press, 1971.

Císcar Pallarés, Eugenio. *Tierra y señorio en el País Valenciano (1570–1620)*. Valencia: Del Cenia al Segura, 1977.

Cohen, Abner. *Arab Border Villages in Israel: A Study of Continuity and Change in Social Organization*. Manchester: Manchester University Press, 1965.

Cole, Donald P. "Alliance and Descent in the Middle East and the 'Problem' of Patrilateral Parallel Cousin Marriage." In *Islam in Tribal Societies from the Atlas to the Indus*, pp. 169–186. Akbar S. Ahmed and David M. Hart, eds. London and Boston: Routledge & Kegan Paul, 1984.

Cortes, Vicenta. *La esclavitud en Valencia durante el reinado de los Reyes Católicos*. Valencia: Ayuntamiento de Valencia, 1964.

Coulson, Noel. J. *A History of Islamic Law*. Edinburgh: University of Edinburgh Press, 1964.

Diccionari català-valencià-balear, inventari lexicogràfic i etimològic de la llengua catalana, 10 vols. Second edition. Antoni M. Alcover, Francesc de B. Moll, Manuel Sanchis Guarner, and Anna Moll Marquès, eds. Palma de Mallorca: Editorial Moll, 1964.

Domingo Pérez, Concepción. "La agricultura de Castellón de la Plana, 1468." *Saitabi* 27 (1977): 221–238.

Domínguez Ortiz, Antonio, and Bernard Vincent. *Historia de los moriscos: vida y tragedia de una minoría*. Madrid: Editorial Revista de Occidente, S. A., 1978.

Doussinague, José M. *La política internacional de Fernando el Católico*. Madrid: Espasa-Calpe, S. A., 1944.

Dufourcq, Charles Emmanuel. *L'Espagne catalane et le Maghrib aux XIIIe et XIVe siècles, de la bataille de Las Navas de Tolosa (1212) à l'avènement du sultan mérinide Abou-l-Hasan (1313)*. Paris: Presses universitaires de France, 1966.

Duran, Eulàlia. *Les Germanies als Països Catalans*. Barcelona: Curial Edicions Catalanes, 1982.

Encyclopaedia of Islam. Second edition. Leiden: E. J. Brill, 1960.

Epalza, Míkel de. "Notas sobre el lingüista Ibn Sidah y la historia de Denia y su región en el siglo XI." *Revista de instituto de estudios alicantinos* 33 (1981): 161–172.

———. "Les Morisques, vus à partir des Communautés Mudéjares précédentes." In *Les Morisques et leur temps*, pp. 30–41. Louis Cardaillac, ed. Paris: Éditions du Centre National de la Recherche Scientifique, 1983.

———, and Enrique Llobregat. " ¿Hubo mozárabes en tierras valencianas? Proceso de islamización del Levante de la Peninsula (Sharq al-Andalus)." *Revista del Instituto de Estudios Alicantinos* 36 (1982): 7–31.

Esposito, John L. *Women in Muslim Family Law*. Syracuse: Syracuse University Press, 1982.

Fattal, Antoine. *Le statut légal des non-musulmans en pays d'Islam*. Beirut: Institut de Lettres Orientales, 1958.

Ferrer i Mallol, Maria Teresa. *Els sarraïns de la Corona catalano-aragonesa en el segle XIV: segregació i discriminació*. Barcelona: Consell Superior d'Investigacions Científiques, 1987.

———. *La frontera amb l'Islam en el segle XIV. Cristians i sarraïns al País Valencià*. Barcelona: Consell Superior d'Investigacions Científiques, 1988.

———. *Les aljames sarraïnes de la governació d' Oriola*. Barcelona: Consell Superior d'Investigacions Científiques, 1988.

Ferrer Navarro, Ramón. "La Plana: su estructura demográfica en el siglo XV." *Cuadernos de Historia* 5 (1975): 67–91.

Furió, Antoni. *Camperols del País Valencià: Sueca, una comunitat rural a la tardor de l'Edat Mitjana*. Valencia: Institució Alfons el Magnànim, 1982.

———. "El País Valencià de l'Edat Mitjana a la Modernitat (segles XIII–XVI)." In *Història de l'Economia Valenciana*, pp. 43–56. Valencia: Diputació Provincial de València, 1983.

———, and Ferran Garcia. "Dificultats agràries en la formació i consolidació del feudalisme al País Valencià." In *La formació i expansió del feudalisme català*, pp. 291–310. J. Portella i Comas, ed. Girona: *Estudi General*, vols. 5–6, 1985–1986

Fuster, Joan. *Poetas, Moriscos y Curas*. Josep Palacios, trans. Madrid: Editorial Ciencia Nueva, S. L., 1969.

García Ballester, Luis. *Historia social de la medicina en la España de los siglos XIII al XVI*. Vol. 1: *La minoría musulmana y morisca*. Madrid: Akal Editor, 1976.

Garcia Càrcel, Ricard, and Eduard Císcar Pallarés. *Moriscos i agermanats*. Valencia: L'Estel, 1974.

García Cárcel, Ricardo. "Las Germanías y la crisis de subsistencias de 1521."

Boletín de la Sociedad Castellonense de Cultura 51 (1975): 281–315.

———. *Orígenes de la Inquisición Española: el tribunal de Valencia, 1478–1530.* Barcelona: Ediciones Península, 1976.

———. "El censo de 1510 y la población valenciana de la primera mitad del siglo XVI." *Saitabi* 26 (1976): 171–188.

———. "La revuelta morisca de Espadán." *Al-Andalus* 41 (1976): 121–146.

———. "La ganadería valenciana en el siglo XVI." *Saitabi* 27 (1977): 79–102.

———. *Las Germanías de Valencia.* Second edition. Barcelona: Ediciones Península, 1981.

García Martínez, Sebastià. *Bandolers, Corsaris i Moriscos.* Valencia: Eliseu Climent, ed. 1980.

———. "La Ribera desde las Germanías a la expulsión de los moriscos." In *Economia Agrària i Història Local: I Assemblea d'Història de la Ribera,* pp. 43–98. Valencia: Institució Alfons el Magnànim, 1981.

García Sanz, Arcadio. "Mudéjares y moriscos en Castellón." *Boletín de la Sociedad Castellonense de Cultura* 28 (1952): 94–114.

Gellner, Ernest, and Charles Micaud, eds. *Arabs and Berbers.* Lexington, Mass: D. C. Heath and Company, 1972.

Gilmore, David D. *Aggression and Community: Paradoxes of Andalusian Culture.* New Haven, Conn.: Yale University Press, 1987.

Ginat, Joseph, *Women in Muslim Rural Society.* New Brunswick, N.J.: Transaction Books, 1982.

Glick, Thomas F. *Irrigation and Society in Medieval Valencia.* Cambridge, Mass.: The Belknap Press of Harvard University Press, 1970.

———. "The Ethnic Systems of Premodern Spain." *Comparative Studies in Sociology* 1 (1978): 157–171.

———. *Islamic and Christian Spain in the Early Middle Ages.* Princeton: Princeton University Press, 1979.

———, and Oriol Pi-Sunyer. "Acculturation as an Explanatory Concept in Spanish History." *Comparative Studies in Society and History* 11 (1969): 136–154.

Goñi Gaztambide, J. *Historia de la bula de cruzada en España.* Vitoria: Editorial del Seminario, 1958.

Goody, Jack. *The Development of the Family and Marriage in Europe.* Cambridge: Cambridge University Press, 1983.

Gual Camarena, Miguel. "Mudéjares valencianos. Aportaciones para su estudio." *Saitabi* 7 (1949): 165–199.

———. "Los mudéjares valencianos en la época del Magnánimo." *IV Congreso de Historia de la Corona de Aragón* I (1959): 467–494.

Guichard, Pierre. "Le peuplement de la région de Valence aux deux premiers siècles de la domination musulmane." *Mélanges de la Casa de Velázquez* 5 (1969): 103–158.

———. *Structures sociales "orientales" et "occidentales" dans l'Espagne musulmane.* Paris: Mouton & Co. and École des Hautes Études en Sciences Sociales, 1977.

———, Jacqueline Guiral, and José Hinojosa Montalvo. *Nuestra Historia,* vol. 3. Valencia: Mas Ivars-Editores, S. L., 1980.

Guiral, Jacqueline. "Les relations commerciales du royaume de Valence avec la Berbérie au XVe siècle." *Mélanges de la Casa de Velázquez* 10 (1974): 99–131.

———. "La piratería, el corso: sus provechos y ganancias en el siglo XV." In *Nuestra Historia*, 3: 267–280. Valencia: Mas Ivars-Editores, S. L., 1980.

Guiral-Hadziiossif, Jacqueline. *Valence, port méditerranéen au XVe siècle (1410–1525)*. Paris: Publications de la Sorbonne, 1986.

Haliczer, Stephen H. "The Castilian Urban Patriciate and the Jewish Expulsions of 1480–92." *American Historical Review* 78 (1973): 35–58.

Halperin Donghi, Tulio. *Un conflicto nacional: moriscos y cristianos viejos en Valencia*. Valencia: Institución Alfonso el Magnánimo, 1980.

Hamilton, Earl J. *Money, Prices, and Wages in Valencia, Aragon, and Navarre, 1351–1500*. Cambridge, Mass.: Harvard University Press, 1936.

Hart, David M. "The Tribe in Modern Morocco: Two Case Studies." In *Arabs and Berbers*, pp. 25–58. Ernest Gellner and Charles Micaud, eds. Lexington, Mass.: D. C. Heath and Company, 1972.

———. "Segmentary Systems and the Role of 'Five Fifths' in Tribal Morocco." In *Islam in Tribal Societies from the Atlas to the Indus*, pp. 66–105. Akbar S. Ahmed and David M. Hart, eds. London and Boston: Routledge & Kegan Paul, 1984.

Hegyi, O. "Minority and Restricted Uses of the Arabic Alphabet: The *Aljamiado* Phenomenon." *Journal of the American Oriental Society* 99.2 (1979): 262–267.

Hess, Andrew C. "The Moriscos: An Ottoman Fifth Column in Sixteenth-Century Spain." *American Historial Review* 74 (1969): 1–25.

———. *The Forgotten Frontier: A History of the Sixteenth-Century Ibero-African Frontier*. Chicago: The University of Chicago Press, 1978.

Highfield, Roger. "Christians, Jews and Muslims in the Same Society: The Fall of *Convivencia* in Medieval Spain." In *Studies in Church History* 15 *(Religious Motivation: Biographical and Sociological Problems for the Church Historian)*, pp. 121–146. Derek Baker, ed. Oxford: Basil Blackwell, 1978.

Hillgarth, J. N. *The Spanish Kingdoms*. Vol. II: *Castilian Hegemony (1410–1516)*. Oxford: Oxford University Press, 1978.

Hinojosa Montalvo, José. "Las relaciones entre los reinos de Valencia y Granada durante la primera mitad del siglo XV." In *Estudios de Historia de Valencia*, pp. 91–160. Valencia: Universidad de Valencia, 1978.

Kamen, Henry. *The Spanish Inquisition*. London: Weidenfeld and Nicolson, 1965.

———. *Inquisition and Society in Spain in the Sixteenth and Seventeenth Centuries*. Bloomington: Indiana University Press, 1985.

Kowaleski, Maryanne. "Local Markets and Merchants in Late Fourteenth-Century Exeter." Ph.D. dissertation, University of Toronto, 1982.

Kriegel, Maurice. "La prise d'une décision: l'expulsion des juifs d'Espagne." *Revue Historique* 260 (1978): 49–90.

Küchler, Winfried. "Besteuerung der Juden und Mauren in den Ländern der Krone Aragons während des 15. Jahrhunderts." *Gesammelte Aufsätze zur Kulturgeschichte Spaniens* 24 (1968): 227–256.

Labarta, Ana. "Reconocimiento de tutela a un mudéjar de Daroca (documento árabe de 1477)." In *Aragón en la Edad Media: estudios de economia y sociedad (siglos XIII al XV)* V: 207–218. Zaragoza: Universidad de Zaragoza, 1983.

———. "Contratos matrimoniales entre Moriscos valencianos." *Al-Qantara: Revista de Estudios Árabes* 4 (1983): 57–87.

Lacarra, José María. "Introducción al estudio de los mudéjares aragoneses." In *Actas del I Simposio Internacional de Mudejarismo*, pp. 17–28. Madrid-Teruel: Consejo Superior de Investigaciones Cientifícas, 1981.

Ladero Quesada, Miguel Angel. "La repoblación del Reino de Granada anterior a 1500." *Hispania* 28 (1968): 489–563.

———. *Los Mudéjares de Castilla en tiempos de Isabel I.* Valladolid: Instituto "Isabel la Católica" de Historia Ecclesiastica, 1969.

———. "Datos demográficos sobre los musulmanes de Granada y Castilla en el siglo XV." *Anuario de Estudios Medievales* 8 (1972–1973): 481–490.

———. "Los Mudéjares de Castilla en la Baja Edad Media." In *Actas del I Simposio Internacional de Mudejarismo*, pp. 349–390. Madrid-Teruel: Consejo Superior de Investigaciones Cientifícas, 1981.

———. *Castilla y la conquista del reino de Granada.* Second edition. Granada: Diputación Provincial de Granada, 1988.

———. *Granada después de la conquista. Repobladores y mudéjares.* Granada: Diputación Provincial de Granada, 1988.

Lapeyre, Henri. *Géographie de l'Espagne morisque.* École pratique des hautes études, Démographie et socíetés, 2. Paris: SEVPEN, 1959.

Lapidus, Ira M. *Muslim cities in the later Middle Ages.* Revised edition. Cambridge: Cambridge University Press, 1984.

Lea, Henry Charles. *A History of the Inquisition of Spain*, vol. 1. New York: Macmillan, 1906.

Levy, Reuben. *The Social Structure of Islam.* Second edition. Cambridge: Cambridge University Press, 1957.

Llorens, Peregrin-Luis. "Los sarracenos de la Sierra de Eslida y Vall d'Uxó a fines del siglo XV." *Boletín de la Sociedad Castellonense de Cultura* 43 (1967): 53–67.

———. "La morería de Segorbe: rentas de su Mezquita a fines del siglo XVI." *Boletín de la Sociedad Castellonense de Cultura* 49 (1973): 303–323.

López de Coca Castañer, José-Enrique, and Manuel Acién Almansa. "Los Mudéjares del obispado de Málaga (1485–1501)." In *Actas del I Simposio Internacional de Mudejarismo*, pp. 307–347. Madrid-Teruel: Consejo Superior de Investigaciones Cientifícas, 1981.

López Elum, Pedro. "La población de la morería de Játiva (1493)." In *Estudios de Historia de Valencia*, pp. 161–170. Valencia: Universidad de Valencia, 1978.

Macho y Ortega, Francisco. "Condición social de los mudéjares aragoneses (siglo XV)." *Memorias de la facultad de filosofía y letras de la Universidad de Zaragoza* I (1923): 137–319.

MacKay, Angus. "Popular Movements and Pogroms in Fifteenth-Century Castile." *Past and Present* 55 (1972): 33–67.

――――. "The Hispanic-*Converso* Predicament." *Transactions of the Royal Historical Society*, 5th ser., 35 (1985): 159–179.

Mateu Ibars, Josefina. *Los virreyes de Valencia: Fuentes para su estudio*. Valencia: Ayuntamiento de Valencia, 1963.

Meyerson, Mark D. "Between *Convivencia* and Crusade: The Muslim Minority of the Kingdom of Valencia during the Reign of Fernando 'el Católico.'" Ph.D. dissertation, University of Toronto, 1987.

――――. "Prostitution of Muslim Women in the Kingdom of Valencia: Religious and Sexual Discrimination in a Medieval Plural Society." In *The Medieval Mediterranean: Cross-Cultural Contacts*, pp. 87–96. M. Chiat and K. Reyerson, eds. *Medieval Studies at Minnesota 3*. St. Cloud, Minn.: North Star Press of St. Cloud, Inc., 1988.

Monroe, James T. " A Curious Morisco Appeal to the Ottoman Empire." *Al-Andalus* 31 (1966): 281–303.

Murphy, Robert F., and Leonard Kasdan. "The Structure of Parallel Cousin Marriage." *American Anthropologist* 61 (1959): 17–29.

Nieto Fernández, Augustín. "Hermandad entre las aljamas de moros y las villas de la governación de Orihuela en el siglo XV." In *Primer Congreso de Historia del País Valenciano*, 2: 749–760. Valencia: Universidad de Valencia, 1980.

――――. "La morería de Orihuela en el siglo XV." In *Primer Congreso de Historia del País Valenciano*, 2: 761–771. Valencia: Universidad de Valencia, 1980.

Patai, Raphael. *The Arab Mind*. Third edition, rev. New York: Charles Scribner's Sons, 1983.

Peñarroja Torrejón, Leopoldo. *Moriscos y repobladores en el reino de Valencia: la Vall d'Uxó (1525–1625)*, 2 vols. Valencia: Del Cenia al Segura, 1984.

Pérez, Joseph, Jean-Paul Le Flem, Jean-Marc Pelorson, José M. López Piñero, and Janine Fayard. *Historia de España*. Vol. V: *La frustración de un imperio (1496–1714)*. Manuel Tuñón de Lara, ed. Barcelona: Editorial Labor, S. A., 1982.

Peris Albentosa, Tomas V. "La estructura de la propiedad agricola en la morería de Alzira (1508–1579)." *Qüestions Valencianes* 1 (1979): 47–92.

Piles, Leopoldo. "La situación social de los moros de realengo en la Valencia del siglo XV." *Estudios de Historia Social de España* 1 (1949): 225–274.

Piles Ros, Leopoldo. *Apuntes para la historia económico-social de Valencia durante el siglo XV*. Valencia: Ayuntamiento de Valencia, 1969.

――――. *Estudio documental sobre el Bayle General de Valencia, su autoridad y jurisdicción*. Valencia: Institución Alfonso el Magnánimo, 1970.

Pons Alós, Vicente, *El Fondo Crespí de Valldaura en el Archivo Condal de Orgaz (1249–1548)*. Valencia: Universidad de Valencia, 1982.

Pons Boïgues, Francisco. "Retazos moriscos." *El archivo* 3 (1889): 131–134.

Redondo Veintemillas, Guillermo, and Luis Orera Orera. *Fernando II y el Reino de Aragón*. Zaragoza: Guara Editorial, 1980.

Regla, Joan. *Estudios sobre los moriscos*. Third edition. Barcelona: Editorial Ariel, 1974.

Reyerson, Kathryn L. *Business, Banking and Finance in Medieval Montpellier*.

Toronto: Pontifical Institute of Mediaeval Studies, 1985.

Ribera y Tarragó, Julián. "La enseñanza entre los musulmanes españoles." In *Disertaciones y opúsculos*. Vol. I, pp. 229–359. Madrid: Imprenta de Estanislao Maestre, 1928.

Roca Traver, Francisco A. "Un siglo de vida mudéjar en la Valencia medieval (1238–1338)." *Estudios de Edad Media de la Corona de Aragón* V (1952): 115–208.

Rubio Vela, Augustín. "Sobre la población de Valencia en el cuatrocientos (Nota demográfica)." *Boletín de la Sociedad Castellonense de Cultura* 56 (1980): 158–170.

Sabbagh, Leila. "La religion des Morisques entre deux fatwas." In *Les Morisques et leur temps*, pp. 43–56. Louis Cardaillac, ed. Paris: Éditions du Centre National de la Recherche Scientifique, 1983.

Salvador, Emilia. "Sobre la emigración mudéjar a Berbería. El tránsito legal a través del puerto de Valencia durante el primer cuarto del siglo XVI." *Estudis* 4 (1975): 39–68.

Sarasa Sánchez, Esteban. *Sociedad y conflictos sociales en Aragón: siglos XIII–XV (estructuras de poder y conflictos de clase)*. Madrid: Siglo Veinteuno de España Editores, S. A., 1981.

Sesma Muñoz, José Angel. *La Diputación del Reino de Aragón en la época de Fernando II (1479–1516)*. Zaragoza: Institución "Fernando el Católico," 1977.

———. "Instituciones parlamentarias del Reino de Aragón en el tránsito de la Edad Moderna." In *Aragón en la Edad Media: estudios de economia y sociedad (siglos XII al XV)*, IV, pp. 221–234. Zaragoza: Universidad de Zaragoza, 1981.

———. *El establecimiento de la Inquisición en Aragón (1484–1486): documentos para su estudio*. Zaragoza: Institución Fernando el Católico (CSIC), 1987?

Sevillano Colom, Francisco. "Las empresas nacionales de los Reyes Católicos y la aportación económica de la ciudad de Valencia." *Hispania* 57 (1954): 511–623.

Solano Costa, Fernando. "Estudios sobre la historia de Aragón durante la Edad Moderna," *Cuadernos de Historia: Anexos de la Revista "Hispania"* 1 (1967): 129–158.

Suárez Fernández, Luis. *Política internacional de Isabel la Católica*, 5 vols. Valladolid: Instituto "Isabel la Católica" de Historia Ecclesiastica, 1965–1972.

Thrupp, Sylvia. "Medieval Industry, 1000–1500." In *The Fontana Economic History of Europe: The Middle Ages*, pp. 221–273. Carlo M. Cipolla, ed. Glasgow: William Collins Sons & Co. Ltd., 1981.

Torres Fontes, Juan. "La Hermandad de moros e cristianos para el rescate de cautivos." In *Actas del I Simposio Internacional de Mudejarismo*, pp. 499–508. Madrid-Teruel: Consejo Superior de Investigaciones Científicas, 1981.

Tyan, Émile. *Histoire de l'organisation judiciaire en pays d'Islam*. Second edition, rev. Leiden: E. J. Brill, 1960.

Vera Delgado, Ana María. *La última frontera medieval: la defensa costera en el obispado de Málaga en tiempos de los Reyes Católicos*. Málaga: Diputación Provincial de Málaga, 1986.

Vicens i Vives, Jaume. *Ferran II i la ciutat de Barcelona*, 3 vols. Barcelona: Tipografia Emporium, E. C., 1936–1937.

Viguera Molíns, María Jesús. "Dos nuevos documentos árabes de Aragón (Jarque y Morés, 1492)." In *Aragón en la Edad Media: estudios de economia y sociedad (siglos XII al XV)*, IV: 235–261. Zaragoza: Universidad de Zaragoza, 1981.

Vincent, Bernard. "Les éléments de solidarité au sein de la minorité morisque." In *Le concepte de classe dans l'analyse des sociétés méditerranéenes XVIe–XXe siècles*, pp. 91–100. Nice: Université de Nice, 1978.

Wasserstein, David. *The Rise and Fall of the Party-Kings: Politics and Society in Islamic Spain, 1002–1086*. Princeton: Princeton University Press, 1985.

Index

Designer: U.C. Press Staff
Compositor: Asco Trade Typesetting Ltd., Hong Kong
Text: 10/12 Times Roman
Display: Helvetica
Printer: Edwards Brothers, Inc.
Binder: Edwards Brothers, Inc.

Compositor:
Text:
Display:
Printer:
Binder: